The Stone Circles of Britain, Ireland and Brittany

THE
STONE CIRCLES

OF

BRITAIN, IRELAND

AND

BRITTANY

Aubrey Burl

Yale University Press • New Haven and London

Some sections of this book were previously published in *The Stone Circles of the British Isles*
Yale University Press, 1976

Designed by Kate Gallimore
Typeset in Times by Best-set Typesetter Ltd., Hong Kong
Printed in China

Library of Congress Cataloging-in-Publication Data

Burl, Aubrey.
      The stone circles of Britain, Ireland and Brittany / Aubrey Burl.
              p. cm.
      Includes bibliographical references (p.) and index.
      ISBN 0-300-08347-5 (cloth)
      1. Stone circles—Great Britain. 2. Stone circles—Ireland. 3. Stone
circles—France—Brittany. 4. Great Britain—Antiquities. 5. Ireland—Antiquities. 6.
Brittany (France)—Antiquities. I. Title.

GN805 .B8699 2000
936.1—dc21
                                                         99-087909

Again
dedicated to the memory of

JOHN AUBREY
1626–1697

of Easton Pierse, Wiltshire

'The Father of British Archaeology'

whose work made 'Those walke and appeare that
have layen in their graves many hundreds of yeares:
and represents as it were to the eie, the places,
customes and Fashions, that were of old Time'.

Contents

Figures

Tables

Preface

This book is a substantially revised version of the writer's *The Stone Circles of the British Isles*, researched from 1964 to 1973, written in 1973–4 and published by Yale University Press in 1976. The introduction has amendments. The early chapters introduce new approaches ranging from the social to the scientific and the remainder of the book is different in content and arrangement. The ancestry of stone circles, their age, methods of construction, the societies that built them, local units of measurement, previously unacknowledged sightlines to the sun and moon, the purpose of the rings, their eventual desertion: all these questions are being answered.

There are more subtle matters that hint at varying ritual beliefs: why true circles were preferred in one region but not in another, some carefully planned, some set out by eye; why ovals were laid out along the western coastlands of Scotland; why the cromlechs of Brittany, those almost unconsidered marvels of the megalithic world, should be elliptical, horseshoe-shaped, even rectangular, but seldom circular. These have been almost unconsidered excitements in the study of the tantalus of stone circles.

It is more than twenty years since *The Stone Circlesof the British Isles* appeared. During that time research has flourished. Since 1976 there have been major studies of megalithic rings in the west of Europe such as works about circles in Britain by Thom, Thom & Burl (1980); Burl (1980) and Barnatt (1989); in Ireland by O'Nuallain (1984a, 1984b, 1995) and McConkey (1987); and in Brittany by Burl (1985).

Regions have been examined: Cornwall by Barnatt (1982); Dartmoor by Turner (1990); the Lake District by Waterhouse (1985); the Peak District by Barnatt (1990, 1998); Wigtownshire by Murray (1981); north-eastern Scotland by Tulloch (1983); and the rings around the Wicklow mountains in Ireland by Churcher (1985).

There have also been books about particular circles: Avebury by Burl (1979), Malone (1989), Ucko et al. (1991); about Callanish by Ashmore (1995); and the Rollright Stones by Lambrick (1983, 1988). Contrasted with this trickle Stonehenge has suffered a deluge. Like a once-dormant volcano it erupted in a fallout of nearly a score of serious works from Niel in 1975 to Bender in 1998, half of them published in the 1990s. These do not include sad improbabilities claiming the ring was linked with celestial haloes, was the temple of King Arthur, was designed on astro-geometrical-arithmetical patterns, was landscaped by Welsh incompetents or was alive with sex-crazed sarsens.

There are also the reviews of henges, the earthen counterparts of stone circles: by Burl (1983); Clare (1986, 1987); Harding with Lee (1987); and Barclay (1989). Lost timber rings, known only by their elusive postholes, have been resurrected and catalogued by Gibson (1998). The present book has profited from these advances, as well as from the discovery of more circles in unexpected places: Auchlee recumbent stone circle in an Aberdeen garden; Machrie Moor XI, Arran; Achmore, Isle of Lewis; and Y Capel, Powys, all buried under peat; and others in Wales and Ireland. Almost four hundred additional sites have been included in the gazetteer. Amongst them are some unusual, apparently derivative rings in the Channel Islands and nearly fifty cromlechs, some of them gigantic, from the coastlands of Brittany.

There have been losses. Kiltierney stone circle, Co. Fermanagh, was destroyed in 1974 during the course of 'farm improvements'. A senseless bonfire cracked the recumbent stone at Dyce in 1998. Beaghmore was vandalised. So was Mitchell's Fold. Conversely there have been many, necessarily partial, excavations that have created a treasure house of information about chronology and ritual. Only mentioned here they include, in Brittany: Château-Bû and Pen-ar-Land; in England: the Devil's Quoits, the Rollright Stones and Stonehenge; in Ireland: Cashelkeelty and Carrowmore; in Scotland: Balfarg, Balnuaran of Clava, Berrybrae, Cairnhall, Callanish, Cultoon, Machrie Moor I and XI, Park of Tongland, Ring of Brodgar, Strichen and Temple Wood; and in Wales the excavation of the Sarn-y-bryn-caled timber ring in Powys.

Despite these important contributions it has not been twenty years of academic tranquillity. Arguments persist. Alexander Thom's controversial theories (1967, 1971, 1978) of a standardised western European yardstick; of Pythagorean geometrical constructions for ellipses, rectangles and horseshoes; and statistical evidence for solar sightlines and intricate lunar alignments for extrapolation still generate disciples, doubters and dissenters. The astronomical battleground remains occupied by steadfast armies, adherents of the precision advocated by Thom facing cohorts of believers in more numerous but coarser lines like those surveyed and analysed by Ruggles (1981, 1984, 1999) and Ann Lynch (1982).

There are also non-combatants. Some archaeologists have preferred neutrality, even passive resistance, to the effort of understanding celestial mechanics and, being prejudiced against the concept of those phantoms of the imagination, astronomer-priests, have contentedly kept their feet – and their minds – on the ground.

But there has also been enjoyment. One of the greatest megalithic pleasures since 1976 has been the centuries-late printing in 1980 and 1982 of John Aubrey's *Monumenta Britannica, Parts 1, II and III*, assembled between 1665 and 1693, an incomparable compilation by that inquisitive antiquarian of notes, sketches and plans of ancient sites. The early eighteenth-century rejection by Oxford University of the Welsh scholar, philologist and archaeologist, Edward Lhuyd's field-notes, the greater part of which were later destroyed by fire, was a huge loss to megalithic studies (Hatchwell & Burl, 1998). Today one realises all the more the debt that prehistorians owe to the preservation of John Aubrey's records and how progress in archaeological thinking was retarded when his book's publication in 1693 was abandoned because of insufficient subscribers. The failure permitted the druidical derangements of William Stukeley (1740, 1743) to influence thinking about the past for almost two hundred years.

Scholars, Stuart Piggott, Anthony Powell, Michael Hunter and John Fowles amongst them, have commented on Aubrey's almost heretical insistence on the superiority of direct observation to the sterile tradition of relying on books. 'What uncertainty doe we find in printed Histories,' he wrote to his disloyal friend, Anthony Wood, in June 1680, 'they...for want of intelligence (things being antiquated) become too obscure and darke'.

He directed the way towards modern archaeological thinking by realising the need for fieldwork and comparative studies. When he 'was asked to write about Avebury and Stonehenge,' remarked Glyn Daniel, 'he begged to be allowed to defer his work until he had seen all the other comparable monuments in England and Wales'. Yet, as John Fowles wryly noted, 'until very recently [he] was generally regarded as little better than an amusing minor tattler'.

John Aubrey was Britain's first great archaeologist, recording antiquities, obtaining information from colleagues about unconsidered remains, brilliantly deducing the prehistoric origins of stone circles. With natural modesty he belittled his achievements. 'What did I do that was worthy, leading this kind of life? Truly nothing, only umbrages [shadows]'. Yet he did acknowledge the value of his work in preserving things overlooked or misunderstood or in the process of being destroyed. 'That which was neglected and quite forgotten and had sunk had not I engaged in the work.'

Which is the reason why this book, like its predecessor, is gratefully dedicated to his memory.

Acknowledgements

I am greatly indebted to many colleagues for information, for advice and for their encouragement in lectures, in the field and in countless public houses. In particular I must thank Tom Arnold, Val Bannister, John Barnatt, Stan Beckensall, Richard Bradley, Mark Brennand, Rodney Castleden, Margaret and Ron Curtis, Philip Deakin, Peter Donaldson, James Dyer, Alex Gibson, Andrew Lawson, Neil Mortimer, Leslie Myatt, Sean O'Nuallain, Oliver Padel, Richard Reiss, Graham Ritchie, Clive Ruggles, Alison Sheridan, Ian Shepherd, Derek Simpson, Cheryl Straffon, Jack Stevenson, Paul Walsh, John Waterhouse, and John Wray.

I must also congratulate, and marvel at, Philip Burton who so knowledgeably discovered the source of 'From Ushant to Scilly is thirty-five leagues' lurking anonymously in the *'Daily Express' Community Song Book* of 1927.

Especial thanks are offered to kindred researchers for the generosity of allowing me to use their personal studies of stone circles: Isabel Churcher for the rings around the Wicklows, Rosemary McConkey for her studies in Northern Ireland, and Andrew Tulloch for his thesis on the recumbent stone circle tradition in north-eastern Scotland.

Numerous institutions and their staff helped me with the provision of books, information, photocopies and offprints: Birmingham Reference Library; Corpus Christi College library, Cambridge; English Heritage; the Institute of Cornish Studies; the *Exmoor Review*; the National Monuments Record; the Ordnance Survey, Southampton; the Royal Society; the Society of Antiquaries of London Library; and the University of Birmingham Library. I also received two generous grants from the British Academy enabling me to undertake fieldwork in the Western Isles and in south-west Ireland.

What merits this book contains have also come from the guidance and expertise of colleagues at Yale University Press: the friendship and endurance of my editor, John Nicoll, and the strict attention and sensitivity of Kate Gallimore.

Finally, the greatest debt is, as always, to my wife, Judith, for her fortitude, forbearance, support, her skills as a navigator and note-taker, her insistence that we should complete the day's project and, simply, her company.

Time Chart

	Stone Circles	Egypt	Europe
BC			
4000 sites	**Neolithic Age**		Earliest Mesopotamian
			Brittany: Megalithic tombs
			Britain: Long barrows
	Early Stone Circles		
3500	Carrowmore		Height of Sumerian civilisation
			Brittany: cromlechs and
			Carnac rows
c. 3200	Castlerigg		
	Stenness		
3100	Stonehenge	Early Dynastic	
	earthwork		
3000	Rollright Stones		
	Stanton Drew		
			c. 2900 The Flood
	Callanish		c. 2800 Maltese temples
	Avebury inner rings		
		c. 2750 Beginnings of	
		Old Kingdom	
		2686 Saqqara stepped	
		pyramid	
	Avebury Outer Circle		
	Bronze Age		Britain: Round barrows
		2575 Giza pyramids	
		Cheops	
2500	**Middle Period Stone Circles**		Early Minoan civilisation
	Stonehenge sarsen		Troy II
	ring		
	Avebury Kennet Avenue		
	Machrie Moor		
2000		Middle Kingdom	Crete: Minoan temples
			Knossos
			Abraham leaves Ur
			1792, Babylon
			Hammurabi

1500	**Late Stone Circles**	Thebes, Luxor	*c.* 1500 Volcanic eruption on Thera
	Drombeg		Growth of Mycenae
	Lundin Farm	New Kingdom Valley of the Kings	
		Karnak hypostyle temple	
		Akhenaton	
		1347 Tutankhamun	
		c. 1235 Exodus, Moses	*c.* 1250 Trojan Wars
	Kealkil	Late Dynastic	Nebuchadnezzar, Babylon
			Israelites v Philistines
1200			David and Absalom
			Solomon's temple
	Abandonment of stone circles		Kingdom of Israel
			Iron Age Halstatt culture
			Etruscan civilisation, Italy
			776 First recorded Olympic Games
			753 Foundation of Rome
			c. 750 Homer born
	Iron Age		Britain: Hillforts

A Note on Dating

Until 1950 there was no accurate method of dating anything unless it was historically recorded in one of the classical civilisations. Since that year, however, radiocarbon analysis of organic material has provided a technique for assessing an object's age. Such Carbon-14 assays are always quoted with a deviation of ±, 1700 ± 50 bc suggesting that the organic object had a 2:1 probability of having died between 1650 and 1750 bc. Doubling the deviation raises the chances to 95.5 per cent. Because of fluctuations in the level of atmospheric radioactivity such determinations do not provide the exact dates once expected of them and by 4000 BC are over six hundred years too low. Such 'dates' can sometimes be tested against historical annals such as those from dynastic Egypt. For early prehistory there is no such assistance.

Since 1966 dendrochronology, the science of tree-ring dating, particularly from the long-lived Californian bristlecone-pines and ancient Irish bog-oaks, has largely overcome the problem. Tables have been devised in which the counted yearly growth-rings are calibrated against C-14 assays obtained from the same wood although reservations continue about the absolute accuracy of the method. In this book the table by Pearson et al. (1986) has been used. There 1700 ± 50 bc becomes c. 2150–2025 BC.

Determinations based on the C-14 process are followed by bc, real years by BC. The laboratory number is also quoted. A typical entry, from an antler at Stonehenge is 2431 ± 18 bc (UB-3788), c. 3030–3070 BC with a midpoint at 3050 BC.

The arcane, almost unintelligible foible of some archaeologists in citing an assay as '4640 ± 60 BP [Before Present year of AD 1950] uncal (GU-4379) calibrated to 3622–3111 BC cal (95.4% confidence, calibrated using OxCal 2.11)' has not been followed here despite its precision. Life is short and the length of a book is finite.

Astronomical dates from celestial events such as the calculable movements of stars are real and thus followed by BC. It is an archaeological misfortune that the positions of the sun and moon have changed so slowly along the horizon over time that their most northerly and southerly risings and settings have hardly moved over the millennia. A solar or lunar alignment, therefore, is of little value for dating an event.

Introduction

This Inquiry I must confesse is a gropeing in the Dark: but although I have not brought it into a cleer light; yet I can affirm, that I have brought it from an utter darkness to a thin mist.

John Aubrey, 1693, 25

To begin a book about stone circles by referring to Stonehenge is like starting a discussion on birds by describing the Dodo. Neither is a typical example of its class. Both are above average in size, of peculiar construction and both represent a dead-end in evolution. They are not representative. Yet Stonehenge was not unique. It had counterparts in Britain, their lintelled uprights enclosing circles many paces across. But these were timber rings and they have rotted into oblivion leaving their one stone imitation to endure and distort peoples' understanding so that, when asked what a stone circle was, it would be Stonehenge that came to mind together with druids and sacrifices, astronomy and astrology, midsummer sunrise, witchcraft, black magic, orgies, and stones with supernatural powers.

Always Stonehenge. Perhaps Avebury might be mentioned, maybe the Rollright Stones or Callanish, probably only the names of circles that happened to be in one's own part of the country.

But ignorance is not the same as indifference. Stone circles attract hundreds of visitors every year, so many that some sites are being unintentionally damaged as the ground is worn down by wandering feet. In 1978 the interior of Stonehenge was closed to the public. In Brittany the Carnac rows from Ménec to Kerlescan are barricaded against visitors by wire-netting and are now overgrown with head-high gorse. A quarter of Avebury was roped off for a season to protect the bank. Fortunately there are less-threatened rings.

On the Ordnance Survey maps are hundreds of 'stone circles', many of them spacious enough to fit around a house, the stones shoulder high, bleached, rutted and lichened by centuries of rain. Every year thousands of enthusiasts walk to these lonely rings hoping to understand what they were because the circles are the wordless memorials of prehistoric people who struggled to raise the ponderous stones for reasons that are only slowly being recovered. Stirred by the mystery of these silent places on the hillsides and moors men and women come to them, stare, puzzle, and often leave disappointed because there is nothing to explain the ring's age or purpose. Only emptiness. There are miles of tiring heather or easier grassland, treacherous peat-bog

Fig. 1. Stone Circles in Britain and Ireland.

or hillsides hindered by drystone walls, flickering butterflies, soaring and wheeling curlews, whinchats, and aggressive oyster-catchers. There is also silence.

At the circle there are, perhaps, a dozen stones, some upright or leaning, others fallen and three-quarters covered with turf and peat. Worn patches of ground show where sheep have grazed or cattle have rubbed against the rough pillars. Nothing else. There is nothing to say where the stones came from, how they were brought to the site, how heavy they are, how many people assembled here, at what time of year, for what purpose and for how long. In the local museum the persistent enquirer may discover a dull pot labelled with the name of the ring. Nothing else.

Near the circle may be a single standing stone or round barrows covering the burials of men and women who may have used the ring. On the skyline there is sometimes the silhouette of a ruined chambered tomb, its tumbled slabs jutting from the overgrown long mound like drowning fingers. Alongside there is sometimes an old cast-metal sign stating that the monument was raised in the New Stone Age around 2500 BC. Confusingly, such notices are rarely updated and '2500 BC' probably should read as an uncalibrated 3000 bc or an approximate chronologically correct 3750 BC.

Such information is seldom available on site and many visits to stone circles end in frustration. On Monday, 30 August 1773, Samuel Johnson irritably dismissed the encircled Clava cairn of Kinchyle of Dores near Inverness. 'To go and see one druidical temple,' he complained, 'is only to see that it is nothing, for there is neither art nor power in it; and seeing one is quite enough.' A few days earlier he had already reacted indifferently to another ring at Strichen considering some mature forest trees 'more worthy of notice'.[1] Pleasingly, ten years later the grumpy fellow did appreciate another ring, 'probably the most ancient work of man upon the Island. Salisbury Cathedral and its Neighbour, Stonehenge, are two eminent models of art and rudeness, and may show the first essay, and the last perfection in architecture'.[2] This was sensitive. There was an art in the planning of many rings whose builders skilfully incorporated delicate features in the design. Such finesse had a long ancestry.

In the centuries around 7500 BC when Britain and Ireland became separated from the European mainland prehistoric communities slowly changed from hunting and foraging to farming. Stock-breeding and rudimentary agriculture were being practised as early as 4500 BC by people of the New Stone Age or Neolithic who relied on flint and stone for their hardest, strongest, sharpest tools and who settled on the easily worked chalk uplands of southern and eastern Britain and north-eastern Ireland. Over decades, centuries, forests were cleared, the heaviest trees ring-barked and allowed to decay, others felled, the undergrowth burnt and raked away to create open stretches for grazing. Huge burial-places were constructed, long earthen barrows with wooden burial chambers in the lowlands, stone-chambered cairns in the west. Revealing their builders' belief in a connection between the sun, the moon and the dead nearly all these tombs faced somewhere between north-east and south-east, the rising places from summer to winter of those celestial bodies.

Human bones were taken to these ossuaries. In later centuries bones were abstracted for the ceremonies of the living. The skeletal remains show the people to have been short-lived by modern standards, the average age for men being about 30–35 years, for women, 25–30 years. Infant and child mortality was high. Early death was commonplace but the locations to which the ancestral bones were carried were extraordinary.

Plate 1. The fossilised ammonite on an entrance slab at Stoney Littleton, Gloucestershire (Photograph: the author).

Many of them, which over the centuries were transformed from tomb to temple, still survive. Chambers of timber long since rotted and collapsed, others of stone often tumbled but recognisable, some almost intact: passage-tombs such as Newgrange in Ireland with its ritualistically carved slabs; Maes Howe in the Orkneys; long mounds like West Kennet in Wiltshire or Stoney Littleton, Somerset (Pl. 1), with the giant impression of an ammonite in an entrance stone chosen perhaps for its mysticism. The sun, the land, river and tree, hill, rock, spirits, everything lived, was vital in this animistic age.

Late in the third millennium BC a widening knowledge of metallurgy in copper and bronze caused changes in technology and in society as privileged families acquired precious objects of rare materials including gold. It is in this Early Bronze Age from about 2200 BC, that archaeologists find rich possessions in the innovative round barrows – murderous bronze daggers, intricately strung necklaces of jet, amber and faience beads – the property of an élite.

During a thousand years of warmer, drier weather farming improved, field-systems took in ever larger areas, populations grew and spread onto higher, less congenial lands such as Dartmoor and the Yorkshire Moors, the settlers worked the thinner soils until, around 900 BC in the Late Bronze Age, a deteriorating climate forced the poorer, less productive uplands to be abandoned. Conflicts between the dispossessed and those in less troubled regions developed into the aggressions of the Iron Age in the first millennium BC when the class of priests and law givers known as the Druids first appeared.

It is in the period between the later Neolithic and the Late Bronze Age, from about 3300 to 900 BC, more than a hundred brief generations, people whose lives were no more than glitters of sunlight on a running stream, that stone circles were introduced, became popular, reached into farther, quieter parts, and were finally abandoned. It was a third of the way through those centuries before the monstrous squatly barred cage of Stonehenge was erected. The monument was still undergoing change over a thousand years later when many of the simpler rings had been deserted or had been wrecked by societies believing that they were no longer of use.

Until 1976 it was the misfortune of most megalithic rings that so much over-emphasis had been paid to Stonehenge, to its date, its anomalous architecture and the controversy over its problematical astronomical sightlines, that other rings were ignored. Even today in the majority of accounts about the prehistory of western Europe the rings are dismissed in a few pages, occasionally even in a few lines. Yet these other rings are much more informative about life in antiquity than Stonehenge.

It was years ago at the end of the Second World War that I first saw Stonehenge, walking in those traffic-free days from Amesbury along two empty miles, passing the Iron Age hillfort of Vespasian's Bank, not seeing a single car on the sunlit Sunday road. It was the only time that I have known Stonehenge deserted but in my inno-cence I was unaware of the luxury. I bought a ticket from a hut alongside the ring and strolled into the empty circle.

I remember staring at the incredible sarsen lintels of heavy sandstone and wonder-ing how it had been possible for people before the mechanical Romans to raise so many tons of stone so exactly, how the standing pillars, the height of three men, could have been erected. I had one slim guidebook, which told me that the sarsens had been lifted by megalith builders from the west who had mingled with vigorous incomers from the east known as Beaker Folk.

The book was sceptically up-to-date in its denial 'that Stonehenge was connected with the Druids and with human sacrifice' and it added one very perceptive observa-tion that 'Stonehenge may come to be regarded not as an isolated monument but rather as the climax of a long chain of stone circles.'[3] This was far-sighted. But the book hardly mentioned astronomy and had nothing at all to say about the function of this gigantic astonishment on Salisbury Plain.

How different fifty years later. Now, for the aficionado, there are full-length books about megalithic rings, research has been widespread, the number of recorded circles has increased from a speculative 200 forty years ago to almost 900 by 1976 and 1,300 today. More is being learned each year. Sadly, the progress has brought attendant problems.

By the 1960s Stonehenge was attracting so many visitors, most of whom did not arrive on foot but in cars, caravans and coaches, that a car park was laid out on the far side of the road. Then in 1968, fearful of accidents as people crossed the busy A344, the Department of the Environment commissioned the architectural horror of a sub-terranean tunnel like an unfinished fall-out shelter to provide access to the site.

Even this did not deter more and more feet, hundreds of thousands of them yearly, strolling around the stones. The chalky soil was eroded: gravel was spread. Then duck-boards. Neither worked. Finally, in 1978, Stonehenge was closed to the public and remains so. Now the sarsens have to be viewed from a roped barricade 70 yards from the circle. The small consolation is an improved shop where one can buy souvenirs, postcards and books. It is a privilege rarely accorded elsewhere.

At Avebury, 18 miles to the north, an enormous circle around two smaller rings inside a vast banked-and-ditched enclosure, there is a pleasant museum and an enterprisingly well-stocked shop selling books and leaflets about this famous circle-henge but after Stonehenge and Avebury there is little else. Thirty-eight miles farther north is one of the legendary rings of Britain, notorious as a meeting-place for witches, but despite this a general guidebook could offer only questions.

> As mysterious in their origin and purpose as Stonehenge, the Rollright Stones have stood on the boundary here [between Oxfordshire and Warwickshire] for thousands of years. Worn by wind and rain and mutilated by man they form two groups, with a solitary stone on a ridge over 700 feet [215 m] high which juts out from the Cotswolds. On this ridge was one of the oldest roads in England, relics of men of the Ages and Stone and Bronze having been found along its route . . . But why did they build this strange Circle. Was it a religious temple where Stone Age men worshipped, or was it a hilltop observatory from which men watched the sunrise and the stars in their courses, to plan the calendar and to ensure the growing their corn in due season? Perhaps, like Stonehenge, it was both.[4]

At the site there is no information. There used to be before vandals interfered. Now there are only the stones, hedged from the lane, shrivelled. Lambrick's excellent book[5] is out of print. A person might think that the stone circle was simply that, a weathered ring put up long ago for reasons lost to our knowledge and that going to one was what Samuel Johnson had said, a waste of time. This would be mistaken. Even the most unprepossessing, least promising site can reward.

On Sheet 84 of the 1:50,000 Ordnance Survey map is Easthill stone circle a few miles from Dumfries. Although conveniently near a lane a visit can be an anti-climax for the untutored. Beyond trees and then uphill for half a mile one comes to a tumble of small boulders in a wilderness of bracken. Some stones are displaced, one is missing. Few rings are less enticing. Yet Easthill has things to tell. Today there are eight blocks. In the mid-nineteenth century there were nine. But the local name for the site is the 'Seven Grey Stanes'. The cautious Victorian Ordnance surveyors reported, 'Druidical circle, supposed'.

Look carefully. There is an outcrop conveniently nearby on rising ground to the west and this was the probable source of the stones. Prehistoric communities seldom went far for their stones. Here none weighs more than half a ton and each could have been dragged and set in place by a dozen workers. Before this they may have cut a shelf into the hillside and piled up soil to create a level platform. The boulders are on a low but distinct flat-topped mound. A hollow at the south-east shows where Canon Atkinson dug fruitlessly a hundred years ago.

Nothing more methodical than simply pacing up and across the 'circle' will prove it to be an oval about twenty-three strides north–south by twenty-one, about 24.7 × 23.8 m, dimensions that are not integers of Thom's Megalithic Yard of 0.823 m. Nor is its perimeter of 76.1 m. The shape, however, indicates the social connections of Easthill.

Around Dumfries are other ellipses also arranged with long axes set towards cardinal points. In size they range from Whitcastles, 55 × 43 m to the enormous Twelve Apostles with an internal area of 5,400 m². It is seventeen times as big as Easthill, 317 m², whose own ring, though small, could comfortably have accommodated sixty people. Even excluding some because of age, sex or illness the number is more than enough to have built the ring.

There is more. An assiduous student would discover probable cupmarks on the eastern block, three of them in a straight line, 25 cm long, perhaps fashioned there to be in line with the equinoctial sunrise. Alexander Thom suggested that the planners had chosen the location so that the midsummer sun would rise over a prominent brae to the north-east and set in a dip to the north-west.[6]

Fallen, disturbed, half-hidden, wordless, yet Easthill contains its own record, offering information about its shape, size, source of stones, its number of workers, its population, its coarse but likely sightlines and the ritualistic beliefs of its builders. Visitors to empty and ruinous circles should not despair.

Not unexpectedly, however, with monuments so old, raised by people without writing, yielding only discarded fragments of antiquity, carrying little decipherable art, many questions survive, many perhaps insoluble. Scientific techniques will help. So will statistical analyses. But ultimately the sharpest insights come from those who, like John Aubrey, think of archaeology as a humanity rather than a pure science, remembering in the words of Sir Mortimer Wheeler, that archaeologists dig up 'not *things* but *people*'. To see the stones as artefacts rather than the handiwork of human beings is to depersonalise the study.

It was claimed that 'Archaeology *per se* is no more than a method and a set of specialised techniques for the gathering of cultural information. The archaeologist as archaeologist is really nothing but a technician'. 'Do you believe that?' asked Wheeler. 'I don't'.[7]

Archaeologists who have accepted themselves as no more than technicians have quite rightly been criticised.

> Ever since the time of Stukeley archaeologists, ever more concerned with the accumulation of factual detail, and less with the wider significance of the sites they investigate, have distracted attention from the possibility of an alternative approach to the problems of the past. Excavation can only test existing theories; and scientists, suspicious of the means by which they are reached, often fail to appreciate the views of poets and visionaries.[8]

This may be so but it must be added that such visionaries, welcome though they are, too often complacently ignore those factual details when constructing their own preferred models of the past. Undisciplined fancy can never be acceptable as a substitute for logic based on fact. Any evaluation of stone circles must begin with the tedious but unavoidable accumulation of data susceptible to physical proof. Selection is not permissible. Omission is impermissible. Distortion is unforgivable. Any hypothetical model of prehistory has to be founded on this premiss. But a qualification is demanded. A model of the past, even imperfect, is positive and far preferable to archaeological pessimism. 'What was the significance of these great stone monuments [circles], and why were they sited where they were? Although self-styled experts on the meaning of stone circles abound, in fact, no-one knows'.[9]

The comment is amazingly misguided. Whoever the abundant 'self-styled experts' may be questions about the situation of stone circles can certainly be answered. And much else has been learned about the rings. In particular, the past twenty years has seen much discovery and explanation.

When *The Stone Circles of the British Isles* was published in 1976 its aim was to state the problems of the rings. Until the publication of that book there had never been a comprehensive survey. It not only provided that but was accompanied by a detailed set of references, bibliography and gazetteer. It was a novelty. Although three centuries had passed since John Aubrey's fieldwork at Avebury and almost 250 years since William Stukeley made his plans and wrote his description of Stonehenge stone circles remained enigmas. Chambered tombs, hillforts, barrows long and round, henges, causewayed enclosures and settlements had been catalogued and classified but megalithic rings existed in anonymity. They were infamous for their lack of finds and while their bleak emptiness deterred the archaeologist the same vacuum attracted the fantast to whom the rings offered an escapist paradise that could not be marred by the presence of facts.

In his poem *Jerusalem* William Blake wrote of 'stony Druid temples' in which men 'reared mighty stones, danced naked around them' but there is no need to look back to the early nineteenth century for reveries of what stone circles might have been. Gullibility is ever-present. So are the credulities of castles in the air without foundation.

In 1976 several books of this nature were quoted. Since then there has been further phantasmagoria such as the claim that at Avebury the Great Goddess was so fanatically adored that her adherents landscaped her image – arms, body, legs and more intimate areas – by laying out '27 Neolithic long barrows and circles arranged over 60 square miles' to delimit the outline of a 'vast goddess figure'. Avebury itself was strategically placed at a very sensitive part of her anatomy. The fact, awkward as always because of C-14 assays, that the landscaping took over a thousand years to complete disconcerted no wishful thinker and very few literary critics.[10]

Ten years later another book was awarded a WABY, 'The Worst Archaeological Book of the Year' by Glyn Daniel, editor of *Antiquity*. It claimed that trying to establish at which latitude in Britain the risings and settings of the sun and moon occurred at right-angles to each other prehistoric surveyors laid out a precise east–west line of circles and standing stones between an experimental observatory on the Preseli mountains of south-west Wales and the Rollright Stones in Oxfordshire.

Discovering that Rollright was both too far north and east the planners recalculated, decided that Salisbury Plain was better and built Stonehenge there.[11] The inconvenient facts that the line did not lie east–west, was not straight, was a far-fetched 140+ miles long, and that even the latitude of Stonehenge was inaccurate apparently upset only archaeologists 'concerned with the accumulation of factual detail'.

The author of another book speculated that at the midsummer sunrise Stonehenge's outlying Heel Stone cast a long shadow onto the Altar Stone at the centre of the ring. This 'phenomenon', astronomically and anatomically incorrect, was interpreted as the long phallus of the Sky God penetrating the womb of the fecund Goddess, Stonehenge, thereby fertilising the earth for another year.[12] The theory was misconceived, based on a fallacy.

Such frivolities are butterflies, attractive but of little weight and short-lived. The mélange is irreconcilable with objective studies and most archaeologists have been reluctant to stray into the lush and lunatic pastures at the edges of their own well-tilled fields. Until recently stone circles were the centres of an unchallenged escapist world.

Attitudes are changing. Megalithic rings can be defined as approximate circles of spaced standing stones. In Britain, Ireland and Brittany they were erected between the Late Neolithic and the final years of the Middle Bronze Age, from the end of the fourth millennium BC to that of the second. They can stand alone but local variations may have banks, ditches, internal or outlying stones, avenues, single long or short rows.

The kerbstones of cairns and barrows do not qualify as stone circles even when they are exceptionally tall and spaced apart but detached rings of pillars standing well outside chambered tombs such as Newgrange in Ireland, the Clava cairns in Scotland and Kercado in Brittany are accepted.

Over 1,300 rings are recorded, some in good condition, many more ruinous or listed as sites at which the existence of a former circle is well attested. They are distributed in highland regions with concentrations in north-eastern and central Scotland, in the Lake District and the south-peninsula, and in northern and south-western Ireland. There are lesser groupings in Caithness, the Outer Hebrides, the Peak District, the Wicklow Mountains and in Wales and Wessex.

They are very rare on islands and where they do occur their architecture is usually strongly affected by the conservatism of island communities. Haltadans on Shetland or the Meayll Hill 'circle' on the Isle of Man are more like the exposed kerbs and cists of megalithic tombs than free-standing stone circles.

The number of 1,300 is arbitrary for it is impossible to establish how many have been removed and forgotten. The spread of farming into marginal lands in the late eighteenth and early nineteenth centuries AD with tenants usually being allotted the poorer soils encouraged the burying, blasting or dragging away of the obstructive stones. Fortunately superstition sometimes preserved a few stones.

At Fortingall in Perthshire three neighbouring rings were toppled into pits in accidental conjunction with a century-old beer bottle. In each case three stones were left standing like a Christian trinity.

It is said that when a farmer wrecked the nuisance of Auchleven circle in Aberdeenshire his herd of cattle was instantly devastated by disease and he was ruined. There are many similar stories and a lot of monuments were saved because of rustic fears of supernatural recriminations. A mediaeval barber was crushed by a vengeful stone at Avebury. And John Aubrey reported that 'One Daniel Healy of Donaghmore in Ireland, having three different times dreamed that money lay concealed under a large stone in a field near where he lived, procured some workmen to assist him in removing it, and when they had dug as far as the foundation, it fell suddenly and killed Healy on the spot'.[13]

A farmer at Auchterhouse in Forfar was more prudent. Even though his scared labourers refused to help he obstinately took away some circle-stones for field-walls. Then a menacing ghost materialised at his shoulder. Virtue replaced vandalism. He replaced the stones.

His was a happier fate than that of a tenant in the lonely hills of Wigtownshire whose devastation of a ring resulted in a series of disasters. Needing lintels for some doors he plundered the Laggangarn ellipse in which two stones had been Christianised by the carving of crosses on them. Desecration was followed by retribution. He was bitten by a mad dog. With agonising rabies and raving in a hydrophobic fever he begged his sister-in-law to kill him and she smothered him between two chaff-stuffed mattresses. Next year she slipped on ice, broke her arm badly and died of infection. As the chronicler of this dismal tale admonished, 'Let all greedy builders take warning.'[14]

Storms have been helpful in protecting antiquities. The 'excavation' of a barrow at Beedon, Berkshire, in 1850 was interrupted by a cloudburst. When the Wiltshire antiquarians, Sir Richard Colt Hoare and William Cunnington began the digging of a Dorset barrow thunder drove them into their trench but 'the lightning flashed upon our spades and iron instruments, and the large flints poured down upon us from the summit of the barrow so abundantly and so forcibly that we were obliged to quit our hiding-place, and abide the pelting of the pitiless storm upon the bleak and unsheltered down'.

Foul weather just as bad accompanied the digging of the Lamlash stone circle on Arran. Even more dramatically the eighteenth-century owner of the Long Meg and Her Daughters circle near Penrith, Lt-Colonel Samuel Lacy, decided to blow up the ring.

> Whilst the work was being proceeded with under his orders, the slumbering powers of Druidism rose in arms against this violation of their sanctuary; and such a storm of thunder and lightning, and such heavy rain and hail ensued, as the Fell-sides never before witnessed. The labourers fled for their lives, vowing never to meddle with Long Meg... All lovers of antiquity must be thankful for the providential throwing of cold water on so wicked a design.[15]

But economics often overcame fear. At Annaside, Cumberland, of a circle of twelve stones standing in 1803 only one pillar remains today. Carbalintober, Co. Londonderry, was destroyed in 1833. Grey Croft, Cumberland, was thrown down and buried in 1820. Even awareness that such antiquities were important was not always enough to save them.

> In a western parish of Cornwall, some labourers were employed in enclosing waste land, when they came across a stone circle, and suspecting it to be akin to others popularly held in veneration, they hesitated to destroy it, and appealed for advice to a mine captain, who decided if noticed in Borlase it should be preserved. The doctor's *Antiquities* being referred to, and no mention of the circle found, it was at once cleared away.[16]

Even the indignation of landowners at the ignorance of their tenants was not always effective. In the 1830s, at Strichen, Aberdeenshire, the circle to which Samuel Johnson had been so indifferent sixty years earlier, was pulled down. Mr Fraser, later Lord Lovat, ordered it replaced. It was. Wrongly. The circle-stones were reset to the south of the recumbent instead of to its north, a transposition suiting the tenant but one that would have been impiety to the ring's appalled builders who had aligned it exactly on the southern moonrise.

The now-spurious site was further demeaned by being transformed into a tea-garden for a sanatorium and hotel. Even worse followed. The abused ring was uprooted in 1965 with no preliminary excavation. Encouragingly, at the request of the people of Strichen the site was carefully dug and restored by the writer and colleagues between 1979 and 1982.[17]

Disappointingly, despite today's awareness of the need for conservation and the increasing wish to safeguard the past, destruction of circles continues. Ignorance may excuse the uprooting of Pabell Llynwarch Pen near Bala around 1750 but not the demolition of Lissard and Kilboultreagh, both in Co. Cork, between 1963 and 1970; Lohart, Co. Kerry was wrongly restored around 1964; Wester Torme, Perthshire, was removed in 1980. Two Peak District rings were vandalised in the late 1980s. The Nine Ladies on Stanton Moor there is under threat from quarrying.

There have been many justifications for modern interference with ancient monuments, 'justification' often being a euphemism for Expediency hiding behind Progress.

Plate 2. A vandalised stone at Mitchell's Fold, Shropshire (Photograph: the author).

The stone circle at Moncreiffe near Perth was moved and re-erected to make room for the M90 motorway. The little ring of Pen y Beacon in the Black Mountains is partly overlain by a car park. Cairnwell in Kincardineshire was threatened with demolition by the need for industrial development. The henge at Goldington in Bedfordshire is buried under a Tesco supermarket. 'Progress' can mean a change for the better; it can also mean a displaced boulder tumbling downhill.

Simple vandalism, perhaps alcoholic, led to many stones of the Beaghmore complex in Co. Tyrone to be pushed over. As recently as 1994 the two biggest stones at Mitchell's Fold in Shropshire (Pl. 2) were bulldozed just as senselessly. Their re-erection cost over £10,000. In the 1960s limestone pillars were dragged onto the lane, fires were lit and property burned down at the Rollright Stones in Oxfordshire.

Even good intentions caused damage. 'Save the Ponys' was painted on Stonehenge, saying more for the compassion than the education of the culprit. Arcane idiocy resulted in cabalistic icons being daubed on Avebury. A misguided sense of mission impelled 'born-again' Christians to depaganise the Merry Maidens by attempting to take away one of the stones in the hope of sterilising the heathen temple. New Age delusions of the power of imaginary fertility rites at the time of the Spring equinox resulted in eight stones being added to the original six at the Doll Tor stone circle in the Peak District, the illegal 'restoration' hacking and wrecking kerbstones and destroying almost the entire east cairn.

Until three hundred years ago these relics of a distant age were safeguarded by indifference, fear and superstition. In 1723 Stukeley grieved at the wanton smashing of Avebury's gigantic slabs. 'And this stupendous fabric,' he mourned, 'which for some thousands of years, had brav'd the continual assaults of weather, and by the nature of it, when left to itself, like the pyramids of Egypt, would have lasted as long as the globe, [has] fallen a sacrifice to the wretched ignorance and avarice of a little village unluckily plac'd within it'.

It is regrettable that our growing understanding not only of their significance but, worse, of their whereabouts has encouraged a bevy of bigots, busybodies and bulldozers to despoil them. It is of little consolation to realise that it has not only been in historical times that rings were affected. Conflicts between prehistoric groups caused damage. During the Bronze Age Berrybrae, a recumbent stone circle in Aberdeenshire, had its stones thrown down and broken and its inner ring-cairn dismantled. Followers of a different creed converted the site into an enclosed cremation cemetery.

A megalithic ellipse at Bryn Celli Ddu, Anglesey, had a passage-tomb built on top of it. Nature also intruded. Cavancarragh, Co. Fermanagh, and Machrie Moor XI, Arran, became engulfed by peat and there will be others still concealed in the bogs that developed during the Iron Age. At Er-Lannic in southern Brittany a third of a megalithic horseshoe and the entirety of a similar fer à cheval alongside it are submerged in the Gulf of Morbihan whose waters have risen some 9 m since Roman times.[18]

Adding uncertainty to the original number of stone circles are imitations such as the bardic rings for Welsh *eisteddfods* like that in the grounds of Plas Newydd, Llangollen put up in 1908. Other modern 'stone circles' can be seen at the megalithic centre in St Merryn, Cornwall, or, complete with centre stone, behind the Two Bridges hotel, Dartmoor. A tidily gravelled recumbent stone circle with internal boulder-burial was constructed in 1988 at Ferrycarrig near Wexford (Pl. 3).

There are also follies. In the decades between 1770 and 1830, the Age of Romance, having a personal 'druidical temple' became a foible amongst wealthy landowners who read macabre gothick novels, such as *The Monk* (1776), *Frankenstein* (1818) and *Melmoth the Wanderer* (1820), in the evocatively gloomy atmosphere of their own shrines and grottoes.[19] Such follies include the early nineteenth-century Druids' Temple near Ilton in Yorkshire, oddly claimed to represent Stonehenge to which it has no likeness. It was, perhaps, a fanciful version of a Neolithic temple in Malta. At Auldgirth, Dumfries, around 1827 a ring was erected by a friend, later enemy, of Robert Burns. On the outskirts of West Rhin, Denbighshire, is a latterday, overgrown Stonehenge, built about 1830 for Major West who could gaze upon it from Quinta House across the valley.

Of all the imitations the most venal and vulgar was the do-it-yourself Stonehenge advertised by William Burrough Hill in 1914.

STONEHENGE. What could be more beautiful, majestic, entrancing and educational than a full-size replica on a lawn of a garden of a few acres? Model A, 1/10 full size may be obtained for 50 gns; Model B, half full size for 250 gns; and Model C, full-size for 500 gns. All prices include crating, packing and plan for fixing.[20]

There is no record of anyone, even someone with a few acres of garden, accepting the offer.

As well as these copies are the sites that never were. Occasionally and by accident a natural litter of stones formed a circle. At Summerhouse Hill near Carnforth in Lancashire a tor collapsed leaving a clutter of stones from which the smaller were removed for the building of a summerhouse on the hilltop. The remaining blocks chanced to create the south-western arc of a vast but irregular stone circle 140 m in diameter, the largest of all rings after Avebury's Outer Ring, and one and a half times

Plate 3. A 'new' stone circle at Ferrycarrig, Co. Wexford (Photograph: Sean O'Nuallain).

more spacious than the gigantic central circle at Stanton Drew, Somerset. Two further blocks farther away were thought to be outliers.[21] Nature not man was responsible.

In the nineteenth century the ruinous kerbstones of chambered tombs were often confused with true circles. Tountinna in the Ara Mountains of Co. Tipperary was mistakenly described as 'a fine stone circle which still bears the name of "The Graves of the Leinster Men" '. Similarly, the Keentagh 'stone circle' near Portaferry in Co. Down is actually a Neolithic burial-mound with decorated kerbstones. In Wigtownshire the Wren's Egg was thought to be a vast but wrecked concentric circle with a central pillar whereas, in reality, it is a glacial boulder with a pair of dumpy stones just to its east.

Because of these problems even to put a notional figure to the number of stone circles once existing is an impossibility. Well over a thousand are known to have existed, the earliest yet known date in Britain coming from the Lochmaben Stane in Dumfriesshire, 2525 ± 85 bc (GU-1591), the latest from Sandy Road, Perth, 1200 ± 150 bc (GaK-787), 790 ± 80 bc (OxA-2683) from Drombeg in Co. Cork and 715 ± 50 bc (GrN-9172) from the Five-Stone ring of Cashelkeelty in Co. Kerry. In calibrated years such a time-span would spread from about 3300 to 900 BC, a period of 2,400 years. This must be considered the longest period over which megalithic rings were set up.

If it is assumed that for every known ring two have been lost there would once have been about 4,000 circles. If it is also assumed that two-thirds were erected during the major phase of building between 3000 and 1300 BC then 2,600 rings were created over 1,700 years, fewer than two circles annually. It is probable that in some centuries there was more rapid growth but there would have been a correspondingly slower development at other times. If there has to be a social model for the development of a stone circle cult it is of the gradual dissemination of ideas amongst societies more accustomed to tradition than innovation.

Yet slow though the growth may have been it was both compelling and enduring. One has only to consider the 18 miles transportation of 50-ton sarsens to Stonehenge to realise how imperative it must have been that such projects were undertaken. At Rudston in Yorkshire Britain's tallest standing stone is a 24-ton monster that would have taken a hundred workers to set up. It had been pulled 10 miles from Cayton Bay to stand at the junction of several cursuses.

Even in historic times rings continued in use. Royal courts were held in some because of their status as traditional meeting places. In 1349 there was a judicial assembly at the recumbent stone circle of Old Rayne in Aberdeenshire. In 1379 the son of Robert II had a court at the standing stones of Kingussie. English and Scottish commissioners met at the Lochmaben Stane in 1398.

Nor did the belief in the powers of stone circles die with the advent of Christianity. Council after holy Council condemned the continuing veneration of stones and demanded their destruction. In AD 658 the Council of Nantes stated, 'As in remote places and in woodlands there stand certain stones which the people often worship, and at which vows are made, and to which oblations are offered – we decree that they all be cast down and concealed.' As late as AD 1560 the Synod of Argyll had a stone circle on Iona destroyed because the islanders worshipped there.[22]

Some rings became the centre of 'the old religion' practised by covens. In 1662 Isobel Gowdie at her trial said that she went to the circle and chambered tomb of Auldearn near Nairn. In 1949 a coven was seen inside the Rollright Stones. The huge block by the Backhill of Drachlaw ring is known as the hag's or witch's pillar.

Such blasphemous stones were so outrageous that a fanatical Breton priest, Jacques Cotteux of Louisfert near Châteaubriant, swore to eradicate the indecent heathen practices by the demolition of every megalith in his parish. Capstones and slabs from dolmens, cists, dozens of menhirs were dragged to the village by his flock to construct the depaganised base of a platform on which holy statues, crosses and plaques proclaimed the triumph of Christianity.

Débris d'un culte sanguinaire	Wreckage of a bloodthirsty cult

De vieux rochers, gisaient épars
    au fond des champs,
	Whose ancient stones lay scattered
	    in the fields,

Nos bras avec amour ont fait
    ce calvaire,
	Our faithful arms have made this
	    calvary,

Oeuvre de Bretons bons croyants.[23]	The work of God-fearing Bretons.

But at Carnac in the Morbihan heathen customs persisted into the last centuries when barren wives went to the great rows of stone whose gift of fertility were attested by generations of mothers. In Finistère betrothed couples would strip at midnight and rub bellies on the protruding bosses of the gigantic Kerloas menhir.

Fecundity, power, protection, such associations and the myths of petrifaction, dancing and musicians, may all contain warped memories of what stone circles were and how they were used.

Chapter One

Early Work on Stone Circles

I know that some will nauseate these old Fables: but I doe profess to regard them as the most considerable pieces of Antiquity, I collect: and that they are to be registred for Posterity, to let them understand the Encroachment of Ignorance on Mankind: and to learne what strange Absurdities Man can by Custome and education be brought to believe.

John Aubrey, 1693, 66

There was little systematic investigation of stone circles until recently. A brief account of research since Tudor times is provided here. Readers interested in more detail should refer to Daniel, 1967; Piggott, 1976, 1989; and Hayman, 1997.[1]

In his *History of the Kings of Britain, c.* 1136, Geoffrey of Monmouth wrote that Merlin moved the Giants' Ring from Mount Killaraus in Ireland to Salisbury Plain where it became known as Stonehenge, and he seems to have confused Avebury with Amesbury which he called Mount Ambrius. Superficially it seems remarkable that he should have claimed the stones to be Irish when some of them did indeed come from a source on the Ireland–Wessex copper-route[2] but in this he was not referring to the small Welsh bluestones but to the great granite pillars near Naas in Ireland, which had been seen by clerics on their way to Kildare Abbey who thought them to be the remains of a circle built by giants and robbed by Merlin to create Stonehenge.[3]

Mediaeval references to prehistoric sites are rare and observations on stone circles were factual: judicial courts were held there or a farmer's land lay near one, and although there was a fourteenth-century reference to the Rollright Stones in Oxfordshire it was only to declare that nothing was known about the ring or its builders.[4] Interference with the stones was unusual, speculation about them even rarer so that although the Church regarded them with suspicion scholars looked on them not at all. Attitudes changed only slowly.

'This monumente seemeth to importe an intention of the memoriall of some matter done in this kinde of exercise, thowgh time haue worne out the maner.' John Norden's comment about the Hurlers stone circles on Bodmin Moor in 1584 reflected the ignorance of past centuries and it was only towards the end of Elizabeth I's reign that visitations and itineraries were being written that would make people more aware of their antiquities. Even so, Norden's work did include novelties such as a sketch of a now-destroyed circle called 'The Nine Sisters' on St Breocks Down.

William Camden published his *Britannia* in 1586 and its first English edition, *Britain*, appeared in 1610. John Speed's *Fifty-four Maps of England & Wales* came out between 1608 and 1610. Sir William Dugdale wrote *The Antiquities of Warwickshire* in 1656, and visited many other parts of the country. Edward Lhuyd, 1660–1709, Welsh antiquarian and philologist, went to stone circles in Wales, Scotland and Ireland and contributed descriptions of them like that of the Druids' Circle near Penmaenmawr to the 1697 edition of *Britannia*. It was from such scholars as well as his own travels that John Aubrey, compiled invaluable notes in his *Monumenta Britannica*.[5]

This increase in curiosity about the ancient remains of the countryside provided the seedbed not only for Aubrey's researches but for less well-known contemporaries like James Garden, Rector of Aberdeen University, who, although he had seen several recumbent stone circles such as Auchquhorthies and Cothiemuir Wood could find nothing 'either in the names of these monuments or the tradition that goes about them, which doth particularly relate to the Druids'. Aubrey himself was realistic about the methods and values of contemporary antiquarians. 'It is said of Antiquaries, they wipe off the mouldinesse they digge and remove the rubbish' but he was hopeful that his own insight was useful 'that these monuments were Pagan Temples, which was not made-out before'.[6]

John Toland, 1670–1722, Irish free-thinker and enquirer into Celtic matters, discussed the question of stone circles with Aubrey and wrote that the latter was 'the only person I ever met who had the right notion of the Temples of the Druids, or indeed any notion that the Circles so often mention'd were such Temples at all', but it was he himself who was most responsible for the myth of an association between stone circles and druids in his *History of the Druids*, 1726. 'I pass to the certainty I have concerning the TEMPLES OF THE DRUIDS, whereof so many are yet intire in those Ilands, as well as in Wales and Ireland; with some left in England'.[7]

The early eighteenth century was an era of neoclassicism and developing science. Into an atmosphere of reason in which Dr Johnson could kick a stone to prove its philosophical existence came a reactionary passion for unspoiled wilderness and the unknown, romantic past. There were Grand Tours to the Continent and lesser tours on which people visited Wales and Scotland instead of merely reading about them. And as more and more stone circles became known it was apparent that they could satisfy all sorts of needs from the scientifically astronomical to the gothic demand for mystery and sacrifice. Satisfying every taste the Druids could be projected as primitive but pure theologians or, more excitingly, as barbarous and bloodstained necromancers.

From Martin Martin's *A Description of the Western Islands of Scotland*, 1703, of which Samuel Johnson stated 'no man writes so ill', Toland read that Stenness and Brodgar in the Orkneys were believed by the natives to be places of pagan idolatry with the sun worshipped in Brodgar, the moon in Stenness whose stones stood in a lunar arc. Toland wishfully deduced the same astronomical content for Callanish in the Outer Hebrides. 'I can prove it to have been dedicated principally to the Sun; but subordinately to the Seasons and the Elements'.[8]

When one adds John Smith's theory in 1771 that the Heel Stone at Stonehenge was aligned on the midsummer sunrise it is clear that William Stukeley, 1687–1765, with his certainty that the Druids were the founders and architects of stone circles and his realisation that the major axis of Stonehenge was aligned to 'the north-east, where abouts the sun rises, when the days are longest . . . being the point where the sun rises, or nearly, at the summer solstice' was the forerunner of today's believers in astronomer-priests.[9] Of Stukeley's work it is sufficient to observe that he, despite his

Plate 4. One of the earliest drawings, 1575, of Stonehenge.

obsession with proto-Christian Druids, more than anyone before him, except for John Aubrey, placed stone circles in a prehistoric context. Others were more vague in their dating:

> I will not forget these stone that are set
> In a round, on Salisbury Plaines,
> Though who brought 'em there, 'tis hard to declare,
> The Romans, or Merlin, or Danes.
>
> Walter Pope, 1676

In 1866 T. G. Bonney confirmed the existence of such chronological confusion in the popular mind. 'In England, everything of unknown origin is instinctively assigned to one of four – Julius Caesar, King Arthur, the Druids or the Devil', adding that Stonehenge (Pl. 4) had variously been considered the handiwork of Boadicea, the Phoenicians as well as 'the later Britons, the Saxons or the Danes'. Inigo Jones had argued that the circles were Roman; Walter Charleton that they were Danish; and Georg Keysler that they were not Druidical but Anglo-Saxon monuments akin to those in his native Holstein.[10]

In contrast to these misconceptions Stukeley (Pl. 5) did insist that Stonehenge and Avebury were simply aggrandised versions of many lesser rings. Unfortunately he later lost his objectivity and became preoccupied with the equally illusory visions of landscaped snake-like avenues of standing stones, suns and moons at Stanton Drew, and Druids.

In the nineteenth century with a gradually increasing appreciation of the distant past those Iron Age lawgivers and bards slowly faded from the circles but little progress was made elsewhere. A dire combination of enthusiasm and curiosity resulted in many destructive diggings in the centres of rings, often unrecorded, which achieved no more than redeposited chaos for later excavators.

Then, after the middle of the century, there was an outbreak of proper fieldwork from newly formed local archaeological societies. During a golden period of some thirty years between 1880 and 1910 circles were visited, measured, planned and recorded all over Britain and Ireland though most investigators looked only within their own county boundaries. Areas were catalogued: Cornwall by A. L. Lewis and by

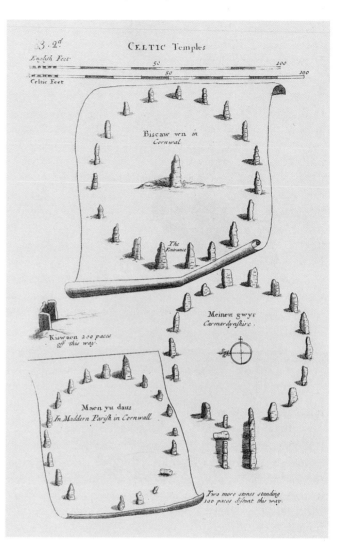

Plate 5. Sketches of stone circles by William Stukeley.

Lukis and Borlase; Cumberland by J. C. Ward and by C. W. Dymond; Derbyshire by J. Ward, by A. L. Lewis and by W. J. Andrew; a multitude of rings in north-east and central Scotland were examined by F. R. Coles while the charming rings of south-western Ireland were plotted by J. P. Condon. There were many other short reports of small groups and single sites.

The late nineteenth century had seen the second great stage of stone circle study but even that period of thirty years was not without its problems. Every epoch has yielded weirdly wonderful ideas. Deciding that the severe plainness of stone circles was only a gaunt vestige of their original form Christian Maclagan anticipated Vayson de Pradenne by over sixty years. In 1937 that ingenious French archaeologist suggested that Stonehenge had once had a roof of timbers. Maclagan's delusion of 1875 was that megalithic rings were the collapsed and vandalised remnants of brochs, those tall defensive stone towers from Scotland of the second and third centuries AD and 'had most probably constituted an important part of the uncemented structure of the dwellings or strongholds of our living ancestors'. A. L. Lewis was quite unconvinced.

'Mr. Maclagan's book appears to have been published at considerable expense to support a view of which he probably has a monopoly, namely that all stone circles are the last remains of circular buildings of unmortared masonry of the *broch* type.'[11]

In the same decades advocates of an astronomical function for megalithic rings attracted the public's awareness. From 1883 onwards the same A. L. Lewis, a devotee of stone circles, produced many papers emphasising the importance of examining alignments and considering the relationship between sites and the hills that surrounded them. In 1906 Sir Norman Lockyer, director of the Solar Physics Laboratory, published his *Stonehenge and Other British Stone Monuments Astronomically Considered* in which he suggested that prehistoric societies had established a solar calendar in which May sunrise had been celebrated as an important time of the year. The publication of a star chronology by P. V. Neugebauer in 1929 enabled students to establish within a year exactly when bright stars had risen in particular areas of the horizon. As an example, in 2500 BC halfway up Britain at the latitude of 55° where Newcastle and Dumfries lie Sirius, *α Canis Majoris*, would have risen at the southeast, 128°, whereas in the same year Capella, *α Aurigae*, rose at the north-east, 33°. The Pole Star, *α Polaris*, was a full 20° from True North at that time.

Investigators such as Somerville in Ireland continued careful research into archaeoastronomy but much peripheral work by surveyors was casual and of little value although its impact upon the popular mind was great. One of its few opponents was Allcroft whose two books in 1927 attempted to prove that circles were not observatories. 'The modern belief that Druidism included astronomy or astrology, or both, is a growth of the last two centuries or so.'[12] Instead, stone circles were moot–or meeting–places of the early British period.

Perhaps the scholarly archaeological climate of the 1930s was not conducive to travels across such troubled waters or post-Druidical skies and except for flickers in local journals stone circles faded as a subject for study. The dubiety of the claims put forward for their more esoteric uses caused them to be banished to the archaeological doldrums already occupied by Atlantis, Druids and ley-lines.

Scholars preferred to remain on the accepted and safe foundations of their discipline rather than venture onto the astronomical quicksands into which stone circles seemed to be sinking. 'So much time and ingenuity has been spent on this matter in the past that it deserves some attention here if only to demonstrate the inadequacy of the arguments upon which it is based,' wrote Atkinson of the connection between Stonehenge's Heel Stone and the midsummer sunrise. Equally dismissive but with considerably more hostility Engleheart ridiculed the notion that alignments might have been built into megalithic monuments. 'Calendar orientation . . . as predicated in any sense of round barrows or stone circles – has no sounder basis in objective fact or logic than had the Druidical, Dracontian, Phallic and other obsolete imaginings.'[13]

The period after 1945 was the time of the third progress. After the field-surveys of the beginning of the century, which themselves were augmented by the work of the Ordnance Survey and the Royal Commission for Ancient and Historic Monuments, more attention was paid to the questions of the age of the circles and, more tentatively, of their function. Few conclusions were reached although the introduction of radiocarbon dating from 1950 onwards promised a firmer chronology than had previously been available through typological models of pottery and artefactual sequences. One of the first 'dates' came from an Aubrey Hole at Stonehenge, 1848 ± 275 bc

(C-602) signifying that there was a 2:1 chance that the charcoal had come from an object that had died between 2123 and 1573 bc. Such an enormous span of time rendered the result almost useless. Modern techniques would reduce the deviation to as little as ±40 bc. But it was the beginning of a scientific method that is now indispensable in the study of ancient material.

By 1960 it was clear that variations in the amount of Carbon-14 in the atmosphere were causing errors in radiocarbon 'dates' that were incompatible with those reliably known from historically recorded objects. The problem was solved through dendrochronology, the science of tree-ring dating, which permitted calibration tables to be created whereby a determination from Stonehenge of 2425 ± 19 bc (UB-3787) was converted to the more accurate bracket of 3085–2920 BC.[14]

In the same decade two books caused archaeological disruption. *Stonehenge Decoded*, 1966, by Gerald Hawkins claimed that there were not only astronomical sightlines built into the monument but that the fifty-six Aubrey Holes around the circle could have been used as instruments for the prediction of lunar eclipses. The fact that the author had deduced these propositions through the use of the novelty of a Harvard-Smithsonian IBM 704 computer persuaded many readers that his theories must be indisputable.

Even more startling were the ideas put forward in *Megalithic Sites in Britain*, 1967, by Alexander Thom, a retired professor of engineering, whose lengthy studies of megalithic settings convinced him that the builders of stone circles and rows of standing stones had employed a national unit of measurement, a 'Megalithic Yard' of 0.829 m; had used Pythagorean principles in the layout of ellipses and other non-circular shapes; and had an erudite comprehension of the movements of the sun and moon. Initially these excitingly revolutionary concepts were accepted but were later subjected to several critical analyses by mathematicians and astronomers who finally expressed doubts about their validity.[15] Although now generally rejected as being over-precise Thom's ideas should be welcomed. They stimulated thinking about yardsticks, shapes of rings and archaeoastronomy that had never properly been considered by archaeologists.

'Every age has the Stonehenge it deserves – or desires' wrote Jacquetta Hawkes and this may explain the technological over-emphasis sometimes attributed to the purpose of stone circles as astronomical observatories and which too often has been based on inadequate or insubstantial data. Such honest but wishful thinking is essentially little different from the Druidical fantasies of previous centuries.

The greatest difficulty in understanding what stone circles were for is in understanding the people who raised them. If Late Neolithic and Bronze Age societies in western Europe were no more than groups of dispersed peasant-holdings, of skilful farmers knowledgeable about sources of stone and flint, gathering together in the autumn for seasonal ceremonies and festivities then circles need be no more than rings used for communal rites, each region being doctrinally separate from the others. What is understood today of the settlements, equipment and social relationships of the time does not contradict this aboriginal interpretation.

Conversely, Britain has been seen as socially coherent, dominated by an intellectual élite of astronomer-priests whose influence extended to north and south, from the Shetlands to Brittany, even into the farthest, isolated valley. What environmental evidence there is points to an age of peaceful existence and drier weather, a time when arcane study of the movements of the sun and moon might have continued without interruption, uninterrupted centuries when the most complex celestial motions were assiduously perceived and used for foretelling even minor perturbations of the moon. During this postulated age religious activities that in the beginning had been simple and communal became more complex, organised in a stratified society of warrior-chiefs and concomitant priests.

If the proposition of a nationally used Megalithic Yard is accepted the idea of a unified Britain must also be accepted. Such a concept does not sit comfortably with the regional variations in the architecture of chambered tombs and of stone circles. Adding to the uncertainty is the entire absence of written records, even of recognisable art that might have provided some indication of the nature and behaviour of rituals such as those seen in the rock carvings of Scandinavia. In western Europe if astronomical lore was recorded the equipment has perished. It may have been memorised much as the Druids of the Iron Age are said to have remembered the thousands of bardic verses of their laws, needing, according to Julius Caesar, some twenty years to assimilate them. Such a length of years may have been a Roman misunderstanding of the 18.6 years of the lunar cycle. Pliny recorded a Druidical rite of gathering mistletoe on the sixth day of the moon, adding that the moon was regarded as a powerful healer. But the physical evidence, if ever it existed, has gone.[16]

Perhaps the monuments are their own record, containing in their stones the measurements, the geometrical designs, the remains of ceremonies, the astronomical orientations whose rediscovery will recreate the regulated activities that once took place in the rings. Equally possible is the suggestion that such 'science' is a modern reaction from Victorian images of Druidical disembowellings on blood-trickling slaughter stones throughout the land.

Only the stones remain to reveal the tenuous truths of what stone circles were. Undecorated, worn by weather, fallen and overgrown, pillars dragged away, these inadequate relics are all that survive for investigators today. Their existence is their reality. There is nothing else.

As John Aubrey wrote: 'These Antiquities are so exceeding old, that no Bookes doe reach them, so that there is no way to retrive them but by comparative antiquities, which I have writt upon the spott, from the Monuments themselves.' 'My head was alwaies working: never idle, and even travelling (which from 1649 till 1670 was never off horseback) did glean some observations.'[17]

Chapter Two

The Origins of Stone Circles

The Romans had no Dominion in Ireland or (at least not far) in Scotland, therefore these Temples are not to be supposed to be built by them: nor had the Danes Dominion in Wales . . . But all these Monuments are of the same fashion, and antique rudenesse: wherfore I Conclude, that they were Works erected by the Britons: and were Temples of the Druids.

John Aubrey, 1693, 129

Introduction

Seven kilometres (4½ miles) west of Tréguier on the north coast of Brittany the massive cairn of Tossen-Keler was excavated in 1963–4. Three-quarters of its circumference was surrounded by a U-shaped kerb of ponderous granite blocks; $33 \times 25\,\text{m}$, a typical Breton *fer-à-cheval* cromlech or horseshoe of stones of which there are only a few in Britain.

It was a Late Neolithic enclosure with a primary date of 2550 ± 250 bc (GiF-280), about 3600–3000 BC. It was also multi-phase. The cairn had been a final addition. The horseshoe preceded it. Three of its fifty-eight blocks bore carvings of chevrons, an axe and a domed 'anthropomorph', motifs perhaps symbolising a weapon-bearing protectress of the dead, art 'bien connu dans les dolmens à couloir du Morbihan'.[1] They had been taken from an abandoned, maybe destroyed chambered tomb. As with other early stone circles in Britain, Ireland and Brittany an open-air enclosure had been erected in succession to an enclosed burial-place at a time when communities were recovering from a long period of disturbance and when new beliefs were supplanting those that had failed. Open-air rings of the sky replaced tombs of darkness and the earth. Such an interconnection between a spacious ring and death is the leitmotif of the debate concerning the origins of stone circles.

Tenuous roots can be distinguished centuries earlier in the orientations of long burial-mounds, in the unroofed assembly-places known as causewayed enclosures, and in the addition of uncovered concave forecourts to chambered tombs. A stone circle was not a sudden innovation. It was like Topsy. It 'just growed'.

Neolithic Burial Mounds and their Alignments

More than a thousand years before the first megalithic ring families of Neolithic farmers had settled on the rich, virgin soils of western Europe. They lived in a self-sufficient existence that only over many generations developed into cohesive societies. Families supported themselves, building their own homes, making their own

Plate 6. Winterbourne Stoke earthen long barrow, Wiltshire. It is aligned NNE towards the most northerly moonrise. (Photograph: the author).

axes and tools of stone and flint, shaping their own hand-coiled pots, their own clothes of soft skins. In isolated farmsteads, separated from their neighbours, each family had its own land-holding. These were short-lived people but they were vigorous and enterprising, converting forest wildernesses into open countryside. They constructed their own family burial-places, wooden cells under long earthen mounds in the lowlands, stone-built chambered tombs on the bouldered hillsides of the west.

Much has been written about the changing burial practices in these tombs, how from the first family vaults with a single cell for men, women and children they developed into clan mausolea with multiple chambers from which skulls and longbones were abstracted for rites of the living, how, finally, some barrows became the sepulchres of one chosen male, these matters have been discussed at length.[2] What has rarely been considered in detail is why the majority of these long mounds were directed towards the eastern half of the horizon.

'The occurrence of orientation in prehistoric structures has long been noticed. It has not, however, received from investigators more than a passing comment such as "the barrow is directed to the eastward" or "the entrance to the chamber faces the north-west" '.[3] Yet the question is of direct relevance to one of the facets of stone circle studies.

The orientation of an earthen long barrow (Pl. 6) was clearly an important consideration to its builders. In southern England 84 per cent of the mounds point somewhere between north-east and south-east with the western hemisphere almost entirely avoided. On Salisbury Plain 90 per cent were aligned between north-east and SSE. With a statistically acceptable base of over a hundred sites the unavoidable conclusion must be that there was an association between death and the east in the minds of Neolithic people. Comparable lunar and solar alignments determined the laying-out of tombs in western Europe.

Predictably, in times of slow travel when territories were separated by miles of unpopulated countryside there were distinct regional differences in the preferred part of the skyline that was looked towards. Bearings of megalithic tombs demonstrate this. Often there is a major concentration of lines bunched tightly together with a looser band directed towards a second arc. Among the Clyde tombs thirty sites faced between 18° and 84°, about 2° apart, where eleven lay between 90° and 124° with an average spacing of 3° (Table 1).

There were some exceptions to the easterly direction. The Clava passage-tombs of north-east Scotland faced between SSE and south-west and their related ring-cairns had a more restricted range from ssw to south-west. The wedge-tombs of western and south-west Ireland had entrances looking between south-west and west. There are reasons for believing that both groups were late in the megalithic tradition but their unorthodoxy does not invalidate the observation that there were chosen directions which have to be explained.

The Carrowkeel passage-tombs of north-western Ireland were aligned in a narrow NW–NNW band, which appears to have been imposed by the situation of the conspicuous Maeve's Cairn on the high summit of Knocknarea mountain miles away to the NNW.[4] Hills considered sacred may also have been the target but such limited points of the horizon do not explain the broad sweeps of the skyline contained in Table 1. An astronomical cause is probable.

Except for the sun stars can be rejected. Neolithic tombs remained in fashion for some 1,500 years from about 5000 to 3500 BC. Although stars do not have unchanging rising and setting positions but move steadily along the horizon year by year not one bright star had a range that corresponded to any of the arcs contained in Table 1. None swung even as far as the short 45° between the ENE and ESE of the Camster cairns. The relatively rapid Capella, α Aurigae, shifted no more than 22° from NNE to ENE over the fifteen centuries. The dazzling Sirius, α Canis Majoris, dawdled only 7° and Deneb, α Cygni, a mere 4° (Table 2).

In contrast the midsummer sun rose each year at the north-east and six months later rose at the midwinter south-east exactly covering the band shown by several of the megalithic enclaves (Table 3). The moon did the same but over a wider arc each lunar month of the year. If the people who raised a long barrow or a stone-slabbed chamber had any celestial interest it was to create a solar or lunar alignment.

The Neolithic was never static. Its social structure, its trading systems, its burial-practices were always modifying, but life was consistent. The family group was its basis, a stone economy its background, and a cult of ancestors its spiritual strength. In funerary rites the sun and moon were essentials. Over the decades everything became more complex but the frameworks of existence remained.

Table 1. Regional Azimuths of Chambered Tombs in Britain, Ireland and Brittany.

Type of Tomb	Region	Preferred Arc	
		Major	Minor
Allées-couvertes	Brittany	E–SSE	NE
Avebury region	Wiltshire	NE–E	SE–SSE
Severn-Cotswold	Wessex	ENE–SE	NE
Clyde-Solway cairns	SW Scotland	NNE–ENE	E–ESE
Wedge-tombs	SW and W Ireland	SW–WNW	NW
Single-court cairns	N Ireland	NNE–SE	W–NNW
Stalled cairns	Orkneys	ESE–S	NE
Passage-tombs			
Dolmens à couloir	Brittany	E–SSE	NE
Loughcrew	Co. Sligo	ESE	ENE
Clava	Inverness-shire	SSW	SSE–SW
Camster	Northern Scotland	ENE–ESE	NE, SE
Maes Howe type	Orkney mainland	E-S-W	NW

STAR	2500 BC	2000 BC	1500 BC	1000 BC
Alderbaran	−2.25	1.03	3.15	5.68
Altair	8.5	7.36	6.51	5.95
Antares	−6.71	−9.51	−12.24	−14.87
Arcturus	45.73	42.76	39.72	36.64
Betelgeuse	−5.06	−2.7	−0.53	1.43
Canopus	−55.43	−54.48	−53.81	−53.37
Capella	28.69	31.41	34.04	36.53
Deneb	36.27	36.49	36.92	37.55
Pleiades	2.4	5.22	8.02	10.77
Polaris	65.05	67.57	70.16	72.81
Pollux	24.67	26.41	27.86	28.98
Procyon	4.55	5.84	6.86	7.57
Rigil	−23.18	−20.71	−18.4	−16.26
Rigil K	−19.03	−16.24	−13.42	−10.63
Sirius	20.85	19.4	18.17	17.19
Spica	12.89	10.52	8	5.35
Vega	42.67	41.44	40.41	39.57

Table 2. Declinations of Bright Stars, 2500 to 1000 BC.

Causewayed Enclosures; Open-air Assembly-places

Early in the fourth millennium BC spacious ditched-and-banked earthworks were thrown up at the edges of settled land in southern England. By prehistoric standards theirs was a brief fashion. Flourishing in 3800 BC nearly all had been abandoned by 3200 BC. These causewayed enclosures, many on rounded hilltops, were a lowland phenomenon from Devon to East Anglia, perhaps even Yorkshire, but with no counterparts on the highlands to the north-west. There were no megalithic equivalents.[5]

The enclosures were most numerous along the Thames Valley westwards to Crickley Hill on the heights overlooking present-day Gloucester. Quite regularly spaced about five miles apart their purpose is contentious, a medley of possibilities: camp, market, cattle kraal, occasional settlement and centres for seasonal festivals, even cemeteries.

Table 3. Times of Sunrise and Sunset in southern, central and northern Britain.

Latitude	Region	Midsummer		Equinoxes		Midwinter	
		21 June		21 March and September		21 December	
		Rise	Set	Rise	Set	Rise	Set
50°	Land's End	51°	309°	90°	270°	129°	231°
55°	SW Scotland	45°	315°	90°	270°	135°	225°
60°	Shetlands	35°	325°	90°	270°	145°	215°

The title is to blame. A term like 'causewayed enclosure' is a desperation by archaeologists trying to make today's words categorise sites that may be similar in appearance but possibly dissimilar in purpose.

A 'causewayed enclosure' was an irregular circle bounded by up to four concentric rings of banks and ditches and covering anything from 3 to 24 acres (1.2–9.7 ha). Some were enlarged, others unchanged. In the ditches of some were a litter of animal bones, flint chippings, excrement covered with soil to reduce the stench, broken sherds. At other sites the ditches held burials of children and tidied collections of human bones as though from corpses exposed to rot inside the earthwork, 'a vast reeking open cemetery, its silence broken only by the din of crows and ravens' at Hambledon Hill in Dorset.[6]

Against the necropolitical chance of all the enclosures being hallowed burial-grounds are scraps of opposing evidence. Autumn gatherings are likely from the presence of hazel nuts at Windmill Hill, Wiltshire, crab apples at Hembury in Devon, and evidence of the culling of young cattle. The presence of non-local objects such as oolitic limestone and Cornish pottery in the chalk landscape of Wessex shows that people from distant parts came together for feasting rather than funerals. The cut meat bones, domestic equipment, flint tools for skinning and dressing carcases all suggest occupation even if only periodical. There are sexual carvings, chalk phalli, 'cups' that may be representations of vulvae, rounded balls like testicles, indications of rituals of magic and fertility, forerunners of practices inside some stone circles.

Many enclosures are so enormous that one must imagine both people and herds inside them. The sites clustering along the 80 miles of the central Thames average about 150 m in diameter, enclosing 18 acres (7.3 ha) of shallow hillside. Such camps were almost ten times bigger than the single-entranced henges that succeeded them. Causewayed enclosures are sometimes seen as the precursors of henges but the two distributions do not overlap neatly and occasionally do not coincide at all. If there was a connection it may have been that of an all-purpose causewayed enclosure from which only the elements of ritual were continued in the low-lying, smaller and more formally designed henge. The terms are to blame.

Some archaeological nomenclature has been unpoetic. The now-forgotten 'parallelithon' does not evoke any image of a Dartmoor double row of standing stones. Other verbiage was pretentious: 'Proto-archaeologue' was an absurd alternative to 'antiquarian'. 'Causewayed enclosure' and 'henge' stand for nothing more than a constructional technique. 'Brick building' is a modern equivalent.[7]

The most economical interpretation of the Neolithic causewayed enclosure is that its basic function was to act as a seasonal assembly-place for scattered communities coming from miles away for feasting, sub-tribal pacts, slaughtering of over-numerous livestock; a temporary shanty town whose high banks kept cattle from straying but which, centuries later, were sometimes converted into defensive ramparts. In the long years of the Early and Middle Neolithic it was an enclosure reflecting the complexities of an expanding social, political and commercial world.

Chambered Tombs and Unroofed Forecourts

In some regions of megalithic tombs a transformation developed, which retained some connection with tradition but which was also a forerunner of the true stone circle. Crescentic forecourts (Pl. 7), some as deep as semicircles, were features of later

Plate 7. The deep crescentic forecourt of the Creggandevesky court-cairn, Co. Tyrone (Photograph: the author).

Clyde tombs in south-western Scotland and of the court-cairns of northern Ireland. On occasion enlarged façades were added to existing tombs. The hemispherical fore-court of Browndod in Co. Antrim is grossly skewed anti-clockwise from the NW–SE axis of the four long chambers as though awkwardly appended to the cairn. At Malin Mor, an over-restored cairn in Co. Donegal, the almost total incurving of the façade was imaginatively and evocatively described as 'lobster-clawed', the tips of the claws leaving only a narrow entrance to a fully enclosed but unroofed courtyard. Such inno-vatory, spacious forecourts permitted more people to join in the rites. What had been undertaken by a few in the dimness of a claustrophobic chamber could now be shared by a community in the light of the open air.

The court-cairn of Ballymacdermot near Newry in Co. Armagh exemplifies the tran-sition. Erected on land cleared by fire and looking southwards towards an undulation of mountains the forecourt dominates the monument. Its eleven head-high, grey-mot-tled spaced stones form more than half a circle 6 m across. The addition of a few more pillars and removal of the eroded and squashed cairn would produce a free-standing megalithic ring. Assays of 2880 ± 95 bc (UB-694), 2765 ± 190 bc (UB-698) and 2345 ± 90 bc (UB-695), centring on *c.* 3500 BC, suggest that this was a site late in the history of court-cairns, the very time that the court was taking precedence over the cairn.[8]

Such outstanding forecourts are known to be ultimate developments in the typology of chambered tombs. In south-west Scotland 'it would seem innately likely that the earliest cairns – representing early settlement – would be associated with land below 150 ft [46 m], and that cairns built at greater heights and probably on soils less easy to till would for the most part mark penetration of the hinterland'. It was those final tombs-cum-courtyard enclosures that were given the roomy and airy forecourts 'culminating in a monument like Carn Ban in Arran, situated at a height of 900 ft [274 m] some six miles from the sea'.[9]

At Carn Ban, wearily reached up a long, coniferous hillside, the difference between the size of the chamber, $9.7\,m^2$, and the area of the semi-circular forecourt, $38.7\,m^2$ is instructive. It allowed four times as many participants to congregate inside the megalithic horseshoe of heavy blocks outside the tomb. An isolated stone beyond the façade's south-eastern terminal may have been one of an intended complete circle attached to the front of the cairn. Such a development did occur in northern Ireland.

There, from Co. Antrim in the east to Co. Mayo in the far west, almost 400 court-cairns are known. Their forecourts range from slight crescents to half-circles and ultimately develop into courts that are completely enclosed. The tomb's chambers lay at the far end of these roofless ovals. It is significant that all thirty-six of these 'full' court-cairns occur only in the west in areas where there are very few stone circles proper.[10] It is as though the presence of open-air courts intimately connected to a megalithic tomb inhibited the introduction of free-standing circles of stone.

Whether in Ireland or Scotland the area of the court, however shallow, always exceeded that of the chamber. Ratios of 4:1 at Carn Ban and at Creevykeel, Co. Sligo; of 5:1 at Blasthill on the Kintyre peninsula; 6:1 at Ballymacdermot, at Ballymacaldrack, 'Doey's Cairn', Co. Antrim, Clontygora, Co. Armagh, and Creggandevesky, Co. Tyrone; 9:1 at Browndod, Co. Antrim, East Bennan, Arran and Mid Gleniron I, Wigtownshire; these are exceeded by the overwhelming 17:1 at Tormore on Arran.

That ceremonies were held in these novel enclosures is indisputable. The full court of Behy, Co. Mayo, had been paved with cobbles amongst which lay sherds, a stone axe and flints. A rectangle of paving was discovered at Clontygora, 'the King's Ring', whose excavation in 1937 'progressed favourably despite political incidents in the immediate neighbourhood'. Black soil and hollows testified to activities at Ballymacdermot. A 'curious arrangement' of a 'lump of quartz in a semi-circle of small stones' was found in the forecourt of Mid Gleniron.

In front of the Browndod cairn was a broken standing stone near which were pits and scattered sherds, an assemblage like that at Cairnholy I on a Kirkcudbright hilltop (Pl. 8). There, facing the gently concave façade, was an area in which five hearths of oak and hazel had burned. 'A sixth fire, large and immediately opposite the entrance

Plate 8. The shallow crescentic forecourt of Cairnholy I, Galloway (Photograph: the author).

to the chamber, was made after a standing stone . . . had been bodily removed. By the hearth nearest to the north portal an offering was made involving the deposition of broken fragments of a pot.'

The rituals in these forecourts were akin to those enacted in earlier centuries inside the tombs, linking them with the past. 'It is tempting to think of the human bones at Ormiegill [Caithness] as part of a removed burial, and to regard the sherds at three Clyde tombs in the same way'.[11] Although out of the darkness and into the light, now for many participants rather than some, the customs of long generations had not been discarded. Then there was change.

The 'Dark Age' of the Late Neolithic

Towards the end of the fourth millennium BC there were decades, perhaps centuries, when a deterioration in established ways of life resulted in a loss of faith. Traditional customs were set aside.

A steep decline in the number of radiocarbon dates between 2500 bc and 2300 bc, about 3200 to 2900 BC in real years, mark a time of crisis.[12] Pollen from previously cultivated areas show scrub and weeds spreading across deserted fields. Forests regenerated. Chambered tombs were blocked up and abandoned. A series of assays from court-cairns record the blocking of their forecourts with rubble: 2445 ± 55 bc (UB-241) from Annaghmare, Co. Armagh; 2680 ± 130 bc (UB-2045) Ballymacaldrack; 2170 ± 300 bc (D-48), Ballyutoag, Co. Antrim; 2625 ± 50 bc (UB-2114), Tully, Co. Fermanagh. A determination of 2240 ± 110 bc (Q-676) from the Clyde tomb of Monamore, Arran, is of same general period around 3300 BC. Only at Ballymacdermot, noticeably far south of the main group in Ireland, are there later dates: 1710 ± 60 bc (UB-207) and 1565 ± 85 bc (UB-705).

Former causewayed enclosures were converted into defended villages with heavy gateways and walls. They were attacked. At Carn Brea in Cornwall, Hambledon Hill in Dorset, Crickley Hill in Gloucestershire burnt-down entrances and savage masses of flint arrowheads are evidence of bitter conflict.[13] Explanations for the troubles have been many. Overuse of land, failure of crops, famine, plague, an expanding population that became too large for the supply of food. Or a more insidious agent, a worsening of the weather.

Measurements of the width of annual growth rings in ancient Irish oaks show a sudden contraction around 3190 BC caused by colder, wetter weather. At the same time, around 3250 ± 80 BC in Greenland, there is evidence of acid rain from volcanic eruptions in Iceland that created dismally miasmic clouds, almost eliminating sunlight. The growth of pines was restricted in Scotland. With water-logged, poorly drained soils the effects for farmers were disastrous and widespread.

In western Ireland blankets of peat smothered the walled fields of Beldberg Beg in Co. Mayo. The consequences for uncomprehending, unprepared societies were appalling. 'We have to envisage the possibility of failed harvests, famine – and no doubt plague and pestilence as well . . . vast tracts of land rendered uninhabitable. In such circumstances the survivors would have been those who were more warlike than their neighbours.' Similar eruptions in the 1620s and 1150s BC may have been equally disruptive.[14]

That such tragedies were seen as warnings from the angry forces of nature and that they led to changes in society is not an over-dramatic hypothesis. There are historical parallels. In January, AD 1362 a five-day-long hurricane uprooted great oaks, demolished houses and wrecked towns in southern England. The gale was accepted as divine punishment for the 'pure synne' of mankind who 'shulde doe the bettre'. In AD 1600 the eruption of the Huaynaputina volcano in Peru cast 'a shroud of dust around the planet'.

In even more recent times 1783 was an uneventful year for achievements, memorable only for the first manned flight in a balloon, the invention of the Montgolfier brothers. But in the summer of that year the Laki volcano erupted ravaging Iceland, destroying cattle, killing a quarter of the population. Across Europe the effects were dreadful.

There were clouds of ash, the stench of sulphurous gases, fogs so murky that the sun could not be seen, violent thunderstorms. Panic and despair followed. The poet, William Cowper, wrote that 'some declare that the Sun neither rises nor sets where it did, and assert with great confidence that the Day of Judgment is at hand', and 'so long in a country not subject to fogs, we have been cover'd with one of the thickest I remember'.

On 12 July the *Ipswich Journal* described the weather: 'There was an uncommon gloom in the air. The dews were very profuse. The Sun was scarce visible, even at mid-day, and then entirely shorn of its beams so as to be viewed with the naked eye without pain.' In Leicester men stared at the 'awful appearance of lightning . . . exhibiting a wonderful spectacle of dreadful magnificence; before eleven o'clock the whole firmament appeared on fire . . . this scene of inconceivable horror continued for nearly an hour'. There was flooding, twenty-four people died, more were badly injured, and there were fires and damage to houses.

Not only northern Europe suffered. The fog was just as thick and hot in Italy and even the summits of the Alps were covered by it. In Naples it was so bad that boatmen could see nothing and dared not leave land without a compass to guide them.

Farmers were ruined. Barley and oats turned brown, rye was mildewed, trees shed leaves, vegetables were shrivelled as though burned by fire and beans became pallid and wrinkled. The ensuing fear and discontent of an ignorant peasantry is considered to have contributed to the onset of the French Revolution. There were other results. 'The weather also had a deep cultural and literary influence. It marked the birth of ghost stories, Gothic novels . . . which owed their atmospheres of terror to the darkness, fog and storms' in them.[15]

If these were the effects that the eruption had upon ordinary people only two centuries ago at a time when scientists such as Benjamin Franklin could explain what had happened how much more frightful must have been the reactions of prehistoric groups, incapable of understanding the calamity, existing in a fragilely capricious spirit-world, knowing only that their once-assured means of communicating with that world had failed.

Comparable climatic catastrophes have been attributed to the impact of comets like the one that exploded over Tunguska in central Siberia in June 1908, devastating over a thousand square miles of forest and tundra. The detonation was heard over six hundred miles away and the force was estimated to have been as powerful as a two megaton atomic bomb.

Similar collisions are suspected in prehistory, one in the centuries around 2300 BC, another about 1200 BC when a dramatic decline in temperature, constant pouring rain, flooding and earth tremors may have led to historic disruptions in Mycenaean Greece, in the new kingdoms of Egypt, Bronze Age Israel, affecting civilisations as far away as the Shang dynasty of China. It may also have resulted in the belief that stone circles were no longer effective intermediaries against natural disasters.[16]

It is unlikely, however, that even many years of cold and rain would have affected Neolithic societies so drastically and lastingly unless life had not already been precariously poised between stability and collapse, the worsening climate exacerbating a discordance that had begun centuries earlier in the mid-fourth millennium. Whatever the answer, as life slowly returned to balance it returned with innovations, new pottery styles, new cults, and the new assembly-places of Late Neolithic open-air henges and stone circles. Old cults waned. Chambered tombs were abandoned because the powers of ancestors had been unable to resist when the spirits of the skies had threatened. People turned to those powerful skies. Unroofed enclosures were constructed.

Coves: Links between Tombs and Circles

In the long transitional period of a Dark Age between the closing of chambered tombs and the introduction of stone circles one structure may have formed a psychological bridge. Known as a cove it was a megalithic chamber without a covering mound, a funerary monument composed of a backstone and two sideslabs but no capstone.[17]

Until the early eighteenth century AD three gigantic sarsen blocks stood inside Avebury like a clumsily built and roofless porch. Stukeley called it 'an immense work . . . which the old *Britons* call a cove'. Despite his improbable ability to communicate with the Neolithic dead it was an apposite choice of name to describe the cell-like structure.[18]

Excavations of coves at Avebury (Pl. 9) and at Beckhampton nearby, at Stanton Drew in Somerset, Arbor Low in the Peak District, at Cairnpapple near Edinburgh and at Stenness in the Orkneys produced no C-14 material or anything dateable and the chronology of coves must be inferential, based on the close resemblance of these rare, unusual monuments to the chambers of megalithic tombs. It is noticeable that 'classical' three-sided coves were erected in areas such as Wessex where tombs had simple, rectangular cells.

About a dozen coves are known, upstanding, three-sided, unroofed and open in one direction, usually the east. There is one inside the Standing Stones of Stenness circle in the Orkneys, another inside Cairnpapple circle-henge, an architectural variation inside Arbor Low circle-henge, two at Avebury, another at Stanton Drew and a possible cove inside the northern horseshoe of Er-Lannic North in Brittany. It is unproven because it is submerged in the Gulf of Morbihan.

Another probably existed near the circle-henge of Meini-gwyr in Dyfed, a site known as Yr Allor, 'the altar', which Stukeley drew as a cove. Today two stones still stand, the taller flat-topped, its companion pointed. A third lies nearby in a ditch. The adjacent stone circle offers support for the belief that Yr Allor had also been a cove, especially as tombs close by at Parc y Llyn and Garn Turne, although ruined, have box-like chambers, the latter also having a funnelled forecourt. Yr Allor is likely to have been a genuine cove.

The experienced Welsh antiquarian, Edward Lhuyd, whose notes Stukeley transcribed, referred to the stones as 'a Kist vaen to y^e N.E. [of Meini-gwyr] abt. 2 Arrows flight distant'. In Camden's *Britannia* he elaborated. 'Three other, large, rude stones, which I therefore note particularly because there are also four or five stones erected at

Plate 9. The two remaining sarsen slabs of the Cove inside Avebury (Photograph: the author).

such a distance from the circular Monument they call *King's stones* near *Little Rolrich* in Oxfordshire.' This comparison with the Whispering Knights portal dolmen near the Rollright Stones adds credence to the suggestion that Yr Allor was a cove.[19]

Two observations can be made about these intermediary and transitory structures. First, no cove is known among groups of passage-tombs with circular chambers such as the Clava cairns of north-eastern Scotland. Coves exist only where there were earlier rectangular chambers in megalithic tombs. The similarity of coves to them is strong making it feasible that coves were imitations of those disused cells. Secondly, they are invariably associated with a stone circle.

There were two basic forms. The Avebury type, consisting of three vertical slabs like a roofless sentry-box, was popular in areas of tombs with a single, sub-rectangular chamber. The Stenness cove was different and the difference itself augments the argument that coves were the inventions of people who now preferred open-air monuments but who wished to maintain rituals previously enacted inside a tomb.

The Stenness cove consists of two front slabs standing in line close together with a third slab set centrally a little behind the narrow gap between them. In plan it resembled the outline of a matador's wide-brimmed, flat-topped hat without its sides. It was identical to the projecting sideslabs and backstone of the chambers in the Unstan stalled cairn a mile to the west of Stenness.

There was a Yorkshire version of these facsimiles near the cliffs at Whitby. Not far from a long cairn whose prominent façade had projecting corners like the fender of a grate archaeologists found a setting so perplexing that it was jovially but frustratedly called a 'Wossit', short for 'what is it?'

Of sturdy oak posts it was sub-rectangular, about 8.5 × 9 m, open to the north-east.

Likened to 'the palisaded forecourt of the Street House neolithic cairn' only 460 m away, in appearance it was 'a cross between the courtyard of a Neolithic tomb and a henge monument'. As with other coves it reproduced the architecture of a burial-place but was uncovered and lacked burials.

The excavator asked, 'Does the Wossit represent the development of ritual traditions which involved the dislocation of elements of ritual from the deposition of funerary remains during the Early Bronze Age?' Dates of 1790 ± 60 bc (BM-2566) and 1750 ± 50 bc (BM-2567), c. 2300–2100 BC, make it later than coves but the motives of its builders seem much the same.[20]

It is arguable that coves were settings raised in conspicuous positions at a time intermediate between the abandonment of megalithic tombs and the erection of stone circles. Later they were incorporated into them. All were associated with some of the largest megalithic rings in western Europe: Stanton Drew, Avebury, Er-Lannic, Arbor Low, Cairnpapple, Stenness. The average interior of these spacious enclosures was some 2,400 m^2, well over nine times the average ring's 260 m^2.[21] Given the likelihood that the bigger the area the more the number of people who used it it is arguable that coves were put up in regions of dense population and were, for a short time, important ritual centres in their own right.

Another version of these reductions of chambered tomb architecture to its most elementary may have resulted in the prostrate block flanked by a pair of tall pillars in the recumbent stone circles of north-east Scotland. This economical three-stone embodiment of the supine slab in front of the two high entrance jambs of passage-tombs such as Newgrange and Knowth may later have been elaborated by being incorporated in a ring of standing stones much as the coves of southern England were modified by the addition of a stone circle.

The Emergence of Henges, Stone Circles and Rings of Posts

In regions where there were no tombs and no ancestors to venerate the building of megalithic rings came early. In the closing centuries of the fourth millennium BC the custom of raising large free-standing enclosures: earth-banked henges in the populated lowlands of easily worked soils, rings of closely set stones as imitations of henges in the harsher west, began and became widespread (Fig. 2).

As with chambered tombs and earthen long barrows there were clear-cut distinctions amongst the design of henges from locality to locality. In the south of Britain the earth or chalk of their ditch was used to heap up an outer bank. In the north-east of England two shallower ditches were preferred with one heavy bank between them. In Ireland, around the Boyne Valley, henges had no ditch. Instead, for material for the bank, the interior of the henge was scooped out around its edge leaving a convex arena like an upturned saucer.

The blueprint for the three divisions was broad but blurred. No two henges were identical. There were minor mutations from place to place so that in southern England with its norm of a single inner ditch and outer bank Stonehenge, always the maverick, had an internal bank, outer ditch and, still visible today, a low outer bank composed of turves stripped off the ground at the beginning of the project.[22] Stone circles were just as variable.

There was no sudden outburst in the building of these assembly-places. Nor was it uniformly spread. Radiocarbon assays from early henges show this. There is a long

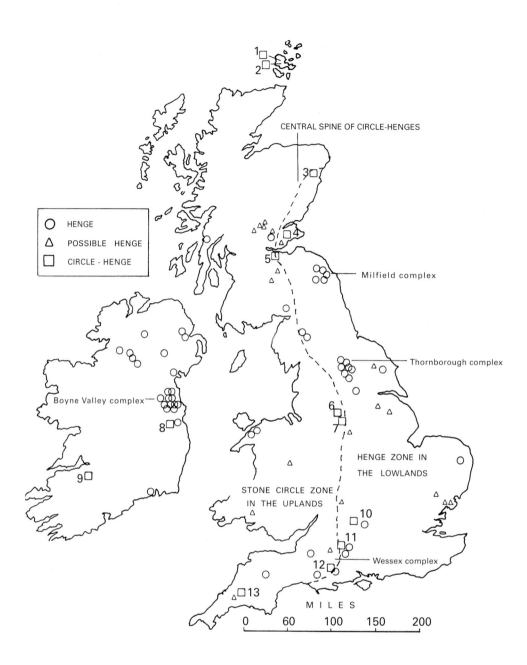

Fig. 2. Henges in Britain and Ireland. Circle-henges: 1. Ring of Brodgar; 2. Stones of Stenness; 3. Broomend of Crichie; 4. Balfarg; 5. Cairnpapple; 6. Bull Ring; 7. Arbor Low; 8. Castleruddery; 9. Grange (Lios); 10. Devil's Quoits; 11. Avebury; 12. Stonehenge; 13. Stripple Stones.

batch from Stonehenge: 2600 ± 60 bc (OxA-4833), 2570 ± 100 bc (OxA-4842), 2510 ± 45 bc (OxA-4834), 2505 ± 40 bc (OxA-4834), 2482 ± 22 bc (UB-3794), 2480 ± 18 bc (UB-3789), 2460 ± 60 bc (BM-1583), 2443 ± 18 bc (UB-3793), 2440 ± 60 bc (BM-1617), 2431 ± 18 bc (UB-3788), 2425 ± 19 bc (UB-3787), 2417 ± 18 bc (UB-3790), 2415 ± 18 bc (UB-3792); and 2470 ± 50 bc (GU-1670) from Balfarg Riding School, Fife. There are others from stone circles: 2356 ± 65 bc (SRR-350) from Stenness; 2525 ± 80 bc (GU-1591) from the Lochmaben Stane, Dumfries; and 2550 ± 250 bc (GiF-280) from the megalithic horseshoe of Tossen-Keler cromlech, Côtes-du-Nord, Brittany, show that the building of unroofed ritual structures in some parts of Britain, Ireland and Brittany was established well before 3000 BC. A 'date' of 2790 ± 150 bc (NPL-220) from Llandegai NE henge, Bangor, offers the possibility that a few rings in Britain could have been built as far back as 3500 BC.

Comparably early assays reveal that in wooded areas rings of posts were put up. A determination of 3075 ± 90 bc (GU-1296) from a structure of uncertain type, possibly a circle of timber uprights, at Temple Wood North, Argyll; three of 2520 ± 50 bc (GU-2316), 2130 ± 90 bc (GU-2324) and 2030 ± 180 bc (GU-2325) at Machrie Moor I, Arran; and 2365 ± 60 bc (GU-1163), 2320 ± 60 bc (GU-1162), 2320 ± 50 bc (GU-1160) and 2085 ± 60 bc (GU-1161) from the first phase at Balfarg, Fife, combine to show that at least in the north of Britain some post-rings were the contemporaries of the first henges and stone circles. The recently exposed tree-trunk ring at Holme-next-the-Sea in Norfolk was constructed around 2050 BC.[23] Henge, stone circle, wooden ring, all were built of what material was most easily found.

To a positive there will be a negative. Opposites exist, sometimes to the confusion of archaeology.

> All things counter, original, spare, strange;
> Whatever is fickle, freckled (who knows how?)
> With swift, slow; sweet, sour; adazzle, dim

wrote Gerard Manley Hopkins in words very apposite to the contradictions provided by some C-14 determinations for stone circles. Some prove that the emergence of megalithic rings began centuries earlier than once thought. Conversely, others are traps for the unwary, offering spuriously late 'dates' for the end of the tradition.

A series of assays from south-west Ireland: 790 ± 80 bc (OxA-2683) for Drombeg; 830 ± 35 bc (GrN-17509) and 945 ± 35 bc (GrN-17510) for Reansacreena, both sites in Co. Cork; and 970 ± 60 bc (GrN-9713) and 715 ± 50 bc (GrN-9172) for Cashelkeelty in Co. Kerry seem to suggest that these rings remained in use as late as c. 1250 BC in the Late Bronze Age.[24] The determinations deceive.

They derived from intrusive burials left in the circles by people of a different cult perhaps centuries after the sites had been deserted. They are no more relevant to the original activities inside the rings than the food-vessel round barrow imposed on the bank of Arbor Low circle-henge; or the passage-tomb squashed between the internal pillar and circle-stones at Callanish; and are no better guides to the age of the rings than the Early Bronze Age cists dug into the Machrie Moor stone circles on Arran. Without reliable organic material recovered from the undisturbed bottoms of stone-holes it must remain safer to consider the major floruit of stone circles to have been between 3200 and 1500 BC. Carrowmore, may be earlier. Some Irish rings may indeed be later but these, at present, must be deemed exceptions.

The fact that Charles Dickens (1812–70) scratched his signature on a window-pane of Shakespeare's so-called birthplace of New Place in Stratford-upon-Avon does not date that late fifteenth-century building. The cremation in a coarseware vessel at Drombeg, with 'dates' wobbling from AD 680 ± 120 (D-62) to 13 ± 140 bc (TCD-38) to 7690 ± 80 bc are probably just as misleading (see chapter 14).

Distribution

As well as the problems caused by the existence of chambered tombs other factors affected the distribution of stone circles. One was geology. It is a truism that stone circles were erected only where stone was available, henges where it was not (Fig. 3). Henges and circles occupied almost mutually exclusive regions determined by the nature of the countryside. Stonehenge must be ignored as a megalithic transvestite, started by a fortuitous glaciation from Wales, the ring's metamorphosis completed by fanatical woodworkers on Salisbury Plain.

As Fox pointed out decades ago in *The Personality of Britain* this country has two major geographical zones, the highlands of older mountainous rocks, up to 1,342 m in height, which make up the entirety of Scotland except for the brief band along the east coast, all Wales and England west of the Pennines down to the Peak District and across to Devon and Cornwall in the south-west peninsula. Stone was freely scattered but the harsh rugged landscape was inimical to large-scale settlement and the stone circles of the highlands were preponderantly for relatively small groups of people.

Quite differently the lowlands offered wide tracts of good soils, peaceful rivers and rounded, low hills. Populations were larger, more stable. To the east of a buckled north-east to south-west boundary from Bridlington to Bournemouth, an area that encompassed the Yorkshire Wolds, the Cotswolds, Chilterns and the Downs, a landscape of hills that seldom exceeded 30 m in height, in this undemanding terrain henges were built, great rings for great numbers of people.

Even excluding the enormous, sprawling earthwork enclosures such as Durrington Walls and Mount Pleasant the average internal area of a henge was about 3,600 m^2, almost fourteen times greater than the 260 m^2 of an ordinary stone circle. This distinction between the social conditions imposed by the geological imperatives of height, rainfall and cultivable land is emphasised in the highland zone by the mini-henges in an alien environment around the Moray Firth. Sites such as Achilty, Cononbridge, Muir of Ord and Wormy Hillock are a shrunken sub-species with arenas of no more than 170 m^2, pygmies when contrasted to the classic henges in the lusher lands a hundred or more miles to the south.[25]

Fox made a complementary observation about the occasional pockets of stone that were present in the lowlands. 'It is to be noted that, while there is practically no building stone for the "dry walls" of hill forts or for megalithic monuments in the lowland save on the limestones . . . which lie on its western and northern margin, the denudation of overlying Tertiary rocks has provided, on Salisbury Plain and the Berkshire Downs, residual masses of sandstone, sarsens – just the right kind of monoliths for early man's constructions, and to their existence the grandeur of Stonehenge and Avebury is due'.[26]

Henges were raised in the lowlands, stone circles to their west and north. Along the watershed that divided the two zones henge and circle often combined with a ring of stones standing along the inner edge of the henge's inner ditch. Known as circle-henges they can be found as far north-east as Balfarg in Fife and as far to the south-west as the Stripple Stones on Bodmin Moor.

Along the intervening spine between them are famous sites such as Arbor Low, the Rollright Stones and the Devil's Quoits in Oxfordshire, Avebury and Stonehenge in Wiltshire. Although firm dating is lacking for the phases of the majority of these

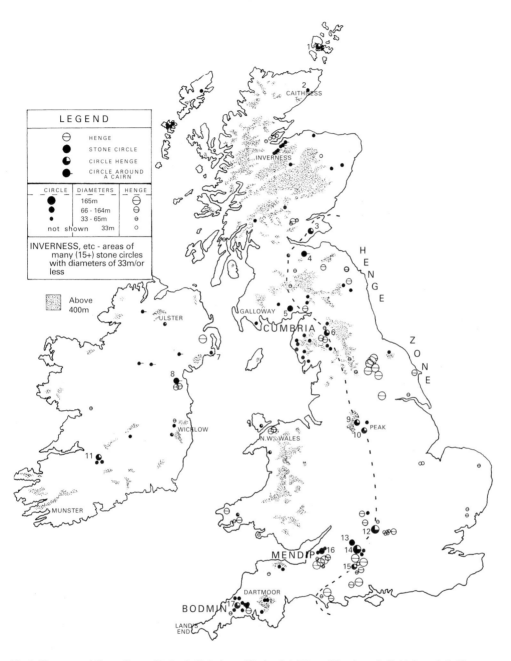

Fig. 3. Henges and Great Stone Circles in Britain and Ireland: 1. Ring of Brodgar; 2. Guidebest; 3. Balfarg; 4. Cairnpapple; 5. Twelve Apostles; 6. Long Meg and Her Daughters; 7. Ballynoe; 8. Newgrange; 9. Bull Ring; 10. Arbor Low; 11. Grange; 12. Devil's Quoits; 13. Winterbourne Bassett; 14. Avebury; 15. Stonehenge; 16. Stanton Drew; 17. Stripple Stones.

hybrid settings it appears that it was the henge that was the primary structure with the stone circle a later addition. That was certainly true at Balfarg, at Cairnpapple and Stonehenge and probably also at Arbor Low where the ring is of an entirely different shape from the henge that surrounds it.

'Such vast perennial memorials, seem rather to be a work of a people settled in their country . . . I am apt to believe, that in most Counties of England are, of have been Ruines of these kind of Temples,' wrote John Aubrey.[27] What he did not ask was why such rings were almost entirely absent from islands, a lacuna to be considered here.

Changes in Cult Belief

It was the emergence of a new and strongly held cult but former traditions were not instantly or easily given up. There was a change from the cramped, gloomy chamber of a tomb to the unroofed, wide ring, a change from darkness to light, from the dead to the living, from the grave to the sky, a change apparently associated with a new form of pottery known as grooved ware. At first there was change only where it was unresisted, in fertile areas but where there was little or no earlier settlement, in regions such as the English Lake District and north-eastern Scotland.

In Ireland the remains of a stoutly-built wooden structure, oval, 9.1 × 8.1 m, with a possible porch at the exact east was found close to the gigantic passage-tomb of Knowth in the Boyne Valley of Co. Meath. Built on earlier layers of domestic rubbish it contained votive deposits of flints from Antrim a hundred miles to the north and a stone axe from Tievebulliagh mountain even farther away. In pits were cattle and pig bones. There were also over four hundred grooved-ware sherds (Pl. 10).

So many unusual vessels, a type of pottery previously unknown amongst the local Carrowkeel and Sandhills pots, demanded explanation. 'Was a void developing as a result perhaps of the passage tomb complex declining under deteriorating climatic conditions, or exhaustion of over-cultivated soil?' The excavator concluded that the combined evidence of stratigraphy and a new style of ceramics 'argue for the emergence of a separate and culturally different phase of prehistory in the Boyne Valley and by extension in Ireland'.[28] This could be widened to include Britain and, without grooved ware but by similar processes of change, Brittany. It was the introduction of a cult that was accepted initially and with least opposition in underpopulated areas.

In upland parts where there were few inhabitants the adherents of the new system of beliefs encountered no resistance. Stone circles were erected. They remained unchallenged. Elsewhere where tombs were numerous the change was slower and sometimes never developed. Gloucestershire with almost a hundred long chambered mounds had no stone circles. The Blackhedge Farm sites at Leckhampton, once thought to be ruinous exceptions, were dismissed by O.G.S. Crawford in *The Long Barrows of the Cotswolds* as 'without the least doubt of recent origin . . . simply boulders which have fallen from the steep cliff above'.

Societies in other heavily peopled parts, closely interconnected by family relationships, continued in their ancient practices and remained unconverted.

The Problem of Islands

Islands epitomised conservatism. Remote from interference their occupants kept to the old ways, rejected innovation. Of the hundreds of islands in the far west of Europe along the Atlantic seaboard from southern Brittany up to the Shetlands only the western isles have many circles. Where there were Neolithic burial-mounds on Belle-Ile off the Quiberon peninsula, the Ile-aux-Moines in the Gulf of Morbihan, the

Plate 10. A grooved-ware vessel. Such pottery was associated with a mysterious cult (Photograph: the author).

Channel Isles, the Isle of Wight, the Scillies, the Isle of Man, the Orkneys, the Shetlands, there is hardly a megalithic ring. Even the 'stone circle' on St Martins shown on the 1:25,000 map of the Scillies is no more than the kerbstones of the denuded Gun Hill chambered cairn.[29]

Of the two hundred or more islands around Ireland, including large land-masses such as Rathlin, Valentia and the Aran Islands not one has a megalithic ring. The Orkneys with eighty passage-tombs and stalled cairns has just two, Stenness and Brodgar, huddling within a mile of each other. And where a form of stone circle was actually constructed on an island its architecture was bastardised by the inclusion of features derived from megalithic tombs such as the cists and passages of the Meayll Hill 'circle' on the Isle of Man. The horseshoes of Er-Lannic on an 'island' in the Gulf of Morbihan, southern Brittany, were erected on a hillock that became half-submerged by a rise in sea level in Roman times.

The reason for this widespread void is clear. Almost ignored by the outside world the inhabitants of many islands lived in isolation, rarely visited, unaffected by novelties. Only the farthest of the western islands of Scotland, the Outer Hebrides, were different. Unlike the others they were not cut off. Lying on the long, busy seaway between the rich and powerful societies of the Boyne Valley and the Orkneys they were constantly exposed to new ideas as voyagers with exotic wares passed in the shelter of their cliffs, dragged their boats ashore at night. Arran, midway between the Scottish mainland and the Kintyre peninsula, and on the sea-route from north-eastern Ireland, knew comparably constant traffic. 'We may imagine these grey seas as bright with Neolithic Argonauts as the western Pacific is today.'[30] A similarly well-travelled sea route between Brittany, southern England and south-western Ireland may account for the peculiar 'cists-in-circles' of the Channel Islands and the 'Cornish' circle on Ile Beniguet.

Even in the Hebrides coexistence was uneasy. On Lewis the small group of little ellipses is on the west coast near Loch Roag miles from the big chambered tombs. Only on North Uist do spacious ovals intermingle with the medley of Clyde long cairns, Hebridean round cairns and Craonaval passage-tombs, a mixing of megalithic structures in time and space almost without parallel in western Europe.[31]

The mainland of Ireland itself may have experienced comparable retardation. With a profusion of strongly established megalithic burial traditions – portal-dolmens along the Irish Sea coast, court-cairns in the north, passage-tombs in the eastern and central regions – the construction of stone circles may have been delayed for centuries.

Sometimes on islands there may have been physical retaliation against what seemed to be blasphemy. The toppling and smashing of a megalithic oval and the deliberate building of a passage-tomb over its ruin at Bryn Celli Ddu on Anglesey reveals a determination to eliminate anything alien to the beliefs of the natives. A diminutive chambered tomb was squashed into the circle of Callanish in the Outer Hebrides. Miles to the east of Callanish the great ellipse of Druim Dubh, 'black ridge', may have been 'intentionally felled in antiquity. The same seems true of . . . the Achmore stone circle' 4 miles to its west.[32]

Cultoon at the south-west of Islay may be a further instance of an intrusive ring being demolished on an island where there were megalithic tombs. Only three stones were standing when Alexander Thom surveyed the site in 1973. Others were prone, half-concealed or completely buried below peat. They lay in an ellipse 41.2 × 33.5 m. Excavations in 1974 and 1975 proved that many stones had never been erected. Some lay by holes that had been occupied, others had no sockets prepared for them. An assay of 765 ± 40 bc (SRR-500) from charcoal in the overlying peat indicated that the work had stopped well before 1000 BC.

The most massive stone, more than 3 m long, lay at the north-east end of the long axis which, to the south-west, pointed to Slieve Snaght mountain in Co. Donegal 55 miles away across the Irish Sea, a peak behind which the midwinter sun set in the decades around 1800 BC.

The undertaking may not have been abandoned through indifference or sloth but because of hostility. 'That some kind of destruction may have been visited on the site was suggested by the fact that one of the uprights had been snapped off short and that no fallen fragments were found next to it.'[33] Some stoneholes had been dug but no stone lay by them as though the erection of the ring had been under way when it was unexpectedly interrupted. With the Clyde chambered tomb of the Giant's Grave a mile away and another one three miles east Cultoon's wreckage may be an example of conflicting rivalries.

Where rings were raised on the mainlands of Britain, Ireland and Brittany antagonism in reverse sometimes occurred. Circles of standing stones were put up around old tombs, confining them, surrounding the wedge-tomb of Clogherny Meenerrigal in Ulster with a ring of boulders. At Rosdoagh in Co. Mayo, beautifully situated above Broad Haven bay, 'is Druids Circles, a ritual monument comprising two concentric circles'. 'It is quite possible that two distinct phases are represented, the first a court-cairn, the second of unknown date, an enclosure incorporating the remains of the megalithic structure'.[34]

On occasion such conversions were resisted and they were left unfinished. Uncompleted rings around great mounds, Kercado in Brittany, Newgrange in Ireland, and around some Clava Cairns in Scotland may be evidence of sacrilege that had been halted.

The 'X' Factor

Within this intricate pattern of development, diffusion and discord the chronology is warped. What may have been the rapid development of circles in Cumbria came more slowly and later in Wessex, never in Herefordshire and the Forest of Dean. Nor were sites the same. The stone circles of north-western Ireland had an origin and a system of ritual different from those of England and western Scotland. A third type of ring with an ancestry in eastern Ireland became established in a broad north-east to south-west band hundreds of miles long, spreading diagonally across Scotland and Ireland. The rectangular or oval cromlechs and the horseshoes (*fer-aux-chevaux*) of Brittany formed another enclave whose arcane practices affected limited but critical areas of southern England.

There was a hypothetical threefold development of stone circles which, when mapped, resembles a long and tilted X-formation across Britain and Ireland. One of the three, possibly the earliest, had a restricted expansion in north-west Ireland. The second and third were extensive in distance and long-lived in time with putative roots respectively in the Boyne Valley and the English Lake District.

If the radiocarbon dates from the Carrowmore cemetery of Co. Sligo have been interpreted correctly then some of the very first stone circles may have developed there from the boulder-circles whose major architectural characteristic was a conspicuous ring of heavy boulders encircling a low and flat-topped cairn. Simplified, comparable settings were constructed north-eastwards up to Co. Donegal. With the entrancing exception of Beltany Tops they are now ruinous.

Forming the 500-mile long NE–SW arm of the 'X' was the recumbent stone circle tradition, originating perhaps from the supine stones outside passage-tombs in the Boyne Valley. It was a custom adopted in north-eastern Scotland, ultimately resulting in the tombs of the Clava group, but initially inspiring the recumbent stone circles of Aberdeenshire. Descendant from them were the Four-Posters of Scotland and, ultimately, the 'multiple' circles and Five-Stone rings of south-western Ireland.

This powerful tradition intermingled with a north-south line of 'entrance' rings at the crossroads of Arran with its ellipses, concentric circles, recumbents and Four-Posters. Extending over 600 miles was a band from the Orkneys down to Land's End. The earliest rings, in the Cumbrian Lake District, appear to be megalithic versions of henges. To the north were roomy ellipses like the Twelve Apostles and those on North Uist that contrast strangely with the mini-ovals of Callanish and its associates only a few miles away. Patchily amongst them were true circles.

To the south of the Lake District varying types of entrance rings occurred in eastern

Ireland, Wales, and southern England where there was also a minor contribution from Brittany in the form of rectangular settings at King Arthur's Hall, Cornwall and the Four Stations around Stonehenge. The horseshoe of sarsen trilithons inside that monument may also have its derivation in the Breton *fer-aux-chevaux*. It is a suggestion strengthened by the existence of Breton carvings – axes, daggers and anthropomorphs – on the stones of the trilithons and of the circle.[35]

The world has a long history of intolerance and desecration. In 1643, just for sport, Roundhead soldiers set hounds to chase cats through the vandalised Lichfield cathedral. 'The rebels intirely ruined all the ornament of the inside, with the brass inscriptions, tombs, etc. and were going to pull down the whole fabric for sale,' deplored William Stukeley in 1712.[36] The basilica of Hagia Triada in Constantinople was converted into a mosque by Ottoman Turks in 1453. Vikings sacked Lindisfarne Abbey on Holy Isle in AD 793, slaughtering the monks. Profanations such as these may have had bloody antecedents at the beginning of stone circle building.

Years ago Gordon Childe envisaged Neolithic missionaries zealously converting natives to the cult of building stone tombs. Theirs was a ministry disseminated by 'apostles of a megalithic faith [who] presumably arrived by the Atlantic seaway'. 'Like Celtic missionaries the megalithic saints . . . sailed the coasts of Scotland, Ireland and the remoter isles inspired by equally unworldly motives.' They were frequently opposed. 'If . . . the [mediaeval] Christian church could be rent by heresies and schisms, how much more might numerous and bigoted sects be expected in the megalithic religion?'[37]

Childe's thoughts may have been even more relevant to the question of the first stone circles in Britain, Ireland and Brittany.

Chapter Three

The Construction of a Stone Circle

*Twas in that deluge of Historie, that memorie of these British Monuments utterly
perished: the Discovery whereof I doe here endeavour (for want of written Record) to
work-out and restore . . . by comparing those I have seen one with another . . . to make
the Stones give Evidence for themselves.*

John Aubrey, 1693, 32

Earth, Wood and Stone

'The builders of the megalithic remains were utterly illiterate, and have left no written
records of their erection,' wrote Fergusson, adding gloomily, 'what is even more dis-
heartening is that in almost every instance they are composed of rough unhewn
stones'.[1]

This was misleading. It implied that just because the stones had not been dressed
and smoothed very little could be learned about their age or construction. On the contrary, so far from being Fergusson's 'rude stone monuments' most stone circles were
the result of careful planning that involved: i. the choice of the most desirable site;
ii. the size of the intended ring; iii. the transportation of heavy blocks; iv. the laying-out
of a circle or an ellipse; v. which was frequently planned using a local unit of
measurement; vi. and the preparation of stoneholes; vii. which often were of a specific
number; viii. some rings contained astronomical sightlines. These were aspects true for
most rings. Also to be discussed are the many variations in architecture such as centre
stones, the construction of concentric circles, entrances, outlying pillars, recumbent
stones, the levelling of sites and alignments to the sun or moon.

The Choice of Site

Several requirements affected the choice of where a stone circle was to stand. A convenient clearing was looked for, perhaps one already opened by earlier people: overlying a former settlement as happened at Er-Lannic in Brittany; or where barley and
oats had been cultivated at Stenness in the Orkneys.[2] Flat land was preferred like that
at Ballynoe in Co. Down but sometimes a slope had to be accepted because the large-
ness of a ring like Fernacre on Bodmin Moor precluded the choice of more horizontal ground. The problem was often overcome by cutting into a hillside to create a
level shelf or by piling up a platform like the one revealed by excavation at Kiltierney
in Co. Fermanagh.

An important consideration was the personal one of how convenient the place was for its users. Small groups would want a ring to be within walking distance of their settlement. Larger rings, intended for the gatherings of dispersed populations, would most sensibly be situated near the centre of a territory. But there is a qualification and cautionary words are demanded. It is a misfortune that the prehistoric record is imperfect. Only rarely is there evidence of where the builders of stone circles lived. Equally absent is proof of where they were buried. The three vital aspects of society: settlement, ritual and burial are elusive companions.

These are major frustrations in the study of stone circles. Such imbalance between life and death in other periods has led to the aphorism that Iron Age people with their hillforts but rare graves lived but never died whereas Beaker people with their round barrows but no homes died but never lived. To this the disgruntled researcher might grumble that stone circle communities never lived and only infrequently died. Even on Dartmoor where rings are often close to hut-circles it cannot be demonstrated that the two are contemporary with each other. Nor is it certain that the cremated human bones interred at the heart of some megalithic ring are those of a person who had participated in the original ceremonies there. As yet the proximity of circle, settlement and cemetery remains inferential.

A second requirement, and an essential one in deciding where a circle was to be erected, was the easy availability of stone. It is a truism that circles were set up only where there was easily accessible stone. Even the megalithic chameleon of Stonehenge conforms, its glaciated Welsh bluestones found a few miles away on Salisbury Plain by woodworkers. Elsewhere people put up rings of stone where boulders and blocks lay conveniently. Little quarrying was done, the splitting of laminated sandstone slabs at Stenness and Brodgar in the Orkneys being splendid exceptions. Free-lying stones had to be found within three or four miles with no steep slopes, marshes or rivers between. Otherwise there could be the earthen banks of henges or rings of posts, some perhaps with lintelled beams across their tops, but there would be no stone circles.

The size of labour forces and the nature of the terrain were always constraints but everywhere monuments were built of the materials to hand. This had been true for the builders of chambered tombs long before stone circles were designed.

> Ireland's early inhabitants did not transport ponderous blocks of stone for great distances. Transport was very difficult and confined to pack-animals and primitive vehicles and boats. In the megalithic tombs of the Neolithic period, the stone used was invariably local: the Lower Paleozoic *greywackes* and fracture-cleaved *sandstones* of the passage-graves of the Boyne Valley and Slieve na Caillighe or Loughcrew Hills; the carboniferous cherty limestone of Carrowkeel, Carrowmore and Knocknarea in County Sligo; and the granite of the portal tombs on the flanks of the Dublin and Wicklow mountains, all are of local provenance.[3]

With the exception of the heavy prostrate block in the recumbent stone circles of Scotland this observation is true of all stone circles.

The Size of Stone Circles

It is arguable that the size of a ring, whatever its shape, was determined by the number of people in the congregation that was going to use it. The immense interiors of some henges and megalithic rings were far in excess of that needed by a few hierophants in ceremonies watched by uninitiated spectators outside the surrounding banks or standing stones. Nor were the henges and rings set in natural amphitheatres from which people on the hillslopes could observe the rituals. The enclosures, whether of earth, timber or stone, are most convincingly explained as combinations of an internal temenos or sacred precinct and an encircling earthwork or ring of stones.

It is another impossibility to know how many people took part in the ceremonies, whether women and children were excluded, whether outsiders were admitted. The writer has made the cavalier assumption that any participant would enjoy a comfortable 1.8 m body-space of outstretched arms, about 2.6 m^2 and that half the interior of a circle would be reserved for the officiants. Should this be correct then Stanton Drew might have had a congregation of almost two thousand people and smaller rings such as the Druids' Circle in North Wales, 25.7 × 24.5 m and Mitchell's Fold in Shropshire, 27 × 25 m between eighty and a hundred. Attractive but less spacious circles like Drombeg in Co. Cork, 9.3 m in diameter, might have accommodated no more than fourteen or fifteen. It must be emphasised, however, that there are no data to support such a hypothesis.

It is noteworthy that the very largest of stone circles stand only just outside henge areas and never well away from them. Stanton Drew Centre, Somerset, is 7 miles NNE of the Priddy henges. The stones of the Ring of Brodgar in the Orkneys were erected inside a henge as much as 149 m from crest to crest of its bank. Long Meg and Her Daughters, Cumberland, is 6 miles north-east of the Penrith henges. There are several henges within a few miles of the incomplete ring around Newgrange. The Twelve Apostles near Dumfries is 17 miles west of Broadlee henge. Such associations of large enclosures, differing only in the material used to construct them, give some indication of the densities of local population (Table 4).

The henge ancestry of early stone circles is supported by the observation that those regions containing many large rings also contain henges. In contrast, areas where there are no or very few henges have only small megalithic circles: south-west Scotland, south-west Ireland, Dartmoor, the Yorkshire Moors, sites late in the series and whose average diameter hardly exceeds 12.2 m. The conjunction of large stone circles and henges and their overlap in the circle-henges along the NE–SW spine of Britain point to a western transmutation into stone of an earlier tradition of circular earthworks.

As could be expected in circles of widely differing periods and erected in a variety of environments there was an immense range in the lengths of their diameters. In total the rings average 20.9 m but this bland statistic conceals the fact that over a hundred sites in the counties of Cork and Kerry in south-west Ireland are only some 7.7 m across with an interior of some 46.5 m^2 whereas ten enormous sites in Morbihan, Brittany, are an incredible eighty times larger with mean diameters of 64 m.

Each country was distinct from the others. In England 91 per cent of the rings averaged 22.4 m. In Scotland 92 per cent were less spacious, some 16.6 m in diameter. Northern Ireland, 83 per cent, and Wales, 75 per cent, were comparable with each other, 15.4 m and 18.4 m respectively. The mean in Ireland, heavily affected by the preponderance of tiny Five-Stone rings in the south-west, was very much smaller, 89 per cent of its sites averaging no more than 9.5 m. The Channel Islands had only a few 'cist-in-circles' from 4.6 m to 9.3 m across. In Brittany there was no peak to the evenly spread histogram of diameters but there was a sharp separation in size between the western and northern coastal sites of the peninsula, 31.5 m, in contrast to the vast cromlechs and horseshoes of the Morbihan which were more than twice as large.

No.	SITE	DIAMETER m	Area m^2
1	Stanton Drew Centre, Somerset	112.2	9,887
2	Ring of Brodgar, Orkneys	103.6	8,430
3	Avebury Centre South, Wiltshire	102.4	8,236
4	Long Meg and Her Daughters, Cumbria	109.4 × 93.0	7,991
5	Newgrange, Co. Meath	107.9 × 91.1	7,720
6	Avebury North, Wiltshire	97.5	7,466
7	Twelve Apostles, Dumfriesshire	86.6 × 79.3	5,394
8	Devil's Quoits, Oxfordshire	76.0	4,537
9	Achnagoul, Caithness	88 × 63	4,534
10	Dorrery, Caithness	73	4,185
11	Balfarg, Fife	*c.* 60	*c.* 2,827
12	Edinkillie, Moray	*c.* 58	*c.* 2,642
13	Aultan Broubster, Caithness	62.5 × 53	2,602
14	Guidebest, Caithness	57.3 × 52	2,340
15	Grange, Co. Limerick	59 × 45.8	2,122
16	Hethpool South, Northumberland	61 × 43	2,060
17	Fridd Newydd South, Merioneth	50.6	2,011
18	Broomrigg North, Cumbria	50.9 × 50	1,999
19	Lochmaben Stane, Dumfriesshire	55 × 46	1,987
20	Whitcastles, Dumfriesshire	54.9 × 43.1	1,858

Table 4. The Twenty Largest Megalithic Rings in Britain and Ireland.

Giving some indication of the numbers of people using megalithic rings in Britain, Ireland and Brittany the great majority, 92 per cent, had an average diameter of no more than 13.7 m. With an internal area of less than 150 m^2 they may have been the assembly-places of about thirty people, a number sufficient to transport and erect the stones but far from an imaginary multitude gathering together in their hundreds.

The Transportation of Stones

Once the site had been chosen and while scrub and weeds were being cleared from it so that the outline of the proposed ring could be scribed out other workers left to drag in stones of suitable bulk and shape. Men seldom had to go farther than a mile or two. They were not obsessed with monumentality. At Merrivale on Dartmoor impressively long blocks of granite lay high on the steep sides of Mis Tor a mile away but, lower down the slopes smaller slabs clustered in dense thousands, blocking any easy way through them. The challenge was refused. Lesser and lighter stones were taken from King Tor instead: it was closer, the hillside was easier. The intervening ground was uncluttered. The outcome was a modest construction characteristic of most stone circles.

Only when a specific length and shape of stone was demanded like the colossal block that was to be the focus of a recumbent stone circle in north-eastern Scotland were exceptions made to this custom of choosing less arduous tasks. The monstrous sarsens of Stonehenge, manhandled over a score of miles across a valley and up the hard gradients of Salisbury Plain, is a unique example of megalithic madness.

Sometimes circle builders used nature to their advantage, integrating a small outcrop in their ring. Exposed bedrock that resembled a tumbled, broken pillar tempted people to include its four pieces of 'pillar' at the south-east of the Ynys-hir ring near Brecon. It made one fewer stone to be hauled in. It may also have been considered that such a blending of the natural with the human gave increased power to the setting. Near Coniston the south-west arc of a kerbed enclosed cremation cemetery on Banniside Moor incorporated a huge natural boulder.

The methods employed to move the stones of ordinary rings are debatable. They may have been pulled over wooden rollers but rollers are not efficient over rough ground. More probably a stone would be lashed onto a sledge and then towed along a trackway of moveable rails, gangs laying lengths down, waiting until the load had passed over a pair, picking them up, carrying them to the front of the line, repeating the process hour by hour.

A combination of rollers and rails was the technique found most practicable in the 1979 experiment at Bougon near Niort in France when a 32-ton block, comfortably flat-bottomed for rollers, was pulled by 230 workers hauling on eight flaxen ropes with twenty men behind levering the stone over level ground. Progress was slow. It was calculated that it would have taken five weeks or more to complete a journey of three miles, no more than 137 m a day,[4] even in winter when the ground was hard with frost.

With rougher, uneven stones a sledge provided a better carriage than rollers. In megalithic rings an average stone weighed between two and three tons and could have been hauled by a score of men. Pieces of prehistoric rope have been discovered in Britain: heather from Skara Brae like the ropes known as 'simmons'; grass, even nettle from the Somerset Levels. Cables made from the inner layers of bark from the small-leafed lime may have been used. Seeped in mud for weeks the reeking material could be separated into ten or twelve thin ribbons and twisted together. It would have been the strongest plant fibre native to Britain.

It is doubtful whether such vegetable ropes were strong enough for a heavy stone and it is likely that cables of plaited leather were manufactured for such work. In historic times thonging of sealskin was sturdy enough to drag horse-drawn ploughs in the Hebrides. Ropes taut with the weight of laden baskets of flint scored deep grooves in the rims of Late Neolithic mine-shafts of Grimes Graves in East Anglia. Strips of rawhide plaited into 15 cm thick hawsers would have had considerable tensile strength as long as they were kept subtle. With a breaking-strain of 1,814 kg per 6 cm^2 a 7.6 cm thick rope of leather would have been capable of withstanding a weight of a third of a tonne.[5]

Whether men or oxen pulled the stone is more easily answered. Oxen are extremely strong but are also 'slow, deliberate and ruminative . . . and their reactions of words of command, or even to more painful stimulation, are notoriously sluggish'. Watching ox-carts at work in the Transvaal an observer noticed that the pace was almost imperceptible, 'so slow that a man could step on and off a cart while it was moving'.

In 1812 the Reverend Sydney Smith, clergyman and wit, recorded his experience with oxen. 'Was advised by neighbouring gentlemen to employ oxen; bought four – Tug and Lug, Haul and Crawl; but Tug and Lug took to fainting, and required buckets of sal volatile, and Haul and Crawl to lie & die in the mud'. He changed to horses. In early prehistory such alternative traction-animals were not available and it may be assumed that the majority of prehistoric stones were shifted by man-power.[6]

The Shape of the Ring

Many earlier writers remarked on the eccentric shapes of the so-called stone circles but it was Alexander Thom who codified the designs and proposed methods by which they might have been set out.[7]

He suggested that there were five important shapes (Fig. 4): the circle, the flattened circle, the ellipse, the egg and the complex, all with a geometrical framework. Thom put forward no order of development but theorised that the reason for non-circular plans was the desire for circumferences that were multiples of a hypothetical national unit of measurement, his Megalithic Yard of 0.829 m. Cowan, having analysed the various shapes, concluded that the most probable order of development was: circle, flattened circle, ellipse and egg.[8] At present this still appears true although the non-circular designs may have been devised earlier than had been thought.

Of the 1,300 or more megalithic rings known in Britain, Ireland and Brittany the approximate proportions are 800 circles, 300 flattened rings and ellipses, and 200 nondescript sites conforming to no recognisable symmetrical shape such as the Beaghmore 'circles' in Co. Tyrone distorted like iron bands torn off a barrel.

Claims for the geometrical construction of ellipses, designed through the use of Pythagorean triangles, has been rigorously examined by Barnatt and Moir, and through practical experiments Barnatt has shown that many may have been set out by eye alone. 'The majority of rings are laid out simply by eye and are found in all regions', the circles in southern England generally being more accurate.[9] Circles would have been the easiest to lay out, requiring only a central peg and a length of rope. It is not surprising that throughout the whole 'megalithic' period most rings were round. Results from the analysis of sixty-five rings in Ireland led to the conclu-

Fig. 4. Examples of Thom's Shapes of Megalithic Rings: a. Merry Maidens, Cornwall; b. Barbrook I, Derbyshire; c. Esslie the Greater, Kincardine; d. Burgh Hill, Roxburgh; e. Kerry Hill, Montgomery (Powys). (b–d, after Thom, 1967).

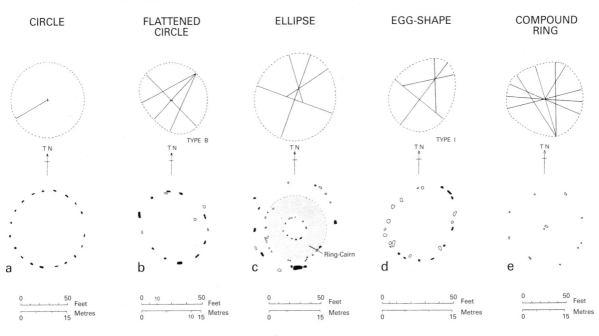

sion that they were not geometrically constructed. Instead, the authors decided upon the 'hypothesis that stone circles are meant to be circular, and locally smooth to the eye'. They concluded that their results were 780:1 times better than Thom's.[10]

Fleming speculated that people sometimes deliberately built non-circular enclosures such as flattened rings and ellipses so that two conditions, unavailable in a true circle, might be fulfilled: the audience could see all the rites; and the principals could occupy visually focal positions facing the spectators.[11] The hypothesis is attractive. Architecturally there is no structural reason for the choice of an oval building such as Woodhenge but aesthetically an ellipse has a feature impossible in a circle, a longer axis. This might, as Fleming suggested, have provided a focus for ceremonies. It might also have defined a sightline towards a celestial event.

The design of ellipses and eggs may have had a mathematically geometrical basis as Thom theorised but sceptics have maintained that much of his 'proof' had no substantial foundation. Despite his contention that an ultimate development of design might have been megalithic rings with several flattened sides it is noticeable that nearly all such sites have continuous boundaries, of earthen banks like Avebury or contiguous stones like the ring-cairn of Delfour in Inverness-shire. It is as likely that they were the result of haphazard construction as of nice mathematics.

The latter argument is supported by the shape of the Moel ty Uchaf cairn in Merioneth in which the ring of touching kerbstones has flattened arcs at north-west, north-east and south-east. Thom claimed that the builders 'started with a circle 14 [megalithic] yds in diameter and therefore $3\frac{1}{7} \times 14$ or 44 yds [40.2 m] in circumference. But this was not enough: they wanted also to have a multiple of $2\frac{1}{2}$ yds [2.3 m] in the perimeter. So they proceeded to invent a method of drawing flattened portions on the ring, which would reduce it to $42\frac{1}{2}$'.[12]

In contrast to this recondite activity there is an empirically persuasive counter-proposal. On the circumference of the proposed ring primary stones could have been set diametrically opposite each other. The intervening spaces could then have been filled in by separate work-gangs keeping as close to the required curve as their judgements allowed. Such groups, each responsible for separate lengths, have been deduced at Stonehenge, Avebury, at causewayed enclosures such as Windmill Hill and Robin Hood's Ball. 'In plan this earthwork is very irregular and seems to have been designed in a series of straight sections.'[13]

So did the timber ring underneath Barrow 41 in the Brenig Valley, Denbighshire. 'This stake and wattle circle was somewhat irregular in plan, consisting really of a series of rather irregular rows of stakes, each row placed end to end to form a rough ring; it is possible that the structure was made in prefabricated sections.'[14]

It is arguable therefore that Thom's complex sites are the results not of intricate designs but of long-established practices for laying out earthwork ditches. This might also account for the flattened rings which may be no more than poorly-executed ovals. If so, megalithic rings had only two basic shapes, the circle and the ellipse.

It is certainly not true, however, that ellipses themselves were no more than circular mishaps. A ring such as Burgh Hill in Roxburgh, 16.3×13.4 m with a ratio of 1.2:1 between its long and short axes has too many small stones standing on or lying across its perimeter to doubt that its builders had intended an oval.

There is even a cultural group of ellipses. There are over thirty, 60 per cent of the rings in western Scotland, from the Twelve Apostles, Dumfries, near the Solway Firth in the south to Ceann Hulavig, formerly Loch Roag, on Lewis in the Outer Hebrides.

Even the recently discovered Wildshaw Burn in Lanarkshire is an ellipse, 50×40 m. It is the shape that binds these rings together, not their size. The interior of the Twelve Apostles is over fifty times greater than the dwarfed Ceann Hulavig.

How they were planned is unresolved. Surveyors considered that the fine ellipse of Machrie Moor I on Arran had been laid out using two focal points halfway between the ring's centre of the ends of the long axis.[15] Being aware of this possibility the clean bedsand was diligently trowelled during the writer's excavations there in 1978–9. Nothing appeared.[16]

Conversely, the Temple Wood South ring in the Kilmartin Valley was said to be egg-shaped and laid out using two opposing equilateral triangles that overlapped at six crucial points. During the excavation 'small upright stone marker-pegs', likened to avocado pears, were located at three of the points 'so confirming the geometrical analysis'. Unexpectedly, there was no mention of them in the subsequent report.[17]

It now seems probable that the majority of megalithic rings were, as Stukeley wrote of Stonehenge, 'not very precise, neither in design, nor construction' and 'done with a sufficient but not mathematical exactness'.[18] Size was a determining factor, shape was important, but niceties such as the neat positioning of stones was of minor interest.

Units of Measurement

It may be assumed that in well-planned circles such as the Merry Maidens in Cornwall the outline of the ring was scraped out by means of a rope attached to a central peg. In some cases the length of the radius may have been a number of Thom's Megalithic Yards (M.Y.) of 2.72 ft [0.83 m] or $2\frac{1}{2}$ times that length in a Megalithic Rod (M.R.) of 6.8 ft [2.07 m].

Thom claimed that measurements were made by these standardised rods which were accurate to 0.76 mm, about the thickness of an active wasp's leg. He thought that such yardsticks circulated widely in western Europe, as far north as the aberrant ring of the Giant's Stones in the Shetlands. Builders of megalithic rings in Scotland, Wales and Ireland used the identical length. Almost nine hundred miles south of the Shetlands the rows of standing stones at Carnac, Brittany, were spaced 5 to 14 M.Y. apart. Despite these assertions it is very hard to accept Thom's confident statement that 'there must have been a headquarters from which standard rods were sent out' because 'if each small community had obtained the length by copying the rod of its neighbour to the south the accumulated error would have been much greater'.[19]

The problems associated with such a concept are myriad. It is not clear how such a measure could be disseminated. Either there was indeed a single centre, perhaps Avebury, where the yardstick was meticulously guarded. In such a case inhabitants of Caithness or the Outer Hebrides, knowing of the rod's existence, had to travel immense distances to borrow it. Or else they waited, maybe for impatient generations, for a travelling surveyor to chance upon their settlement. And how the rod was preserved so immaculately remains unexplained.

The idea that circle-builders did have a yardstick was first mooted by William Stukeley in 1723 or 1724 when he deduced that the dimensions of Stonehenge were based on multiples of a Druid's Cubit of 20.8 ins (53 cm) 'most probably deriv'd from Noah and Adam'.[20] Seventy years earlier Inigo Jones thought that the ring was Roman. It could not have been raised by natives, 'a savage and barbarous people, knowing no use at all of garments'. Preoccupied with his classical erudition Jones overlooked the ambiguity in that his architects had used not the Roman pes (foot) of 11.664 ins (29.6 cm) but Imperial Feet in their design. He supposed that Stonehenge was 110 English feet (33.5 m) across. But by an unfelicitous coincidence the sarsen ring's true diameter of 29.6 m, was exactly 100 Roman pedes, something that Flinders Petrie was to realise three hundred years later.[21] Neither Stukeley nor Jones was right and Petrie's calculation was a chronological irrelevance.

Since Stukeley further erroneous units have been computed. The ruined foundations of a round house near Hestingsgot in south Shetland were supposed to contain evidence of a 'Hestingsgarth Foot' of 12.96 ins (32.9 cm), a measure also claimed for the much-abused Stonehenge as well as Avebury, Stanton Drew and others. Ludovic Mann speculated that Bronze Age toolmakers worked in an Alpha Foot of 14.85 ins and a Beta of 13.28 ins (37.7, 33.7 cm).

In 1976 Maria Reiche, doyenne of researchers into the Peruvian desert lines of Nazca, concluded that an identical unit of measurement 4 ft 3 ins (1.34 m) 'with slight geographical variations' had been used both in Peru and in at least twenty-three British stone circles. She persistently amended the unit however and 'between 1949 and 1984 she offered no few than *nine* distinct suggestions for this "Nazca Yard" ranging from 84 meters all the way down to 32.5 centimeters'.[22] Such indecision simply emphasises the difficulty of recovering any precise length from imprecise material.

Measuring-sticks undoubtedly did exist in prehistoric Europe. One of hazel was found in the Danish Bronze Age tumulus of Borum Eshoj near Aarhus beside a tree-trunk coffin. It measured 79 cm and had three notches cut at 15 cm intervals. A second, of oak, was recovered from Borre Fen, 1.35 m long, divided into eight equal parts of 16.9 cm. Of Borum Eshoj it was written, 'There can be little doubt that it was a Bronze Age measuring rod marked out in feet, which was used in the construction of the coffin – possibly also in the laying out and erection of the mound'.[23]

Amongst other body-measurements the foot has frequently been taken as a convenient length. The sixteen 'fingers' of the Greeks equalled a foot of 12.17 ins (30.9 cm) and the Roman foot was 11.664 ins (29.6 cm). The Trelleborg Vikings used a variant of this, 11.56 ins (29.4 cm). The mediaeval French *pied* was 12.79 ins (32.5 cm) but the Parisian was 12.78 ins (32.5 cm). Study of megalithic monuments in Brittany convinced Merlet that a 'Gallic pied' of 31.75 cm (1 ft ½ ins) had been the chosen length.

Hicks has plausibly suggested that it was flexible body-yards, the distance from nose to tip of an outstretched arm, about 1 m, that prehistoric people employed, each community having their own subtly individual version of this. 'Very similar sets of body-based measurements have been found . . . to be used not only in Europe . . . but also throughout much of the world, including Melanesia and among the American Indians. This suggests either their very great antiquity or their obviousness.' Thom's Megalithic Yard of 0.83 m might then be seen as one of many regional measuring devices.

Ratios of the human body, famously demonstrated in Leonardo da Vinci's sketch of a naked man, 'human figure in a circle, illustrating proportions', arms aloft, legs apart, contained in a perfect circle, show what a range of lengths were available from a source that did not differ greatly between people of average dimensions.[24]

Such measurements are more relevant to the proportions of megalithic monuments than the artificiality of the metric system. The metre theoretically was one ten-millionth of the distance from the Pole to the equator. It was not. It is scientific but not sympathetic. Although illegal in France since 1837 many country people there still

Diameters in metres of innermost to outermost rings at Woodhenge

	F	E	D	C	B	A
	11.7	17.6	23.4	29.3	38.1	43.9
Short Foot 29.2 cm (11½ inches)	40.1	60.1	80.1	100.2	130.4	150.3
Megalithic Yard 0.83 m (2.72 ft)	14.1	21.2	29.5	35.3	46	52.9
Beaker Yard 0.732 m (2.402 ft)	16.0	24.0	32.0	40.0	52.1	60.0

Table 5. Three Hypothical Units of Measurements at Woodhenge.

think in pre-Napoleonic measures, three *pied* to the metre, *le pouce* for the inch or thumb, eggs sold by *le douzaine*, and meat by *le livre*. Some farmers calculate the area of fields not by the hectare by *la perche*, the old perch, pole or rod. The rod, long-forgotten, was the length of the left feet of sixteen men lined up heel to toe as they came out of church, 5.03 m (16 ft 6 ins) in all.

Body-measurements like these are of considerable antiquity: the inch, the width of a thumb; the handsbreadth or palm of 7.6 cm or 10.2 cm (3 or 4 ins); the foot, 30.5 cm (12 ins); the span of outstretched fingers about 22.9 cm (9 ins); the cubit which was the length of the forearm, 45.7 cm (1 ft 6 ins); the yard; and the fathom of extended arms, 1.83 m (6 ft). These would inevitably vary between communities, possibly originally based on the body of a leading man and, unless recorded in abiding stone, of which there is no record, modulating over the years as a yardstick became worn or another person's proportions were adopted.

The human body provided an obvious variety of lengths. Common sense indicates that practical considerations would demand longer measures when large structures were being planned and it is likely that multiples of a short body-length were devised like the English Rod. Thom proposed a Megalithic Rod of 2.07 m, 2½ Megalithic Yards. For Avebury Stukeley postulated that 'a staff of 10 foot, four inches, and a little more than half-a-inch [3.16 m], becomes the measuring-reed . . . being six [Druid] cubits'. On the island of Malekula in the New Hebrides, now Vanatua, the anthropologist, Bernard Deacon, recorded that natives had a 'rod' of a stick or creeper composed of five basic units of a span when building.[25]

Cautious evidence is emerging that yardsticks were used in early prehistoric Europe. The first persuasive data were assembled by Maud Cunnington following her and her husband's excavation of Woodhenge in 1926–7 (Table 5). The site, close to Stonehenge, consisted of 156 postholes of six ellipses which were meticulously planned by their nephew, Lt-Col. R. H. Cunnington. The respective long diameters were: 11.7, 17.6, 23.4, 29.3, 38.1, 43.9 m.

Wondering if a unit of measurement had assisted the builders Maud Cunnington found that a 'Short Foot' of 11½ ins (29.2 cm) fitted well, the six diameters being 40, 60, 80, 100, 130 and 150 Short Feet in length. 'Counting from the fingers of two hands is a natural one and was used in early times by many different people; the length of the human foot as a unit of length is equally obvious, and naturally varied slightly'.[26]

Although they were innovative her figures were not as accurate as she claimed. All were a little in error. Nor was the Megalithic Yard more compatible. But both were sufficiently close to stimulate further examination and the writer found that a 'Beaker

Yard', so called from the pottery discovered on the site, of 0.732 m produced perfect multiples of 4 for five of the six diameters, the 38.1 m feasibly being a minor mistake for 38.064 m, a mismeasurement of less than 6 mm whose adjustment would have resulted in a multiple of 52 units. Cunnington noted that the spacing between the six rings was a regular 2.92 m or precisely 4 Beaker Yards.

In other regions there may have been other preferred lengths, 95 cm in central Scotland and in south-west Ireland, figures that can only approximate to reality because of the inadequacy of many of the available plans for stone circles and also because the rings were the work of human beings with as many imperfections as people today.[27]

There is, nevertheless, some independent corroboration of a yardstick. Scrutiny of the design and size of the monumental Irish passage-tomb of Newgrange in the Boyne Valley led Powell to deduce a standardised unit of 13.1 m, 'a length which bears no relationship to any variant of the megalithic yard', but which had been chosen to determine the shape of the mound, and the plan of the passage and cruciform chamber. It might also have been used at the nearby tomb of Knowth.[28]

Applying the length to the various dimensions of Newgrange yielded one multiple of 6 × 13.1 m, 78.6 m, from the tomb's entrance at the south-east to the finely decorated kerbstone 52 opposite at the north-west. There were three multiples of 5, three of 4, one each of 3, 2, a width of 1 across the passage, and a tiny one of ½, 6.6 m, from side-chamber to side-chamber inside the tomb.

These are significant figures, relating as they do to critical lines and widths 'all built around a rigid frame comprising two 4:5:6 triangles and one 3:5:6 triangle. These give the monument its distinctive "heart" shape'.

It is likely, however, that 13.1 m was a 'rod' rather than a fundamental unit. It was probably an elongation for the laying-out of long distances multiplied from sixteen day-to-day 'yards' of 0.82 m, a length quite close to Thom's Megalithic Yard. There is a curiosity. As can be seen in Table 6 there seems to have been an identical counting-base of 4 to that at Woodhenge, eight units for the ½ Rod, forty-eight for 3 Rods and up to ninety-six for the long 6 Rods. It will be proposed later that simple counting-systems based on 3, 4 but rarely 5 were quite widely employed in the erection of stone circles. There were also preferred numbers of stones in the rings.[29]

At present it would seem both that yardsticks were known with individual but comparable lengths in separate communities and also that elementary counting-systems were in existence. These will be considered in the regional chapters that follow.

Table 6. The Boyne 'Rod' and the Boyne 'Yard.'

Boyne Rod Multiples of 13.1 m	m	Boyne Yard Multiples of 0.82 m
6	78.6	96
5	65.5	80
4	52.4	64
3	39.3	48
2	26.2	32
1	13.1	16
½	6.6	8

The Erection of Stones

'Let us consider for a moment what was the procedure in building a simple megalithic monument,' wrote T. E. Peet, 'When the stones were once on the spot it is not hard to imagine how they were set upright with levers and ropes.'

It may not be hard to imagine. Indeed, Fergusson deemed the construction of Stonehenge 'child's play' because the colossal ring of sarsens 'was erected leisurely' but such casually dismissive remarks evade the necessity of describing the digging of stoneholes, their shape and required depth, the use of clay, lubrication, the levers and ropes, the knowledge of how many workers were needed for each task, the overseers, the pre-shaping of the stones and the patterning of holes around the ring (Pl. 11). Quite frequently the holes were laid out, arguably by eye, in opposing pairs so that in the finished monument the stones were not always regularly spaced but often did stand opposite another on the far side of the ring. Imagination is not a satisfactory substitute for understanding.[30]

Once a stone was on site it was dragged to its place in the circle. Its hole had been prepared by the cutting and hacking of the ground with stone or flint axes, the topsoil shovelled out by ox shoulder-blades attached to wooden shafts, carried away in wickerwork baskets, the rougher, harder lumps of chalk or gravel or resistant stone manhandled off the site. Fractures of arms and legs, the distortions of arthritic joints, are evidence of physical strain induced by Fergusson's 'child's play'.

The hole was not a mere pit. Unless the bedrock was unmalleable, yielding only to hours of back-breaking pounding with heavy, blistering mauls, its depth would be

Plate 11. The monstrous 'Swindon' stone at Avebury's northern entrance. It weighs about 40 tons (Photograph: the author).

Plate 12. The cumbersome Goggleby stone, Shap (Photograph: the author).

decided by two factors. It had to be about a quarter the length of its pillar because if it were shallower the stone might not be held firmly. There was a second complication. Sometimes a ring of stones graded in height was intended, perhaps rising up towards the south-west, and then a more sensitive relationship between the length of the pillar and its fellows on either side of it would affect the deepness of its cavity.

Where stones were of more than one or two tons the near side of the hole would be ramped so that the block could be manoeuvred more easily and safely down the slope before being hauled upright against the vertical back of the pit. To reduce damage as the stone's base grated against the rear of its hole saplings stripped of their bark and greasy with oozing sap might be pile-driven upright tightly against the pit's back as anti-friction devices. Stake holes for this were uncovered at Stonehenge. At other sites 'the saplings may never have been driven into the virgin soil', leaving no trace of their existence.[31]

On occasion there was a further refinement. Across the bottom of some holes a thick layer of moist clay was paddled down. There have been varying explanations. A short while after the stone had been set up inspection of the clay would reveal whether the pillar was properly balanced in the layer, held perpendicular by temporary props. A gap growing between it and the clay would show that it had shifted. Alternatively, 'the stone must have largely found its own equilibrium [on the clay] after which its own weight would have kept it upright'.

During the 1973 excavation and re-erection of the inverted boulder of the Goggleby Stone at Shap (Pl. 12), six tons of bulbous granite, it was noted that 'the smooth interface of clay layer 5 and the monolith would provide a perfect surface for the stone to slide over'.[32]

Eventually the stone was pushed and levered down the ramp. When its end was resting at an angle of about 50° against the back of the hole it had to be levered upwards until it reached an angle of some 70° from the vertical. Then with stout ropes wound around its top men would drag it upright. With a pointed base like the Goggleby Stone's this demanded animal strength but little engineering expertise. Most boulders, slabs and blocks did not naturally possess such a characteristic. Men created one.

At Old Keig, a recumbent stone circle in Aberdeenshire, Kilbride-Jones saw that a shapely pillar flanking its recumbent was not flat-bottomed but sharply angled where a big triangle of bits and pieces had been roughly hammered off one side leaving its base 'keeled' like the downturned beak of a parrot. Margaret Stewart recognised similar shaping at several rings in Perthshire.[33] Fallen stones at many circles reveal the same technique that reduced the friction as the lifted stone's centre of gravity passed in front of this fulcrum or point of leverage. To allow for the 'beak' the back of many stoneholes had a deeper hollow to accommodate the extension.

At 70°, three-quarters of the way to the perpendicular, the stone was exerting a resistance of a fifth of its dead weight. Physical trials have shown that for a short while a man can pull 100 lbs, 45.4 kg. A cubic foot $(0.028 \, m^3)$ of granite weighs about 162 lbs, 73.5 kg. A straightforward calculation shows that an average 1.8 m high circle-stone, about 2.4 m long, and 1 m wide and thick would require a work-gang of twenty-four plus perhaps four or five other workers wedging the slowly rising block from behind.

$$\frac{(72 \, \text{c.ft} \div 5) \times 162 \, \text{lbs}}{100} = 24 \text{ men}$$

Once upright and held in place by timber supports but still only precariously balanced heavy chockstones were jammed into the gaps at the hole's sides, bashed down, more forced in on top, often so effectively that the pillar has remained unmoved through four or five millennia of rain, gusting winds and eroding snow and ice.[34]

Other than keeling it was rare for a stone to be shaped or trimmed in any manner. As always, its carpentry methods distinguished Stonehenge. Elsewhere it was suspected that the stones at the Hurlers three rings on Bodmin Moor had been hammer-dressed *in situ* and around them chippings formed what appeared to be a deliberate, but actually accidental, floor. Some flanking stones in north-eastern Scotland also were fashioned so that they would stand snugly against their recumbent.

Shaping was not a widespread custom, yet aesthetics are noticeable. Unaffected by humans the stones were sometimes selected for their differing appearance, tapering top against flat, tall against low, slender against plump. At Machrie Moor I on Arran granite boulders and sandstone needles alternated around the ring. And in circle after circle the practice prevailed of setting the unweathered, smoother face of the stone towards the interior of the ring.

'Rude stone monuments' the unsympathetic Fergusson called them. The poet, Andrew Marvell, was closer to the beliefs of the makers of these majestic rings:

> Choosing each stone, and poising every weight,
> Trying the measures of the breadth and height,
> Here pulling down, and there erecting new,
> Founding a firm estate by proportions true.[35]

The Number of Stones

Because of the fragmented state of many rings, tumbled, broken, robbed, it is often impossible to be sure of the original number of stones (Pl. 13). Uncertainty becomes despair in circles like Hampton Down in Dorset where a photograph of 1908 showed sixteen pillars. By 1964 there were twelve more. Worse came. Excavation in 1965 proved not only that the real prehistoric ring had been erected some distance to the east but had never contained more than eight stones.[36]

Plate 13. The eight standing stones of the Nine Stones, Bodmin Moor. Originally there may have been thirteen (Photograph: the author).

Despite this archaeological nightmare communities in Britain, often widely scattered, did have preferred numbers for their ritual centres. Perhaps thirteen stones for the little ellipses around Loch Roag on the island of Lewis. In south-western Ireland reliable estimates revealed that two-thirds of the rings were built of nine, eleven or thirteen stones. In the English Lake District several of the second-phase rings such as Grey Croft contained twelve. In the south-west peninsula of England many minor rings of Dartmoor were composed of thirty to thirty-six stones. In Cornwall, twenty-six to twenty-eight were the vogue on Bodmin Moor and nineteen to twenty-two at Land's End. Barnatt has pointed out that in that part of England the larger rings, 30 m or more across, tended to have between twenty-seven to thirty-two stones.[37]

Elementary counting-systems based on simple roots such as 3 or 4 but rarely 5 are detectable and it was they rather than the length of the circumference of a ring that decided the number of stones that would be raised along it. Over 70 per cent of the primary recumbent stone circles in north-eastern Scotland were made up of ten or eleven standing stones as well as the supine recumbent whether the perimeter was as short as the 56 m of Dyce, its stones spaced about 5.2 m apart, or as long as the 80 m of Sunhoney, with gaps of 7.3 m between the stones.[38]

Such numerical choices were decidedly regional (Pl. 14). Only sixty miles separates Alford at the heart of recumbent stone circle territories in Aberdeenshire from Aberfeldy to the south-west in Perthshire but there rings of ten or more stones are hugely outnumbered by the cluster of four-, six- and eight-stone circles.

What cannot be doubted is the liking for twelve-stone rings, which represent no fewer than 12 per cent of the quantifiable circles in Britain and Ireland. It has been suggested that the popularity of this number was based on its many factors of 2, 3, 4 and 6 and the ease with which it lent itself to the partition of a ring into quadrants, thereby facilitating the laying-out of the stoneholes.[39] It is noticeable that the circle of fifty-six Aubrey Holes at Stonehenge was probably designed by arranging closely set

Plate 14. The eleven stones of the Nine Stones or Maidens, Belstone, Dartmoor. The ring is also called the Seventeen Brothers (Photograph: the author).

pairs of postholes at north, east, south and west, and then filling each of the intervening arcs with twelve more holes.[40] Like the putative counting-system at Woodhenge and Newgrange a radix of 4 would have been an easy one to use. Five would have been computed 4 + 1, eleven 4 + 4 + 3. Errors frequently developed when numbers above twenty were required.

With such practical but undemanding numeracy it could be predicted that rings of four, eight, twelve and sixteen stones would be quite common and they do represent one in three of all the sites in Britain and Ireland where sufficient stones survive for their original number to be estimated.

Astronomy

Adding complication to complexity many rings had solar or lunar sightlines built into them. The subject is the most contentious in the study of stone circles. Belief in the astronomical purpose of circles received its most fervent advocacy in Lockyer's *Stonehenge and Other British Stone Monuments Astronomically Considered*, 1906. He contended that people set out the major axis of a ring towards a place on the skyline where a heavenly body, sun, moon or star, appeared. Other uncritically enthusiastic writers gave the same credence to alignments from the centres of circles, from one circle to another, to outlying stones, to mountain peaks and notches, even to cairns, standing stones and chambered tombs despite their being a thousand years older than the ring. Recent scholars, Thom, MacKie, Ruggles have been much more demanding in their work.

'Evidence' of a sightline in a single site is inadequate. It could be fortuitous. To ascertain alignments beyond doubt it is necessary to find them repeated in a large group of similar monuments in a restricted area, a principle established by the writer as long ago as 1969. The recumbent stone circles of north-eastern Scotland proved ideal rings for such research.[41]

It is only after the most rigorous analysis that an alignment should be accepted for, statistically, the odds are in favour of a good line occurring fortuitously in almost any circle. Examining an ellipse like Grey Croft in the Lake District, about 27×25 m in dimensions with twelve stones and an outlier there appear to be so many lines and so many possible targets that to discover nothing would be improbable unless sharp criteria are applied.

There are two questions about prehistoric astronomy, whether it existed with deliberate sightlines to the sun, moon or star or whether this is an illusion created by deceptive coincidences at Stonehenge and elsewhere. The second question is more subtle. If the lines did exist, what were they used for? Were there astronomer-priests scientifically studying the heavens or were the lines symbolical, for the dead or for the spirits of an Other-World?

Proof of an alignment demands the presence not only of a celestial target but also both an artificial backsight where an observer stood and a foresight towards which he looked. In stone circles it is assumed that the backsight was on the axis and that the foresight was man-made and remarkable such as a tall stone, or a decorated slab, an outlier or a row of standing stones. The existence of a convenient notch unindicated by any of these features is inadequate. 'Whereas it is logical to suppose that a row of stones or a pair of archways were designed to point to some celestial object . . . it is unjustifiable at the present time to assume that natural objects were so used . . . The problem is greatly alleviated by rejecting markers that are distinctly non-homogenous, such as a burial-tumulus viewed from a stone circle.'[42]

There is an alternative condition of accepting astronomical alignments and that would come from a single-phase monument in which there are several, unequivocal sightlines. Stonehenge would not qualify because its alignments were laid out over at least three phases. Godmanchester, a huge timber trapezoid in Cambridgeshire would. Its five radiocarbon assays indicate that it was constructed during a single phase ranging from 3965 (OXA-3370) to 3525 BC (OXA-3369) and it has been calculated that it contained some fourteen alignments towards midsummer, equinoctial and mid-winter sunrises and sunsets and midsummer and midwinter lunar events.

The criterion needs strict application. There is little qualitative difference between hypothetical alignments using a mélange of stone circles, cairns, standing stones and hill-slopes and the chimerical ley-lines fabricated out of the innocent countryside from the wishful 'alignments' of circles, hill-forts, mediaeval crosses and dew-ponds. Even outliers can be misleading. At Grey Croft Thom suggested that the pillar, no more than 1 m high, was nicely aligned on the setting of the bright star Deneb, α Cygni. With a declination of +36°.3, a combination of latitude, horizon height and azimuth (the compass-bearing), this would have dated the ring within a few years of 2300 BC, rather late for a site containing a broken Group VI stone axe. Worse, the situation of the stone is untrustworthy. The pillar had been buried around 1820 by a tenant farmer and only re-erected in 1949 by pupils of Pelham House school.[43] Its precise position within a foot or two before its disturbance is unknown.

This is not a quibble. The stone stood 33.5 m from the middle of the ring. If, instead of sighting over its low top an observer had looked to its left-hand or right-hand side there would have been a difference of nearly four centuries of where Deneb set beyond it on the distant horizon, the declinations changing from 36°.29 to 36°.49. The variation would be even greater if the stone has been somewhat misplaced. Fortunately, this is a dilemma of almost complete irrelevance to the megalithic monument under discussion. Alignments to stars other than the sun are not apparent. The targets were the sun or moon and those bodies moved so little across the skyline in the centuries between 3200 and 1000 BC that delicate definitions are impossible.

Despite the considerable handicap of being unable to look directly at the sun its movements were steadfast and easy to understand. It rose at the north-east at midsummer and over the following six months moved day by day southwards until reaching the south-east at midwinter. Its settings were as predictable, from south-west in the dead of the year to north-west when the weather was warmer and the trees were in leaf. Although prehistoric people may not have been aware of it these solstitial, or extreme, positions varied according to the latitude, the hours of summer daylight at latitude 50°, Land's End, being two hours fewer than those at latitude 60° at the Shetlands over 700 miles to the north because the sun was longer in the sky there. The reverse applied in winter when the Shetlands received just over four hours of daylight, Land's End nearly seven.

The sun is simple. The moon is not. Although, like the sun, it swings backwards and forwards from north to south along the horizon whereas the sun takes a year to complete its cycle the moon takes only a month, waxing and waning from full moon to crescent to invisibility in a fortnight. Its revolving crescents may have seemed magical to prehistoric people, its tips pointing to the west when waxing and gradually turning towards the east as it waned. And unlike the regularity of the sun it was doubly inconstant. At midsummer the full moon was at the south, illuminated by the sun at the north. At midwinter it was at the north. It and the sun were like searching partners, always circling, never meeting, in a stately, slow pavane, beautiful but baffling. Even more bewilderingly, the moon oscillated.

At both north and south its extreme risings and setting expanded and contracted over a period of 18.61 years. In the centre of Britain, at latitude 55°, one year the full midsummer moon at the south-east rose at its maximum position around 148° but in each of the following nine years it rose 2° to 3° farther north until finally it appeared no closer to the south than 124°, its minor standstill. Then it began its long return to its major rising. So involved was this lunar cycle together with its rapid monthly movements and frequent ascents in daylight when it could not be seen that it would have taken years, perhaps generations for observers to accumulate the knowledge of just where the lunar standstills would occur.

This is not to deny the astronomical awareness of the people who laid out the stone circles and henges of western Europe. Conversely, it is not intended to suggest that their alignments were anything more than approximate. The precision sometimes implied for them seldom existed and then perhaps only by accident.

Many of the earliest monuments of Britain were in some way connected with the movements of the sun or moon but the 'accuracy' of their alignments could be as coarse as ±5°, quite distinct from the few seconds of arc that have been claimed for some megalithic sites. The majority of earthen long barrows had their burials at the higher end which was customarily somewhere between NNE and SSE, the arc of the rising moon between its extremes. A related but solar interest can be detected in the arrangements of chambered tombs.[44] Fieldwork has convinced the writer that it is not possible to determine the bearing of these weathered mounds to better than ±2°.

From the researches of investigators over the past decades it is becoming clear that the builders of many stone circles, sites of ceremony and calendrical gatherings, continued to refine the alignments whose recorded positions were passed down, presumably orally, from generation to generation.

There is a fact firmly to be established. Had the intention of prehistoric societies been to construct an astronomical observatory they would not have designed a circle. A line of stones or a horseshoe of pillars for computations would have been more efficient. A circle is an enclosure. It would have been an effective fence demarcating the sacred and profane worlds but its plan militated against an exclusive use for solar or lunar observations and the prediction of eclipses. Whatever astronomical purpose it contained was only a part, perhaps minor, of its function.

There is a gloss. The flimsiest of hints exist that some alignments may contain disrupted records of a prehistoric calendar. Because of the relative predominance of a seemingly significant batch of solar declinations Thom suggested that they implied the existence of an annual calendar of sixteen months. 'When we find indications of the same declinations in Cumberland, Lewis, Wales and Caithness we must consider the possibility that the calendar dates throughout this wide area were in phase.'[45]

The data are far from steadfast. The alignments were extracted from a variety of sites: disparate chambered tombs, a diversity of stone circles, and rows differing in length and numbers of stones. Few of the monuments were in perfect condition. Some of them were shattered. All of them were scattered. What superficially seems convincing diminishes when examined more carefully. Choosing for each declination just one of several stone circles listed by Thom exposes the uncertainty (Table 7).

Dispersion is more obvious than decision. The rings range from northern Scotland to England and central Wales. Some are plain, some contain cairns, one has a recumbent block. Their alignments are composed indiscriminately of sightlines from circle to circle, from circle to an outlier or to the indicated foresight of a mountain peak, from stone to stone and from circle to stone row.[46] The calendrical interpretation may be valid but the evidence for it is weak.

To re-establish a calendar from such wreckage is akin to an attempt to build a delicate grandfather clock out of spare parts collected from the rubbish dumps and scrapyards of far-flung towns. Yet from the imperfect evidence eight declinations do seem to emphasise risings and settings of the sun around ±16° and ±24°. They coincide with the major 'Celtic' festivals of the summer solstice sunrise and sunset, +24°; the May

Table 7. Solar Alignments from Midsummer to Midwinter. Thom, 1967, Table 8.1.

Alignment	Site	Thom's No.	County
Midsummer sunrise	Esslie the Greater	B2/4	Kincardine
Midsummer sunset	Loupin' Stanes	G7/4	Dumfriess
Lughnasa sunrise	Cauldside Burn	G4/14	Kirkcudbright
Beltane sunset	Nant Tarw	W11/4	Brecks
Imbolc sunrise	Sheldon of Bourtie	B1/8	Aberdeen
Samain sunset	White Moss NE	L1/6d	Cumberland
Midwinter sunrise	Temple Wood	A2/8	Argyll
Midwinter sunset	Loch Buie	M2/14	Mull

Day sunset of Beltane, +16°; the early August sunrise of Lughnasa, +16°; the sunrise of early February, Imbolc, −16°; sunset at the beginning of November, Samain, −16°; and the solstitial sunrise and sunset of midwinter, −24°.

There is one fact. Although some festivals such as Imbolc and Lughnasa are only faintly represented amongst the declinations the two solstices were strongly emphasised whether at Stonehenge, Ballochroy, Newgrange or elsewhere. Midwinter, moreover, was recorded almost twice as heavily as midsummer, its sunset taking precedence over dawn. It is clear that the turning points of the year, particularly the time of change from darkness and cold to light and warmth, were of very great importance to prehistoric people.

The data are flimsy as gossamer. But stiffening comes from the impression that these pagan celebrations were taken over by the Christian church after it had failed to eradicate them. The summer solstice became the Feast of St John the Baptist; Lughnasa was changed to Lammas, the Harvest Festival; Imbolc to Candlemas and the Feast Day of St Brigid, herself a heathen goddess. Samain was converted to All Saints and All Souls Day; and the important midwinter solstice was celebrated as Christmas.

Yet amidst all this upheaval and purification it is interesting to notice that the exhortations and condemnations of the Church had no effect on the May Day orgies of Beltane, the time of licentious and promiscuous revelry. Beltane with its possibly phallic maypoles and sexual freedom proved significantly too enjoyable for Christianity to destroy.

In the conflict between animal pleasure and spiritual purity pleasure prevailed. What to missionaries was debauchery was, to its participants, a means of communion with nature to ensure the fertility of the earth, acts of sympathetic procreation between men and women. That it could also be intensely pleasurable encouraged its continuation which, changed and vulgarised, persisted into the early seventeenth century and beyond.

> Thus the Robin and the Thrush
> Musicke make in every bush.
> While they charm their pretty notes
> Young men hurle up maidens cotes.[47]

It was the one heathen festival that Christianity was unable to convert. Indeed, the reverse occurred. St Walpurga of Wimborne, Dorset, and abbess of the double monastery at Heidenheim in Germany died on 25 February 779. Years later her bones were transferred to Eichstätt between Nuremberg and Munich on the inauspicious date of 1 May, the day of Beltane.

Perhaps she had been regarded as a protectress of crops as the three ears of corn on her images suggest, and in the rural mind she may also have been regarded as the embodiment of fertility. Whatever the cause it resulted in the day of her translation being celebrated as Walpurgisnacht when witches in the Harz mountains copulated with demons at the time of the burgeoning Spring. Centuries later peasants would dance in the fields on 'her' day to make the crops grow tall.[48] Pagan rituals of fecundity, Christianity and prehistoric ceremonies of creation intermingle in activities that may survive as remembered wisps of a long-discarded calendar.

Conclusions

The mechanics of stone circle building are gradually being recovered. Their general shape has long been recognised. Almost three hundred years ago in 1726 knowing of the Rollright Stones John Toland wrote that 'These Temples *are Circles of Obeliscs* or erect stones, some larger, some narrower, as in all other Edifices, some more and some less magnificent. They are for the greatest part perfectly circular.'

Although unspecific about methods of design this was more respectful than Fergusson's judgement a hundred and fifty years later. 'The circle at Rollright is a sort of monument that the boys of any of our larger schools could set up in a week.' He was wrong. Yet a reverse opinion following the publication of Alexander Thom's hypotheses was almost as over-stated.

'Britain is dotted with ring-shaped monuments whose ground-plan appears crude – at first glance. Closer scrutiny reveals that they are perfectly symmetrical, in fact, their very oddness seems not only intentional but the product of careful calculations. But what those calculations were is a puzzle that tantalises scholars.'[49]

'Tantalising' is exactly right. The 'careful calculations' are indeed a tantalus, a frustration of searching for an answer that is unobtainable because it did not exist. The circles tease and confuse because they are contradictions of complexity and coarseness, seemingly identical but always individual and with a panoply of 'furniture' that changed from district to district.

Not every ring was plain. There are the refinements of central stones that are not central, concentrated in two major groups three hundred miles apart in south-west Scotland and south-west Ireland. There are portalled entrances in Cumbria, concentric circles around the North Channel, avenues in Wessex, long rows on Dartmoor. There are outlying stones, scatters of glittering quartz, internal cists, burials, ground scorched red where pyres once burned. There are sightlines to sun and moon and to hills and mountains, perhaps the dwellings of the gods.

None of these is a tantalus. They are real. What their significance was to their builders is a difficult problem but not one that has to remain unanswerable. 'What song the Syrens sang, or what name Achilles assumed when he hid himself among women, though puzzling questions, are not beyond of all conjecture,' decided Sir Thomas Browne.[50] Nor are the mysteries of stone circles.

Century by century blood-stained Druids have been converted into meditative Druids and then into astronomer-priests investigating celestial minutiae who have today been re-transformed into societies that erected the circles to protect their world, people who believed in an other-world of strong, sometimes malicious forces, powers that could be placated and manipulated through long-proven rituals and offerings. It was not science that consoled men and women. It was supplication.

Chapter Four

Function: *Calendars, Cults and Sex*

The matter of this collection is beyond human reach: we being miserably in the dark, as to the oeconomy of the invisible world, which knows what we do, or incline to, and works upon our passions and sometimes is so kind as to afford us a glimpse of its prae-science.

John Aubrey, 1696, xv

Function

The most important question about stone circles, of course, is what they were used for, what happened in them, and this can still not be answered completely. Archaeological material, literally material and therefore voiceless, provides only the frailest evidence upon which to base any speculation about the nature of prehistoric social practices. Fleming's comment that 'many prehistorians fall into the trap of saying "it is to do with ritual", therefore it must be connected with unknowable and irrational ideas (in my own frame of reference), therefore I cannot hope to understand it'[1] is symptomatic of the frustration, sometimes exasperation, of having to cope with ghosts, the discarded remnants and rubbish of the past, the objects lost and forgotten, with no inherent message, out of context, the feeblest specks of what once existed, sounds silent and gone forever.

'Ritual and religion,' wrote Orme, 'are taboo subjects in archaeological circles, denounced by the brave and avoided by the sensible; only a perverse few continue their studies in this dangerous field'.[2] This is correct. Yet there are reasons for optimism. Ritual can be recognised by its dissimilarity from the activities of the mundane world. 'In a "ritual" context, items could come into association which would never be mixed in day-to-day life, or could be treated in thoroughly abnormal ways', and 'ritual represents a situation in which a microcosm of the world can be manipulated within a bounded analytic space'.[3]

The rituals of prehistoric peoples may be incomprehensible to us or they may be understandable but this is not the problem. The difficulty is to be certain that we can identify and define those beliefs from the fragments of tangible associations that remain. Speculation is easy. Realisation is almost impossible for an extinct society. Firth has written of the elusive meanings of modern Polynesian feasts even when they have been explained to European anthropologists, Evans-Pritchard remarked 'that we have to account for religious facts in terms of the totality of the culture and society in which they are found ... They must be seen as a relation of parts to one another within a coherent system, each part making sense only in relation to other institutional systems, as part of a wider set of relations.'[4]

If this is so despairingly true of extant primitive communities where custom may still be physically observed and participants spoken with then how much harder it must be to re-establish a prehistoric religion from which all the practices, taboos, social codes, ceremonies have gone, leaving only the fallen stones and broken artefacts. The archaeologist must speculate even to assess the size of an ancient population. He must be yet more daring to propose a framework of kinship and tribal relationships because his models will be founded on anthropologically dubious parallels. To say anything detailed about religion within this vague society is virtually wishful thinking. But archaeology is a tool of history, a study of mankind, and attempts must be made even if the theoretical structure has been pronounced jerry-built.

Comfortingly, it is possible that some clues concerning early religion are available from the knowledge of later prehistoric groups whose ritual practices were historically recorded by classical authors such as Julius Caesar though even here one should accept that all 'history' is a one-sided interpretation in which misunderstanding, prejudice and partial knowledge affect the 'knowledge' passed down to us.

Calendars

Centuries after the abandonment of stone circles the Celtic Druids of the Iron Age may have recorded the relationship between the sun's and moon's movements on the Coligny bronze calendar, discovered in 1897 40 miles north-east of Lyon. This fractured first-century AD tablet carried a table of sixty lunar months probably of the sidereal length of 27.3 days. Two more intercalary months were added to it.

Written in the Gaulish language but in Roman lettering each month was divided into a 'good', waxing half and a 'bad' or ANMAT, waning fortnight. Being based on the completed revolutions of the moon the periods were slightly shorter than the Gregorian calendar month, losing an average of fifty minutes daily although in September this was reduced to twenty minutes allowing the full moon to be seen in the early evening for several nights in succession, the farmer's Harvest Moon. It has been calculated that the Druidical 'Golden Year' was accurate to within two days of the moon's 18.61 year cycle. Possible precursors of such a calendar were probably known in Late Neolithic times and are discussed in chapter five.

Some ratification of the existence of a prehistoric lunar calendar comes from the old Irish thirteen month-year: 21 January, the month of Brigit, the tripartite goddess, later to become the Christian St Brigid, abbess of Kildare; 18 February, Gwydion, the magician; 18 March, Bran, voyager to the Underworld; 15 April, Arianhod, sister of Gwydion; 13 May, Olwen, daughter of the king of giants; 10 June, Dagda, 'the good god'; 8 July, Cuchulainn, superhuman war-hero; 5 August, Mannan, son of the sea-god; 2 September, Sadv; 30 September, Paluc, owner of a mythical cat; 28 October, Gwyn, Lord of the Dead; 22 November, Cailleach, a lovely young woman horrifyingly transmuting into an old hag; 23 December, Ceridwen, the enchantress.[5]

Such signs of cultural continuity are not an argument for inhabiting stone circles with Druids. Caesar in Book VI, Section 14, of his *Gallic War* wrote 'It is believed that their rule of life was discovered in Britain and transferred thence to Gaul'. It is entirely possible that the ancestry of these priests and lawgivers extended back well before Celtic times, stemming from Neolithic and Bronze Age societies much concerned with seasonal fertility ceremonies.[6]

Of late it has been suspected that many Iron Age hillforts were not only for defence but may have served as focuses for large-scale ceremonies just as the earlier causewayed enclosures and henges had done. The construction of forts like Maiden Castle, Dorset, and the Trundle, Sussex, on the sites of Neolithic earthworks might have arisen from the wish to perpetuate traditional meeting-places. Hunsbury hillfort, Northampton, was within a few hundred metres of the causewayed enclosure at Briars Hill. Richard Feacham speculated that '*Medionemeton*, "the Middle Sanctuary", known to have existed near the Antonine Wall in Scotland, may have been located at Cairnpapple (West Lothian), where excavation of a Neolithic henge monument showed that this sacred spot continued to be revered in the Bronze Age and also in the Iron Age when four humans were interred in long stone cists'. So far from breaking with the past there is clear evidence of continuity of custom into the Celtic Iron Age.

Ritual shafts, similar to those of the Iron Age but unequivocally dated to the Bronze Age have been excavated at Wilsford in Wiltshire and Swanwick in Hampshire, the latter with traces of dried flesh in it.[7]

It is also permissible to suggest that the corpus of astronomical knowledge held by the Celts had a primitive origin in the orientations and sightlines known in the long burial-places and stone circles of the Neolithic just as the four great Celtic festivals developed from customs in which the months of February, May, June, August, November and December were celebrated in megalithic rings three millennia before the Celts.[8] There is certainly a notable correlation between the postulated Iron Age provinces of the British Isles and architectural regions of stone circles which, presumably reflect broad geographical territories as suggested in this book.

Early stone circles contain simple orientations to solar or lunar extremes, marking the times when ceremonies of propitiation or purification were to be held. Such meetings for the appeasing of the elements survived in Europe into the Middle Ages and later, being held at special occasions of the year, usually Spring and Midsummer but, in north-western Europe, often at Hallowe'en (31 October) and Whitsun (early May). In the hills around Callendar in central Scotland on the night before May Day, less than two hundred years ago, people would cut a turf-circle on the hillside large enough to accommodate the celebrants. A bonfire was lit and an oaten cake broken up, one portion blackened with charcoal, and everything put in a bag. Blindfolded each person took a piece. He or she who drew the dark one was to be the token sacrifice. Similar rituals continued in Wales, Scotland and Ireland until late in the eighteenth century. In England, on the first Saturday after 1 May the great May Queen festival was held in Bromley, Kent and at Knutsford in Cheshire, and May Poles were set up in many villages and towns, a very distinctive one still standing at Welford near Stratford-on-Avon.

On other occasions, at Lent, villagers would leap through bonfires to help their crops ripen, blazing torches of straw were carried into the fields and effigies burnt as offerings. Such gatherings and seasonal activities are likely to have an antiquity reaching back to the first farmers.

George Long wrote that 'there can be no doubt that the Beltane customs in Scotland on the first of May, and the Bonfires on Midsummer Eve, do actually date from the pagan worship of Baal and of the human sacrifices which characterised that dreadful cult'. Baity elaborated: 'In general, the evidence appears to indicate that astronomical lore, astra and deity symbolism, and seasonal rituals set by astra events and considered essential to successful agriculture and stock breeding were part of the Neolithic mixed farming tool-kit, and 'the great emphasis on the summer solstice rituals in areas where the megalithic cultures were evident does imply a possible connection'.[9]

Cults

To the calendrical implications of stone circles can be added that many of them were associated with an axe-cult. Two stone axes were deposited at Llandegai henge and one of bronze at Mount Pleasant earthwork enclosure in Dorset. Concentrations of stone axes have been noted around Avebury and the Ring of Brodgar, Orkney. Stone and bronze axes were unearthed at Mayburgh henge near Penrith.

Such a cult was widespread in Europe. Several instances of the axe being associated with the sun are known in countries as far apart as Spain and Sweden. At Troldebjerg, Denmark, a hearth in a Middle Neolithic long house covered a pit with pot and an axe with its cutting-edge upwards. 'No doubt the ritual . . . centred around the axe in association with the kindled fire,' wrote Maringer. 'Both must have been symbols of the sky god who had sway over lightning and fire. It is the same god to which the peasant made offerings by placing them in the soil of his field, burying them in the earth, or hiding them under a stone'.

Even in the last century farmers in western Europe believed that stone axes lying in their fields were thunderbolts and talismen. In Germany an axe is still considered an object of fertility. To the Neolithic mind an axe used to fell trees, to till fields and which struck sparks might have been considered to contain generative powers and have a kinship with fire. A place where axes were bartered or exchanged would thus be not only a meeting place and a market but also a temple in which trade and ritual went hand in hand.

The axe became the embodiment of the forces of nature, especially at important times of the year such as midsummer or midwinter. It was a long-lasting cult, enduring well into Celtic centuries. Model axes were found at the ritual centre of Woodeaton, Oxfordshire, built in the Romano-British period.[10]

An axe-cult gives extra significance to the famous carvings at Stonehenge, all in cardinal positions, as well as another at the recumbent stone circle of Drombeg in Co. Cork. In Brittany motifs of shafted and unshafted axes were ground out on western stones in line with the equinoctial sunset at the horseshoe of Er-Lannic, another was found at the *fer-à-cheval* of Kergonan, both in the Morbihan, and a fine axe in relief was noticed in the *fer-à-cheval* of Tréguier, Côtes-du-Nord.

In Brittany many of the great Carnac Mounds such as Le Moustoir and Tumulus St Michel held sumptuous grave-goods including miniature 'axes' of lovely callais or serpentine, perforated to be hung around the neck like spiritual forebears of Christian crucifixes.[11] Such non-functional 'axes', like those of chalk at Stonehenge and Woodhenge, are indications of a widespread cult.

The deposits of actual stone axes at the northern *fer-à-cheval* at Er-Lannic reflect this. The horseshoe seems to have been raised on a former *atélier* for the production of axes, an observation in keeping with the hypothesis that circles and the axe-trade were sometimes interconnected. The tallest stone at the south and cupmarked pillars close to solar positions reveals Er-Lannic as an example of the intermingling of ritual, social activity and trade in a megalithic ring. Supporting evidence for these interlocking roles comes from the stone axe discovered as a stray find in the Castlerigg ring. Revealingly, a broken Group VI axe lay by the south stone in the Grey Croft stone circle.[12]

Known as elf-shots as late as the nineteenth century AD the prehistoric stone axe was placed in cattle-troughs to protect animals against ill-health. It was used as a charm against the pangs of childbirth in Scotland. The connection with a sky-god is clear for in western England the axes were thought to be thunderbolts and in an interesting link with fire cottages in Ireland often had a stone axe placed in their rafters as protection against lightning.[13]

Although the belief in an axe-cult in stone circles is justified the same is not true of a pan-European religion that worshipped a mother-goddess, the 'hag' or old woman. Because of a profusion of female figurines, engraved plaques and carved stones these have been interpreted as a goddess cult over Mediterranean and western European lands. Such a female deity has been identified in regions as far apart as Anatolia and Ireland, often represented not as a complete figure but symbolically by her eyes. 'It was a sometimes awe-inspiring face, dominated by excessively big eyes under arched brows.' Hence the name of 'Eye Goddess'. Carved motifs, supposedly of eyes or eyebrows but perhaps outlines of flying birds caused Gordon Childe to write of stones that 'disclose the chthonic deity to whose bosom the faithful dead returned'. Robert Graves in a collation of fancy speckled with fact, *The White Goddess* ('a silly book. I wish I'd never written it'), envisaged the passage-tomb of Newgrange as the home of Dagda who may 'be equated with Osiris, or Adonis, or Dionysus, who was born from a fir and mothered by the horned Moon-goddess Isis, or Io, or Hathur.'[14]

Such analogies are exaggerated. What persuasive evidence there is of such a guardian of the dead seems limited to France, particularly Brittany, whereas in Britain she has no carvings and in Ireland the art in the passage-tombs is more solar-orientated. Analysis of Boyne motifs make the goddess-interpretation unlikely whereas the 'sun-dial' stone at Knowth and the incidence of the midwinter sunrise roofbox at Newgrange clearly demonstrate an interest in solar events.

'As the evidence stands, there are two great provinces of megalithic stone-cult art: Brittany and Ireland, and although both share with the [Iberian] peninsula a basic symbolism, both display such emphatic and large-scale divergent achievements that they cannot have replied solely on that one southern source.'[15] Stone circles are unlikely to have been temples of the mother goddess. The activities within them were more probably directed to fertility practices.

Dancing

That these included dancing is an assumption that cannot be proved although such communal activity is well recorded amongst primitive societies. Frazer gave many examples of ring-dancing around a maypole in Europe at the leafing-time: around bonfires at Lent when in Switzerland and elsewhere burning wheels like sun-discs were rolled down hills and when witch effigies were burnt on hilltops. On the Isle of Man a wren was killed at the winter solstice and buried. Then the people would dance in a ring. Such circular group-dances were customary at important divisions of the year.

Plate 15. A sixteenth-century sketch of a Virginian indian dance.

It is intriguing to learn that many of the ceremonies of the American indians left the same sort of material that is discovered in British ritual sites (Pl. 15). At the time of the first fruits in August or September a whole Creek village would undergo a process of purification. During the festival that followed warriors danced around a fire. Finally, men and women together formed three rings to dance once more around the fire before bathing in running water to free themselves of their past sins. The Seminole indians performed similar rites.

Much of these ceremonies would leave no trace but there is comparable evidence in some British circles of seasonal gatherings, of bonfires, of rites at sunset, of associations with water. In the pre-literate Neolithic and Bronze Ages no direct record survives, even oral, of the activities inside megalithic rings but it is of interest to find a firm connection with dancing in the names of many circles. Both the Trippet Stones and the Merry Maidens, like several other Cornish rings, are reputedly young girls turned into stone for dancing on the Sabbath. At Stanton Drew a wedding party was petrified for dancing on after midnight on the Saturday. Athgreany in Co. Wicklow is supposedly a group of dancers and their piper who suffered the same fate for their sacrilegious merry-making.

Stonehenge was known as the Giants' Dance. Haltadans in the Shetlands was 'the limping dance'. The Merry Maidens in Cornwall was also known as 'Dans Maen', the stone dance. In Brittany at Les Demoiselles, Langon, girls were petrified for dancing on the Sabbath. Such associations between rings of standing stones, merrymaking and dancing were widespread in south-west England and Brittany.[16]

In the ditch around a round barrow at Winterbourne Whitchurch in Dorset the group was worn smooth by dancers' feet. At the barrow of Sutton 268, Glamorgan, dancers had circled the burial before the barrow was heaped over it.[17]

Some musical instruments have survived such as the simple pipe of a perforated swan's leg from the Wilsford 23 barrow in Wiltshire and the nine-piece pan pipe from a shaman's grave at Przeczyce in Poland. It is likely that the Neolithic pottery drums from the Trichterbecher cultures of northern Europe provided the rhythmic background for festive dancing like that proposed for stone circles.

Music was probably vital to the ceremonies. Experiments have shown that drumming inside tombs like Camster Round, Caithness, and recumbent stone circles such as Easter Aquorthies, could have created resonating sounds and vibrations that evoked an eerie atmosphere. Inside the dark burial-place the stale air, smells, skeletons and corpses 'combined with echoes and possibly resonance, these elements could have amounted to a remarkable and affecting experience'. By association drumming and the playing of wind instruments inside megalithic rings may have heightened the awareness of death and the forces of the other world.[18]

The tenuous data favour some form of dancing in the rings. Witchcraft at the Rollright Stones, at the Auldearn Clava tomb in Scotland, perhaps at Long Meg and Her Daughters, contribute something because if Murray were correct witchcraft was in part a post-Christian survival of pagan customs although 'the fancies of the late Margaret Murray need not detain us. They were justly, if irritably, dismissed as "vapid balderdash" by C. L. Ewen in *Some Witchcraft Criticisms*, 1938'. Yet mediaeval demonology did contain 'scattered fragments of paganism'. In witch-covens, 'the dances were the rapid, sexually exciting dances of the fertility cults. They were undoubtedly ancient and pre-Christian.' At her trial in 1662 Isobel Gowdie, whose coven of thirteen witches had met at the now-destroyed stone circle around the Auldearn Clava cairn in Inverness-shire asserted that the 'Devil always takes the Maiden in his hand next him when we would dance Gillatrypes'.[19]

As it is very likely that the horned or antlered 'god' of the Bronze Age was ultimately transmuted into the Devil of the witches in Christian times his existence in such contexts is another indication that dancing was a part of prehistoric religious practices. Evidence of the Christianisation of pagan rituals may survive in the well-known Horned Dance held in early September at Abbots Bromley, Staffordshire, as part of the annual Lammas Wake, itself possibly a relic of the Celtic harvest festival of Lughnasa.

Communal dancing would not preclude an axe-cult which could have been an integral element of the ceremonies as rock-carvings at Bohuslän in Sweden reveal. And merely because dancing is well-attested amongst early societies does not mean that a megalithic ring in which it took place could not be elegantly designed.[20]

Much of the opposition to the geometrical and astronomical hypotheses of the late Alexander Thom have been based on the improbability of Neolithic peasant farmers being capable of such erudition. Similar objections have been aimed against the later Druids as Pythagorean philosophers. 'We know that the Celts at this period, say 80 bc, were still practising divination by human sacrifice and preserving the skulls of slain enemies by nailing them as trophies to the porches of their houses. Is it possible that they were at the same time living on the rarefied levels of Greek philosophy?'

To which the answer must be affirmative. A miserable domestic, even savage way of life and the possession of a high intellect are not incompatible states.

As a people the Celts have always had a natural feeling for learning and intellectual exercise. It is an aspect of their temperament that has amazed and intrigued outsides who have come into contact with them, and have found such a marked contrast between their frequently crude and often careless domestic arrangements and the refinement and elegance of their use of language and appreciation of linguistic subtlety.

In the same way the reeking midden around the Neolithic village of Skara Brae did not necessarily render its inhabitants incapable of abstract thought. Indeed, the reverse has been argued, that it and other settlements such as Durrington Walls, occupied by users of arcane grooved ware, were the centres of a privileged class. 'The filthy state of the rooms . . . need present no obstacle to the theory that they were the residences of a small élite . . . supported by the agricultural population.' Rather than a miserable village on the coast 'could Skara Brae and Rinyo [a similar settlement on Rousay] have been the residences of some of these wise men and their families who were engaged in astronomical, ceremonial and magical work in the Orkney islands?'[21]

Yet before the student of the Late Neolithic sees it as a Euclidean Utopia he should recall the quite extensive evidence for fertility cults in British early prehistory whose practices would probably be obscene to modern thought, and try to reconcile these with Thom's astronomical magi. It is important to remember that many recorded Celtic customs like the horned god date back to at least the Bronze Age when the stag, and perhaps the bull, were representative of the sun. The survival of horns and crotals from the votive hoard of Dowris suggests a bull-cult there in the later second millennium BC.[22]

It may therefore be necessary to envisage ceremonies of animal symbolism performed in megalithic rings by shamans or witch-doctors. If there is any validity in the triple assumption that Celtic beliefs were descended from earlier traditions; that parallels may be made between other primitive people and British Bronze Age societies; and, thirdly, that surviving artefacts are informative about Neolithic and Bronze Age usages, then the evidence is strong that religious rites in stone circles were very much concerned with fertility, their fulfilment emanating from acts of sympathetic magic related to animals.

Sexual Activity

A stone circle starkly simple on its hillside today may be transformed into a prehistoric Mount Palomar without difficulty but the wealth of Celtic animal mythology and the images on Scandinavian rock-carvings warn that it may be necessary to have the stones illuminated by night-fires and inhabited by antlered shamans holding axes on high, raising finger-spread hands, performing acts of fertilisation with domestic animals and with humans.

'The belief that it is possible to influence the fertility of the land and the abundance of crops by sexual intercourse on the part of human beings is too familiar to need elaboration' and 'In prehistoric times it would seem that the Sky-father Earth-mother fertility ritual was enacted, doubtless by human instruments and agents of the respective god and goddess, to enhance the fecundity of the soil and the reproduction processes in nature generally.' 'The association between men and animals is also made clear in a number of scenes of bestiality. In one from the Val Camonica, a man is penetrating what appears to be a donkey.'[23]

The shaman would 'become' the sun-god himself by imitative actions, practices more expected of bone-rattling witch-doctors than of Thom's grave and dispassionate mathematical astronomers. Body-painting was known as the lumps of red and yellow ochre from Mosley Height, Skara Brae and elsewhere testify.

Sex was not unknown or unwelcome to prehistoric societies. Masturbation has been inferred from the postures of some Maltese clay figures. Previously accepted as arrow-straighteners or 'ritual batons' some short, cylindrical Palaeolithic artefacts have been speculatively reinterpreted as erotic dildoes. Farming and fecundity went together.

> I see this obsession with fertility reflected in Neolithic monuments. Tall stones were erected, over which the 'life-giving' sun could be seen to rise. At midwinter, in some places, the rays of the sun then penetrated artificial mounds via long passages – as at Newgrange in Ireland. Interpretations of the megaliths have often downplayed their anthropomorphic and sexual aspects. For me they are clear evidence of the invention of 'Mother Earth', the gendering of earth as female.[24]

The physical evidence of entrances to circles, of avenues leading to them, may confirm such beliefs.

If it is considered that sexual symbolism is implicit in the deliberately differing heights, shapes and positioning of stones then it is likely that both men and women participated in the rites. There is certainly a consistency in the opposing of flat-topped and pointed stones in the entrances and in the 'high-and-low' sides of avenues to make the supposition a feasibility. If, moreover, these interpretations are correct it becomes a probability that avenues led to circles rather than away from them, lines of approach with men on the right, women on the left. Here the physical evidence ends. What happened inside the circles must still be left to the imagination.

Much early religion was naturalistic, concerned with nature and its effects, sometimes requiring a shaman to intercede with nature on behalf of the community, less a witch-doctor than a medium who would dance himself into a drum-beaten ecstacy before passing into a trance.

> A fire burns on the ground. Framed against the night by the red glow of the flickering flames, the shaman begins to move rhythmically, drumming, dancing, leaping and singing. The little bells on his robe tinkle, his iron ornaments clatter, and the Tungus sit there in the dim light, their attention rivetted on his every move. The shaman's excitement communicates itself to the circle of spectators, and the larger the audience, the stronger the empathy between them and him. They all know each other, being inter-related and members of the same clan. Drawn together by the combination of night and firelight, they allow the monotonous rhythm of the drums to waft them irresistibly from the everyday world. The excitement mounts, leaping like a spark from one man to the next, until all are near ecstacy and each is at once spectator and performer, doctor and patient, hammer and anvil.[25]

Many of the Plains indians of America had a form of Sun Dance – which had little to do with sun-worship – that was prompted by the need for supernatural assistance. It involved slow, communal dancing in a circular enclosure around a 'killed' tree, the hardly moving 'dancers' going without food or water until they drifted into a trance. The Great Basin indians, both men and women, also danced around a tree, singing songs about the animals they hunted. Even the post-Christian Ghost Dance was a desperate attempt to invoke the old powers to bring back the buffalo and the indians' dead tribesmen.

The dancing is gone. What does survive in Britain is evidence of fertility beliefs dating back to the Neolithic: from flint mines, from causewayed enclosures and henges.

Plate 16. 'Female' and 'male' sarsens in the Kennet Avenue, Avebury (Photograph: the author).

Both at Grimes Graves and at Blackpatch a realistically carved chalk phallus lay in the pits. Other chalk phalli were discovered at Windmill Hill and, in bone, at the Trundle. Chalk figurines came from Windmill Hill and Maiden Castle, Dorset. A large chalk phallus was found in a shaft at Maumbury henge. Of the same Late Neolithic period, from a repaired section of the Bell trackway in the Somerset fens came the hermaphroditic ashwood figure with breasts and developed penis described discreetly as a 'god-dolly'. Another male figurine, of pine, was unearthed at Dagenham, Essex, possibly of the Bronze Age, with a hole for a detachable penis very like the Late Bronze Age wooden figures from Roos Carr, Yorkshire. Four of them stand on a ship and may be compared with the Bronze Age rock-carvings from Ostfold and Bohuslän which have tentatively been linked with 'the hypothetical epiphany of the sun-god at a Spring festival'.[26]

Standing stones (Pl. 16), especially those at the centre of a circle, have frequently been described as representations of phalli for fertility rites. So might the small carving from the nuraghe culture of Sardinia which shows 'three naked women dancing a wild dance round a stone'. Standing stones, sometimes associated with deposits of stone axes, have been found in the forecourts of chambered tombs, sometimes apparently chosen for their evocative shape, and such pillars have been interpreted as sexual symbols. If the pillars inside stone circles were indeed phallic representations then it becomes all the more likely that at such sites rituals of generation took place.[27]

Drink and Drugs

When considering prehistoric ways of life it is essential not to think of the people as simplified versions of ourselves, engaged in meetings governed by decorous behaviour. Their beliefs, values, customs and cultural background were different. They were superstitious, conservative, dependent on tradition, with little comprehension of the world's natural laws, and relying almost totally on ritual for protection. Neither propriety nor sobriety were obligations to be respected when people gathered at stone circles or other ritual enclosures. Alcohol and other stimulants quite possibly determined the conduct inside the rings.

An unlikely trio of an Iron Age Archdruid, Captain Cook, and Dr Crippen might seem out of place in this debate but not if the plants associated with the three men are listed instead. Meadowsweet, *filipendula ulmaria*, was one of the Druids' sacred plants. Fruit of the lime provided the vitamin-C that diminished the effects of scurvy amongst James Cook's eighteenth-century crews. Henbane, *hyoscyamus niger*, a hallucinogenic and poisonous herb could induce fantasies of flying. It also killed Crippen's wife. The prehistoric existence of concoctions that included all three plants reveals something of the nature of the proceedings in stone circles.

Alcohol was known. The small-leaved lime tree, *tilia cordata*, was both a chandlery and a distillery for Neolithic man. Once widespread in England along streams and valleys from the Thames to the Humber, flourishing in oak forests,[28] the fibrous bark of the shapely, grey-trunked trees was excellent for twining into strong ropes. More pleasurably, the lime's dull yellow flowers emitted a wonderful scent and attracted bees. Honey had long been known for its sweetening properties and from a drained honeycomb an intoxicating drink could be fermented in the form of mead, a name derived from the promiscuous Irish goddess, Medh, 'she who makes drunk'.

Sweetened with the juice of the tall creamy meadowsweet flowers, 'Queen of the meadows', the drink was both palatable and strong. 'The smell thereof makes the heart merrie, delighteth the senses'.[29] The dried leaves of bog-myrtle, *myrica gale*, were sometimes added as a preservative.

In a barrow at Egtved in Denmark the corpse of a young girl was provided with a lugged birch-bark bucket whose interior was darkened with a brown crust. Analysed 'as a mixture of beer and fruit wine' – meadowsweet, clover, wheat, bog myrtle, cow- or cranberry and lime-honey – the liquid had been ale fortified with mead, 'a strong festive drink' like others at Nandrup Mors, also in Jutland, and Bregninge.[30]

In a cist at Ashgrove, Methilhill, Fife, a beaker placed by the face of an elderly individual had spilled over, its alcoholic contents lost. Mead or methilhillated spirits? At the circle-henge of Balfarg in the same county a handled beaker capable of holding two pints was set by the hands of a corpse of a young man, 'intended to make this person's journey to the underworld a little less cold and cheerless.'

All a Neolithic brewer needed was barley for cakes to be mixed with water and yeast to be fermented into beer, a hearth and a big, fireproof pot like a typical flat-bottomed grooved-ware bowl. With capacities up to six gallons the pottery has been found all over Britain. On Orkney the vessels were 'heavily gritted with volcanic rock, which would have allowed them to withstand the constant heating and cooling necessary for a successful brew'. Adding meadowsweet extended the drinkable condition of the beer for several weeks. The weed was plentiful on Orkney.[31]

Alcohol was not the only stimulant. In a compelling understatement it was remarked that 'The cord used to decorate beakers was hemp or cannabis, which was combined with alcohol to produce a strong cocktail.'[32] Henbane also was picked and treated for its enhancing effects upon the mind. 'A plant of this family has now been associated with a set of cultic paraphernalia long recognised as typical of British Neolithic religion: Grooved Ware pottery, and the sort of ritual structures with which it is often associated. These folk, with their astronomical alignments and ceremonial enclosures, surely are the nearest prehistoric equivalents to 1960s hippies; and in Scotland, we can now put a name to the mind-bending drug these Neolithic hippies used: it was henbane, *Hyoscyamus niger*.'[33] In the late tenth century AD a woman buried in the Fyrkat Viking fort, Denmark, had over a hundred seeds in her belt-pouch.

A member of the *solonaceae* family it was a drug associated with madness and delirium. Growing in abundance on dry, sandy places, with stalks 0.6–1 m high and with prickly, sticky leaves it gave off a foetid, offensive smell. But its creamy, sheathed flowers were attractive, stellate and coloured white around red like a Tudor rose in reverse.

At the suspected mortuary structure at Balfarg Riding School in Fife excavators recovered a grooved ware bowl with a residue adhering to its sides of black henbane, meadowsweet, deadly nightshade, *atropa belladonna*, hemlock, *conium maculatum*, which, in the analyst's words, was 'an elaborate use of potent plants, or a dangerous or careless misuse of them'. 'It seems that the mix is normally coarse and crude. A consistency of a coarse porridge with added pottage (potherbs) and flavouring is indicated', a draught that without exaggeration 'may be deemed ritually "charged" and dangerous'.[34] It was, and 'porridge' was the clue.

Henbane makes a witch's brew that should never be drunk, only used with caution as 'an outward medicine'. To drink henbane is to die but an old saying of witches tells that 'to smear hemlock is to fly'. Hence the porridge. What had been recovered from the vessel was not a drink nor a food. It was an application.

In 1960, having read a formula for a witch's 'flying' potion *in Magiae Naturalis* (1560), by Johannes Baptista Porta, Dr Erich-Will Peuckert of the University of Göttingen, together with a colleague risked what could have proved a terminal experiment. Onto their foreheads and armpits they rubbed an unguent of deadly nightshade, thornapple, henbane, wild celery and parsley mixed in a base of hog's lard, everything measured in the proportions specified.

'Both passed into a trancelike sleep for 20 hours during which each had nearly identical dreams of flying through the air to a mountain top and participating in erotic orgies with monsters and demons . . . It is probable that mediaeval witches who used such ointments believed that they actually had such experiences.'[35] With the same plants easily gathered in the prehistoric countryside it is just as possible that similar experiences were known and enjoyed in ancient times, perhaps identical to the reported shaman spirit-flights to the realms of the dead.

Conclusions

Neolithic and Bronze Age ritual enclosures had a multiplicity of purposes: as family shrines, for seasonal gatherings or as trading-places. Widespread across western Europe in space and time, stone circles are unlikely to have been colleges for dispassionate musings on the nature of the universe. Dancing, drums and drugs may have been the ingredients for the rites.

The paucity of finds from the circles means only that whatever the activities inside them they did not demand permanent and tangible offerings being buried there. Astronomical observations would leave little except the stones themselves. Neither would the dancing of a community engaged in their imitative rôles of god and animal and human. So far from astronomy and magic being mutually exclusive they were quite possibly complementary in the ceremonies inside stone circles. It is unlikely, however, that these were occasions of pure science as has sometimes been claimed.

Chapter Five

The Earliest Stone Circles

Mr Toland assures me that in the northern parts of Ireland are severall such monuments of Stones standing circularly, set in the quarter land of Rathseny in the parish of Clunmeny in the Barony of Inesoen, and in severall other places.

John Aubrey, 1693, 127

Introduction

The earliest of all stone circles may be in the north-west of Ireland. Somewhat mis-leadingly termed 'boulder-circles' the open-air rings at Carrowmore in Co. Sligo are transitional forms of unroofed enclosures between Neolithic passage-tombs and the true stone circle.

Irish passage-tombs being a source for the origins of some stone circles is an elusive possibility. These mounds with an orthostatic passage leading to a sepulchral chamber are widespread in Ireland. More than 1,450 Irish megalithic tombs are known, court-cairns, portal dolmens, wedge-tombs. Among them, as well as many scattered sites, the Boyne-type cruciform-chambered tombs of which Newgrange, Co. Meath, is the best-known, are concentrated in five great cemeteries: 40 tombs in the Boyne complex, Co. Meath; 25 at Loughcrew in the same county; 13 at Kilmonaster, Co. Donegal; 12 at Carrowkeel, Co. Sligo; and well over 40 still surviving at Carrowmore, also in Co. Sligo.[1] With the exception of a controversial assay of 3780 ± 85 bc (LU-1840), *c.* 4650–4500 BC, from Carrowmore, the earliest fully accepted date came from habitation material under the small Knowth B with a date of 2928 bc ± 150 bc (UB-318), *c.* 3850–3500 BC.[2]

As well as the geometric art for which the Boyne and Loughcrew groups are famous, these tombs have large and contiguous kerbstones which, before the piling up of the cairn, must have made an impressive ring whose diameter was not always deter-mined by the length of the passage. A cairn of 24.4 m radius, for example, would have sufficed to cover the passage and chamber at Newgrange but, instead, the designers deliberately laid out a vast ring 86.3 × 59.7 m across, perhaps either to incorporate a second, smaller mound, or to make an enclosure large enough for all the participants before the completion of the cairn. At Knocklea, Co. Dublin, a stone circle was actu-ally concealed by the mound of the passage-tomb. It may be that there were two stages in the building of such chambered tombs, the first dedicatory or propitiatory rites within a stone ring, followed by the completion of the tumulus.

It was seldom that people of open-ring traditions lived side by side with the Irish passage-tomb builders. Such co-existence was unusual. Sometimes circle and tomb could be adjacent as happened near Dowth, Co. Meath, where a henge and the possible chambered tomb of Cloughlea were close together. Sometimes the passage-tomb people adopted the idea of an enclosure to put round their tomb, a combination found at Newgrange and in many of the Clava tombs of north-east Scotland. Oliver Davies in discussing the affinities of the Castledamph stone circle, remarked that some stone circles might have been put up by 'descendants of the passage-grave folk, the circular peristaliths of whose cairns may have degenerated into free-standing circles'.[3]

Nevertheless, stone circles are rare in areas of Irish passage-tombs although chambered tombs with circles around them do occur in peripheral areas. Near the Boyne there is not only Newgrange but the tombs of Killin Park, Co. Louth; Killycluggin, Co. Cavan; and Ballybrolly, Co. Armagh, all inside freestanding circles. There are also many simple cairns within circles in this part of Ireland, including the destroyed Vicar's Cairn, Co. Armagh, 40.2 m across, with over fifty stones in the circle, one having concentric circles carved on it in passage-tomb style. In 1797 the monument was almost complete but by 1868 the stone circle had been removed and today the cairn exists only in a mutilated form with some of its kerbstones in the adjacent field-bank.

In Ireland the people of passage-tomb customs and those of the open circles held inimical beliefs. They rarely mingled. The builders of the tombs seem motivated by a cult of the dead unrelated to the large, open rings which acted as foci for dispersed groups. The dichotomy probably resulted from a hostility between one set of people and another that would explain the infrequent overlap of stone circle and passage-tomb.

Before 3200 BC in the Late Neolithic the two cults remained independent and it is only well into the third millennium that circle and burial were freely combined to create the composite Bronze Age cairn-circles and kerb-cairns of the western coasts of Britain.

The Carrowmore 'Passage-Tomb' Cemetery, Co. Sligo

Of the five great passage-tomb cemeteries from the Boyne group in the east to Carrowkeel and Carrowmore in the west four are relatively homogenous. The exception is Carrowmore with its anomalous circle-like structures. Labelling its exceptional rings as *Stone Circles* on the Ordnance Survey maps early surveyors were percipient. Many of the so-called kerbed cairns and chambered tombs in this poorly protected megalithic cemetery are embryonic rings, forms transitional between the heavy kerbs of cairns and the true free-standing stone circle.

On a limestone plateau and in the shadow of the towering Knocknarea mountain to the west with the cold nipple of Maeve's Cairn outlined on its crest, over sixty sites survive of a hundred or more (Fig. 5), others demolished during the course of gravel-digging. They concentrate in an area about $1\frac{1}{4}$ miles from north to south and some three-quarters of a mile wide.

Fig. 5. The Carrowmore Cemetry, Co. Sligo.

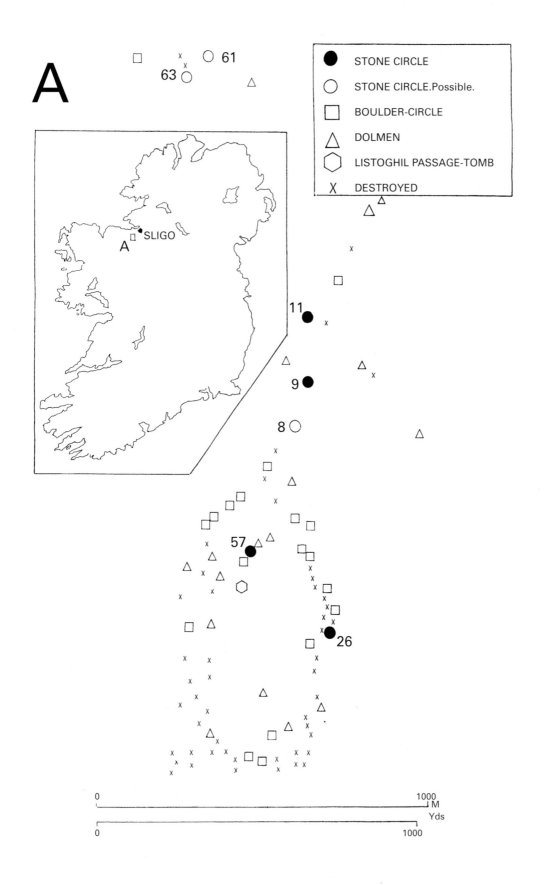

A

STONE CIRCLE
STONE CIRCLE.Possible.
BOULDER-CIRCLE
DOLMEN
LISTOGHIL PASSAGE-TOMB
DESTROYED

63
61

SLIGO
A

11
9
8
57
26

0   1000
                                          M
                                        Yds
0   1000

In 1983 Kitchen observed that 'Another noteable feature of the Carrowmore tombs is the apparent absence of a covering mound or cairn. It has generally been accepted that the tombs were originally covered and that the boulder-circle acted as a surrounding cairn ... The present writer's observation has failed to discern any visible evidence of cairn material within the circles. In the four sites excavated recently no evidence was found to suggest that a cairn or mound either of stone or turf had ever existed.'[4] To this should be added the fact that the stones either stood on the ground or were set in shallow hollows with nothing to prevent them being disturbed by a heavy internal cairn had it ever existed.

Twenty-two boulder-circles survive, rings of stones surrounding roughly circular flat-topped platforms. Sometimes the ring is concentric with smaller stones on the inside. 'Boulder-circle' is a term preferred by Kitchen to stone circle 'because of the latter's rather specific connotations'.[5] To the contrary, the sites should be accepted as genuine forms of megalithic rings.

Carrowmore is an extensive though ravaged complex of chambered cairns, easily the largest concentration of megaliths in Ireland. In 1837 Petrie counted sixty-four monuments and estimated that 'originally there could not have been less than double that number'. Nearly all the monuments were despoiled and plundered in the last century, disturbed by local people needing stones and gravel.

Unlike its supposed counterparts Carrowmore is not a hill-top cemetery but lies on a low-lying gravel ridge in a landscape of low hills on a limestone plain. Fergusson was impressed. 'Carrowmore is more accessible than Carnac. The inns at Sligo are better than those at Auray ... The scenery near Sligo is far more beautiful than that of Morbihan, yet hundreds of our countrymen rush annually to the French megaliths ... but no one thinks of the Irish monuments.'[6]

Few of the sites are genuine megalithic tombs. Most are boulder-circles of local gneiss. Inside some is a dolmen with a capstone or a covered chamber. The majority have no trace of a central structure.

There is only one classic passage-tomb, no. 51, Listoghil. It is centrally placed in a rather higher position than the other tombs. Its stone cairn about 40 m in diameter has a disturbed chamber under a big limestone capstone. Circular motifs and a cup-and-ring mark had been carved on its roof slab.[7]

Four sites were excavated at Carrowmore between 1977 and 1979.[8] The investigations suggested that the small, passage-less tombs on their low knolls were probably very early burial-places of immigrant farming families. From such uncomplicated monuments, their central burials spiritually protected by a ring of contiguous boulders separating the dead from the profane world, gradually developed the idea of an open stone circle.

All four were boulder-circles with internal features (Pl. 17): a small chamber or cist in no. 4; a dolmen inside no. 7; a central cremation without any structure at no 26; and a cruciform chamber in no. 27. None had the passage of the classic Irish passage tomb. A series of radiocarbon dates was obtained from three of the sites. They are the oldest radiocarbon dates for Irish megaliths. There was no date for the primary construction of the third site, no. 26.

Site 27, the southernmost of the four, on a little mound is another boulder-circle, but with a blotchy, despoiled cruciform tomb inside it. It was excavated in 1978–9 when a series of C-14 assays provided dates of 3090 ± 60 bc (LU-1698), 3050 ± 65 bc (LU-1808) and 2990 ± 85 bc (LU-1818), with an average of 3043 bc, in real years

Plate 17. Carrowmore 4 boulder-circle with an internal boulder-burial (Photograph: the author).

bracketed between an early 3900 BC and a late 3650 BC, either date very early for stone circles in Britain and Ireland. This was the latest of the Neolithic determinations from Carrowmore, causing the excavator to remark that 'It is also likely that this may show the end of the primary building of megalithic monuments at Carrowmore'. Enclosing the tomb but well spaced away from it and with no sign of an internal cairn is a ring of thirty-seven boulders, heavy and close-set, 20.7 m N–S by 19.5 m.

To the north Site 26, against a quarry, was excavated in 1978. It is a completely free-standing circle of thirty large, rounded stones, originally perhaps thirty-eight, 16.2 m N–S by 14.6 m. A central cremation was discovered.

Beyond Site 26 the next excavated ring, Site 4, is a boulder-circle, the fourth of a line of increasingly spaced monuments extending to the NNE for almost three-quarters of a mile, by the end of which the sites had become true stone circles. The twenty-eight stones of Site 4 stand in an oval about 12.5 m E–W by 11.6 m. They surrounded a long cist from which an assay of 3800 ± 85 bc (LU-1840), c. 4650–4500 BC, came. Such an early date is controversial. A second assay of 2370 ± 75 bc (LU-1750), c. 3150–2950 BC, came from contemporary material.

Just ESE of Site 4 is Site 57, a free-standing ring of thirty-three heavy boulders, eight of them in an adjacent field. It is a big site 16.2 m N–S by 15.1 m. The stones are massive, 1.8 × 1.1 × 0.9 m, weighing four to five tons each. It would have taken perhaps a score of workers to move them into position. The interior is a platform of cobbles but inspection shows that the 'Kerb' stones do not support the platform, but lie on and against it.

The next site, excavated in 1977–8, the dolmen of Site 7 with its tall, capstoned, polygonal chamber stands on a manmade platform. Thirty boulders, some of them fallen, surround the chamber. A central posthole, perhaps not contemporary with the chamber, gave a date of 3290 ± 80 bc (LU-1441), c. 4150–3950 BC. Significantly in

Plate 18. Carrowmore 9 stone circle (Photograph: the author).

terms of its stone circle affinities the western stones of its encircling ring support the platform but those at the east, although against it stand free.

Well to the north, 260 m away, is Site 9 (Pl. 18), a free-standing ring, with only eight of its exceptionally big and well-spaced stones surviving. There is no trace of a platform on which the stones could have stood. The ring is 13.7 m N–S by 12.5 m. It has a huge block at the south-west. In any other county or country this setting would be recognised as a stone circle.

Site 11 to the north, almost at the end of the cemetery, is another spacious ring, here with only five stones of which one is the adjacent field. The highest is at the WSW. It is noticeable that the farther these open rings are from the megalithic tombs the less closely set are their stones and the bigger the rings become, Site 11 being no less than 21.3 m E–W by 19.2 m. They had become recognisable stone circles.

There is a christianised boulder-circle with crosses and a Madonna on the eastern outskirts of Sligo itself. It has been converted into a secular traffic island.

Later Stone Circles of the Carrowmore Tradition

Early though it was the particular Carrowmore combination of a flat-topped cairn lying inside a free-standing ring of tall stones never developed. Perhaps inhibited by the presence of unsympathetic court-cairn societies there are few, if any, successors to the tradition outside Co. Sligo.

Less then sixty miles to the south-west in Co. Mayo there is the mutilation of a stone circle at Inishowen overlooking a delightful view of Lough Mask and the mountains. Edward Lhuyd saw it in 1700 and William Stukeley copied the Welshman's notes, ''tis 29 Paces diameter'. The description is vague. Near Ballinrobe was a flat-topped platform about 22 m across and 4 m high. It supported a ring of numerous stones, two of them exceptionally tall. The site may later have been transformed into a rath by the construction of an outlying double-banked earthwork. The level cairn is reminiscent of Carrowmore and so are the shouldering stones but the evidence is too slight for certainty.[9]

By an odd coincidence John Toland, 1670–1722, an Irishman born in Co. Donegal, free-thinker and scholar of Druidism, informed John Aubrey of another Inishowen stone circle, not in Co. Mayo but near his birthplace. It was, he wrote, the sanctuary of the Druidess Gealcossa, 'white legs', who inhabited the 'mount in Inisoen aforesaid in the county of Dunegall . . . On this hill is her grave, and hard by is her temple; being a sort of diminutive Stonehenge; which many of the old Irish dare not even at this day any way prophane.' He may have been referring to the wedge-tomb and nearby circle of Carrowreagh but, if so, like so many of the stone circles of the county the site has been wrecked beyond recognition.[10]

One at Bocan, Glackadrumman, is in such disarray that little can be said about it. Only seven stones are erect, others are down or broken around a sub-circular area about 18.3 m in diameter. In 1816 it was reported that 'graves' with 'earthen urns' had been found there.[11]

The better-preserved ring at Beltany Tops (Pl. 19) shows clearer affinities with Carrowmore. No one has questioned its status as a stone circle yet here are all the Carrowmore features of contiguity, internal platform and comparable size.

On the level top of a rounded hill not far from Raphoe with its Druid Bookshop this fine circle, one of the best in Ireland, stands around a level-topped cairn 1 m to 1.2 m high. There is a possible outer bank. When Somerville visited the ring in 1909 it surrounded 'a flat circular space' but in the 1930s when Oliver Davies went there

Plate 19. Beltany Tops 'Carrowmore' stone circle, Co. Donegal (Photograph: the author).

'the platform had been recently and unscientifically excavated, and been left in dreadful confusion'.[12] The chaos remains visible in the hummocks and hollows of turf.

In a true circle 44.2 m across some sixty-four stones remain of an original eighty or more so closely set as to be reminiscent of the Carrowmore boulder-circles 57 miles to the south-west. The comparison is made closer by the waves and roughs of the small stones spread across the interior. This platform, the kerb-like standing stones, the drum-like cairn inside are all paralleled at Carrowmore making it possible that Beltany Tops is a ring not only transitional between late passage-tombs and early stone circles but might even be one of the very first of those open-air rings. It could well date to before 3000 BC.

Its stones range in height from 1.2 m to 2.7 m, the tallest at the WSW shaped like a grazing mammoth. It faces a triangular slab across the circle 1.4 m in height whose inner face is copiously decorated with forty-three or more cupmarks. At the north of the ring a large and square stone stands 2.1 m high. A tall outlier 20.4 m to the south-east is 1.9 m high. Altogether four, maybe five, stones have carvings: the outlier, stones at the north-east, north-west and NNE, and a doubtful pillar at the south-west. Except for the heavily decorated slab all the markings are on the outer faces.[13]

Beltany Tops is perhaps the most intriguing 'astronomical' site in the north of Ireland. Somerville suggested that several solar alignments existed at the site. Looking from a tall stone at the north-west, 'conspicuously greater and higher than its neighbours', the outlier 64.6 m away stands edge on in line with the midwinter sunrise over Betsy Bell mountain 28 miles away. Another line across the circle looks towards the prominent hill, Croaghan, 7 miles to the south-east, above which the sun rose in early November at the Celtic festival of Samain. A third orientation, towards Argery hill-top 4 miles away, records the equinoctial sunrises.[14] Three solar alignments built into a ring might seem convincing proof that they were intended. 'Beltany also has an alignment with the sunrise of the winter solstice. If the weather is right on the day, the sight of the sun rising in a valley of the Sperrins on the horizon and lining up with some of the principal stones in the circle can be just as magical an experience.'[15] There are, however, reasons for doubt.

Somerville's hypothesis implies that the circle-builders deliberately searched for a location where three notable landmarks stood in line with the equinoctial, Samain and midwinter sunrises, something difficult to achieve even today with the aid of detailed maps. Nor should hills by themselves be accepted as foresights which should be manmade. Only the outlier at Beltany conforms to this rule and the evidence for its solstitial sightline is suspect. The line does not pass through the centre of the ring but some 3.4 m to its north although there was nothing in the circle to obscure the view. The backsight and outlier could have been set up 1.8 m farther to their west where the alignment would have crossed the middle of the circle and still coincided 'with a hill-summit seen against the sky, at some little distance. The azimuth of the line is (exactly) that of sunrise on the day of the Winter Solstice.'[16]

The best alignment at Beltany Tops is that from the great pillar at the south-west to the cupmarked stone (Pl. 20). Although 1.2 m wide this triangular stone has a peaked top that defines the sightline neatly, leading the eye to a small but conspicuous hill-summit of Tullyrap 5 miles away where the sun rose in early May. 'The azimuth of this line, in any case, is precisely that of sunrise on Bealltaine (6th May); and it is important to note that the present name, "Beltany Hill", gives the almost exact pronunciation of

Plate 20. The cupmarked 'Beltane' stone at Beltany (Photograph: the author).

the Gaelic name of this "May Day" celebration. This seems a very convincing proof of the connexion of the Circle with the date found by orientation'.[17]

Cupmarks in many megalithic rings do seem to have been associated with lunar or solar positions. Analysis of the eight cupmarked recumbent stone circles in north-east Scotland – Arnhill, Balquhain, Braehead, Cothiemuir Wood, Loanend, Loanhead of Daviot, Rothiemay and Sunhoney showed that eleven decorated stones stood in line with an extreme of the sun or moon, one aligned on sunrise, three on the minor southern moonset, two on the major southern moonrise and no fewer than five on the major southern moonset. Statistically this is too complete a correlation to be coincidental and it must be accepted that in those circles the cupmarks were astronomically placed.[18] The same could be true at Beltany Tops where the cupmarked alignment had a declination of +16°.6 very close to sunrise in early May.[19]

The problem at Beltany Tops is that the alignments are good but they cannot be tested against similar sites because none exists. Beltany is a unique circle. It stands between the heavily kerbed 'passage-tombs' of Carrowmore, Co. Sligo, to the west, from which it was quite possibly derived, and the Ulster rings of semi-contiguous stones to the east. In neither complex are cupmarks known except at atypical rings such as Millin Bay, Co. Down; Kiltierney, Co. Fermanagh; and at Castledamph, Co. Tyrone, where an intrusive cist may have had a cupmarked slab. Without such external confirmation of its alignments, Beltany must remain a debatable archaeo-astronomical candidate.

If Beltany Tops was indeed a ring derived from the Carrowmore tradition it had no apparent partners anywhere in northern Ireland. As in other regions where there was an innovative stone circle the creation of others may have been hindered, discouraged, resisted by native users of chambered tombs. As well as wedge-tombs on the Inishowen peninsula there were hundreds of court-cairns spread across northern Ireland and many of them were undoubtedly contemporary with, even earlier than Beltany Tops. Radiocarbon determinations indicate that some were standing before 3800 BC when the Carrowmore cemetery was developing. Dates from before 3600 BC have come from Ballymacaldrack, Co. Antrim; Ballymacdermot, Co. Armagh; from Tully, Co. Fermanagh, and from Creggandevesky, Co. Londonderry.[20]

Beltany may have been the finest of the Carrowmore rings but it was the last of its line.

Chapter Six

Sanctuaries and Depots: *Rings with a Difference*

I have . . . occasionally made this following Collection, which may perhaps some time
or other fall into some Antiquary's Hands, to make a Handsom Work of it. I am heartily
sorry I did not set down the Antiquities of these parts sooner, for since the Time afore-
said many Things are irrecoverably lost.

John Aubrey, 1680, 1

Dissimilarity and Proximity

It is unusual for megalithic rings that are entirely different in appearance to be close
to each other. When there is a concentration of circles in any region it is normal for
them to share architectural traits. Size may vary. Style does not.

There are many instances in which multiple sites coexist, especially in the south-
west of England: in pairs like the Grey Wethers on Dartmoor, sometimes in threes
like the Hurlers, the Thornborough henges in Yorkshire and the Stanton Drew rings
in Somerset, even the unfinished four Priddy henges near Cheddar but always the
rings resemble each other and may be regarded as either being erected over a period
of years or having a variety of functions for rituals at particular times of the year.

In southern Brittany five vast and different but now fragmentary cromlechs
lay within 3k (2 miles) of each other. At Carnac the egg-shaped and inverted eggs
of Ménec East and West, the unknown design of the lost Kermario and the two
megalithic horseshoes of the angular north-facing Kerlescan South and east-facing
Kerlescan North were erected only a kilometre ($\frac{1}{2}$ mile) apart. Even omitting the excessively spacious Kerlescan North, $240 \times 200\,\text{m}$, $48{,}000\,\text{m}^2$, the average interior of the
others was $4{,}225^2$, capable of accommodating over a thousand people. It is unlikely that
the neighbourhood of Carnac contained a population five times that number. It is more
plausible that the enclosures were calendrical, constructed as places of assembly for festivals at the summer solstice, the equinoxes and the midwinter solstice respectively.[1]

Understandably, except for architectural similarities such as recumbent stones or
portalled entrances, which indicate a cultural unity between rings stone circles have
customarily been studied as individual sites. Because of this it has rarely been asked
why some rings stand close to others, sometimes within walking distance, but yet are
architecturally quite dissimilar.

It is a question that was first considered in the early eighteenth century. Just before
then, in 1694, James Garden had written to John Aubrey telling him of 'two rounds' on
Orkney, the great circles of the Ring of Brodgar and the Standing Stones of
Stenness, that natives called 'the ancient Temples of the Gods'. Nine years later, however, in his book about the western isles of Scotland Martin Martin enlarged upon

this. The rings were 'Places design'd to offer Sacrifice in time of *Pagan* Idolatry; and for this reason the People called them the antient Temple of the Gods . . . Several of the Inhabitants have a Tradition, that the Sun was worshipped in the larger, and the Moon in the lesser Circle'.

He did not explain why this should be but John Toland did. Repeating the tradition 'that the Sun and Moon were worshipt: which Belief of theirs is very right, since the lesser Temple is semi-circular'. Visually the rings were unlike each other. Brodgar, although some stones had fallen, was a complete circle. Stenness had only four stones standing in a semi-circle open to the east like a lunar crescent It was the first attempt to account for the difference although on Orkney the dissimilarity had been caused not by design but by weather and the opportunism of men removing handily fallen stones.[2]

Stenness and Brodgar had been of the same fashion, circle-henges that varied only in size. The same was true of Stanton Drew not far from Bath, a 366 m long line of three circles. When William Stukeley visited the rings with John Strachey in 1723 he was intrigued by the circles, the central one a huge 112.2 m across, another a much smaller 44.2 m, and a third collapsed 29.6 m ring and ruined avenue in such disarray that he thought it to be the remains of five concentric circles from 95 m to 27.4 m in diameter. Believing, wrongly, that the middle ring had thirty stones he deduced that it represented the days of a month and was a Solar Temple. The smaller ring with twelve stones was a Lunar Temple, and the third 'quincuple' in which he was misled by the confusing muddle of fallen circle and avenue stones was 'consecrate to the five lesser planets', a Planetary Temple.

Two hundred years after him Ernest Sibree followed the same approach but with contrary interpretations. The thirty-stone circle did represent the days of the month but of the lunar month. The twelve-stone ring stood for the months of the year and therefore was a Solar Temple. Recognising Stukeley's 'concentric' ring was in reality an eight-stone ring it was the Temple of Venus 'because 8 solar years of 365 days are the equivalent of 5 Venus periods of 584 days'. The arithmetic was impeccable. The interpretation was not.[3]

In passing, it should be noted that if Neolithic and Bronze Age people did divide the year into months these would not have been the twelve of the Julian calendar, from *mensis Ianuarius* to *mensis December*, introduced by Julius Caesar in 46 BC but, instead, based either on the thirteen of the moon or the sixteen 'epochs' of Alexander Thom which the present writer has suggested might be reduced to eight prehistoric periods, later christianised, of: 5 February, the 'Celtic' Imbolc which became the Christian Candlemas; 23 March, the vernal equinox and the Annunciation of the Blessed Virgin Mary; 8 May, Beltane, and Whitsun; 21 June, the midsummer solstice, the Feast of St John the Baptist; 9 August, Lughnasa, Lammas, Harvest Festival; 23 September, autumnal equinox, Feast of St Matthew; 6 November, Samain, All Souls, All Saints, Martinmas; 21 December, midwinter solstice, Christmas.[4]

Whether at Stanton Drew or at the great circle of Brats Hill on Burnmoor in the Lake District where smaller pairs of stones lie only a few hundred yards away at White Moss and Low Longrigg the rings are simple, plain, disparate only in size. Such combinations are quite unlike the medley of circles, ellipses, a concentric, Four-Posters, a Five-Stone ring and deviant recumbent stone circle gathered on Machrie Moor on Arran, or the huddled cluster of a cairn-circle, variant recumbent stone circle, an ellipse and embanked stone circle standing in four adjacent fields at Cong in Co. Mayo, like a Bronze Age interdenominational centre of amorphous sects.

Two reasons can be offered for these incoherent aggregations. They may have been erected as staging-posts on busy trade routes, or at the sources of desirable material, good stone for axes, copper or tin for metal artefacts. There is evidence to support both suppositions.

Trade and Traffic

The island of Arran was a maritime crossroads. It was a meeting-place for travellers between Scotland and Ireland, a haven safely reached across the 16 miles of the Firth of Clyde, before a carefully attained landing in Ireland, voyagers sheltered by the hills of the Mull of Kintyre, waiting for good weather before crossing the 20 miles of open sea in the North Channel.

From the Scottish mainland there was a good bay at Brodick and then a demanding 3-mile climb along the only pass across central Arran, the String that rose steeply before softening into a gentler slope down to an expanse of flat land crossed by the Machrie Water and protected to the west by the 139 m high rocky felsites of Torr Righ Mor, 'the great hilly ridge'. There were beaches ideal for shoring boats, the white pebbly strand of Machrie Bay and, less than 4 miles to the south, the golden-brown sands of Drumadoon Bay and the tiny harbour of Blackwaterfoot.

The effect of such a desirable resting-place was cosmopolitan. On the triangular machair of fertile alluvium and sandstone on Machrie Moor several chambered tombs were built. Early Neolithic Scottish round and long Clyde cairns at Tormore lay close to an Irish type of passage-tomb at Carmahome, its circular chamber and wsw-facing passage perhaps a forerunner of the Clava Cairns at the far north-eastern end of the Great Glen.[5] The mixture of architecture displays the conflicting influences to which Arran was subject.

The Neolithic saw the importation into Scotland of Group IX porcellanite axes from Tievebulliagh mountain, Co. Antrim. Significantly, many have been found on the far side of the country. 'There is a remarkable concentration in the northeast, particularly in Aberdeenshire . . . In this northeastern district seventeen axes of Irish origin were identified and another six have subsequently been added.' Another concentration occurred around the Clyde estuary, including two from Arran itself.[6] Sherds of Irish pottery akin to Lyles Hill ware were excavated at the Aberdeenshire recumbent stone circle of Loanhead of Daviot.

Rather than a diminution the Early Bronze Age saw an increase in traffic. 'Scotland, as so often in the centuries that followed, was much more strongly influenced by Irish practice than the rest of Britain, both in terms of numbers of halberds and the proportion of examples of Irish type.' Food-vessel bowls of Irish style are known in Scotland, 'where they may have been inspired by the Irish potters'. Beautiful lunulae of gold from Irish workshops have been found in Dumfries, Peebles, Perthshire, Ayr or Lanark and as far to the north-east as Moray. There are Irish products on Arran itself, food-vessels, a lunula from Kiscadale, a lock-ring at Whitefarland, cup-ended ornaments in Ormidale and Whiting Bay.[7]

The stone circles on Machrie Moor are so different in their building styles that the group is unlikely to be entirely insular in origin and their dissimilarities are best explained by traditions from outside the island. Their concentration on the moor may be evidence that the whole south-west littoral had combined into one great 'chiefdom' epitomised by a 'stupendous' round cairn at Blackwaterfoot 'a hundred and fourteen feet over [34.8 m] and of vast height', thought to be the largest in Scotland. One of its several cists contained a two-rivetted bronze dagger with a ribbed gold pommel, a combination like that from Collessie Cairn in Fife and the weapons in the Normanton Down barrow cemetery of the Wessex culture in southern England. It is chronologically in keeping with food-vessels from the circles themselves and a crescentic jet necklace from the Tormore cairn nearby.[8] Such evidence may be examples of an Early Bronze Age chieftain society responding to the sea-trade in prestigious wares, receiving gifts in return for protection. It would have been across Machrie Moor that traders, merchants and migrating groups passed on their way to or from Ireland.

On the rich five square miles, 3,200 acres (1,295 ha), of the moor six stone circles, Sites 1 to 5 and 11, bunch together like cattle in the rain in one small and irregular triangle of four acres (1.6 ha), a cramped eight-hundredth of the moor, no ring being farther than 180 m from another. With related, more isolated but never far-off sites they offer a remarkable non-conformity of styles: plain circles, some of low granite boulders, others of tall sandstone pillars, ellipses, a concentric, a probable 'Irish' Five-Stone ring, and an outlying ordinary circle that was converted into a complex ring-cairn. There are also Four-Posters, and a variant 'Aberdonian' recumbent stone circle, all within 2 miles of each other.

Three of the circles at the heart of the group stand in a 190 m long line from Site 1 at the ESE to Site 3 at the WNW. Two, Sites 2 and 3, may be the work of Arran natives, insular rings containing central cists probably added to sites erected as early as 2400 bc (c. 3000 BC). It is noticeable that the putatively 'foreign' circles were put up well away from the line. Site 4, possibly of Irish origin, 77 m to the south, and Site 5, a concentric similar to others in north-west England, 137 m to the south-west. More detached still were the diminutive Four-Posters of Ballymichael Bridge and Machrie Burn, outlying examples of a concentration in central Scotland. The most remote circle, Auchagallon, is arguably an ill-remembered copy of the recumbent stone circles of Aberdeenshire almost 200 miles to the north-east of Arran.

Machrie Moor I, a ring of two phases, lies at the east of a line of three rings. Its long-decayed timber concentric ellipse had affinities with similar rings in the English Lake District. It was excavated by Bryce, in September 1861; by the writer in 1978 and 1979; and by Haggarty in 1985 and 1986. In this chapter the emphasis, as with the other rings on Machrie Moor, will be on the regional information provided by its architectural relationships. The results of excavations and dates will be discussed in more detail in chapter thirteen.

The outer ring was a ragged oval of posts with a long axis of about 19.5 m. It enclosed a more regular ellipse with an inner horseshoe open to the north-east. In shape and material it was akin to the rings of posts at Oddendale North in the Lake District, 1,100 m NNW of the better-known concentric of stone. Its dimensions of 18 m and 12 m had similar proportions to Machrie Moor I, 1:1.1; 1:1.2, whose three radiocarbon assays indicate that the posts were erected around 2900 BC when the Late Neolithic period was merging into the formative years of the Early Bronze Age. At some time the posts were replaced by an ellipse of six squat granite boulders alternating with five smaller sandstones, a sixth being missing at the north-east.

Not far to its west Site 2, a simple circle, was the first to be dug by Bryce on 24 May 1861. Originally of seven or eight tall sandstone pillars from Auchencar two miles to the north they stood in a circle 12.8 m diameter. Three survive, the biggest 5.3 m high. From the central of two cists inside the ring came a tripartite food-vessel and four flint

Plate 21. Machrie Moor XI stone circle under excavation, 1979 (Photograph: Mick Sharp).

arrowheads, from Co. Antrim 40 sea-miles to the south-west. It is likely that both the cists and the flints were secondary deposits.

At the western end of the line, 100 m away, only one stone of Old Red Sandstone of Site 3 stands. The ring would have been rather similar to Site 2 but was an irregular ellipse or egg, 16.3 × 15.4 m, SSW–NNE.

To the south-west of this wrecked circle Site 4 now consists of four low granite stones but quite possibly there had been a fifth in a north-west gap where a mutilatingly wide and deep trackway was cut into the peat. If so, the ring would have been a true circle *c*. 6.4 m. Its features are suggestive. The very lowest stone of its granite boulders is at the south-west. On the far side of the ring the north stone is a higher, heavy triangular boulder and its partner to the east is as big but flat-topped. In their shapes and stature the setting closely resembles the portals of a south-western Irish Five-Stone ring where such 'entrance' blocks stand opposite the lower recumbent. In this Site 4 is like Circle 275 on Penmaenmawr in north Wales halfway between Arran and south-west Ireland and with some fifty rings in Cork and Kerry.

On the hypotenuse of the megalithic triangle, between Sites 4 and 1 is Site 5, the largest of the Machrie Moor rings. It is a concentric circle like others from north-west England where Oddendale, Gunnerkeld and the Druid's Temple lie on the outskirts of the larger, more monumental circles of the Lake District. It is an irregular ellipse 18.1 × 11.6 m known as 'Fingal's Cauldron Seat'. One of its stones has a hole where Fingal is rumoured to have tethered his dog, Bran.

The last of the six rings, Site 11, was discovered in the mid-1970s by probing in the 1 m depth of overlying peat. It was excavated by the writer in 1978 and 1979 (Pl. 21) and by Haggarty in 1985 and 1986. On land that had previously been cultivated a ring of ten posts had been set up in an irregular ellipse apparently formed by two linked semi-circles, 14.7 × 12.9 m. This ephemeral structure was replaced by a circle of nine unimpressive sandstones and a granite block in a shapeless ring about 13.6 × 12.2 m in which no planned geometry is discernible. Inside the ring a symbol of conjoined triangles like a diablo quoit had been incised on a large boulder. Like Sites 2 and 3 this was a plain ring and perhaps one of the ritual centres of people from Arran itself.

Outside the main group there were other rings. Half a mile to the west Site 10 was a large, open and exactly circular site that was subsequently converted into a complex ring-cairn. There were also Four-Posters, 'circles' best known in central Scotland at sites like Lundin Farm in Perthshire. Ballymichael Bridge Four-Poster, 'christianised' by the removal of its north-west stone, was 1,200 m east of the group with the Machrie stream between. One and a half miles north of the group was the tiny and unobtrusive Machrie Burn, separated from the other rings by the Machrie Water.

On the coast almost 2 miles north-west of the Machrie Moor cluster was Auchagallon, a variant recumbent stone circle with an ancestry in north-east Scotland. Fifteen local red sandstones stand in a ring about 14.9 × 14.1 m across inside which a central cist was reported. The stones are from 0.9 m to 3.2 m high but the tallest was the west flanker standing to the wsw of the 'recumbent', 1.8 × 1.5 m long, much longer than the others which average 76 cm in length. Alongside it the east flanker is 1.7 m high. The combination of an internal cist and possible cairn, south-westerly orientation and recumbent slab firmly links Auchagallon to the recumbent stone circle tradition.

The circles on Machrie Moor cannot represent territorial areas for there are six of them within a few paces of each other. Their differing diameters, and therefore their internal areas, their varying shapes from circle to ellipse to non-geometrical, their structures including a concentric, the distinct choices of either low granite boulders or thin, sandstone pillars, all argue against a single overall design. The congerie appears to be a mixture of local styles intermingling with mainland Scottish rings both near and far, north-western English and Irish.

If they were raised by bands of incomers from overseas it would not have been for the acquisition of valuable local material. There was little on the island except for pitchstone. Pitchstone is like obsidian, 'perhaps the finest vitreous rock in Britain'. A working-site is known at Invercloy, Corriegills, just south-east of Brodick, a 320 m long ridge, of dark-green almost black pitchstone. Along the western side of Arran there are composite dykes along the Tormore shore. Implements made of pitchstone have been found as far away as Tweeddale, perhaps reaching that region via the Biggar Gap, and as far east as Fife. Others have been discovered in the Cairnholy I chambered tomb, Kirkcudbrightshire The distribution, though limited, reveals Arran's outside contacts.[9]

Pitchstone was best suited for smaller implements, blades and flakes and was exploited from Mesolithic until well into Bronze Age times. But for axes, hammers and the like it was in competition with stone and flint. Stone axes of epidotised tuff from the Group VI axe factory in the Langdale mountains of Cumbria have been found on Arran. So have others from the Irish Group IX site of Tievebulliagh, Co. Antrim. Flint also was imported, probably from northern Ireland.[10]

Two observations should be made about the situation of the six Machrie Moor circles. All of them were isolated from any domestic settlement and burial areas. Eleven hut-circles, two chambered cairns, a round cairn and a standing stone lie to the west of the group, separated by a ridge which lay diagonally between them. Ten more hut-circles and two cairns form a second group to the north of Machrie Water.

The location of the circles was also chosen for its ceremonial and calendrical aspect. Machrie Glen is the only pass across central Arran and all six circles were in sight of a prominent notch to the north-east where the glen divides into two steep valleys. Four 'are sited so that the notch is intersected exactly on midsummer morning' and the two others, 3 and 4, are only slightly out of position. 'It explains why all six circles are located in only one restricted area of the three zones of prominence on the moor.' Only Site 10, the complex ring-cairn was badly situated.[11]

The notch was the key. The midsummer sun rose there and even the somewhat misplaced circles 3 and 4 would have seen the sun within five minutes of its rising. 'Presumably in the context of ceremonial astronomy this would have been almost equally effective.'

Arran was not the honeypot of a prehistoric Klondyke attracting prospectors from hundreds of miles away. It was more feasibly a convenient market-place with voyagers from distant parts converging there at an agreed time of year, the summer solstice. The circles can be seen as gathering places in which the combination of architectural styles from outlying regions and the calendrical association of midsummer had modern parallels in the stone axe trade in aboriginal Australia. 'The tools were traded along known routes by stages and that these journeys were arranged to coincide with seasonal festivities of magical and social significance.'[12]

There are logistical considerations inherent in this interpretation. Sea-travel was probably by shallow-drafted, wicker-framed boats lined with cow-hide, seams sealed with pitch. With their upcurved, lifting bows, the craft rode the waves well and although slow, covering no more than 30 to 60 miles daily, they were stable. As much as 11 m in length they could carry a crew of twelve to fifteen rowers.

For spiritual protection their bows may have had eyes painted on them like the 'oculi' on modern Portuguese *saveiros* and Maltese fishing-vessels. 'The eye, known as the oculus, came to be painted on the bows of ancient ships. It represents the face of the god who was, it was hoped, safely upon board to protect the ship and crew.'[13]

Being light the boats were easily beached. But although comfortably dragged ashore and sometimes carried from river to river across dry land to avoid dangerous currents portage would have been impracticable over long distances. On Arran it is likely that seamen and traders arrived, left their boats by the coast, assembled with other groups on Machrie Moor, exchanged goods, took part in the trucial ceremonies, and returned home. The desirable articles they had brought would be passed from community to community on the mainlands over many far-flung miles.

The size of rings gives some hint of the numbers in the midsummer assembly. On the increasingly unprovable assumptions that a. people actually occupied the rings; b. that each had a body-space of about 2.6 m^2 and c. that the rings were too small for the luxury of a privileged space for a 'priest' the statistics are displayed in Table 8.

The island of Arran lay conveniently between the Scottish and Irish mainlands and provided a safe meeting-place for visitors from those countries and from England. The island of Lewis in the Outer Hebrides may have served a similar purpose for craft crossing the seas from eastern Ireland to the Orkneys, two wealthy and powerful regions that shared architectural and artefactual features. 'The evidence from the Boyne Valley shows quite strong links with the Orkneys.'[14] The connection might explain the assemblage of disparate rings around Loch Roag.

The waters between the mainland and the eastern coasts of the Hebrides could be challenging with strong tidal races around the Mulls of Galloway and Kintyre and

Circle	Size	m^2	Occupants allowed 2.6 m^2 each
I	14.4 × 12.7	144	55
II	15.2	182	70
III	15.6	191	74
IV	6.4	32	12
V	11.6	106	41
XI	13.6 × 12.2	130	50

Table 8. Hypothetical 'Populations' of the Stone Circles on Machrie Moor, Arran.

equally powerful currents around the Kyle of Skye.[15] The Gulf of Corryvreckan between Jura and the wrinkled shores of Scarba was notorious for its whirlpool 'like an open cauldron sucking and disgorging its draughts, so that its roar is like distant thunder'. When winter gales raged in from the west and met a flood tide the sea turned into an unnavigable confusion of white water swirling and rearing in every direction at once. The gulf was presided over by the *Cailleach*, the old hag who decided the fate of any vessel that dared enter it. It is rumoured that St Columba navigated the torrent when it was at full flood, calming the waters 'with words alone'. Less influential seamen avoided it.

The seas to the west of the Outer Hebrides were preferred with plentiful coves and protected beaches. From the south there was a less testing route to the west, following the coasts of Tiree, Coll, Rhum, passing through the Sound of Barra and northwards along the Atlantic shores of the Uists and Harris and Lewis.

One twilight in 1933 Alexander Thom sailed into 'East Loch Roag, that beautiful secluded inlet, to the north-west of the Island of Lewis. I was seeking a quiet anchorage . . . [and] after dropping anchor, as we looked up there was the rising moon with the stones of Callanish silhouetted on it.'[16]

He may have had the same experience as a Greek mariner in the fourth century BC. The Greek historian, Diodorus Siculus, quoted part of a lost history by Hecataeus of Abdera (fl. *c.* 320 BC), which is most sensibly interpreted as a statement that an explorer around northern Britain had seen a 'Spherical temple' on an island where 'the moon as viewed from this island appears to be but a little distance from the earth', a lunar event unique to the 58° North latitude of Callanish.[17]

Callanish, the 'spherical temple', has an immensely high internal pillar, perhaps originally a single standing stone to provide a conspicuous landmark for seamen. Within a mile or so are three other but different rings: Ceann Hulavig, an oval with a central stone; Cnoc Ceann a'Gharaidh, perhaps an embanked ellipse; and Cnoc Fillibhir with concentric ellipses. It is a collection of dissimilar rings comparable with the mixture on Arran and may have resulted from the arrival of crews from southern Scotland, Ireland and England taking welcome shelter on the long voyage to the Orkneys.

Sanctuaries and Sources

Staging-posts such as Arran, Lewis and elsewhere can account for certain aggregations of variously designed rings standing near to each other. Proximity to a source of a desirable substance like workable stone for axes may explain the existence of equally dissimilar sites.

Until two hundred years ago there was a peculiar huddle of stone circles in Shropshire. Just west of the Stiperstones, that remarkably jagged ridge of bleakly white quartzite tors littered with a chaos of rocks on which the Devil sits in mist and storm, there were as many as five rings spread over 2 miles in a buckled NNE–SSW line. Some were low-lying in what is now marshy ground. Two stood high on the dry heaths of Stapeley Hill. There were small stones, tall stones, central stones, perhaps an outlying stone, even a Four-Poster. Only one circle has endured the centuries well.

Three of them, Hoarstones, Mitchell's Fold and the Whetstones were large rings with interiors of around 465 m², one and half times the national average. In complete contrast to this excess the two remaining sites, Druid's Castle and the dubious Shelve were pygmies, barely one-eighth the size of a normal ring.

Like butterflies attracted to a buddleia the builders of these rings were drawn to the area by an outcrop of picrite at Cwm-Mawr by Corndon Hill immediately south of the circles. Picrite was a stone excellent for the manufacture of perforated, wooden-handled maces, battle-axes and axe-hammers and from about 1650 bc (c. 2000 BC) products of this Group XII axe-factory near Hyssington were distributed widely in central Wales but also reaching thinly into Wessex, the Peak District, Yorkshire and Anglesey.[18] This varying density, strongest in Wales, weakest in north-east and south-west England, was reproduced in the architecture of the circles, which were principally of Welsh forms.

At the northern end of the circles the 'ring' near Shelve church may be spurious. It was uncharacteristically small, no more than 9 m across, and the Ordnance surveyor considered it 'a fortuitous arrangement of natural boulders and cleared stones'. To its north-west, however, the Hoarstones site, 'a dreary spot', changeably known as Marsh Pool, Hemford and Black Marsh, is authentic. It is inconspicuous, its 38 to 40 local doleritic boulders lower than the stalky tufts of grass in the boggy field. On the perimeter of an ellipse 23 × 19.8 m the stones are irregularly graded to the southeast. The distinctive feature of the ring is its taller, typically not quite central pillar, 1.1 m high.

A mile and half to its SSW, also close to a trackway along the western slopes of Stapeley Hill but on much higher, drier ground, the denuded ring of Mitchell's Fold is quite different (Fig. 6). Being so temptingly near the track much of its western arc has gone. It is reported that a farmer took a stone for a step in his cowshed but the almost instant eruption of a thunderstorm that night led to predictable panic, repentance and replacement.

Even before robbery there were fewer stones than Hoarstones, perhaps no more than twenty in an oval with a longer SE–NW axis, a shape and orientation common to many megalithic rings in central and northern Wales.[19] Because of theft the exact dimensions are problematical, Hartshorne offering a confident and Grimes a tentative 27.4 × 25.9 m, Lewis 28 × 26.2 m, and Stukeley 28.4 × 25.9 m, 55 and 50 of his Druid's Cubits. Thom concurred, the longer diameter, 28.2 m, being just over 34 Megalithic Yards and the perimeter, 34.8 m, an almost precise 42.[20]

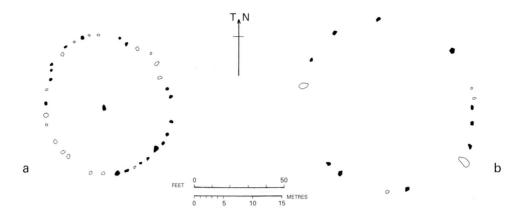

Fig. 6. Two Shropshire (Salop) Stone Circles: a. Hoarstones; b. Mitchell's Fold.

In 1752 James Ducarel wrote of an easterly entrance composed of two man-high stones 1.8 m apart. Today the taller at the south-east stands 1.9 m above ground. Its partner, 2.4 m long, has fallen but would have been of comparable height. As the seven other standing stones average no more than 53 cm high the pair would have framed a conspicuous approach to the ring. Ducarel's later gloss that the two portals had a lintel across them like a trilithon at Stonehenge was fanciful and false. A low, cubical block on a cairn about 75 m to the south-east he thought to be 'the altar'. It has also been considered an outlier but if so one of stunted proportions.[21]

Not far to the south of Mitchell's Fold was the enigmatic ruin of the Druid's Castle, also called Mitchell's Fold Tenement, that Lhuyd mistook for Mitchell's Fold itself, calling it 'Medgel's Fold'. Of this probable Four-Poster, no more than 6 m square, the last stone was uprooted in 1878 when farm buildings were being extended. Whereas on Arran the Four-Posters were geographically and chronologically peripheral to the major group of Late Neolithic rings the known Early Bronze Age dating of this type of 'circle' conformed neatly with the period of the Shropshire axe-factory.[22]

The last of the circles, the Whetstones at the south of the line, was finally demolished around 1870, the majority of its stones having been blown up a decade earlier. Even when the antiquarian, Hartshorne saw its 'mutilated fragments' in 1841, only three leaning stones remained in the low-lying, wet ground, the biggest 1.2 m long. The ring had been a large one with an estimated major axis of 30 m but there is no account of its shape or of any significant architectural feature.

Shapes matter. So do features. On the assumption that the varied Shropshire rings were trading outposts of communities wishing to acquire stone of good quality for hard-wearing tools and prestigious regalia it is arguable that the Corndon sites had counterparts in settlements elsewhere in Wales and England.

Mitchell Fold's entrance is reminiscent of 'Cumbrian' rings to the east in Wessex. Nor were Hoarstones' ellipse, central pillar and stones graded in height unique. Another oval with a centre stone lies on Kerry Hill only 12 miles to the south-west. Banc-du with its off-centre block of Fowler's Arm Chair is a further 8 miles in the same direction. Rings with stones markedly rising in height are more distant. Two, Brisworthy, graded to the north, and Fernworthy, graded south, are on Dartmoor 130 miles to the ssw. A third, Gors-fawr, stones rising in height towards the south, by the Preseli mountains in south-west Wales is 90 miles from Hoarstones but, maybe significantly, is not far from the coast and Cardigan Bay from which weathered nodules of Irish flint were collected and taken across Wales.

It is also close to the Group XIII axe factory whose shafted implements, of the same period as Corndon's, were dispersed in two clear-cut directions: eastwards to Wessex where several axe-hammers were found near Stonehenge's Aubrey Holes; and northeastwards in Wales to Radnor and Montgomery. In Shropshire itself an axe-hammer was discovered at Chirbury within a mile and a half of Mitchell's Fold.

This bipartite distribution may account for the juxtaposition of another stone circle against Gors-fawr, but one of no similarity to it, the embanked and portalled Meinigwyr which may have been the entrepôt at the beginning of the Wessex network. Unlike Gors-fawr it had no resemblance to Hoarstones.[23]

Evidence for contacts between Four-Posters is less equivocal still. The Druid's Castle had kindred rings in Wales. With two other Welsh Four-Posters, the Four Stones, Walton, to the ssw and the Cwm Saesan stones near Rhayader to the southwest, the 'Scottish' trio stand at the corners of an isosceles triangle with a 20-mile wide base and sides of 25 miles.

Mitchell's Fold with its tall portals is best seen as an outlying example of others in north Wales such as the Druids' Circle above Conway Bay near the Group VII factory at Graig Lwyd. Even there on Penmaenmawr alongside a source of desirable augite granophyre there was megalithic variety. Not far to the north-east of the embanked Druids' Circle is the 'Irish' Five-Stone ring, Circle 275; a ring-cairn to the south-west, Circle 278; and the nearby ruined, plain rings of Red Farm and Cors-y-carneddau.

Two questions must be asked about the builders of the Corndon rings and the picrite they wanted: how it was distributed and what was exchanged for the stone. If the products were taken southwards it was probably along the previously mentioned trackway on Stapeley Hill, later used by stage-coaches. It passes just west of Hoarstones and Mitchell's Fold and then by modern Church Stoke to the river Clun 11½ miles away. Many flints have been found in the area, particularly in the vicinity of Pen-y-Wern cairn-circle 1½ miles south-east of Clun

To the west a line of standing stones along hills acted as landmarks from Rock Hill, to Black Hill with its large prostrate stone. East of Camp Field was another, 4.3 m long that was buried around 1865. Nearby was another slab, the Whitcott stone whose diamond-shape was envisaged as 'female'. It signposted the way to a ford. At Pontylinks, 2 miles west of Clun, in 'Stone Meadow' was a gigantic block, 2.4 m long, 2.1 m wide and 1 m thick, some fifteen tons of monstrous basalt that eight horses failed to move. At the second attempt the iron chains broke and there was a violent thunderstorm.

There were further stones: the Old Stone at Beguildy and the Heartstone, the most important menhir in the area, erected at the junction of trackways.[24] From there axes and hammers could be transported across central Wales to Cardigan Bay in an exchange network that had early Irish bronze axes carried one way, picrite implements in the other.

In an easterly direction from the Hoarstones group of rings it is likely that the finished implements were taken on men's shoulders or by sledge 2 miles southwards to the pass between Corndon and the Stiperstones and then for some 50 miles by boat between the hilly slopes and forests of the boisterously narrow West Onny river before flowing into the languorous and lovely valley of the Onny and Teme down to the Severn just south of present-day Worcester.

> In valleys of springs of rivers,
> By Ony [sic] and Teme and Clun,
> The country for easy livers,
> The quietest under the sun.
> A. E. Housman, *A Shropshire Lad*, L

Some axes reached Wessex and it may have been from there that good flint was taken to Shropshire. 'A collection of at least 10,000 flints found locally; had been brought into Clun Museum, with a further 3,000 collected by the late Mr. Jonas Cooper from Clunbury parish.' It has been estimated that at least a thousand large cores reached the area each year, the majority from Wiltshire.[25]

What appears true for the mixture of rings at Corndon, Penmaenmawr, even the Preselis seems also applicable to the three henges connected with the axe-factories of the English Lake District. There an abundance of fine-grained tuffs occurred on the scree-slopes of the Langdale mountains and it has been possible to plot the tracks along which the roughly shaped cores were carried some 8 to 10 miles from those often dangerous places to grinding and polishing sites where suitable sandstone was available. The best-known site, Ehenside Tarn, was within 3 miles of the Ringlen Stones, a circle near Egremont, but the ring was demolished in the nineteenth century and little is known of it. Several other sites, however, were also close to the great stone circles of Cumbria: Portinscale to Castlerigg; the Hunsonby 'floors' to Long Meg and Her Daughters; and Clifton and Belmont to the Penrith henges of Mayburgh, King Arthur's Round Table and the Little Round Table. In their architectural diversity but geographical proximity these earthworks are cultural counterparts to the Shropshire and Welsh conclaves already discussed.[26]

Mayburgh with a circular plateau 88 m across and with one, east-facing entrance and vast bank of water-worn cobbles was quite unlike the King Arthur's Round Table 350 m to the ESE. That enclosure is earth-banked, with an ungeometrically oval interior, 54 × 48.5 m and with two entrances on a SE–NW axis. And neither Mayburgh nor King Arthur's Round Table was similar to the Little Round Table about 150 m to the south, 'made contrariwise to the former,' wrote Stukeley contrasting it with the "Arthurian" henge, 'consisting of a low rampart' with an outer ditch and inner bank some 48 m from crest to crest broken by one NNE entrance. Its last vestige disappeared just before 1881.

In its construction Mayburgh is most closely paralleled by henges in Ireland for whose banks the builders scraped out a shallow scoop around the edge of the interior creating a low, domed plateau like an upturned saucer. Mayburgh's interior may have contained an aggrandised version of a Four-Poster but three of the black pillars of volcanic ash 'were blasted and removed by orders of a person who seems to have been at that time the farmer of this place: one of the men employed in the work having hanged himself, and the other turning lunatic, has given fair opening to vulgar superstition, to impute these misfortunes to their sacrilege in defacing what they suppose was formerly a place of eminent sanctity.'[27]

In contrast to Mayburgh the 'English' henge of King Arthur's Round Table can be matched with sites in Yorkshire to which many Langdale axes were transported. There are kindred earthworks at Cana, Castle Dykes, and Nunwick. The similarity is heightened by the presence of a cremation trench inside King Arthur's Round Table, a feature frequently found in the long barrows of the Yorkshire Wolds.[28] Excavated by

Plate 22. An aerial view of Mayburgh 'Irish' henge, Westmorland (Photograph: Jean Ward).

Collingwood in 1937 and then by Bersu in 1939 a long trench lay on the axis of the henge. In it the remains of a corpse consumed by a fire of hazel wood rested under a collapsed cairn of stone slabs. It was a form of burial exactly matched in Yorkshire 'flu cremation' barrows such as Willerby Wold and East Heslerton.

Mayburgh (Pl. 22) seems an Irish enclosure, King Arthur's Round Table one from Yorkshire. The Little Round Table resembles neither. With its atypical outer ditch it had few things in common with a conventional, externally banked henge but it was not unlike structures of previous centuries, the Neolithic causewayed enclosures of Wessex and southern England. It may not be an entire coincidence that just such an ancestry has been proposed for the initial chalk and turf earthwork phase of Stonehenge.

The anomalous appearance of the Little Round Table alongside the 'foreign' rings of Mayburgh and King Arthur's Round Table, the three gathered together outside the ring of mountains, adds to their interpretation as depots for the acquisition and distribution of stone axes. An axe from the Langdales was found inside Mayburgh and Stukeley reported the discovery of a 'brass celt' there, almost certainly a bronze axe ritualistically deposited in the entrance.

> We shall consider the possibility that it was through the aggregations that took place at such sites that the axes first changed hands . . . The major concentration of these sites was in the Eden Valley, towards the opposite ends of the routes to north-east England . . . The same distribution of sites continues to the north, with a second group of henges and early stone circles around the Solway Firth. It has long been suggested that these monuments might have played some part in the movement of Group VI artefacts.[29]

There is an impression of activity, very slow but increasing year by year, extending into decades and centuries, of bands of travellers from Yorkshire, maybe driving herds of cattle through the Stainmore Gap in the Pennines, exchanging beasts and hides for axes, of other men from the south establishing long distance trails along rivers and valleys, bringing flint from the chalklands of Wessex.

From this comes a question. It is understandable that people from Yorkshire and southern England should accept an assembly point to the east of the Langdales as a convenient place to meet. This would appear a contradiction for seafarers coming from Ireland and the west. It could be argued that Mayburgh should have been at Workington or Whitehaven on the coast rather than by Penrith on the far side of the mountains.

The paradox has an explanation. The 'Irish' Mayburgh is not a replica of the henges 200 sea-and-land miles away in the Boyne Valley of eastern Ireland, earthen, twin-entranced and irregular in design. It more nearly approximates to the Giant's Ring at Ballynahatty just south of Belfast, circular except where a steep slope forced a flattening of the circumference, with a probable single entrance at the north-west, a construction of gravel and small boulders, and about 213 m from crest to crest of its great bank enclosing a domed plateau. Mayburgh with its overpowering wall of stones and boulders dragged from the nearby river was a faithful copy.

Fine Antrim flints were shaped and finished in the shelter of the Giant's Ring and it may have been such implements that were sailed across the 120 miles of the North Channel and the Solway Firth before following the River Eden 30 miles southwards to Penrith. Eastern Cumbria was easier than western for the journey. Rivers were highways. Mountains were walls. The presence of Group VI axes in northern Ireland may be evidence of exchange.[30]

Conclusions

If the explanation is correct that the combinations of adjacent circles and henges so different in type at Corndon, Penmaenmawr and Penrith was because they had been built close to a source of good stone then it is noticeable that clusters do not occur near the first axe factories such as Groups IIA, IVA, XVI and XVII in Cornwall. These were being exploited as early as 3250 bc (c. 4000 BC) long before any stone circle or henge was erected.

There was no closely meshed gathering of rings there. The henge of Castlewich was not far from the Group IV factory on Balstone Down near Callington but there was no other henge or stone circle near it. No circles pressed around the Group XVII site at Kenidjack north of Land's End. The postulated outcrop of greenstone along the shores of Mounts Bay at Penzance was unattended. The Merry Maidens stone circle was 3 miles to the south of its nearest point, Boscawen-Un 3½ miles to the west and Boskednan the same distance to the north-west. These were scattered rings and their locations imply separate territories rather than a purpose as staging-posts or entrepôts for the trade in stone axes.[31]

For the early axe-factories there may have been an alternative means of disseminating their products. 'Like the majority of the sources, many causewayed enclosures were themselves situated in locations which were peripheral to the main areas of contemporary settlement. Indeed, a number are situated on or near to sources of raw material.'[32] Amongst their other functions causewayed enclosures may have been outlying market-places for the reception and exchange of diverse goods, stone axes among them. If so, the apparently inexplicable Little Round Table would have been a monument in direct line of descent from them.

Several significant revelations about stone circles emerge from this study. The first concerns chronology. Collections of varied rings adjacent to each other near sources of good stone may be assumed to be of the same period as the floruit of the axe factory. For the Langdales one might infer that as the calculated range of exploitation was from *c.* 3000 to 1800 bc (*c.* 3700–2200 BC)[33] then the Penrith henges could be placed within those centuries of the Late Neolithic. For the Group XIII site near Corndon the rings of Mitchell's Fold and elsewhere would have been erected much later between 2000 and 1800 bc (*c.* 2500–2200 BC) in the Early Bronze Age.

For the Lake District sites of Group VI the great stone circles in the mountains themselves would be earlier than the henges on their outskirts, put up at a time when exploration and exploitation of the Langdale scree-slopes was fully established. The distances separating the rings in the central region are approximately eight to ten miles. This is the distance from the factory sites at Scafell Pike, Glaramara, Pike o'Stickle and others[34] to either Castlerigg to the north or to Brats Hill to the west; from Castlerigg to Elva Plain or to the destroyed Motherby ring; and between Brats Hill and either Grey Croft or Swinside. Eight miles from Motherby are the three Penrith henges and that distance separates them from Long Meg and Her Daughters to the north or from Kemp Howe to the south. The vast but devastated Grey Yauds was 8 miles north of Long Meg. The regularity indicates that among other purposes the rings acted as staging-posts, the miles between them about the number to be covered by a heavily laden, stolidly plodding ox.

Although clusters of rings near axe factories can be considered coterminous with the factories it does not follow that in any group the sites are close contemporaries. For the Group VII circles on Penmaenmawr with dates attributed to 2750 to 1800 bc (*c.* 3500-2200 BC) it is likely that the Druids' Circle was many years, probably centuries, older than the tiny Circle 275. The same temporal difference is probable between the large rings of Hoarstones and Mitchell's Fold against the diminutive Four-Poster of the Druid's Castle.

A second insight provided by the occasional bunching of sites is that such rings were places of assembly in trucial areas agreed and accepted by both natives and incomers. Extrapolating from the astronomical evidence on Arran it would seem, and commonsense would suggest, that gatherings would occur at predetermined times of the year. This implies the existence of calendars, solar or lunar. If travellers from Bridlington in Yorkshire where so many Group VI axes have been found were to arrive in the Lake District at a particular month, a journey of some 150 miles, driving cattle and lumbering oxen, they would have allowed weeks for the trek. There is no implication of a penalty clause for late arrival, but tardiness could result with axes of the highest quality having been allocated to more punctual competitors.

The directly east, 'equinoctial' entrance at Mayburgh and the east–west long axis at Long Meg and Her Daughters a few miles away, both in the Eden Valley and close to the Stainmore Gap, are in keeping with the idea of autumnal gatherings when the summer work at the axe factories was at an end. On the far side of the mountains the disturbed ring of Elva Plain also has an east–west alignment. Gift exchange and periods of non-hostility to strangers demanded both sanctuaries and rituals at mutually acceptable times of the year to sustain them.

There is also the question of how the axes were distributed. There has been much debate over whether products were taken to distant areas by their makers or whether purchasers came from those areas to obtain the tools. From the disparate architecture of the stone circles and henges at the sources the latter explanation is more feasible.

Patterns changed. In the formative period of trade and exchange axes were carried over many long miles from source to settlement. In later times the stages were shorter. In the earliest centuries axes and adzes and ard-shares may have been transported by sea and river directly from Cornwall to Wessex and East Anglia. 'Such direct contact, over distances of several hundred kilometres has already been implied for Groups I and VI [Cornwall and Cumbria] whose relative frequency distribution patterns are not factory centred . . . Each of the three big factories [1, VI, VII] owed its growth and development to direct contact and bulk "trade" with major centres of population at a considerable distance from them.'[35]

This did not apply to later sites of stone for perforated implements such as the Group VIII of south-west Wales whose implements were limited to the south and centre of that country; or to the Group XIV of Nuneaton, restricted to the Midlands; or Group XV of the southern Lake District or Group XXVII of the Southern Uplands of Scotland, all of which had distribution areas close to their source.[36]

Nor was it relevant to the Bronze Age copper mines at Great Orme on Anglesey or Mount Gabriel in Co. Cork; or the elusive lodes of tin in Cornwall.[37] There were no clusters of stone circles, large or small, against them.

Whatever truth there may be in these speculations it has been known for many years that there was a correlation between regions of early stone circles and axe factories and the distribution of their products. This is especially obvious in the study of the fine megalithic rings of Cumbria, the subject of the following chapter.

Chapter Seven

The Stone Circles of Cumbria

This searching after Antiquities is a wearisome task . . . But methinkes it shewes a kind of gratitude and good nature to revise the memories and memorialls of the pious and charitable Benefactors since dead and gonne.

John Aubrey, 1670, 17

The Distribution of Circles in Britain and Ireland

The majority of the large stone circles are to be found along the western coast of Britain, especially in England in Cumbria and Cornwall. There are outlying examples on the east coast of Ireland. Intermingled with these are later and smaller rings that often contain burials. Some of the little Cumbrian sites will be referred to in this chapter.

The coastal distribution of these large circles is better understood when it is realised that for prehistoric man travel by water was often easier than across land. Seaways were preferable to the dense, trackless forests and widespread swamps of the countryside where even the higher routes along hill ridges might be cut by lateral valleys and swirling rivers.

A boat, moreover, was better than one's back for carrying a load of heavy stone axes and it has been noticed that the distribution of axe factory products was 'almost entirely riverine. It would seem that almost every river, tributary, coastal area and island was embraced in this ubiquitous trade'.[1]

And not only rivers. The seas along the western shores carried settlers and traders from Brittany to Ireland, from Ireland and from Galloway to the Orkneys. The more treacherous tidal races and currents could be by-passed by short portages across isthmuses like that between Luce Bay and Loch Ryan or the Crinan peninsula. The building of small, southern-derived megalithic tombs along these coasts and their later incorporation under eastern-inspired long mounds bear witness to the sea-crossings of those early people. The importance of Cumbria with the most mountainous region of England, the Lake District, is shown by its use by Neolithic groups passing through the Stainmore Gap in the Pennines on their way from Yorkshire to Northern Ireland, or going northwards through the Tyne Gap towards south-west Scotland. What sort of craft was used for sea voyages is unproven. Dugout canoes were unsuitable. Experiments intimate that lightweight, timber-framed, skin-lined vessels up to 8 m long, buoyant and flexible, and capable of bearing ten people up to 90 miles a day may have been used with their considerable benefit of being easily beached.

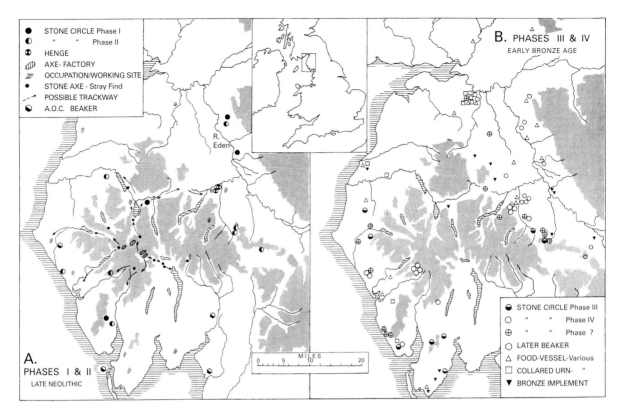

The legend in the map reads:

STONE CIRCLE Phase I
   "   "   Phase II
HENGE
AXE- FACTORY
OCCUPATION/WORKING SITE
STONE AXE - Stray Find
POSSIBLE TRACKWAY
A.O.C. BEAKER

R. Eden

A.
PHASES I & II
LATE NEOLITHIC

MILES
0   5   10   20

B. PHASES III & IV
EARLY BRONZE AGE

STONE CIRCLE Phase III
   "   "   Phase IV
   "   "   Phase ?
LATER BEAKER
FOOD-VESSEL-Various
COLLARED URN- "
BRONZE IMPLEMENT

Fig. 7. The Distribution and Hypothetical Phases of Cumbrian Stone Circles.

The combination of maritime activity and the outgoing trade in stone axes made the diffusion of stone circles along the western coasts of Britain almost inevitable. Once the first megalithic rings were erected, probably in Cumbria itself, it was always likely that other regions would have rings built in them, not as facsimiles but fundamentally of the same origin as those in north-western England, large, uncluttered, circular and of many stones. In and around the mountains there was an almost complete absence of chambered tombs and long cairns. The great megalithic rings were built without opposition.

These Cumbrian circles are some of the most splendid in Britain and Ireland (Fig. 7). One of the finest at Castlerigg near Keswick (Pl. 23), seen in the morning with its tall entrance silhouetted against the mountains of Blencathra and Skiddaw, revives something of the awesome impression it must have made in prehistoric times. There is the meadow-wide space of Long Meg and Her Daughters; the close-set pillars of Swinside with its double portals; the tumbled pink boulders of Kemp Howe slumped grotesquely against the railway; Gunnerkeld, to be seen from the modern motorway; and the stones of Grey Croft, the quiet Irish Sea just to its west, the incongruity of the Seascale nuclear power station and its dumps in brutal ugliness to the north. Far to the south is the concentric ring of the Druid's Temple overlooking Morecambe Bay, bracken hiding its low outer circle, turf covering the burnt patches and the cremations and the pit where a tiny urn was left.

Such a variety of architecture makes this part of Britain a good starting point for a study of stone circles. Useful general reviews of the rings can be found in C. W.

Plate 23. The mountainous setting of Castlerigg (Photograph: the author).

Dymond, 1881, 1891 and 1902; R. G. Collingwood, 1933; and J. Waterhouse, 1985.

Cumbria is a self-contained area bounded on the west by the Irish Sea, on the north by the Solway Firth, on the east by the Pennines and on the south by Morecambe Bay. Yet on a clear day one can see from its highlands to Ireland and to south-west Scotland. Despite the central dome of mountains it was an attractive region to prehistoric settlers for the marine gravels along its coastline offered well-drained, fertile soils, and it was along this littoral that some of the first people settled at sites such as Ehenside Tarn, Seascale, and perhaps Skelmore Heads, Ulverston. Analysis of buried pollen grains has revealed a slight decline in the number of elm trees from the later fourth millennium BC perhaps because of intensive grazing of farm animals, a decline that became marked from about 3300 BC at the time when the Lake District 'factory' of Group VI was being actively worked.[2]

Immigrants from Ireland or other travellers by sea would be attracted by the coastal plain. People from the east would come first to the sandstones and rich earths of the north–south Eden Valley which soon became the major thoroughfare and it was along this valley that Bronze Age smiths and other travellers passed from the mid third millennium onwards. Yet it was neither along the coast nor along the River Eden that the earliest circles were put up. They were erected in and around the central dome, a mountainous district seemingly inimical to settlement but whose valley floors with their rich loams provided good if limited grazing. The reason for the choice was the connection with the stone-axe industry and henges.

	DIAMETERS		
Site	Shape	m	m²
Brats Hill	Flattened	32 × 25.9	651
Broomrigg North	Circle?	50.9 × 50	1,999
Castlerigg	Flattened	32.9 × 29.9	773
Elva Plain	Circle	33.5	881
Grey Yauds	Unknown	47.5	1,772
Lamplugh	Unknown	*c.* 31	755
Long Meg and Her Daughters	Flattened	109.4 × 93	7,991
Studfold	Oval	32.8 × 25.9	667
Swinside	Circle	28.7	647

Table 9. Dimensions of the large Lake District Megalithic Rings.

The Dating of the Cumbrian Circles

Amongst the features of early henges are circularity, an unbroken enclosure except for a single entrance, portal stones and an open central arena not more than about 61 m across. These traits in Cumbrian circles were probably in imitation of henge banks. There are still hints of banking at Castlerigg, Swinside and Long Meg.

With a mean diameter of 48 m, the rings encompass two and a half times the average area in Britain and Ireland. A counting system based on multiples of 4 and a 'yard' of about 0.8 m (2 ft 7 in) may have been used in the layout of these very large sites. The diameter of Swinside conforms to 36 of such a unit; 40 m at Brats Hill, 40.6 m Castlerigg and Studfold, 43 m at Elva Plain as though the measure was an accepted but not rigorously applied length in terms of region-wide accuracy (Table 9).

Unlike the majority of circles elsewhere the rings were formed of many stones, perhaps sixty at Swinside, over seventy at Long Meg and Her Daughters, eighty-eight at the Grey Yauds, as though to create the effect of a continuous 'wall' of stone as megalithic replicas of the banks of henges, uninterrupted except for the entrance. The Lake District rings also have entrances, sometimes just a wider gap at Studfold, more elaborately at Long Meg and at Swinside where two outer portals were set up. They were subtly related to alignments, either to a cardinal point or to a calendrical event.

In shape the rings are either circular or have a flattened arc. Waterhouse has noted that where a side straightens, at the north-west at Brats Hill or east at Castlerigg, it was where the land began to fall away. At Long Meg the distortion happened where the slope levelled out. Topography rather than Pythagorean geometry appears the cause of these deviations.

The Cumbrian circles also have entrances (Fig. 8). These openings were sometimes little more than a wider gap flanked by tall pillars. Occasionally they were decisively formed by the addition of an adjacent pair of stones outside the gap, like portals. Showing the strength and extent of the tradition both types of 'gateway' were constructed outside the Lake District in rings probably associated with the distribution of stone axes. Gapped entrances were put up in Westmorland, at Irish circles around the

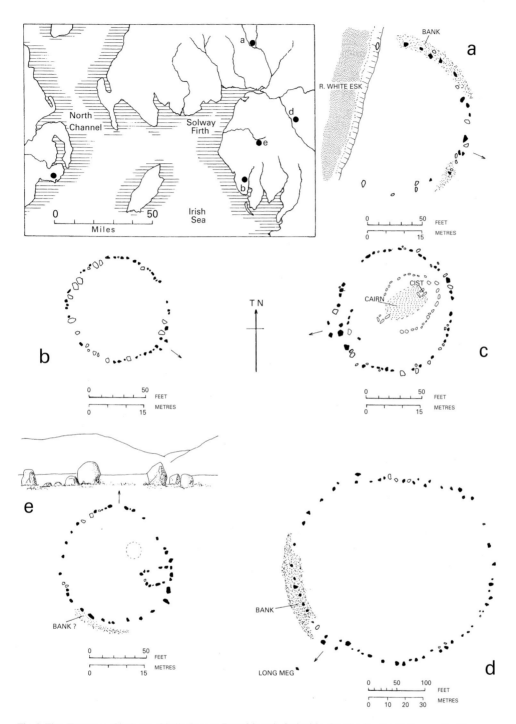

Fig. 8. Five Entrance Circles: a. Girdle Stanes, Dumfriess; b. Swinside, Cumberland; c. Ballynoe, Co. Down; d. Long Meg and Her Daughters, Cumberland; e. Castlerigg, Cumberland.

Wicklow mountains and the Sperrin hills, even as far to the south in England as Land's End. The more elaborate portals were as widespread: at the Girdle Stanes and Loch Buie in Scotland; at Ballynoe in Ireland; the Druids' Circle in north Wales; and the Rollright Stones in Oxfordshire. The addition of yet more pairs beyond these portals resulted in the short avenues of rings like Stanton Drew in Somerset.

There may once have been external portals at Castlerigg. Stukeley, who saw the ring in 1725, wrote that 'at the north end is the kistvaen [a rectangular setting] of great stones' of which the outer pair may later have been removed and buried to allow ploughing closer to the circle.[3]

Several sites like Castlerigg, Swinside, Long Meg and Brats Hill, all in Cumbria, possess such characteristics and, tentatively, they may be assigned an early place amongst the stone circles. Ballynoe, Co. Down, directly across the Irish Sea from Swinside, shares many of these features. Middle Neolithic Carrowkeel pottery was found there.

The stones of these great rings are not graded in height, are unshaped except for their keeled bases and usually lack art. Except for Castlerigg and Brats Hill they have no internal 'furniture' such as a centre stone or a cove. The exceptions to this are the enigmatic rectangles, one surviving at Castlerigg, the other destroyed at Brats Hill. The two rings share an astonishing likeness in situation and architecture.

They are almost equidistant from Sprinkling Tarn at the centre of the Langdale sources of tuff, perhaps a hard day's travel from it. Castlerigg is about 11 miles NNE along the easier, gently winding valley of the Derwent. Brats Hill is ten demanding miles to the SSW along precipitous mountain ridges, past Broad Crag, Scafell Pike and Scafell Fell, down the steep Hardrigg Gill to Burnmoor Tarn and the plateau of the Eskdale Fells. The resemblance between the rings is so remarkable that it is as though they were planned by the same group of people, designed as the first depots for the reception of freshly shaped roughouts brought from their mountain sources.

Although separated by fifteen savagely difficult miles they almost duplicate each other in size, shape, number of stones and inner quadrilateral. The diameters of Castlerigg are 32.9 × 29.9 m, of Brats Hill, 32 × 29.5 m, and both have a flattened arc. Alexander Thom superimposed their plans to demonstrate their almost perfect conformity. Even the number of stones, about 42, was common to both sites.

The similarity is emphasised by an internal setting unique to them. Inside Castlerigg, joined to the tallest, radially set pillar at the south-east, is an unexplained rectangle of low blocks, 4 m wide and extending 8 m into the ring. Making the comparison between the Keswick ring and its counterpart on Burn Moor even closer, 'when this spot [Brats Hill] was first visited by Mr. Wright of Keswick, 29 years ago [1827], the easternmost cairn was surrounded by a parallelogram of stones similar to that in the Keswick circle, very few of which now remain'. A convincing interpretation of the reason for these rectangles has still to be found.[4]

The age of the arguably primary rings in Cumbria remains conjectural. It is possible to construct a diagnostic scheme in which early traits are added in Column A, and presumably later features such as small diameters, concentric circles, centre stones, ovoid shape and banking listed in Column B. The subtraction of the totals gives a crude but apparently reliable indication of the chronological relationship of the circle (Table 10). Artefacts from the later rings are of the Early Bronze Age or later suggesting that the principles behind the diagnosis were valid. The majority of burials

Table 10. Analysis of chronological traits in the Cumbrian stone circles.

SITE	EARLY TRAITS								LATE TRAITS									GRAND TOTAL	FINDS
	Diameter 27 m +	20+ stones	Stones 1 m + high	Entrance	Outlier	Circular or Flattered	Surrounding bank	+ TOTAL	Diameter –21 m	10–15 stones	Stones –1 m high	Concentric	Centre stone	Associated circle	Oval	Embanked	– TOTAL		
Phase 1. c. 3100–2900 BC																			
1 Castlerigg	1	1	1	1	1	F	1	7	×	×	×	×	×	×	×	×	0	+7	Stone axe
2 Long Meg	1	1	1	1	1	F	1	7	×	×	×	×	×	×	×	×	0	+7	
3 Swinside	1	1	1	1	1	C	×	6	×	×	×	×	×	×	×	×	0	+6	
4 Grey Yauds	1	1	1	?	1	C	×	5½	×	×	×	×	×	×	×	×	0	+5½	
Phase 2. c. 2900–2500 BC																			
1 Brats Hill	1	1	×	½	1	F	×	4½	×	×	×	×	×	×	×	×	0	+4½	Antlers
2 Elva Plain	1	1	×	×	1	C	×	4	×	×	×	×	×	×	×	×	0	+4	
3 Gunnerkeld	1	1	1	×	×	C	×	4	×	×	×	1	×	×	×	×	–1	+3	
4 Kemp Howe	×	1	1	×	½	?	×	2½	×	×	×	×	×	×	?	×	–½	+2	
5 Grey Croft	×	×	1	×	1	F	×	3	×	1	×	×	×	×	×	×	–1	+2	Group VI stone axe
6 Gamelands	1	1	×	½	×	F	×	3½	×	×	1	×	×	×	×	1	–2	+1½	
7 Ash House Wood	1	1	×	×	×	?	×	2½	×	×	1	×	×	×	?	×	–1½	+1	
8 Broomrigg North	1	×	×	×	½	?	×	2	×	×	1	×	×	×	?	×	–1½	+½	
Phase 3. c. 2500–2000 BC																			
1 Studfold	1	1	×	×	×	×	×	2	×	×	1	×	×	×	×	0	–2	0	
2 Oddendale	×	1	×	×	×	C	×	2	×	×	1	1	×	×	×	×	–2	0	
3 Casterton	×	1	×	×	×	C	×	2	1	×	1	×	×	×	×	×	–2	0	Beaker burial?
4 Kirk	×	½	×	×	½	C	×	2	×	×	1	×	×	×	1	×	–2	0	
5 Blakeley Raise	×	×	1	½	×	?	×	2	1	1	×	×	×	×	?	×	–2½	–½	
6 The Beacon	1	½	×	×	×	×	×	1½	×	×	1	×	×	×	1	×	–2	–½	
7 Wilson Scar	×	1	×	×	×	×	×	1	1	×	1	×	×	×	×	×	–2	–1	Flints
8 Lacra South	×	×	1	×	×	1	×	2	1	1	×	½	×	1	×	×	–3½	–1½	Flints
9 Kopstone	×	×	½	×	×	×	×	½	×	×	½	½	×	×	×	1	–1½		
10 Druid's Temple, Birkrigg	×	1	×	×	×	×	×	1	×	×	1	1	×	×	0	×	–3	–2	Pennine urn
Phase 4. c. 2000–1500 BC																			
1 White Moss NE	×	×	×	×	×	C	×	1	1	1	1	×	×	1	×	×	–4	–3	
2 White Moss SW	×	×	×	×	×	C	×	1	1	1	1	×	×	1	×	×	–4	–3	
3 Gretigate NE	×	×	×	×	×	×	×	0	×	1	×	×	×	1	0	×	–3	–3	
4 Low Longrigg NE	×	×	×	×	×	C	×	1	1	1	1	×	×	1	×	×	–4	–3	
5 Moor Divock 4	×	×	×	×	×	×	×	0	×	1	1	×	×	×	×	×	–3	–3	Food-vessel
6 The Cockpit	×	×	×	×	×	×	×	0	×	×	1	1	×	×	0	1	–4	–4	
7 Lacra NE	×	×	×	×	×	×	×	0	1	1	1	½	1	1	0	×	–6½	–6½	Overhanging-rim urn
8 Bleaberry Haws	×	×	×	×	×	×	×	0	1	1	1	×	×	×	0	1	–5	–5	Flints

1 = a feature of the ring. × = the ring does not contain the feature.

occur in the later sites although this factor was not considered in the analysis. It should be noted, however, that internal burials could be secondary intrusions. There are remains of small cairns inside Castlerigg and Brats Hill. Two great mounds once existed inside Long Meg and Her Daughters.

Because there have been so few reliable excavations the dating of stone circles is difficult. Only ten have been subjected to modern investigation: three at Lacra, 1947;

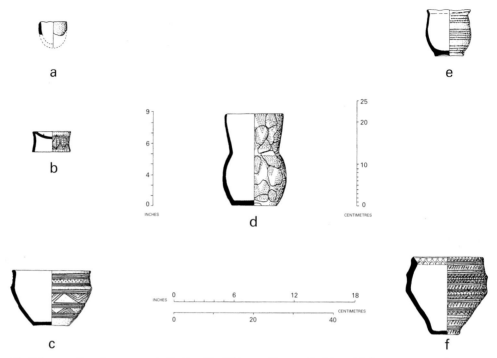

Fig. 9. Some pottery from stone circles,: I: a. Neolithic cup, Grange, Co. Limerick; b. vase-support, Er-Lannic, Brittany; c. grooved ware bowl, West Kennet Avenue, Avebury, Wiltshire; d. S3/W beaker, Grange, Co. Limerick; e. B/W beaker, The Sanctuary, Wiltshire; f. food-vessel, Machrie Moor 4, Arran.

the four rings of Broomrigg A, B, C and D, 1948–50; Grey Croft, 1949; Wilson Scar, 1952; and Gretigate, 1960. To these may be added Mosley Height, Lancashire in 1950. As the C-14 method was not widely used until late in the 1950s there is no assay for any of these sites.

In general it is the smaller, later Cumbrian ring with its cremation that has provided artefacts (Figs 9 and 10). From Broomrigg C, a small ring, came a Pennine urn, indigenous to north-western England, a plain pygmy cup, thirteen jet beads and a V-perforated jet button. There were also two bronze fragments, perhaps from an awl, 'the only bronze recorded from the excavation of a Cumbrian stone circle'.

All these belong to the Early Bronze Age. From Lacra D came an inverted collared urn. At the Druid's Temple, Ulverston, another urn was discovered, a sandstone disc with funerary associations and a lump of red ochre, possibly for body-painting. Two tiny circles on Moor Divock yielded a food-vessel covered in herring-bone decoration of Yorkshire style and a collared urn. Indeterminate flints have been recovered from other rings.

These objects belong within a period from about 2300 to 1700 BC. The only earlier implements are Group VI stone axes at Castlerigg and Grey Croft. From that site came a Bronze Age jet ring. Other than these there is no known dateable material and the chronology of the Cumbrian megalithic rings remains provisional.[5]

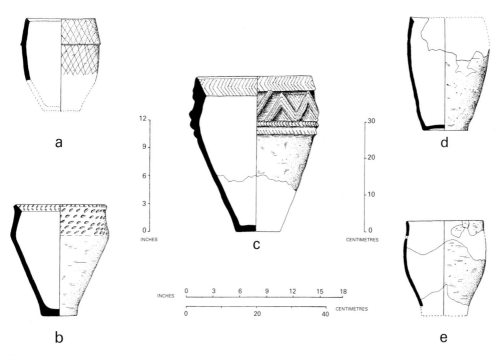

Fig. 10. Some pottery from stone circles II: a. Collared urn, Lacra D, Cumberland; b. enlarged food-vessel, Druids Circle, Caernarvon (Gwynedd); c. encrusted urn, Glenballoch, Perthshire; d. flat-rimmed urn, Sandy Road, Scone, Perthshire; e. late prehistoric urn, Drombeg, Co. Cork.

Situation of the Cumbrian Stone Circles

Most of the great circles stand in situations easily approached by dispersed groups unlike the later rings which occupy hillside positions either in the upper Eden Valley or in south-west Cumbria. Some of the early sites like Grey Yauds are in natural passes with steep fells a mile to its east and the wooded Eden Valley 2 miles westwards and 150 m lower. Others were close to rivers, Kemp Howe being a few hundred metres from the River Lowther. Some were in valley bottoms. Gamelands lies at the foot of Knott Scar on the fertile lowlands around Orton and the River Lune.

This propensity for well-drained, easily accessible sites ultimately doomed many rings. Grey Yauds, 'jades', either worn-out horses or disreputable women, perhaps synonyms, over 47.6 m across, was destroyed when the common was enclosed and today only the outlier survives. Kemp Howe, a 24.4 m circle, once had an avenue of stones leading southwards to it from a small barrow. The ring was tumbled when the railway was laid. With the enclosure of the common in 1815 the avenue was ruined and only a few huge blocks like the Goggleby Stone and the Thunderstone remain. The tumulus in Skellaw Field, 'the hill of skulls', was levelled at the same time. In the *Gentleman's Magazine*, 1824, someone wrote, 'When the antiquary now views the remains of this remarkable monument he cannot but regret at what perhaps, he may call the barbarous treatment it has met with'. Gamelands was no luckier. A ring 42.1 × 35.1 m in diameter of granitic glacial erratics, the whole interior was ploughed in 1862, some stones buried, others blasted into fragments.[6]

The size and situation of these great rings support the belief that they were intended for large concourses of people. Quite different are the upland and remote locations of the later rings, many of which cluster together like tombs in a necropolis. On Askham Fell, 320 m O.D., on a wide and exposed plateau the Moor Divock complex consisted of small stone circles, avenues, ring-cairns and barrows. None of the five circles was more than 14 m across and one, excavated by Canon Greenwell in 1866, contained a Yorkshire food-vessel. The entire megalithic group is strung out along a mile of moorland and is best explained as a familial cemetery used over several generations with ritual and sepulchral monuments intermixed. Hut circles in the vicinity may be rare examples of the living places of the circle users.

Somewhat similar is the Lacra group on a limited plateau overlooking the Duddon Sands. The first circle was badly damaged but the second, 16.2 m in diameter, had a low central cairn covering a turf stack over a fire-reddened patch by which were pieces of cremated bone mixed with birch and ash charcoal. The third ring also had oak charcoal. The most complicated site was Lacra NE, 18.3 × 15.6 m, with a possible central stone and a debatable avenue extending WSW with an opposing single line of stones running ENE from the circle.

By the north-western stone was a broken and inverted overhanging rim (OHR) urn around which lay oak and hazel charcoal showing that the urn had been laid in its shallow pit during the autumn. Like Moor Divock the Lacra circles with their hint of seasonal ritual may be considered the handiwork of a small family group. Whether the rings were simple burial places is problematical. Cremated deposits in stone circles could have been for supplicatory purposes.

A circle in which ritual and sepulchral may have integrated was Oddendale, a concentric ring on the weatherblown top of Hardendale Fells. The outer ring is 26.2 m across, of low stones and encircles a contiguous kerb, 7 m in diameter, which edged a mound covering cremated bone and burnt material. A single stone, almost exactly at the east, stood midway between the rings.

The farther south one goes in this region the more the stone circle tradition overlaps with that of enclosed cremation cemeteries and ring-cairns of the second millennium, monuments in which deposits of cremated bone were placed within a pennanular bank. Such hengiform sites are common in the southern Pennines at sites such as Banniside Moor, Lancashire, with its five pits, cremations and large stone at its south-west; or Blackheath, Yorkshire, an earthen circular bank with several cremations and Pennine urns. At Mosley Height, Lancashire, a circle of eighteen large boulders was irregularly spaced on a stony bank enclosing a paved arena 12.8 m across under which were cremations, urns, grain-rubbers and stone hammers of the Early Bronze Age, everything in pits haphazardly arranged around a little central cist holding the cremated bones of an adult female. Such a site has demonstrable affinities with enclosed cremation cemeteries and with stone circles.[7]

So, to a lesser extent, has the Druid's Temple on Birkrigg Common in Lancashire-North-of-the-Sands (Fig. 11). This concentric circle, 26.5 m and 8.4 m in diameters, superficially resembles the earlier rings but excavations in 1911 and 1921 revealed the entire interior to be roughly paved like Mosley Height. And like that site it contained cremations, one with a delicate inverted OHR urn, only 15 cm high.

The Druid's Temple may have been the ritual centre of people whose settlement lay only half a mile to the north on the slopes of a limestone hill. There, at Urswick 'Stone Walls', was a spacious stone-walled oval enclosure covering 1½ acres (0.6 ha)

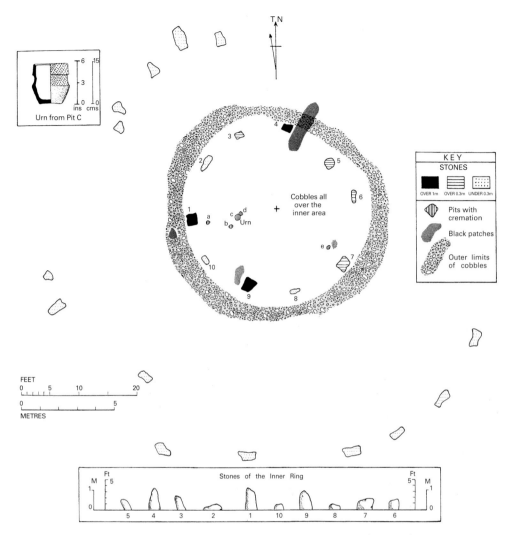

Fig. 11. The Druids Temple, Birkrigg Common, Lancashire-north-of-the-Sands (Cumbria).

with paddocks and pens for animals, a large circular hut and four smaller. Just north of the site was a long cultivation terrace.

The living were accompanied by generations of the dead. To the west were barrows, one rectangular containing seven cremations, three in cordoned urns, another mound with ten cremations, there is a dislodged cist and, close to the Druid's Temple, a round barrow 12 m across covering three inhumations, one with a bronze awl, the burials enclosed in a low stone circle that was covered by the barrow. All this was Bronze Age but the area had been occupied before that. A mile and a half to the north is the fallen ruin of Skelmore Heads, a Neolithic chambered tomb with a massive capstone. The so-called 'burial-chamber' of Tosthills two miles to the west is no more than a natural, rocky outcrop.[8]

This digression indicates the variety of stone circles in any region, a diversity of architecture, function and cultural intermixing against which the analysis of the earlier rings may be better judged. It is from their own comparative uniformity and purpose as communal rallying places that they can be differentiated from other megalithic rings.

The Early Stone Circles

The diameters of the first stone circles are smaller than the ancestral henges, averaging 48 m against approximately 73 m. This is because of the width of henge banks and ditches. The internal areas are little different in area. A direct comparison between a henge and a nearby stone circle of comparable dimensions, King Arthur's Round Table near Penrith, and Grey Yauds 7 miles to the NNE is revealing. The 91.4 m henge has an earthen bank about 10.4 m wide and some 1.2 m high. Its soil came from an inner ditch 9.8 m wide and 1.2 m deep. The rather irregular internal plateau, about 51 × 46 m, was some 1,840 m². It has been calculated that it took about 55,000 man-hours to complete the double-entranced henge.

Grey Yauds, a great ring destroyed in the later nineteenth century, was 'a nearly exact circle' 47.5 m in diameter, its interior of about 1,750 m² being about the same size as King Arthur's Round Table. The eighty-eight granite stones of the ring were local. Between 1.2 m and 1.5 m in height they weighed three to four tons and demanded teams of twelve to sixteen men to drag them up the gentle gradient to the site. If the time for locating suitable stones, levering them onto sledges and rails, lashing them securely, dragging them half a mile uphill, digging their stoneholes, setting them up and jamming them tightly with chockstones, were to take only one eight-hour day for each stone it can be calculated that work would have taken just over 11,000 man-hours. (88 stones × 8 hours × 16 labourers), only a fifth of the time taken to construct the henge.

The statistics are misleading. In theory one man alone could have dug the ditch and heaped up the bank of King Arthur's Round Table although even toiling eight hours every day with no weekend breaks or holidays the task would have taken him nineteen years. Conversely, one man could not have put up the heavy stones of Grey Yauds. The minimum work-force of sixteen could have finished setting up the circle in three months. Assuming more sensible gangs of about fifty for each site with days missed for bad weather and unavoidable chores elsewhere King Arthur's Round Table could have been raised in six months and Grey Yauds in about a fortnight.

Exactly how early the majestic stone circles of the Lake District were remains inferential as no closed finds have come from them. During successive periods in the Lake District incoming people occupied different areas. There were the Neolithic miners and traders of the Group VI stone axe industry within a crude time-span of 3750 BC to 2250 BC (3000–1800 bc); and food-vessel and beaker users of the Early Bronze Age; and the people with whom cinerary urns and bronze implements are associated from about 2250 BC to 1550 BC (c. 1800–1300 bc). The large stone circles can persuasively be linked with the first of these and given a speculative origin towards the end of the fourth millennium BC.

Their distribution is significant. They 'command access routes into the Lake District mountains'. The probable high trackways used for transporting the stone axes from their mountain sources follow several routes along which roughed-out axes have been picked up including five unpolished axes from the Pike of Stickle in the Langdales themselves, 'a cache (lost or forgotten) of finished roughouts originally intended for "export" to one of the axe-grinding sites on the Cumbrian coast or in Furness'.[9]

Plate 24. The surviving stone of a possible Four-Poster inside Mayburgh (Photograph: the author).

Several of the rings lie close to such paths. Swinside is at the coastal end of the high route from the Great Langdale factories down the Duddon Valley. Elva Plain is close to Derwentwater and the Bassenthwaite hills out towards the Cumbrian coast. Castlerigg, often misnamed the 'Carles' or 'husbandmen' through a misreading of Stukeley's 'Carſles', is magnificently placed for travellers coming northwards down Borrowdale to go either north-west along Derwentwater or to turn east towards the Penrith henges, themselves at the focus of the mountain pass and between the rivers of Eamont and Lowther. Long Meg stands on the way towards the Tyne Gap and north-eastern England where so many Group VI axes have been found.

'It may be remarked, in passing, that several stone celts have been found in and about the Vale of St. John.' In 1901, lying in the peat at Portinscale, not far from Castlerigg, four rough-outs and a finished axe lay near a pile of chippings and a thick log stump with a battered top, a 'Celt maker's manufactory'. Axes have been recovered near Long Meg and Her Daughters and near Swinside. Others came from the circles themselves, part of one just beneath the turf at the entrance to Mayburgh (Pl. 24). Stukeley recalled that 'in ploughing at Mayborough they dug up a brass celt', which suggests that the henge continued to function as a distribution centre well into the Early Bronze Age. A stone axe was in a pile of stones taken from the Hird Wood ring. Three have come from Castlerigg. In 1856 Benjamin Williams reported that 'a rude stone club', perhaps one of the heavy, broad butted 'Cumbrian' axes up to 38 cm in length, 'and [a] stone celt there were made of the hypersthene greenstone and the greenstone chirt of the neighbourhood'. A third one, unfinished, was found inside the circle in 1875. Yet another, unbroken, lay by the disturbed stonehole at the exact east of the Grey Croft stone circle.[10] Their relationship to trackways and to polishing sites has already been noted.

The distribution of the supposedly early rings is different from later cultural groups such as the users of beakers. These fine funerary vessels first appear in the archaeological record in Britain around 2500 BC. There was little connection between their users and the early axe factories. In Cumbria there were two major styles, an earlier of all-over-corded (AOC) around the south-west coast, probably not reaching Cumbria before 2400 BC and never penetrating the central massif. The other, more numerous type is concentrated in the Eden Valley. It was composed of Northern beakers, particularly the late N3 short-necked forms. So far is it unlikely that these pottery styles were connected with the axe factories that it has been deduced that the liking by their users for shafted battle-axes actually led to the decline of the Lake District industries whose epidotised tuff was unsuited to perforation. Only the Coniston Grits of the much later Group XV manufactory survived the disruption with its production of shafted battle-axes, and axe-hammers.

The sepulchral food-vessels of the Early Bronze Age, their enlarged versions, related encrusted urns and some Irish bowls are again concentrated in the Eden Valley and its tributaries with a slight scattering along the western coast to the north and south of the Solway Firth. The other enlarged and encrusted food-vessels and Irish bowls are spread along the western littoral. Nowhere are they found in the mountain passes.

Similarly, the collared urns in Cumbria were found along the south-west coast. Nor, except for the single bronze axe near Keswick, does any of the earlier Bronze Age metalwork lie within the mountains and it must be concluded that like their beaker and food-vessel counterparts the people possessing these copper and bronze artefacts preferred the more easily travelled areas. The recent discoveries of northern style beakers at Levens Park, of food-vessel sherds at Mecklin Park and urns at Aldoth and Greystoke only confirm the peripheral distribution of these Bronze Age vessels.[11] It is the elimination of such late associations that encourages the belief that the first stone circles were Neolithic in origin.

Although today there are few early circles along the west coast R. G. Collingwood noticed the correlation between the axes and the rings and wondered whether the western absence had been caused by the construction of timber rather than stone circles. There has, moreover, been considerable demolition of stone circles along that coast where a strip of land only about a mile or so wide is available for agriculture. As well as the vanished site of the Ringlen Stones near Egremont there were the three sites at Gretigate dynamited and partly buried in the nineteenth century. Further south there were three other great rings: Annaside, Hall Foss and the Kirkstones which were recorded in the eighteenth century but which have since been demolished.[12]

Despite this geographical lacuna it is arguable that the presence together at the heart of the Lake District of axe factories and great stone circles is not accidental but an indication that the two were contemporary and functionally connected. It is a hypothesis supported by the distribution of the rings, by finds of axes inside them and by radiocarbon dates.

Two of these came from Great Langdale itself at the small site of Thunacar Knott, one of 2730 ± 135 bc (BM-281) from charcoal associated with stone tools and chippings, another of 2524 ± 52 bc (BM-676) from a similar context. These centre on 3400 BC in recalibrated years showing that the Langdale factories were being worked some five and a half thousand years ago. It is feasible that rings such as Castlerigg, so close to the stone sources, are of the same general period.

Other determinations ranging from 3010 ± 300 bc (C-462) to as late as 1580 ± 150 bc (BM-68) came from Ehenside Tarn, a settlement near Egremont. Group VI axes were found there. In corroboration of an early date for the rings there is a further assay of 2525 ± 85 bc (GU-1591) from the Lochmaben Stone disrupted ellipse a few hundred yards from the Solway Firth which, at low tide, could be crossed to England four miles away. The internal size of this oval, about 1,970 m², commensurate with the spacious Cumbrian rings, and its relative proximity to the Langdales suggest that it may have been put up somewhat later than the circles of the central regions at a time when Group VI axes were reaching south-west Scotland.[13]

Astronomical Lines

Adding architectural complications to chronological complexity many of the rings had sightlines to the sun built into them and, as has been discussed, this subject of astronomy is one of the most contentious in the study of stone circles. If these circles were for a concourse of people at special times the large rings might expect to have conspicuous circumferential stones or outliers marking major solar positions, such orientations being not for esoteric calculations but more probably for seasonal observances, the summer or winter solstices or the vernal and autumnal equinoxes when the sun was midway between its northern and southern extremes. Autumnal gatherings are suspected in the causewayed enclosures, the putative ancestors of henges, and the earliest stone circles may have had something of the same purpose. What astronomical alignments they contained would be calendrical.

In Cumbria the sightlines were usually determined by the entrances to rings, sometimes emphasised by an outlying pillar, and they were solar (Pl. 25). It was noticeable that in a study of eighteen sites Thom proposed only nine for astronomical use, of which just four were concerned with the sun: Castlerigg, L/1; Swinside, L1/3; White Moss, L1/6d; and Long Meg and Her Daughters, L1/7. The remainder had a multiplicity of targets including the moon and the stars of Antares, *α Scorpii*; Arcturus, *α Boötis*; Deneb, *α Cygni*; and Pollux, *β Geminorum*, whose alignments Thom considered established by outliers (3), by stone to stone across the circle (4) and by circle to

Plate 25. The restored Blakeley Raise, Cumbria. Thom believed it to be aligned on the northern moonset (Photograph: the author).

circle (10). Only the entrance at Swinside was considered as a foresight.[14] Entrances consistently define the times of 'Celtic' festivals, midwinter sunrise at Swinside, midwinter sunset at Long Meg and to the cardinal point of north at Castlerigg.

It is quite common to discover that the cardinal positions of north, south, east and west were marked by larger stones in these great rings. At Long Meg two massive blocks lie close to east and west, opposite each other. At Elva Plain the longest stone is at the west, the shortest at the east. At Swinside there is a high, tapered pillar at the north, and a less tall flat-topped stone at the south. At Brats Hill the highest is at the south.

There is evidence in prehistoric Britain of an interest in these cardinal positions. Of Wessex beaker burials Lanting and van der Waals wrote, 'A N–S orientation must have been the rule in this area . . . Men were buried with their head toward the North, usually lying on their left side facing East . . . Women were usually buried with their head toward the South, lying on their right side, thus also facing East.'

In Yorkshire an early north–south orientation was replaced by the custom of aligning the body east–west, but with sex discrimination continuing with men having their heads at the east, women's at the west. 'A similar pattern appeared in food-vessel burials with men lying on their right side, women on their left, but still facing southwards.'[15] It is remarkable how often these rough cardinal alignments occur. It is also remarkable how crude they were, sometimes varying as much as 5° from the meridional line. There is an explanation.

A sightline to the north was of no calendrical relevance. Neither sun nor moon ever rose or set there. But north was midway between the annual north–eastern and north–western risings and settings of the sun and, every nineteen years, of the major midwinter moon. Prehistoric communities may have aligned the long axis of their ring upon that magical midpoint. Had the north–east to north–west skyline been level the orientation would have been to true north.

Nature not only abhors a vacuum. She also detests flat horizons, and with hills or mountains higher to north–east or north–west the rising sun would have appeared later to the east and set sooner to the west 'pulling' the observed midpoint away from north. Modern astronomers understand this. Prehistoric people neither knew nor cared. The alignment that they wanted and achieved was one to the middle of the sunless and moonless gap.

Such a 'north–south' line could have been defined over no more than two or three sunny days. An 'equinoctial' alignment would take six months from midsummer to midwinter for just one sighting. This may account for the astronomical fact that for every suspected equinoctial sightline there are at least half a dozen north–south orientations.

In the absence of explanatory evidence modern man is denied the likelihood of rediscovering the cosmology of early people. One may note that the Egyptians acknowledged the importance of a particular stellar group, the northern circumpolar stars, 'those that know no destruction', or 'those that know no weariness'. Such stars that never disappeared below the skyline were symbols of the dead who had triumphed over death and had passed into eternal life. To the Egyptians the north became a place of everlasting blessedness because there was no death there. Other prehistoric people, albeit with different interpretations, may also have looked on the north with awe and incorporated lines towards it in their monuments.

It has been claimed that outlying pillars were for astronomical use. Such stones are known in Cumbria from Grey Yauds down to Cheetham Close, Lancashire, but of the seventy or more established outliers in the British and Irish rings there are no constant orientations amongst the forty-two that have been properly surveyed. Instead, some may have been territorial markers announcing that the land was occupied, or alternatively acting as signposts for passers-by. This is feasible for the King Stone at the Rollright Stones in Oxfordshire.

In Cumbria the outliers at Long Meg, Elva Plain, Grey Croft and Brats Hill were all placed where they would be helpful as directional pillars. Long Meg stands on a ridge above the valley and is visible even from low down the slope. Elva Plain has steep slopes to north and south and the outlier points south–westwards along the hogback that runs west towards the coast.

The 'outlier' at Castlerigg is probably an erstwhile circle-stone, probably from the west side where there is a wide space, that was buried outside to allow farm-wagons access into the ring for harvesting. In 1769 the elegaic poet, Thomas Gray, saw wheat growing there and even today ridge and furrow is still conspicuous in the field. Later the stone was dug up and dragged to the edge of the field because it was damaging ploughs. At no time did it have an astronomical function.

Outliers are unsatisfactory foresights. Portalled entrances are better. A stone to one side of the circle's entrance and the portal beyond it created an unequivocal sightline with no need to locate the centre of an open ring. At Swinside (Pl. 26) the southern-most entrance-stone and its portal had an azimuth of 134°.5 and a declination of –24°.6 which at that latitude is very close to midwinter sunrise. As similar portalled phenomena occur in Ballynoe in Co. Down, the Girdle Stones in Dumfriesshire, at the Druids' Circle in North Wales and the Rollright Stones in Oxfordshire it is becoming clear that such enhanced entrances not only formed an impressive approach to the circle but were also deliberate astronomical devices.[16]

The Anatomy of Long Meg

What has been claimed for archaeo-astronomical alignments in megalithic Cumbria can be emphasised by examining the ring of Long Meg and Her Daughters. With the exception of the gross enormity of Avebury's Outer Circle this is the fourth largest of all the rings, exceeded only by Stanton Drew Centre, the Ring of Brodgar and Avebury Centre South. Long Meg stands at the edge of the wide sandstone terrace above the east bank of the River Eden, six miles from the Penrith henges across the river, within three days' walk of the Langdale factory sites and lying on the northern riverine route to the Tyne Gap.

Measuring some 109.4 m north–south by 93 m its seventy or more lumpish, bulbous boulders, all local, were put up on ground sloping steadily down to the north. There, where the ground levels out, the arc straightens in a line of tumbled boulders. Thom considered the site to be one of his geometrically designed Type B flattened rings but the explanation is more mundane. Aerial photography shows that the straightish arc abuts the southern side of a sprawling ovate enclosure, 220 × 190 m into whose ditch several of the circle-stones had slipped.

The enclosure might explain the presence at the head of the slope of Long Meg (Pl. 27), a thin and high pillar of sandstone, different from the local boulders and brought there from a source over a mile away to stand conspicuously on the ridge where even today, despite intervening walls, its tip is still visible to passers-by on the

Plate 26. Swinside, Cumbria. The portalled entrance is just left of centre at the far side of the ring (Photograph: the author).

lower slopes of the Eden Valley. In the beginning the monolith quite possibly was a territorial marker for the settlement on the far side of the hill from the river.[17]

Over-casually, or perhaps wishfully, it is a popular belief that the flattest, decorated side of the pillar faces the circle but it does not. It looks towards the ENE, 64°, a full 20° off the line to the centre of the ring, suggesting that the subsequent circle was awkwardly interposed between the enclosure and Long Meg with the intention of ensuring that the stone could be used as an astronomical gnomon.

'Long Meg' was a mediaeval catch-phrase applied to any long and slender object, 'to persons very tall, especially if they have *Hop-pole-heighth* wanting *breadth* proportionable thereunto', very apt for the high but scrawny pillar of red sandstone standing south–west of the ring of seventy stones or so. A legend tells that the twelfth-century 'wondrous wizard', Michael Scott, metamorphosed Meg, a local witch, and her coven into stones. Another more secular account claims that the circle-stones were Meg's daughters or even her lovers. If a piece were broken off Meg she would bleed. Scott also endowed the stones with a mystical power so that no one could ever count them accurately, an arithmetical embargo familiar as far away as the Countless Stones in Kent.[18]

Eighteen metres from the outlier is the portalled entrance at the south–west of the ring. Nearby there are questionable stretches of banking. The stones of other large rings in the Lake District may also have been set in cobbly banks. Despite ploughing

Plate 27. The outlier of Long Meg to the south-west of the stone circle (Photograph: the author).

traces remain at Castlerigg and Swinside. It is a feature apparent in related rings as far apart as the Girdle Stones in Scotland, the Druids' Circle in Wales and the Rollright Stones in England. The combination of numerous closely set stones, entrances and banking may again disclose the vestiges of an ancestry from henges.

The heaviest stone, the monstrous east boulder resting opposite another almost as bulky, weighs about thirty tons and could have been hauled and levered into place by a gang of about 150 men. Yet a ring such as Long Meg, enclosing some 8,000 m² was probably meant for many more than that. Factors affecting the location and size of towns today: accessibility, good soil for farming, water, applied equally to the situation and size of stone circles and a circle's area can be taken as a rough guide to the ring's population. In their proportions the great Lake District rings mirror the density of modern populations which themselves have been largely determined by the fertility of the countryside. Keswick near Castlerigg had a population in 1971 of 5200. Penrith close to Long Meg had over 12,000 and this may explain why the latter ring is so much bigger than Castlerigg. The existence of many villages, hamlets, farms and fields in the neighbourhood of Long Meg is in poignant contrast to the few scattered habitations on the fells near Keswick and Castlerigg.[19]

Astronomy affected the plan and choice of the stones. As in other great rings of Cumbria there were two alignments, cardinal and calendrical. The monsters facing each other are not exactly due east–west but slightly ENE–WSW. One assumes that a midpoint between the midwinter and midsummer sunsets was obtained by sighting on those events and marking the position central to them. With land higher to the south–west than to the north–west this, as in so many of these 'cardinal' settings, caused a theoretical error of a sightline some 3° south of true west. To the community that laid out the line there was no error.

The calendrical sightline was to the midwinter sunset and involved a circle-stone, the portal beyond it and Long Meg. Although Long Meg's outlying stone could act as a foresight to indicate the midwinter sunset an observer would have found it difficult to locate an unmarked backsight at the centre of an irregular ring 93 m across. Portal stones solved the dilemma. At Long Meg the circle-stone on the western side of the entrance and the portal beyond it were in direct line both with the tall outlying pillar rising behind them and with the midwinter setting sun beyond it. The three stones created a neat sightline for the observer.

There is an interesting aside. In 1983 Martin Brennan described how the rising sun on its cycle from midsummer to midwinter casts a shadow day by day in a clockwise spiral around a tree, stone or post. On its return from midwinter to midsummer the shadow would be anti-clockwise. It is remarkable that amongst the clutter of almost eradicated carvings of cups, concentric circles, arcs, gutters and lines carved on Long Meg's broadest, smoothest surface the three large spirals carved are all anti-clockwise (Fig. 12).

Interestingly, a spiral was noticed at Castlerigg in September 1995. Forty-eight centimetres in diameter it was carved on a stone of the circle at the east end of the unexplained rectangle. The stone alongside it bore a lattice pattern. Because the south–eastern horizon was slightly higher than the north–eastern the midpoint between the midsummer and midwinter sunrises was slightly south of true east. The stones were set there, not at 90° but 2° to 3° to the south. The 'sunrise' spiral was clockwise.[20]

Burial and Continuity

A final question of these great Cumbrian circles is the presence of burials and cairns inside some of them. Often placed in a stone-lined cist and accompanied by flint artefacts and a Bronze Age vessel there is a strong likelihood that these human deposits were inserted into a circle that was already ancient.

Because bones had been discovered in many rings Colley March argued in 1888 that a stone circle 'had some close relation to the dead', that burials were always 'numerous in its neighbourhood' and that 'stone circles were secure repositories for dead bodies during the time required for the bones to be stripped of their flesh.'[21]

An abandoned ring could have been transformed into a hurdle-lined mortuary-house but nowhere is there proof of such a supposition. What can be observed, however, is the manner in which cemeteries of Bronze Age round barrows developed around some of the great rings, Stonehenge and Arbor Low being two examples. This suggests that the ring was the forerunner of these necropoli and has become the focus of funerary rites.

In Philemon Holland's 1610 English edition of Camden's *Britain*, it was reported of Long Meg and Her Daughters that 'within that ring or circle, are heapes of stones, under which, they say, lye covered the bodies of men slaine. And verily there is reason to thinke that this was a monument of some victory there achieved, for no man would deeme that they were erected in vaine.' John Aubrey added credulous details. 'In the

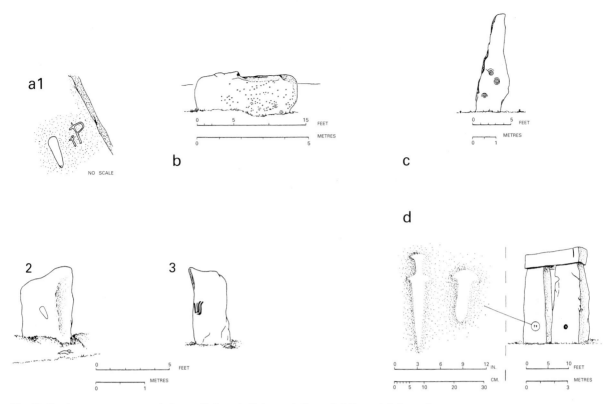

Fig. 12. Carvings on some stone circles:. a. Er-Lannic, Brittany: 1. Stone 2; 2. Stone 1; 3. Stone 3;
b. Rothiemay recumbent stone, Banffshire; c. Long Meg outlier, Cumberland (after Harvey, 1948);
d. Stonehenge, Stone 53.

middle are two Tumuli, or Barrowes of cobble-stones, nine or ten foot high . . . Quaere
Mr Robinson the Minister there, about the Giants bone, and Body found there. The
body is in the middle of the orbicular stones', suggesting that the cairns had been
cleared away to allow ploughing inside the ring.[22]

The placing of a burial within a circular enclosure is known at other North Channel
sites like the henges of the Giant's Ring, Belfast; Longstone Rath, Co. Kildare; and
Ballymeanoch, Argyll. In the latter case the eccentrically placed ditched barrow and
its two cists is likely to be the intrusive work of Beaker users some time in the mid-
second millennium. The same invasive element occurs at Cairnpapple, West Lothian
and at Dun Ruadh, Co. Tyrone, in both of which secondary tumuli were built inside
older earthworks. Burial cists were also added to Balbirnie stone circle, Fife. The fire-
reddened patches in circles such as Lacra may be the relics of pyres, the object of
which may have been not only to consume the remains of the dead but also to invoke
a sympathetic bond with the sun.

This is an interpretation far removed from the funebrial explanations of earlier
writers to whom Bronze Age stone circles with their interments were the sepulchres
of mighty chieftains, yet it would provide a continuum from the rites of the earlier
megalithic rings, ceremonies enacted by smaller groups no longer journeying to distant centres but performing modified but analogous rituals within their own more
modest monuments.

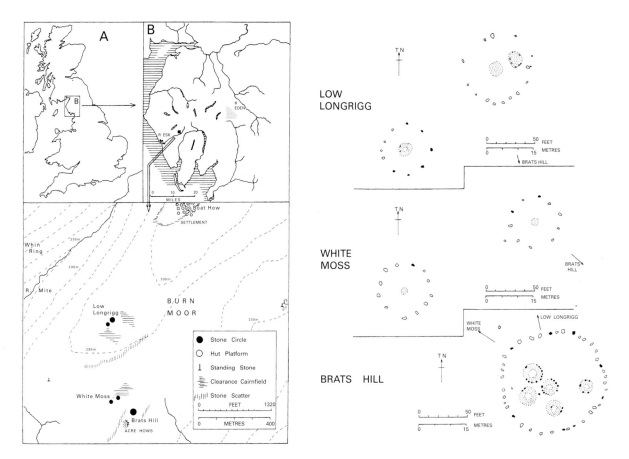

Fig. 13. The complex of stone circles on Burn Moor, Eskdale, Cumbria.

In most of the large Cumbrian rings such a transformation is not obvious although there is frequent evidence of cremation, fragments of charcoal and slivers of bone were the only finds from Swinside. At Studfold, a ring more oval than the others, 32.8 × 25.9 m, there was a low cairn 4.6 m from the focal point of the ellipse. It can be presumed to be secondary to the ring. No finds are recorded from the excavation.[23]

More helpfully, at Brats Hill on Burn Moor (Fig. 13) five cairns lay in the southern half of the ring. As there are four other circles nearby on the plateau it is worth considering whether the group is transitional between the early and the late traditions. Unlike many of the great circles Brats Hill is reached only after a hard walk up Gill Bank from the village of Boot in Eskdale, a three-quarter mile struggle up a stream bed ascending a gradient of 1:5. The great circle stands to the west just below Brats Hill knoll. It measures 32 × 25.9 m, being flattened at the NNW where the ground falls away. Of its forty-two stones most are now down, the tallest 0.9 m high standing at the south. Ten metres to the north–west is an outlying stone no more than 0.3 m high. There may have been an entrance at the north–west.

The five internal cairns from 6.4 m to 7.6 m in diameter were retained within kerbs of fourteen stones. When two were opened in 1827 each had a dome of five large stones covering human cremations, animal bones and antlers. What temporal relationship they had to the construction of the circle is unknown but as a cluster it is likely that they were raised consecutively with the first being that just south of the circle centre. The others crowd around it leaving almost the entire north–east of the interior open. Kindred concentrations of cremations in one half of a site have been noticed at the Old Parks barrow, Kirkoswald, at Cairnpapple henge, and at two of the Dorchester mini-henges, Oxfordshire. The two certain ploughed-down cairns inside Castlerigg also lie well to the north of the circle's centre. In the case of Brats Hill it is useless to speculate whether the cairns represent succeeding generations or the deaths of important persons, singly or collectively, or even sporadic offerings in the years when the weather had been bad. What can be inferred is that the cairns were concentrated in the south–west of the ring because the participants in the ceremonies wished to face in that direction.

About 130 m north–west of Brats Hill are two much smaller rings lying NE–SW on White Moss, the south–western site 16.6 m across with a cairn at its centre. Thirty metres to the north–east is a second, better-preserved ring, 15.9 m in diameter. It also contains a cairn.

Hardly a quarter of a mile to the north of White Moss is another pair of rings at Low Longrigg. The south–west site from which both White Moss and Brats Hill can be seen is an inconspicuous stone circle 15.2 m across with an inner cairn. Eighteen metres north east is a second ring, all its stone prostrate, an ellipse 21.6 × 15.2 m, with two cairns. The dissimilarity in size and shape of the two sites suggest that they had been built successively.[24]

Surmises on the interconnections of such sites and Brats Hill, even between themselves, is a matter for the visionary rather than the archaeologist although the fact that Brats Hill can be seen from Low Longrigg but not the reverse implies that the smaller ring was the later.

The warmer, drier weather of the Bronze Age together with a postulated increase in population caused people to settle on previously less desirable land in many of the highlands of Britain and Ireland until a deterioration in the climate and over-exploitation of the thin soils compelled the abandonment of those marginal regions. Signs of occupation can be seen on moors whose modern acidic soils offer no sustenance. From Burn Moor tarn itself came palynological evidence of a decrease in oak forest from about 2000 BC onwards and an expansion of grassland and weeds. The absence of cereal pollen shows that the clearances were the handiwork of cattle-grazers rather than agriculturalists. The smaller circles could have been the manifestations of settlers attempting to extend their territories to land that even in their time provided little encouragement, and if the rings were indeed built in sequence that could be a sign of the gradual widening of tree-felling and stone clearance to create wider areas for grazing.[25]

In the vicinity of both pairs of rings are overgrown clearance cairns, none large, but testimony to the farming that once took place on the now peat-covered moor. A droveway and a line of hut-circles on a platform settlement to the north by Boat Howe may have been homesteads of the pastoralists who raised the White Moss rings. Similar conglomerations of little cairns in Northumberland were considered to be the results of removing stones from newly made fields. Other cairnfields have been noticed in Cumbria on high ground against field-systems 'on the now agriculturally impoverished areas of the southern fells'. On the Yorkshire Moors they are often south-facing on dry ground and belonging to 'a late period in the history of the moorland when the original forest soil had been truncated by erosion and surface stones were becoming a problem'. In the vicinity are overgrown clearance cairns, none large, but testimony to the farming that once took place on the now peat-covered moor.

In 1974 an excavation by the writer of a small cairn near Low Lowrigg confirmed its non-sepulchral nature. If broad chronological parallels may be made between Yorkshire and Cumbria then the small Burn Moor circles could belong to a period in the late centuries of the second millennium when people were making desperate endeavours to obtain a living from the ever wetter, ever colder moor. From 1200 BC the worsening weather produced the beginnings of swampland conditions, which forced people away from the inhospitable upland.[26]

Long before then, in a secondary phase of stone circles history, the propensity for constructing concentric rings of numerous stones and with entrances continued on the outskirts of the Lake District at sites such as Gunnerkeld, Shapbeck and Oddendale at the east and at the Druid's Temple to the south. It was a form of architecture that may have influenced the design of many rings in Northern Ireland where at Broughderg and Beaghmore G the circles have obvious entrances and where the majority of others in the Sperrin hills have a multitude of low, cramped boulders.

In Cumbria, however, the more general tendency was towards a preferred number of twelve stones, not closely set like those in the great rings but well spaced. Twelve was chosen irrespective of the diameter. At Grey Croft the metre-wide stones were 5.8 m apart, at White Moss SW and Blakeley Raise, 3.6 m from each other but at White Moss NE only 3.2 m. Even more tellingly, in the timber concentric rings at Oddendale both rings contained twelve posts even though the outer diameter of 18 m much exceeded the 11.9 m of the inner.

A similar repetition of twelve stones was prevalent in south–west Scotland as far to the west as Wigtownshire 'and it may be supposed that there was a tradition of building 12-stone rings along the coastlands of the North Channel'.[27]

Nothing was static. Stone circles changed as society changed. With an increasing demand for implements perforated for the shafts of prestigious maceheads and battle-axes, utilitarian axe hammers, prospectors searched for stone like picrite and quartz dolerite that was susceptible and straightforward for drilling. The Lake District tuffs were not and the Langdale industry went into decline. Its tools were 'almost exclusively axes, with a few perforated specimens'. It is an understatement. Of 1,059 Group VI products identified in Britain from Land's End to the Moray Firth only two were maceheads, three were axe hammers and there was a disc with a central hole. The remainder, 99.99 per cent, were undrilled axes.[28]

Production, slowed, stopped. With the recession great stone circles were no longer needed as staging-posts, entrepôts, cosmopolitan meeting-places for travellers from distant parts. Rings erected in the Early and Middle Bronze Ages were usually for local clans, even single families that continued the tradition of assembling at the sacred precinct of their shrine or *fanum* at particular times of the year.

Perhaps, in even later centuries, the ancient rings whose first purpose had long been forgotten received burials, the living honouring the departed by interring them in the hallowed places of their forefathers.

Chapter Eight

The Stone Circles of Northern Ireland and the Wicklows

Mr. Gethyng of the Middle Temple assures me that in Ireland are severall Monuments of Stones standing circularly as at Stonehenge Kynnet etc.

John Aubrey, 1693, 121

Introduction

Arguably Cumbrian in inspiration the idea of circular rings with entrances became widespread. It was grudgingly adopted northwards into western Scotland, enthusiastically southwards into north Wales, the Midlands and the south-west peninsula of England, and westwards into northern Ireland where the earliest of these derivative rings may have been erected at Ballynoe 5 miles from Dundrum Bay in Co. Down.

Large open circles are rare anywhere in Ireland even along the east coast where influences from Scotland, Wales and England were strongest and where the majority of henges and uncluttered rings are to be found. The indigenous passage-tomb custom of combining tomb and temple in one monument was not easily reconciled with the concept of the simple, open ceremonial circle, so that where such intrusive monuments were built near passage-tomb domains tombs were quite often added to them, sometimes many years later.

Voyagers, Trade and the Irish Sea

Eighty miles of Irish Sea separated England and Scotland from north-eastern Ireland but the crossing was made easier by the Isle of Man (Pl. 28) halfway between the Duddon Sands and Dundrum Bay a few miles from Ballynoe. In fair weather experienced navigators could travel confidently and would have reached the island from Cumbria in a summer's day, paddling long, skin-lined boats capable of five knots an hour across the almost tideless waters. 'Boats rather larger than the *curraghs* of west Ireland would have been the most suitable or pioneering settlers, more similar to the whaling *umiaks* of the Eskimo, around say 32 ft long [9–10 m] with 8 paddlers or rowers and one to steer . . . Boats of this kind would have been adaptable, and superlative in difficult waters.'[1]

Tides in the Irish Sea, averaging 1–3 knots, were seldom a hazard although Spring tides in the North Channel could reach a difficult 3–5 knots for light boats. Conversely, flood tides to the south of the Isle of Man produced slack water over wide

Plate 28. Meayll Hill aberrant stone circle, Isle of Man (Photograph: the Manx Museum).

stretches making progress comfortably undemanding.[2] From the Isle of Man the silhouetted peak of Slieve Donard in the mountains of Mourne guided the seafarers westwards towards Dundrum Bay. Returning, they would have steered towards the even more dominant outline of Scafell.

Men had been crossing these waters from south-west Scotland and north-west England early in the Neolithic as the 'Scottish' architecture of chambered tombs like Cashtal yn Ard and King Orry's Grave on the Isle of Man and Dooey's Cairn, Ballymacaldrack, in Co. Antrim, with its atypical cremation trench, confirm.

Trade and exchange of good stone and flint for tools explained the connections. 'It is clear that Neolithic people did not simply randomly pick up stones and make them into axes, but that in many cases specific rock types were carefully chosen.'[3] Routes were established. Alliances were made. Sanctuaries for the safety of incomers and natives were constructed, judiciously situated for seasonal gatherings. On either side of the Irish Sea two productive sources of stone vied, the porcellanite of the Irish Group IX Tievebulliagh and Rathlin Island factories, and the epidotised tuffs of the Group VI Langdale production centres. Group IX axes have been found in England, eight in Yorkshire where stone was scarce and flint plentiful but only one in Cumbria where stone was abundant but good flint unobtainable. Cumbrian axes are almost as rare in Ireland.

The north-east corner of Ireland, an irregular rectangle from Loch Foyle to Strangford Lough, from Coleraine to Downpatrick, some 2,500 square miles of rich chalk farmland, 150 miles of ragged coastline, was open to the sea and influences from the north, east and south. Forty miles to the north brought voyagers to the Mull of Kintyre and Arran. The same distance eastwards took them to the Isle of Man, and a further 40 miles to the Lake District. Southwards from the Isle of Man a journey of 70 miles carried traders to Anglesey and North Wales.

The results in Ulster were cosmopolitan and predictably uneasy with suspicion between opposing groups of chambered tomb cults and equally between them and the users of stone circles. In that cretaceous landscape were some wedge-tombs, most of them near the sea, portal dolmens, more evenly distributed, and over a score of passage-tombs, the majority like Carnanmore clinging by their megalithic fingertips to the coast. 'There are several passage-grave cairns along the coast of NE Antrim and there was evidently a colonisation by passage-grave builders.'[4] The most numerous of these tomb types were the thirty or more indigenous court-cairns widely spread across the countryside. Not surprisingly in such a medley of chambered tombs stone circles were few and late. Conservatism ensured that.

'It is clear that there was an intensive exchange or trade network in place in the Neolithic between the islands of Britain and Ireland.'[5] Axes were the clue. The statistics are informative. From the Group IX sources of porcellanite, a very hard speckled blend of dolerite and basalt, thousands of roughouts, some extracted by fire, have been recovered from high up Tievebulliagh Mountain overlooking Cushendall near the north coast. Across the sea at Brockley on Rathlin Island more axes were manufactured.

The island with its black and white cliffs of basalt and chalk could be dangerous. Men in their laden boats had to take care crossing the short miles of Ballycastle Bay to the mainland. At spring tides just after the new moon when the water was highest there were grippingly swirling currents above a deep gully in the Sound. Known as the Cauldron of Breicin or Slough Na More it was said that Breicin, grandson of Niall of the Nine Hostages, was caught in the maelstrom and perished. Fifty curraghs went down with him.[6]

As well as more than a thousand Group IX axes discovered in Ireland nearly two hundred are known in Britain as far away as Kent and Northumberland in England, over eighty in Scotland, some in Arran from which about two hundred pieces of pitchstone were taken to Ireland, puzzling because although sharp the material was inferior to the native Irish flint.[7] The axes reached as far north as Aberdeenshire, the Hebrides and the Orkneys but not, significantly, to areas much closer in Scotland: none in Dumfries, one in Kirkcudbright, two in Wigtownshire. Those were Group VI domains with versions of Cumbrian circles in them.[8]

Conversely, a few Group VI Lake District axes are known in the Irish rectangle, usually near the coast in the counties of Armagh, Down and Antrim where in a house and flint-knapping site by Ballygalley Bay hundreds of thousands of flint chippings were recovered with two broken Group IV axes during the excavation of 1989.[9] Assays of 2880 ± 117 bc and 3045 ± 75 bc, calibrated to a bracket of *c.* 3990–3640 BC, testify to Anglo-Irish contacts in the early Neolithic.

Not all 'axes' were tools. Some from Tievebulliagh were unusable. From 20 cm to 38 cm long and weighing up to 100 lbs they 'would have required the likes of Finn McCool to wield'. These were symbols of power, prestigious regalia like the beautiful maceheads of later centuries. Even protectively magical. One was placed under the doorstep of an old farmhouse at Killamount, Co. Wicklow.[10]

North-Eastern Ireland

The stone circles here are a jumble of great and small rings, some early, most of the Bronze Age. Geology and Neolithic settlement were the causes. There were marked contrasts in landscape and type of stone circle between the counties of Antrim and Armagh north of the mile-wide Dundonald Gap between the Castlereagh and Braniel Hills. Through the gap the River Elter flowed into Co. Down and the rings near Strangford Lough. The steep basaltic hills, glens and waterfalls of Antrim and the lowlands of Armagh were geographically and culturally separate from the Mountains of Mourne and the drumlins of Co. Down.

On the assumption that there was resistance to change on the part of megalithic tomb users it is arguable that the few circles were late, set up only when the tombs had been abandoned. Worse, the rings in the counties of Antrim and Armagh are either destroyed, dubious or dismal. There was a highly doubtful concentric, an unlikely 45.7m across, at Ballyrickard More close to the coast near Glynn. Its supposed central pillar was no more than 84cm high. Also in Co. Antrim was the reputedly 'Druidical circle' at Slievenagh. More interesting sites existed in Co. Armagh where another Druid's Ring at Ballybrolly near Armagh surrounded a portal dolmen 'like a chair of whinstone with stones around on three sides'. The destroyed circle of Vicar's Cairn did enclose a cairn. That ring with its ring-marked stone had gone by 1868. Its hilltop cairn survives, reduced and disfigured.[11]

The stone circles in Co. Down are just as mixed but more rewarding. Mullaghmore, well inland near Newry, is a stray. It is a 'Scottish' Four-Poster, its four stones standing on a 3.8m circle around an internal pit with a cremation and a bucket-shaped pot. Its nearest relative is the delightful Glentirrow in Wigtownshire, 40 miles away across the North Channel. Four-Posters elsewhere in Ireland are far to the south in the counties of Wexford, Cork and Kerry.[12]

Twelve miles to the east of Mullaghmore, by the coast, the five boulders of Newcastle one fallen, form a gigantic oval 45.1×42.7m laid out at the foot of a steeply wooded slope within 300m of the sea. The ring may be a fabricated antiquity of the Romantic Revival. Equally, in size, shape and coastal position the ruin could be a variant of the ovals of south-west Scotland or North Wales. Well to its north are the excellent circles of Ballynoe and Castle Mahon the first of Cumbrian descent. Near them Millin Bay is a megalithic curiosity.

Ballynoe, Co. Down

'The actual sequence of events that led to the final appearance of the Ballynoe circle (Pl. 29) has so far defied all attempts at reconstruction and we seem to have a monument spanning several different building phases, beginning in the Neolithic and continuing into the Early Bronze Age.'[13] The first observation is suitably cautious. The chronological deduction is debatable.

Ballynoe is a true circle with a diameter of 29.9m, its interior of 700m^2 capable of accommodating well over a hundred participants. Originally there may have been as many as seventy, almost contiguous, stones in the ring up to 1.8m high, of local Ordovician grits and granites, which litter the local slopes. The tallest, biggest stones are at the north and south with four more forming a portalled entrance at the wsw. There are pairs of 'outliers' just outside the ring. They may be no more than casual

Plate 29. Ballynoe stone circle, Co. Down (Photograph: the author).

erratics, misaligned on the circle, both at the NNE, 30 m apart, and at the SSW, separated by 38 m. Neither is in line with the circle's centre. There are at least nine other scattered boulders in the field.

The circularity, the size, the close-set stones, the cardinal orientation, the entrance are all Cumbrian traits. Ballynoe, in fact, is almost a duplicate of Swinside a hundred miles away across the Irish Sea. It is likely that Ballynoe, whose name, 'the new settlement', is remarkably apposite, is a 'Lake District' stone circle (Table 11).

Not unexpectedly in a 'Cumbrian' ring there is a solar alignment to the west through the circle- and portal stone forming the north side of the entrance. At that latitude and with a raised skyline of 2° the entrance is finely aligned on the place halfway between the midwinter and midsummer settings of the sun.

Cumbrian connections in this part of Ireland are shown elsewhere by the henge of the Giant's Ring, Ballynahatty, near Belfast, 20 miles north of Ballynoe, because that enormous earthwork is duplicated in shape and construction by the cobble-banked henge of Mayburgh near Penrith.

Ballynoe was excavated in 1937–8 by van Giffen who unfortunately left detailed fieldnotes for only the 1937 season before his death in 1973. A good report from what could be gleaned from the rather skimpy notes was published by Groenman-van-Waateringe and Butler in 1976.

Table 11. Comparisons between Ballynoe, Co. Down and Swinside, Cumberland.

	Ballynoe	Swinside
Shape	Circular	Circular
Diameter	29.9m	28.6m
Number of stones	65–70	55–60
Tallest stones	North, South	North, South
Entrance	Portalled at WSW	Portalled at SE
Site	Levelled	Levelled
Astronomical	'Equinoctial'	Midwinter
Alignment	Sunset	Sunrise

It is the interior of Ballynoe that has generated controversy. Within the ring there is a partly kerbed long mound lying east–west. Cists with cremations lay at both ends. Near them were baetyls, smooth rounded balls, meteoric stones often associated with fertility and with death.[14] Just inside the entrance at Ballynoe is a short arc of six stones alongside an apparent raised platform. The excavation left the majority of questions about the nature of the site, single- or multi-phase, the type of the structures, date, unanswered.

There has been no lack of speculation. Macalister thought that the monument was the remains of a concentric circle, an outer ring 30 m in diameter enclosing an elliptical ring, 18 × 13 m. Herity suggested that the long mound had been raised by Beaker intruders. Later with Eogan he considered that there had been a primary passage-tomb later enclosed by a stone circle with outliers. Eogan visualised the long oval mound as a small passage-tomb built over a court-cairn. Harbison speculated that the stone circle may 'well have been the final building stage' Evans had a different approach, proposing that 'influences from several sources were probably reaching this region of entry from overseas'. The present writer believes that there were four distinct stages, an initial stone circle followed by two prehistoric phases of interference and alteration culminating in historical robbery.[15]

As in so many megalithic rings native burial-places were inserted into an outlandish shrine, an intrusion suggesting either an early abandonment of the stone circle or a recrudescence of the persisting antagonism between opposing sects. At Ballynoe it began with the building of two kerbed cairns, possibly small passage-tombs, the larger eastern oval approximately 17 × 15 m, quite feasibly the primary tomb at its entrance would face the customary east. Five baetyls were set against the kerbstones where a sherd of Carrowkeel ware also lay. The smaller, round 'passage-tomb' with a likely western entrance was about 11 m in diameter. It effectively blocked the entrance of the circle.[16]

Locally, such desecration was not unique. The Vicar's Cairn inside its stone circle was kerbed. In Co. Down there are other kerbed round cairns at Ballyskeagh and Rowreagh.[17] It was a commonplace practice throughout Britain and Ireland to impose tombs and barrows onto existing stone circles and henges, there being a well-known instance at Arbor Low in the Peak District, even an entire passage-tomb at Callanish. No fewer than five cairns, each with fourteen kerbs, huddle like timid gatecrashers inside the Brats Hill circle in the Lake District.

If this had been all at Ballynoe there might have been little debate about the sequence of events. There was, however, a second disruption. The two tombs were levelled and their kerbs partly dismantled to accommodate a long, sub-rectangular mound, 24 m in length by 9 m wide and 1.5 m high, like a variant court-cairn. To make room for it seven or eight kerbs were removed from the west side of the much-levelled east cairn.

Its partner was more savagely treated. To allow the mound to extend to the western edge of the stone circle four-fifths of the cairn's kerbs were uprooted leaving only the short arc of six stones as a decorous terminal to the mound.

Van Giffen came upon a tripartite cist there like three segmented chambers, the capstones missing, probably taken away to permit ploughing in historic times. On the Isle of Man the cists set like short passages inside the 'circle' of Meayll Hill also lacked capstones, the convenient and conspicuous slabs ransacked for buildings and for repairing walls in recent centuries.

Ballynoe's cists held cremated bones of young adults. So did a cist or cists at the eastern end. The three western cists must belong to the long mound because their eastern end protruded beyond the kerbs of the earlier cairn. There was a rather similar series of cists in the weird monument of Millin Bay 11 miles north-east of Ballynoe on the far side of Strangford Lough.

The mound at Ballynoe contained features reminiscent of the Audleystown dual court-cairn 10 miles to the north and Ballynoe's 'facsimile' with its two sets of terminal chambers reaffirms the hostility that could persist between the opposing users of round passage-tombs and long court-cairns.

Uncertainty must persist over the sequence of events at Ballynoe but if the ring were based on English models its builders would not have set it up around anything. Such rings were open and uncluttered. It is more feasible that the cairns and the long mound were secondary and intrusive. There are parallels beyond those already cited. A stone circle was destroyed to make way for a passage-tomb at Bryn Celli Ddu on Anglesey. It is fortunate that the fine megalithic ring of Ballynoe was only despoiled, not destroyed.

In its beginning one might visualise a powerful band of settlers, strong enough to withstand attack, ambitiously hoping to establish a trading-station for the dissemination of Lake District axes. If so, they were unsuccessful. One might suppose that an alien stone circle was erected close to the sea by incomers who had time to fetch stones, put them up, use the ring for a generation or two before their site was taken over. But even the interruption of the passage-tombs did not know lasting tranquillity. Only the builders of the aberrant court-cairn created a truly enduring monument. The people of a nearby circle may have been luckier.

Four miles west of Strangford Lough, 'the violent inlet' where tides can race at ten knots through the constricted mouth of the bay, the circle at Castle Mahon is 21.3 × 19.8 m in diameter, its six lowish stones widely spaced, the tallest no more than 1.1 m high at the north-east. The 1953 excavation found that a broken stump at the WNW had a pit by it with some slabs of shale, oak charcoal and nine nondescript Western Neolithic sherds.[18] Against the ring's centre a large, steep-sided pit was reddened by a fierce ashwood fire that had been extinguished by cramming clay over it. People had then set up a large block in the pit, resting it on four thin shale slabs before filling the hole with loam and oak charcoal. Charcoal was strewn thickly on the ground. The only bone to be discovered lay in a neat cist just north of the fire-pit. In it hazel charcoal covered the intensely burned bones of a child. With it was a well-made plano-convex flint knife, also burned.

Parallels for the rites inside Castle Mahon are widespread and Bronze Age. Cullerlie, Aberdeenshire, had a central fire-pit. Monzie, Perthshire, had evidence of a strong fire and a tiny cist holding the burnt bones of an adult and child. Reansacreena, an embanked recumbent stone circle in Co. Cork, had a central pit. Three metres to its north was a second pit with a shale slab over a cremation and this may reveal something of the practices at Castle Mahon because it appeared that a central stone had been removed from the first pit.

Several rings in Co. Cork, Maulatanvally and Templebryan among them, have low central stones. The Reanascreena pit could have held a similar stone before its removal and the filling of the cavity with earth and charcoal. At the centre of the fine ring of Croft Moraig in Perthshire was 'a flat natural boulder, embedded in the old surface, and near it a shallow hollow . . . with a sparse scatter of comminuted charcoal in the filling, suggestive of a hearth'. Across the Irish Sea the henge at Bryn Celli Ddu, Anglesey, had a central pit whose filling had been 'put in around a central feature such as a stone or wooden post which was later withdrawn or which decayed'.

At Castle Mahon the largest stone, aligned north–south, was not removed but was pushed over by the people who had built the circle and lit the fire, perhaps having used it for some dedicatory ceremony. With no silting around it must have been toppled almost immediately. Then the pit was filled with charcoal from a different fire. Imagination allows an impression of flames in May when the ash trees came into leaf, the setting up of the stone then, months later, the burning of oak with its acorns, the tumbling of the stone and the filling of the pit with scraped-up earth and charcoal. The Atlantic distribution of centre stones has already been referred to as a practice that reached back to Neolithic times. At Castle Mahon the circle is more probably of the Early Bronze Age but the Western Neolithic sherds may indicate a date in the third millennium BC in the centuries when northern and south-western Ireland were connected by the trade in copper ores.

Comparisons can be made between Castle Mahon and British rings such as Grey Croft in Cumbria with its central autumnal deposits of charcoal and cremation, even with the Druids' Circle in North Wales with its internal pits and child cremations but the parallels are not close. The people who built Castle Mahon erected their own Irish ring with no strong allegiances to external traditions. So did the natives who constructed the idiosyncratic Millin Bay 'circle'.

Hard by the coast of the Irish Sea Millin Bay is a sepulchral oddity, a phantasmagoric combination of a megalithic circle, a semi-circle, long cist, baetyls and slabs, a pre-Frankenstein creation designed by an absentee committee.

A cairn-covered long cist was surrounded by an irregular oval bank lined with contiguous stones, some of which had carved motifs like those in the Loughcrew passage-tomb cemetery.[19] In the cist were disarticulated bones of some sixteen individuals of whom about twelve were children. Care had been taken to stack skulls and long bones tidily, even to the extent of replacing teeth in their sockets – sometimes wrongly. The monument is a good example of how the connection between death and ritualism preoccupied the prehistoric mind. Nothing but unstratified sherds of Carrowkeel ware dated the site but there are vague affinities with the cairn at Old Parks, Kirkoswald, Cumbria and even more loosely with the Balnabraid cairn on the Kintyre peninsula of Argyll, both with material of the late third millennium BC. If Millin Bay is of the same chronological horizon it would once again emphasise the variety of contacts around the Irish Sea in the Early Bronze Age.[20]

The Wicklow Mountains

Further 'English' stone circles, large, circular and with entrances may have been constructed in the Wicklow mountains of eastern Ireland a hundred miles south of Ballynoe and far beyond the passage-tomb cemetery of the Bend of the Boyne. The same Cumbrian traits can be seen, although more weakly, in the stone circles there. They are few. Sometimes burial-places were put up inside them. It may have happened at the henge of the Giant's Ring near Belfast with its off-centre portal-dolmen and at Dun Ruadh, Co. Tyrone, where cists and cairns were added to an oval ring.

Henges and stone circles intermingled below the steeper, north-western slopes of the granitic Wicklows. The famous copper lodes and the fabled Wicklow gold lay

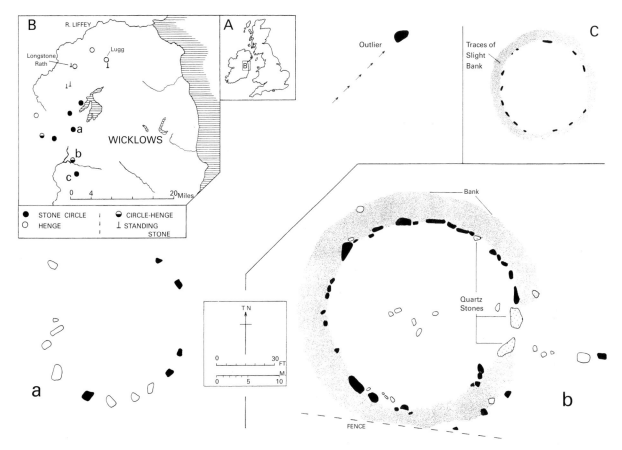

Fig. 14. Three stone circles in Wicklow: a. Athgreany; b. Castleruddery; c. Boleycarrigeen. (a. and c. after plans by J. Patrick).

many miles to the south-east in the drab wastes around Arklow. A 22-ounce gold nugget was discovered in 1795, probably washed down by east-flowing streams. Its source remains untraced. The circle builders, however, were more attracted to the fertile soils of the Curragh than to the presence of mineral deposits.

Within 15 miles of Naas are hengiform monuments; several stone circles; passage-tombs perched like Seefin on hill summits; portal dolmens, with two characteristically flat-topped uprights and a pointed pillar on which the capstone was swivelled into position, one at Haroldstown, Co. Carlow, the other at Browne's Hill covered with an incredible boulder weighing 100 tons; and three of the tallest standing stones in Britain and Ireland: Craddockstown West, 4.4 m high, Longstone Rath, 5.3 m tall and Punchestown, a towering pillar of granite 6 m high, stones so immense that mediaeval clerics from England thought they were the remnants of a colossal stone circle, the Giants' Dance, that Merlin had robbed to build Stonehenge. There are also the stone circles of Athgreany, Boleycarriggeen, Castleruddery (Fig. 14), Broadleas, and a possible 'Cork-Kerry' Five-Stone ring at the now-destroyed Ballyfoyle.

There is an obvious distinction between earth and rock in the Wicklow plain. On the rich soils near the Bog of Allan there are henges with wide banks at Longstone Rath; at Lugg near Dublin with its rings; at Carbury where the sites seem late and atypical; and at the Curragh itself, now a racecourse, where there are at least two henges. Site 4, 33.5 m across with entrances at east and west, had a central oval pit in which it seemed a young woman had voluntarily been buried alive.

In contrast, the few stone circles are in the western foothills, several of them affected by the henge tradition of an encircling bank. The stone circle most closely resembling the ditchless Irish enclosures is Castleruddery in the western Wicklows near Baltinglass. This little-known ring near the Slaney has a stone-lined bank, an easterly entrance, huge portal stones of quartz, and an open space about 29 m across. It has no ditch and its earth bank must have been scraped up from the interior.

Other stone circles in the Wicklows also have banks. Boleycarrigeen, the Griddle Stones, 14 m in diameter, near Baltinglass, stands in a north–south pass between the mountains, its twelve ragged slabs inside a low bank and seemingly graded, the tallest, 1.8 m high, to the east where a gap may indicate a rudimentary entrance. Further north is the shattered Tournant on its platform; the Piper's Stones in Co. Kildare, ruined and overgrown with pines, Broadleas with its contiguous, low boulders, and the circle-henge of Brewel Hill, 'the Piper's Chair'.

Neither Boleycarrigeen nor Athgreany are easily paralleled in this part of Ireland, and although lack of excavation, even of meticulous fieldwork, makes assumptions about these rings hazardous it is probable that they resulted from contacts with north-west Britain where, in Cumbria, stone circles with banks and entrances are also known.

Rings in and around the Sperrins

In contrast to the cosmopolitan north-east corner of Ireland or the large rings of the Wicklows the circles to the west were different. In the long crescent like a waxing moon of the Sperrin mountains where Sawel rises to 680 m passage-tombs almost vanish, court-cairns and portal dolmens flourish, and the multitude of late stone circles, a group in Co. Fermanagh, a crowd in Co. Londonderry and an explosion in Co. Tyrone, are not duplicates of the great Lake District rings like those of Co. Down. They more nearly resemble the smaller, later Cumbrian circles of low but numerous stones and the boulder-circles of Carrowmore to the west.

The Sperrins are a ridge of high, rounded hills dividing north-west Ulster from the north-east. Theirs is an area barricaded by Lough Neagh to the east and Lough Foyle and its river to the west. 'This is a region of cultural survivals where innovations, particularly agricultural changes have been slow to appear.' It is a tract of heathery bog-land with creeping brambles of white-flowered cloud-berries, expanses of sombre moors and deep, wooded valleys.

There are very nearly a hundred and fifty stone circles in the Sperrins. Unlike the earlier distribution of Mesolithic and Neolithic occupation sites and tombs in northern Ireland they were built inland on low hillsides. If their construction is to be attributed to incomers then these probably approached from the north from Lough Foyle and through the Butterlope Glen into the rising, rounded countryside, much of it now peat-covered, of Cos. Londonderry and Tyrone, an infiltration by people seeking land in an undeveloped part of Ireland.

During the Bronze Age many different groups settled on these weak soils: early and late beaker-users from south-west Scotland, from north Wales, makers of northern English food-vessels, of native Irish bowls, even some collared-urn communities from the east and south whose custom of urned cremations was adopted by the food-vessel group. 'Short sea-crossings made Ulster . . . the region where intrusive elements were strongest and the region where fusion with native elements produced distinctly insular cultures.' This is clearly true of the stone circles whose architecture displays a mixture of sources.[21]

Rings in the Sperrins were frequently built on protected southern slopes on a small plateau or terrace. They tended to be spaced about 5 miles apart in little territories above the forests of the lowland plain, and in general they are of low stones, small in diameter averaging only 11.7 m across, some like Ballybriest, Dooish and Toppan so diminutive that a healthy sheep could leap over them. The rings increase in average size from north to south, Co. Londonderry, 10.2 m; Co. Tyrone, 12 m and Co. Fermanagh 13.9 m. The best-known group, the seven sub-circular circles at Beaghmore, have a mean diameter of 13.2 m.

Most of the 'rings' are irregular and unmegalithic. Many remain unknown below the creeping peat and it is likely that a complete map of their distribution would explain much about land-use and territorial patterns in the Irish Bronze Age. But unlike any other region in Britain and Ireland many are composed of numerous stones. Almost half of the inland rings have forty-five or more close-set and overgrown football- to beach-ball-sized boulders whereas in other regions it is unusual to find a circle with more than twenty stones. Such a dissimilarity suggests a possible development from the contiguous kerbstones of the boulder-circles in the Carrowmore cemetery of Co. Sligo 80 miles south-west of Sawel Mountain.

Some fourteen sites have been investigated, as early as 1852 at Clogher to as late as 1987 at Dun Ruadh and the artefacts recovered indicate a Bronze Age floruit for the majority. A Neolithic cache of flints which might have pre-dated the circle at Cuilbane and shouldered Neolithic bowls at Beaghmore C are rarities among the urn and amber beads from Kiltierney, the flints deposited at Gortcorbies NE in a 'ceremony of consecration', the urn and food-vessel from the adjacent ring there, and the nondescript flints, pits and cremations from other sites. The Irish bowls from Dun Ruadh underline the Bronze Age associations of the rings. Late radiocarbon dates from the Beaghmore complex and from the secondary ring-cairn at Dun Ruadh of 1503 ± 48 bc (UB-3048), c. 1875–1750 BC, provide confirmation of the second millennium BC development of many rings in the Sperrins whose architecture displays a widespread mixture of sources.[22]

There are plain rings but they are outnumbered by a hotchpotch of styles. Many are associated with cairns or cists. Twenty or more are close to chambered tombs or round mounds. Others have internal cairns and/or cists and burials in them. Ervey in Co. Londonderry surrounds a portal-dolmen and Clogherney Meenerriggal in Co. Tyrone contains a wedge-tomb. There are at least seven and perhaps as many as a dozen concentric rings like Corraderrybrock, Gortcorbies NE and Castledamph South, two or three central stones, other rings with stones graded in height, a variant form of recumbent stone circle, a possible 'Cork-Kerry' Five-Stone ring at Aghatirourke in Co. Fermanagh. Others with avenues stretch in a 16-mile long line north-westwards towards Strabane, leading to cairns like those on Dartmoor and in Caithness and Sutherland in the far north of Scotland. A number, particularly in the eastern Sperrins have double lines of stones that lead tangentially to their ring: truncated at Knocknahorna, an avenue at Davagh Lower, splayed at Beaghmore. A cluster at Broughderg in Co. Tyrone have pronounced entrances. A relationship distant in time but architecturally related to the portalled entrances and short avenues of Cumbria and Wessex seems probable in the absence of closer counterparts.

If this were not sufficient variety then three-quarters of the sites are closely adjacent to another in pairs, threes, fours, fives, even nines, a multiplicity that became an obsession in Co. Tyrone. There was a kind of communal fanaticism in this profusion of paired and multiple rings such as the three pairs at Beaghmore, a fashion that became almost zealotry in the central counties. There were no pairs or multiples in the east in Cos. Antrim, Down or Armagh. But there were many in Cos. Londonderry and Tyrone, increasing further south until the custom faded out in Co. Fermanagh to the west of Tyrone where among sixteen sites, there was only the set of three rings at Montiaghroe.

Quite differently, Co. Londonderry on the north coast has eight associated sites out of eighteen, 44 per cent: five associated at Aughlish, four at Ballybriest and Corick, three sets of threes and two pairs. The custom was even stronger in Co. Tyrone, with no fewer than twenty-one linked sites, forty-nine or 80 per cent of the sixty-one rings being grouped: fives at Broughderg and Tremoge, fours at Culvacullion, Doorat and Glassmullagh, and, at Copney and Moymore, a bewildering nine shoulder to shoulder as though afraid of the dark. There are also three groups of threes and a gaggle of thirteen pairs.

A feature only recently recognised that distinguishes the sites with double lines is that it is usual for the rows to be 'high-and-low', one side of the line having stones noticeably taller than those of its partner. At Moymore a short row of stones has stones half as tall again as those in the long row against it. The two Aughlish circles have tangential avenues of similar 'up-and-down' sides. So has Altaghoney. It is an architectural foible most apparent in the Beaghmore complex where short rows of tall pillars are juxtaposed against long and meandering lines of knee-high stones. Whether male and female symbolism is implicit in the distinction between one side and the other tempts the mind given the cognate opposing of heights or shape or flat top opposite pointed in so many pairs of standing stones.[23]

There are also a few Three-Stone rows, rare in the west, more frequent in central regions where a circle at Tremoge has three enormous slabs lying alongside it. Towards the east coast in Co. Antrim such settings stand as isolated monuments with no circle, a fact implying an independent origin for the lines, again a probable late development from the concept first of portalled entrances, then avenues, then long single lines until the ultimate economy of two, three upright pillars entirely free from any megalithic enclosure.

Amongst the Sperrins, part heather, part stalky grass, dreary moors of boggy upland, heavy with peat, one comes almost by accident to the rings, unobtrusive even when they lie by roadsides like Corick near a ford a few miles south of Draperstown. On a drab hillside near a ford across the Sruhanleanantawey stream in the Crockandan hills the circle is the survivor of a former group of five. A 1.3 m stone stands near the centre. As though the landscape were not desolate enough for the ring it has been further blemished by a rutted and overgrown track that limps through it.

Nearby are the remnants of a second stone circle. Close to it are six stone rows, some short, some long, three arranged north–south, two pointing to the NNW, the sixth to the NNE. Twenty long paces away is a spatter of standing stones that may be the wreckage of a chambered tomb or an equally ruined large cist. Once the handiwork of a family working the impoverished land here their ritual monuments have been so smothered by peat that many of the stones in the rows were 'located only by prob-ing'.[24] Regrettably, the condition of Corick and its appearance is only too characteris-tic of many of the stone circles in the Sperrins.

This is not true of the best-known rings here, the seven distorted circles at Beaghmore. They are enigmatic, their interrelated circles, cairns and rows having no obvious pattern. Once buried beneath peat the site was half-uncovered in 1945–9 and 1,269 stones revealed.[25] Further work was undertaken in 1965 and a hearth was revealed near the easternmost ring, E. Over sixty flints, including a scraper, and two worn sherds lay there. Charcoal provided an assay of 2185 ± 80 bc (UB-608), *c.* 2900–2600 BC, from this pre-circle period of occupation.

The monuments were built on a terrace of light, sandy soil overlooking a wide, birch-covered valley to the north-west whose river flowed into the Foyle and the sea 30 miles to the north. Near Beaghmore are the concentric Aghascrebagh, two rings at Davagh, the three of Tremoge, the graded Beleevna, the Broughderg circles with their entrances and, just to the west, the multi-phase ring-cairn of Dun Ruadh.

Some of the stone rows at Beaghmore pass over straight stretches of rubble, the col-lapsed walls of Neolithic fields. That agriculture had taken place here was shown by analyses of pollen revealing a decrease in pine forests accompanied by an increase in heathland and weeds of cultivation such as plantain.[26] Around 4000 BC clearances for farmland were made by people using carinated Neolithic vessels, some of which had their interiors brushed smooth, perhaps by the use of rush leaves. The people had apparently performed their rituals in a type of Goodland site, burying deposits of pot-tery and charcoal in shallow pits.

At Goodland, overlooking Murlough Bay, Co. Antrim, miners had dug nearly two hundred pits for flint, ending with 'the deliberate and repeated placements of portions of the extracted nodules in [the] pits with a matrix of habitation débris including deliberately broken pots'. The deposits of earth, stones, charcoal, flints and the sherds of over 260 pots was believed by the excavator to be 'the scraped up traces of aban-doned settlements'. One pit with Sandhills ware was dated to 2625 ± 135 bc (UB-320E), *c.* 3500–3225 BC.[27]

Rituals at Beaghmore changed. Over the years crop-growing gave way to the rais-ing of cattle. Late in the fourth millennium the site was abandoned and the land reverted to forest. Over the centuries the climate became warmer and by 2500 BC heaths had replaced much of the woodland although even then peat was forming on these ill-drained uplands whose then soils supported only bog-mosses like yellow sphagnum, cotton-sedge and rough stalks of heather. By 1000 BC peat was everywhere, glistening with pools left by the grey rains, its dying vegetation rotting and rising against the stones of rows and circles built on the Bronze Age moors.

At Beaghmore (Pl. 30; Fig. 15)), 'the moor of birches', there are isolated cairns, three pairs of circles with intervening cairns and long and short rows, and an isolated circle also with cairn and row. At the east four splayed rows crawl up the slope to a dainty cairn whose cist contained a porcellanite axe. Rings A and B flank the cairn. Well to the west are the biggest 'circles', C and D, with optimistic diameters of 16 m, in reality 17.1 × 15.9 m if deviations are ignored and 16.8 × 16.2 m with the same proviso. Ring D touches a cisted cairn with two stone rows. The buckled Ring C looks as though it had been set out on a dark night of rain. At its north-east its stones curve out to encompass a flat natural stone. At the south-west it has a convex alcove of three cir-cle-stones standing on a bank of pebbles. Below the ground of the circle were pits with

Plate 30. Rings F–G, Beaghmore, Co. Tyrone (Photograph: the author).

Fig. 15. The complex of stone circles at Beaghmore, Co. Tyrone.

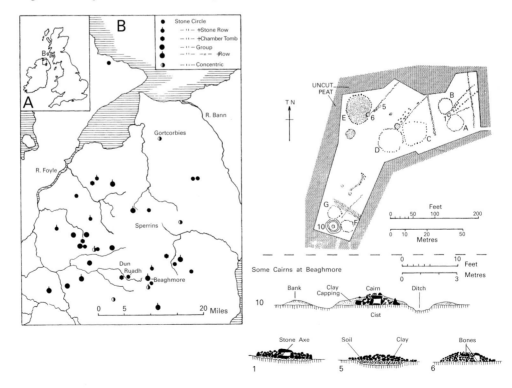

hearths, charcoal, flint and broken sherds, the remains of a Goodland ritual site, part of which had been indifferently incorporated into the later ring.

To the north-west is another little cairn with the usual long and short rows. In it was a miniature corbelled cist with a cremation. On top was vegetation gathered from the nearby bog: fungus, moss and birch twigs. A flagstone had been placed on this and on the stone were the cremated fragments of a skull. Such a separation of skull from body was noticed in an urned cremation in the round barrow of Winterbourne Steepleton 4a in Dorset, and at Sutton 268 in Glamorgan.[28]

Circle E at Beaghmore absorbs this cairn like an amoeba ingesting. Unlike the other rings it is megalithic for some of its stones are chest-high. The interior is embedded like a fakir's bed of nails with 884 upright, sharpish small stones. A few miles to the south-west there are others of these 'dragon's teeth' circles, studded with stones at Copney. Their central cists had been robbed in prehistory.

Near Beaghmore E is a large cairn in which an oak branch lay in a pit, a practice very similar to the branches found in Celtic ritual shafts. Well to the ssw is the final excavated pair of circles although others almost certainly exist hidden in the peat on either side of the lane. Between the two rings a cairn has a bank and an inner ditch. Both the rings respect the cairn's ditch. Circle G has an entrance at its south-east like the little rings by the Broughderg river 2 miles to the north-west.

Charcoal under the cairn between F and G yielded an assay of 1535 ± 55 bc (UB-11). Peat from the ditch gave another date of 775 ± 55 bc (UB-163). The cairn's construction must lie between the two determinations, probably closer to the first and this is indirectly confirmed by a deposit of patinated flints near the end of the circles' single long row. They had been stuck upright in the soil where Charcoal provided a determination of 1605 ± 45 bc (UB-23). Together the determinations suggest that the circles belong in the approximate chronological bracket of 1900–900 BC, and arguably from the evidence from other rings, within a century or two of 1700 BC.[29]

At Beaghmore crude astronomical alignments have been deduced. Archie Thom examined ten of the tangential lines. Only two produced reasonable declinations, both to the midsummer sunrise. The other eight offered nothing. 'In general the fairly short rows do not point to any obvious markers or foresights on the horizon. As for the remaining rows the average declination indicated is too low by about one lunar diameter . . . Were the erectors beginners and learning about the moon's movement or were the rows put there for other purposes?', Thom asked.[30]

Neither may be true. Thom surveyed only to the north-east because the opposite skyline was so close that any change in vegetation would have had a considerable effect upon the calculated declination. Yet if one end of the Beaghmore rows was more significant than the other it was the south-west. Every row had a cairn there and the rows led uphill towards it and the burials that it contained.

Today the Beaghmore rings lie on a monotonous peat moor but previously the countryside was very different. When the stones were set up there was heath but there was also forest, hazel, birch, even oak as the branch from one of the cairns demonstrated. Pollen analysis indicated that quite dense patches of woodland grew close to the circles, changing the horizon from the bland, low distances of today into high and dark skylines.

Given the rising ground to the south-west even low-growing hazel within 90 m of the rings would have raised the skyline to 3°. A stand of birches a quarter of a mile from the circle would have had the same effect. So would mature oaks half a mile away. It is credible that the Beaghmore rows were aimed towards the midwinter sunset at the south-west, linking death with the setting sun, a conjunction known in other rows linked to cairns such as Ballochroy. At a latitude of 54°.7 and the assumed horizon height of 3° those rows that point most directly to their cairns at Circle A, B; C, D; E; and F, G have declinations respectively of –23°.1, –24°.5, –23°.9 and –22°.5, all of them except the last close to the midwinter sunset declination of –23°.9 around 2000 BC.

From this presumed existence of solar sightlines it is probable that a declination of –22°.5 from the F, G row was not because of carelessness but because it acted as a useful forecast of the approaching winter solstice. It was the declination of sunset in early December and January, warning people of the year's ending and of the propitious returning of the sun towards the times of longer daylight and improving weather. Other primitive societies have divided their year into 'months' in this way and the Beaghmore rows may have provided just such a calendrical function.[31]

There has been no explanation of why six of the rings are in pairs. At present the most feasible but unprovable solution would be that the circles were intended for complementary activities, something encouraged by the linking paving between the three circles of the Hurlers on Bodmin Moor, Cornwall. The Beaghmore complex retains many enigmas. Yet its date is quite well established and its paired rings, their interposed cairns, the long and short rows, the entrance to Ring G, all these features are known in the later Cumbrian circles such as Low Longrigg, Moor Divock, Kemp Howe, Gunnerkeld, and it may be that it was from those traditions that the ceremonies enacted in the rings of the Sperrins largely derived.

Mysteries exist at Beaghmore. Despite their unimpressive irregularity the rings possess alcoves or recesses like those at the Stripple Stones in Cornwall. Another bulges at almost the exact west in the fine ring of Beltany Tops in Co. Donegal. In Circle C there is a distinct apse 2.1 m deep at the south-west. There are others in all the rings except for the solitary Circle E. They may have been recesses for the officiating priest or shaman.

A cairn by the Drumskinny ring, Co. Fermanagh (Pl. 31), 30 miles west of Beaghmore also has an alcove. Excavated in 1962 this 14 × 13 m oval of rough stones is in a fenced corral through which hens scuttle, some of its stones deep in the reed grass of the scrubby field. It could not be dated.[32] A single sherd of Western Neolithic ware lay near a stone at the east. Otherwise, only crude flints were found. Even the cairn to the WSW had no deposits, nor did the row of miniscule stones leading to the cairn from the SSE. But the cairn did have a diminutive elliptical setting of upright stones at its centre and a pronounced alcove at an azimuth of 290°.

Like those at Beaghmore this has no obvious purpose. It may, however, provide an oblique method of dating Drumskinny. A very similar cairn was excavated at Wind Hill in Lancashire, 10.4 m across, with an alcove at its east and an oval stone setting at its centre. Two cremations were uncovered, a flint scraper and knife, a pebble hammerstone and a V-perforated lignite button, a typical beaker assemblage of around 1900 BC. In the same manner the complex platform-cairn, Brenig 51, Merioneth, had a semi-circular cairn containing a collared urn inserted at its north-east. A C-14 assay of 1470 ± 70 bc (H-802), c. 1800–1710 BC, is not far in time from Wind Hill. If Drumskinny is of the same period it belongs in the same chronological period as Beaghmore.[33]

Plate 31. Drumskinny circle and row, Co. Fermanagh (Photograph: the author).

A considerable problem of the Sperrin rings is the question of the contemporaneity of circles and adjacent cairns. At Gortcorbies NE, Co. Londonderry, a concentric circle, 13.5 m and 4.6 m in diameters with its tallest stone at the east had a central cist with hazel, willow and oak charcoal in it. The cist had been set in a heavily burnt area inside the inner ring. A cairn with a food-vessel, an N/NR beaker and quartz pebbles overlay the circle at the east and was clearly secondary to it. A time around 2000 BC would not be inappropriate. But the relationship of the circle to a large cairn just to the south-west is uncertain.[34]

A similar conflation of different monuments exists at Clogherny Meenerriggal, Co. Tyrone, where seventeen tallish stones set in rubbly paving were arranged in a 16.2 m circle around a wedge-tomb in a round cairn. One assumes that the tomb is the earlier. A quarter of a mile to the east on a mountain shelf above Butterlope Glen is the western of a pair of circles at Clogherny, 12.2 m in diameter of well-spaced uprights. There was an almost central posthole. Pits around it were empty but hazel charcoal seems to have been scattered about the interior. To the ENE of the circle was a fallen outlier with white pebbles lying by it.[35]

Although there is a common pattern of cremation, of charcoal and of burnt areas in these rings it would be unwise to claim close cultural links between them. The superficial similarity was modified by local practice but it might explain the discovery of stone axes at several sites, a hammerstone at Gortcorbies, the Tievebulliagh axe at Beaghmore. Five other stone axes, four of them Group IX, came from the neighbourhood of the circles. It is possible that these artefacts are the relics of an enduring axe-cult.

In parallel, the unusual ring at Kiltierney, Co. Fermanagh, not far from Lough Erne, quite possibly was related to the Scottish recumbent stone circle tradition and its destruction in 1974 during farm 'improvements' was a grievous loss to Hiberno-

Caledonian archaeology, especially when one remembers the other 'Scottish' ring in northern Ireland, the Four-Poster of Mullaghmore some 50 miles east of Kiltierney.

Kiltierney was one of a group of monuments. At the north was a ransacked passage-tomb. The stone 'circle', 11.1 × 10.2 m, stood 230 m to the south-east. On its slope men levelled a platform for the ring's fifteen ungraded stones, the tallest at the ESE, cupmarked. Of red sandstone it 'must have been brought from a distance', perhaps deliberately imported to incorporate this alien, decorated pillar into the circle.

At the wsw a low slab 1.8 m long but only 0.9 m high was flanked by two higher stones in an arrangement very like that of the Scottish recumbent stone circles. Adding strength to this interpretation outside the recumbent was a crescent of pebbles and rock fragments like that at Strichen in Aberdeenshire.

The ring was ultimately converted into an enclosed cremation with five burials, an inverted cordoned urn, three beaker-like sherds, stone beads and pendants. It was a transformation almost identical to the changes at Berrybrae, Aberdeenshire whose adaptation was dated to 1500 ± 80 bc (HAR-1849) and 1360 ± 90 bc (HAR-1893), a span of about 1825–1575 bc. Similar changes of nearly the same dates occurred at the henge, later a ring-cairn, at Dun Ruadh, Co. Tyrone.

Excavated first in 1935–6, then re-examined in 1987 Dun Ruadh was a multi-phase site. As at Beaghmore it seems that there had been a Goodland 'sanctuary' there. The excavators came upon many stone-filled pits with charcoal, flints and Neolithic Grimston/Lyles Hill and Ballymarlagh sherds of north-eastern Ireland styles. Upon this simple site a henge was raised in the years 2137–1940 bc (1700 ± 65 bc: UB-3045). Erected in a forest clearance the enclosure, about 53 m from crest to crest, had the unusual feature for Ireland of an inner ditch. There was an entrance at the ssw rather than the more common eastern side.

The henge was abandoned. The forest regenerated. Then using the decaying henge as a base a ring-cairn was built on its remains. Charcoal provided a date of 1503 ± 48 bc (UB-3048), c. 1877–1703 bc. In thirteen cists were Bronze Age Irish bowls and a Hiberno-Scottish food-vessel, a type of pot common on both sides of the North Channel. One cist inserted in the bank contained the burials of a thirty-year old woman and a four-year old child.

Either with the wish to destroy the open inner plateau or because they wished to use this sanctified area for different purposes people set up a spacious, off-centre horseshoe setting of fifteen thin slabs. Two more stones formed an approach at the ssw aligned on the henge entrance. The rectangular cists were placed at random around the stones. Everything was finally covered with the ring-cairn with its paved passage and cobbled centre.[36]

There were other changes and contrasts. Even within a group of stone circles there is evidence of contradictory traditions. At Castledamph overlooking the low Glenelly valley in Co. Tyrone there are two contiguous rings whose stones become especially tall where the sites touch, a feature duplicated only at the tangential megalithic horseshoes at Er-Lannic in southern Brittany. A hundred metres south of the Castledamph pair is a ruined concentric circle. Just to the west is a long line of big standing stones like those on Dartmoor. Like them, it marches uphill to a cairn. The line is almost exactly north–south and has a subsidiary parallel row of lower stones, a reminder of this increasingly recognised 'high-and-low' feature.

It may have been the replacement for an initial line of posts. Excavation revealed three deep pits like postholes alongside it much as the converging line of stones of the Alignements du Moulin, Ille-et-Vilaine, Brittany, had postholes in them.

At Castledamph the north end of the stone row flanked the circumference of a concentric circle around the cairn. The 4.6 m-wide space between the outer and inner rings of the circle was set with cobbles as though for mourners or celebrants to move or dance around the cairn whose cist held the burnt bones of an adolescent. A misplaced cupmarked slab may have been the cist cover.[37]

Such flooring has been claimed in several Lancashire and south Cumbrian rings like Bleaberry Haws, only 5.2 × 4 m, which was nefariously dug into in the absence of the proper excavator. The interior was covered with cobbles. There was a cairn nearby. At Mosley Height rough paving covered pits and cists with cremations and Bronze Age tripartite Pennine urns. A small ring at the centre held the burial of a young woman. The concentric circle of the Druid's Temple on Birkrigg Common near Ulverston had similar cobbling. Cremations, one with a dwarf collared urn, were found in the inner ring. By them were lumps of red ochre, perhaps once used for body-painting.

A remarkable number of concentric circles in the north of Britain have such cobbled interiors. From south-west Scotland, another region that affected northern Ireland, on Machrie Moor, Arran, the excavator of Circle V reported that 'under the thin sward we found a complete floor of stones, of various sizes, mostly small, but placed without any such arrangement as would be found in a pavement'. At Temple Wood South, Argyll, the surface was covered with a layer of boulders 15 cm to 23 cm thick. Although at Castledamph the penannular cobbling may have been for ceremonial dancing no interior was more inappropriate for such movements than the blisteringly spiky setting inside Circle E at Beaghmore. They were more probably intended only as coverings for the sealed, burnt pits, cists and cremations that were so widespread in Middle Bronze Age Britain.

Conclusions

The story of stone circles in northern Ireland is one of increasing insular development. At first much exposed to influences from England and Scotland and limited to a coastal fringe in later centuries a widespread native tradition developed.

The Ballynoe stone circle may be an excellent version of the primary Cumbrian rings. Mullaghmore a few miles away may be Scottish in inspiration. So may Kiltierney but that ring also contained local variations. The rings of north-eastern Ireland have been described as a jumble and that is what they are, a mixture of designs and styles that became ever more localised as the centuries of the Late Neolithic passed into the later phases of the Bronze Age.

Beyond the coasts the inland rings of the Sperrins contain elements from England, Scotland, and very probably from north-western Ireland and the Carrowmore cemetery but their idiosyncracies are their own. Multiple circles merging together like frogspawn at Moymore have no counterparts outside the Sperrins. The splendid splayed 'high-and-low' rows of the hillsides are more numerous in this part of Ireland than anywhere else and rather than being an introduction from outside they are arguably homegrown. Ultimately they may have affected the layout of the famous avenue at Callanish in the Outer Hebrides.

Puzzles persist. It is still not clear why so many circles were set in complexes of two or more. Apses or alcoves have not been investigated. Astronomical alignments, almost certainly coarse rather than precise, have rarely been considered. Lack of research hinders clarification of these monuments. Their disrepair impedes progress. 'Many Irish prehistoric remains are, in extent and rude grandeur of construction, unmatched by the same class of monuments in Great Britain,' wrote Wood-Martin rather ambiguously.[38]

Chapter Nine

The Stone Circles of Western and South-Western England

I am apt to believe, that in most Counties of England are, or have been Ruines of these kind of Temples.

John Aubrey, 1693, 127

Introduction

Cumbrian-type entrances were also adopted in England. The process was evolutionary. Entrances with two outer portals were transformed into short avenues by the addition of extra pairs as at Stanton Drew. At other sites yet more pairs were set up resulting in the long and impressive lines of the Kennet Avenue at Avebury. Miniature versions of these grandiose avenues were erected on the south coast in Dorset. On Dartmoor the avenues were succeeded by double and single rows of standing stones. There, on the western edges of the moor, the rings degenerated into what were no more than huddled enclosures for a cairn to which as much as a mile of standing stones led. These changes from simple entrance to single, long row evolved over the four hundred miles that separated north-west from south-western England.

Both the national and the various regional distributions of entrances, avenues and rows give credence to this interpretation of stone circle development. It is the length of time involved that remains unclear. Two rings, one 300 miles north of the Lake District, the other the same distance to the south, may have been very different in date. In the Orkneys, the circle-henge of Stenness with its northern entrance had an assay of 2356 ± 65 bc (SRR-350) from charcoal at the bottom of its ditch, making it likely that the ring was erected before 3000 BC. It is improbable that the Merry Maidens in Cornwall a circle with an eastern entrance, was as early.

Despite the tradition's strength its rings were not evenly spread. There was a paucity of stone circles along the Welsh Marches, none of significance in Cheshire or Staffordshire, some in Shropshire already discussed, none in Herefordshire and Worcestershire where the geological sub-strata of soft Lias and Keuper marls was inimical to the construction of megalithic rings, nor in Gloucestershire whose plethora of chambered tombs inhibited the building of alternative ritual monuments. It was only far away from Cumbria in Somerset that the first impressive stone circles are to be seen.

The Three Rings of Stanton Drew, Somerset

Below Wales, by the side of the Bristol Channel, is the largest stone circle in western Europe after the outer ring at Avebury. Two much smaller rings flank it. Stanton Drew, 'the homestead by the stones', was, in Stukeley's words, 'vulgarly called the Weddings . . . that upon a time a couple were married on a Sunday; and the friends and guests were so prophane as to dance upon the green together, and by a divine judgement were thus converted into stones'.[1] Other legends attached to the rings. John Wood, the Bath architect, making a plan in 1740, was warned by villagers that the stones could not be counted. 'A storm accidentally arose just after, and blew down Part of a Great Tree near the Body of the Work, the People then thoroughly satisfied that I had disturbed the Guardian Spirits of the metamorphosed Stones.'[2]

Perhaps the successor to a wooden structure the site consists of three circles in a 366m long line, the central an enormous 112.2m in diameter, surrounded by a ditch and bank with a north-eastern entrance. Two smaller rings lie to its north-east and ssw. They lie near the River Chew, Broadfield Down rising steeply to the west, the Mendips to the south. With the remains of two avenues, a cove and an outlying stone the group is remarkably similar to Avebury thirty prehistoric miles of forest and marshes to the east. The stones are a brecciated mixture of local sandstones and limestones from a source 3 miles away near Dundry.

On a low river-terrace this once-great site is disappointingly unobtrusive, its very spaciousness and toppled stones reducing its impression. The coarse, fallen blocks do not assist the imagination. Early in the eighteenth century 'a late tenant, for covetousness of the little space of ground they stood upon, buried them for the most part in the ground: he was justly punished, for the grass at this time will not grow over them'.[3]

Following C. W. Dymond's earlier planning of 1872 and 1874 his 'new and accurate instrumental survey' of 1894 established the three as true circles, the diameters of the smaller rings being an uncontroversial 29.6m for the north-east ring and 44.2m for the slumped, grass-covered ssw setting. The original numbers of stones are estimated as eight and twelve respectively. The central ring is more problematical. Often regarded as an ellipse Dymond proved it to be circular. Of about thirty-six stones, some now missing, others lying in disorder a tentative diameter of 112.2m seems acceptable, rather bigger than Avebury's southern circle.[4]

Given stone numbers of 8, 12 and 36 and the measured diameters a counting-base of 4 may have been employed using a unit of measurement of approximately 0.92m, 32 units for the north-east ring; 48 for the ssw and some 124 for the great circle. For laying out such huge rings the builders possibly found it convenient to use a Rod of 3.68m, four times longer than the yardstick, sixteen lengths being required for the arduously laid-out central ring, another multiple of 4.

From the north-east ring a short but disrupted avenue, whose eight stones suggest that three pairs had been added beyond the portals, slopes down towards the River Chew (Pl. 32). From the central circle a second avenue, 50m long but of only three pairs, joins the first where the land falls abruptly and where the river may once have flowed.

Beyond the church and 300m to the wsw of the central circle is a disturbed cove facing south-east. The backstone has fallen outwards but the two sideslabs are erect and from their shapes it can be seen that the three pieces came from a single block.

Plate 32. Fallen avenue stones at Stanton Drew. Notice the light line of an avenue extension on lower ground leading to the River Chew in the background (Photograph: Neil Mortimer).

High on a ridge a third of a mile NNE of the rings lies Hautville's Quoit, a shattered and neglected stump behind a hedge by the roadside. When John Aubrey saw it in 1664, 'a great roundish stone, of the shape of a coyte', it was 3.2 m long, 2 m wide and 30 cm thick. Sixty years later Stukeley recorded a second stone nearer Chew Magna and the pair may have been trackway markers along the ridgeway.[5] Like Long Meg the Quoit may also have acted as a territorial pillar, informing travellers of a settlement in the wooded and well-watered valley below them.[5]

During his planning John Wood noticed that the complex had been landscaped. The centres of the north-east and great circle were in line with the distant cove and the ssw and great circles were aligned on the outlier. An orientation from the north-east ring to the ssw circle was aligned on the most southerly setting of the moon.[6]

No reliable excavations of the circles are known. When a stone fell in the middle of the seventeenth century the meaningless 'crumbes of a man's bones, and a round bell, like a large horse-bell, with a skrew as the stemme of it' were found in its stonehole.[7] It can only be conjectured that the rings at Stanton Drew probably spanned a period from the later centuries of the fourth millennium BC into the formative years of the Early Bronze Age when, apparently, they were abandoned. They stood at the centre of a 14 mile-wide ring of eleven chambered tombs, 46 per cent of the total in a triangular area of 300 square miles. The distribution suggests that the rings were a Late Neolithic focus for clan gatherings that replaced the meetings at funerary shrines of individual families in previous generations.[8]

If so, their function did not last. Stanton Drew was slighted. The bank was demolished, backfilled into the ditch, levelling it. There are fewer than fifty round barrows in the vicinity, a mere 10 per cent of those in that part of Somerset, all at the outer limits of the 7-mile radius. There were some 460 round barrows in the region but emphasis had shifted to the Priddy henges a few miles to the south-west. There, in a rectangle of no more than 50 square miles, were some 300 round barrows, 65 per cent of the total.[9] Just as Avebury had been supplanted by Stonehenge so the stone circles of Stanton Drew gave way to the henges in the Mendip hills.

The Stone Circles of Exmoor

Only forty miles separate Stanton Drew from the Brendon Hills on Exmoor to the south-west but it is like moving from the giants of Brobdingnag to the pygmies of Lilliput. Stranded on the western outskirts of megalithic Britain Exmoor is an enigma. In graceful contrast to the rough jaggedness of Dartmoor the folds of its heather-covered moors and valleys are a delight. Its stone circles are not. The area of the moor is three-quarters that of Dartmoor to the south, 265 square miles against 365, and as Dartmoor has some seventy rings Exmoor should, in theory, have about fifty. It contains just two plus a plough-damaged henge at Parracombe.

Geology and competition were the causes. Erosion of Dartmoor's granite tors created millions of blocks, heavy, thick, long, perfect material for a stone circle. There was no granite on Exmoor whose Devonian slates and Hangman grits broke naturally into slabs so small that a grazing lamb could conceal them. This shortage of big stones limited the construction of chambered tombs to the jumbled boulders of Battle Gore on the north coast near Watchet, a sepulchral surprise that was explained as the Devil having thrown them from Dunster 5 miles to the west. The imprint of his hand can still be seen on a leaning pillar.[10]

Stone circles were as rare and as ruined. Porlock, 2 miles from the north coast slumps near the edge of the moor, the majority of its forty or more closely set stones neglected and fallen in a 24.4 m circle. In its shape and numerous, huddled stones it resembles a pocket-sized 'Cumbrian' ring, an observation that gaps at the north-west and south-east like tumbled entrances do not discourage although they could as well be the result of robbery for the nearby road.

Withypool 6 miles to the south, composed of perhaps a hundred pale, grey grits, is a circle 36.4 m across, a diameter that diminishes what stature its unimposing stones have. There are wide spaces at the north and west and narrower ones at the east and SSE. Gray noted the 'general irregularity of the stones and in this arrangement there is a marked similarity between the three circles' of Withypool and the vast rings of Stannon and Fernacre on Bodmin Moor 60 miles to the south-west, circles that may also be of Cumbrian descent.[11]

Between Withypool and Porlock is the controversial site of Almsworthy, its stones lost in blowing bracken and grass. Gray imagined it as three concentric ovals, the outer measuring 34.1 × 28.7 m. Of the sixteen supposed stones of this ring only six exist, only three of the central ellipse, 26 × 19.8 m, and four of the inner, an inconsistent circle 12.8 m across. Way reinterpreted the site as the remains of stone rows like others on Dartmoor, and Almsworthy probably was indeed two adjacent sets of three short lines similar to Corringdon Ball 50 miles to the south.[12]

The stone circles and the rows exist in what is one of the most intriguing and most unconsidered prehistoric regions in Britain and Ireland. Because its monuments are so unspectacular their unique nature has been almost ignored despite being described by Camden an astonishing four centuries ago 'wherein, there are seene certaine monuments of anticke worke, to wit, Stones pitcht in order, some triangle wise, others in a round circle'. There were also pairs of stones, short rows, minilithic squares and oblongs (Table 12).[13]

There is a profusion of Bronze Age relics on Exmoor, standing stones, three or four hundred round barrows, scores of linear settings; rows, rectangles, triangles, nearly all of them north of the Chains, a long marsh-fringed ridge of hard red sandstone that

Type of Site	Certain	Possible	Total
Pair of Standing Stones	8	3	11
Three-Stone Row	4	3	7
Four-Stone Row	3	1	4
Long Single Row	6	2	8
Long Double Row	16	6	22
Multiple Rows	8	1	9
TOTALS	**45**	**16**	**61**

Table 12. Stone Settings on Exmoor (after: Quinnell & Dunn).

stretches east–west across the moor. Culturally it separated influences from Dartmoor to the south from others to the north. The abundance of these almost unmentioned abbreviated settings may explain the lack of stone circles, the northern inhabitants of Exmoor resisting such innovations, preferring lines to rings. South of the Chains double rows like White Ladder have affinities with rows on Dartmoor. Shorter settings do not.

Beyond the Bristol Channel and the Atlantic seaways, the pairs of stones and the short Three-Stone and Four-Stone rows have counterparts much farther away. There are pairs at Land's End and short rows in south-west Ireland. Challengingly there are more distant versions of both in Finistère and Côtes-du-Nord in Brittany two hundred sea-miles to the south. Whether there is a genuine archaeological connection has not been investigated.[14]

The Stone Circles of Dartmoor

On Dartmoor, a lozenge-shaped granitic mass of some 365 square miles, there was considerable occupation in the third millennium BC. There are the slightest of signs of Mesolithic and early Neolithic activity around the edges of the moor which around 3100 BC had 'some growing bog on high ground . . . and . . . continuous forest which had only temporary clearances in it'. But by the Late Neolithic and Early Bronze Age on the higher moor 'some stone circles may have been set in an almost treeless landscape similar to that of today'.[15]

The seventy or more stone circles of Dartmoor present problems. They are divided between a smaller group of large free-standing circles mostly at the moor's north-eastern corner, the driest and most-sheltered region and the nearest to Wessex. To the west, the south and the inhospitable centre of the moor are dozens of smaller rings, termed 'encircled cairns', surrounding low mounds. They are usually associated with long double or single rows of standing stones. The almost complete absence of C-14 assays and dateable artefacts leaves the chronology of Dartmoor rings in limbo. The large sites of the north-east may belong within the first quarter of the third millennium BC, c. 2800 BC. The insignificant rubble-banked, dwarfed settings of the south-west could be as late as the decades around 1700 BC, over a thousand years of stone circle development and adaptation on the moor.

The big open circles Scorhill, Buttern, Grey Wethers and others were put up near rivers. A few like Sherberton at the east or Brisworthy at the south-west stand in

Plate 33. The fine but little-known stone circle of White Moor Down, Dartmoor (Photograph: the author).

isolation but there are eight spacious rings within 4 miles of each other at the north-east of Dartmoor from the restored White Moor Down at the north down to the reconstituted pair of the Grey Wethers. Averaging 23 m across and of many stones they possess traits akin to those of the Cumbrian sites.

Most of them: White Moor Down; the two Butterns; Scorhill; Fernworthy and the Grey Wethers are quite evenly spaced, standing at intervals of 'a fairly consistent 2 kilometres [1¼ miles] suggesting each was constructed as part of a comprehensive design and hence contemporary in planning and execution'. Closely comparable boundaries demarcating territories occurred in the later layout of reaves (a Devon word, used by archaeologists, for field boundaries) in the same part of Dartmoor. An exception, the enormous but fragmented ring of Mardon Down, some 38 m across, is farther away north-east of Moretonhampstead.

With the circles occupying areas of some 800 acres (325 ha), allowing 2½ acres (1 ha) per person for sustenance and assuming that land lying fallow or unsuitable for cultivation would render three-quarters of the region unproductive annually each circle may have had a population of fifty to a hundred people, up to a thousand men and women there at the beginning of the Early Bronze Age.[16]

At White Moor Down (Pl. 33), confusingly renamed 'Little Hound Tor' by Butler, there may be a gapped entrance at the north-west where no stonehole was found during the re-erection of 1896. It abuts the present trackway. A comparable but equally uncertain southern entrance may have existed at the despoiled splendour of Scorhill where two great blocks lie side by side against a barbarous cart-track. Between Scorhill and Fernworthy the peculiar Shovel Down SE with its four concentric rings, the outer only 9 × 8.6 m in diameter, is approached by an avenue of stones that culminate in the collapsed flamboyance of a 3.5 m long pillar and 2 m long triangle of granite weighing over four tons, powerful 'male' and 'female' slabs that once framed the entrance to this unusual ring.

Such physical evidence strengthens the possibility of sexual symbolism which seems implicit in the differing heights, shapes and positioning of stones, and makes it likely that both men and women participated in the rites. There is a consistency in the opposing of flat-topped and pointed pillars at the entrance to a ring, in the 'high-and-low' sides of avenues to make the supposition worth consideration. If these interpretations are correct it becomes a likelihood that avenues led to circles rather than from them, lines of approach, men on the right, women on the left. What happened once inside a ring must still be left to one's imagination.[17]

There is illusory art at Scorhill. Carved 'breasts' like those in some Breton *allées-couvertes* exist on the inner face of the tallest stone. They deceive. About 5 cm across and protruding 2 cm or so from the surface they are geological bosses, amygdales, almond-shaped cavities bulbous with crystals. Similar excrescences can be seen on stones lying on the moor, even on the perforated Tolmen, 'toll-maen' or 'holed stone', in the River North Teign nearby. Yet even though natural their magical appearance may have led to the inclusion of the 'decorated' pillar at Scorhill.

From that tapering 2.2 m high stone the 1.6 m tall outlier at White Moor Down can be seen 2 miles away, approximately in line with the most northerly moonset, an astronomical alignment which, if a prehistoric reality, implies considerable interconnection between the communities of the two rings.

Three miles south of Scorhill the Grey Wethers (Pl. 34), or 'sheep', is a pair of circles 6 m apart which, because of a nineteenth-century restoration give a good impression of their original appearance. Arranged north–south, 31.6 m and 35.5 m in diameter, they stand near the crest of a slope with Sittaford Tor to the west, its clitter of collapsed granite blocks being the source of the circle-stones. South of the crest the land falls to the deep valley of the East Dart a mile away, and the North Teign is only three-quarters of a mile to the north. The situation suggests that the site of the rings was chosen to be in a pass between the heads of the rivers.

Nor were other rings casually placed. Although their builders faced the customary constraints, needing local free-lying stone and having to be close to their settlement they still chose the situation of the rings with care. Large 'territorial' circles such as Scorhill and Sherberton were 'invariably sited so that they can be seen on the skyline when approached from river-valleys, but are overlooked by higher areas of ground from one or more directions . . . in locations resembling that of Castlerigg', another revelation of their Cumbrian ancestry. Often located on watersheds between major

Plate 34. The paired Grey Wethers, Dartmoor (Photograph: the author).

rivers the waterways permitted easy access, even over long distances, to those great assembly-places.[18]

There is evidence of rituals. At the paired Grey Wethers the presence of ashes shows that fire played a part in the ceremonies. At Brisworthy there was charcoal. At Fernworthy, a mile north-east on another hill, the interior was strewn with it. Unusually, the stones of this ring are graded in height with the tallest, 1.2 m high, significantly at the south. The gradual rising in height towards one arc of a circle has become recognised amongst southern rings. The same phenomenon can be seen at Brisworthy on the far side of the moor. Grading also exists at Gors Fawr in Pembrokeshire.

The only groups of stone circles to be consistently graded are the Clava Cairns, the recumbent stone circles of north-eastern Scotland and their smaller counterparts in south-western Ireland. Fernworthy, Brisworthy and Gors Fawr may be dispersed outliers of a Cornish tradition. Grading also can be seen in several stone circles both on Bodmin Moor and at Land's End in Cornwall.

At Fernworthy at least five kerb-circles, some with low stone rows, existed around the circle, presumably set up when the ring was already old. A spoiled double row approaches from the south leading to a cairn 9 m from the circle. Another double row starts 90 m to the north, going towards a round barrow. One of the kerb-circles excavated in 1897 covered a rock-cut pit in which there was a fine, long-necked S2/W beaker, pieces of a probable two-rivetted bronze dagger, a V-perforated lignite button and a flint knife. This nearness to a stone circle of a Beaker burial demonstrates the fascination that megaliths had for the users of such pottery even at a time when beakers had been known in Britain for four centuries or more. The Fernworthy beaker is unlikely to have been made before 2000 BC.[19]

The large Dartmoor circles contain in their pairing, in their territories, and in their crude north–south lines at the Grey Wethers and Fernworthy the major traits of megalithic rings in south-west England. The charcoal in some may be the remains of sweepings from bonfires or pyres. One unexpected fact, already noted, is that irrespective of their size they contain approximately the same number of stones, between thirty and thirty-six. Similar arithmetical consistency although with different numbers occurs also in Cornwall on Bodmin Moor and at Land's End, implying elementary numeracy.

Over the centuries stone circles changed. During the Early Bronze Age the landscape in occupied areas like Dartmoor changed from a patchwork of woodland clearings into wide, deforested tracts on which people settled. Over five thousand hut-circles are known on Dartmoor. In general, the bigger such as Kestor near Scorhill are spread amongst stone-lined fields in the drier north-east of the moor. The majority of the smaller, frequently inside spacious walled cattle enclosures or pounds, are in the south-west.[20]

People can be glimpsed. Six miles east of Sherberton, at the very edge of the moor, Foales Arrishes was a village of large huts and small rectangular fields spreading over 25 acres (10 ha). The arable settlement was partly excavated in 1896 when flints and sherds of decorated pottery were recovered. One of them inspired Baring-Gould to an emotive reminder that it was humans that were being recovered: 'The decoration is here and there made with a woman's fingernail. Consider that! Some poor barbarian squaw five thousand years ago fashioned the damp clay with her hands and devised a rude pattern, which she incised with her nails. She is long gone to dust, and her dust dispersed, but the imprint of her nails remains.'[21]

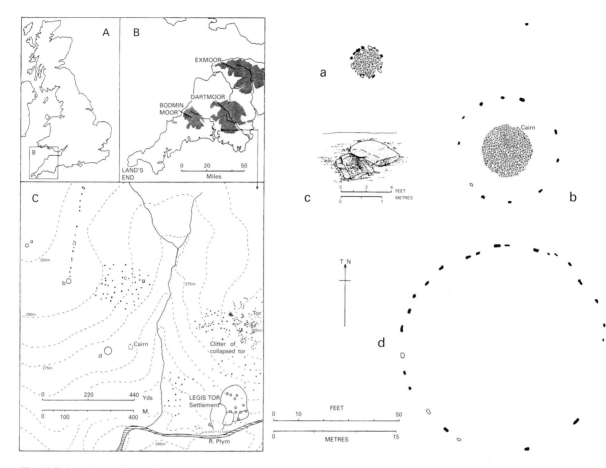

Fig. 16. Brisworthy and its environs, Dartmoor, Devon. a. Ringmoor kerb-circle; b. Ringmoor cairn-circle and stone row; c. Ringmoor cist; d. Brisworthy stone circle. (a., b., d. after Davidson & Seabrook, 1973; c. after Worth, 1953).

It is an archaeological sadness that despite so many hut-circles, some like those at Merrivale, Down, Tor, Drizzlecombe and elsewhere within a brief walk of a stone circle, it remains impossible to be sure that the men and women who lived in the dwellings were the people who used the rings. There is no dating evidence. Settlements, however, even in overgrown collapse and decay, do provide clues about the evolution between early circle and occupation site. The great ring of Brisworthy (Fig. 16) stands on an east-facing slope just north of the River Plym. The circle can be seen from the Legis Tor pastoral pound 550 m to the east although it is not conspicuous against the hillside.

The pound which eventually covered just over four acres (1.7 ha), had high drystone walling to keep out wild animals and to prevent cattle from straying. Of the four interconnected compounds the southern is the earliest, a mere a quarter of an acre (0.1 ha), a single hut attached to its wall. At Legis Tor there are almost fifty hut-circles altogether, some paved, one with two steps at the entrance, all with stone walls that once supported a wigwam-like roof of branches and turves. Several dwellings contained pottery of the early Trevisker style, 'a second millennium pottery tradition from south-western England seen as a local version of the southern Deverel-Rimbury tradition'.[22] There have also been claims for Neolithic sherds inside the pound.

Legis Tor is now a tumble of stones jumbled in confusion but once cattle grazed by the river, children shouted in excitement, smoke rose, people talked by their homes. Only the ruins, the broken pots, the tools they mislaid, flints, pot-boilers, a broken spindle-whorl, remain as clues to their daily life.

Legis Tor pound and Brisworthy stone circle may never have been used by the same people. Or maybe the people of the earliest settlement built the circle. Physically this would have been possible as the heaviest circle-stone weighed only one and a half tons but the fact that there was only one hut in the pound accommodating no more than seven or eight people makes it unlikely that they would have needed such a spacious ring. It is as feasible that Brisworthy was a focal centre, one congregation of its widespread community being the Legis Tor settlers.

Often such pounds have the hybrid circle-rows near them and it is quite possible that these were contemporaries. Legis Tor has Ringmoor half a mile north-west. The row, double in parts, is 530 m long and climbs easily to the NNE towards a circle with its tall southern stone. The ring with its internal cairn was restored in 1911 when five extra stones were dragged off the moor to complete it. With the changing customs and contracting societies of the mid-second millennium BC the great circle of Brisworthy may have been abandoned in favour of a less impressive but more desirable all-purpose monument combining procession, ritual centre and burial.

By 2500 BC the expansion of farming land for crops or cattle led to an idiosyncratic but vigorous culture blended from many sources. The pastoral population on the south-west and west produced a form of hybrid monument that cannot be perfectly matched anywhere in Britain or Ireland, the well-known combination of encircled cairn and stone row.

Almost one hundred of these long Dartmoor lines: avenues, single, double and multiple rows are recorded as well as six or seven on Exmoor including the 50 m line at Exe Head south of the Chains, 'a collection of stones more nearly recalling the *Dartmoor* stone rows than any other group which we have seen on *Exmoor*.'[23]

Some of the lines on Dartmoor are in good condition. Most are robbed for walls and roads and now discernible amongst the tussocks of sour grass only by enthusiastic searchers for these are not megalithic monuments and their once knee-high, weathered stones have been half-engulfed in peat. Nor are they consistent. Some are single rows, as many are double and more than a dozen are multiple, often composed of groups of three lines, and to compound disarray some consist of single, double and treble rows intergrouped in a confusion whose components are difficult to disentangle.

Lengths vary. Apart from the 2 miles of Stall Moor, probably the conjunction of three separate rows that merge on the reedy, eroded river banks near Erme pound, the longest line is the single row on Butterdon Hill, 1,973 m of little stones that lead from a great fallen menhir to an encircled cairn. The shortest complete setting is the 14 m-long double row at Penn Beacon SW. In passing, it should be added that like the sequential addition of extra sections to avenues like Avebury it is possible that several of the Dartmoor rows such as Stall Moor were multi-phase thus explaining their irregular layout. In his broad-ranging study of Dartmoor's megaliths Turner observed of these wandering lines that their 'longitudinal extensions may be indicated by changes in alignment'.

Plate 35. The triple row and cairn-circle at Cosdon, Dartmoor (Photograph: the author).

Perhaps a fifth of the rows begin at a tall terminal pillar. Certainly 80 per cent of them, and all the single rows, are set along easy gradients and culminate in a small round cairn at the end of the row near the crest of the slope. As one walks along a ridge between streams and sees the distant cairn, its focal position emphasised by the stones increasing in height as they near it, one can imagine that these were processional ways affording a dignified approach to the sacred area, the single rows perhaps economical versions of the more monumental double lines which themselves were diminished variants of the great Wessex avenues (Pl. 35).[24]

They were not for astronomical observations. They are too low, too far-stretched across the waves of moorland, too sinuous for one to sight along them. Despite North's implausible contention that they contained alignments as early as 2700 BC for Rigel, α *Centauri*, setting at Corringdon Ball to as late as 1500 BC for Capella, α *Aurigae*, or Pollux, β *Geminorum*, at Drizzlecombe, the observable fact is that the stones are too low at either site for any star observations, especially at night, the only time that stars can be seen. The chronology moreover is, in Piggott's famous phrase, 'archaeologically unacceptable'. The first is too early for Corringdon Ball. The second post-dates the laying-out of the extensive Dartmoor territorial reaves. North was confident, 'The rows were simple and the custom of building them lasted more than a

Plate 36. The Down Tor cairn-circle and stone row, Dartmoor (Photograph: the author).

thousand years'. Perhaps. The writer's own researches led to the conclusion that the fashion of laying out rows on Dartmoor endured for no more than some five centuries from about 2100 to 1600 BC. There is no direct evidence. Only Cholwichtown has been properly excavated and its little pit contained nothing but acidic soil which gave no hint of its age.[25]

Four in five of the rows have cairns at their head but only half of these have stone circles of unimposing stones around them although those at Down Tor (Pl. 36)or Ringmoor or Stall Moor stand statuesquely on their wild, empty hillsides. The last, known as the Dancers, and even more hopefully as Kiss-in-the-Ring, has a 1.7 m high pillar alongside the ring. It is visible from the tall Staldon row one and a quarter miles away across a valley and from it Staldon can be seen distinctly on the skyline.

The majority of the little cairns on Dartmoor, however, have neither row nor circle attached to them and it is arguable that these cairn/circle/row accretions are the results of a mixture of traditions. As well as cairns unassociated with other features there are circles without cairns and cairn-circles without rows. There are also rows at Staldon and Black Tor and Merrivale without terminal cairn or circle and which may have served to demarcate territories or non-secular areas. The paired Merrivale double rows, now divided by a tin-miner's soggy leat have a stone circle on one side and a group of hut-circles on the other. The rows used to be known as the Plague Market for it was here in 1625 that country-dwellers left food for the stricken inhabitants of Tavistock of whom 575 were to die.[26]

The fact that some rows exist by themselves and that others are set askew to the centre of their circle encourages the belief that many were additions to existing circles. Some were undoubtedly planned as units, the earlier perhaps in the south-west for although circle-rows exist both in the south-west and the north-east there are subtle differences.

Concentrated in the 15 square miles of a right-angled triangle at the south-west corner of the moor are more than a dozen embanked stone circles whose morose stones and wretched bank enclose a yet-more inconspicuous cairn or cist. They seem one more example of the merging of styles on Dartmoor. Their distribution overlaps that of the misleadingly named 'stone rings' and 'ring-settings', which owe more to the ring-cairn and henge architecture with their surrounding bank and almost complete lack of standing stones. They are late. Excavation of a cairn-cemetery with two of these settings at Shaugh Moor in 1977 provided seven assays: 1480 ± 80 bc (HAR-2213); 1290 ± 80 bc (HAR-22140); 1570 ± 70 bc (HAR-2216); 1480 ± 80 bc (HAR-2219); 1480 ± 90 bc (HAR-2220); 1400 ± 70 bc (HAR-2221) and 1450 ± 90 bc (HAR-2285), averaging 1450 ± 80 bc, calibrated to a bracket of *c.* 1850–1650 BC, very late in the megalithic history of the moor.[27]

The Stone Circles of Bodmin Moor

Less than 20 miles west of Dartmoor but divided from it by the River Tamar and 10 miles of prehistoric forest and swamp is the granite moor of Bodmin, once a tree-covered upland out of which rose the northern crags of Brown Willy and Rough Tor. There is high rainfall here and exposure to the chilling Atlantic winds but today the purplish grassy turf makes for good walking and several of the Bodmin stone circles, still well preserved, merit inspection by anyone prepared to stroll a mile or two into the moor. There are sixteen rings. Duloe in the south, 11.9 × 11.3 m, is the smallest (Pl. 37). Fernacre in the north is the largest with diameters of 46 × 43.3 m.

Except for Duloe, some small rings like Altarnun and the important site of the Hurlers they tend to congregate around the north-west and, like the big Dartmoor rings, are close enough together to be local centres rather than focuses for widely spread communities. Also like Dartmoor there appears to be some standardisation in the number of stones (Table 13). It has been speculated that the two most northerly sites, Fernacre and Stannon were the earliest because they had far more stones, more closely set, which with their flattened arcs may be signs of an indirect Cumbrian connection. There is no proof. Their irregularity like that of the Stripple Stones and King

Plate 37. The quartz pillars of Duloe stone circle, Cornwall (Photograph: the author).

Area	Quantum	Site	Diameter m	Approximate No. of Stones	Perimeter	Spacing
Dartmoor	30–36	Buttern ESE	24.5	30	77	2.6
		Fernworthy N	18.3	30	57.5	1.9
		Grey Wethers N	31.6	29	99.3	3.4
		Grey Wethers S	35.5	33	111.5	3.4
		Scorhill	26.2	36	82.3	2.3
		Sherberton	30.1	36	94.6	2.6
Bodmin Moor	26–28	Craddock Moor	39.3	27	123.5	4.6
		Goodaver	32.7 × 31.5	28	100.7	3.6
		Hurlers NNE	34.7	28	109.0	3.9
		Hurlers Centre	41.7 × 40.5	28	131.3	4.6
		Hurlers SSW	31.9	26	100.2	3.9
		Leaze SE	24.8	28	97.9	2.8
		Stripple Stones	44.8	28	140.7	5.0
		Trippet Stones	33.1	26	104.0	4.0
Land's End	19–22	Boscawen-Un	24.9 × 21.9	19	73.7	3.9
		Boskednan	21.9	22	68.8	3.1
		Merry Maidens	23.8	19	74.8	3.9
		Tregeseal E	21.8 × 21	20	64.7	3.2

Table 13. Preferred Numbers of Stones in Three Regions of South-Western England.

Arthur's Down sets them apart from more regular circles such as the delightful Trippet Stones.

Around Bodmin Moor there was a mixing of many traditions with two henges near the south coast, a circle-henge with a single south-west entrance on the moor itself, and in a 10-mile long stretch of stone circles a variety of shapes, sizes and architecture including six true circles, two flattened circles, an egg-shaped ring, three circles with centre stones, three possible outliers, a circle around a barrow and a group of three associated circles. In a letter of 10 November 1749 to William Stukeley his Cornish colleague William Borlase wrote, 'I found in a short time that though we had few remains about us of striking beauty or magnificence, yet we had a great variety of monuments here which were of the most remote antiquity'.[28]

Of the circles to the east and south of Bodmin sites like Smallacombe, so similar to many of the smaller Dartmoor rings and likely to be of that tradition, Altarnun and the reconstructed Goodaver need no description though Altarnun for its charming isolation is rewarding. Even the little circle of Duloe with its Bronze Age ribbon-handled urn and its charcoal-strewn interior can be overlooked although its tall quartz pillars make it a neat and attractive site to visit. But the three circles to the north of Liskeard do require consideration (Fig. 17).

'The neighbour Inhabitants terme them *Hurlers*, as being by a devout and godly error perswaded that they had been men sometimes transformed into Stones, for profaning the Lords Day with hurling the ball,' wrote Camden in 1610. A few years earlier Norden had elaborated: 'The Cornish-men, as they are stronge, hardye, and nymble, so are their excercises violent, two especially, *Wrastling* and *Hurling*, sharpe and seuere actiuities . . . The first is violent, the seconde is daungerous', going on to explain the name of the circles as 'certayne stones raysed and sett in the grounde of some 6 foote high and 2 foote square [2 × 0.6 m]; some bigger, some lesser, and are

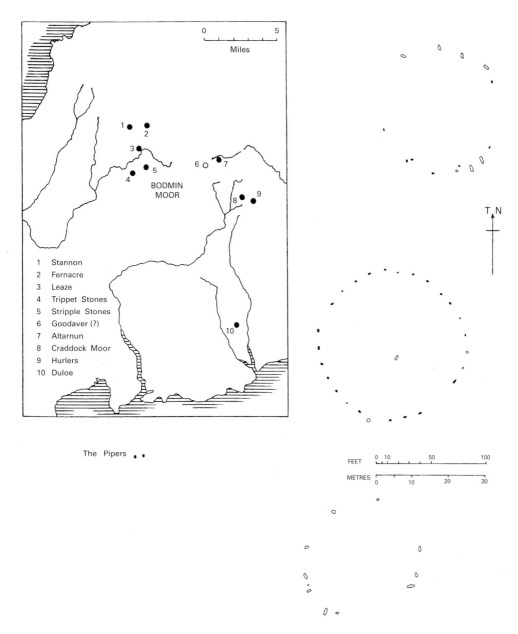

The Pipers

Fig. 17. The Hurlers, Bodmin Moor, Cornwall.

fixed in such stragling manner as those Countrye men doe in performing that pastime *Hurling*.[29]

Few sites are so important. Few stand in such dispiriting surroundings in a tin-mine scarred landscape of derelict buildings and dreary industry. They lie battered, one almost demolished, on a NNW–SSW line, their diameters from north to south being 34.7 m, 41.7 × 40.5 m and 31.9 m. The north circle was paved with granite and a stony pavement, 1.8 m wide, lay between it and the central ring. That circle, whose taller stones rise to the south, has an off-centre pillar. Uncommonly its granite stones, blocks packed in their holes to hold them secure, were smoothed by hammering, their shattered crystals spread over the interior. During the 1936 excavations a pit with crude paving but with no circle-stone was discovered on the southern arc linking the ring to its neighbour.

An indication of slight grading was noticed by Barnatt, the northern ring having its tallest stones at the SSE and the mutilated southern possibly at the ESE. As this is the direction of the downward slope Barnatt wondered whether the grading was an indication of the direction from which people came to the sites.[30]

Low on the inner face of a stone at the north-west of the northern ring may be a carving of three concentric circles about 38 cm across. They are indefinite, perhaps imaginary. But the stone stands at 296°, an azimuth which towards the rising skyline creates a declination of $+16°.7$, that of the Beltane or May Day sunset. Should the motif be real it is a very rare instance in southern Britain of megalithic art and astronomy combining, although axe-carvings have been claimed at Boscawen-Un at Land's End.

Just WSW of the central circle stand two stones, the Pipers pointing downslope towards the River Fowey 2 miles distant. Like so many other open rings the Hurlers were built in a pass, here between the Fowey and the River Lynher, the steep sides of Stowe's Hill and Caradon rising to north and south.

Not unexpectedly, no artefacts were found to date the Hurlers. Nor are there hut-circles nearby. Trethevy Quoit, a splendid portal dolmen is 2 miles south. Although there are more than a score of round barrows within a mile of the Hurlers there are only two within half a mile, one being the famous Rillaton Barrow whose unique, ribbed gold cup of the Early Bronze Age was discovered in 1818, misplaced, and later discovered in the dressing-room of King George V.

Grouped circles like the Hurlers are common in the south and south-west of England from Avebury down to Tregeseal on Land's End yet there has been hardly any debate about the reason for these juxtapositions.[31] In Somerset there is not only Stanton Drew but the destroyed and forgotten pair of rings on Claverdon Down, Bath. There are also the four henges of Priddy in the Mendips. On Dartmoor are the Grey Wethers and the two rings at Buttern. Bodmin Moor has the Hurlers, the tiny circles of King Arthur's Down and two rings at Leskernick. Further south in Cornwall there is Wendron, the Merry Maidens and Boleigh, and the trio at Tregeseal.

It has been noticed how this multiplication of sites became almost a paranoia in northern Ireland but there has been little speculation about the reasons for the groupings. One might begin with an arbitrary definition that rings are conjoined if the distance between them is no more than twice the diameter of the smallest ring. This excludes the three circles at Stanton Drew, the wreckage of Buttern ESE and WNW which are almost half a mile from each other, and even the Merry Maidens and its 'partner', Boleigh, 220 m to the south-west. Also eliminated is the 'pair' at Leskernick, separated by almost a quarter of a mile and by the fact that the northernmost 'may be a fortuitous group of stones'.[32] Seven of these multiple settings, however, are close enough together to be accepted as intentional conjunctions.

The rings in these multiple complexes stand side by side. At Avebury the distance between the south and north rings is 20 m. At Priddy in the Mendips the three southern henges are equidistantly spaced 59.4 m. On Dartmoor the two Grey Wethers are 6 m apart; the three Hurlers on Bodmin Moor 24.4 m and 27.4 m; the nearby pair on King Arthur's Down, 3 m; at Wendron near Land's End, c. 18 m; and Tregeseal c. 23 m. The average spacing for the ten gaps between the rings is 18.1 m. Even the now-destroyed pair of rings at Bathampton on Claverdon Down, Bath, were close together.[33] Explanations for the contiguities have been few.

Thom thought that the angle formed between the centres of rings might have been arranged astronomically so that an observer in one circle might have his eyes directed towards another and then to a position of the sun or moon. The results were unimpressive. Nothing was found at Wendron, his site no. S1/10. There was one improbable target and two unlikely dates of 1860 BC and 1800 BC at the Hurlers, S1/1, for the rising of the bright star Arcturus, α Boötis, an inaccurate alignment on the setting of the minor southern moon at the Grey Wethers, S2/1, and a sightline at Avebury, S5/3, to the setting of Deneb, α Cygni, whose proposed declination of 36°.5 occurred in the years around 2000 BC, eight centuries too late.[34]

If astronomical considerations were not the cause then it might be thought that only guesswork remains, an uncertainty of whether the rings had different functions, one for men, the other for women, or for calendrical assemblies at different times of the year, or for ceremonies associated with birth and death, or for other even more arcane possibilities. Fortunately, a careful inspection of the sites diminishes the problems.

Rings in any of these settings are rarely of the same size or shape. Often the associated circles are of different diameters, 35.5 m and 31.6 m at the Grey Wethers, 18 m and 16.3 m at Wendron. Their shapes vary, circular and oval both at King Arthur's Down and Tregeseal, perhaps even a circle and a horseshoe at Avebury. Where there are three or more circles their centres do not lie in a straight line as though they had been laid out as a unit. At the Hurlers the centre of the ssw ring at the end of the 125 m long line lies 8 m to the east of the alignment. At the three henges at Thornborough in North Yorkshire, 'almost in a straight line', the middle earthwork is 32 m to the east of the line between the NNW and SSE enclosures. At Priddy the centres of the three henges form a 475 m line from which the central henge deviates by 7.3 m to the west. Even more exaggeratedly the unfinished fourth henge is a full 67 m off line.[35]

The accumulated data implies that rather than being contemporaries or substitutions the assemblages consist of additions to permit more elaborate ceremonies. The succession is clear at the two well-separated Llandegai henges near Bangor in North Wales. A fire-pit near the middle of the north-east henge contained charcoal from which an assay of 2790 ± 150 bc (NPL-220) was obtained. A cremation deposit outside the one entrance gave a determination of 2530 ± 145 bc (NPL-2240), the two radiocarbon 'dates' converting into a bracket of about 3700–3050 BC in real years.

The double-entranced henge to the south-west had a cremation outside its farther entrance. From it came an assay of 1790 ± 145 bc (NPL-222), c. 2350–2000 BC. Even at their closest the calibrated dates for the two earthworks are seven centuries apart and could, at an extreme, have differed by almost two thousand years.

Whether at Llandegai, Thornborough or at the Hurlers it appears that the complexes were accretions. The absence of slighting is an implication of changing needs in which the initial enclosure was not abandoned or destroyed but had one or more rings raised by it as customs changed over the centuries.

In the south-west peninsula these associated groups lie between rivers at suitable positions for converging people and traders. It is possible that at the Hurlers as at Stanton Drew the large central circle was the first of the three, its partners being added at a later time to accommodate a larger population or to allow more complicated rituals, to permit the beliefs of separate cults or for ceremonies at varying times of the year. Speculation is synonymous with fancy. Hints of ritual complexity come from the paved area between circles, from the missing stone in the central ring as though participants were to pass from one enclosure to another. Conjectures may miss answers.

Eight miles north-west of the Hurlers are the two circles of the Trippet Stones and the Stripple Stones, the first of three groups within a mile and a half of each other, Leaze and the two rings on King Arthur's Down in the centre, and the three immense near-circles of Louden Hill, Stannon and Fernacre at the north-west end of the line. The six stand in an area of 4 square miles between the heights of Brown Willy, *bron wennyly*, 'swallows' hill, and Hawks Tor. All of them are of local granite.

'Cumbrian' rings may exist at the north-west edge of the moor where there is a quadrangle of land at three of whose corners rise the startling hills of Garrow Tor, the weird and abrupt elegance of Rough Tor and, to their east, midway between them, Brown Willy silhouetted like the snout and lumpy body of a submerging crocodile, skull thickly pimpled with rocks. The area is not large. Its longest side is only two miles from end to end but on those once-fertile 1,250 acres (500 ha) are barrows, cists, outlines of prehistoric fields, droveways, four hundred or more hut-circles. Streams separate the secular from the sacred, running deeply between the settlements and three vast megalithic rings, Stannon at the west, Fernacre to its east and Louden Hill to its south. They are enormous. Over sixty rugged granite blocks surround Stannon's wavering ring, enclosing more than 1,300 m². The equally distorted Fernacre is even bigger, nearly 1,600 m². Louden Hill, more symmetrical than the others but disastrously wrecked, is over 1,500 m². Even assuming that half their interiors were set aside for the ceremonies of shamans/priests/witch-doctors/proto-Druids, and allowing comfortable body-space for onlookers each of the rings could have accommodated over three hundred people, when an overall population in that restricted region was of a thousand men and women.

It is unlikely. On the improbable assumptions that the hundreds of hut-circles were occupied at the same time, that all were for human use rather than many for cattle or the storage of grain, and that each sheltered four people, a series of increasingly unlikely propositions, the demographic statistics imply a total of 1,600 men, women and children. A realistic reduction to a quarter of that number would still leave four hundred people, sufficient for one of the three circles but not for all.

It is arguable that if the rings were contemporary rather than successive like Victorian gorsedds such as those at Llangollen in 1858, Beaumaris in 1859 and Denbigh in 1860[36] – against which the architectural similarities, particularly between Stannon and Fernacre, militate – then the trio may have been intended as centres for rituals at different times of the year. The tors are the key.

'A trinity of hills', A. L. Lewis called them. 'Hills and mountains have been associated with sun worship and with temples in other countries. It is therefore reasonable to suppose that they have similarly been associated in this country.' Reverence for conspicuous landmarks might explain the presence of three capacious rings within a mile or so of each other. They have an architectural relationship with the distant Cumbrian circles in size, asymmetry and numerous stones, as many as sixty-eight at Stannon. To these can be added the existence of solar sightlines that emphasise the empathy between the sun, the landscape and the prehistoric mind.

On Bodmin alignments to tors were discerned by Lewis in 1892, later on the eastern side of the moor by Lockyer who, despite the inconvenience when 'a hail-storm made observations difficult' discovered significant sightlines from the circles of the Trippet and Stripple Stones. The rainy, cloud-darkened stark heights seem to have fascinated, perhaps awed, the people living below them.[37]

The recently discovered havoc of the Louden Hill ring on a ridge between Stannon and Fernacre had a crude alignment to the midwinter sunrise over Garrow Tor. So had Stannon which additionally was due west of Brown Willy over which the sun rose at the equinoxes. To the north-east it appeared in a prominent notch on Rough Tor in May and November, the festivals of Beltane and Lughnasa.

Fernacre's situation was even more arcane. It stood at the exact crux where north–south and east–west intersected, Garrow Tor peaking to the south, Rough Tor to the north. Across that meridional line the equinoctial sun rose over Brown Willy. Opposite it the southern slopes of Louden Hill marked sunsets at the equinoxes. Men must have prospected almost fanatically to find so propitious a site. Its spectacular landscaping suggests that Fernacre was the first of the triumvirate of rings.

T. S. Eliot wrote of 'old stones that cannot be deciphered' and of 'the still point of the turning world'. Fernacre's lifeless stones may have been the still centre of its builders' lives. The ring was perhaps what a *kiva* was to the Anasazi indians of New Mexico. These were buildings with doorways to north and south but circular because they duplicated the circle of the skyline. It was a place where earth and sky met and where the four directions of the world were reproduced, 'a metaphor of the cosmos in stone . . . an image of time and space'.[38]

> At the round earth's imagin'd corners, blow
> Your trumpets, Angells, and arise, arise
> From death, you numberlesse infinities
> Of souls . . .
>
> John Donne, *Holy Sonnets, VII*

It is possible to imagine but not to prove that there were seasonal gatherings, people in their hundreds assembling at Fernacre in the Spring and Autumn, at Stannon in May and November, at Louden Hill at the midwinter solstice, waiting at dawn for the sun to appear above the gloom of the lightened edges of the rocks and for their leaders to conduct irrecoverable rites of fecundity and supplication, possibly both useless and repugnant to the modern mind but which to those long-dead men and women ensured the continuance of their world.

Between Stannon and the Hurlers is Leaze, meaning 'clearings' or 'pastures', overlooking the River De Lank, well-preserved despite the miserable wall that thrusts through it. Nearby are the two dainty rings on King Arthur's Down. Farther south is an almost perfect circle, 33 m in diameter, with stones well above height for Cornwall. The Trippet Stones or Dancing Ring is one of many megalithic sites in Cornwall whose name stems from a puritanical condemnation of sabbatical dancing.

Leaze, the Trippet Stones and the adjacent circle-henge of the Stripple Stones appear to have some standardisation in the number of their stones. This tendency was noticed on Dartmoor and occurs again in the Land's End rings.

In the first edition of this book it was postulated that on Dartmoor, Bodmin Moor and at Land's End the larger stone circles, whatever their circumference, were constructed of a chosen number of stones, 30–36 on Dartmoor, 26–28 on Bodmin Moor and 20–22 at Land's End. As a generalisation this remains true but, as Barnatt has pointed out, 'doubt can be cast on this theory'. Noting the irregularity of some rings, the number of missing stones and the variation in their spacing he quite properly questioned whether it was possible to offer anything so numerically exact. The writer agrees. Nevertheless, for Land's End rings a deliberate nineteen has been fervently advocated.

> Most circles in West Penwith have 19 stones, and although the number at circles like Tregeseal has varied over the years between 10 and 20, the balance of probability is that there would originally have been 19, the same as Boscawen-Un and the Merry Maidens. Nineteen would have been an important number for a people who celebrated the path of the moon through the great lunar cycle.[39]

What does remain true is that neither the radius nor the circumference was important to its builders other than that the enclosure should be spacious enough for its users. Numbers of stones did matter but varied all over Britain and Ireland. In Inverness-shire and Aberdeenshire many circles had twelve stones. So do some rings in Cumbria. In Perthshire there are groups of six- and eight-stone circles as well as the tiny Four-Posters whose counterparts with an additional recumbent block may be the Five-Stone circles of Co. Cork. This regional conformity may have owed less to arithmetical judgement than to a perpetuation of a tradition whose numerical inception does not appear to be induced by an awareness of metonic cycles or the prediction of ellipses. It is a standardisation that does not exist in the putatively early Cumbrian rings, like Swinside, which possess many stones.

It may not be an accident that another ring, as irregular as Fernacre and Stannon, is only 3 miles directly south of the former. The Stripple Stones is a circle-henge, the only one in the south-west peninsula. Two single-entranced henges are known near the south coast: the circular Castlewitch with a south entrance close to the Balston Down greenstone axe-factory; and the oval Castilly with a northern entrance 18 miles west. Neither is more than 12 miles from the Stripple Stones, suggesting that there might have been an expansion of henge-building from the south towards the rock-strewn moor.

Suggestive the name of the Stripple Stones may be but there is nothing unseemly about it. Although the charming circle of the Trippet Stones, girls turned to stone for dancing on the sabbath, is only half a mile away, and the Nine Maidens at Altarnun just 6 miles to the ENE, despite the legend of the petrified Merry Maidens, *dans-maen*, 'the stone dance', at Land's End, it would be a misinterpretation of a place-name to envisage lovely young women in fetching nudity treading moonlight measures inside the circle. Such activities are not unknown, even today. When the late Peter Pool, student of linguistics and amateur archaeologist, was clearing a path to the Boscawen-Un ring he was flabbergasted to see a number of naked women dancing and chanting inside the stones. He coughed discreetly. Perhaps too discreetly. Only when their rites were completed to the party's unclad satisfaction did the celebrants disperse.[40]

Encounters like that, however, are not to be thought of at the Stripple Stones. Rather than a titillating 'unclothed' the word 'Stripple' mundanely means 'dry earth', turves cut from waterless places for securing and protecting drystone walls. On the cold and arid ridge of the Stripple Stones sods rather than Salomes are the clue.[41]

The Stripple Stones ring lies sadly desolate below Hawk's Tor, its bank overgrown, its stones collapsed, a field-wall built contemptuously through it. Yet when it was excavated during a wet July fortnight in 1905 Harold St George Gray managed to make a good plan. As usual, there was a wide ditch within the circular bank which was flattened at the north-east like Stannon and Fernacre. There was a single wsw entrance.

There were three apsidal alcoves, termed demi-lunes by the excavator at the west, NNE and east, the largest at the NNE being about 11.3 m wide by 4.6 m deep. Analogous recesses were recorded at the Durrington Walls earthwork enclosure, Wiltshire, and at a barrow near Amesbury and, of course, in northern Ireland.[42]

Inside the bank of the Stripple Stones was a 44.8 m diameter stone circle of twenty-eight stones, its centre some 1.2 m north-east of the centre of the henge. The stones are rough granite from the nearby tor and up to 3.1 m high but rarely set more than about 0.8 m deep in the ground. Only four now stand. All the investigation found were three flint flakes, burnt flints and some fragments of wood in the northern section of the ditch.

The prostrate 'central' pillar was set up 4.3 m SSE of the middle of the ring. Three postholes just to its east and a fourth to its west may have been trial pits by workers experimenting to find a particular position. The place finally chosen was in line with the entrance, perhaps to act as a pillar to guide visitors to the ring. There is another, more exotic explanation. The stone could have acted as a backsight from which an observer looked towards the sides of the three 'demi-lunes' much as people had looked to the edges of Cumbrian entrances. If so, the apses may coarsely have defined the major northern moonrise, the equinoctial sunrise and the May Day sunset.

As Stukeley replied to Borlase in 1749, 'the druids always celebrated their public sacrifices exactly at the four great quarters of the year, the solstices and equinoxes, and that they might be exact therein, they set up observatorys by great stones'.[43]

Astronomical complications like these demanded a well-judged position for the stone, explaining the trial-and-error procedures evinced by the postholes. An error of only 0°.6 would have changed the angles by nearly a degree, a problem trebled by the desire for three, independent sightlines. If this tentative hypothesis is wrong one is left with the apparently inexplicable apses, the four postholes and the 'misplaced' centre stone. Depressingly, the builders may simply have been incompetent or indifferent to exactness. Societies in antiquity were often quite undedicated to the minutiae of design.

Before leaving Bodmin Moor a most un-British megalithic monument should be noted. It is half a mile WNW of the pair of little rings on King Arthur's Down which 'appear to align exactly with King Arthur's Hall, but this is just out of sight and may be a coincidental arrangement'. King Arthur's Hall is an earth-banked neat rectangle, 47 m north–south by 20 m described by Norden as 'situate on a playne Mountayne . . . a stange or Poole of water'. It is internally lined with closely set stones of alternating low flat-topped slabs and long, lean pillars like the parapet of a disjointed battlement. There is an entrance at the south-west corner, some rough paving at the north-west and at the centre of the south side is a stone that projects at right-angles from the bank, pointing northwards.

With a dished interior up to 60 cm lower than the surrounding moor the enclosure is frequently water-logged and has been likened to an empty swimming-pool.[44] This technique of scooping out material for a bank has already been noted at Mayburgh and was a method widely used in the construction of henges in Ireland. It is almost unknown in Britain. Like the Grange henge in Co. Limerick the stones at King Arthur's Hall rest against the bank rather than revetting it. They are embellishments.

Comparisons have been made with Welsh earthworks in Pembrokeshire: the sub-rectangular Ffynnon-brodyr the nearby ovoid of Dan-y-coed and the warped circle of Fynnon-newydd, but apart from their suspected hollowed centres the analogies are weak. There are no stones, the ENE–WSW axis is wrong and they are grossly different in size. It is the symmetrical oblong and the cardinal orientation that are critical. Prehistoric rectangles and horseshoe-shaped settings are almost alien shapes in Britain and Ireland but widespread in megalithic Brittany. Not 6 miles from King Arthur's Hall there is a massive D-shaped horseshoe of low stones on East Moor.[45] With little more than a hundred miles of the English Channel between Roscoff in northern Brittany and the south coast of Cornwall it is possible that King Arthur's Hall is neither Roman nor mediaeval but a late Neolithic/Early Bronze Age Breton monument.

Its rectangle is paralleled in southern Brittany where the reconstructed parallelogram of stones at Crucuno near Carnac was cardinally aligned, east–west, with sightlines to the equinoxes. Nearer to Cornwall, in Finistère, were the now-lost granite quadrilaterals of Parc ar Varret, perhaps informatively 'the field of the dead', and Lanvéoc on the Crozon peninsula, uprooted in the nineteenth century but planned and sketched before it was destroyed. It also lay east–west. On Ushant, 'from Ushant to Scilly is thirty-five leagues', there is a restored megalithic horseshoe, *fer-au-cheval*, at Pen-ar-Land.

'During the late third and early second millennia bc Cornwall would appear to have been more in touch with Ireland and Brittany than with the rest of England'. It could be that in the centuries when gold and tin were being exchanged across the seas from Ireland and Cornwall incomers from Brittany, traders or merchants, raised their own place of assembly and sanctuary, practised their own rites, in an area long-established by natives as a sacred part of the landscape.

It is a possibility strengthened by the discovery of a large, seemingly Breton stone axe of un-Cornish dolerite in the Tamar estuary 'which might be viewed as a direct Breton import into the south-west'. Across the English Channel the little island of Béniguet off Le Conquet once had an 'English' stone circle, an oval 25 × 15 m quite unlike the cromlechs in Brittany but closely comparable with Cornish rings such as Boscawen-Un and Tregeseal East. Early contacts between Brittany, Ireland and southern Britain are proven with finds of Breton artefacts in Wessex. Given fair weather crews and cargo in long, wicker-lined boats could cross the sea in two days. This could account for the existence of the 'Cornish' Ile Beniguet ring. It could also explain the existence of the 'Armorican' King Arthur's Hall.[46]

The Stone Circles of South-Western Cornwall

The further to the south-west one travels the smaller the circles become. At Land's End, 60 square miles of low granitic hills and downs the larger sites are only 18.3 m to 24.4 m across. In some cases even smaller monuments, doubtful as true stone circles, are close to them. There appear to be four major regions of occupation, each with a large ring: the south-east with the Merry Maidens; central Penwith with Boscawen-Un; the north-west and the three Tregeseal rings; and the North Downs where Boskednan was built. A long way to the east, between Land's End and Bodmin Moor, two further rings were erected on Wendron Down near the Camborne Group XVI greenstone axe factory.

Tantalising evidence has been uncovered of a former timber circle at Caerloggas between Bodmin and Land's End. It had three distinct phases. First there was a concentric 25 m circle of embanked posts, the south-west entrance being marked by bigger uprights. The ring was replaced by a simple embanked circle and in turn this was succeeded by a ring-cairn probably of the Early Bronze Age from the finds of a metal dagger and a piece of amber. The discovery of two pits, one with specks of cremated bone, and a spread of white pebbles and quartz by a central moorstone inside the circle shows the ritual nature of this long-lived and much altered site whose changes warn that stone circles may not themselves be the uncomplicated structures that they seem. One is also reminded that an ephemeral material like wood may have been as widely used as stone by people who never considered the imbalance that this would cause on archaeological distribution maps.[47]

Today the margin of cultivation in the Land's End peninsula is around the 120–140 m contour and it is interesting to observe how the stone circles, well over four thousand years ago, were erected on the 105 m contour or higher where, perhaps, the forests of the coastal plateau were rather less dense. A facile typological sequence might impute a steady advance from the south coast to the higher northern ground. The Merry Maidens, 98 m O.D., is 1 mile from the sea. Boscawen-Un, 128 m O.D., is 3 miles; Tregeseal, 165 m O.D., 6 miles; and Boskednan, 220 m O.D., 8 miles. But even if such a sequential penetration did occur there is nothing to say how long it took. Circumspectly one can suggest that the four rings are culturally related.

They have similar numbers of stone. And, providing a distant link with Lake District rings, there are rudimentary entrances in the form of wider gaps to the west at Boscawen-Un, and to the east at the Merry Maidens, a circle 23.8 m in diameter, sometimes known as the Dawn's Men.

Not far to the north-east is a pair of the tallest stones in Cornwall, the Pipers, 4.6 m and 4 m in height which were never visible from the circle even when an intervening wall was temporarily dismantled to facilitate an astronomical survey.

'Dawn's Men' has nothing to do with sunrise. It is a corruption of *dans maen* or 'stone dance', a story of nineteen girls dancing on a Sunday who were petrified for their sin, the pipers who played for them being similarly punished.

Tom Lethbridge – Glyn Daniel described him as 'one of the last of that invaluable band of dilettante scholars and skilled amateurs of whom we have had so many in Britain' – in what was even at his most enthusiastic an eccentric moment, attempted to date the Merry Maidens by holding a pendulum over one of the stones which 'soon felt as if it were rocking and almost dancing about. This was quite alarming'. By counting the pendulum's gyrations he arrived at a date of 2540 BC for the construction of the ring. There is no independent verification of the result of this unorthodox experiment but even with the most sceptical opinion about the paranormal it must be admitted that the 'date' could be strangely close to the truth![48]

Further inland the 24.9 × 21.9 m flattened circle of Boscawen-Un, 'the elder tree on the downs', besieged by gorse, has been excellently restored. It has a tall 'central' pillar, leaning almost 30° from the vertical and as erratically off-centre as that at the Stripple Stones. Internal stones like those are unusual in the south-west although they do occur, as if by selection, in the bigger sites like the Hurlers Centre, the Stripple Stones and Boscawen-Un, the most spacious of the Land's End rings.

It is around the coasts of the Irish Sea that the most imposing centre stones occur in henges such as Longstone Rath, Co. Kildare, or stone circles like Glenquickan in Kirkcudbrightshire. It is possible that standing as it does in a landscape of standing stones Boscawen-Un's pillar preceded the ring which was put up around an ancient stone in the same manner as the magnificent stone inside Callanish in the Outer

Hebrides, originally set up as a landmark for seafarers and only later having a rather unimposing stone circle set up around it.[49]

When Boscawen-Un was trenched around 1864 no deposits were found at its base. The diggers believed 'that it was carefully placed in its leaning position'. More sensibly Stukeley thought that 'somebody digging by it to find treasure disturbed it'.

Of the remaining great Land's End circles the now-spoiled trio at Tregeseal, 'Catihael's farm', were set exactly east–west of each other. Boskednan, 'the house by the reeds', in the middle of North Down has a small cairn overlying it on the southeast. In its cist were fragments of a handled urn with twisted cord decoration. The two tall pillars at the NNW of Boskednan were possibly intended to frame Carn Galva which dominates the horizon, yet another example of ritual landscaping.[50]

The large Land's End circles are spaced about two to three miles apart. Around them the countryside contains three-quarters of the chambered tombs in western Cornwall whether entrance-tombs like Brane and Treen or portal dolmens capped with vast capstones at Zennor and Lanyon Quoit, relatives of Trethevy Quoit which Norden, c. 1584, described as a 'litle howse raysed of mightie stones, standing on a litle hill within a feilde'.[51]

The contiguity of chambered tombs and stone circles carried no implication that the tomb builders were connected with the rings but it may indicate the extent of land usage in the Late Neolithic and Early Bronze Age of Cornwall. Most of the smaller circles are more widely dispersed. Of over two hundred round barrows, the majority of which belong to the Bronze Age, fewer than half are close to the large circles, suggesting that the rings were earlier. This is not true of the many standing stones, three-quarters of which are within a mile of the circles. In particular, to the south it is noticeable how many of the menhirs stand at the head of little valleys near the edge of the downs like boundary markers.

A study by Frances Peters of nearly a hundred stones, some known only by documents or by field-names, concluded that there were two major groups, all very visible on the higher slopes, a northern around 170 m O.D. and a southern around the 100 m contour. In seventy-three cases 'stones that seemed intervisible on the maps could be seen from one another on the ground'. They had been 'purposely positioned along contours, possibly marking the boundary of one type of land or land use' and the fact that some could be seen from as far as a mile away 'suggests a more than local significance'.[52] Their lines were far from straight.

A radical difficulty in the search for the age and purpose of the circles is to determine which is, in fact, a ceremonial enclosure. The Nine Maidens at Porthmeor, which Thom identified as a ring of his Flattened B design was probably a dilapidated hut-enclosure. And of Botalleck in St Just Thom wrote, 'The layout of some of the multiple sites was apparently very complicated as is shown by Borlase's plan of the Botallek circles reproduced by Lockyer. One of the circles is evidently of the flattened type.' Lockyer was enthusiastic, 'the most remarkable multiple circle on record – alas! It is only on record, for every stone has gone to build an engine house'. The restored engine-house of the mine, closed in 1912, perches at the cliff-edge 60 m above the bursting waves, its abandoned shaft plunging nearby 500 m to the sea-bed.

Industrial archaeology it is. Arcane stone circles they were not. Described as a 'curious cluster' in which 'there was some mystical meaning' by Borlase the Botallack sites were almost certainly walled compounds and hut-circles with no esoteric design – except by accident.[53]

A recent and surprising discovery was that the Men an Tol, sometimes known as the Devil's Eye, the famous holed stone out on the moors near the Boskednan ring, had been part of a stone circle. Until 1992 it was generally believed that the 1.1 m rectangular slab with a 53 × 46 cm bevelled hole through it was the central feature of a simple 6 m long line, flanked by a tall stone to its east with a second to the west, a third prostrate by it. Speculation that it had originally been the 'portholed' entrance to a chambered tomb was mistaken. The nearest examples of such distinctive tombs were nearly 200 miles away at Rodmarton and Avening in Gloucestershire.

An excavation, by W. C. Borlase before 1885, yielded one flint. In the same year Lukis recorded a fifth stone 10 m to the north-west with another lying nearby. The brilliant but tragic artist, John Blight, had noticed them in 1864 and was the first to conjecture that the monument was the skeleton of a stone circle. He was ignored. The hole was too exciting in its own right.

As early as 1700 the slab was 'famous for curing pains in the back by going through the hole, three, five or nine times'. Naked children could supposedly be immunised from scrofula and rickets by being passed through it three times towards the sun and then dragged anti-clockwise, 'widdershins' three times around it. Paradoxically, its curative powers caused ill-effects. Too many people came. Too many wriggled through. Pushed over, turned around, the ground around it trampled, muddied, churned, the precarious slab was threatened by unintended vandalism.

Probing by the Cornwall Archaeological Unit located evidence of a true circle 17 m to 18 m across, once of some twenty to twenty-two stones, numbers characteristic of Land's End rings. Other researchers recalculated the number of stones as nineteen, and claimed that from the middle of the ring the Men an Tol, whether standing radially to the circumference or along it, was in line with the major rising of the southern moon.

The perforation was probably natural. Lying on a nearby tor a saucer-like boulder had been exposed to a million rains whose waters gathered, seeped, eroded the centre away. Marvelling at the phenomenon people had taken it, improved the hole and incorporated the magical block in their circle. Then decades, perhaps centuries later the northern edge of a burial-mound was laid reverently on it much as a cairn had overlapped the eastern side of Boskednan half a mile away. Four thousand years later, on Bonfire Night, 1999, so-called 'Friends of the Stones' burned the slab with napalm to make it better 'or at least more aesthetically pleasing'. Genuine friends despise the arrogance.[54]

The Cornish stone circles appear related to the other great rings to the east and north of England. There are no essential differences. All the features of the other circles are to be found here, circularity, entrances, even grading. Barnatt noticed the gentle difference in the heights of stones, tall opposite low both on Bodmin Moor and at Land's End.[55]

Visions of an invasion of circle-builders into Cornwall are needless for there was already a sizeable population there in the early Neolithic, from the evidence of stone-axe sources at Mounts Bay, St Ives and Marazion where outcrops of suitable stone were being exploited and axes exported as far as Wessex in the fourth millennium BC. The products were not carried far overland but were taken by sea to Wessex. There the traders competed with others from Cumbria and it is easy to perceive how this intermixing of distant people contributed to the spread of the idea of stone circles. Such conceptual models could even have been derived from a knowledge of the gigantic circle-henge at Avebury in whose vicinity so many axes from Cumbria have been found.

In spite of the disappointingly scanty evidence it appears that the rites in these Cornish circles did not differ substantially from those in the even larger circles of the north. The very absence of finds shows that material gifts, unless of food or drink, were not part of the ceremonies. The presence of charcoal testified to the lighting of fires outside the rings but the flames illuminate only the writhing shadows of the people, and the opaque light from the sunset or the sunrise does no more than sharpen their distant silhouettes and touch the rigid stones and the heavier blackness of the countryside and forest around them.

Some small clue to their beliefs comes with a study of the north–south and occasional east–west lines noticed earlier in the Cumbrian rings and customary in the entrances of henges in the south-west. These lines, which may be axial and used in the initial setting-out of the circles, are also apparent in some of the larger rings of the south-west where the tallest stone was placed near the south in sites like the Hurlers and Fernworthy. It is possible that the east–west relationship of the Tregeseal sites was deliberate.

But what is not instantly obvious is that many Cornish circles have their tallest stone to the west between ssw and NNW. The difference in height is not conspicuous but is consistent and would have been known by the builders. These non-equinoctial alignments cannot be fortuitous and may have been connected with the times of sunset in late Autumn and early Spring, periods inconsequential to agriculturalists preoccupied with sowing and reaping but times that:

> do deeply concern the European herdsman; for it is on the approach of Summer that he drives his cattle out into the open to crop the fresh grass, and it is on the approach of Winter that he heads them back to the safety of and shelter of the stall. Accordingly, it seems not improbable that the Celtic bisection of the year into two halves at the beginning of May and the beginning of November dates from a time when the Celts were only a pastoral people.[56]

Hence the celebration of Hallowe'en or the eve of Samain at the end of October, the time of kindling of fires, and when 'the souls of the departed were supposed to revisit their old homes'. The Celts reckoned their periods of time by the number of nights, not days, day always following night, so that the setting of the sun was of more significance that its rising.

Even to imply that Celtic festivals, historically recorded over a thousand years later than the last stone circle, might have origins in Neolithic beliefs is problematical, especially as even the Celtic rites are imperfectly understood. But certain elements are pre-Celtic and even an austere recital of what is known of the pre-Christian festivals helps to repopulate the rings with people rather than metempiric abstractions, and reminds the reader of the intimate interplay in early religion of the animal and supernatural worlds.[57]

Of the four annual Celtic festivals: Imbolc or Oimelg, Beltane, Lughnasa and Samain, Beltane on 1 May was the celebration of the god Belenus, 'one of the more ancient and widespread Celtic gods associated with pastoralism' whose name supposedly means 'the shining one'. At his festivals Druids drove cattle between two fires, perhaps as symbolic offerings to the sun. The other major pastoral celebration of the year was held on the night before 1 November. Samain was the time of malevolent spirits, often in the form of birds of prey when all the forces of the Other World were loosened. Then both countryside and humankind were threatened, the god mated with the raven-goddess, doom-ridden, and sacrifices had to be solemnly performed to ward off the evils that came with the decline of the sun.

Of the beliefs and customs that impelled the building of stone circles few tangible clues survive. One consistent element has been the recognition of alignments to cardinal points. Many rings are too badly damaged for any certainty of their design but high stones stand at the south of the Hurlers, at the west at Stanton Drew and there are equinoctial lines at the Stripple Stones, Tregeseal, Boscawen-Un and the Merry Maidens. Approximate north–south orientations are usual in the south-west peninsula, feasibly obtained by bisecting the distance between the rising and the setting of the summer sun for there was no Pole Star to sight upon at that time. Because of the precession of the equinoxes Polaris was some 30° away from North in 3000 BC. Between that date and about 2300 BC Thuban, α *Draconis*, shone dimly there and between 1500 and 300 BC only the faint star Kochab, β *Ursae Minoris*, was close to the pole. As late as the time of the Greek astronomer, Hipparchus, fl. *c*. 160–124 BC, Polaris was still 12° away and even today is about 54′ from North. It will move closer over the next hundred years.[58]

People earlier than the Celts may have shared comparable though perhaps simpler animistic beliefs translated into rites inside stone circles of the late fourth millennium, people for most of the year isolated from other groups, their lives depending on their crops and their cattle. They could ensure the continuation of their lives in part by their own muscular efforts. To these they added superstitious safeguards, a skull from a tomb, the creation of an arcane circle, the lighting of fires, watching the skies for signs that the sun was returning, repeating regularly the ceremonies that had always been successful.

Fires at rings like Brisworthy and the Grey Wethers offers a frail connection with the later bonfires of fecundity in mediaeval Europe. The nocturnal leaping through the flames, the carrying of burning torches around the fields, the feasting, the token sacrifices may be as illusory as they are attractive. The absence of human remains except as secondary deposits and of other material offerings leave only the tantalising supposition that communication with nature was expected to be direct and had no need of buried gifts. At the most only the sweepings from a fire – a pyre? – were brought into the ring perhaps accompanied by dances as evanescent as the snows of years gone by, with axes brandished ephemerally in the air, with thoughts that were never written down. The robed priest, masked witch-doctor, the shaman, the sacrifice, the tethered beast, the whirling dancer, maenadic women, solemn assemblies, orgiastic sexuality for the fertility of the earth – nothing remains.

Conclusions

Before leaving the circles of south-western England and turning to those of Wales it will be appropriate to summarise what has been claimed for these native monuments. The paucity of artefacts makes dating speculative but the single C-14 assay from the Lochmaben Stane, the links with the stone-axe industry, the associative relationship of chambered tombs at Stanton Drew, the scarcity of round barrows indicates a pre-Bronze Age origin, and at Land's End, all point to a Late Neolithic floruit for many of the great stone circles.

The larger sites are best interpreted as assembly-places for scattered groups, not centres for adjacent settlements. Later, with the increasing fragmentation of Bronze Age societies smaller circles were erected for individual families.

In the south-west peninsula multiple circles are quite common amongst the larger from Avebury and Stanton Drew southwards. These double, even quadruple complexes, often near water and in passes, may have been the result of ring being added to ring or of centres being used for gatherings at various times of the year. The fact that these multiple sites are limited in number and usually near trackways or rivers suggests that they were places where native and stranger could meet.

The southern distribution of megalithic rings in England finishes in Cornwall. There is no stone circle on Lundy Island west of Bideford Bay or on any of the Scilly Isles beyond Land's End.

Chapter Ten

The Stone Circles of Wales

Mr. Camden much studied the Welch language, and kept a Welsh servant to improve him that language, for the better understanding of our Antiquities.

John Aubrey, 1680, 51

Introduction

Of over 1,300 stone circles in Britain and Ireland Scotland contains almost four-tenths, England and Ireland each have about a quarter but Wales has only 6 per cent, hardly eighty rings, few of which are comparable in size with the great circles of the Lake District, their nearest region. Nor do they have an individuality of their own. There is no such thing as a Welsh stone circle, only stone circles in Wales, a form of megalithic anarchy caused by the topography of a country whose mountains, deep valleys and fast-flowing rivers created geographical zones that even today remain almost remote from each other.

Traces of Cumbrian influences are observable, less pronounced, more divergent the farther they are away from the Lake District. A fallen but 'classic' portalled entrance formed part of the Druids' Circle near Conway, ninety miles from Keswick. An avenue, splayed, minute and meandering led towards the tiny ring of Rhos y Beddau not far from Llandrillo but 120 miles from Cumbria. Seventy further miles south another avenue, even more splayed and not even directed to the circle dwindled uphill at Cerrig Duon close to Llandovery. Short rows at the nearby sites of Trecastle Mountain and Nant Tarw may have been emasculated versions of what in the beginning had been the stately, dignified approaches to proud megalithic rings like Avebury and Stanton Drew.

Even these bastardised descendants of Cumbrian traditions were exceptions. The farther away the more idiosyncratic the rings became. Some, like Fowler's Armchair on Banc Du mountain in Radnor (Powys), perhaps the highest circle of all, 475 m O.D., lie desolate under moorland winds far from pass or major river in parts where few strangers ever came. Others like Pennybridge or Penbedw Park or Pen y Wern stood alongside trackways or riverine routes and their architecture was derived from the lands from which people travelled. Most of them were small. The largest at Fridd Newydd South, Merioneth (Gwynedd) is only 50.6 m in diameter. The average is 18.4 m.

In each region, south, central, north, there are different types of ring with different architecture. Even earlier in the Neolithic this had been true with areas susceptible to outside rather than internal influences, affected by customs from Cumbria, Wessex, Ireland, even Brittany. In his meticulous 1963 overview of the Welsh sites Grimes recognised these divisions and categorised the rings into those with outlying stones, those with avenues, those inside henges and embanked stone circles. Other good studies can be found in Roese (1980b) and Briggs (1986).

There were four major areas: Pembrokeshire (south-west Dyfed); Merioneth (Gwynedd); the mountains of Mynydd Epynt in central Wales; and the north coast of Caernarvon (Gwynedd), where several rings were built near the Group VII axe-factory of Graig Lwyd.

Because the majority of the circles were Bronze Age there was less resistance to their erection in occupied regions already settled in the Neolithic. Megalithic tombs existed there, portal dolmens like Carreg Samson, 'the most perfect cromlech', in the south-west; long cairns such as Pipton in the Mynydd Epynt; the multi-phase cairn and cells of Dyffryn Ardudwy, in western Merioneth; or the side-chambered Capel Garmon near Llanrwyst in Snowdonia.

In Wales the major distinction amongst the rings is architectural, between those that are simple and those in which the stones stand in banks. To this can be added the fact that some rings were close to sites of stone axe production. A third factor, however, one that has hardly ever been remarked upon, is shape. There are circles and there are ellipses. Shape and alignment go together. In true circles an orientation could be marked by grading the heights of the stones, or by adding an entrance, or by the use of an outlier. In non-circular rings it could be established along the long or short axis. All these variations exist in Wales.

Grey Hill

Twenty miles NNW of Stanton Drew, across the Severn Estuary and remote from any other ring in Wales, the ruinous and isolated stone circle of Grey Hill is a worry of uncertainties. Unusually set on a hill patchy with bracken, it may have been embanked, perhaps once had a central pillar or an off-centre cist under a cairn, and from it a broken line of standing stones led to three Bronze Age cemeteries of cairns and barrows. Such a vestigial link between circle and burial-place may have been a fading version of the more definite combinations, like those on Dartmoor, in which avenues and rows, megalithic rings and cairns blended ritual and death together.[1]

South-West Wales

The open oak forests of the south Welsh coast had attracted crop-growers and pastoralists in the fourth millennium BC as chambered tombs like Tinkinswood near Cardiff or the Nevern group of portal dolmens like Pentre Ifan near Cardigan show. Beneath the Coygan Camp hillfort, Carmarthen Bay, lay remains of a settlement dated to 3050 ± 95 bc (NPL-132), c. 3900–3700 BC. Neolithic timber houses at Mount Pleasant, Glamorgan, Clegyr Boia, Pembrokeshire, or a stopover trading-post on the sand dunes at Merthyr Mawr Warren near Porthcawl with broken stone axes from at least four 'factories' tell the same story of Neolithic land-use and sea-trade along this quiet and lovely coastline. An axe-flake of rhyolitic tuff from the factory on Ramsay

Island, Pembroke, Group VIII, at the extreme south-western tip of Wales, discovered at Coygan, suggests an early use for this source. The rather later, famous site of Carn Meini, Group XIII, in the Preseli mountains with its spotted dolerite used not only for the battle-axes, maceheads and axe hammers that were briefly bartered in Wales and occasionally in Wessex also provided the notorious Stonehenge bluestones whose transportation will be discussed.

Yet despite this millennium of activity there are few circles or henges here, one little group near the Preselis and perhaps four other rings recorded along the hundred miles of coast. In the far west was Pennybridge, destroyed in 1918, alongside a trackway near the great barrow-cemetery of Dry Burrows. In south-east Wales is Grey Hill. Between there is only Mynydd y Gelli, 'tree mountain', with a possible internal cist, and the cairn-circled Y Naw Carreg, 'the nine stones', demolished in the First World War. Legend claimed that its stones could not be counted, which does not reflect well on the local teaching of arithmetic. Young people would gather to count the stones 'on a Sunday about Midsummer', recorded the Royal Commission *Inventory* for Carmarthenshire.

The one concentration of circles can be seen at the south-west foot of the Preselis just where voyagers between Ireland and England might cross the peninsula to avoid the currents and wild seas around St David's Head where strongly westerly winds drive waves into rocky coves and spray bursts against the cliffs. A safer passage could be made between Fishguard and Carmarthen Bays, passing by the brooding Preselis where rings like Meini-gwyr, 'the leaning stones', stand.

Signposted with a plan and reconstruction drawing this 18 m ring once had about seventeen tall stones of which two remain, set in a low, stone-lined clay bank 36.6 m from crest to crest with a narrow entrance, also stone-lined at the west. There is no ditch. In front of the entrance was a pit holding only grey clay and much fine charcoal, but food-vessel people had later lit a fire on top of the disused bank and thus provided evidence that Meini-gwyr had probably been built during the late part of the third millennium BC.[2]

It stood in a vibrant ritual complex. Within a 500 m radius there was a cairn-circle to the north, a ring-cairn and three mounds to the south-west, a now-uncertain embanked stone circle and probable ring-cairn to the north-west. Two hundred metres to the west beyond the entrance, is the contentious site of Yr Allor, 'the Altar', possibly a Three-Stone row, more probably a cove.

Edward Lhuyd, the Welsh antiquarian, saw it and his notes were transcribed in the 1695 edition of Camden's *Britannia*. Stating that the entrance to Meini-gwyr was lined with stones he added 'and over against this avenue, at the distance of about 200 paces, there stand on end three other large, rude stones' comparing them not with a line of stones but with the three-sided chamber of the Whispering Knights portal dolmen near the Rollright Stones in Oxfordshire. In 1717 Stukeley copied Lhuyd's notes and misreading them sketched the stones as a 'Kiswaen 200 paces off this way' to the north rather than the west, illustrating them as the two sideslabs and backstone of a cove resembling others at Avebury and Stanton Drew. As Lhuyd had quite clearly likened them to the cove-like setting of the Whispering Knights Stukeley was wrong in direction but arguably correct in interpretation. Yr Allor was a cove.

What remains there is a pair of standing stones some two hundred metres west of Meini-gwyr, a metre part, the southern 2 m high and flat-topped, its partner, 1.5 m in height and typically pointed. The third stone, 3.9 m long, lies in a nearby ditch.

Plate 38. Gors Fawr, Pembrokeshire. The Preselis are in the background, far right (Photograph: the author).

Excavations at the site in 1991 and 1992 found little, but 2 m to the south was a small ring of pits of which the east had held a post, the south an urn and the central a cremation. It is yet again an indication of how death, offerings and cardinal points mingled in the prehistoric mind.[3]

Twelve miles west of Meini-gwyr was Letterston III, another embanked circle, this of twenty stones, 12.2 m in diameter. That distance beyond its eastern entrance of big, radial stones was a ritual pit filled with oak and ash charcoal comparable to the pit at Meini-gwyr. Quartz had been spread over the ring's interior. Letterston may have belonged to the same period for eventually, when its stones were loose, perhaps fallen, people heaped a huge turf mound over it after an urned cremation had been placed between its neglected portal stones.

How closely the Beaker groups in south Wales were associated with the later trade in stone axes from the Preselis is uncertain although several funnel-necked S2/W vessels with bar-chevron decoration have been found in this region and at Stonehenge, a type of pot that may not have been made much before the eighteenth century BC. As Clarke wrote, these people show 'a distinct interest in the henge and stone circle monuments, especially those with free-standing uprights' and he hypothesised that it was they who introduced circle-building into central and south Wales as copies of forms that they had seen in the west. It may have been these rather late groups or users of the earlier elegantly shaped W/MR beakers who used the megalithic ring of Gors Fawr less than 2 miles from Carn Meini in the Preselis.[4]

Gors Fawr (Pl. 38), 'the great marsh', is a true circle close to Meini-gwyr but quite different from it. Its stones are graded with the tallest at the south. Otherwise it is a plain ring like two others on the far side of the Severn estuary a hundred miles south-east on Dartmoor. Fernworthy, also circular, has stones graded to the south and Brisworthy to the north. Although three such dispersed rings can hardly be deemed culturally connected it is of interest that a Group XIII macehead from the Preselis was discovered at Sidmouth near Dartmoor.

Two tall stones 14.6 m apart on a NE–SW axis, stand 134 m to the NNE of the stone circle. Respectively 1.7 m and 1.9 m high the northern stone is low, scrawny, tapered, its partner taller, thicker, flat-topped rectangular block, another instance of opposing heights, shapes and tops of paired stones.

Bushell, who did a lot of fieldwork in the Preseli region in the early twentieth century, thought the ring to be like an exaggerated sundial with the stones set at 24° intervals for calendrical purposes – an observation that was inaccurate – and imagined from a scatter of natural boulders a chimerical avenue directed towards the outliers and the rising of Arcturus, *α Boötis*, in 1420 BC. Thom considered the outliers to contain their own axial alignments on midsummer sunrise over the nearby Foel-drych hilltop and, in the opposite direction, to the midwinter sunset. Yet it was Bushell who likened the Preseli region to a prehistoric Westminster which, in the sense of a cult-centre, it may well have been.

Unromantically, Briggs demurred. 'Mynydd Preseli is in fact a range of low, unremarkable and thinly populated hills, the "awesomeness" of which is directly attributable to the establishment of its geological connection with Stonehenge.'

This is true. Yet to stand on those pedestrian hills with their outcrops like fossilised pin-cushions and clenched fists of rock, and to look across the moorland and the distant fields with their standing stones, circles and chambered tombs is to be aware of a land deep in antiquity. One remarks what the eye of the mind beholds.[5]

Hardly 5 miles to the west of Gors Fawr is the damaged Dyffryn Syfynwy ring on an ENE slope overlooking a deep valley. The tall, jagged stones, many fallen long ago, stood in a 22 × 18.9 m oval around a low cairn. This once impressive ring is now ruinously confused, stones lying on the cairn which itself has been despoiled.

There is an indelible myth about the Preselis. It is frequently asserted that there had been an epic transportation of bluestones from those hills to Stonehenge because they were a landmark to seafarers from Ireland, 'a sacred mountain' whose stones possessed virile and unearthly powers. It is unlikely. As will be argued later, despite the protestations of geologists glaciation is a better explanation for the presence of bluestones on Salisbury Plain. Everywhere else in Britain and Ireland local people used local stones. But for mundane, not magical reasons. Slabs were chosen because they were the closest. Rhyolite, plain and spotted dolerite, the popular 'bluestones' from the Preselis, were selected for the standing stones and circles of the neighbourhood. Even the portal dolmen of Pentre Ifan with its tall uprights and one of the largest and heaviest capstones in Wales was a mixture of unspotted dolerite and various rhyolites. The tallest pillar of the Dyffryn Syfynwy ring was a cleaved rhyolite. Its companions also were rhyolites but 'visually different'. Gors Fawr had eight spotted and four unspotted dolerites. Other 'bluestone' rings in the immediate area may have been destroyed. Such indiscriminate motleys suggest that it was not the stones' birth on a magic mountain that attracted working-parties. The stones were not talismanic. They were convenient.[6]

The West Coast

Far north of the Preselis is another region of megalithic rings, the coast around Tremadoc and Barmouth bays to the east of the Lleyn peninsula, another major area of Neolithic settlement. Pollen analysis has shown a portal dolmen at Dyffryn Ardudwy near the sea to have been built in a clearing amongst thick hazel woods that had already been disturbed by earlier farmers. Less than 2 miles to the east on what is now bleak upland peat two embanked stone circles were erected in a stretch of west alder woodland. The land had been first attacked by man in the Neolithic, then more widely cleared for agriculture in the third millennium before, slowly, the soils, mutilated by the clearances and then by the grazing of cattle degenerated into open bogland that persists to the present day.

Many axes from the Group VII Graig Lwyd axe factory near Penmaenmawr have been found in the vicinity of these Ffridd Newydd circles on the Hengwm moorland whose surrounding mountains offered prospectors copper, lead and gold. Major trackways defined by standing stones guided traders across the uplands from west to east, from Ireland through the mountains to the south-flowing rivers that led to Wessex. One track beginning at Llanbedr just south of Harlech has a 3.4m high monolith on the flat land at the tidal limit of the Afon Artro marking a safe landing-place for voyagers. From there the track climbs north-eastwards into the high, empty wastes, tall stones marking the route past Bala Lake and finally to the Severn. Another, lesser track may have threaded south-eastwards from Llanbedr, past the Hengwm circles to Cerrig Arthur, another embanked ring that lay on a prehistoric way from Barmouth Bay.[7]

On the moors to the north-east of the Carneddau Hengwm dolmens the two Fridd Newydd rings were built close together. Hardly noticeable now, both were embanked stone circles, the northern 32.9m in diameter with an outer 1.5m wide ditch. No holes had been dug for its stones which were simply propped up by the bank. They have gone. To the south was a larger ring, 50.6m across, its low stones set strangely in the outer edge of the bank. Both were excavated in the autumn of 1919. The south yielded only small sherds of apparent late beakers from a south-east stonehole but the north ring had a fire-pit near its centre filled with red ash heaped on a flat stone and covered by another. Another oval pit may have been a grave, its bones dissolved by the acidic soil. Nearby were eighteen rusticated beaker sherds similar to those from the adjoining circle.[8]

These paired rings are less than half a mile from Llecheiddior, an egg-shaped ring, 19.8 × 15.2m, of short stones also supported in a stony bank. Not far to the south of Ffridd Newydd is yet another embanked oval, Cerrig Arthur on a site cut into the hillside. Such monuments shade imperceptibly into ring-cairns whose stones are not as pillar-like but which, nevertheless, are set in banks and which in turn are sometimes indistinguishable from stone-lined enclosed cremation cemeteries like Banniside Moor in Lancashire.

A good example of a complex ring-cairn in Gwynedd is the terraced Moel Goedog West, 7.6m, embanked and kerbed with twelve low stones. Excavation located an empty central pit. Other pits had held cremations, an enlarged food-vessel, a collared urn, and a series of radiocarbon assays ranged from 1685 ± 70 bc (CAR-165) down to 1495 ± 70 bc (CAR-161), c. 2150–1750 BC with a midpoint around 1875 BC. 'As the C14 phases from all phases of this monument are statistically inseparable the demonstrated sequence of events probably took place over a maximum of a few hundred years.'[9]

Unlike circle-henges in which the stones of the circle stand independently inside the henge true embanked circles with their stones actually set in the bank are relatively uncommon in Britain and Ireland, about fifty being known. Pobull Fhinn and Loch a Phobuill on North Uist are the largest. Five sites in Ireland, including Grange and Castleruddery average 24.7m across their banks. In Wales there may be as many as a dozen including the probably spurious Ysbyty Cynfyn. What concentrations of embanked stone circles there are occur in the adjoining counties of Derbyshire, twenty, and Yorkshire, eleven. It is noticeable that in central and northern England embanked stone circles, complex- and simple ring-cairns intermix on the moors. One large ring occurs at Gamelands in Westmorland, 42.1 × 35.1 m, a site having affinities with the Druids' Circle in Gwynedd. Much more characteristic are little rings like the Nine Ladies in the Peak District, 11.5 × 10.5 m, and the Twelve Apostles, 15.9 m across, on Ilkley Moor.

Embanked stone circles may have been variants of the circle-henges along the spine of Britain along the Pennines on the watershed between stoneless henges to the east and open stone circles to the west. For the Welsh embanked circles Roese did indicate a comparable relationship between them and the Welsh circle-henges, the small embanked rings being found not in the central hills and mountains but in proximity to the coast, sometimes no higher than 150 m O.D., overlapping the low situations of the circle-henges themselves.[10]

Embanked circles do not form a coherent group in Wales. Those in the south are different in size, design and architecture from those in the north. It is the southern sites that occupy low situations. They are circular with banks but no ditches and with a single, stone-lined entrance facing either east or west. The best known is Meini-gwyr. Such rings appear aligned on the equinoctial sunrises or sunsets and their apparent connection with the trade in stone axes hints that as a group they belong to the Late Neolithic/Early Bronze Age transition.

As will be seen the embanked stone circles of North Wales are different. They are not circular but oval and do not face east or west but are aligned ESE–WNW. In the same area around Snowdonia are plain rings which are also elliptical showing that this was a preferred and deliberate shape for communities in this part of the country. The shape and the common axis provide insights into the thinking of their builders.

In the embanked circles wherever in Britain or Ireland there is repeated evidence of burials, perhaps as dedications, even sacrifices in the Bronze Age. Although quite early beaker material came from the Grange ring, Co. Limerick, elsewhere the finds are of the Bronze Age: food-vessels from Cunninghar, Clackmannan, and the Druids' Circle; rusticated beakers from Ffridd Newydd; collared urns from Danby Rigg, Yorkshire and Nith Lodge, Ayrshire; Pennine urns from Mosley Height, Lancashire and Todmorden, Yorkshire; pygmy cups from Nith Lodge, Mosley Height and Todmorden, associated with faience beads at the two latter sites. It is improbable that such consistent Bronze Age artefacts should be secondary deposits in these dispersed rings and it is safe to regard the majority as late in the history of stone circles particularly as the complex ring-cairn of Barbrook II, Derbyshire, with its two Pennine urns, contained charcoal dated to 1500 ± 150 bc (BM-179), c. 2000–1625 BC.

Whether such rings originate from circle-henges like Grange remains unclear although the stone-built entrances at Meini-gwyr, at Letterston may have been constructed in imitation of earlier orthostatic passages. The impact of henge architecture must have been strong in eastern districts of Britain and may account for some of the eccentricities of embanked rings in the Peak District and in Yorkshire just as Fullerton in Aberdeenshire may have had its stones set in a bank to resemble the circle-henge of Broomend of Crichie a mile away.

Nearby 30 miles south of Ffridd Newydd is what could be a ravaged circle-henge, ditchless, like several others along these western coasts. At Ysbyty Cynfyn near

Cardigan one stone still stands in a bank which now surrounds a church. It has been supposed that this was a pagan monument that had been Christianised, something that did happen in Llandysiliogogo church in the same county where a megalithic stone actually supports the pulpit.

Convincing doubts have been expressed about the 'ring' at Ysbyty Cynfyn which may be nothing more than a bogus tourist attraction invented around AD 1800 when the church and its cemetery were being repaired and altered. The circle was not mentioned in reports of 1755 and 1796. A description of the churchyard in 1804 mentioned only one 'large, upright stone'. It was as late as 1807 before the 'large druidical circle or temple' was recorded. Perhaps just before then the other four stones to the east of the big one were introduced as enticements for visitors.[11]

Elsewhere in this region there is the oval Cefn Coch on a ridge near Tremadoc Bay within a mile of the doomed Cwm Mawr ring 'blown up in recent times'. There are occasional well-scattered rings like Pen y Stryd. Far inland along the Dovey valley, 15 miles from any other circle, are the associated rings of Cerrig Gaerau and Lled-Croen-yr-Ych, 'the width of the ox-hide' because it was believed to be the burial-place of a bereaved ox at whose death his hide was stretched out and surrounded by standing stones. Both circles stand on a broad, flat saddle in the mountains of Powys. The large stones of Cerrig Gaerau, 21 m across, are fallen but some of the lesser pillars of Lled-Croen-yr-Ych, still stand in an oval 24.7 × 22.9 m. There is a low outlier standing edge on 31.7 m to the south-east. Such paired sites have sometimes been interpreted as successive if their shapes and sizes differ. The presence of the unusual megalithic ring at Cerrig Gaerau so far into the centre of Wales does point to the mixture of influences there.

Mynydd Epynt

In the worn, smoothed hills of Mynydd Epynt in south-central Wales are similarly paired sites whose major trait is the existence of adjacent alignments. At Nant Tarw (Fig. 18), or 'the bull stream', Thom's misnamed 'Usk River', on an extensive flat terrace overlooking former marshland are two unobtrusive rings within 90 m of each other. The ESE is an oval 20.7 × 19 m, its biggest pillar only 90 cm high at the south-east end of the major axis but not on Thom's theoretical perimeter. Well to the west but close to the western ring, is a long, fallen monolith with a small stone by it. Being so uneasily close to that site it suggests that the east ring and its outlier may have preceded the other only to have any sightline blocked by its successor. At that latitude the alignment to the fallen stone would have been close to sunset in early November, the time of Samain.

The WNW ring is an ellipse 20.7 × 17.8 m. Over a hundred metres to the WNW is a massive prostrate boulder with two much smaller beyond it, a collapsed Three-Stone row. Thom calculated that from the centre of the ellipse to the stones the azimuth of 285° produced a declination of 10°.1 but the proposed alignment on the setting of the bright star, Spica, α Virginis, in 1900 BC is unconvincing.[12]

Three and a half miles NNE of Nant Tarw across the Usk valley, near a Roman road and camps are two more rings on Trecastle Mountain, again dissimilar to each other. The ENE is 23.2 m across, of inconspicuous stones with an off-centre mound inside it. Close by the second much smaller ring, only 7.3 m in diameter, is ruined and incomplete. To its WSW is a wretched short alignment crawling towards the circle, its stones

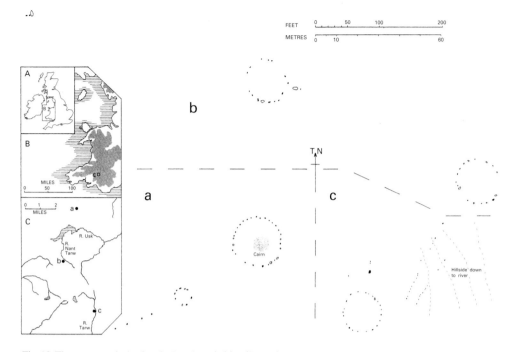

Fig. 18. Three stone circle sites in Brecknockshire (Powys): a. Trecastle Mountain; b. Nant Tarw; c. Cerrig Duon. (After Grimes, 1963).

just perceptible in the wet ground. Even allowing for a rise in the ground level it is unlikely that such a setting could have been laid out for astronomical purposes. It is significant that although proposing three solar sightlines in these rings, his 'Y Pigwn', Thom overlooked this 'row' altogether.

It is with the third site, Cerrig Duon, 'the black stone', four miles SSE of Nant Tarw in the narrow and dark Tawe valley that one purpose of these idiosyncratic rows is shown. Thom's 'Maen Mawr' is an egg-shaped ring, whose geometry, either his Type I with a perimeter of 57.3 m or Type II, 58.2 m, and diameters of 18.8×17.6 m has been strongly criticised.[13] It stands on a platform above the river Tawe immediately to its east. Although its stones are low only 9.1 m to the NNE there is a massive rectangular block, 1.8 m high and measuring 1.5×0.9 m along its sides, more than five tons of fine-grained sandstone. Like the outlier at Nant Tarw this stone, the true Maen Mawr, 'great stone', has two little stones in line with its axis behind it. It may mark the rising of Arcturus, α Boötis, in 1950 BC. It is more probably directional.

It can be seen from a considerable distance to the south and also to the east across the river even when the ring itself is out of sight. From the north it stands out solidly on the near horizon against the far-off hills. About half a mile northwards on the eastern valleyside is another standing stone, Forest Fawr, 2.1 m tall, set like a playing-card, its long axis pointing directly to Maen Mawr. Less than 185 m beyond this stone, following its alignment, one comes past the shoulder of the hill and Maen Mawr can be seen on its spur. Its usefulness as a guidestone is apparent.

No finds are recorded from these lonely rings and at first they seem entirely unaffected by any outside influence. That this is not so is revealed by the detached avenue at Cerrig Duon, 45.7 m long, narrowing as it nears the ring but not directly in line with it. Today it is only just detectable even in the short grass but it does follow the easiest line of approach up the hillside from the river 20 m below.

The only other avenue connected with a Welsh stone circle is at the oval Rhos y Beddau, 'the moor of graves', 11.4 × 10.5 m, a ring of little stones on a steep hillsides in Montgomery, Powys. An avenue overgrown with heather and almost lost in it as it creeps towards the ring. It is an odd approach. It is not joined to the ring, it is not aligned on the centre, and its southern stones are higher than those on the north. A third of the way along it changes direction. It is probably of two phases, put up by people who, although they knew that circles and avenues went together, treated them as separate elements.[14]

Avenues of standing stones connected to stone circles are a feature of several north Wessex rings where they were arguably a development from shorter settings like the portalled entrances to Cumbrian rings. Timber double rows which may be analogous are recorded from Neolithic burial sites such as Kemp Howe and Kilham in Yorkshire as well as at henges, Lugg in Co. Dublin being an example. Earthen versions exist at Stonehenge – which once may have had stones in the bank – at Arbor Low in the Peak District and maybe also at the Bull Ring in the same region.

Other circles with avenues occur rarely in Scotland: Broomend of Crichie in Aberdeenshire, Callanish on the Isle of Lewis, and more commonly in England in Westmorland, the eastern marches of Wales and in the north-east of Dartmoor, the overall distribution suggesting some relationship with the Lake District to the north. As many of these avenues lead up the easiest slope from a river their deliberate association with water must have been a factor in the minds of their builders, the two linked short avenues at Stanton Drew becoming all the more significant in this context.

Even more remote than Cerrig Duon or Nant Tawr is Ynys-hir (Fig. 19), 'long island', on a bleak ridge on Ministry of Defence land deep in the mountains at a height of 396 m O.D. It is a perfect circle 18 m in diameter. The stones were shallowly set with only a few packing-stones so that by the time the ring was excavated in 1940 they had nearly all fallen. There were no dateable finds. One stone-lined posthole was discovered 1.5 m inside the ring near the south-east stone.

On its knoll in a bland landscape the ring has been slightly damaged by a shell-hole. Like Gors Fawr some 50 miles to the west the little stones are graded with the tallest, widest and heaviest between the south and ssw. The builders of this lonely circle

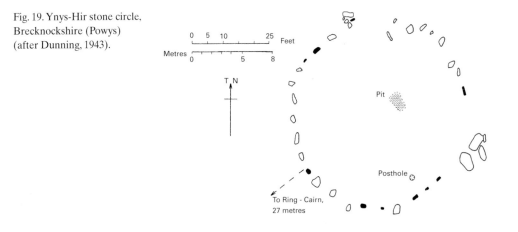

Fig. 19. Ynys-Hir stone circle, Brecknockshire (Powys) (after Dunning, 1943).

incorporated a jutting outcrop that looked like three fallen slabs at the south-east. Similar integration of a natural feature is known elsewhere. A stone circle was erected around an earth-fast boulder at Leskernick SE on Bodmin Moor. A huge boulder was used as a kerbstone at a ring-cairn on Banniside Moor, Lancashire.[15]

Just to the south-west of the circle was a ring-cairn which had been converted into a barrow by newcomers who placed Bronze Age pottery including a small, coarse pygmy cup in it. At the centre was a pit with a token cremation and charcoal under a flat stone like that at Ffridd Newydd. Ring-cairns alongside stone circles have been noticed elsewhere in Wales but their distribution is by no means identical, overlapping only in the north and south-west of the country.[16] Their juxtaposition at Ynys-hir may be attributed to the use of the same territory by people at different times. There is just such a pairing at the drab Cheetham Close, Lancashire, where a 15.5 m circle and a 22 m ring-cairn were built alongside each other.

Other pairings occur on Extwistle Moor, Lancashire. At Danby Rigg on the Yorkshire Moors a stone circle lies near a multitude of clearance cairns and a large ring-cairn in a contiguous uncleared area flanked to north and south by deep, defensive ditches. Half a mile separates stone circle from ring-cairn. We have no knowledge of whether they were contemporary, built by the same people, had the same purpose or were for complementary practices.[17]

A similar but closer association occurs 13 miles east of Lampeter at Cefn Gwernffrwyd deep in the mountains. There a shattered circle, about 24 m across, slumps within 60 m of a larger ring-cairn whose builders, like so many others, showed an interest in the south-west quadrant by setting a huge stone there. Tangential to the ring-cairn is a Three-Stone row akin to those at Cerrig Duon and Nant Tarw 15 miles to the SSE.

Twenty miles north-east of Ynys-hir is another group of rings around the heights of Radnor Forest: Rhos Maen; the oval of Gelli Hill, 21.3 × 19.5 m with an outlier on the western skyline; the heather-thick Six Stones; and lower down the Lugg valley the Four Stones near Walton, reported by Camden to be a circle ruined in the reign of King John but, in fact, a good Four-Poster a surprising 300 miles south of central Scotland where such rings flourish. It is part of a thinning southwards of these neat circles; Aucheleffan and others on Arran; the Three Kings and the Goatstones in Northumberland; the Druid's Altar near Grassington and perhaps the two High Bridestones, all in Yorkshire; Gibbet Moor in the Peak District, and as far south-west as Lettergorman in Co. Cork.

The Four Stones are rounded lichen-marked boulders from the volcanic Stanner Rocks 2 miles to the south. They stand at the corners of an irregular rectangle about 2.2 × 1.7 m but on the circumference of a perfect circle 2.9 m in diameter. Proving the site's Scottish ancestry there are three cupmarks on the south-west stone, a very rare form of megalithic art in Wales. It is noteworthy that at Llanerch Farm only 5 miles to the west is a boulder on which there are some thirty of these alien carvings.

Since first being recognised as a Four-Poster in the mid-1970s others of these Hibernian nomads are suspected in and around Wales; Bryn yr Aran near Hafod and Carno; the Druid's Castle in Shropshire, 25 miles north of the Four Stones; Cwm Saesan, 20 miles north-west near St Harmons, once an oblong of two large and two low stones; and Cwmdu, 'black valley' the same distance to the south. Ley-hunters will be disheartened to learn that the line is straight. Almost. The cause of this meagre spread of northern rings late in the Bronze Age is obscure.

Not far from the Druid's Castle in Shropshire are the two circles of Mitchell's Fold and Hoarstones discussed earlier. Eleven miles to the south-west the Kerry Hill ring lies near the Clun-Clee trackway, an important prehistoric route between the Irish Sea and the Severn Basin from Early Bronze Age times, used for the dispersal of perforated axe hammers and articles of bronze until 'with the onset of wetter conditions its use declined: from the Late Bronze Age the district was either deserted, or isolated, the older levels being sealed in parts by the growth of hill-peat'.[18]

Pen-y-Wern may have been a circle on this route. Kerry Hill is farther to the west on a southern hillside. Like Mitchell's Fold it is a large site but of irregular shape. Termed a compound ring by Thom it has a maximum diameter of 26.5 m. It has only nine stones, some thin slabs, some great boulders but none more than 53 cm high. A 1.2 m-long pillar lies near the centre. This, the central stone at Hoarstones, the reputed counterpart at Mitchell's Fold, may be related to others in Wessex. Connections through trade certainly extended northwards along the Severn valley from Wessex.

Other clusters of centre-stone circles exist in south-west Scotland and in Cos. Cork and Kerry, Ireland, but it is unlikely that there was any direct contact between places so distant from a remote ring like Kerry Hill whereas the Clun-Clee trackway by which it lay did extend westwards to the Birmingham plateau and then south into Wessex where rings such as Avebury and Winterbourne Bassett had central pillars. Links between Wessex and east Wales along the edges of the Severn Valley do much to explain common architectural features like central stones and avenues.

Thom, having analysed the plan of Kerry Hill as a compound ring, remarked 'On the ground this is a very unimpressive site, but when it is surveyed and the geometry studied it turns out to be another member of the group we are examining . . . while the axis is not east and west the line KT is very nearly due north', a cardinal direction frequently noticed in the Cumbrian rings. It has, however, been suggested that the ring may be a modern, and spurious, version of a gorsedd in which central stones are obligatory.[19]

North Wales

The megalithic rings of North Wales have benefited from two sharp but generally overlooked insights. The first, of the mid-eighteenth century, recognised that the stone 'circles' were in fact ellipses. The second, well over a century later, showed that there was an astronomical explanation.

The first unconscious discovery about ellipses was made by the Welsh antiquarian, Richard Farringdon, in whose manuscript, *Snowdonia Druidica* of 1769 is his record of Cefn Coch (Pl. 39), a ring 23 miles south-west of the Druids' Circle and now almost entirely removed. In the eighteenth century it was in better condition and Farringdon planned it, terming it 'The Druid Ellipsis' of fourteen stones, measuring 44 and 36 Druid's cubits.

His concept of the cubit came from Stukeley's idea of a Druidical rod 53 cm long that had been used in the construction of Stonehenge. Farringdon accepted this in his analysis of Cefn Coch and the accuracy of his dimensions should not be accepted uncritically. There was, however, no reason for him to turn the ring into an ellipse and certainly no motive for giving it an alignment of ESE–WNW as his plan shows.[20] The orientation is akin to the others in north Wales. So is the shape. It is significant that in

The Druid Ellipsis at Cefn Coch

P. 19

Distance 80 paces

Solitary stone

Plate 39. Farringdon's plan of the elliptical Cefn Coch in 1769.

western Scotland to the north of those mountains the large rings also are ellipses. The reason for this choice of design would not be made clear until the beginning of the twentieth century.

It is their shape that distinguishes the embanked circles of northern Wales. Alexander Thom postulated that prehistoric communities laid out ellipses so that the circumference could be an exact multiple of the unit of measurement used in measuring out the diameter, something impossible in a circle whose perimeter would be 2×3.1416 times the length of the radius. For the Druids' Circle he claimed that the long and short axes measured 31 and $29\frac{1}{2}$ Megalithic Yards of 0.829 m and that the perimeter was 95.047 M.Y. 'It would have been quite impossible for the builders to detect the discrepancy in the hypotenuse (1 in 3800). From their point of view the perimeter was also perfect with an error of only 1 in 1500.'[21]

There is an alternative explanation. Unlike the uniformity of a true circle an oval has the advantage of two distinct axes, long and short, and either could be used to provide an alignment across a ring without the need for a taller stone or an outlier. Barnatt and Moir suggested that there were no intentionally non-circular rings, only circles set out casually by eye. The evidence does not support this. There are two enormous regions in Britain where ellipses predominate, north Wales and western Scotland, and the ovals in them are too many to be fortuitous.

The most dramatic confirmation that a long axis had been aligned on a celestial event came from the timber rings of Woodhenge, Wiltshire, excavated by Maud

Cunnington in 1926–7. The SW–NE axis of the six ellipses of posts passed over the grave of a slaughtered child near the centre of the site and was in line with the midsummer sunrise. In Scotland, the unfinished oval of Cultoon on Islay had its long axis pointing south-westwards towards Slieve Snaght mountain in Co. Donegal behind which the midwinter sun set. 'It is difficult to deny that the position of the Cultoon elliptical ring was chosen to obtain this exact relationship and the design of the ring confirms this.'

Seeming support for this interpretation of a long axis in non-circular rings as an indicator for an astronomical event comes from a site hundreds of years older than those in Britain and two and a half thousand miles away at Nabta in the Sahara Desert. In that small egg-shaped stone 'circle' the WSW–ENE long axis lay in line with the solstitial sunrise. By non-British coincidence a north–south alignment was incorporated, perhaps to guide prehistoric nomads crossing the desert. Nearby stone rows and an isolated 'phallic' monolith formed part of this remarkable complex.[22]

The same use appears true of the long axes in the large rings of North Wales and Anglesey, the Roman 'Ynys Mona', an island that may have been settled quite early by circle and henge people. Only 8½ miles away across the Menai Straits cremation pits in the henge of Llandegai I were dated to 2530 ± 145 bc (NPL-224) and 2470 ± 140 bc (NPL-221), c. 3400–3000 BC, a time when the exploitation of axe sources from the augite granophyre of Graig Lwyd had already begun.

Prehistoric Anglesey being an island with well over a score of chambered tombs it is predictable that stone circles would be few and damaged. Even the presence of Bryn Celli Ddu, the Bryn Gwyn stones and two possibly imaginative Four-Posters cannot prove Ynys Mona an exception to the rule that islands and stone circles do not go together. Chambered tombs like Barclodiad y Gawres and the heavily capstoned Lligwy dolmen dominated. Circle-builders were unlikely to be welcomed.

The island, for all the glories of its megalithic tombs, is a stone circle tragedy. Its two once stupendous rings are spoiled beyond recognition. The pair of surviving blocks at Bryn Gwyn are reputedly the largest standing stones in Wales. The taller is a thin 4 m high, gross boulder, a metre taller than its eastern companion. It has been claimed these are the remains of a 12 m ring, probably oval in the typical shape of rings in north Wales, once surrounded by a ditch and outer bank. In the 1695 edition of Camden's *Britannia* the great Welsh antiquarian, Edward Lhuyd, wrote, 'Farther west-ward . . . there are stones pitch'd on end, about twelve in number, whereof three are very considerable, the largest of them being twelve foot high'. Just to the east was Castell Bryn-gwyn, a henge that was used well into the Bronze Age.

Seventy years later the ring was a wreck. In 1766 the Rev. Henry Rowlands mentioned only three large stones and a stump. Intriguingly, in his fanciful sketch of a druidical grove at Tre'r Dryw not far away he seems to have drawn two 'Scottish' Four-Posters near the Bryn Gwyn circle. As there was an 'Irish' Five-Stone circle on Penmaenmawr both Anglesey and the north coast of Wales may have been another of those accessible sanctuaries and entrepôts open to merchants and traders from over-seas. Typical of the fate of stone circles on the island they have vanished.[23] So has the megalithic ring of Bryn Celli Ddu.

Today a finely restored passage-tomb covers the catastrophe of a circle-henge levelled and smashed by the tomb's builders. Around 3000 BC a prestigious circle-henge had been constructed, an earthen bank and ditch surrounding an oval 19.2 × 17.4 m. Of the original sixteen standing stones the tomb builders removed five stones, buried one and toppled and smashed the remainder with heavy mauls.

The ring had been dramatic. In it cardinal points and a solar line were integrated. The two largest stones were at the north and south. By the north quartz fragments lay. By the south was the cremation of a young girl, possibly a dedicatory sacrifice. The burnt bones of a second, maybe another offering, were placed at the west. A central pit had held a stone or post.

In 1908 Sir Norman Lockyer visited Bryn Celli Ddu which at that time was an exposed ruin. He took a bearing down the collapsed passage, the 'creepway', and found that, allowing for the hill on the north-eastern horizon, it faced the midsummer sunrise. Because the site was not excavated and restored until 1928 he could not know that the tomb had been deliberately built on top of the ellipse whose long axis had been in line with the solstitial sunset to the south-west, an axis that had been respected by its destroyers but in reverse, to the eastern half of the horizon as was customary in chambered tombs.[24]

In north Wales the majority of the oval rings have long axes lying ESE–WNW but it was always the western direction that was significant. It is true of the Druids' Circle, of Cerrig Pryfaid, of Llecheiddior, even of the Westmorland ring of Gamelands which, like the Druids' Circle, was of Cumbrian ancestry. These ellipses have an orientation around 294°. At the Druids' Circle a tall stone stands there with a sudden ridge behind it. At Cerrig Pryfaid there is an outlying stone to the WNW. The alignments are informative. They are in line with the May Day sunset, the occasion of the 'Celtic' fire-festival of Beltane. The clustering of alignments in these Welsh ovals towards this important occasion is not likely to be random.

Because of the shape, unlike the circles of the Lake District it is just possible that the ovals of North Wales and south-western Scotland and the Hebrides were influenced by Irish traditions. Henges in the Boyne valley of Co. Meath, sites like P and Q, are 'oval rather than circular', the oval shape predominating 'in the four largest sites reaching diameters of 180 m to 280 m'. It is feasible but at present only the most frail of suggestions as to how astronomically useful an ellipse was reached Britain quite early in the Neolithic and was adopted to south and north of the English Lake District by native people both in Wales and in south-western Scotland.[25]

The ovals of Bryn Gwyn and Bryn Celli Ddu were Neolithic but the Four-Posters, if they were real, were Bronze Age. So were the majority of the circles in North Wales. Dates from them prove this when trade between Wales, Ireland and England was strong. Circles on long-established trackways, standing stones guiding travellers from one to the other, are records of the constant visits and departures. Axes from Graig Lwyd were plentiful in Wales and many reached Wessex, the east and west Midlands, and Yorkshire. The ways were marked. In the absence of navigable rivers men walked. There was little transportation by sea. Only one axe is known in Scotland, none in Ireland.

The Druids' Circle stood half a mile south of Graig Lwyd. Two miles away the well-preserved ring of Cerrig Pryfaid stands on a southerly route, an outlier marking the way past cairns towards the great block of Bwlch y Ddeufaen and the needle-like pillar of Picell Arthur or Arthur's Spear near Caerhun and onwards towards the River Conway.

Far beyond it there is a problem. Thirty miles east of Penmaenmawr five big stones remain of the NE–SW half of a 29.9 m true circle on the side of a valley at Penbedw Park, 'the chieftain's grave', near Cilcain, Clwyd. They stand on the route from Yorkshire, past modern Chester, across the Conway to the Clwydian hills, Rhuddlan and Graig Lwyd. Six trees have been planted where stones may have stood in the empty arc from south-west to north-east and there is a thick, 1.6 m high outlier 220 m to the west towards the mountains, the forested valley of the Clwyd and then the steep hillsides of the Cambrian highlands. It is a convincing scenario but the ring may be a folly. It was first mentioned in the late eighteenth century when Pennant wrote, 'In the meadow below the house is part of a druidical circle'. The ring is certainly suspiciously situated in full view of Penbedw Hall about half a mile to the WNW. And of the five stones two are set atypically across the circumference.

Three matters, however, favour its antiquity. It does stand near a known trackway. If it was a folly it is odd that its romantic designer should have omitted the six stones nearer the house. To the contrary, tradition claimed they were the most convenient and were removed to be built into the Hall. Thirdly, the Royal Commission surveyors calculated that from the circle the outlier would have stood in line with the equinoctial sunsets. None of it is conclusive but it should not be ignored. Circle or facsimile is unresolved despite the nearby round barrow from which sherds of an enlarged food-vessel were taken in 1860.[26]

Much closer to the Druids' Circle on Cefn Coch, the red ridge that stands above the great headland of Penmaenmawr, there is a broken line of cairn-cemeteries, mounds, ring-cairns and stone circles across the junction of three moorland tracks, which themselves are defined in places by standing stones. Just east of Graig Lwyd at least twelve monuments crowd along half a mile of the track. The chief of them is the famous Druids' Circle.

A mile to its east the small ring of Hafoty lies half-collapsed on the flank of a mountain ridge. The trackway from England passes through this circle, then by the cemetery of small cairns and on to the knee-high stones that are all that is left of a ring, maybe once as much as 30.5 across, near a ruined cairn at Red Farm. The trudging path climbs slowly westwards over half a mile of rock and grass to Circle 275, too prosaic a name for such a miniature delight, four low boulders and an even lower, longer one at its south-west.

Quite unexpectedly, being so far from its homeland, this is an 'Irish' Five-stone ring, 3.1 m in diameter, to which many visitors pay no attention in their haste to reach the Druids' Circle (Pl. 40). Yet when it was excavated during a cold, wet May in 1958 it produced compelling evidence of its origins. Between the east and south stones were crude spreads of stones like a bank. The interior was covered with quartz and near the centre was a shallow pit densely packed with quartz. The diameter, the number of stones, the quartz all recall the diminutive Five-Stone rings of south-west Ireland, tiny settings in the Boggeragh hills of Co. Cork like Carrigagrenane, Knocknakilla or Knockraheen with their quartz. In Co. Kerry an equally squashed ring at Cashelkeelty provided assays dated to the end of the second millennium BC. The known trading contacts between Munster and north Wales during the Bronze Age seems to have led to the laying out of a little Irish ring on these Welsh moors on the major trading route between Ireland and eastern England.[27]

Farther west, 145 m beyond the Druids' Circle is Circle 278 almost hidden in a dip, an irregular ring-cairn about 16 m in diameter, its central space walled with flat-topped stones. The interior was empty except for a fire and a female cremation by a south-east slab. Opposite was another area of burning and a slab-covered pit with a small, collar-decorated urn of the Primary NW series, but no burial.[28] The tallest stone had stood at the SSW. On the other side of the central space was 'an elaborate setting

Plate 40. Circle 275, Penmaenmawr. The Druids' Circle is on the skyline (Photograph: the author).

of stones that looked rather like a small armchair' which the excavator surmised 'might have been intended to support the base of a wooden image or totem', possibly akin to the 'pulpit' at Millin Bay across the Irish Sea in Co. Down. Two radiocarbon assays were obtained from Circle 278, 1520 ± 145 bc (NPL-11) and 1405 ± 155 bc (NPL-10), spanning the years from *c.* 2000 to 1500 BC. Such dates, analysed from wood lying beneath the bank, relate only to the erection of the monument and not to the subsequent activities within it.

More stone circles, tumbled and almost unrecognisable, may have stood to the west of Circle 278 but it is the evocative Druids' Circle to its east that compels attention (Fig. 20). Whereas the ring-cairn lurks in a hollow the grand stone circle stands picturesquely, hard by the trackway, its stones upright and bleak against the skyline. Some of the granitic monoliths are nearly 1.8 m high and despite the despoliation of treasure-seekers and the blasting operations of nineteenth-century wall builders the ring retains a wild grandeur.

It was charmingly described in the reign of Charles I (1625–49), on the moor

standeth the rarest monument that is to bee found in all Snowdon, called y Meini Hirion [the long stones]; ytt standes . . . above Gwddwglase, uppon the playne mownteyne. This monumente standes rownd as a circle compassed about with a stone wale, and within the wale close unto the wale are longe greate stones rownd aboutes the circle standynge uppon there endes in the grounde, that a man woulde wonder where in these partes such stones weare to bee found, and how they weare so sett uppon there endes in the grownde.[29]

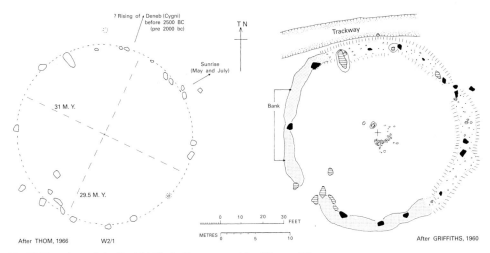

Fig. 20. Two plans of the Druids' Circle, Caernarvonshire (Gwynedd).

Having erected the thirty pillars the Late Neolithic workers piled up a boulder bank 46 cm high and up to 1.7 m wide all around the ring except at the wsw where a 2.4 m wide gap with two massive portals formed an impressive entrance exactly like those of their Cumbrian antecedents. Once birches had grown in the locality. Even when the ring was put up a few trees probably stood near the trackway that today can be made out as a hollow trail that goes directly by the north side of the bank, protected from the sea-winds by a rise in the ground. The Druids' Circle appears to have been situated at the juncture of several such tracks, a fact that points to its status as a meeting-place.

In plan Thom defined it, his 'Penmaen-mawr', as an oval 25.7 × 24.5 m, 31 and 29½ of his Megalithic Yards of 0.829 m, on a major WNW–ESE axis. The excavator, however, thought it was flattened against the trackway. There is a small standing stone exactly at the north at that point. It is almost a metre inside Thom's hypothetical perimeter which takes no cognisance of the concentric bank. Had the builders wished to erect their ring as close to the track as possible then the 'misplaced' stone becomes explicable as a reluctance on their part to set it on an ancient route.

Griffiths, the excavator, thought the major axis to be not ESE–WNW but wsw at the entrance to ENE where a tall and perhaps artificially shaped stone, no. 16, and a peculiar outlying stone stand. The outer face of Stone 16 has a little shoulder which 'local tradition, ever ready to take full advantage of the opportunities offered by the circle, states . . . was the "altar" on which the slain bodies of infants were placed during sacrificial ceremonies'.

Like other great rings the interior of the circle is uncluttered but near the centre the capstone of a fine cist was uncovered. Quartz lay round it. In the cist was an inverted enlarged food-vessel and the cremated bones of a ten to twelve-year-old child. To the WNW was a pit with another enlarged food-vessel containing a second child cremation, here with a small bronze knife. A third pot stood in another pit from which a slight trench led south-west to a hollow lined with overlapping sandstone hones on which there was a badly preserved cremation.[30] Such whetstones, like cult axes, may have been worn as amulets. A tiny perforated example was discovered with a cremation at Ffridd y Garreg Wen, Clwyd. Others, also holed, are known from Y Graig Fawr, Tanrallt Farm and Glydfa in the same county of Flintshire.[31]

The location of the Druids' Circle on its vital east–west trackway and its enclosing bank are suggestive of eastern and northern influences. Embanked rings are frequent in the Peak District of Derbyshire and in Yorkshire. In Wessex they are virtually unknown. At Carperby near Aysgarth in west Yorkshire are the weathered stones of an embanked oval 28 × 23.8 m, its fallen pillars of local gritstone up to 1.2 m long. They lie on an overgrown bank. There is a low, disturbed mound at the centre. At Gamelands in Westmorland the flattened ring, some 42.1 × 35.1 m, has a reduced bank in which forty stones once stood. There was a south-east entrance. Ploughing around 1862 dragged up the stones of a probable cist.

The Druids' Circle, so attractively placed, may be regarded as a monument in which two traditions combined, embanking from the east, a portalled entrance from Cumbria to the north. A third tradition, perhaps a secondary one, was the inclusion of burials within the ring. The spectacular cairn-circle of Bryn Cader Faner, a combination of a low cairn from which well-spaced stones emerge prominently, dramatically sited on the skyline with tall pillars leaning spikily from its overgrown mound like a megalithic coronet is a hybrid phenomenon often observed in the later rings of Wales.[32]

But the significance of the child burials is obscure. Elsewhere, at Pond Cairn, Glamorgan and the Aber Cwmddyr ring-cairn, Cardigan, there are child burials, the latter having 'within the central area the unburnt body of a headless child'. At Bedd Branwyn cairn, Anglesey, 30 miles west of the Druids' Circle, amongst other burials there were three separate deposits of infants' ear-bones. Within the barrow at Treiorwerth nearby there were the ear-bones of a six-year old. 'It is suggestive of some unpleasant ritual, probably sacrifice, accompanying the funerals of certain special individuals.' The one piece of bone in the central ritual pit of the Bryn Celli Ddu passage-tomb was the burnt ear-bone of an adult. Directly across the Irish Sea the central cist at Castle Mahon contained a child's cremation. There were others inside Millin Bay. Other sacrifices are suspected from Bronze Age cist burials in Ireland.[33]

It must be wondered whether the child cremations at the Druids' Circle are similarly the evidence of sacrifice like the slain child at Woodhenge in Wiltshire, relics of a darkening past that the visitor to a stone circle should be aware of, informing him that he may be standing not in a scientific observatory or contemplative chapel but in a macabre enclosure of death where people, fearful in a precarious world, offered fire and human beings in return for their own safe-keeping. Today's sunshine may delude the modern mind.

Chapter Eleven

The Stone Circles of Western and Northern Scotland

A book entitled 'A Description of the Isles of Orkney' . . . makes mention of two rounds sett about with high smooth stones or flags about twenty foot above ground . . . the largest is 110 paces diameter, and [they are] reputed to be high places of worship and sacrifice in Pagan times.

James Garden to John Aubrey, 4 May 1694

Introduction

Immediately across the Solway Firth from the great stone circles of the English Lake District a second line of impressive megalithic rings extends 300 miles northwards along the western coast, starting in Dumfriesshire, reaching the Outer Hebrides, Caithness, the Orkneys and culminating in the quaint sub-circles of the Shetlands.

The line is a mixture. In it are true circles, several with entrances like those of Cumbria: the Girdle Stanes, Loch Buie and, in the far north, Stenness and Brodgar. They are a minority. Three in five of the sites are ellipses, well-designed geometrically, not accidents, long and large ovals in south-western Scotland and North Uist, dainty miniatures on Lewis (Table 14).

Entrance Circles in Scotland

Here and there in western Scotland are true circles with portalled entrances like those already described in Cumbria. A cultural connection is likely.

Near Langholm in Annandale, 40 miles north of Castlerigg the River North Esk has cut away nearly a third of the 39 m circle-henge of the Girdle Stanes that stands, tree-ringed, in an inconspicuous hollow, its grassy outer bank showing clearly at the north. Several stones lie in the river. On the far side of the ring is a tumbled south-eastern entrance with portal stones. The diameter, the situation, numerous stones, bank and entrance are characteristic of a 'Cumbrian' ring intended for the needs of dispersed groups. Not unexpectedly it contains a solar alignment. Across the northernmost circle-stone and portal of the entrance towards the high hills, the early November sunrise of the 'Celtic' Samain occurred.[1]

A survey made on Good Friday, 1911 claimed two solar lines towards natural features and two others on Capella, *α Aurigae*, for 1360 BC, *c.* 1100 bc, and 2150 BC, *c.* 1775 bc, but these were not critically established, and the latter was considered 'unacceptable' because it was aligned on one of two outliers 128 m to the north-east on a rise, one stone being low, the other almost buried so that it could not be used as a sighting

County	Ovals	Circles
Dumfriess	Lochmaben Stane	Girdle Stanes
	Twelve Apostles	Kirkhill
	Whitcastles	
	Whiteholm Rigg	
	Windy Edge	
Ayrshire	Nith Lodge	Molmont
Lanarkshire	Wildshaw Burn	
Argyllshire	Temple Wood North	Pobull Burn
	Temple Wood South	Strontoiller
Islay	Cultoon	Lossit Burn
Mull		Loch Buie
		Tenga
Tiree	Hough East	Hough West
Skye	Snizert	
North Uist	Carinish	Cringraval
	Pobull Fhinn	
Benbecula		Suidhealchadh
		Sealg
Lewis	Cean Hulavig	Airidh Sleitinish
	Callanish	Loch Raoinavat
	Cnoc Ceann a'Gharaidh	Priest's Glen
	Cnoc Fillibhir	
	Druim Dubh	
	Na Drommanan	
Orkneys		Ring of Brodgar
		Stenness
Shetlands	Loch of Strumm	
NUMBER	22	16
AVERAGE DIAMETER	30 × 26.3	31.2
AVERAGE AREA	638 m²	764 m²

Table 14. Shapes of Rings along the Western Coasts of Scotland. The figures are misleading. Whereas the majority of the ovals are large, most of the circles are small. By subtracting the total areas of the two Orkneys rings, 9,190 m², the average area of the circles falls to 217 m², barely a third that of the ovals.

device.[2] A sinuous possible line of standing stones wanders from these outliers and around a knoll to the megalithic oval of the Loupin' Stanes nearly half a mile away.

Other lonely circles like Strontoiller by Loch Etive in Argyll or Loch Buie on Mull, like strangers in a foreign land, demonstrate how far apart the settlements may have been in this unfriendly region of rock and water.

Loch Buie, miles to the west of the only chambered tomb on Mull at Port Donain, is one of the most delightful of true circles. On the south coast by a bay in the Firth of Lorn it was erected on unusually fertile soil for the island, the so-called Garden of Mull. In the 'Field of the Druids' it stands in a landscape of distant, dark mountains and nearby crimson rhododendrons. It is a small ring, only 13.4 m across. One of its nine stones was removed before the visit of the Welsh antiquarian, Edward Lhuyd, in

Plate 41. An outlier and the lovely ring of Loch Buie, Mull (Photograph: the author).

1699, but has been replaced and the circle is an example of megalithic perfection. There are Cumbrian hints of its ancestry. The tallest of its svelte pillars, 2.1 m high, is a flat-topped 1.2 m-wide block that stands at the west. The lowest is very close to True North. These cardinal positions, a putative solar alignment and a probable portalled entrance at the south-east are reminiscent of the traits noticed in Lake District rings such as Swinside.

The well-preserved Loch Buie circle (Pl. 41) has a low outlier at the south-east far too close for discriminating astronomical use, and a taller slab set edge-on 36 m to the south-west, well-placed both for observing the midwinter sunset and for directing people towards the sandy shores of Loch Buie half a mile away. Like the outlier at Long Meg it may have combined ceremonial and practical functions. 366 m NNW another stone stands close to the entrance to the only good pass through the Torosay mountains and is most probably directional in character.

After Loch Buie there were few geometrical circles until the Orkneys are reached 200 miles of sea NNE of Mull.

The Scottish Ellipses

The stone circles of south-western Scotland (Fig. 21) fit persuasively into Late Neolithic contexts and are similar to those in Cumbria in their size, situation and architecture. Within a few miles of the Solway Firth is the seventh largest megalithic ring in Britain, the Twelve Apostles just outside Dumfries, divided by a hedge, spoiled in atmosphere by the road that edges the fields in which it stands. Typically it is low-

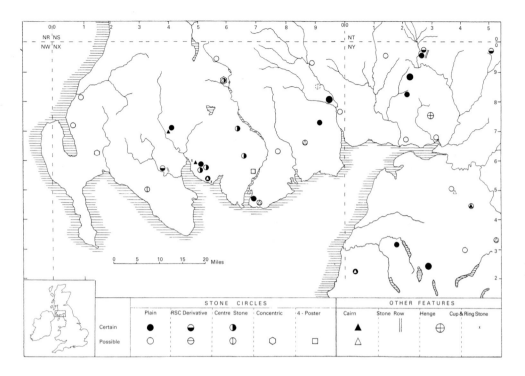

Fig. 21. The distribution of stone circles around the Solway Firth.

lying between Cluden Water and the River Nith in the southern part of the valley, 6 square miles of flat, fertile ground with hills closing in the east and west, and in an excellent position to be the focus for a large and scattered community.

This 86.6 × 79.3 m diameter ellipse had a long axis very close to north-south, 1.5°–181.5°, maybe directed to place halfway between the midwinter sunrise and sunset. The ring of eleven stones, the tallest at ENE and WSW, should be regarded as a northern outlier of the Cumbrian group, only 50 miles by land along the shores of the Solway Firth from Long Meg. Over a hundred Group VI stone axes from the Lake District, have been found in south-west Scotland, many in the locality of the Twelve Apostles.[3] A mile away by the Nith was another circle of nine large stones, 'unfortunately, and without the knowledge of the proprietor, Peter Johnston, Esq., of Carasalloch, they were broken up and applied to the purposes of building'.[4]

The answer to why a circle of eleven stones should be called the Twelve Apostles may lie in a letter from H. M. Survey quoted in the Ordnance Memoirs of 1850. 'There should be only 11 stones. The drawn plan shows only this number; but there turns out to have been an accidental blue spot on this plan which has been reproduced by the zincography on the published plans.' It is likely, however, that twelve was the original number. Locally it was said that a nineteenth-century farmer had dragged the stone away to make room for his plough. When rebuked he replied that it was only Judas that had been removed.

It is striking to see the resemblance between this circle and the Broadlee henge 17 miles to the east. Their diameters are very similar, Broadlee being 79.2 m across. The henge has entrances at NNW and SSE, an orientation similar to the long axis of the

Twelve Apostles. Both lie between rivers and are low-lying at the south of a river valley in level countryside. As Broadlee is only 30 miles north of Penrith it seems likely that both henge and stone circle had fundamentally the same purpose, the materials of their construction simply mirroring the local geology.

Another huge ring, Whitcastles, 54.9 × 43.1 m, with its largest stones at north and south, is a collapsed ruin at the foot of Little Hartfell Hill. As well as this and other open sites like Easthill there is also the pear-shaped block of the Lochmaben Stone on the shores of the Solway Firth looking across the estuary towards Cumbria. The name probably derives from *Locus Maponi*, and the site may have been used well into Iron Age and Roman times as a shrine of the hunter sun god whose Celtic name was Maponus,[5] once more confirming the long use of some stone circles and the continuity of tradition whereby customs were perpetuated even by later incomers to the district.

Once there was a megalithic oval here, about 55 × 46 m. All that now survives is this enormous 2.4 m boulder and another forming part of a stile nearby. In 1841 the Reverend James Roddick wrote: 'On the farm of Old Graitney... was seen not many years ago a number of white stones placed upright circling half an acre of ground in an oval form. One of them, the largest, is all that now remains, as some suppose, of a Druidical temple, the rest having been removed for the cultivation of the soil.'

The stone on its terrace, conspicuous from Redkirk Point sea-lapped to the south-west, is the one survivor of a ring whose builders, perhaps, saw the axe traders coming from the Lake District mountains to the autumnal assemblies at territorial centres like Broadlee henge, the Twelve Apostles and Whitcastles at a time when people still gathered to celebrate, trade, reaffirm laws and worship in such rings, whether at the southern Cheetham Close, Lancashire, with its outlying stone, or at the northern Girdle Stanes.

In this part of Scotland the oval shape was preferred not only in stone circles and henges but even in the late enclosed cremation cemeteries such as the Whitestanes Muir group, 12 miles north of the Twelve Apostles, where the sites were oval or egg-shaped. Site I with its eight cremations was dated to 1360 ± 90 bc (GaK-461), *c.* 1750–1570 bc.[6]

Remote from the others, almost 30 miles north of the Twelve Apostles the Wildshaw Burn near Crawfordjohn, discovered in 1991 when the A74 was being upgraded to motorway status, shares the characteristics of a large oval, about 50 × 40 m, aligned near to north–south, its forty stones all prostrate suggesting that the ring had been left unfinished or, significantly, 'destroyed in antiquity'. Alignments to the midwinter sunrise and midsummer sunset have been claimed for the outlying ellipse.[7]

As noted in chapter two deliberate demolition was also suspected at the large oval, 41.2 × 33.5 m, of Cultoon on Islay, abandoned at some time before 950 bc. Its long axis had been set in line with the midwinter sunset around 1800 bc but stones were prostrate, others missing or broken. Islay is, of course, an island. There are at least five Clyde chambered tombs on it.[8]

Miles to the west Neolithic people had settled in the fertile Kilmartin valley of Argyll with its notable linear cemetery, henge, standing stones and the stone circles at Temple Wood. Carvings of flat bronze axes and halberds, patterned cist-slabs and the discovery of later beakers and food-vessels show that the area was flourishing during the Early Bronze Age, and it may have acted as a convenient staging-post for trade-goods being taken northwards from southern Scotland and Ireland.

The northern ring was a small oval, 10.5 × 10 m, which may have succeeded a wooden structure dated to 3075 ± 190 bc (GU-1296). The ellipse is likely to have been much later. Immediately to its south was a second ellipse, 13.5 × 12.5 m with conjoined spirals carved on a northern stone. Burial cairns with inhumations were added accompanied by a late N3 beaker, flint arrowheads and a scraper.

It was not enough. Like Ballynoe this disturbed site suffered further alteration, kerb-cairns were set up in the interior and a thick bank enclosed the entire monument. Six radiocarbon assays ranging from 1090 ± 55 bc (GU-1297) to 857 ± 50 bc (SRR-530), c. 1350–1050 bc, showed how prolonged a life this abused site endured.[9]

It is of interest to find that the oval shapes, and possibly the alignments, persisted along the western coasts of Scotland: at Cultoon; at the eastern ring of Hough on Tiree, 39.6 × 32.9 m and its less certainly elliptical western partner; in the big rings of North Uist; and on Lewis, Callanish probably being an oval rather than a flattened ring. In this it would be in keeping with its three neighbours of Cnoc Fillibhir, Cean Hulavig and Cnoc Ceann a'Gharaidh. In northern Scotland there are gigantic ellipses in Caithness. The tradition extended to Orkney where Stenness is an oval. Its neighbour, the Ring of Brodgar, is a true circle.

The Western Isles

Unlike the comparative uniformity of the southern megalithic rings the stone circles of the Western Isles contain a diversity of architecture. In them may be found several outliers and centre stones, a few concentric circles and at least one avenue. Integrated with these features was an increasing custom of placing burials within the rings which themselves are rather smaller and frequently non-circular. The fact that the majority of the sites were erected close to the Atlantic explains this variety for it could be expected that their builders received ideas from the south and from Ireland via the trade in Tievebulliagh stone axes.

There is a very informative contrast between the distribution of axes on the Scottish mainland and in the western islands. On the mainland Lake District outnumbered the Irish products by eleven to one (134:12). But twice the number of Irish axes were recovered from the islands.[10]

No henges are known in these islands. Nor are there many large circles. There are either clusters of rings like the groups at Machrie Moor, Arran, and on Lewis, or individual circles on Coll and Tiree, Mull, central Argyll, Skye and North Uist, a pattern suggesting smaller, more isolated settlements whose position was often determined by the demands of the sea route.

Just as the forests and swamps of the countryside hindered journeys so the seaways of Britain and Ireland encouraged the careful traveller. Early prehistoric settlements in the north-west were frequently alongside coasts and estuaries or by navigable rivers. Trails were rare on land and not wide enough for pack animals. To travel, people used water, crossing land only to avoid dangerous tidal races and currents. It is possible to reconstruct a route from south-west Scotland up to the Orkneys.[11] The scatter of circles lies alongside it.

From the Solway Firth travellers crossed from Luce Bay in order to bypass the perilous Mull of Galloway, and from there journeyed north to the Kintyre peninsula. No sensible seaman would have risked the Mull of Kintyre whose furious races inexorably destroyed any open boat in bad weather. So men moved up the protected eastern waters of the Kilbrennan Sound, passed to the west of Arran, and accepted the inconveniences of the short portage from Loch Fyne to Loch Crinan. It was at the northeast of this narrow, much-crossed neck of land that Neolithic people had settled in the fertile Kilmartin valley with its notable linear cemetery, henge, standing stones and the stone circle at Temple Wood, a compelling collection of monuments for the archaeologically minded visitor. Carvings of flat bronze axes and halberds, patterned cist-slabs and the discovery of later beakers and food vessels show that the area was flourishing during the Early Bronze Age.

This was not the route taken by the leather-sided and shallow-drafted vessels from Ireland and Scotland on their way northwards to Orkney. Earlier tragedies warned seafarers to avoid the fatal Gulf of Corryvreckan, 'the pock-marked cauldron', between the islands of Jura and Scarba, 'rough island', where the narrow channels create irresistible races.

In 1947 George Orwell and three young companions nearly drowned off the wrinkled coast of Scarba when they misjudged the tide. The hidden barrier of a rock pinnacle causes violent whirlpools. 'When winter gales are blowing in from the west to meet a flood tide Corryvrechan becomes an unnavigable confusion of white water crashing in all directions at once.' 'Any small craft . . . that is swept there by the flood (and there is no turning back) against the seas raised by a westerly gale, has little chance of survival in the terrific seas that break from the whirlpool for several miles to the west.'[12]

Instead, the Atlantic seaways were preferred, moving from large island to large island, 27 miles of open water between northern Ireland and Islay with its three stone circles, keeping close to western shores, by-passing Jura and Colonsay, as many miles again to Mull ignoring Tyree and Coll.

Voyagers did not land on the clouded and infertile island of Rum, anglicised as 'Rhum' in the late nineteenth century, not landing at the 'wet desert', cold, mountainous, with heavy rainfall, and whose few Neolithic settlers compensated for the climate with an alcoholic mixture of milled oats, heather honey and meadowsweet, a brew like homemade parsnip wine. It failed to entice boats as they moved over the 40 miles to Skye.[13]

There are no more than four possible circles known on the 600 square miles of Skye, two of them by Loch Slapin, the first protected bay on the island from Ardnamurchan. Here voyagers may have waited for good weather before crossing the deep, storm-swept Minch that led them to the Outer Hebrides and ultimately to the Orkneys. And in this nerve-testing way the stone axes and the finer bronzes were carried sporadically from island to island, perhaps passed from settlement to settlement across waters that had become a major seaway between eastern and northern Ireland, south-west Scotland and the distant Orkneys and Shetlands.[14]

At the south of the Outer Hebrides there are few chambered tombs and no stone circles on the southern islands of Barra and South Uist but it is remarkable to learn that on the latter island modern parish boundaries 'date from as long ago as the pre-Roman Iron Age', a continuity that may even reach farther back into the centuries of the Bronze Age.[15]

Only on North Uist are there large ovals with long diameters of over 37 m. The true circle is rare in these islands along the Atlantic coasts. Space forbids more than a mention of these great rings along the south coast.

'An early settlement of the Hebrides, centred on North Uist, and represented by tombs of the Clettraval type, would seem likely.' In this jigsawed landscape of fresh-water lochs, low hills and inlets, bays and channels with long stretches of sandy machair the Clyde-type chambered tombs were erected on the upland moors of North Uist, 'the most fertile of the Outer Hebrides to this day'.[16]

Primary megaliths like the Clettravel long cairn provided a stratified pottery sequence from early plain wares, through Beacharra and Hebridean styles, Unstan vessels, grooved ware and late beakers, and an indication of their early date comes from their proximity to known Neolithic settlements. The Clyde tomb of Geiriscett by Vallay Strand is within a mile of the fenced house and animal pen of Eilian Domhnuill with its thousands of Unstan sherds. Some 5 miles to the east the long cairn of Barpa na Feannag is not far from Eilean an Tighe, 'the island of the house', with its masses of early Beacharra pottery.

The chronology of chambered tombs in the Hebrides remains conjectural but it seems that in time the Clyde tombs with their segmented chambers were succeeded by local Hebridean passage-tombs with a distinct demarcation between passage and chamber. The North Uist large ellipses were probably later still, maybe no earlier than 2700 BC at the uppermost.

Neolithic contacts between the Outer Hebrides and Ireland are reaffirmed by the discovery of an unused porcellanite axe on Lewis. Lying in peat and, from its pristine state, apparently deliberately deposited as an exotic votive object the axe had a well-preserved hawthorn shaft. The find from Shulishader on the Eye peninsula of eastern Lewis was dated to 2520 ± 95 bc (OxA-3537), c. 3389–2914 BC, with a midpoint around 3150 BC.[17]

The large megalithic ellipses of North Uist in the south of the island are unlikely to be as early. Each of them is near not to a Clyde chambered tomb but to a Hebridean type, Carinish, 43.1 × 39.8 m, is half a mile west of the long cairn of the same name. Loch a Phobuill, 39.6 × 35.1 m, is close to Craonaval with its tall peristaliths. And Pobull Fhinn, 37.8 × 28 m, by the lochside, is half a mile south-west of the fine Barpa Langass round tomb with its secondary beaker sherds. Such associations are interesting on two counts. The first is the atypical juxtaposition of tomb and circle as though antagonisms had been overcome. The second is that the circles by sea inlets are spaced about 1½ miles from each other and may have served areas but 320 acres (130 ha) in extent, areas that would have supported only a small agricultural population so that stock-breeding must also have been part of the economy of these people. Hints that this was so come from the bones of a calf, sheep or goat, and water fowl found at Rudh' an Dunain tomb, and the animal bones excavated at the Neolithic settlement at Northton on Harris. The large chambered tombs point to the needs of many people. In conclusion, all these rings and the ruinous Cringraval, about 36.6 m across but of uncertain shape, stand on low plateaux and have their long axes approximately east–west with the tallest stone at the east. Their unencumbered interiors, their size, shape and positions present unequivocal parallels with the circles of south-western Scotland.

These great ovals, their interiors averaging 823 m³, are almost five times as spacious as the four diminutive ellipses, 171 m³, near Loch Roag on the Isle of Lewis less than 50 miles to the north. Even including the larger Lewissean sites of Druim Dubh and Na Drommanan the North Uist rings still exceed their northern cousins by a factor of more than three. It is thought the Uist sites were for settled and large communities whereas those on Lewis were more comparable to transitory overnight stops on a Wells Fargo trail, backwater centres for a few natives and occasional seafarers.

The island of Harris and Lewis is known to have been settled since Neolithic times. Dates of 2461 ± 79 bc (BM-705), *c.* 3300–3050 BC, for birch forest clearance, and 1654 ± 70 bc (BM-706), *c.* 2100–1950 BC, for an oval beaker house have been recorded at Northton. Outside contacts are confirmed by finds of other beakers in the Hebrides, by a bowl from the North Uist habitation site of Eilean an Tighe exactly like others from the Orcadian tombs of Unstan and Mid Howe, and by the discovery of two Irish Group IX stone axes on Lewis.[18]

Lewis was noticeably different from North Uist. Chambered tombs and stone circles did not mingle there. Hebridean passage-tombs like Garrabost are on the east coast near or on the Eye peninsula where the Neolithic axe was found at Shulishader. The ellipses were built on the far western side of the island. The only convergence of tomb and ring occurred at Callanish when an intrusive and non-Hebridean tomb was inserted into an old megalithic oval.

The small oval rings cluster around the shores of Loch Roag, a rare and magnificent bay sheltered from Atlantic gales by the island of Great Bernera and providing safe beaching for crews on their voyage northwards. Along the western coasts tall standing stones announced the havens of safe landing-places.

At Loch Roag the sandy beaches and dunes give way to the machair, level stretches of rich, calcareous soil, before reaching the rocks and mountains of the interior and the area around Loch Roag was very attractive to prehistoric man. It is not surprising to find a group of circles here spread along 2 miles of the coast in the depths of the bay. None is more than half a mile from the sea. An exception is the one true circle of Achmore, a large inland ring 41 m in diameter, separated from the others 6 miles to its west.

There, Ceann Hulavig, once known as Garynahine, is an oval, 13.3 × 9.5 m, set NW–SE with a low central stone and cairn. Further north the largest surviving ring, Cnoc Ceann a' Gharaidh, formerly Loch Roag, is close to the seashore. It is an oval about 21.6 × 18.9 m on a north–south axis and has an eccentrically placed cairn. Just inland from it Cnoc Fillibhir is a concentric ring, 13.7 × 13.1 m in diameter, its inmost tall stones arranged in a NW–SE oval. All were built of the oldest rock in Britain, Lewissean gneiss, grey and streaked with thin, twisting lines of quartz like fine-grained wood. In these rings there appears to have been a preference for thirteen stones, an observation which has led to the suggestion that the number was arithmetically linked to the lunar months in a year.

Half a mile away, across a small bay, is one of the finest circles in Britain at Callanish. In recent years it has been ludicrously and linguistically misnamed 'Calanais' as though that were an ancient Gaelic form. It was not. Like many place-names on Lewis the original 'kalladarnes' was Old Norse, 'the headland from which a ferry can be hailed'. There is another 'Callernish' at a headland on North Uist.[19]

The thirteen unworked stones of Callanish (Pl. 42) form a small ring, 13.4 × 11.8 m, which with its thin pillars, chambered tomb, avenues and rows, has long excited the imagination since Martin Martin described it as 'ye Heathen temple' in 1695, wherein the Druid priest officiated by the imposing centre stone. Following the mid-nineteenth-century excavation by Sir James Matheson it has been seen as a deliberately despoiled astronomical observatory by Somerville; as a calendrical computer by Hawkins; as a fusion of burial and ceremonial architecture by Daniel; and by Thom as a lunar and stellar site susceptible to the most refined observations. Its chambered tomb has been well described archaeologically by Henshall; and its history excellently

Plate 42. Callanish, Lewis, Outer Hebrides (Photograph: Derek Simpson).

documented by the Pontings. A controlled excavation by Ashmore in 1980–1 found that the ring had been erected on an area of earlier arable cultivation, barley having been grown there in lazy-beds.[20]

The site is visible from a considerable distance for it stands on a promontory quite near the highest point where there is a rocky knoll. From the circle the waters of the surrounding lochs can be seen to east, west and north although the sea is almost totally hidden by higher land. The rudder-like pillar inside Callanish, almost 5 m high was quite probably erected as a navigational marker like the high seaside menhirs of Clach Mhic Leoid and Borvemore on Harris to the south and the 5.8 m tall Clach an Trustal stone 16 miles up the coast to the north-east, visible from a long way out at sea. The orientation of the Callanish stone does not respect the long axis of the ring and was originally probably a 'sailors' stone' with its broader face looking out to sea as a landmark.

The stones of Lewissean gneiss came, if local legend can be trusted, from a stone-strewn ridge near Loch Baravat a mile north-east of Callanish, perhaps close to the now-destroyed ellipse of Na Drummanan.[21] Even the largest, the central pillar 4.8 m high, weighs no more than seven tons and would have needed no more than thirty or forty workers to haul and erect it.

The tall stones are held upright in their holes by small packing-stones. The 'centre' stone is about 1.2 m north-west of the true centre and is at the back of a diminutive chambered tomb of Orkney-Cromarty type like the remote and tiny Nev Hill and Hona Hill on South Ronaldsay 150 sea-miles to the north-east beyond the dangerous waters of the Pentland Firth. The connection between them and Callanish is unexplained. Like them the Callanish tomb has a short passage and two little chambers divided by projecting slabs barely 0.9 m high.[22]

It was discovered deep beneath the peat in 1857 when only scraps of cremated human bone were unearthed from the chamber. It is accepted that the aberrant tomb is secondary much as some of the other Lewis cairns were added to circles, and just as the passage-tomb at Bryn Celli Ddu, Anglesey, was built over a circle-henge intimating that sometimes stone circles were deliberately altered or even destroyed by passage-tomb builders. Prehistoric destruction of circles is not unknown.

It is likely that despite being termed a flattened circle Callanish was intended to be an ellipse like its neighbours. It is noticeable that its tall central pillar is aligned north–south whereas the ring has a long NE–SW axis suggesting that the two are not contemporaries. If men planning to create an oval laid out a ring swinging a rope from the base of a venerable stone then, as the opposing arcs of the rope were extended to each side of the pillar, the ends of the rope would become shorter and shorter until they began to pull in on themselves. Where that occurred the two ends would be marked and the points connected producing a ring with a straightened side, one of Thom's flattened circles.

Running NNE from the circle is a damaged and slightly splayed avenue of high stones, 83 m long and terminating in two higher stones set at right-angles to the others like some of the 'blocking' stones at the end of the rows on Dartmoor. The western side of the avenue is higher than the eastern, a characteristic of the Irish 'high-and-low' double rows, something not surprising knowing of other Irish associations on Lewis. Also hinting at a dual phase of construction the tall stones decline in height away from the circle but then, halfway along, rise towards the terminal pillars as though an extension had been made to a shorter avenue.[23]

A single row of four stones leads exactly west for 9 m. Another, of five stones, extends 15.4 m towards the ENE; and what was probably intended as an avenue but is now a single row of five stones in a 22 m line leads southwards gently uphill towards the knoll of Cnoc An Tursa 91 m away.

Even on a drizzling day the stones straggle proudly along their ridge, stark against the western sky, and when the sun is shining the nearby houses hardly intrude upon the imagination, the setting of loch and hillside, sky and circle blend so indivisibly together.

Archaeologists have been taciturn about Callanish, seeing in it an enigma not easily solved by traditional methods. In contrast, astronomers have welcomed the challenge, finding in each stone row the possibility of a good celestial alignment. Toland believed the circle and its avenue were landscaped versions of the sun and the moon. Somerville thought the north avenue to be directed towards the rising of Capella, α *Aurigae*, between December and May in 1800 BC, the west row aligned on the equinoctial sunset, and the east on the Pleiades in 1750 BC. Hawkins observed that the latitude of Callanish is close to that at which 'the moon at its extreme declination remains hidden just below the southern horizon', and at Callanish the moon would appear just to skim the horizon each eighteen to nineteen years if looked at along the south row in 1500 BC. Thom commented on the re-erection of some avenue stones and showed that the south row was set out almost precisely towards the meridian, 180° 1′, that the east row could have been orientated on the rising of Altair, α *Aquilae*, in 1760 BC, and the NNE avenue on Capella in 1790 BC, although such a star at its rising would be so faint as to be almost unnoticeable. In a later work Thom added that an observer looking down the NNE avenue towards the SSW would have seen the moon's maximum setting along the slope of Mount Clisham 16 miles away on Harris.[24]

The avenue at Callanish does seem to define lunar and solar alignments. It is credible that these were intended by the Callanish people but it is almost unbelievable that references to the sightlines should exist in a first-century BC classical text, a reference first noticed by John Toland in the early eighteenth century. 'Particularly the great Iland of Lewis and Harries, with its apendages, and the adjacent Iland of Sky; which in every circumstance agree to the description that DIODORUS SICULUS gives of the land of the *Hyperboreans*.' Toland emphasised the Greek's references to harps, the moon, a round 'Temple', and the 'peculiar Dialect' of Erse 'which in every circumstance agree to the description' of Lewis.[25]

The Greek historian Diodorus Siculus, of Sicily, quoted from a lost history by Hecataeus of Abdera, a verse-chronicle with later interpolations.[26] It appears to claim that an early voyager, maybe Pytheas, sailing around northern Britain had seen a lunar 'spherical temple' on an 'island no smaller than Sicily'. In its path across the sky 'the moon as viewed from this island appears to be but a little distance from the earth' an event unique to the latitude of Callanish. Diodorus added that 'the god' visited 'the island every nineteen years', the 18.61-year cycle of the moon.

The latitude of 58° north is critical. Nowhere farther south in Europe could the major moon between its rising and setting seem to skim the horizon. It would rise much higher in the sky. Not until 58° south of the equator, around Cape Horn, does the same lunar phenomenon occur. A Mediterranean voyager, perhaps the legendary Pytheas, must have seen such a low moon at Callanish or some other 'spherical temple' at that northern latitude and to the writer's knowledge there is none in Norway or southern Sweden, just one or two megalithic rings in Scotland, Guidebest in Caithness, the Ring of Brodgar on Orkney, both of them several miles inland from the coast.

Stonehenge has repeatedly been identified as the 'temple' but this is wrong. Its latitude is five hundred impossible miles too far south for the moon ever to brush the skyline. Just as germane, the circle had been converted from a lunar to a solar monument at least 1700 years before the Greek voyager.[27]

Callanish, because of its latitude, and its lunar alignment is a better candidate for the monument that some adventurous seafarer saw. With his ship hugging the safety of the coasts of western Scotland, following its inlets, the tall stones of Callanish would have been as dramatically visible as they were to Alexander Thom over two thousand years later. In August 1933, he sailed into Loch Roag. 'We stowed sail after dropping anchor, and as we looked up there was the rising moon with the stones of Callanish silhouetted on it. I did not know how near we were to the main site of the Callanish megalithic monuments, the Stonehenge of Scotland.'[28] The same stark stones may have astonished a Greek crew.

The astronomy is enigmatic. Diodorus wrote that when 'the god [the moon] visits the island every nineteen years', it would dance 'continuously the night through from the vernal equinox until the rising of the Pleiades'. This has been considered astronomical nonsense because at the time of the Spring equinox the Pleiades were in conjunction with the sun 'and would rise unseen shortly after sunrise'.

Somerville's 1909 plan indicated alignments towards the Pleiades, to True South and to the equinoctial sunset. At Callanish the western row with an azimuth of 266° was aligned not towards the equinoctial sunrise but to the sunset, the slight WSW bearing being caused by the higher skyline to the north. Diodorus did not write that the Pleiades rose 'at' the Spring equinox but that the moon danced from the solar equinox 'until' the appearance of the lovely cluster of stars, 'The Seven Sisters'. They would first become visible 'at their dawn easterly rising, which coincided with Beltane, on May Day'. According to Frazer, 'In Hesiod's time Greek corn-reaping began on the morning rising of the Pleiades, which then answered to our 9th of May.'

However corrupt the chronicles of Diodorus Siculus they do appear to record that special significance was given to the period of five or six weeks between the equinox of late March and the beginning of May, the time for the planting of crops and the welcoming of the sun's returning warmth. The Pleiades, one of the most obvious of all stellar groups, have been observed and used world-wide by farmers because of their calendrical value, and 'in particular [people] have commonly timed the various operations of the agricultural year by observation of [their] heliacal rising or setting'.[29]

If the 'spherical temple' was not Callanish it is a remarkable coincidence that it was only the moon, the equinox and the Pleiades that Diodorus mentioned. Callanish seems associated with all of them. The avenue was directed towards the southern moonset; the eastern row was oriented on the equinoctial sunset; and although other stars are feasible targets the eastern row could have been aligned on the Pleiades, the third of the heavenly bodies specified by Diodorus.

Somerville's plan was somewhat inaccurate. A survey by Glasgow University's Department of Geography in 1974 amended the azimuth of the east row from 77°.8 to 76°.5. The new declination of 7°.8 meant that the Pleiades were rising in line with the ENE row around 1550 BC, c. 1375 bc. Excavations in 1980 and 1981 that recovered local Hebridean pottery, late beaker and grooved ware sherds and from which seven radio-carbon assays were determined, ranging from 2260 ± 50 bc (AA-24966) to 215 ± 50 bc (AA-249), c. 2900–2750 BC, suggest that the circle was erected in the later Neolithic around 2825 BC, the avenue added later, the three short rows even later around 1700 BC in accord with current thinking about their floruit. The 'astronomy' supports this. Implausible though it appears the words of Diodorus Siculus may contain memories of ancient rites that endured into the Iron Age long after 'peat started to form . . . in the earlier half of the 1ˢᵗ millennium BC'.[30]

There are other legends about Callanish.[31] They tell of a great priest-king, adorned with mallard feathers, who came to Lewis with a fleet and had the stones erected by black slaves, many of whom died. Another folk-story told of a nineteenth-century antiquarian who as a boy visited the island and met an old man in whose childhood people went to the stones secretly, especially at Midsummer and on May Day. 'His parents had said that when they were children people went openly to the circle but the Ministers had forbidden all that so now they went in secret for it would not do to neglect the stones . . . And when the sun rose on Midsummer morning "Something" came to the stones walking down the great avenue heralded by the cuckoo's call.'

A voice so thrilling ne'er was heard,
In spring-time from the Cuckoo-bird,
Breaking the silence of the seas
Among the farthest Hebrides.
William Wordsworth, *The Solitary Reaper*

The cuckoo is the harbinger of Spring, and its call may have become associated with the time of the Beltane May Festival.

The combination of ceremonial and astronomical practices at other sites has been suggested and it may be that such a fusion took place at Callanish. What is certain is that the construction, despite its complexity, contains only architectural traits well known elsewhere, its centre stone having a counterpart at Ceann Hulavig 2 miles away. Avenues are rarer in the north but 'high-and-low pairs of rows like those at Callanish are commonplace in the Sperrin mountains of northern Ireland at rings such as Beaghmore and Broughderg in Co. Tyrone, or Formil in Co. Fermanagh. With Irish porcellanite axes having been found in Lewis an Irish origin for at least part of Callanish is likely.

Callanish was probably never finished. Of the grandiose design involving a circle with four radiating avenues only the NNE avenue was completed. It is significant that these stones are nicely aligned downhill towards Tob na Faodhall, the Bay of the Ford. Legends associating stone circles with water are common.

Whereas there is no obvious association with water in earlier Neolithic ritual monuments like the chambered and unchambered long mounds or causewayed enclosures, there is a marked change in the later henges in which 'many of the sites have been chosen for their proximity to streams'.[32] Such a transference from the former hilly locales to low-lying situations may have been occasioned by the increasing importance of water in the religious practices of Late Neolithic and Early Bronze Age people.

Of the remaining structures at Callanish only one stone of the east side of the south avenue was put up. The south sides of the east and west avenues were completed, the other sides never started. That the project was abandoned and that these were not meant as single rows is indicated by the fact that the axial lines of the four intended avenues would have met at the circle-centre whereas the present single rows converge on a point well away from it.

Why the work was discontinued can only be speculated. Perhaps passage-tomb builders deliberately desecrated the circle as others had done at Bryn Celli Ddu. Prosaically people may have become discouraged by the work still to be done, or the death of a leader may have removed the driving-force for their labours.

Callanish today epitomises most of the problems connected with stone circles. Its shape, its centre stone, its intrusive tomb, its astronomical lines merge into contradictions that may be modern over-complications. We should, perhaps, view the circle and its avenues as the result of solitude working upon the religious fervour of people whose lives were limited by their own island. As has been said of the Maltese temple-builders, 'this lonely people . . . in the midst of a boundless sea under a boundless sky in a world without beginning and without end, royally free and yet captives, may have concentrated increasingly on the mystic realms of the hereafter'.[33] Born of this seclusion came a monument whose architecture made it as insular as the elongated island tombs of the Orkneys, its seeds gathered from distant sources, its conception nurtured in the long, uninterrupted days on the sea-wrapped Hebrides.

Northern Scotland

Despite the large number of Orkney-Cromarty chambered tombs in Caithness there are few megalithic rings whether large or small. It seems as though the builders of the Camster tombs of the Orkney-Cromarty group with their side-slabbed chambers would not erect circles. In the Orkneys both Maes Howe cruciform-chamber tombs and Camster mounds co-exist, but the only circles are near Maes Howe on the mainland, never on the outlying islands like Rousay where Camster stalled cairns predominate.

In Caithness the tombs outnumber the megalithic rings by a factor of $8:1$[34] but the pattern of distribution is similar to that on North Uist. Often a ring is close to a group of tombs and it is possible that they were the later foci for people in the locality. Aultan Broubster, Broubster and Dorrery stand against a score of tombs near Loch Calder. Achnagoul was erected at the heart of a smaller collection, including Garrywhin, near Dunbeath. But no ring is close to the famous Camster Round and Camster Long cairns nor to a concentration of tombs near Sordale Hill. The ceremonial relationship of circle to tomb here persists in obscurity.

There are few large rings here but those that do exist are enormous, three ellipses, two great circles, open rings in passes and with large stones at the west. They thus fall into the same category as the other ceremonial circles of the south and may owe their existence to their comparative nearness to the Atlantic route.

They are so vast that five of them: Achnagoul, Aultan Broubster, Dorrery, Forse and Guidebest, averaging $3184\,m^2$, are amongst the twenty largest rings in Britain and Ireland. They are three times more spacious than the huge ellipses on North Uist and the biggest of all, Achnagoul encloses $4354\,m^2$ and could have contained six Stonehenges or thirty-five Callanishes.

The best known of these giants is Guidebest, so close to the Burn of Latheronwheel that the river has cut away the ground up to the circle itself. This ruined ring, surrounded by gorse bushes and in an inconspicuous hollow of pasture land, is $57.3 \times 52\,m$ in diameter. It has its tallest remaining stone, $1.5\,m$ high, at the west on the very edge of the burn's high bank. A few stones of another large circle at Forse survive some miles from Camster. Yet others have been found by Leslie Myatt. As well as Achnagoul there is Aultan Broubster in the low land between Loch Calder and Forse Water to the west. It is $62.5 \times 53\,m$ and, despite being badly damaged, appears to be flattened to the north-east. The tallest stone, $1.0\,m$ in height, stands at the west. Small cairns have been built close to these circles. At Aultan Broubster there is even one near the centre but there is no reason to consider it any more than an addition. Another circle, Achany in Sutherland, half-sunk in peat, $26.8\,m$ across, forty miles south-west of Guidebest near Lairg, has five boulders still in situ on the circumference of what seems to be an oval in a remote glen by the Gruidie Burn. In shape and situation it is quite different from the large Caithness circles.

Of the smaller sites little can be said. Lack of proper excavation leaves it uncertain whether some might not be the ruinous kerbs of erstwhile cairns. Several of them like Aberscross, The Mound, have cists or cairns inside them. This obscure $7.3\,m$ circle has its most massive stone at the west and a tall, thin pillar opposite. Originally there were six stones, a number apparently preferred by the builders of rings in the region. Now the natural platform on which The Mound stands at the foot of Craigmore hill is half-covered in bracken and bushes, the hillside littered with boulders. Overhead, electricity cables stretch along the valley of the Fleet.

In May 1867, Lawson Tait cut an east–west trench across the site. At the exact centre there was a buried human cremation without pot or implement, the heads of a half-burnt humerus and radius showing it was an adult whose remains had been placed here on the covering slab of an oval stone cist aligned east–west. Despite evidence that this had never been disturbed it held only half a centimetre of rainwater on the rock bottom. Nor were there any deposits at the bases of two circle-stones. If anything had been interred in the circle the acidic soil had destroyed it.

Three widely dispersed sites in Sutherland, Auchinduich, Cnoc an Liath-Bhaild and Dallharraild, possess the feature not recorded elsewhere, except at the strange site of Bowman Hillock near Huntly, Aberdeenshire, and Maughanclea, Co. Cork, of having their stones set at right-angles to the circumference, surely another example of a local custom. These rings in their lonely river valleys are very small, not more than 9.1 m across, the first being a concentric.

Cnoc an Liath-Bhaild, a ruinous ellipse approximately 9.1 × 7.1 m around a now-gone 6.7 × 5.2 m, has the suspicion of a low cairn at its centre. A pronouncedly taller circle-stone stands at the west against a background of smoothed moorland hills. Note should also be made of the recent discovery of a questionable 12 m circle with massive central boulder at Clachtoll by the coast in western Sutherland.[35]

Two badly damaged circles, one ring-marked, stood on the eastern slopes of Learable Hill, Sutherland, in Strath Ullie, one of the infrequent passes between the east and north coasts. The circles are not remarkable but one stands near to a complex of standing stones, cairns, parallel and splayed rows.[36]

The stone rows of Caithness and Sutherland, which occupy roughly the same areas as the Orkney-Cromarty tombs, particularly around Lybster on the coast, differ from those of Dartmoor in one respect. Whereas the latter are always parallel those in northern Scotland may be either parallel or splayed. Yet they have common traits with those in Devon. They are on hillsides, often connected to an unencircled cairn or cist, and are built of unobtrusive stones unlikely to have been chosen as sighting devices. The settings contain as many as twenty-three rows at Mid Clyth and these, like their southern counterparts, are composed of several groups, usually in threes.[37] The orientations vary. With their short lengths, averaging about 34.7 m and their ankle-high stones they appear to be parochial variations as peculiar to the region as the megalithic horseshoe-shaped settings like Achavanich and Broubster, 15 miles apart in central Caithness, which too possess the local trait of having stones at right-angles to the perimeter. Another horseshoe setting, this time concentric, of hoary, moss-grown stones within two parallel rows, may have stood by the coast at Latheronwheel 5 miles south of Achavanich. It was shattered for dyke building a century ago.[38] Horseshoe settings in stone, timber or earth are known along the east coast of Britain from Caithness down to Norfolk where Arminghall's post structure was dated to 2490 ± 150 bc (BM-129), c. 3400–3000 BC.

There are many other horseshoes, 'fer-aux-chevaux', in Brittany from Tréguier in the north to Kergonan on the Ile-aux-Moines in the south. Solar and lunar alignments have been detected in them.[39]

In Britain Achavanich, 'the field of stones', by Loch Stemster is the finest and best-preserved of these unusual settings. Close to the pathetically damaged Camster cairn of Achkinloch it is a large site, 68.6 m long and with an open south-eastern mouth 26 m wide. These proportions are comparable to the great Caithness ellipses and it is arguable that that is what horseshoes, whether in Britain or Brittany, were, abbreviated forms of megalithic ovals from which one end had been truncated to make a clear-cut entrance. In Brittany, at Kerlescan and elsewhere a broad fer-à-cheval stands alongside an equally broad oval cromlech.

Achavanich possesses unusual features. Its impressive stones stand at right-angles to the circumference like jutting cogs, a rare custom but one that was used by the three small Sutherland circles. At Achavanich the stones on the east are taller than those on the west, a variant of the 'high-and-low' rows already noticed at Callanish and widespread in Ireland. It is also clear that as in Breton *fer-aux-chevaux* and at Stonehenge it was the curved head rather than the open end that was the focal point of the horseshoe. In most sites this was usually manifested by stones rising in height towards that position. At Achavanich there is no grading but a large cist was placed there just as rows on Dartmoor and in northern Ireland led uphill to a cairn or cist. Some of those rows were celestially aligned. At Achavanich whose long axis lay about 162°–342° towards a low skyline the site may have been laid out to be in line with the most northerly setting of the moon.[40]

Orkney

Only 8 miles of sea separate Dunnet Head, the most northerly point of the Scottish mainland, from the stark cliffs of Hoy, an island off south Orkney, but they are some of the most dangerous waters in the British Isles. Over the centuries raging waves have smashed deep ravines along the coasts of the Pentland Firth where the tidal races of Rispie and the Boars of Duncansby swirl and rush at ten overpowering knots.

To the south-east of Dunnet Head even today guidebooks warn, 'Boating. Very dangerous between Dunnet Head and Freswick Bay'. To the south-west of the Head at St John's Point with its nesting kittiwakes and petrels the Merry Men of Mey is the worst of these turbulences, a havoc of white water so terrifying that the Admiralty Guide reports that 'the extreme violence of the race, especially with w. or NW. gales, can hardly be exaggerated'. 'Even in fine weather there is a breaking sea . . . but with a westerly swell there is a terrific turmoil right across the firth'.[41]

Yet in boats hardly more than heavy canoes men from the Scottish mainland and from eastern and northern Ireland had been daring these hazards for a thousand years before two great stone circles were erected on Orkney in the years following 2800 BC. At this extreme of the Atlantic sea-route are the two most northerly circle-henges of Britain and Ireland, the Standing Stones of Stenness and the Ring of Brodgar, the third biggest of all megalithic rings.

Not one of the nine islands from South to North Ronaldsay has a stone circle, probably because on them are over fifty chambered tombs, mainly stalled cairns, fifteen on Rousay, nine on Eday. Only on Orkney itself are there megalithic rings, significantly constructed at the middle of a 9-mile line of five Maes Howe tombs from the Howe at the east to Quanterness. They are at the very heart of the island.[42]

Stenness and Brodgar stand a mile apart at the ends of a narrow isthmus dividing the lochs of Stenness and Harray. Both sites are impressive, Brodgar having a 103.6 m circle inside a rock-cut ditch 123 m in diameter, and Stenness a 61 m ditch around the remains of a probable ellipse, 32.3 × 30.6 m, aligned SSE–NNW.[43]

Both circles have stones of great size. Brodgar is in much better condition with many of its stones having been re-erected whereas Stenness has only four of its original twelve remaining. It is tempting but maybe misleading to see this site and Brodgar as separate meeting-places at the edges of social areas divided by the isthmus. To the contrary, what data are available indicate that the rings were successive, the larger taking over the rôle of the smaller as an increase in population demanded a more spacious enclosure.[44]

Which of the two is earlier is not proven although there are reasons to suppose that Stenness with its single northern entrance preceded the Ring of Brodgar, larger, farther to the north, with opposed entrances at north-west and south-east. Near Stenness are five Neolithic Maes Howe tombs but only a few Bronze Age round cairns. Differently, near Brodgar are only Bookan and the Stones of Via passage-tombs but some twenty round cairns and a long mound.

From their astronomical surveys the Thoms deduced that many of the cairns had been arranged to be lunar backsights to distant peaks and an improbable date of 1560 ± 100 BC, c. 1350–1150 bc, was calculated. Brodgar is unlikely to have been an observatory. The weathered, untidy mounds are not persuasive as meticulously devised celestial mechanisms and the 'targets' towards the minor positions of the moon, always difficult to detect, ten to its risings, four to its southern setting, are not convincing. It is only proper, however, to record that the entrances at Brodgar, centred on 127° and 307°, may also have been directed towards the minor moon, that at the south-east looking towards cairns F33 and F36 and the minor moonrise over Mid Hill three-quarters of a mile away.[45] More arguably, the propinquity of Bronze Age cairns around Brodgar and their scarcity at Stenness may be a coarse guide to the relative chronology of the two rings.

The argument is treacherous but the differences in the type of neighbouring monument and their own architecture in these Orcadian circle-henges, as well as their positions, point to Stenness as the earlier. Other evidence also favours this.

Quantitative analysis of the work involved and the size of the rings points to Stenness being the earlier. An estimated 14,100 m³ of rock was quarried from Brodgar's ditch but only 1,860 m³ from Stenness, a ratio of almost 8:1. Brodgar demanded 80,000 man hours contrasted with 12,500 man-hours at Stenness, a factor of over 6:1. The vastly different areas of the rings, 8,430 m³ inside Brodgar contrasted with the puny 760 m³ at Stenness, a factor of 11:1 demonstrates that Brodgar was intended for a much greater number of people.[46]

Radiocarbon assays also help. At the centre of Stenness excavation has uncovered a small stone rectangle of slabs edge-on in which a post had stood. To the north-west were two stone holes and, beyond them, the ploughed-out remains of a little timber construction with a date of 1730 ± 270 bc (SRR-592). Cremated bone was found. The two stones had later been deliberately pulled from their sockets and the holes backfilled. Radiocarbon determinations of 2238 ± 70 bc (SRR-351) from this area and of 2356 ± 65 bc (SRR-350) from animal bone in the ditch suggest Stenness was constructed late in the third millennium bc in the Late Neolithic, c. 3100–2775 BC, a period in keeping with the belief that such great circles are early in the history of megalithic rings. The damage to the stones and the removal of others may have resulted from prehistoric destruction of an old sanctuary when the new one, at Brodgar, was constructed some centuries later.[47] It was huge, capable of holding an assembly of some 1,600 people comfortably, well over ten times the capacity of Stenness.

From a ditch terminal at Stenness came some sherds of grooved ware. Such Late Neolithic pottery has been found in many ritual sites including early Wessex henges, and elsewhere in Orkney at Skara Brae only 6 miles to the north-west. But at Brodgar the sole finds during the restoration of 1906 and the very limited investigation of 1973 were a rough stone axe and a quartz hammerstone.

Brodgar has entrances at the south-east and north-west but Stenness has an apparent north–south axis similar to the meridional lines observed in other great circles.

Interestingly, particularly tall stones stand at west and south in Brodgar, also marking cardinal points. North-south, east-west, sunrise and sunset were seminal directions to the people of the Maes Howe chambered tombs, to the settlement of Barnhouse near Stenness and to Stenness itself. For years the magnificent 3 m-high Barnhouse pillar was known to record the sunset from Maes Howe ten days before the winter solstice.[48] What was not known was the existence of a Neolithic settlement comparable with the famous site of Skara Brae.

Dogs have been useful in archaeology. In 1940 in the Dordogne region of central France a little dog, Robot, fell down a pit which opened into the startling Palaeolithic art gallery of Lascaux. In the same year at Thame in Oxfordshire another dog scratching amongst weeds unearthed a Reformation hoard of ten silver groats and five gold rings. Over forty years later at Barnhouse in a field a little south-east of the ring of Stenness when archaeologists were despairing of finding anything more than flint scatters a dog became trapped in a rabbit burrow. Digging it out revealed the wall of a 'Skara Brae' type of house.[49]

Excavations beginning in 1986 uncovered fifteen houses with others still lying untouched, rectangular with round corners, narrow entrances, central hearths, dressers, beds. Phosphate analysis revealed intimate details of domestic life. In the beds to the left of the entrances there were traces of urine, hinting that this was where mothers with their infants had slept.

There was also a singular house over four times the average in size, containing no beds, only a hearth and a dresser. It had been kept scrupulously clean. One might speculate that this had been the dwelling of a head man or a building used as a meeting-place but it is equally feasible that it had been the sacred precinct of a priest concerned with a study of the heavens. At Skara Brae one 'house' could be locked only from the inside, and MacKie interpreted the entire settlement 'as the architecturally unusual residences of a specialist élite group supported by the agricultural population', likening the buildings to 'the monastic sites of the Early Christian period'.[50] The Barnhouse structure may also have been for arcane purpose for it was noticed that its long entrance passage with an external hearth had been set in line with the midsummer sunset.

In the settlement hearths and the sky went together. The sides of the oblong fireplaces were roughly aligned on the midsummer sunrise, in reverse also on the mid-winter sunset and, probably entirely by coincidence, the moon. Midsummer sunrise and midwinter sunset oppose each other everywhere but in the latitude of 58°.9 the midsummer sunrise and the minor rising of the southern moon occur almost at right-angles to each other, 39° and 129°, depending on whether the horizon heights are the same to north-east, south-east, south-west and north-west. They are not. There are low horizons of about 0.2° to the north-west and south-west but that to the north-east is more than twice as high, 0.5°, and to the south-east almost five times, 0.9°. This would not invalidate the belief that local people had aligned on the midsummer sunrise but not with precision.[51] The rectangularity of the hearths made the lunar 'alignment' an astronomical inevitability.

Just to the north-west of Barnhouse, inside the circle-henge of Stenness, there is another structure, a unique form of cove. It consists of two broad slabs in line and close together. A third slab stands a metre or so behind at the middle of the gap between them. It is identical to the projecting sideslabs and backstone of the chambers in the Unstan stalled cairn a mile to the west of Stenness. It is another instance of the transitional stage between the end of the chambered tomb tradition and the onset

Plate 43. Orkney. The Comet Stone with the Ring of Brodgar behind (Photograph: the author).

of stone circle building. Inferentially, the circle-henge at Stenness would have been erected around this ancient open-air assembly-place.

If Stenness and Brodgar do stand at the edges of their territories then it is significant that each has an outlier between it and the isthmus, at Brodgar the Comet Stone (Pl. 43) on a low platform 137 m to the south-east of the ring, the names coming from the belief that the completely circular Brodgar was a representation of the sun whereas the crescent of the imperfect Stenness was the moon.[52]

Outside Stenness the spectacular Watch Stone, 5.6 m high, stands at the narrowest part of the land. There once was a second outlying pillar. About 140 m north of Stenness there had been a large slab, Odin's Stone, 2.4 m tall, with a hole through it 1.4 m from the ground. It was destroyed in 1814 by a newcomer to the island. There had been other naturally perforated blocks in Orkney, one broken up on Papa Westray, fragments on Stronsay, heathen centres destroyed by ministers enraged that their flocks should go reverently to such pagan abominations. One clergyman on North Ronaldsay wrote that 'he had seen fifty of the inhabitants assembled there on the first day of the year, and dancing with moon light, with no other music than their own singing'. It was also said of Odin's Stone that when the moon was full a local farmer desiring to acquire magical powers went to the stone for nine months in succession, each time going nine times around the stone on his bare knees before making his wish while looking through the perforation. To Christian pastors such deplorable blasphemies had to be terminated.[53]

The discovery of a rough stone axe and a quartz hammerstone at Brodgar is a reminder that people using stone circles appear to have regarded the axe as a sun-symbol, a religious object to be used in their ceremonies. One may comment on 'the large number of broken axe-hammers found on Mainland in Orkney around the Stenness circles, suggesting that here too we may be concerned with a similar phenomenon of a Henge attracting the products of axe-factory sites'.[54]

The Shetland Islands

Many isolated and tempestuous miles of sea north-east of Orkney the emaciated islands of the Shetlands saw the emergence of an insular form of Neolithic chambered tomb, the heel-shaped cairn, oval with a deeply concave forecourt, in design like the houses of the living in the Shetlands. Over a score of these tombs are known from the south to the north of the islands, intermixing with simple box-like cists for the dead and with such a concentration it is predictable that stone circles in the Shetlands would be both few and strangely distorted versions of megalithic rings on the British mainland. Although seven are listed in the Gazetteer all are dubious.

The so-called stone circle of Haltadans or Hjalta-dans, 'the limping dance', is typical of the warped island architecture, an aberrant mixture of a megalithic ring and a chambered cairn. It is a 11.3 m wide ring of twenty-two large blocks on edge, 'rough serpentine boulders' of the locality. Within the circle is an earthen circle about 8 m across with a 1.5 m wide entrance at the south-west. Two tall stones stand at the centre. A characteristic compromise between open ring and burial-place it is feasibly interpreted as a denuded circular kerbed cairn built by people with vague notions of an open-air ring.

It is known locally as the Fairy Ring. There are opposing beliefs about the site. Some believe that the stones are girls petrified for dancing on the Sabbath. Others claim that the blocks are ugly, surly trolls who frolicked there in the moonlight until dawn turned them into stone. The pair of pillars in the middle are the fiddler and his wife. Five hundred metres to the NNW are three cairns with heavy kerbs known as the Fidlers Crus or enclosures.

Chapter Twelve

The Stone Circles of North-Eastern Scotland

They did see ashes of some burn't matter digged out of the bottome of a little Circle (sett about with stones standing close together) in the center of one of those monuments which is yet standing near the Church of Keig in the Shire of Aberdene.

James Garden to John Aubrey, 15 June 1692

Introduction

Whatever their architectural idiosyncracies until this part of the book stone circles have been interrelated, open rings for ceremonies that involved the sun, the lighting of fires, the carrying of axes, rituals of fertility held at special times of the year. Whether in Cornwall or in Caithness a fundamental commonalty appears, an underlying sameness about their use however much local variation might affect the designs. The sharpest difference arises from the recognition that the large, plain Late Neolithic rings probably encompassed rites by all the people, whereas from the beginning of the Bronze Age the smaller rings and their internal features imply a visual concentration upon one person, maybe a richly apparelled priest or headman.

But with the circles of north-east Scotland there is a different tradition with different architecture, with a restricted distribution around the Grampians, a tradition in which the deposition of the dead was an essential component.

It was the beginning of the second arm of the 'X' distribution described in chapter two. Apparently starting in north-eastern Scotland it more probably had its origins in the early Neolithic funerary traditions of eastern Ireland. Once established it covered 500 miles from north-east to south-west over a period perhaps as long as two thousand years, ending with the stone circles of Cos. Cork and Kerry, some of which may have been erected as late as 1250 BC. The architectural feature that distinguishes the Scottish rings is the presence on their circumference of a large, level block lying flat between the two tallest pillars of the ring, the recumbent and its flankers.

Recumbent Stone Circles

Clustered in the foothills of the Grampians along the coastal plain is a remarkable group of stone circles, the recumbent stone circles (RSCs) of Aberdeenshire and neighbouring counties (Fig. 22). These circles have a ring of stones graded in height, the two tallest set between the SSE and the south-west of the ring flanking the recumbent (Pl. 44). Inside the circle there may be a ring-cairn in whose central space human

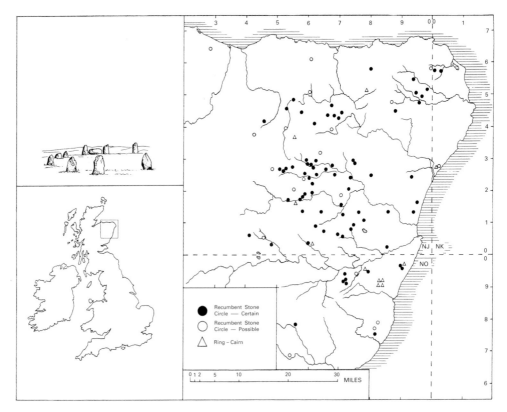

Fig. 22. The distribution of recumbent stone circles in north-east Scotland.

cremated bone was deposited. For centuries the unique recumbent stone has intrigued antiquarians.

Grading the height of stones was a form of architecture that was almost the norm among the RSCs of north-east Scotland and south-west Ireland. The Scottish historian, Boece, c. 1465–1536, knew of them. 'In the times of King Mainus . . . huge stones were assembled in a ring and the biggest of them was stretched out on the south side to serve for an altar . . . In proof of the fact to this day there stand these mighty stones gathered together into circles 'the old temples of the gods' they are commonly called – and whoso sees them will assuredly marvel by what mechanical craft or by what bodily strength stones of such bulk have been collected to one spot'.[1]

The circles do indeed evoke our marvel even today when, nearly five hundred years after Boece, we can normally see only tatters of toppled stones testifying to nineteenth-century demolition. Midmar was 'christianised' by being enclosed in a churchyard where it stands today. So was a ring near Kintore where the churchyard at Kinnellar 'has been the site of a Druidical temple, several stones of which of great size and weight, tho' fallen, yet remain above ground, and others have sunk in the earth. It is a matter of surprise by what process such weighty masses have been transported from such distance as they must have been,' wrote a minister in 1845.[2]

Some stones from Culsalmond were similarly 'depaganised'. Others were simply destroyed. In 1860 there was a large circle at Holywell, also known as Sunkenkirk, like Swinside in Cumbria. In the following year the tenant farmer hauled away 500 cartloads of small boulders. Two cists and an urn with cremated bone were dug out of its interior. The circle-stones were dragged off for barn foundations. One with at least thirty cupmarks was retrieved in 1879 and is now embedded in a stone wall at Tofthills farm. Nothing else survives.

Yet the group within a rectangle about 50 × 30 miles centred on Alford demands attention. The restricted enclave, the eccentric architecture, the consistent burials, the enigmatic relationship with the Cork-Kerry circles 500 miles away in south-west Ireland, provide the archaeologist and astronomer with substantial clues about their function and about the people who built them. Moreover, they and the related rings in central Scotland are the only group that quite regularly had dateable artefacts placed in them. Yet answers remain elusive.

It is frequently a problem to establish the original structure. Some circles have been destroyed. Most, like Wantonwells or Kirkton of Bourtie, have been catastrophically damaged. Sometimes, as at Nether Corskie, only the two flanking pillars are left like a half-dismantled Hollywood set. Or just the recumbent and flankers at South Ley Lodge, reminiscent of an elephantine head. Even where there are the stones of the outer circle at Rothiemay or Easter Aquorthies the smaller kerbs and stones of the cairn have gone. There are seventy-five confirmed sites with a further twenty-eight suspected. These are far from plain rings. They vary in their 'furniture'. Most have stones rising towards the ssw; there is a restricted range in the number of stones, nine to eleven plus the recumbent; some have cup-marks; there are scatters of quartz pebbles; ring-cairns; cremations; and pits with burnt material in the central space. But amongst all these features one is unique and dominant: it is the recumbent, often of a different kind of stone from the pillars of the ring, which makes these circles unique.

Sharples has drawn attention to the similarity of the recumbent and its flankers to early Neolithic timber mortuary structures like Pitnacree in Perthshire no more than

Plate 44. The prehistoric Midmar Kirk RSC in its twentieth-century churchyard (Photograph: the author).

70 miles south-west of central Aberdeenshire. They have been interpreted as 'a rectangular zone defined by two substantial timber uprights at each end . . . This created a subterranean timber box into which was placed human remains. The box was probably covered with a moveable timber lid'.[3] In recumbent stone circles the flankers would represent the upright posts and the prostrate block the timber coffin.

The analogy is attractive but weakened because if the solid recumbent was the megalithic equivalent of a wooden coffin corpses could not be interred there. They would have to be laid on it. For many recumbents this would be an impossibility. Some are too narrow. Others have a pronounced peak at their middle preventing anything from being set there.

If the origin of the recumbent does not lie with these wooden counterparts an answer may stem from the decorated supine stones outside the entrances of passage-tombs in the Boyne Valley of eastern Ireland. Outside Newgrange the Entrance Stone with its five enormous carvings of spirals was laid in front of the passage. At Knowth, a mile to the north-west a 3.1 m long stone decorated with concentric rectangles had been set outside the entrance. Architecturally these blocks have affinities with the coves known in some circles and henges, which have been visualised as skeletal versions of the box-like chambers in megalithic tombs.

Several of the smaller 'satellite' tombs around Knowth also have slabs blocking the entrance: Knowth 2, 4, 8, 13, 14, 15, 16, 17 and 18, Knowth 16 being dated to 2449 ± 67 bc (BM-1078), c. 3250–3050 bc, sufficiently early for the inauguration of the recumbent stone tradition in Scotland to begin around 3000 bc.[4]

Contacts between north-east Ireland and north-east Scotland are well attested during the third millennium bc. Lyles Hill pottery has been found in Aberdeen cairns like East Finnercy. More tellingly still, there are eighty known Group IX axes from Tievebulliagh, Co. Antrim, in Scotland. Significantly, they are distributed along the south-east route through Scotland via Loch Lomond, central Perthshire into the Grampians where over a score are known, eighteen of them in Aberdeenshire.[5]

There are 'entrance stones' along the route between the Boyne Valley and north-eastern Scotland. North of Newgrange the Irish stone circle at Clogherny Butterlope, Tyrone, has a supine stone at the east. It is possible that once this stood erect but a significant number of white pebbles were found by it. Kiltierney in Co. Fermanagh also had a recumbent stone. Prostrate stones analogous to those in Ireland are also to be found outside the 'entrances' of some Scottish cairns and stone circles: Auchagallon on Arran and Torhousekie in Wigtownshire. At Kintraw in Argyll a 14.6 m cairn had been covered in brilliant white quartz crystals very much like the sides of Newgrange. Set in its graded kerb was a blind south-west entrance of projecting stones. Two metres away lay a long stone. At Culcharron, 20 miles north of Kintraw at the mouth of Loch Linnhe, a small cairn with graded kerbs had a blind entrance at the ssw beyond which stretched a cupmarked stone, 1.8 m long, parallel with the kerb. Quartz chippings had been strewn around the stone. Croft Moraig stone circle by Loch Tay on the direct route to Aberdeen has an outer bank at the ssw of which lies a 2.1 m-long cupmarked stone. Many quartz pebbles were discovered in the circle.

On the reasonable assumption that the 'supine stone' custom reached northeast Scotland from Ireland an RSC can be seen as a combination of traditions, that of the plain stone circle coming together with the intermixing of settlers, traders and incomers in the first centuries of the third millennium. The fusion of this tradition with that of placing a prostrate stone at the entrance to a ritual monument could have been

Plate 45. The uncouth block of the Carlin Stane, a half-forgotten version of a recumbent stone (Photograph: the author).

the origin of the characteristic RSC, the first of which may have been the primary megalithic monuments in this part of Scotland, 'concentrated in areas with strong Neolithic presence'.[6]

Indeed, it is possible that in some cases the recumbent and flankers were erected but had no stone circle added to them. There are no circles at Auchmallidie, Braehead, Cairnton, Clochforbie, Druidsfield, Dunnideer, Nether Corskie, South Ley Lodge, Wantonwells. Potterton may be another example.

If there were a coalescence of recumbent and ring it is likely to have been in the low foothills around Alford. Here there seem to be the earliest RSCs, their graded stones set around a perfect circle from 18.2 m to 24.4 m in diameter with tall flanking stones alongside a recumbent 4 m or more long, usually placed between south-west and south. Often there was an inner ring-cairn. Later RSC-builders occupied peripheral areas to north, east and south down to the River Dee. These smaller rings, sometimes distorted, are composed of lower, ungraded stones and, peculiarly, the recumbent and its pillars were frequently placed not only well inside the circle and attached to the cairn but also set between south and SSE. Such sites as Garrol Wood or Auchquhorthies are very different from the 'classical' RSCs like Cothiemuir Wood or Castle Fraser on its long hillside.

The most grotesque of these distortions still stands at Cairn Riv near Turriff where the recumbent tradition was almost literally turned upside down and sideways. The enormous and bulbous 14-ton, 2.6 m-high Carlin Stane (Pl. 45), 'the old hag's pillar', rises between two much lower, slighter blocks only 1.3 m and 60 cm high respectively. The experienced Fred Coles understood the weird transformation: 'This boulder, unshapely and most unusual in height, should be accepted as the Recumbent Stone of the Circle that certainly once existed here.'[7] It was the final deformity of a long-established but ultimately no longer comprehended tradition.

Altogether in widely separated districts of north-east Scotland: Insch, Old Deer, Midmar and others, there may have been about fifteen RSCs initially. With developing land-clearance and productivity it is likely that the population gradually expanded and might have caused over any century an increase of 50 per cent in the numbers of RSCs built by migrants whose ancestral territories could not support the extra people. Such an increase, slow at first, would accelerate so that after 500 years there would have been well over a hundred circles. In 1911 Alexander Mackie in his

Aberdeenshire claimed that 175 circles were known of perhaps an original two to three hundred. Good records of over a hundred still survive, a mixture of well-preserved, mutilated and demolished rings.

Half of the RSCs would be of increasingly aberrant forms. It is instructive to find that many of these putatively late sites do lie at the extremes of RSC country and to realise that even before outlying rings like Garrol Wood were being constructed some of the earliest RSCs could have been abandoned because of the deterioration of the soil *c.* 2000 BC after several centuries of exploitation.

By the mid-second millennium in Britain there can have been few vast areas left of unused, fertile, easily worked soil. Once a whole district had been settled any large band of migrants had few options: forcibly to take over land already occupied; to split into family groups that might search for unexploited glens and uplands; or to travel together to distant, hitherto unexplored parts, something that might be forced on them by the hostility of other people reluctant to allow strangers to settle on their borders. Trade and prospecting for stone and metal ores had extended the knowledge of seaways to most parts of the British Isles including the undeveloped countryside of south-west Ireland. Some RSC groups may have journeyed here. Others drifted into southern Scotland or northern England. Yet others mixed with neighbouring people of different beliefs, and monuments lacking a recumbent stone but strongly influenced by RSC customs were built.

At Berrybrae and Strichen there was prehistoric vandalism. Stones were smashed or toppled, cobbles of the ring-cairn became a bank covering the ruined stone circle. Charcoal from it gave dates of 1500 ± 80 bc (HAR-1849) and 1360 ± 90 bc (HAR-1893), *c.* 1900–1550 BC. The grotesquely hideous N3 beaker found with the charcoal suggested that Berrybrae had been converted into an enclosed cremation cemetry by intrusive beaker and food vessel users. At Strichen a hut-circle, dated to 1140 ± 60 bc (BM-2316), *c.* 1470–1350 BC, was erected by newcomers inside the ring.[8]

Within the rough rectangle of 140 square miles at the middle of the RSC lands there are at least twenty-eight RSCs. Most are Late Neolithic. If ten belong to the period of colonisation the total population then might have been some 500–800 people, virtually a sub-tribe. This demographic hypothesis can partly be tested by examining the RSCs around Old Deer near the River Ugie in Buchan, north-east Aberdeen, to see if the proposed populations are compatible with the numbers needed to build the rings. The seven sites might have had as many as three to five hundred men, women and children, perhaps eighty or more able-bodied labourers. The rings lie in a triangle of 17 square miles, the farthest only 8 miles apart. They are related by their characteristic stony banks which are possibly transitional between ring-cairns and the low banks of enclosed cremation cemeteries.

Loudon Wood, a circle 18.5 m across, and Strichen, 12.1 × 11 m, were possibly the primary rings in the area with a joint population of about 120 people at most. Loudon Wood's recumbent stone, 3.1 × 1.2 × 1.2 m, weighed no more than twelve tons and could easily have been moved up its slight hillside by forty people. Flecks of charcoal, sherds of coarse pottery, quartz fragments and deposits of cremated bone suggest that the activities at Berrybrae were essentially no different from those in the earliest RSCs of previous centuries.

Assumptions about the development of architectural forms are untrustworthy but the fact that the theoretically later RSCs do occupy outlying districts whereas the earlier are central offers some corroboration of this morphological frame-

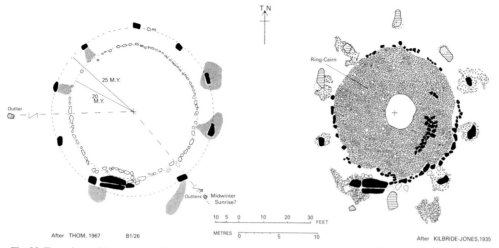

Fig. 23. Two plans of Loanhead of Daviot recumbent stone circle, Aberdeenshire (Grampian).

work. Artefacts provide firmer props. From early RSCs came some early pottery. Loanhead of Daviot had Neolithic and AOC beaker sherds. Old Keig and Old Rayne also had fragments of beaker, often in secondary positions, the latter site containing a fine archer's wristguard of pale green polished stone, broken in half but still showing the three perforations for its wrist-binding. It was most probably associated with an N/MR beaker of about 2400 BC or later. In contrast, the later RSCs have no early material, only pieces of coarse urn or perforated axe-hammers of the mid-second millennium.

At Loanhead of Daviot (Fig. 23), a finely preserved RSC now in state care, Late Neolithic round-based pottery including Irish-derived Lyles Hill ware was found, a combination that points to a construction date not long after 3000 BC. Elsewhere coarse flat-rimmed bucket-shaped pots were produced over as long as a thousand years so that discovery of these plain sherds at Loanhead is not chronologically helpful. Nor are the fragments of a 'clay urn with incised decoration' at the tiny quartz RSC of North Strone, or the urns of 'thick massive paste' at Castle Fraser except to suggest a crude terminal date in the mid-second millennium for the later circles. It must suffice, with our present knowledge, to say that RSCs were being erected in north Scotland between about 3000 and 1500 BC.

For the builders of these circles it is clear that it was the recumbent stone that was of the greatest importance. Despite the care apparently put into some features of RSC construction the circle itself was regarded as no more than an enclosure demanding little care in its construction. Once the three major stones had been carefully set in place, perhaps with the co-operation of neighbouring families, the recumbent being too heavy to be moved by just a few adults, the circle was often added later in a more casual fashion.

Many of the earliest circles in the heartlands around the Bennachie hills stand on the 105 m contour on the protected southern slopes of soft hillsides. Although nearest-neighbour analysis shows an apparently random distribution each circle seems to have its own territory, several with long river frontages and with an overall area, including steep wooded hillsides, of about 4 to 6 square miles. Within these are deep pockets of well-drained, fertile, sandy loam and brown earths, patches of 74 to 200 acres, an average 125 acres being capable of supporting about sixty people if their economy were supplemented by hunting and stock-grazing in the woodlands and clearances. The RSCs are invariably close to but never on these rich soils.

There is a fascinating piece of testimony to long-lasting folk-memory about the choice of these sites. On 15 June 1692, writing about the RSC of Auchquhorthies in Kincardineshire, James Garden informed John Aubrey that 'There was a tradition that Pagan priests of old dwelt in that place [Auchincorthie]' and 'that the Priests caused earth to be brought from other adjacent places upon peoples backs to Auchincorthie, for making the Soile thereof deeper, which is given for the reason why this parcel of land (though surrounded with heath and moss on all sides) is better and more fertile than other places thereabout'. It was unknowing testimony to the excellent judgement that prehistoric people made when seeking good land.

Nothing is known of their settlements. Hut-circles in the neighbourhood of RSCs such as Huntly, Culsalmond, Wheedlemont, Potterton and others are unexcavated and undated and could well be a thousand or more years later than the rings.[9]

Several considerations affected the choice of a site: the nearness of land suitable for growing crops; the availability of stone; and the need for a view to a far horizon. Many RSCs were built on hill-shoulders where the few trees that interrupted the horizon could easily be felled. Today a distant circle is often visible from lower ground but in antiquity forested valleys would probably have obscured a site whose present conspicuous position could be a phenomenon never considered by its builders.

Generally a secondary consideration was the availability of stone. At Dyce the stones came from a nearby quarry. At Hatton of Ardoyne there is an outcrop 45 m away. At Old Keig and Auchquhorthies the stones are presumed local. At Whitehill, however, the reddish porphyritic pillars were dragged from their hill-shoulder source to the spur on which they now stand and this task, involving much difficulty, shows that the position of the circle was of major importance.

So was the bulk of the recumbent. At many sites it is petrologically different from the other stones and had sometimes been brought from afar. It does not follow that this was for ritual reasons. Such a massive block might not be available locally. At Dyce, Loanend, Auchmachar, Easter Aquhorthies and several other RSCs the recumbent is 'foreign', the Old Keig stone coming from somewhere in the Don valley 6 miles away. This block of sillimanite gneiss is gigantic, $4.9 \times 2.1 \times 2.0$ m, and weighs about fifty-three tons. Though much of the journey from source to circle was over flattish ground the final haul had to be made uphill for nearly half a mile at a gradient of 1:14. This must have demanded the strength of well over a hundred people, an effort involving several communities for the occasion. At Balnacraig the recumbent weighs fifteen tons like those at Balquhain and Cothiemuir Wood. At Dyce and Kirkton of Bourtie they weigh twenty-four and thirty tons respectively. It is clear that the circle-builders were obsessed with the need for an impressive stone.

They were also determined to have the upper surface of the stone horizontal. Experiments with a ranging-pole and a long spirit-level have shown that the recumbent is almost exactly level, the one exception amongst the eleven sites examined, Easter Aquorthies, being at a ring where the recumbent stone has tilted forwards. At rings such as Loudon Wood, Midmar Kirk, Old Keig and Aikey Brae where the bottom of part of the block is visible it is possible to see how the neatly horizontal top was achieved.

Plate 46. Midmar Kirk recumbent stone and flankers. Chockstones can be seen supporting the tapering base of the recumbent (Photograph: the author).

Recumbent stones were not rectangular but had tapering bases (Pl. 46). Once dragged into its pit the narrower end of the block could be levered up and down. By placing a water-filled vat on the stone the workers would raise or lower the end of the slab until no water spilled from the container. Then small boulders and large stones were jammed beneath the sloping base so securely that even thousands of years later the recumbents have remained horizontal. What remains unclear is why the work was undertaken. From the interior of the ring the recumbent does not form an artificial horizon because usually the natural skyline rises above it.[10]

The smaller, local circle-stones caused little problem either in transportation or in erection although care was taken in the early sites to ensure the heights were graded down from the recumbent. In those rings the preferred number of stones was often ten or eleven plus the recumbent itself irrespective of the length of the circumference. In later circles such as Candle Hill, Insch, there could be as few as nine. Only North Strone has more than thirteen.

Once at the site some stones were 'dressed'. This is especially true of the flankers where it is easy to see how they were shaped to fit the configuration of the recumbent. The beautifully smoothed pillars at Cothiemuir Wood or at Midmar belie their Victorian description of 'rude stone monuments'. The bases of many stones were 'keeled' or stone-hammered into a rough beak to facilitate their tipping and erection.[11]

Some of the central RSCs had a couple of stones projecting behind the recumbent, a feature sometimes known as a platform but which may be a representation of the passage in a chambered tomb. Still more have the remnants of a bank in which the circle-stones were set. Aikey Brae on a little hilltop has a well-preserved bank. Other banks up to 3 m wide and 1 m high have been recorded at Old Keig and Sunhoney. Aikey Brae, with no trace of an inner cairn, was the only excavated RSC to have no deposit of cremated bone at its centre. Long before 1881, 'during a long summer day', labourers delved nearly 2.4 m into the centre of the circle but there was 'no trace of evidence that the soil had ever before been disturbed'. It is said that 'the party only stopped digging when bedrock was struck'. Archaeology was fun in those enthusiastic days. Numerous small cairns around the RSC were also vainly demolished 'and the day closed without any trace of graves'. Charles Dalrymple who oversaw this operation plunged into the hearts of at least five other RSCs in the mid-Victorian decades.[12]

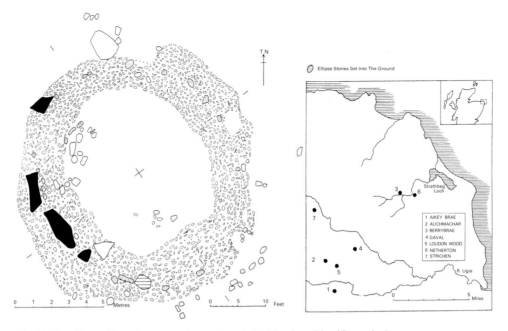

Fig. 24. The ellipse of Berrybrae recumbent stone circle, Aberdeenshire (Grampian).

Not only was the top of the recumbent made horizontal. It is known that at some circles such as Castle Fraser and Loanhead of Daviot the site was levelled. At Nether Balfour, a ring dug away and destroyed around 1845, an observer noticed that 'the ground on which the circle stood was sloping, and within the circle it had been levelled by removing the earth on the upper side, so as to present a bank nearly perpendicular, of not less than five feet [1.5 m], gradually decreasing to the east or lower part, where it became level'.[13]

Then the circle was laid out. Nearly all the rings were truly circular and it may be presumed that the plan required nothing more than a central stake and a rope to inscribe a ring around it. A radius of 9 m to 12 m would cause no appreciable eccentricity through the dragging of the radial rope over rough ground. There is, however, no proof of a standardised measuring-rod being used. Multiples of Thom's Megalithic Yard of 0.829 m vary from fourteen at Ardlair to thirty-four at Rothiemay with no significant peaking around any number. The unit, moreover, seems too long. At fifteen of the seventeen measured RSCs the diameters fall short of the suggested M.Y. multiple, the deviations ranging from −36 mm at Yonder Bognie to −39 cm at Easter Aquorthies with an average discrepancy of −18 cm or 1/5 M.Y. The relevant sites are Bl/5, 1/6, 1/18, 1/23, 1/26, B2/1, 2/2, 2/3, 2/4, 2/6, 2/26, 2/17, 3/1, 3/7, 4/4. Only Westerton and Esslie the Lesser, BI/ 16 and B2/5, have diameters exceeding it.

Interestingly, the perimeter of the elliptical Berrybrae (Fig. 24), 13 × 10.7 m, using Thom's formula for calculating its length, is the product of 2.8658 multiplied by the long axis of 13 m = 37.45 m or almost exactly 18 Megalithic Rods of 2.07 m, an error of less than 19 cm in almost 13.5 m. Unhelpfully, other RSCs in the same region, all of them true circles, show little conformity with the megalithic yard. Although Netherton with a diameter of 17.4 m is 20.99 M.Y., Aikey Brae is 17.4 M.Y., Loudon Wood, 22.4 M.Y., and Strichen 17.6 M.Y.[14]

One strange feature of a few circles to the east of the Correen Hills near Alford is the reputed presence of a causeway leading to the site on the side opposite the recumbent, the readily recognisable sandstone slabs probably coming from a source at Terpersie a few miles away. These RSCs within 6 miles of each other are on the extreme west of the enclave. At Crookmore, atypically in a hollow, the causeway led from the north-east. The Clatt circles of Bankhead and Hillhead also had lengths of paving, the latter of stones 'so close that it was difficult to put in the pick'. At Nether Balfour there 'were remains of about 20 yards [18.3 m] of road paved with flat stones, evidently leading to the circle from the NE'. All these causeways were unarchaeologically stripped in the mid-nineteenth century so that the accounts are not reliable, but their consistent position around the north-east suggests a relationship with the north-east approaches at some of the Cork-Kerry MSCs of south-west Ireland where there had been constant trampling of the soil around the portalled entrances of recently excavated circles.[15] Dowsing at Tomnaverie has given hints of an avenue.

One facet of these complex rings that has hardly been commented upon because it became apparent only when centuries of accreted grime and lichen were removed from the stones of Easter Aquorthies was that its builders had been very conscious of colour. The stones on the west were pink porphyries, those on the east dark grey, except for the one against the east flanker which was a red jasper. Both the flankers were light grey whereas the recumbent was a deep red granite block from the Bennachies, its gently smoothed outer face striated with veins of quartz.

So conscientiously had the colours been arranged, as at Castle Fraser, that it appears a form of symbolism of a nature like that in the two passage-tombs of Balnuaran of Clava, Inverness, where the backstones of the burial-chambers were a deep red. At Easter Aquorthies the vestigial remains of a ring-cairn and probable cist are reminders that death was present there also.

White was another required colour. Quartz is commonplace in RSCs but not indiscriminately scattered. The local mineral provided an impressive 3 m-high outlying pillar just to the south-east of Balquhain. The 'dolls' house' of North Strone had ten of its pygmy stones of quartz, four were pinkish and two were grey granites. At Berrybrae quartz was strewn densely on the platform against the inner face of the recumbent. At Strichen its broken fragments had been spread in a wide crescent on the far side of the ring from the recumbent where it would have glowed luminously at the times of full moon. It is to be wondered whether those moonlike bits were thought to be pieces from the moon itself, bonding the stone circles with a place of death.[16]

Having set out the circle the recumbent was levered into its hole on the chosen part of the circumference, and this statement carries with it a plague of controversy. So consistently is the recumbent stone in the south-west quadrant of the circle that its position must have been deliberately chosen, most probably decided by the astronomical superstitions of its labourers. RSCs have been studied for this possibility. Eighteen years after A. L. Lewis in 1888, Lockyer predicated some alignments on either Capella, *α Aurigae*, or Arcturus, *α Boötis*. A speculative farrago in 1921 by Bishop Browne, added May Day, midsummer and midwinter to the unlikely candidates. Thom found little of moment in the circles although the orientations he did note for four rings were either solar or lunar.[17]

All these suggestions were unconvincing. Preoccupied with risings and settings every investigator, including this writer in 1976, was misled. Of the known RSCs in Scotland almost forty, a statistically strong number, are sufficiently undamaged for their azimuths or compass-bearings to be determined. The midpoints of the recumbent stones all lie between 157°.5, SSE, at Garrol Wood at the south-east of the RSC territory, and 235°.5, south-west, at Tomnaverie at the far west. The fact that these extreme azimuths occur in circles at the very edges of the distribution of RSCs is yet another indication of the 'pebble-in-a-pond' development of these rings.

Over four in five azimuths of RSCs lie between 160° and 210° far south of where the midwinter sun or southerly midsummer moon would rise or set. Three are above 230° well to the north of the midwinter sunset.[18] No star or planet can be fitted to all the azimuths. Capella rose and set along the northern horizon, not the south. Although around 2500 BC Rigel, β Orionis, and Sirius, α Canis Majoris, did set around 225° they both moved northwards away from the RSC alignments in the following centuries. The lengthy and complicated cycle of Venus was too far to the south to explain the azimuths around 230°.

This elimination of solar, lunar, stellar and planetary risings and settings implies either that no astronomical considerations dictated the location of a recumbent stone or that risings and settings of celestial bodies are irrelevant to the problem. The answer was very simple and discovered by the writer in 1980 when he realised the significance of the southern moon's cycle.

The four arcs of the northerly and southerly risings and settings of the moon were explained in chapter three, [87–8], varying in width from latitude to latitude. In north-east Scotland the major southern moon with a declination of −29°.177 in 3000 BC would have risen as far south as 155° and set at 205° on a horizon at eye-level with the circle. A hilly skyline of 3° could reduce this arc to as little as 172° to 198°. Over the nine following years the risings and settings of the moon moved farther to the north until at its minor positions its extremes were about 127° for rising and 233° for setting. Having reached these minima it then returned year by year to its major risings and settings, the entire cycle taking 18.61 years. 'God, what a dancing spectre seems the moon,' admired George Meredith.

Amazingly, four centuries ago Boece knew of the connection between the recumbent, the moon and human cremation. 'The biggest [of the stones],' he wrote, 'was stretched out on the south side to serve for an altar, whereon were burnt the victims in sacrifice to the gods'. The ritual included a monthly sacrifice and 'that is why the new moon was hailed with certain words of prayer, a custom which lingered very late' as though people were still going to the circles in historic times.[19]

The azimuths of the RSCs lie between 157°.5 and 235°.5 with a wide gap between 220° and 231°. This suggests that the recumbent blocks were often laid in line with the southern moon not at its rising or setting but when it was up in the sky. For believers in scientific archaeoastronomy this presents a difficulty. In Aberdeenshire thirty-four well-preserved RSCs have an average diameter of 18.6 m and a recumbent some 3.4 m long. Such dimensions result in a 10° wide 'window' from the east to the west flanker when seen from the far side of the ring and over 21° wide from the central space of the ring.

On occasion such a broad 'sightline' was refined by the choice of a recumbent with a pronounced peak at the centre of its top or, more rarely, with a deep depression like a gunsight. Such stones are exceptions. To the users of the circles it may have been the steady procession of the moon above the recumbent that was wanted rather than a particular moment, minutes of moonlight when quartz glowed luminescently and when nocturnal ceremonies were performed.

The majority of the recumbents lie in the arc between the moon's major rising and setting but four face the area where the minor moon was descending. One reason for this unusual, and elusively difficult alignment being chosen can be explained at the adjacent RSCs of Sunhoney and Midmar Kirk. Just over a mile to their south-west Craigour mountain rose 260m above them, the angle of the skyline, more than 7° high, so steep and close that the major southern moon never appeared above it.

The sun was almost entirely disregarded by the builders of these rings. Midwinter sunrise around 139° was well to the north of 157°.5 and its setting near 222° occurred in the wide gap between the moon's major and minor settings.

Different regions reveal individual preferences. In central Aberdeenshire just north of the landmass of Mither Tap and the Bennachie range many of the RSCs have azimuths just to the west of due south when the moon was highest in the sky. A few miles to the west where the fine RSCs of Castle Fraser and Cothiemuir Wood are to be found there is a greater concentration on the major moonset.

Far to the north-east in the Buchan corner of the county the orientations are to either side of due south. These rings seem late. Aikey Brae, on a hilltop, is a ring 16.6 × 12.8 m in diameter, aligned 185.5°. Berrybrae, excavated by the writer between 1975 and 1978 is an ellipse with its recumbent exactly on the short axis at 231° in line with the minor southern moonset. Loudon Wood had its recumbent at 184°; and Netherton, 185°. In the early nineteenth century the RSC at Strichen had been mistakenly re-constructed with its recumbent apparently at the north. It had formerly lain at the SSE, 161°. In Kincardineshire, south of the River Dee, it was the rising moon to the east of south that was chosen. These circles are generally small with ungraded stones and with recumbents placed well inside the circumference of the circle.

There are clues that builders of RSCs first decided upon the alignment and then positioned the recumbent to be in line with it. In many cases that stone and its flankers do not stand on the perimeter of the ensuing ring but at an erratic angle inwards from it, rarely at a right-angle to the ring's centre, as though after an initial dedicatory ceremony a rope had been stretched from an arbitrary centre and scraped out a circle that usually started at the west flanker. It is also noticeable that the even later internal ring-cairn often has a centre different from the stone circle.[20]

Some RSCs have cupmarked stones and these stand in celestial positions. They occupy only a limited range of five stones from the pillar east of the east flanker to the stone west of the west flanker, the majority being on the recumbent stone itself.[21] Arnhill had two cupmarks there in line with the major moonset. Balquhain had one on the same target, four on the east flanker to the major moonset and twenty-five on the stone west of the west flanker towards the minor moonset. Braehead had four on the recumbent also linked with the minor moonset; Cothiemuir Wood's recumbent had three or four towards the major moonset; Loanend two on the recumbent and the minor moonset; Loanhead of Daviot, twelve on the east flanker, idiosyncratically on the midwinter sunrise; Sunhoney, thirty-one on its recumbent, all of them concentrated on the eastern half of the slab, in line with the minor moonset.

Most copious of all was Rothiemay in Moray. Two stones were decorated on this mutilated ring. Two were on the stone east of the east flanker, calculated to be in line with the major moonrise; and an amazing one hundred and nineteen, including a cup-and-ring mark, were carved on the ponderous recumbent in line with the major moonset.

A mile to the south-west of Rothiemay on the Hill of Avochie there is a massive block whose dimensions of 3.4 m long, 2.7 m wide and about 70 cm high suggest that it is a recumbent whose circle-stones have been removed. It may have faced ssw. On its surface are over sixty cups and sixteen cup-and-ring markings.

Added to these archaeological uncertainties are the human beings themselves, subject to all human frailties, idleness, forgetfulness, indifference, misunderstanding, incompetence. A stone circle affected by any of these circumstances would have errors that cannot be realised but which inevitably ruin neat analyses. With resignation researchers must acknowledge that perfection is unachievable.

When the embanked stones and the recumbent fenced off an open space, the builders performed the first rituals under the midsummer sky, setting up a large crib of wood either in or just outside the circle, a corpse being beneath it. The pyre was lit. Fanned by the wind the fire flamed and flared until everything was transmuted into split and splintered bones, charcoal and ashes. The wide patches of burnt earth at Loanhead of Daviot, Old Keig and Hatton of Ardoyne with its reddened stones demonstrate the heat of the blaze. Carefully the bone-fragments were collected and, at Loanhead, one piece of bone, one broken sherd and one lump of charcoal were deposited in a small pit alongside the burnt-out pyre. Then, keeping the other human remains separate, the rest of the pyre and pottery, perhaps deliberately broken, was religiously buried by the circle-stones. The customs in RSCs suggest the cremations were dedicatory offerings rather than burials.

It is possible that a small rectangular timber structure at the centre of Loanhead of Daviot was the focus of the ceremonies during the early years of the stone circle and that the ring-cairn was a much later addition. It may have been a "mortuary house" whose four shallow holes lie at the corners of a rectangle 1.2 × 0.6 m arranged NW–SE at the very middle of the central space. These holes were extremely shallow but this may be because the pit was subsequently cleaned out by the people who built a fire in the south–east corner.

In his excavation at Old Keig Childe noticed comparable fissures 'but considered they were natural as they were sealed beneath a clayey layer which held bones, sherds and a hearth much like Loanhead'. Since then other enigmatic rectangles, sometimes of wood, sometimes of stone, have been noted at sites as far apart as Stenness, Orkney; at the Sands of Forvie, Aberdeenshire; Mount Pleasant, Dorset, and Balbirnie, Fife. In the excavation report of the latter, Graham Ritchie discussed the affinities of such structures.[22]

Perhaps years after the pyre had been scraped up the central ring-cairn was built within the stone circle at Loanhead of Daviot. Such cairns, averaging 13.4 m across, with kerbstones graded towards the recumbent, were inconspicuous. Whitehill RSC had kerbstones 61 cm high but sometimes the 'cairn' consisted of little more than a floor of stones. At its centre there was a space, usually circular, about 4.9 m across, and it was here that cremated bone was placed, often within a pit.

A few examples of such burials must suffice. Within the central space some pits were lined with stones. Others were simply cut into the soil. At Ardlair two flat stones were arranged 'like a roof' above a pit with a cremation. At Hatton of Ardoyne a large pit was paved with small boulders and held a cremation and a fire-reddened urn. Old Keig's pit, a rectangular trench that cut through a burnt area, was shallower. In it was dark earth, charcoal and cremated bone. There is record of a time before 1692 when they 'did see ashes of some burnt matter digged out of the bottom of a little circle

...in the centre of one of those monuments...near the church of Keig', probably not the RSC of Old Keig but Cothiemuir Wood which was closer to the old church.[23]

No pits were discovered at Castle Fraser, Sunhoney or Auchquhorthies. The central space at the first had a paving of stones under which was black mould, charcoal and cremated bones. At Sunhoney eight deposits of burnt bone were found in the same area. Most of the stones surrounding the central space were fire-marked. The cairn was only 31 cm high. And in Auchquhorthies' centre was charcoal, half-burned ashes and urn fragments. Only very occasionally in RSCs were quartz pebbles strewn about. The heaping of soil in these centre spaces or in the pits, mixed with the charcoal and pottery, an apparently meaningless act, could have a symbolic essential, a form of sympathetic magic, to ensure the continuing fertility of the land.

It is a long way in miles and in centuries from the fine RSCs of central Aberdeenshire via the putatively later, aberrant circles of Kincardine down to the Late Bronze Age RSCs of Cork and Kerry. To visit Loanhead of Daviot or Tomnagorn, planted with young conifers, or the walled-in Easter Aquorthies, is to see good 'blueprint' circles with large recumbents. Further south outlying sites like Garrol Wood in the dim green light of the trees, or Colmeallie, Angus, wrecked, neglected and littered with farm rubbish, or Esslie the Greater is to see circles belonging to a time when the strength of the tradition was declining. Yet it is at Auchquhorthies in its wide field near the coast that perhaps the best-preserved ring-cairn and circle survives.

At circle after circle in these Scottish hills the tall stones have not been moved from where their prehistoric builders placed them over 4,000 years ago, where the fires burned and where, in succeeding years, further human bones were put in the middle of the circle. There was no dancing here. There is no space within the stones and the platform would have been an obstruction. No priest predicted an eclipse. The recumbent is far too long to provide a finely aligned sighting-point. The orientations are lunar, the ceremonies the times when fires were lit, perhaps more bodies incinerated. At Loanhead of Daviot 5 lbs (2.3 kg) of comminuted bone lay in the central space. They were not all adults. Over fifty fragments belong to the skulls of children between two and four years old. It is not possible to know whether these were victims of an epidemic, or a famine, or were sacrifices, although the indications of annual rites diminish beliefs in RSCs as family cemeteries.

It has been claimed, although the account is uncertain, that the antiquarian, Sir John Graham Dalyell (1775–1851) reported 'that about ten people were burned to death at Loanhead in one single execution for the crime of witchcraft', which, if true, made death by fire almost a custom at the ring. And certainly death was an intimate of such rings, as Robert Louis Stevenson understood:

> Grey recumbent tombs of the dead in desert places,
> Standing-stones on the vacant wine-red moor,
> Hills of sheep, and the homes of the silent, vanished races,
> And winds, austere and pure.
>
> 'To S. R. Crockett'

In those hills and homes prehistoric customs were local and persisted from the earliest centuries down to the middle of the second millennium BC even during the moving and mixing of peoples. Such movements are detectable.

There are many other rings of stones in north-east Scotland, often small ovals, which from their graded stones appear related to the RSC tradition. In general they

Plate 47. Cullerlie stone circle and internal cairns (Photograph: the author).

stand at the edge of the RSC districts and, from such burial finds as the decorated urn from Holywell, a cordoned urn from Rappla Wood or the tripartite food-vessel from North Burreldales, seem late. They are very varied. Sheldon near Inverurie may have been an incipient RSC without a recumbent stone. Rappla Wood's little circle stands on a stony platform. Farther south in Kincardine two of the four ring-cairns at Raedykes had stone circles around them. Noticeably, as in south-west England, there is often a standardised number of stones, six or eight being common, five or seven rare. Such circles are frequently graded on a sw–ne axis. Of the central sites Shethin, much ruined, was almost perfectly circular, about 3.8 m in diameter, with the tallest stone at the south-west. South Ythsie was a flattened circle, 5.8 × 3.4 m, with its largest stone at the south-west. Further south Image Wood was an oval six-stone site graded to the north-east; and Thorax, Banff, is 6.8 × 5.4 m of six stones which are not properly graded although the most massive block stands at the wsw and has twenty-two cup-marks.

Cullerlie (Pl. 47; fig. 25), proudly standing on the flat expanse of Leuchar Moss, not far south of the main RSC district, has eight boulders in a circle 10.1 m across, roughly graded to the nnw. At the centre was a small cairn with eleven kerbstones. The central, capstone-covered pit was 'much reddened, and there was charcoal at the bottom to a depth of 25 cm. Some of the charcoal was as large as a closed fist, and against it were fragments of calcined human bone. The pit had obviously contained a fire'.[24] Around this cairn were seven others, six with cremations. The ceremonies within this ring were like those of the earlier RSCs: the site had been levelled; the stones were erected, a fire of willow-branches lit within, ashes settling at the bases of the stones and around the uncovered kerbs; cremated bone was placed within these with oak-charcoal in five cairns and hazel in another showing they were probably not contemporary; then the cairns were built. From the excavation at Cullerlie and from inspection of the other small rings it seems the majority may be seen as later developments from the RSC tradition of central Aberdeenshire.

In the same way the occasional rectangles of four stones in north-east Scotland known as Four-Posters appear to have the same ancestry.[25] They also are graded towards the south-west or north-east. Most commonly found in Perthshire they have no good prototypes there whereas in Aberdeenshire the sites like Backhlll of Drachlaw East, a six-stone circle, 8.5 × 7.4 m, graded to the south-west, has two small stones at its north and south, the removal of which would leave a good Four-Poster. Of six stones of South Ythsie two are noticeably shorter than the others. At Glassel, Kincardine, the oval 5.9 × 3.3 m has five stones, one to the south of the others which stand at the corners of a rectangle, the tallest at the southwest. Such circles are generally outside the central districts of RSCs and, from the urns at Newton of Montblairy, Broomend of Crichie and Tuack are of the Bronze Age. Diameters of the large Aberdeenshire Four-Posters, Howemill and the Hill of Bucharn, or Craighead, Kincardine, are much greater than those in Perth but are commensurate with those of nearby six- and eight-stone circles like Cullerlie. It is likely that Four-Posters have an Aberdeenshire ancestry.

These sites are not as far away from the RSCs as the very small ovals nor some of the multiple sites like Melgum at the extreme south-west, three large circles of tiny

Fig. 25. Five small stone circles in Britain and Ireland: a. Cullerlie, Aberdeenshire; b. Nine Ladies, Derbyshire; c. Nine Stones, Winterbourne Abbas, Dorset; d. Castle Mahon, Co. Down; e. Drumskinny, Co. Fermanagh. The variety of architecture and ritual in the stone circles is shown in these plans. (a. after Kilbride-Jones, 1935; d. after Collins, 1956; e. after Waterman, 1964).

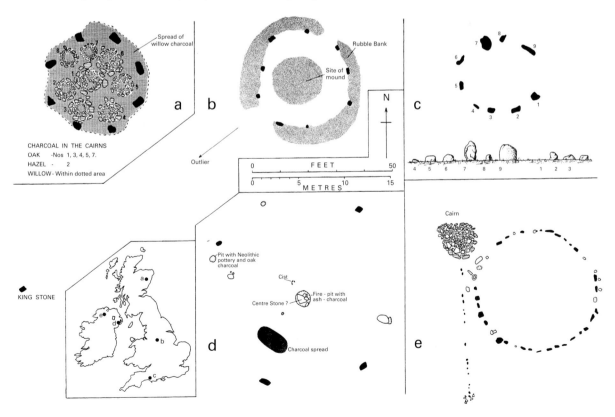

stones, or the three kerb-cairns at Logie Newton, mounds with massive kerbs, which have many blocks of white quartz amongst them. Standing high on Kirk Hill near Huntly, they have been called 'the most remarkable Druidical circle in the parish'. In appearance they are akin to the ring-cairn tradition.

It would seem that not only was north-east Scotland subject to influences from Ireland but also from the south-east whence the idea of some ring-cairns may have spread northwards. It is also probable that the tradition of building henges came from this direction for these earthwork enclosures are to be found all along the coast of east Britain with some very early sites like Arminghall, Norfolk, being known in the south as early as 2490 ± 150 bc (BM-129). There are many in north-eastern Scotland. Several small hengiform rings are recorded in the north-east, some like the Muir of Ord on the Black Isle, Ross and Cromarty, and, as well as some isolated examples, another group around Inverurie at the confluence of the Don and Urie.

Here there are three insignificant enclosures hardly 12.2 m in diameter at Tuack, Fullerton and Cairnhall, two with stone circles, and the more spectacular though wasted circle-henge of Broomend of Crichie, its bank 35.5 m across, with north and south entrances through its outer bank. Inside are the remains of a six-stone circle, 13.7 m in diameter, which was probably added to the henge. There were cremated bones in pits or cists by each stone, some in cordoned urns of the sixteenth or fifteenth centuries bc. During Dalrymple's excavation of November 1855, a sandstone battle-axe was found by a small circular cist in front of the north-west stone and this also has an early third millennium BC horizon.[26]

The encroaching town, a quarry, a housing estate, a juxtaposed main road, railway and a factory chimney have diminished Broomend's setting yet it retains a defiant dignity despite both this and the despoliation it has suffered whereby four of its stones have been taken. An interloper was added from a bank destroyed during the building of the railway. It was a seventh-century AD Pictish symbol stone with well-preserved carvings of a questionable elephant, crescent and V-rods. The avenue that led from a sandbank at the south very close to four cists with three N2 and an N3 beaker, one with a horn ladle in it, of the earlier second millennium has effectively been demolished even though originally it was an 18.3 m-wide double row of over a hundred stones running 412 m to the circle-henge and some 40 m beyond to a larger circle at the north, probably an RSC which was destroyed during the construction of the Aberdeen turnpike road in the late eighteenth century.

In the late seventeenth century James Garden of Aberdeen saw the rings before their disturbance. 'I remember to have seen on the highway betwixt & Invernery [Inverurie] nine miles from Aberdene two small stone monuments consisting of two circles of stones a piece, with a trench or dry ditch, which in the one was without both the circles of stones which it encompass'd [RSC and inner ring-cairn?], & in the other betwixt the two circles, and one of the two monuments (I do not remember which) had two entries (or interruptions in the Ditch to the ground inclosed by it wherof the one was nearly opposit the other' (the two henge entrances at Broomend?). He did not mention the avenues although they were still conspicuous sixty year later when Maitland saw them.[27]

The central burial at Broomend was unusual. At Fullerton nearby, five pits had been dug through a fire-marked patch and held a skull and inhumed and cremated bones. At Tuack, a mile away, four small pits with burnt bones had been set around a flat central stone. At Broomend, 46 cm down, was a layer of burnt material on top of a

4.6m wide tapering pit filled with cobbles. Nearly 1.9m down, the stones rested on three heavy slabs that made the top of a cist in which was a skull and leg bones as well as a deposit of cremated bone. It is rather like another pit at Old Parks Cairn, Kirkoswald, Cumbria over 200 miles away. Yet the builders of these earthen rings in north-east Scotland had clearly picked up the custom from the RSC users of placing death-offerings at the centres of their ritual sites. Despite the absence of pottery and artefacts from Broomend's medial pit, one is again reminded of the variety of burial traits amongst these Scottish stone circles.[28]

From the north-eastern corner of Scotland with its flurry of recumbent stone circle elements of the tradition spread north-westwards towards modern Inverness and south into Perthshire, as far west as the island of Arran and ultimately into Ireland.

The Moray Firth

Mutatis mutandis. The Latin tag, 'things have been changed that had to be changed', must be applied firmly to alterations in the later megalithic styles of north-eastern Scotland. The recumbent tradition extended southwards into central Scotland. It also spread north-westwards but with drastic modifications. Unpredictably, of all its elements: recumbent stone, stone circle, grading, ring-cairns, emphasis on the south-west, cupmarks, quartz, it was the first two traits that became unpopular. The recumbent disappeared. The circle became an optional extra. Death in the form of ring-cairns with graded kerbs, occasional cupmarks and internal burials took over. So did the architecture of megalithic tombs.

The fashion of stone-circle building was in decline. To the north-west the farthest certain RSC from the rings' heartland around Insch is Rothiemay 13 miles to the NNW. But possibly farthest of all was Innesmill, the De'il's Stanes, 30 miles to the north-west near Elgin. It was a large circle, 33.5m in diameter but it has been disrupted and only five of its original nine stones still stand, graded towards the south. Two others are prostrate. A WSW stone has several cupmarks. The recumbent, if it existed, has gone. Fred Coles believed the site had been an RSC because of the nineteenth-century observation by the Minister of Urquhart, 'Near Innes House are nine tall stones in a circle, two of them at the entrance to the "altar" '. Around 1840 another stone circle nearby was 'broken up and carted away to build cattle sheds'.[29]

Elsewhere there were only plain stone circles and ring-cairns with or without stone circles. The recumbent stone vanished. In the outlying Kincardineshire RSCs, well to the south-east of Insch, the process of elimination had already begun. Recumbents at Auchqhorthies and Garrol Wood were part of the ring-cairn rather than of the stone circle, both being a full 2m inside the ring and attached to the internal cairn. In even later rings the block was fully absorbed in the cairn and became no more than a larger or a cupmarked kerbstone between SSE and south-west. The outcome can be seen miles away in the ring-cairns of Inverness-shire, the heavy south-western block of Delfour, the cupmarked boulders at Balnuaran of Clava Centre, Culburnie, Culdoich and Tordarroch.[30]

Today one can see the ruins of ring-cairns and passage-tombs, some of which were composite monuments much as cathedrals are structures of successive styles. A magisterial synthesis of data on these and other Scottish chambered tombs is presented in Audrey Henshall's 1963 and 1972 volumes.

At the eastern and southern edges of the distribution of RSCs there was an outward spread of ring-cairns, circular with a circular central space but without recumbent stones. In Kincardineshire two ring-cairns without circles are close to RSCs. Cairnwell was adjacent to Auchqhorthies and Old Bourtreebush. At Clune Hill an RSC and ring-cairn almost touch each other. Other ring-cairns without circles were built at the extremes of the RSC enclave. Among them are Cairnmore 20 miles to the NNE, the Sands of Forvie on the east coast, and the two central rings at Raedykes 25 miles to the south-east.[31]

These were riverine distributions. Almost 30 miles west of Insch the central reaches of the Spey Valley became a centre for these 'new' ring-cairns. Gownie near Aberlour was perhaps reached by emigrants travelling northwards along the River Deveron, moving westwards along the coast and settling far along the fertile sides of the River Spey. Here great ring-cairns like Marionburgh, surrounded by spacious stone circles, were constructed in the tight valley between the Cairngorms and the Monadliath mountains to the west. There was a limited group of cairns: the Doune of Dalmore overlooked by the little, presumably late, passage-tomb of Upper Lagmore with a possible ring-cairn at the foot of the hill below. Well to the south around Aviemore were more ring-cairns in a line from Tullochgorm to Altlarie 7 miles to the south-west near a long cairn. An informative difference in size is apparent: ring-cairns averaging 15 m across with a 7 m wide central space, the smaller passage-tombs only 13 m in diameter and containing a small chamber no more than 3.7 m from side to side. The presence of short cists and food vessels suggest a period at the beginning of the Early Bronze Age around 2000–1950 BC as C-14 determinations from Newton of Petty and the Balnuaran of Clava passage-tombs and ring-cairn confirm.

Proposals that a priest or shaman could have concealed himself in the central space, uttering warnings and prophecies as though emanating from a disembodied spirit, are ill-founded. With the average height of a cairn no more than a metre no human being, even a midget, could have hidden himself from view.

To the west of the Spey there were no sites in the high, wild country along the Findhorn but along the Nairn and by the Inverness Firth around Drummossie Moor, along 30 miles of riverside, were ring-cairns, some enormous like Gask with a fragmented stone circle once 36.6 m in diameter but comfortably matched by the three rings at Balnuaran of Clava, 31.6 m, 31.7 m and 34.8 × 31.5 m respectively.

The broad Inverness valley at the head of the Great Glen dividing Scotland from south-west to north-east is seminal to a study of the stone circles of the Clava group. Sheltered by mountains, with low rainfall on the rich soils of the Moray Firth, it must have appeared to Neolithic arrivals ideal for settlement. During the earlier part of the second millennium BC peoples of two distinct beliefs encountered each other, their differing ritual monuments uneasily overlapping. From the east, along the coast and spreading down the river-valleys of the Spey, Nairn, and the headwaters of the Ness on Drummossie Moor came the builders of ring-cairns. From the north, from Sutherland and southwards from the Black Isle on Ross and Cromarty came people to claim land on which to build tombs of the rectangularly chambered Orkney-Cromarty tradition.

Strangely, although the land was fertile there had been little earlier settlement. Great mounds at Easterton of Roseisle and Boghead near Fochabers had been raised by Neolithic settlers, perhaps infiltrating the region from the south-west along the Caledonian Valley as numerous Irish sherds of Lyles Hill ware suggest. Pits in the remnants of a lightly built house at Raigmore near Aviemore, many centuries later covered by a Clava ring-cairn, as well as some anomalous determinations, yielded nine radiocarbon assays calibrated to the bracket of 4833–1440 BC. Five primary dates from Boghead, ranging from 3081 ± 100 bc (SRR-685) to 2873 ± 60 bc (SRR-684), c. 3950–3600 BC, are of the same early period.[32] Present knowledge sees these as small, isolated communities whose influence was slight although signs of agriculture have been discovered under and around some cairns such as Culdoich and Raigmore. It was only with the incoming of Early Bronze settlers that the land became strongly inhabited. The contrasting architectural styles of the two immigrations from north and east suggest the ring-cairn was the first-comer. 'On distributional grounds they [Orkney-Cromarty] can be seen to have arrived after the Clava tomb-builders were well-established'.[33]

Known as the Clava, 'burial-place', cairns because of the important pair of passage-tombs and adjoining ring-cairn at Balnuaran of Clava near Inverness one of the most controversial problems has been the question of their origin because of their three distinct elements of chambered tomb, ring-cairn and stone circle. Ring-cairns are widespread in northern Britain but it is only within the Clava tradition that they occur in stone circles.[34] A plausible explanation is that ring-cairn builders from the east converted some of their monuments into chambered tombs as secure places for their dead, adopting much of the north Scottish Orkney-Cromarty architectural styles but rejecting those traditional rectangular chambers in favour of their own circular central spaces thus creating their own unique and atypically late tombs.

Several of the Clava cairns have been excavated from 1828 onwards; Corrimony, Druidtemple and Kinchyle of Dores in 1952; Balnuaran of Clava Centre some time after 1857, and again in 1953 with Culdoich. C-14 assays from Newton of Petty 1975–6 and from the Clava sites in 1996 confirmed the late development of these sites with even later disturbance around 1250–800 BC.[35]

Some time around 1650 bc, c. 2000 BC tomb-builders and ring-cairn devotees may have met on The Aird west of the River Ness. There are the remains of three Orkney-Cromarty tombs there including Belladrum South with a heretical round chamber as though infected by cultural styles from the east. There are two good ring-cairns, Bruiach and Culburnie and six other 'Clava-type' monuments, too ruinous to be classified. The proximity of the region to the Beauly Firth at its north caused Gordon Childe to write that the 'degeneration takes the form of the suppression of the entrance, leaving eventually a ring cairn within a stone circle'. Henshall resolutely claimed the reverse. The only Clava passage-tombs are 14 miles to the south where the River Enrick flows into Loch Ness. Carn Daley was at its mouth, the fine Corrimony 9 miles down the lateral valley.[36]

The Ness seems to have been a barrier. Even ignoring the density of Clava cairns along the west bank of the Nairn there is still a ring-cairn at Cullearnie just east of the Ness, no fewer than six other Clava cairns and passage-tombs at Dalcross and Druidtemple. Against this there is just one Orkney-Cromarty cairn at Carn Glas on Essich Moor, less than 2 miles from a third Clava passage-tomb, Kinchyle of Dores which the testy Samuel Johnson denigrated in August 1773. It was, wrote Boswell, 'a very complete specimen of what is called a Druid's temple . . . Dr. Johnson justly observed that to go and see one druidical temple is only to see that it is nothing, for there is neither art nor power in it. And seeing one is quite enough'. Johnson did not bother to record it, unaware that a bowl-shaped pit in the chamber held human remains, 'a scatter of cremated bones'.[37]

In their heyday both Clava ring-cairns and chambered cairns had deserved better than the ignorance of the unimaginative Johnson. The passage-tombs have straight passages leading through a round cairn to a circular, exactly central chamber. The ring-cairns are uninterrupted, stony penannular banks with large kerbstones, enclosing an unroofed central space. Both types have graded kerbs highest around the ssw, and many have graded stone circles about 24.6 m in average diameter, their builders perhaps using a unit of measurement about 0.84 m long and quite close to Thom's Megalithic Yard of 0.829 m.

There is no other collection of chambered tombs in Britain, Ireland or Brittany set inside circles, only atypical sites like Newgrange in Ireland or Kercado in the Morbihan. Three-fifths of the Clava circles had twelve stones. Estimates are possible at nineteen sites. Three seem to have been enclosed within ten stones. Others may have had 8, 9 (two), 11 or 13 stones but the remaining ten had 12-stone circles although their circumferences varied from 72.9 m at Aviemore ring-cairn to 104.4 m at Balnuaran of Clava North-East.

Yet, perhaps because of the existence of a strong chambered tomb ethos the stone circle became an increasing absentee. Although impressive megalithic rings were raised at Balnuaran of Clava and elsewhere other circles seem to have been begun, left unfinished, others no more the vestigial remnant of a token pillar.

As always there are uncertainties. Nothing can be claimed for Cantraybruiach and Culduthel for today those sites are no more than denuded arcs of kerb-quadrants. Two fallen stones and several stoneholes at Grenish ring-cairn near Loch of Carraigean are evidence of a former circle there, reputedly once the coronation place for Pictish kings. But two stones at Dalcross, one at Culdoich South and none at all at Altlarie, at Avielochan, at Raigmore or at the isolated ring-cairn at West Town near Loch Duntelchaig show how little enthusiasm remained for the former necessity of a stone circle. The absence was neither accidental nor the result of robbery. The stonehole of a once 3.7 m-high but now fallen pillar at the Culdoich North ring-cairn was excavated without result in 1982 'but a resistivity survey coupled with a limited examination in the area failed to reveal further stones or stone sockets'.[38]

There was a surprise. Although set at the customary south-west of the site the tall block, with two cupmarks near its base, had not been positioned in line with any significant celestial event. Although similar art on kerbs at the east and west may have been related to equinoctial risings and settings the declination of the stone, about $-20°.5$, was related neither to sun nor moon in terms of those bodies' extremes. In this its erectors were unlike compatriots at Delfour miles to the sse who raised a 3 m high, shouldered pillar outside the ring-cairn, placing it nicely to mark the midwinter sunset.[39]

There are reasons for believing that the design of a passage-tomb was of considerable concern to its builders whereas some of the increasingly outmoded ring-cairns were less carefully planned. Generally the passage-tombs are smaller than the ring-cairns, and their chambers never exceed 4.9 m across whereas a ring-cairn's central space could be as wide as 10.7 m. Yet both share the unique traits of a ssw orientation: cupmarking, stones graded in height, and most have a surrounding stone circle. The tombs have more compatible designs than the ring-cairns for, where the original plan may be inferred, the majority of their cairns and outer rings were regular circles. In contrast, there is a complete medley of designs amongst the 'circles' of ring-cairns from ovals to eggs and the cairns are often of a different shape again, including two, Bruiach and Cullearnie, that are simply irregular.[40]

It is arguable that passage-tombs of the Clava tradition were chambered cairns built on top of the inner edges of ring-cairns whose great penannular bank formed the outer rim of the so-called 'platform'. The chambers of such hybrid monuments had to be small because the builders, unaccustomed to erecting walls and roofs, lacked the skill to corbel and span the width of the average ring-cairn's central space. A drawn section of the excavation at Corrimony appears to support this contention that a ring-cairn had formed the basis of the monument. At the Balnuaran of Clava passage-tombs the excavator commented on the manner in which the passages sloped down to the central chamber. Of Avielochan Henshall observed that 'it seems probable that it has been constructed in a natural hollow' as the passage seemed to slope downhill.[41]

Before looking into their purpose it is worth asking how many people were involved in their construction. At most cairns the stones are not heavy. The biggest kerb at Gask, the largest ring-cairn, weighs about half a ton. The west circle-stone at Balnuaran of Clava North-East, a sandstone block 3.4 m long, weighs seven tons and over level ground fifteen people could have moved it implying a minimum community of about thirty. One may guess at a total of fifty Clava cairns built over a period as long as three or four centuries. It is likely that the majority were put up in the later centuries as the population increased, and this might indicate that only two or three tombs belong to the early phases with a population of less than a hundred.

Within some cairns there are other signs of ritual: deposits of quartz pebbles, cremated bone, a cist with a skull. The discovery of quartz pebbles is another probable indication that a site belongs within the RSC tradition. Few circles in Britain and Ireland have had quartz strewn inside them. Most occur in north-eastern Scotland. In Inverness, Corrimony and Druidtemple had bits of quartz; in Aberdeenshire, Castle Fraser contained quartz pebbles; so did Corrie Cairn and Culsh. Further south in Perthshire several sites like Croft Moraig and Monzie had fragments of quartz littered around their stones.

Like the ancestral Aberdeenshire RSCs several Clava sites, mainly ring-cairns, have cupmarks, small and shallow basin-shaped depressions made by grinding the surface with a harder stone. Only at Corrimony and in the two Balnuaran chambered tombs are there cupmarks, either in the chamber, the passage or on the circle but in six ring-cairns the diverse positions of the carvings, anywhere from east round to NNW, is divided between three circle-stones and eight kerbs. The common association with burials and their presence on stones supposedly facing the sun suggests that cupmarks were symbols of fertility. Very few circles in the British Isles are cupmarked, only just over 1 per cent of those outside north-east Scotland. But in that area there are forty-two cupmarked sites, 21 per cent of the regional total, a proportion increasing the nearer the circles are to Inverness. In Perthshire 13 per cent of circles are cupmarked, 19 per cent in Aberdeenshire, 43 per cent in Inverness.

There is the vaguest of evidence that cupmarks were made on stones with solar or lunar connections. The alignments are not good. One of the most heavily decorated, a kerb at Tordarroch was very roughly in line with the minor southern moonset but as originally it had faced inwards against the body of the cairn it is likely to have been a reused slab like another stone at Balnuaran of Clava North-East (Pl. 48). The 'astronomy' is likely to be illusory.[42]

This conflict between possible solar orientations and the impossibility of their ever having been used may be reconciled if they are considered to have been for the dead to whom the intervening cairn would literally have been immaterial. A 6 m thickness

Plate 48. A cupmarked kerbstone in the Balnuaran of Clava NE passage-tomb (Photograph: the author).

of cobbles, or the absence of a passage, or cupmarks invisible in the darkness, would be of no moment to the dead. Such a connection between death and the sun accords with the discovery that the roof-box over Newgrange's entrance would have admitted sunlight to the central chamber at the winter solstice even when the tomb entrance was sealed.

Astronomical interests undoubtedly are probable elsewhere. Whereas most Neolithic tombs, including those of the Orkney-Cromarty group, had their entrances between north-east and south-east the passages, kerbs and tallest circle-stones in the Clava cairns occur in an arc between sse and wsw. The passage-tomb mounds were up to 3.1 m high, a height that would preclude sightings being taken across the circle. This is important, for claims have been made that the consistent south-west alignment of the Clava lines show their builders to be much concerned with the midwinter sunset, and it is the Clava tradition that offers strong support for the belief that astronomical orientations were essential parts of the religious ceremonies of prehistoric people in Britain. Care is demanded.

At the latitude of 57° with a solar declination of about 23°.9 between 2000 and 1500 bc midwinter sunset can rarely have been more than 2° or 3° south of 222° and never at the south, 180°, or even ssw at 202°.5. The western arc of Clava passage-tombs is wider than that solar range, from 184° just west of south to 232° at the wsw. If slipshod builders of an average cairn 13.4 m in diameter had intended to sight their entrance on the midwinter sunset they would have made a vast error of at least 2.3 m, about 6 per cent of the circumference, if their tomb faced even ssw.

The alignments of all but three of the seventeen ring-cairns are more restricted, clustering between west of south and south-west, 190°–220°. The moon remained the preferred target. It is possible to recover alignments from twenty-one sites and amongst them there are three declinations towards the minor southern moon and thirteen on its major positions, the majority towards its setting. Against this there were only six alignments on the sun, one towards the midwinter sunrise at Culburnie, others to the midwinter sunset at Delfour and Marionburgh, and at Gask where a combination of cupmarks on a kerb and a circle-stone beyond it marked the line. Of all the passage-tombs only the two at Balnuaran of Clava had their passages directed to the setting winter sun.[43]

In this the cairns differ from the Orkney-Cromarty tombs of which four in five have azimuths between the north-east and the south-east, the arc between midsummer and midwinter sunrise. At the very south of the distribution of the tombs, in Ross-shire, the closest to Clava territory, the alignments are concentrated around the east with two concentrated bands, one to the north, the other to the south of east within a month either side of the equinoctial sunrise. No Clava cairn had a setting related to the equinoxes.[44]

Thom has suggested that observers once squatted in the chambers of these cairns to observe the midwinter setting sun but the length and lowness of the passage would have prevented such a sightline. The alignment did exist as the Balnuaran of Clava passage-tombs reveal but inspection shows that it was not for the living. From the chamber there is a narrow rectangle of light at the entrance, its top formed by the outermost capstone of the passage, its bottom framed by the distant horizon. Too low to be seen by anyone sitting in the chamber it was through that aperture that the midwinter sun shone onto red stones at the back of the burial-chamber before sinking into night at the end of the year.[45]

Two sites in State Care can easily be visited. Corrimony passage-tomb in Glen Urquhart has a stone 'circle', 21.3 m in diameter, surrounding a 15.5 × 14.5 m cairn built on an artificial mound 0.6 m high of small stones capped by flat slabs, perhaps an underlying ring-cairn. Broken quartz had been strewn around the kerbstones during the cairn's construction. A 10 m-wide gap in the stone circle at the ENE revealed a cobbled area indicating that the space was intentional as if intended as a 'window' towards the May Day sunrise. The passage entrance at the south-west led to a corbelled chamber, now roofless, 4 m across. On the floor was a slabbed area set on sand in which the excavators detected the stain of a crouched inhumation. A big slab on top of the cairn may have been the chamber's capstone and its probable underside has many cupmarks, perhaps a reused decorated standing stone like the bigger of two capstones in the Kerveresse passage-tomb near Locmariaquer in Brittany with scores of cupmarks 'like a starry sky', some made before the slab was set in position.[46]

The second site is the splendid Balnuaran of Clava cemetery near Culloden battlefield, Inverness (Fig. 26). Here there are two passage-tombs and an intermediate ring-cairn on a bent NE–SW line about 122 m long. Recently detected ring-cairns in the immediate neighbourhood are signs that today's complex was once the heart of a great prehistoric necropolis.

The south-west passage-tomb has a graded stone circle 31.7 m across in which there is a NNE gap reminiscent of Corrimony's cobbled gap but of no discernible astronomical importance. Like that site the cairn is built on a mound. The entrance, between two large kerbstones, is at the south-west. Cupmarks survive on a stone on the east side of the passage and on the first stone on the west in the chamber. In 1828 or 1829 two probably flat-rimmed pots were discovered, one containing cremated bone. There were later excavations by Piggott, 1952; and Bradley in 1996 who recorded that the midwinter sun would have shone down the passage onto carefully selected dark, red stones in the back wall of the chamber like symbols of death. In 1923 Somerville recorded that in all three of the Balnuaran sites 'there is one stone slab, larger and better trimmed than the remainder, which is given special importance', all of them in line with 'sunset on Samhiun "All Hallows" – the half-quarter day of November' and the grim Celtic festival. He also pointed out that whereas the stones in the eastern half of the cairn were rough those on the west were better-

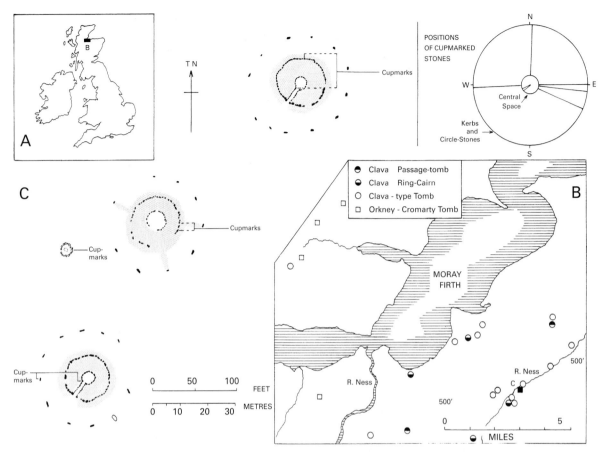

Fig. 26. the complex of two passage-tombs and a ring-cairn at Balnuaran of Clava, Inverness (Highland). The small kerb-cairn is to the west of the ring-cairn.

trimmed flat-sided slabs or pillar-stones, a deliberate contradiction that again may have been tokens of life and death. It may even be that the sun and moon were similarly regarded as life and death, light and dark, warmth and cold, the two balances of existence.[47]

Cupmarks, quartz, composite structures, sunset, moonset, chosen colours, a contrast in texture, death, despite the insensitive Johnson's scepticism these places were never without art or power.

The central site is a ring-cairn, its stones graded towards the south-west inside a stone circle 31.6 m. Radiating out from it to three circle-stones are three enigmatic cobbled settings. An astronomical interpretation has seen the north-western ray aligned on the sunsets of early May and August, declination +14°05, the ESE towards the equinoctial sunrise, +0°.6, and the SSE line poorly aligned upon the most southerly moonrise, −26°.3, an 'error' of almost 4°. There are also cupmarks on two eastern kerbs. When excavated in 1953 the central area was found to be blackened by charcoal amongst which was a thin spread of cremated bone.

The north-east site is another passage-tomb with a 16.5 m cairn also on a wide platform. Around this at ground level is a fine stone ring 34.8 × 31.5 m across. There is a notably cupmarked kerbstone at the NNW. In the passage is another cupmarked stone.

One can only record at the Balnuaran complex evidence of the same rites seen elsewhere: cupmarked stones, cremations, stone circles enclosing areas for ritual, and assume that here also were sites magically used by early settlers for supernatural protection against the terrors and misfortunes of their lives.

To the people who raised the heavy chambers for their dead the surrounding stone circle, if ever it was built, was no more than a barrier against the decay of the profane world outside, a defence, a protection for the bones that lay in the tomb. It is one of the whimsicalities of prehistory that the people themselves have gone, leaving only the stones and 'microscopic scraps of bone' at Avielochan, 'a few bones' and 'a quantity of calcined bones' at the Balnuaran of Clava passage-tombs. At Daviot, around 1820, 'a cist was found containing a skull and other remains which were carefully replaced'. Excavation at Culdoich recovered flecks of skulls, longbones, ribs, digits of a middle-aged man and woman whose burnt bones had been 'broken up deliberately after the cremation' for reasons that only the people could explain.

The people have gone. Saddest of all these unremembered deaths was that of a lightly built man, lying on his right side inside Corrimony. Nothing was left of him except some 'grey, purplish-black and white stains' on the sandy floor of the chamber. Above him, in the blackness, was the capstone and its cupmarks. Around his burial-place, was the stone circle. Its stones endure.

More than a hundred years before Samuel Johnson another doctor, medical rather than honorary, Sir Thomas Browne, was understanding, 'When the Funerall pyre was out, and the last valediction over, men took a lasting adieu of their interred Friends, little expecting the curiosity of future ages should comment upon their ashes.' Browne respected those vanished societies. 'Nor were they confused or carelesse in disposing the noblest sort, while they placed large stones in circles about the Urnes or bodies which they interred.' And unlike Johnson he reached out to the people. 'Beside to preserve the living, and make the dead to live, to keep men out of their Urnes, and discourse of humane remains in them, is not impertinent.'[48]

Just west of the Balnuaran of Clava cairns is a small kerb-cairn, architecturally related to them and with a close similarity to some sites in Argyll. At Clava the 3.7 m oval of fifteen close-set stones is flattened at the NNE and the tallest stones are between south-east and south-west. There was a probable inhumation in a central pit where quartz pebbles had been scattered. The comparison between the diameters of such a kerb-cairn and others like Achacha and Strontoiller in Argyll or Monzie, Perthshire, which average about 4.5 m, and the central spaces of Clava passage-tombs and ring-cairns averaging 4.0 m and 6.7 m respectively is apparent. The contiguity of the stones is like the Clava stone-lined interiors. It is not far-fetched to perceive that one development from Clava passage-tombs was the construction of these small kerb-cairns based on the model of the central space, retaining not only its diameter but its graded heights of stones and astronomical alignments, diminutive and derivative cult sites of later Bronze Age families.[49]

Perhaps the very last of the Clava passage-tombs is to be seen at Carmahome, 250 miles to the south-west on the west coast of Arran near Kilpatrick. The heavily kerbed cairn is small, no more than 5.3 × 4.3 m with a wsw-facing passage leading to a small, round chamber. Typically, there is no stone circle although the Machrie Moor rings are only a few miles to the north.[50]

Closer to the great Balnuaran sites are smaller monuments such as Auldearn in Nairn perhaps once a ring-cairn within a stone circle about 17 m in diameter. Only three stones remain. The ring is dubiously associated with Isobel Gowdie, a young, red-headed wife accused of witchcraft for having held covens at the site in 1662. Around Inverness freestanding stone circles are few. There is one 5.2 m ring at Torbreck, and at Templestone in Moray there is a minute Four-Poster, besieged by over-reaching gorse bushes. The ruins of a circle about 58 m across have been found at Edinkillie, Moray, quite close to a ford across the River Divie in a pass between the hills. Its recent discovery, like that of Aultan Broubster, Caithness, and of others in south-west Scotland, emphasises how easily even great megalithic rings may be overlooked in unpopulated country.

Chapter Thirteen

The Stone Circles of Central and South-Western Scotland

The retrieving of these forgotten things from oblivion in some sort resembles the Art of a Conjurer.

John Aubrey, 1670, 4

Central Scotland

Fifty miles from the aberrant Blue Cairn RSC by the River Dee is a cluster of small circles at the mouth of the Glenshee pass in Perthshire. It includes the petite depaganised Four-Poster of Spittal of Glenshee whose trinity of Christianised stones perch on a glacial drumlin like a trio of tiny seabirds on the back of a basking whale.

From their grading towards the south-west, their cupmarks and their burials, such Four-Posters appear related to the Aberdeenshire RSCs, perhaps derived from intermediate rings such as Raich, South Ythsie and the 'oval' of Backhill of Drachlaw, four of its six stones much taller than the others.

The scarcity of circles along Strathmore suggests that had there been any movement of people from the north-east it was not along the coastal strip but deep along the Dee to Glen Clunie near Braemar, then southwards on the long ascent between the mountains to the summit of the pass, often snowbound in winter, then down the twisting glen to the hills around Blairgowrie. Today it is the highest main road in Britain. In the second millennium BC it was an important route from north-east Scotland.

The concentration of little circles near Glenshee shows this. There are at least six within 4 miles of each other, high on the western slopes of the Forest of Alyth, a mixture of Four-Posters, six-stone circles and a larger ring of nine or ten stones at Broad Moss. In the same region are standing stones, hut-circles and enclosures, cairns on the steep, dividing hillsides, and here as on Dartmoor or in Caithness there arises the impression of families settling on tracts of unexploited land late in the second millennium bc, around 1500 BC.

The varied Glenshee group is a microcosm of Perthshire in which circles, ovals and rectangles intermix. Some stand in the desolate landscape north of the Tummel, or in the lowlands around Perth, or on the lovely hillsides overlooking Loch Tay. Still others suffer in inappropriately reconstituted surroundings: Ferntower on a golf-course; Ardblair with a road running through it; Moncreiffe alongside an estate-drive; and

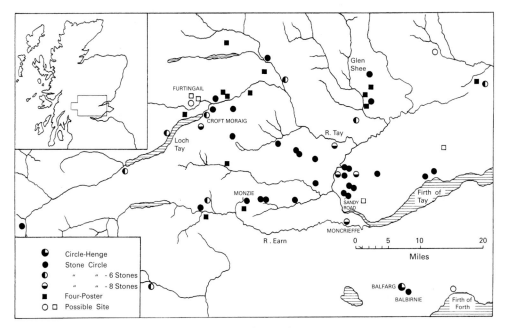

Fig. 27. The distribution of stone circles in Perthshire (Tayside).

Scone heatherset in the patio of Graystanes Close with modern houses and a sub-urban sideroad around it.

Tigh-na-Ruaich in a cottage garden is one of a distinctive group of six-stone circles to be found almost exclusively in the west of Perthshire, although there are prototypes in Aberdeenshire. Despite their ruinous state they appear to be graded, Ardblair to the west, Wester Torrie and others to the ssw, Tigh-na-Ruaich to the north-east, and, supporting a belief in their north-eastern origin, the farther west they stand the smaller their diameter and the more oval their shape. One of the best preserved is at Killin at the far south-west of Loch Tay, an oval, 9.5 × 8.5 m, with a massive stone at the ssw. Some like Machuinn, another graded oval by Loch Tay, and Pitscandlie stand on mounds, a feature to be noticed amongst the Perthshire Four-Posters. Like so many of the rings dug into in the nineteenth century little is known of their contents. At Pitscandlie the mound was attacked and a 46 cm square of sandstone was found with two rough concentric circles scribed on it. An 'urn' was buried near one of the stones. At Tigh-na-Ruaich four huge urns filled with bone were discovered. One of the exca-vators in 1855 noted that the soil within the ring was darker 'as if saturated with blood'. More prosaically he probably saw the outcome of charcoal and burnt bone scattered in the central area.

The Four-Posters of Perthshire (Fig. 27) and nearby counties are more centrally placed than the six-stone rings, although there is a far eastern example at Balkemback, Angus. They were built on hill-terraces like their ancestral RSCs and predictably were graded though sometimes the largest stone was at the north-east just as the Cork MSCs had their high portal stones opposite the recumbent rather than alongside it. The 'rectangles' whose four stones always stand on the circumference of a circle, average 14.7 m² in area, smaller than their Aberdeenshire counterparts, 17.2 m², and were occasionally erected on an existing barrow at Lundin Farm (Pl. 49), in a

Plate 49. Lundin Farm Four-Poster on its natural mound (Photograph: the author).

kerbed mound at Na Carraigean, or on an artificial platform at Dunmoid.[1] No fewer than thirty-seven of the 101 have been dug into although only twenty-one reports exist, most of them skimpy. In ten rings bones and cremations were found.

Amongst them, Clach na Tiompan, seems late in the tradition. It is very small, its grading uncertain, and it lies in the remote reaches of Glen Almond far from any other Four-Poster. Yet even here there were quartz pebbles. Highest of all is Clachan an Diridh, 'the stones of the ascent', beautifully and dramatically situated, its 'huge standing-stones, grey with the moss of ages'. Its mountainous position awed visitors but also puzzled them. 'Surely, if ever the pre-historic circle-builder (supposed to be a Star-and-Hill worshipper) sought for a noble panorama within which to rear some rude image of Stonehenge, this were the very spot . . . And yet what he did erect are only four great, unshapely and somewhat squat, and very rough boulders in the centre of a slight mound,' wrote Coles who was the first to recognise the rings as a special form of stone circle.[2]

Burial relics varied elsewhere. At Glenballoch a cordoned urn filled with bone was 'protected by stones built round it in a beehive form'. At Dunmoid there was a stone cist containing a human thigh bone, at Carse Farm I a pit had been made by a stone, and at Lundin Farm a cremation pit was dug into a beaker barrow. Most of the pottery, the Dunmoid 'urn', a collared urn from Carse Farm, another from Lundin excavated in 1962, and the cordoned urn from Glenballoch, are of the mid-second millennium BC. ApSimon has pointed out the similarity of this cordoned urn to another from the famous cairn of Lyles Hill, Co. Antrim. Both urns have applied chevrons running round the neck below the rim, but the Glenballoch pot was a ceramic tragedy. The two ends of the zigzagging chevron do not link but through an unhappy miscalcuation terminate asymmetrically, a sad conclusion for a vessel that may offer evidence for the expansion of Scottish customs into Ireland during the second millennium.[3]

It was an expansion revealed by a spread of Four-Poster builders southwards: at Bagbie, Kirkcudbrightshire, south-west Scotland; the Goatstones, Northumberland, northern England, and, in the restlessness of the Bronze Age with the endless seeking for unoccupied land, like ever-diminishing clouds of rain Four-Posters were erected on Arran. There was an uneasy drizzle of rings in the hills and mountains of central

Wales, and a few like the last drops of a shower in the far corner of these islands in south-west Ireland in sites such as Robinstown Great, Co. Wexford and Lettergorman in Co. Cork.

A word concerning these semi-megalithic migrants should be added about Fortingall East and West, 7 miles west of Aberfeldy. These are two of three megalithic sites close together on a terrace overlooking the River Lyon. Before excavation in 1970 they seemed to be Four-Posters from each of which one stone had been removed. Digging revealed that in reality they were sub-rectangular settings of eight stones with the largest stones at the corners. Flecks of charcoal and cremated bone were recovered. Both sites had had five stones deliberately overthrown and deeply buried presumably in the nineteenth century from the presence of a Victorian beer-bottle under one stone. Whether the smaller stones had been added to two juxtaposed Four-Posters is difficult to say but paired eight-stone circles are fairly common in central Scotland, and the Fortingall settings may be the results of a mixing of traditions. They stand by what may be a ruined and idiosyncratic RSC once about 23 m in diameter.[4]

They could well be related to a larger, perhaps late, group of circles of which over half stand unusually on low land west of the Sidlaws. Some of these are eight-stone circles. The site at Murthly Hospital is 10.1 m in diameter, graded to the south-west, and contained a collared urn. Grading was also true of the oval Bandirran now in a wood, and the tiny, devastated Colen, with cupmarked south-west and ssw stones, high on a hillstep above the Tay.

Moncreiffe, 13 miles south of Murthly, was also circular and graded. In it lay a profusely cupmarked stone which reputedly had once been in a central barrow with a cremation. At this site meticulous excavations revealed the superficiality of judging stone circles on their surface appearance. Moncreiffe had undergone several alterations. The first monument was a small, single-entrance henge with a timber setting rather like the first phase of Croft Moraig 25 miles to the north-west. Within the henge a later ring-cairn was built surrounded by standing stones, a burial monument which in turn was replaced by an even larger ring-cairn over which there was a heavy scatter of broken quartz. Around this cairn with its flat-rimmed ware was a circle of eight stones perfectly graded towards the south-west and between at least four of these the builders had placed recumbent stones like a turreted battlement. Whatever the relationships of this complex monument later people had not hesitated to despoil it. Metallurgists cleared away part of the ring-cairn, smashed much of the pottery, and used the space for bronze and iron working. The ring has been re-erected nearer Moncreiffe House to permit the construction of the M90 but survives still as a vivid memorial to the confusion of interests of prehistoric people.[5]

Elsewhere in east Perthshire there is even less uniformity. Only Faskally Cottages is graded. In other rings the ssw orientation vanishes, there are many ovals and there are paired sites like the dishevelled kerb-cairns, 2 m apart, at Tullybeagles or the two at Shian Bank, both ovals, which had pillboxes built by them during the Second World War. Thom considered that a south-east to north-west alignment from their centres was directed towards the midsummer sunset.[6] What is likely in these individualistic rings with their haphazard number of ungraded stones, their dwarfed shapes, their unpredictable mixture of banks and outliers, their proliferation on low land, is that they are late, almost at the end of the megalithic tradition.

This is supported by the pair of Sandy Road rings at Scone only one and a half miles wsw of Shian Bank, one of which now survives in a modern housing estate.

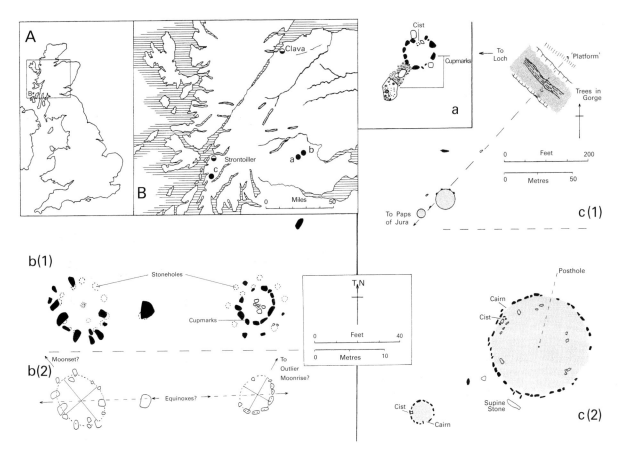

Fig. 28. Three Scottish sites: a. Monzie, Perthshire; b. Fowlis Wester, Perthshire; c. Kintraw, Argyll. (b1. after Young, Lacaille & Zeuner, 1943; b2. after Thom, 1971; c1. after Thom, 1971; c2. after Simpson, 1969).

Excavated in 1961 the western oval had a central pit with a broken, nondescript, flat-rimmed urn half-filled with a token cremation and lumps of charcoal that gave a date of 1200 ± 150 bc (GaK-787), c. 1650–1300 BC. This low ring is many centuries from the monumental RSCs of Aberdeenshire. Coupled and presumably late rings of easily handled boulders have been noticed elsewhere in Britain and Ireland. It is not reasonable to suppose that there was a single, underlying cause for all such pairing. Some rings may have been successive because, for some reason, the first site was no longer adequate.[7]

This may be the explanation for the two rings on the upland wastes at Fowlis Wester near Crieff (Fig. 28) which are related to the Clava-derived kerb-cairns of Argyll. There is a very similar site at Monzie (Fig. 28), 3 miles WSW, around Milquhanzie hill. This type of monument whether in Perthshire, Argyll or Inverness has contiguous kerbs graded W–WSW, is small and often has cupmarkings, scatters of quartz pebbles and outlying stones standing in significant astronomical positions. There is customarily a central burial deposit, usually near an area of burning.

At Fowlis Wester, on the highest point of the scruffy moorland ridge, the builders set up two stone rings. The eastern one enclosed a kerb-cairn. The west circle was begun by the people digging shallow pits into which they put white pebbles. The circle-stones were set in these inadequate holes and very soon tumbled or were toppled

Plate 50. The decorated outlier and kerb-cairn of Monzie (Photograph: the author).

from them. The ceremonies in the ring were like those in north-east Scotland and included the lighting of fires, deposition of charcoal and of bone. The excavators' plan of the stone holes show the ring to be circular, 7.3 m across, and Thom's supposition that the site was an ellipse, $8.3 \times 6.2 \times 5.2$ m, directed towards the midwinter maximum moonset is erroneously based on the present position of the fallen stones explaining why 'no foresight now appears on the horizon'. It once again reminds the archaeologist of the dangers inherent in accepting plans without excavation.[8]

Exactly east of the circle is the stone hole of a huge, prostrate outlier. Just beyond this is the eastern circle of low stones enclosing an 5.9 m kerbed circle resting on quartz chippings amongst which are some implements perhaps from west Scotland. The ssw kerb has three cupmarks hidden beneath the old ground surface. A small fire had burned on the laid clay floor and the expected lumps of charcoal and burnt bone were covered by some stone slabs which themselves were overlain with black earth and quartz capped with small stones. To the NNE, 11.3 m away, a 1.8 m outlier stands edge-on to the site in line with its axis and the cupmarked kerbstone and pointing downhill to the distant River Almond and the major northern moonrise.

The seemingly unremarkable kerb-cairn at Monzie (Pl. 50) in a broad, flat field is similar. Two of its stones have cupmarks. Quartz lay around its kerbs. At its centre an intense fire of hazelwood had reddened the earth and in a tiny cist at the north the bones of an adult and a six-year-old child had been placed. Three metres from the site at the south-west there is a remarkable outlier connected to the kerb by a rough causeway. This irregular 1.8 m-long boulder is decorated with forty-six cupmarks, cup-and-rings, nine double, one triple, there are two grooves and a pair of joined cups. Such so-called 'Galician' art is probably of great antiquity in Britain and examples such as that at Monzie may have been taken and broken from earlier monuments to incorporate the 'magic' into new settings. The style is entirely different from the more geometrical motifs of the Irish passage-tombs.[9]

Kerb-cairns like Monzie in their architecture and rites are almost indistinguishable from others in Argyll and Inverness. It has been noticed how the builders of those ring-cairns and chambered tombs displayed an interest in the movements of sun and moon so that it is not unexpected to find analogous observations in these kerb-cairns, although here the alignments are revealed through the positions of cupmarked stones and outliers. In many cases one end of a line was determined by a cupmarked stone, the other by the outlier which was sometimes, as at Fowlis Wester, lined up like a playing-card with its thin edge towards the cairn to provide a sharp sighting-edge. This may have been true also at Monzie where the marked stone has probably fallen sideways, perhaps even have been dragged a little to the south. A cupmarked kerb and the tallest kerb stand opposed on an east–west axis and the tiny cist is due north.

If the interpretation of these simple solar and lunar sightings is correct then two comments should be made. The invisible cupmarks at Fowlis Wester, like others in Clava cairns, imply that the alignment was fundamental to the construction but was not for the living. The distances between kerb and outlier are, moreover, too short for unambiguous sightlines, never exceeding 11.6 m, too wide a visual error.

At Fowlis Wester there seems to be a pair of complementary rings, one aligned on the major midwinter moonrise, the other on the solar equinox. The solar alignment is obstructed by the eastern encircled cairn. It may be supposed that the sun-line was no longer important and, with indifference, the kerb-cairn builders set up their new monument alongside a site whose antiquity they respected but whose orientation was no longer of any interest. It is of note, however, that comparable pairings of solar and lunar alignments have been analysed by Ruggles in western Scotland in the short stone rows of the Kilmartin Valley and elsewhere.[10]

Nothing datable has come from any of these kerb-cairns, only two rim-sherds of flat-rimmed ware at Monzie. They are assumed to be late. They may reveal how an interest in astronomical observation deepened over the centuries of the second millennium from lines on the most simple solar movements to include lunar orientations.

Presenting quite a different problem is the imposing stone circle of Croft Moraig, Perthshire (Pl. 51; fig. 29), excavated in 1965, at the north-east end of Loch Tay on the route between north-east and west Scotland. Here the revealed sequence of phases emphasises the naïveté of assuming that the visible features of any circle are contemporary.

Around 3000 BC fourteen posts were erected in a horseshoe setting 7.9 × 7 m open approximately to the south and akin to others in Brittany and a few along the coasts of Britain and Ireland.[11] Around it was a shallow ditch. It is not known whether this structure was roofed or whether the posts were painted or carved. It may be relevant to mention that not far away in Glen Lyon there still exists a stone-built shrine that was unroofed and which may once have protected a wooden idol. There were others in Brittany.[12]

At Croft Moraig when the uprights weathered some were replaced more than once and it is tempting to visualise a freestanding timber setting with a central, flat boulder beside a hollow containing burnt bone. Just inside the 'entrance' and 3.4 m outside it were two posts aligned north–south. Outside the ditch and exactly east were two short rows of postholes. Such equinoctial and north–south alignments recall the layout of many stone circles in the Lake District and south-western Scotland. At this stage Croft Moraig resembled Bleasdale, Lancashire, where eleven posts enclosed an 11 m circle with a central pit containing urns, charcoal and burnt bone. A double row of posts at the ENE marked the entrance. An assay from one of the posts gave a date of 1810 ± 90 bc (NPL-69), c. 2500–2100 BC.[13]

Plate 51. Croft Moraig, Perthshire (Photograph: the author).

Croft Moraig was later translated into stone, the posts being replaced by eight stones, graded towards the ssw, arranged in a Breton horseshoe 7.9 × 6.4 m, the NNE stone being cupmarked. Some hollows in the interior and the ditch were stone-filled and had charcoal-laden earth and Neolithic sherds, fine ware and also flat-rimmed, that came possibly from the first phase whose position the stone-builders seem to have duplicated. Around the stones they threw up a stony bank. A long stretch of it has been robbed but at its ssw is a 2 m long supine stone with twenty-three cupmarks on its upper surface. It is in line with the major southern moonset.

Fig. 29. Croft Moraig, Perthshire (Tayside). Phases of development (after Piggott & Simpson, 1971).

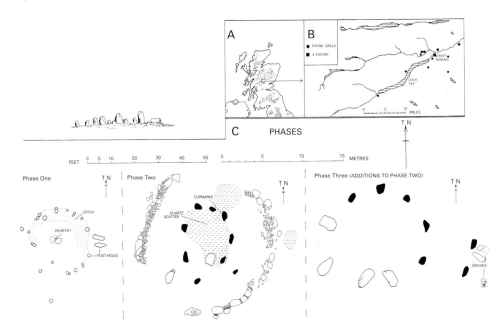

Finally a 12m circle of twelve large, ungraded stones was set up inside the bank round the megalithic horseshoe. A portal formed of a pair of big outlying stones was set up at the ESE to form an imposing entrance. In front of each pillar was an empty hole which may have held an inhumation long since destroyed by the acid soil. By the northern stone, and at the north-east of the outer circle, and within the horseshoe were dense scatters of quartz fragments.

Half-hidden by the hedgerow and by farm-buildings, diminished by tall trees, Croft Moraig is one of the most informative stone circles in Britain and Ireland. Its Neolithic timber ring is one of the earliest known and may have affinities with the tradition that caused east–west lines to be incorporated into many early stone circles. But later the site was adapted by people following the RSC custom of grading stones, scattering quartz, cupmarking and aligning towards the ssw. The trait of placing a supine stone there may have derived from western Scotland rather than from Aberdeenshire. There are 'Aberdeenshire' circles nearby. The etiolated remains of an RSC have been mentioned at Fortingall South, 3 miles to the west. Another may exist at the 49m Coilleachur on the slopes of Craig Formal 3 miles to the east by the Urlar Burn. The regular spacing may reflect territories.

The variety of stone rings in Perthshire and the distribution of monuments along the hillsides of Loch Tay reveals the movement of people and ideas passing along this prehistoric route from Strath Tay through Glen Dochart down to Loch Lomond and southwest Scotland.[14] Croft Moraig reflects this unrest in its several phases.

South-Western Scotland

At the mountainous head of Loch Lomond, 20 miles west of Kinnell in the Tay valley, is the marshy Inverarnon concentric circle, 31.1 m and 21.6 m across, which, like Coilleachur, may have RSC affinities. It stands on the route along which traders, prospectors and settlers may have passed. Yet for a hundred miles in the south there is hardly another circle.

Early prehistoric man appears to have by-passed the heavily forested lands of Ayrshire and the Clyde valley. Even the earliest of the chambered tombs, the late-fourth-millennium Bargrennan group with their small rectangular chambers and round cairns were built to the south in western Galloway. Other long-cairn builders who crossed the Pennines from eastern England settled in the eastern foothills between the rivers Liddel and Nith where sites like Lochhill, dated to 3120 ± 105 bc (1–6409), c. 4000–3750 BC, testify to early occupation around Dumfries. Ultimately the two sepulchral traditions intermixed to produce some of the characteristic Clyde long-chambered tombs whose elaborate concave facades inspired by Irish prototypes, may not have been added before the late third millennium.[15]

Yet despite this Neolithic activity it was not until the Bronze Age that man affected the country around the Clyde estuary. Pollen analysis from Bloak Moss near Stewarton in Ayrshire shows only the slightest disturbance of the forest cover during the third millennium whereas between 1400 and 1000 bc, c. 1700–1000 BC, there were at least three fifty year-long phases of tree clearance, occasionally for cereal-growing, more frequently for the grazing of livestock.[16] Bloak Moss is only a few miles from the possible enclosed cremation cemeteries of Gotter Burn, from Blackshaw Moor circle, and, most interestingly, not 5 miles from a damaged Four-Poster, the Four Stones, near Dunlop, from which cremated bones were dug around 1816. This site, like the Four-

Poster at Aucheleffan, Arran, and the graded six-stone ring with central cist at Lamlash on the same island, bears witness to the dissemination of ideas and people, from the north-east and central Scotland during the early second millennium BC.

The main concentration of identified circles along this inhospitable coastline lies between Luce Bay and Liddesdale. There are three major divisions: an eastern group whose large open circles like the Twelve Apostles may be of Cumbrian origin; a coastal group with central stones; and an inland cluster of unusual sites that appear to be related to RSCs. They include the lonely Torhousekie far to the west in Wigtown. Such a mixture reminds one of the mosaic of social beliefs that could exist even in a small area and of the difficulty in separating them chronologically. Unlike the ceramically rich RSCs of Aberdeenshire the Galloway circles have yielded almost nothing, pot, bronze, flint or burial. Conclusions about their dating in general remains inferential.

Kirkcudbrightshire and Wigtownshire

Unlike the open sites there are a few centre-stone circles halfway along the southern coast west of the Dee. The theoretical foible of erecting a stone within a circle was, in reality, the reverse, the laying-out of an inconspicuous ring of low stones around an ancient standing stone like that at Boscawen-Un or at Callanish. It was rare for a true circle to result from the awkward construction.

Circles with centre stones (Fig. 30) appear to be late and frequently have a cremation deposit at the foot of the centre stone whether in a henge or a stone ring. Although little is known of the practice in stone circles, at Longstone Rath, Co. Kildare, a 5.3 m granitic stone stood in a rock-cut basin at the centre of a henge with entrances to east and west. The central area had been flagged and this paving bore the detritus of numerous small fires. By the pillar a collapsed 2.4 m long cist, arranged NE–SW, held two well-cremated bodies which, from the signs of fire, had been burned in situ on a pyre of oak and hazel. With them were fragments of coarse pottery and a type of bone wristguard sometimes associated with Northern beakers.[17]

Similar deposits by centre stones occur in stone circles. At the circle-henge of Tisbury, Wiltshire, the central burial pit contained cremated bones and a pot now lost. At Callanish the chambered tomb had been squashed between the stone and the surrounding circle. It has already been noted that the tall pillar had acted as a navigational marker long before the non-circular ring of stones was set up around it. At the neighbouring Ceann Hulavig the stone had been surrounded by a later cairn. At Lacra D, Cumberland, with its central stone a Bronze Age overhanging-rim urn was buried at the north-west of the ring. Even at the great circle-henge of Avebury four ritual pits were discovered to the north of the Obelisk in the southern circle, and 'an urn full of bones was found towards the centre of the southern temple in 1880 . . . by Mr Pratt'. The passage-tomb of Bryn Celli Ddu on Anglesey had been built over a demolished circle-henge with a central pit or stone.

Although centre stones are not found in the earliest areas for circles nor in north-east or central Scotland, it would be dangerous to assume they can be used to date a site for they are not necessarily contemporary with their surrounding bank or circle. At Stonehenge the Altar Stone may have been set up at a time different from the other bluestones, the majority of which came from a different Pembrokeshire source. The belief that circles of stone were occasionally placed around an earlier pillar is strengthened by Thom's observations that no stone stands at the exact centre of any site.[18]

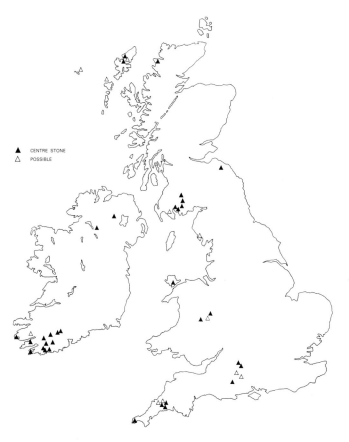

Fig. 30. The distribution of stone circles with centre stones.

There are several stone circles with rather unimposing centre stones in Cornwall and in south-west Ireland where the Cork-Kerry MSCs are to be found. There are others in Wiltshire, Shropshire, Northern Ireland and on Lewis. But the most concentrated group, now regrettably ruined, is in south-west Scotland. At these little rings in the hills around Cambret Moor and the Water of Ken the circles are composed of unobtrusive, rounded stones whereas the interior pillar is distinctly bigger. The best-preserved ring, Glenquickan near Creetown, has a stone 1.9 m high which stands in a cobble-strewn circle most of whose enclosing stones struggle for visibility in the thin, spiky grass. At Claughreid nearby, the 10.7 × 8.8 m oval also has low stones whereas the fallen stone at the centre is 1.7 m long. And at Lairdmannoch the circle itself at the south-east of a large cairn is virtually submerged in the lochside peat, and the 1.6 m centre stone lies half-covered beneath the creeping turf. The same may be said of three other centre-stone rings recently discovered at Loch Roan, Stroangassel and Eldrig Loch with its pointed Carlin Stane.

Such monuments can never have been conspicuous and were probably for local ceremonies. The circle-stones are demarcations. They are too close-set for dancing, their rings are too small to admit a big congregation and, like some of the other late megalithic rings, they are associated with cremation rites, the centre stone possibly providing a focus for the chief participant or perhaps itself embodying the religious symbolism required for the rituals.

The association of late megalithic ring and burial is further demonstrated by the adjacent cairn at Lairdmannoch, by the vestigial cairn suggested by Glenquickan's cobbles, and is valid for other small south-west Scottish sites without centre stones. The shattered monument of High Auchenlarie actually has the remnants of a platform-cairn inside it. Twenty-three metres to the south a cupmarked stone lies on a hillock against the background of the sea. The wretched slabs of Drannandow poke from the ground near Drumfern cairn. Further inland still, just beyond a heather-grown swamp, the great cairn of Cauldside Burn, cist and all, overshadows a circle of thin slabs.

One hundred and twenty metres north-east two stones, the taller fallen, lead to an overgrown ring-cairn, and, crossing the stream and continuing up the stone-walled hillside, one finds one of the most perfect decorated stones in Scotland, a 58 cm sixfold spiral carved on a heavy sub-rectangular block which also bears cupmarks. The stone may have been chosen because it overlooked a pass through the hills.[19]

This is a rare area where passage-tomb and 'Galician' rock-art overlap.[20] Such intermingling is infrequent in cup-and-ring stone districts but Galloway possesses not only the densest group of cup-and-ring marked stones in the British Isles but at least six well-executed spirals suggesting direct coastal settlement from Ireland. This maritime contact is also recognised through the dissemination of cordoned urns, of food-vessels, and of mid-second millennium metalwork from Ireland, a trade whose Hiberno-Scottish background may be highlighted by the observation that the concentration of virtually all decorated stones in Galloway, including spirals, are within 8 miles of a copper source.[21]

Increasingly during the second millennium in Wales, Cumbria, and Ireland stone circles and cairns were combined to make composite monuments, and the centre-stone circles of Galloway appear to be one manifestation of this mingling of sepulchral and ceremonial practice along the coasts of the Irish Sea. That they are late sites emerges from their low perimeters, their diameters averaging only 13.4 m, their occasional ovals, factors they share with cognate monuments in this part of Scotland, the enclosed cremation cemeteries like the Whitestanes Muir group, Dumfriesshire. Nith Lodge, Ayrshire, an embanked stone ring, 9.1 × 4.6 m, had three buried cremations associated with tiny pygmy cups and a collared urn and stone battle-axe both of which belong to the centuries around 1700 BC. Beoch, nearby, had nine large kerbstones around an egg-shaped enclosure with a late northern beaker. The Thieves, sometimes considered to be a ring-cairn, is more probably the savaged remains of an embanked stone circle.[22]

As elsewhere, the megalithic ring had been adapted to surround a series of cremation deposits at a time when the initially distinct architectural forms of henge, stone circle and kerbstone were being conflated in a bewilderment of regional types. Unlike the kerb-cairns and the RSC sites there are few signs of astronomical activity in the Galloway hill-bound rings. It may be assumed that theirs was a socio-sepulchral function for kinship groups living by the rivers and lochs of southern Scotland.

Not far from Castle Douglas there is a possible Four-Poster, Park of Tongland, at the highest point of a hill. Its history was complicated. When Fred Coles saw it in 1884 there were only two standing stones. Between them lay a third and 'on examining the ground carefully, the remains of another' was made out. Years later when a stone fell the site was excavated in 1987 and the stump of the fourth stone was found under the litter of a central cairn. Investigation showed that what had originally been a simple pair of stones like others in south-west Scotland had pyres lit by them and pits dug to receive the cremated bones.[23] A crudely circular cairn was heaped over the cemetery. Then two more stones were set up, converting the monument into a Four-Poster.

Seven radiocarbon assays ranging from 1610 ± 50 bc (GU-2382) to 1090 ± 50 bc (GU-2381), and averaging 1484 ± 50 bc, c. 1850–1750 BC, from the pits, and two from the construction of the cairn, 1430 ± 60 bc (GU-2375) and 1440 ± 50 bc (GU-2376), c. 1800–1700 BC, together with the presence of collared urns and an accessory cup confirm the Bronze Age date suspected for such late rings.[24]

Finally there are, in the extreme east of the region, three or four megalithic rings deep in the hills that climb above Eskdale and Liddesdale in the Cheviots, 20 miles from the sea, peculiar ovals of low stones with two startlingly tall pillars in their south-west quadrant, perhaps orientated towards the midsummer moon. The exaggerated architecture and the orientation implies a distant relationship with RSCs. The builders, whatever their ancestry, probably approached from the valleys to the south-west rather than along the Tweed-Teviot rivers of south-east Scotland where there are no comparable sites in the 1000 square miles of occupied country.

The ellipse of Ninestone Rigg, Roxburgh, stands on a barren moorland hill, grassy tufts obscuring the ring except for the two tall pillars with a half-hidden stone like a coy recumbent between them. Its azimuth of 211° coincides with the major southern moonset. It is like another oval curiously, with the same name – the Nine Stones – at Winterbourne Abbas, 300 miles south in Dorset where two vast blocks 1.8 m and 2.1 m high flank a low stone at the north. This site has the expected north–south axis of southern circles, but it does resemble the Roxburgh ring in its architecture, shape and size. It is possibly coincidental that the Grey Mare and Her Colts, a long chambered tomb with concave façade like some Clyde long cairns of south-west Scotland, is only 3 miles to the ssw.

Ten miles from Ninestone Rigg across the high pass of Sandy Edge an egg-shaped ring of many stones was built alongside an outcrop almost at the brow of the steep Burgh Hill. It has been ruined but alone among its little stones a 1.5 m pillar remains, fallen, at the south-west opposite a 1.1 m-long, low, thin slab in appearance like a Cork recumbent stone. This 'recumbent' and the prostrate pillar are on the main axis of the site which was 'well explored but yielded nothing of a sepulchral nature'.

Across the bleak uplands to the west the Loupin' Stanes, Dumfriesshire, is another oval, this time of twelve stones set on an artificial platform rising to the south-west. Two enormous stones tower at the wsw. Just to the north-west and to the east may be the ruins of other rings. An erratic line of standing stones meanders southwards towards the Girdle Stanes circle-henge 550 m down river, a line that may be the result of the linking of two stone circles of entirely different origins. Further south still near Langholm, the Seven Brethren on Whiteholm Rigg, also has its lowest stones at the north-east, but here, instead of two discrepantly high stones, there seems to be a normal grading in height towards the south-west in this oval that stands at the edge of a terrace overlooking the long, lovely valley of the Water of Milk. The shape and grading probably relate it to the nearby open circles of Dumfries and Galloway, a supposition strengthened by the position of a pygmy outlier, prostrate at 358°.2, indicating a north–south alignment.

Quite different from those rings is the solitary Torhousekie (Pl. 52), a superb site far to the west by Wigtown Bay.[25] This circle, in State guardianship, was built on the Machars, an area of calcareous sandy soil and drumlins that would have provided

Plate 52. Torhousekie variant recumbent stone circle in the Machars near Wigtown Bay, SW Scotland (Photograph: the author).

excellent farming land. It is not only one of the best-preserved sites in Britain, it is also one of the most important being almost certainly a variant RSC whose location may indicate something of the spread of customs from north-east Scotland.

On a manmade platform of earth and small stones nineteen local granitic boulders, graded towards the ESE, were set on the circumference of a flattened circle 21.4 × 20m. The largest stone weighs about six tons and would not have required many people to move it. Within the circle is a smallish central stone between two big boulders and that this setting is a variation of a recumbent stone and its flanking pillars is confirmed by the presence of a D-shaped ring-cairn attached behind it to the WNW.

Torhousekie is unlike any other circle in south-west Scotland but has many resemblances to the later RSCs of Kincardine whose recumbents and pillars were placed at the SSE and set well inside the stone circle. The position of the ring may be the result of a search for copper ores in the early centuries of the bronze industry.

The site can be seen as one facet of influences emanating from north-east Scotland, the NE–SW arm of the X-factor, influences that included the making of pottery like the Glenballoch urn in Ireland, and that impelled the construction of Four-Posters in Northumberland, on Arran, in central Wales and south-western Ireland. As the Cork-Kerry MSCs of south-west Ireland are also sometimes found near copper lodes it may be speculated that prospectors, whose ceremonies were performed in circles with recumbent stones like those in north-east Scotland, ultimately reached the cupriferous regions of Munster and built their own individual forms of RSC. Torhousekie, Auchagallon on Arran, Kiltierney in Co. Fermanagh and the diffusion of Four-Posters are intermediary indications of this movement. As in south-west Ireland there are not only little and late MSCs but also Five-Stone circles like Four-Posters with recumbent stone attached, and with several true Four-Posters such an equation seems feasible. The attractive ring of Torhousekie provides illumination of travel and communication in the early centuries of the Atlantic Bronze Age.

The Island of Arran

Hardly a mile from the west coast of this hilly island, 'the high place', and joined by a mountain pass, The String, to eastern Arran there is a rare expanse of flat land crossed by the Machrie Water. Within this attractive patch of alluvium and sandstone is an intriguing collection of stone circles. On the rich 5 square miles of Machrie Moor six stone circles, Rings numbered I–V and XI, crowd together in one small and irregular triangle of less than 5 acres (1.6ha), no ring being farther than 300m from another. With other more isolated but never far distant sites they offer a remarkable variety of styles: a good circle, site II, and a bad one, XI; ellipses, I and III; a probable 'Irish' Five-Stone ring, IV; a concentric, V; an outlying true circle converted into a complex ring-cairn, X; three Four-Posters; and a variant 'Aberdonian' recumbent stone circle, all crowded together as though the megalithic world of Britain and Ireland had assembled here like a hypermarket of prehistory.

The circles had been built well apart from any area of settlement. There are perhaps a dozen hut-circles, not all contemporary, a few hundred metres to the west but they are separated and obscured from the rings by a ridge. There are a few more across the Machrie Water to the north-west.[26]

Three of the Machrie Moor circles were dug into on a bright day in May 1861, by James Bryce[27] and two, those with tall sandstone pillars, II and III, were discovered to contain cists with Bronze Age food-vessels. In late September Bryce returned on another lovely day and excelled himself by opening five more sites before nightfall. Only two cists were found, with one food-vessel, some more arrowheads and a little bronze awl.

The differing diameters of the rings from 6.4m up to 18.1m; their various shapes of circles, ovals and eccentrics[28] including a concentric ring placed higher than the others; the alternations of low, obese granite blocks and thin, sandstone pillars; their six cists: all argue against a single, overall design. The intricacy of the shapes, even without the artefactual data, indicates a time when the laying out of megalithic rings was well established. The variety is explicable. It has been argued in chapter five that a mélange of traders and prospectors from Scotland, England and Ireland led to Arran becoming a cosmopolitan staging-post for the bustle of voyages from all directions Fig 10.

Machrie Moor I, one of the farthest from the coast, was partly excavated by Bryce, in September 1861. He was more fortunate than the present writer who began the excavation of three circles, I, X and XI, in 1978 only to encounter typical September western weather for two successive seasons with almost continuous rain limiting the work merely to a few frustrated days. The consolation was the uncovering of an unsuspected ring, XI, which had been preceded by a timber circle/cum-ellipse/cum-guesswork – of no definable shape.

More successful excavations by Alison Haggarty in 1985 and 1986 revealed that Site I, an ellipse, had been erected on the site of a long-abandoned and rotted timber ring which had affinities with similar rings in the English Lake District. The site had been raised on land previously occupied and farmed. C-14 determinations from pits provided dates of 2870 ± 50 bc (GU-2321); 3550 ± 70 bc (GU-2320) and 2820 ± 70 bc (GU-2315), a span from about 3900 to 3750 bc. Associated Grimston/Lyles Hill Neolithic sherds were found,[29] probably left by builders of Clyde chambered tombs. Two, Tormore and Moss Farm, stand on the moor itself. Such cairns were built on hillsides by pastoralists and continued in use into the early third millennium BC. A date of 2340 bc ± 110 (Q-676), *c.* 3150–2850 BC, came from Monamore from material laid down just before the tomb was blocked, and some of the mounds, already old, may have had elaborate orthostatic façades and trapezoidal cairns added during the Late Neolithic period.[30]

The outer timber ring of Site I was a ragged oval about 23 × 19.5 m and enclosed a good circle, 14.5 m diameter, of closely set posts like a fence. Inside it was a small but heavy and perhaps roofed horseshoe-shaped setting that faced north-west. Late Neolithic grooved ware was discovered. Charcoal from postholes gave dates of 2520 ± 50 bc (GU-2316); 2030 ± 180 bc (GU-2325); outer, of 2130 ± 90 bc (GU-2324), a general period of 2900–2650 BC.[31]

The rings were abandoned. Agricultural activity followed with signs of deep, long ard-marks across the site, evidence of intensive ploughing. More change followed. The long-forgotten postholes were rediscovered and replaced by an ellipse of six squat granite boulders with five intervening smaller sandstones, a sixth being missing at the north-east. In an off-centre pit an inverted urn held the cremated bones of a person between twenty and thirty years of age.

Just to the north-east of Ring I the dull tops of two little stones of Machrie Moor XI nudging through the heather were first noted in 1864 but forgotten until relocated by Roy and colleagues in the early 1960s and published by Mackie in 1975. Initial, water-logged excavations by the writer in 1978 and 1979 were followed by an exploration by Haggarty in 1985 and 1986. As with Site I there were traces of pre-circle agriculture and then the erection of a ring of ten posts in an irregular ellipse 'planned' by the laying-out of two semi-circles, 14.7 × 12.9 m. Grooved ware, impressed pottery and beaker sherds provided indications of Late Neolithic activity that included more farming of the land before a stone 'circle', approximately 13.6 × 12.2 m, was constructed of nine sandstones and one granite block. It proved impossible to demonstrate any form of geometrical design except that the irregular layout of the stoneholes crudely coincided with the irregularity of the earlier timber ring. At the centre was an empty pit but one adjacent pit contained the cremation of a thirty-year-old individual in a leather bag, accompanied by flint flakes, knives and scrapers of local pitchstone. Inside the ring a large boulder had conjoined triangles incised on it like an angular egg-timer. An assay of 1740 ± 50 (GU-2323), *c.* 2200–2050 BC, from a charcoal layer through which a stonehole cut, implied that the ring had been set up some time after 2100 BC.[32]

Machrie Moor II, 61 m WNW of Ring I, was the first to be dug by Bryce on 24 May 1861. It had been a plain circle, 12.8 m in diameter, originally of seven or eight tall sandstones from Auchencar 2 miles to the north, the tallest standing 5.3 m high. It suffered and only three now stand. Two pillars lie inside, one rounded and perforated in an attempt to convert it into a millstone. Within the ring Bryce found two cists, the central with a tripartite food-vessel, and, significantly, four flint arrowheads, from Co. Antrim 40 miles to the south-west across the North Channel. Bryce returned 'on a most brilliant and genial' day on 26 September 1861, to see if there were a second cist as in Site 3. There was. But it was empty.

Machrie Moor III is 122 m WNW of II. Only one stone, of Old Red Sandstone, stands with the stumps of three others showing, their snapped-off upper parts, up to 4.3 m long, buried. It had been similar to its partner, an irregular circle, about 16.3 × 15.4 m. Bryce came upon two cists, the central with flint arrowheads and a nondescript sherd.

To its south the other cist contained the blanched 'very perfect' skull and bones of a twenty-two year-old individual.

Perhaps the most challenging in its origins is Machrie Moor IV to the south of III. Four low granite stones form a warped rectangle but just to the north-west a trackway had been cut through the peat. It is arguable that a fifth stone had lain there. If so the site would have been a quite good circle about 7.5 m across with a central cist containing bone, a bronze awl, a tripartite food-vessel and three flint arrowheads. But it is the architecture that excites.

The lowest stone is at the south-west. Opposite is a heavy triangular block partnered by a thick, flat-topped boulder in the manner of 'female' and 'male' portals facing a recumbent in the Irish Five-Stone rings of which over fifty are recorded in the counties of Cork and Kerry. The components are the same, the arrangement of the stones is the same. The internal diameter of 6.4 m is twice that of the average 3.1 m in south-western Ireland, a difference in size perhaps occasioned by the greater number of men in a sea-going crew contrasted against the few members of a family in the hills of Munster. Three hundred and fifty miles of sea separate south-western Ireland from Arran but that such distances could be travelled is shown by the undoubted Five-Stone ring of Circle 275 in north Wales nearly 250 miles from Cork.[33]

To the west of IV is Machrie Moor V, the largest ring. It is a concentric with an inner ring of eight granite stones in a true circle 11.6 m, and an outer of fifteen smaller in an irregular ring about 18.1 m. Comparable settings exist in north-western England at the Druid's Temple, Gunnerkeld, Kirkstones and Oddendale.

The two rings were stripped of turf by Bryce who discovered only a disturbed and empty central cist. Locally the site was known as 'Fingal's Cauldron Seat' because the stones were thought to have supported the cooking-pot of the supernatural Irish giant, Finn mac Cumhal. A south-eastern stone has a ledge with a hole through it used by Finn to tether his dog, Bran.

At Machrie Moor X, a complex ring-cairn 1000 m WNW of the main group, the great northern kerbstones had been piled onto the cairn to make room for a wide farmtrack and Bryce decided it was too disturbed to be worth investigation. Excavation by the writer showed that its cairn was enclosed in a perfect circle, 21.7 m in diameter, of thin sandstone slabs. A bank of closely packed stones of local granite surrounded the ring. Inside was a doughnut-shaped cairn with an open central space that had been filled with sand and scattered boulders. A mass of distinctive, small red bits of sandstone had been laid over the entire cairn.

The layers of differently coloured stones in cairns is known elsewhere. A barrow at Charlton Marshall in Dorset was built of alternating layers of flint and chalk. The empty grave of Huish Champflower in Somerset was covered in thick bands of turf and brushwood. On the Yorkshire Moors a barrow at Saintoft was composed of various hues of sand. Not far away another mound, wrote the Reverend J. C. Atkinson, 'consisted of clean, water-worn pebbles and nodules of half a dozen different varieties of stone, such as could have been derived only from the bed of a beck running its course to the sea through a moor-valley some two and half miles distant'. A barrow on Wapley Moor contained a thick layer of white sand that 'must have been brought from a distance of seven miles'.

Remembering the mixture of grey granite and ochre sandstones of Circle I it is possible that they geologically symbolised Arran itself, Jones describing it as 'a barren northern mountainous region of white granites and schists; and a fertile southern lowland region of red sandstone'. Several megalithic tombs on the island such as Clachaig and Giants' Graves contain both types of stone even though some were not local.

'At Carn Ban, for example . . . on a granite hillside, the main megaliths forming the chamber were of granite, but the drystone walling which gave height to the chamber were of sandstone, while the lintel slabs were of alternating slabs of granite and sandstone.'

Jones continued, 'In many cultures, red and white are thought of as symbols of the red blood or flesh and white bones of the human body, an idea which would be particularly apt in the case of tombs built to house the dead,' an interpretation already offered for the Clava tombs of Inverness. 'On Arran, however, it may be that white and red also symbolised the land itself, the white of the north and the red of the south.'[34]

Emphasising the mixture of influences to which Arran was open, 1¾ miles northwest of the group and by the sea is another stone circle at Auchagallon with a stone suggestive of a derivation from north-eastern Scotland. Fifteen irregularly spaced local red sandstones form a ring 9 × 14.1 m in diameter, with a gap at the north-east. It is littered with small stones and cobbles. In 1910 Thomas Bryce was told by Archibald Sim that 'in his youth the enclosed area was flat and free of stones'. He recalled a central excavation 'many years ago', when a cist was exposed but could remember nothing of its contents.

The stones of the ring are from 0.9 m high. The two tallest, 3.2 m and 1.7 m at the west, flank a 'recumbent' 1.8 m high and 1.5 m broad, much longer than other stones which average no more than 76 cm in width. The remains of an internal cairn, the westerly orientation, the grading and the recumbent are strongly reminiscent of a variant Scottish RSC.[35]

On Arran there are simple circles at Lamlash and elsewhere, and there are RSC-derivative Four-Posters, a fine example being at Aucheleffan, its superb view towards the sea-girt pyramid of Ailsa Craig now obscured by drab Forestry Commission conifers. There are other Four-Posters including Ballymichael Bridge east of the Machrie Moor rings and the little Machrie Burn 1½ miles to the north of the group.

Three of the Machrie Moor circles are set in line, pointing roughly to a conspicuous stone on a ridge a quarter of a mile west. This would direct a traveller towards the concealed Machrie Bay, but the line could never have been used astronomically because the horizon is obscured by Beinn an Tuirc mountain 10 miles away on Kintyre and there is no hill-notch. But Barnatt and Pierpoint demonstrated that the circles had been erected in a significant area. 'At midsummer the sun would have risen at a prominent notch on the skyline; visually this notch is centrally placed at the head of Machrie Glen for all six circles.'[36] It was a special place.

The distribution of the Clyde chambered tombs on the island provides support for the interpretation of Machrie Moor as a seasonal meeting-place for natives and strangers from Scotland, England, Wales and Ireland. The score of cairns lie quite regularly spaced about 2 miles apart around the southern coast: Glenrickard, Monamore and others at the east; East Bennan at the south; the Tormore tombs at the west. The intrusive Clava cairn of Carmahome is atypically isolated at the south-west. The majority of the tombs 'are within 500 metres of land probably suitable for agriculture in the neolithic period . . . and this encourages us to think in terms of . . . roughly equal territories based upon this arable land'.[37]

In contrast to this spaced pattern amongst the chambered tombs the large stone circles on Machrie Moor cannot represent territorial areas for five cluster tightly within 275 m of each other. Smaller rings here and there on Arran: Lamlash, Kildonan, South Sannox; Four-Posters like Shiskine and Glenree may have been Bronze Age family shrines, spread in individual areas, but the rings on Machrie Moor are too close together, are too varied in their design, to be explained as native centres. Theirs was a Babel of foreign tongues.

Not 3 miles from them to the south-west Pennant saw 'a stupendous cairn 114 feet [35 m] over, and of vast height' in 1772. It rose above the sea at the mouth of a valley. It was enormous. Later estimates made it as much as 60 m across. Over the years its stones were removed for dykes, drains, houses, even a horse-mill, until nothing was left and in 1900 workmen uncovered the sandstone capstone of a short cist whose slabs were 'so regular as to suggest that they had been hewn; and set exactly vertical and parallel to one another'. No bones were found, nor pottery, but there was a three-ribbed bronze dagger with a gold pommel like another in the immense cairn of Collessie in Fife, a cairn so huge that even using three carts and a large workforce over eight days it was only 'when fully a thousand cart-loads of stones had been lifted and conveyed off the site, we began to realise the magnitude of the task we had undertaken'.[38] The cairn at Blackwaterfoot may have been even bigger, a statement of massive power at a time when there were no carts and when everything had to be achieved through the raw muscles of men and animals.

The circles belong to the centuries around 2500 BC. It is feasible that the burial at Blackwaterfoot was an example of a chieftain society responding to the sea-trade in prestigious wares of the Bronze Age, cargoes of raw materials: flint, copper ores; manufactured articles; poundingly heavy axe-hammers of hard stone, bronze weapons; luxuries of jet, amber, faience beads, the community proud of their leader's personal display of grandeur and might. It may have been such a person that had been interred in the mountainous cairn.

Close to the cairn, at Drumadoon Bay, were small and safe sandy beaches and a tiny tidal harbour sheltered by the Kintyre peninsula, an ideal landing-place for trading seafarers. Tribute and gifts may have been demanded from the incomers in return for promises of safety at the sanctuary of Machrie Moor. It is the kind of question that prehistorians should ask but the kind that archaeology cannot answer.

Chapter Fourteen

The Stone Circles of the Republic of Ireland

The Kingdom of Ireland he hath surveyed, and that with exactnesse . . . and those that he employed for the Geometricall part were ordinary fellowes . . . that circumnambulated with their 'box and needles' not knowing what they did.

John Aubrey, 1680, 238–9

South-West Ireland

Copper was the cause. Attracted by the prehistoric Yukon of cupriferous Munster people came from Cornwall, Brittany, Aberdeenshire to obtain the ores that were available in the counties of Cork and Kerry. The intermixing of customs from southern England, western France and northern Scotland are explicable as the result of prospecting for copper in the late third and second millennium BC. 'The copper resources of the peninsulas and of Killarney were regarded as an attractive part of the potential of Kerry by prehistoric metalworkers.'[1]

Copper mines existed at Ross Island in Lough Leane, Co. Kerry, in use from 2400 BC onwards and from which the earliest copper may have come, and in Co. Cork at Derrycarhoon near Schull on the Mount Gabriel peninsula where six copper-mine shafts contained grooved egg-shaped mauls of grindstone up to 40 lbs (18 kg) in weight. Fourteen assays from Mount Gabriel spread from 1500 ± 120 bc (VRI-66) down to 1180 ± 80 bc (BM-2336) indicating prolonged mining on the peninsula from 1800 BC onwards. From another mine at Ballyrisode came twelve polished stone axes, one of green chloritic grit.[2]

Inevitably the region was affected by traditions from outside. From Cornwall, 200 sea-miles ESE from south-western Ireland came the tradition of adding centre stones to stone circles (Fig. 30). Thirteen or more Munster circles have these, indicating the mélange of beliefs that resulted here during the second millennium BC. Most of these stones are lower than those of the circle and some, at Templebryan and Carrigaphooca, are quartz chosen perhaps because of their brilliance. Elsewhere at the hedge-bound and thistlegrown Maulatanvally and Gortanimill observers have commented on the whiteness of the central stone. Even the ruined Derrynafinchin in a remote valley by Bantry Bay has a vivid quartz block by its central boulder-cist. Although the centre-stone circles of south-west Scotland should not be forgotten, Cornwall would seem the most probable source for such an introduction of centre stones. People knowing of Cornish circles like Boscawen-Un with its large off-centre pillar, or the Hurlers Centre, or the Stripple Stones circle-henge, could well have

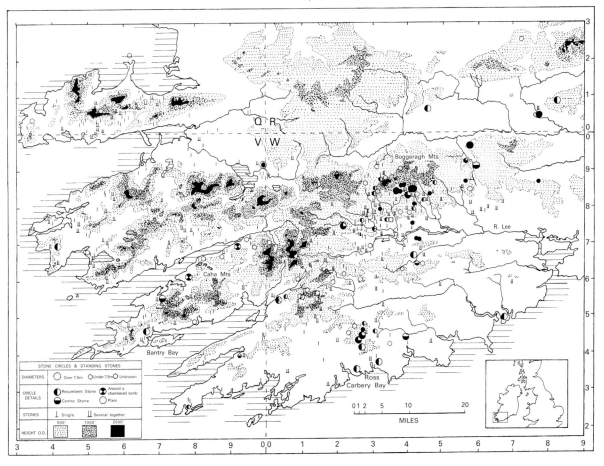

Fig. 31. The distribution of stone circles in south-west Ireland.

added such a feature to the otherwise alien MSCs they encountered in the counties of Cork and Kerry.

Both Cornish and Welsh stone axes have been found in Ireland, particularly along the eastern coasts and it is possible to speak of a 'network of contacts across the Irish Sea which would have facilitated the development of regional exchange networks in the Bronze Age when the Cornish alluvial tin sources appear to have been a vital complement to the copper lodes in south-west Ireland.[3] Such sites, domestic, ritual and industrial show not only the wide extent of activity here during the second millennium but also the variety of custom.

Amongst them were burial-sites including the megalithic wedge-shaped chambered tombs whose origins reached back not to the often-quoted rectangular and ungraded *allées-couvertes* of Brittany but to the trapezoidal, graded *sépultures en V* with terminal cells like the three Liscuis passage-tombs near Rostrenen, Côtes-du-Nord, whose dates range from 3190 ± 110 bc (Gif-3099) to 1730 ± 110 bc (Gif-4075, *c.* 4500–2000 BC, comfortably earlier than Labbacallee, the largest of the Irish wedge-tombs where, in the gallery, lay the headless skeleton of a woman, her skull being found with a male skeleton and a child in a superimposed layer. Intriguingly, the modern name is a corruption of 'Leaba Caillighe', the 'Hag's Bed'. Determinations of 1855

± 45 bc (GrN-11359), 1830 ± 70 bc (OxA-2759) and 1680 ± 70 bc (OxA-2766) suggest that the tomb was in use around 2350–2000 BC, many centuries after Liscuis. Five assays from Altar wedge-tomb at Toormore Bay, near whose entrance was a hoard of a tin-bronze axe and some unalloyed copper, averaged 1123 ± 60 bc, c. 1450–1350 BC,[4] even later than Labbacallee.

As well as the 'intrusive' centre stone architecture and the 'foreign' wedge tombs there were also alien stone circles. The southernmost tip of the NE–SW 'X' distribution ended in south-western Ireland where rings of the Scottish RSC tradition were constructed. There is an architectural grace-note. There, because the recumbent is no longer a heavy block but a thin, upright slab, the terms 'multiple-stone' circle, and 'axial' rather than 'recumbent' have been preferred and will be used here.[5]

The axial stones are thin slabs rather than heavy blocks. There is nothing as impressive as the great squared stone at Cothiemuir Wood. Even Drombeg has a recumbent that, although 2.1 m long, is only 46 cm thick. This is the one stone here to be cupmarked, two carvings being placed on its upper surface. Noticeably, however, the stones have tops that are not only level but also horizontal, another indication of their Scottish ancestry.

The writer is convinced that the many architectural similarities between the Scottish and Irish rings make an origin from Scotland likely. This belief is strengthened by the existence of variant RSCs, Five-Stone rings and Four-Posters like Mullaghmore in Co. Down between north-eastern Scotland and Ireland, and by the presence in Cork and Kerry not only of many little Five-Stone circles resembling Four-Posters with a recumbent added but also of genuine Four-Posters like the one recently recognised at Grousemount, deep in the Derrynasaggart Mountains of Co. Kerry, and another isolated at the very south-east of Ireland, like the only survivor of a shipwreck, at Robinstown Great in Co. Waterford. Dates deep in the second millennium BC from multiple stone circles (MSCs) such as Drombeg add credence to the hypothesis that the Irish sites were a late development from sources in Scotland.

The rings are unusual. In them all the components of their Scottish forebears exist: the recumbent, the flankers, the interest in the south-west, human remains, quartz, cupmarks, the ring-cairn but it is as if some megalithic meccano set had been dismantled, its pieces later reassembled incorrectly, the flankers opposite the recumbent, the ring-cairn outside the circle. But the elegance and the symmetry survived.

Well over a hundred rings are known in Cos. Cork and Kerry (Fig. 32).[6] There are studies by Condon (1916–18), Somerville (1930), Barber (1972), Burl (1976), and, above all by O'Nuallain (1975 and 1984a). Nearly all the sites are small. What is considered to be a large circle here is about 8.5 m in diameter with 42 per cent between 8.5 m and 9.5 m. The bigger sites tend to be placed along the coast in low-lying country with a concentration around Ross Carbery, the very largest at Breeny More, 14 m wide, 14 miles to the north-west in the hills by Bantry Bay. In contrast, the smaller circles are generally inland near the Boggeragh Mountains and ranges to their west.

Many of the bigger circles have a recumbent or axial stone in their south-west quadrant, have tall portal stones, are graded, and contain occasional cupmarks or quartz pebbles. But their pillars are set opposite the recumbent, their grading is 'back to front', they lack an internal cairn, and in consequence their direct connection with Scottish RSCs has been questioned, the doubts being strengthened by the 500 miles of

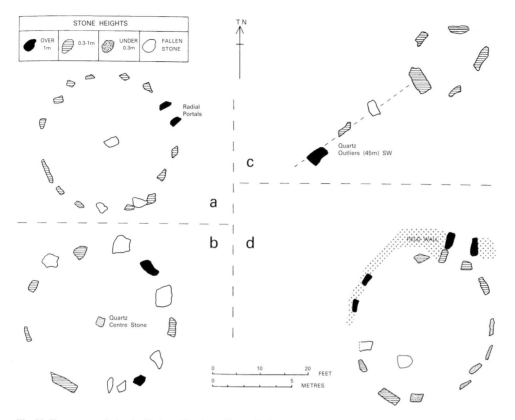

Fig. 32. Four stone circles in Cork: a. Carrigagulla SW; b. Currebeha; c. Knockraheen; d. Carrigagrenane SW (after Barber, 1972).

land and sea between Aberdeenshire and Co. Cork. Yet if the Irish sites have a separate ancestry it is unclear. The almost unique graded heights, the recumbent stone, cupmarks and quartz are persuasive links between Scotland and Ireland, particularly when the intermediate presence of the RSC of Torhousekie in Wigtownshire, the Five-Stone ring of Circle 275 in North Wales and Four-Posters like the Four Stones, Walton in central Wales are recalled.

The circles in which RSC elements are most obvious are those in coastal positions like the gorse-grown Bohonagh; or Drombeg (Pl. 53) overlooking a warped chessboard, and Breeny More. Their diameters range between 3.4 m and 14 m. The number of stones varies between seven and nineteen, two-thirds of them having 9, 11 or 13. This is in contrast to the inland sites which frequently have only five stones and where diameters can be as little as 2.3 m.

Little was permanent in prehistory. Whatever the tradition time, distance, forgetfulness, misunderstanding caused change. In Ireland the recumbent stone was affected. What began around Ross Carbery as a straightforward slab in the south-west quadrant altered the farther away the ring: lumpishly at Kenmare 24 miles to the northwest where the recumbent and the portals are hardly distinguishable from the other circle-stones; diminutively at the dainty Lissyviggeen 32 miles to the NNW; an upright pillar at Ardgroom 40 miles to the west; and amnesiacally at Cong 130 miles away where the square recumbent and its honeycombed flanker were set at the north.

Plate 53.Drombeg multiple stone circle, Co. Cork (Photograph: the author).

Of the 'classic' recumbent stone circles the biggest coastal group is near Ross Carbery. Three sites, Templebryan, impressive in its tree-lined field, Drombeg and Bohonagh are very close to the coast suggesting early colonisation here. Though they are mainly on low-lying land and inconspicuous, most, like Drombeg on a terrace overlooking the sea, are still placed on hill-slopes, often on spurs commanding wide views. Miles further inland other circles are small, the Five-Stone rings of Cappaboy Beg NW, only 2.3 × 1.8 m, or its immediate neighbour to the south-east, a trapezoidal Four-Poster, 4.5 × 2.2 m, far away in the Sheehy Mountains.

Another group, with distinctive portal stones, is found on the north coast of the Caha peninsula, Ardgroom being only half a mile from the harbour on an open height 30 m above the shore. The impression is of settlement by people approaching from the sea, perhaps after several seasons of cautious reconnaissance of the unknown wilderness. Some of these sites contain other features – central boulder-cists or stones, or an extra pair of stones outside the portals – which may be additions to the original MSCs, adaptations by people of differing beliefs.

Other groups occur near Bantry Bay. Such a distribution makes it probable that the primary colonisation of Munster by RSC builders was along the south and south-west coasts by settlers searching for the light, brown earths that were easy to clear and farm.

The stone circles of inland regions are somewhat different. Though there are some large MSCs they often show considerable variation from the 'classic' form and their distribution is related to the River Lee and its tributaries, standing on easily worked soils above the valley bottoms. The sites resemble those in Perthshire. This similarity is heightened by the presence of pairs of stones by some of the circles.

It is tempting to think of the few large inland RSCs as 'parent' sites from which the smaller circles may have developed. The position of Derreenataggart at the extreme south-west of the Kenmare peninsula; of Gortanimill close to the Sullane along which settlers seem to have come; of Carrigagulla near to the Slaney, another settlement route; all these MSCs are situated where incomers might first have settled.

The larger sites are circular and have diameters much the same as some southern Scottish RSCs: Binghill, 10.4m, and Ardlair, 11.6m, in Aberdeenshire. Many of the stones in these circles are 1m high but inland sites like Carrigagrenane, well away from the coast, Gortanimill and Carrigagulla have no stone as high as this. An increase in the number of stones accompanied by a diminution in height is a general feature of later circles and, like their shapes, may be a factor in evaluating the relative chronology of megalithic rings. It may be significant, therefore, that the coastal rings tend to be circular whereas those inland are sometimes oval or just misshapen.[7]

The recumbent or axial stone in the Munster series remains in the south-west quadrant and is usually long and flat-topped. These are not massive blocks. Horizontality was more important than size. The only huge slabs conveniently to hand were unsuitably shaped egg-like boulders.

The longest of the recumbents is the 2.3m stone at Derreenataggart looking between its portals to the hill-surrounded bay below. It is noticeable that Carrigagulla and Gortanimill have recumbents smaller than the average despite their being built in the country where stone was more plentiful than by the coast.

Unlike the Aberdeenshire RSCs the recumbents have no flanking stones. It is the larger coastal circles that are most like the Scottish RSCs with their recumbent stones, grading and tall pillars but, unlike them, the pillars are erected opposite the recumbent, like entrances or portal stones. A similar arrangement may have existed at the strange oval at Burgh Hill, Roxburgh. Many of the Cork inland MSCs have these north-east portals set radially at right-angles to the circumference. Such pillars average only 1.4m in height although those at Drombeg, Bohonagh and Derreenataggart, perhaps amongst the earliest, are over 2.4m high. Not surprisingly, it is at Gortanimill and Carrigagulla that the lowest portals occur. From these stones the circles grade downwards towards the recumbent which, sometimes, is taller than its neighbouring stones. Yet a stone at Bohonagh had its top shaped to slope upwards towards the adjacent recumbent. This was even more noticeable at Drombeg where three stones had sockets whose depths had been graduated in order to give a sloping effect to the tops of the stones up towards the recumbent. It was at the same MSC that a huge lozenge-shaped stone at the NNE had been dramatically placed alongside a very thin pillar like the 'male' and 'female' stones in the Kennet Avenue, Wiltshire, which could be forms of fertility symbolism.[8]

Albeit rearranged, all the architectural traits of Scottish RSCs exist in the Cork sites. Such variation could be expected if a long period had passed during the years of colonisation before settlers had leisure once more to build their ritual monuments. Case argued that any cultural system transmitted from one area to another in this way will be an inexact copy and not identical with that of the homeland. This seems true in the case of the Cork-Kerry MSCs.[9]

At Drombeg, Fahy discovered that the site had been stripped, levelled and a gravel floor laid, 10 cm thick on the west. So intent were the builders on achieving a level surface that boulders had been removed and their pits filled with small stones. Beneath the gravel were burial pits. Drombeg is the only Irish MSC yet known with such a floor but at Bohonagh the site also was levelled with a step cut into the hillside like Nether Balfour, Aberdeenshire. Around the portals and the recumbent were stony areas. Maulatanvally may have been strewn with sandstone. Quartz pebbles had been spread around the portals of Knocknakilla.[10]

Only four of the large RSCs have been satisfactorily excavated. All contained central pits with cremated bone. At Bohonagh a low, central mound covered a shallow, carelessly dug pit holding soil, pebbles and fragments of bone. The embanked MSC at Reanascreena had an irregular central pit, filled with soil but no deposit. Instead, 3.1 m to the north was another small pit with a flat piece of shale over five or six pieces of burnt bone. The excavator speculated that the pyre had been to the east of the site as there was a heavy concentration of charcoal there. The very few bone fragments under the shale suggest a token deposit similar to that in the primary pit at Loanhead of Daviot, Aberdeenshire.

At Drombeg there were two central pits. In the larger was bone and some flat-rimmed sherds like Knockadoon ware of the Early Bronze Age. The second pit had only a few charcoal flecks. It was possible to reconstruct the sequence of events. The pot had been broken before its deposition and perhaps wrapped in a cloth while hot burned bones were placed in it. Then it was put into the larger pit. Some sweepings from the pyre were added. The pot was pressed into place and a pinch of charcoal added before the pit was filled. Such rites are very like those known in Scottish RSCs.

A comparable cremation was discovered at the ruined Five-Stone ring of Cashelkeelty built on previously cultivated land. At the centre of the circle a slab-covered pit held the burnt bones of a 25–30-year-old individual. Flint arrowheads, scrapers and an ard point were recovered from the site of an adjacent but demolished MSC of the same name.[11]

Two sites, Reanascreena and Glentane East, are surrounded by banks and ditches. Similarly embanked stone circles are far to the north-west at the gigantic Grange henge and two others near Lough Gur, Co. Limerick. Just to the south is Lissyviggeen, Co. Kerry, a seven-stone circle 4.0 m across within an earth bank about 20 m from crest to crest. These sites, however, are low-lying whereas Reanascreena was built near the summit of a hill. In the counties of Kildare and Wicklow on the south-east coast of Ireland are several embanked circles on hilltops in situations reminiscent of many Irish passage-tombs including some in Co. Wicklow like Seefin and Baltinglass Hill. Stone circles such as the Piper's Stones, Kildare, or Castleruddery and Tournant, Co. Wicklow, are on summits and are embanked. The former has many features in common with Grange. At Reanascreena there may be a fusion of traits from chambered tombs, henges and MSCs.

The finds from the RSCs are limited to the broken pot from Drombeg, three small flints and four shale fragments from the same site, and a chisel-ended flint found outside Bohonagh's portals. There was also a perplexingly late C-14 assay from Drombeg's charcoal, of 13 ± 40 bc (TCD-38). This was later recalculated as an even more improbable AD 600 ± 120 (D-62). A further date of 790 ± 80 bc (OxA-2683) also seemed to be very late but has been buttressed by others from Reanascreena: 830 ± 35 bc (GrN-17509) and 945 ± 35 bc (GrN-17510), and is conformable with assays from the Five-Stone ring at Cashelkeelty: 970 ± 60 bc (GrN-9173) and 715 ± 50 bc (GrN-9172).[12]

There is a problem. The pottery associated with these assays is the flat-bottomed coarseware of the Late Bronze Age, a period in keeping with the assays. It does not follow that this was the time when the surrounding stone circle was built or even when it was functioning as a conventional megalithic ring.

Like the internal food-vessel cremations at Machrie Moor or the flat-rimmed urn at Sandy Road in Perthshire the Irish determinations derive from material that could well be secondary to the elevation of the ring: an intrusive cremation at Drombeg, another at Reansacreena. The Cashelkeelty assay came from charcoal on the old land surface 'and overlying stony layer'. None came from stoneholes. Such radiocarbon results do not necessarily coincide with the erection of the stone circle or even the period when it remained in use as a place of assembly.

It is more probable that the 'dates' are anachronisms coming from much later burials deposited in the ring by people of different beliefs who regarded the ancient, abandoned structure as a fitting shrine for the interment of one of their dead. It is equally probable that coastal MSCs such as Drombeg were constructed in the centuries around 2000 BC rather than a millennium later. The rough pottery found in them may be as relevant to their erection as his name carved by Lord Byron on the Parthenon when that temple was already two thousand years old.

Turning from the large coastal RSCs to the smaller, inland sites, these still retain RSC traits though only tenuously. The recumbent survives sometimes in a debased form hardly distinguishable from the other circle-stones. A lot of these circles have an outlier or a pair of stones by them either like a double entrance or at right-angles to the circle like a short row and are reminiscent of the Perthshire paired stones at the Four-Posters of Lundin Farm and Ferntower. It is noticeable that the Irish pairs at Clodagh, Kealkil, Knocknakilla and others stand tangentially to their rings like some of the Welsh short rows.[13] Many of the sites, like Carrigaphooca, Macroom, are about 3.2 m across and of five stones including a westerly recumbent. 'To the east of the castle is a large stone placed upon a high rock, secured by wedges of other stones, and near it, the remains of a druid altar, encompassed with a circle of stones pitched end-ways.' The majority lie in the Boggeraghs where the Laney, Delehinagh and Dripsey flow into the Sullane. Each area has at least one large RSC but a riverine penetration from the east is probable rather than one overland from Ross Carbery, and the inland builders are likely to belong to a separate immigration.

Because of the retention of the recumbent stone in the Five-Stone sites, parallels may be made between them and Scottish Four-Posters, especially as in Perthshire the average diameter of eleven Four-Posters was 4.9 m, and in Cork twelve Five-Stone rings averaged 3.2 m. The suggestion that the Five-Stone circle is basically a Four-Poster with recumbent stone retained is supported by the presence of indisputable Four-Posters at Lettergorman and elsewhere. One may even have stood at Barratrough near the picturesque Streamstown Bay in Co. Galway, an astonishing 140 miles north of Ross Carbery.[14]

Plate 54. Knocknakilla, Co. Cork. Leaning and prostrate pair of outliers with the Five-Stone ring behind. A radial-cairn is on the right (Photograph: the author).

Despite the wide distribution of the Five-Stone rings few excavations are recorded, Cashelkeelty has already been described. At Knocknakilla (Pl. 54) no artefacts were found in the hurried half-day of digging but a paved area was noticed around the outside of the stones and, like Corrimony and Castle Fraser in north-east Scotland, there was a concentration of quartz pebbles by the portal stones.

At Kealkil no burial was found. Instead, at the centre of the site below a slope worn through with patches of naked rock there were two shallow trenches crossing each other. 'They evidently served to contain two wooden beams which, we may suppose, served to support an upright post at the point where they crossed.' O'Riordain noted that the portals would have made a foresight through which the alignment past the central post and over the supposed recumbent stone would be almost exactly north; and that a sighting along the edge of the recumbent to the side of a lately fallen member, once 5.3 m tall, of a pair of outlying stones 1.6 m apart, would have provided an easterly orientation. Later, O'Nuallain recognised that the true axial stone, the smallest in the ring, lay at the customary south-west.[15] Kealkil is noteworthy as a site in which RSC architecture was combined with the preoccupation of builders of open circles with north–south and equinoctial lines, another example of the mixing of influences.

The one feature that distinguishes these circles from those in Scotland is the absence of any internal cairn although ring-cairns do exist alongside several circles. Just to the ESE of Kealkil was a radially kerbed cairn, 8.9 m in diameter, from which the only finds were three bits of scallop shell. The site is considered a form of native ring-cairn like those at the Maughanclea Four-Poster, at Knocknakilla and

Knockraheen. Without excavation these ruins cannot be resolved but it is interesting that they occur alongside diminutive Five-Stone rings.

There have been claims that, like Kealkil, other Cork circles had an astronomical function. From an examination of five large RSCs Somerville suggested that Drombeg's recumbent would indicate the midwinter sunset, and Bohonagh's the equinoxes. He could find no good alignments at Reanascreena, Carrigagrenane or Maulatanvalley. Fahy, the excavator of Drombeg and Bohonagh agreed with these conclusions though he carefully noted that Drombeg's alignment did not pass through a distant hill-gap but to one side of it. Reanascreena elicited only the comment that the recumbent may have marked a near-miss on the equinoxes if an error of 12′ may be considered 'near'. But the azimuth of 258° is akin to the wsw lines noticed in many Cornish stone circles, and may be related to them as the presence of 'Cornish' centre stones in other Cork rings and Kealkil's north–south lines intimate.

The very lengths of the recumbents make it unlikely that the builders intended a precise sightline. At Bohonagh the stone is 1.8 m long. As the circle is only 9.9 m across there is a broad angle of vision over the diameter to the width of the recumbent of about 10°. As, in that latitude, the sun moves 3° along the horizon weekly, Bohonagh's recumbent could be used to determine a three-week 'equinoctial' period in March and September but nothing more precise. This may have been the builders' wish but it is difficult to prove. At Drombeg the angle is about 14° because the stone is longer and the variation is for five weeks from mid-December to mid-January rather than precisely to the midwinter solstice.

In a computerised analysis of thirty Irish RSCs Barber suggested that seventeen contained orientations on the sun, moon and Venus. Many of the large rings like Drombeg and Gortanimill had such lines. Of the exceptions ten had postulated stellar alignments. Three others were apparently related to no celestial event. There has been criticism of these widely spread results.[16]

Without further systematic fieldwork, recording horizon heights and azimuths from one side to the other of the axial stones, no unarguable conclusions about sightlines can be offered. Yet from a study of the plans of Somerville, 1930; Fahy, 1959–62; Barber, 1972; and O'Nuallain, 1984a, and the technically superior surveys of thirty-one sites by Patrick between 1972 and 1974 there are indications that the stone circles, large and small, did have coarse alignments built into them. With azimuths to the midpoint of the recumbent slab ranging from 188° at Clogboola to 276° at Dereenataggart there is an obvious interest in the south-west quadrant from about 190° to 270°, the area of the western sky where both the midwinter sun and the midsummer moon would set.

In the years around 1500 BC and at the latitude of Ross Carbery, 51° 35′, the midwinter sun would have set below a skyline level with the observer at 229°, and the southernmost midsummer moon at 219°. With an elevated horizon of 5°, not uncommon in the hills and mountains of south-western Ireland, these directions would change to 237° and 228°. The settings of the minor southern moon would have been 239° and 246° respectively. All that can be stated with such unsatisfactory data is that only ten of the thirty-one azimuths fall within this bracket.

It is of interest, however, that the entrances of many of the wedge-tombs in Cork and Kerry faced the settings of the major and minor southern moons with a few more looking towards settings just north of west. There is also a closely-knit batch between 253° and 290° as though looking towards the mid-year sunsets.[17] Eight of the stone circles also occupy that range. It is possible that the builders of stone circles simply followed long-established regional traditions by casually setting their axial stones to be in line with lunar and solar settings.

Maybe before the mid-second millennium BC people from outside the region and with a half-forgotten Scottish ancestry arrived off the coasts of Munster, moving inland along the rivers, searching the wooded hillsides for easily worked land. The bulk of the circles are sited on the now marshy soils of the highland areas of the south, the thin stony earths of the underlying sandstone. Before the developing peat bogs they would have provided ground well suited to peoples who did not have the heavy plough to farm the alluvial soils of the valley floors. This at once explains the distribution of the circles. The builders penetrated inland along the river valleys until they came to soils light enough to cultivate with the equipment they possessed, probably no more than the spade. Their upper limit would be set by the poor, infertile soils of the higher slopes.[18] In this the rings resemble the Scottish RSCs also set on hillsides above the valleys. But everything seems half-size, their diameters, their 'territories', and everything seems rearranged as though the individual parts of the architecture: the recumbent stone, its orientation, the flankers, the grading, the ring-cairn, were remembered but not their relationship.

Around Ross Carbery the large coastal circles like Drombeg, Bohonagh and Templebryan are 4 to 6 miles from each other, close to convenient bays. A little farther inland six more rings, including Carrigagrenane, Reanascreena and Maulatanvally, crowd into a narrow strip of only 4 square miles. On the Beara peninsula large RSCs like Derreenataggart, Ardgroom, Shronebirrane, Drombohilly and Lohart stand some 3 miles apart. And in the foothills above Bantry Bay eight coastal rings were erected 2 to 3 miles from each other. Although it is not known whether all these neigh-bouring rings were contemporary it is not unreasonable to think of each having an approximate territory of 1 square mile, of which perhaps a third was cultivable. This is about a quarter the area for the Scottish RSCs. If the same demographic equation from Scotland were applied to the Cork circles it would suggest that the Irish rings were used by groups of no more than about thirty people who understandably built rings about half the circumference of those in Aberdeenshire, the relative arenas of the interiors being 1:5. That so few workers could have built a typical stone circle is not contradicted by the size of the heaviest recumbent, that at Derreenataggart, measuring $2.2 \times 1.5 \times 0.4\,m$ and weighing no more than 4 tons, easily moved by sixteen people. Drombeg's recumbent weighs even less, hardly 2 tons. Even the prostrate outlier at Kealkil which must have weighed about 4 tons was re-erected in the Spring of 1938 by only six labourers albeit 'with much difficulty' and with the aid of modern blocks and tackle.

The density of these Cork RSCs, like those in north-east Scotland and in Northern Ireland, is very different from the uncrowded distribution of many circles in lowland Britain and implies different systems of land-owning, perhaps of independent families rather than fiefdoms or tribal areas communally worked.

These largely forgotten circles deep in the Boggeraghs or along the storm-drenched rocks of the western bays once were the most needed centres of people's lives, places that combined the mundane earth with the imagery of the night sky, where a first burial sanctified the area, where people trod or danced around the portal stones as the layers of thick humus at Drombeg and Bohonagh testify, much as others may have done along the north-east causeways of some Scottish RSCs, looking towards the darkening, lowering horizon and the setting of the sun or moon. Now only the stones and the secrets survive.

There are few stone circles in the far west of Co. Kerry, well-scattered sites whose architecture is often a mixture of circle and burial structure, the recumbent tradition persistent but ever more idiosyncratic. Around the Caha peninsula some RSCs like Dromroe or Gurteen have central boulder-cists, enormous slabs supported above ground by three or four low stones. It seems unlikely that they belong to the original circle because their heights customarily match that of the recumbent stone and would hinder any sightline. As they frequently occur without a circle along the coasts of Cos. Cork and Kerry, concentrated in the west at the heads of Kenmare and Bantry Bays, their origins probably differ from those of the RSC-builders. No finds are recorded in Kerry but charcoal from a pit beneath the heavy capstone at Cooradarrigan gave an assay of 1130 ± 35 bc (GrN-15716), *c.* 1426–1266 BC, dates contemporary with the stone circles.[19] Similar overground cists in Scotland at Moleigh, Argyll, or Collessie, Fife, held bronze daggers so that a second millennium date is probable.

A megalithic ring, Kenmare near Dromroe, surrounding a boulder-cist with a mighty seven-ton globular capstone is characteristic of these late axial stone circles. The ring is of interest for, unlike any other in Munster, it is egg-shaped and bigger, measuring 17 m east–west by 15 m. Kenmare is a unique MSC but does have some resemblance to another egg-shaped ring, Burgh Hill, Roxburgh previously noted for its affinities with the RSC tradition.

Further north is the tiny circle-henge of Lissyviggeen. Near Galway Bay is Masonbrook, 'The Seven Monuments', its stones set in a 21.3 m earth bank. Excavations in 1916 suggested that part at least of the central mound might be modern. In the extreme west of the Dingle peninsula was the broken-up Meenanare or Glen Minard ring once described as 'a remarkable pile of druidical stones where tradition says ancient chiefs dispensed justice'. Nothing remains.[20]

What do remain are intruders. In that seabound corner of western Europe there was not only a majority of native monuments but evidence that strangers, maybe merchants and craftsmen, had been allowed to raise their own heathen sanctuaries.

In the bustle of trade and traffic in the Bronze Age, with copper taken from Cork and Kerry, gold from the Wicklows, tin from Cornwall, intricate goldwork from Brittany, equally stylish lunulae made by Irish goldsmiths and sent to Britain and Brittany, foreign stone circles appeared in places overseas.

What seems to have been a Land's End megalithic ellipse was set up on an island off the coast of Finistère. A multiple-stone circle (MSC) with an internal boulder burial can still be seen on Jersey alongside an *allée-couverte*. Most unexpected of all, a Four-Poster, more Scottish than Irish, was erected in the heart of Brittany at Saint-Just, its heavy pillars predictably standing on a conspicuous round cairn. The cairn covered a Neolithic passage-tomb, a Breton *dolmen à couloir*.

If not fully cosmopolitan the Bronze Age world on the busy edge of Europe was never entirely parochial.

Western Ireland

The village of Cong, 'the isthmus', in Co. Mayo, with its remains of a fine Augustinian abbey was a holy place long before Christianity. Between the large and lovely loughs of Mask and Corrib it lies in a landscape of limestone caves, stalactites and subterranean rivers. Such weird contortions of nature may have made the area seem magical to prehistoric people. To the west are the wild mountains and glens of Joyce's Country. To the east is the plain where the mythical Tuatha dè Danann defeated the fabulous Fir Bolg at the legendary first battle of Moytura.

Cong is a quiet place. Its seventh-century monastery was replaced by a twelfth-century Romanesque abbey, now ruined but whose splendid western façade lingers as a memorial to the skill and artistry of its mediaeval craftsmen. Unknown to them the region had been venerated many long centuries earlier.

In 1700 the Welsh antiquarian, Edward Lhuyd, returned to Ireland on his protracted itinerary through Britain, Ireland and Brittany. He came to Cong. 'Within half a mile of Kyng in a field on the Right side of the Road as you go to Ballinrobe in ye County of Mayo [are four stone circles]. They are within a ston's Cast of Each other'. He was wrong about the distance. The rings are a full mile north-east of Cong. But he was right to recognise and sketch their individuality.

They form the corners of a NNE–SSW oblong very roughly 140 m square. They stand in three fields in three townlands and they are all different, cut off from each other by hedges like the demarcated chapels of a Bronze Age ecumenical conference centre. It is a theological irony that these pagan stones are approached through a field by Deanery Place, the home of the Dean of Tuam. Cong Rectory is on the opposite side of the road. Christian churchmen were taking no chances.

In an overgrown paddock by Deanery Place is the western ring, a tidy, open ellipse of flat-topped stones, possibly graded towards the south-west. Over a hundred metres to the south-east is a ravaged embanked circle whose few remaining boulders line the edge of a stony bank. Just as far away to its north-east is a wrecked cairn-circle, grossly overgrown with weeds and scrubby trees, only four of its grey stones left at the western edge of a prominent cairn.

It is the northernmost ring that is the marvel (Pl. 55), a variant multiple stone circle whose vaguely informed builders not only misplaced the axial stone and its flankers but seem altogether to have overlooked other architectural elements. It is a well-proportioned circle, about 16.2 × 15.9 m across, erected on a platform cut into the natural slope. Inside the ring is a kerbed cairn. Eighteen of probably an original thirty stones still exist. At the north is the axial stone, a neatly rectangular block, 1.3 m long, 0.9 m high, with flankers on either side of it. Across the ring at the south-west one of the two portals has gone but to the workers its south-eastern partner must have seemed imbued with a weird power for its inner face is pockmarked with a honeycomb of deep depressions like the handiwork of an obsessive cupmarker. The stone circle is a wonder, far from its ancestry in south-west Ireland, shadowed in tall, lean trees, enduring in a region where megalithic rings are scarce.[21]

Elsewhere are few other good rings, Rosdoagh, the embanked Rathfran or Summerhouse Hill, and Killadangan below the slopes of Croagh Patrick in one of whose niches the midwinter sun sets. 'The sublimity of its appearance and its nearness to a populous plain make it the holiest mountain in Ireland'. Other rings may be found here but this was never a rich area of stone circles because passage-tombs remained the traditional ceremonial sites. Even to the east in Co. Tipperary circles are scarce. At Reardnogy More, a 4.5 m ring lay near the bottom of a hill on which was a short Four-Stone row. And in the Timoney Hills, spread across 100 acres, nearly three-quarters of a former 400 stones stand and lie in confusion after the depredations of road-makers. Sixteen supposedly but almost certainly wrongly form the arc of a 61 m circle with a yet more improbable cove at its centre.[22]

Yet amongst this unpromising landscape there is the wealth of Lough Gur, 12 miles

Plate 55. Cong N, Co. Mayo. A weirdly attractive version of a multiple stone circle (Photograph: the author).

south-east of the Shannon estuary.[23] Here where low-crowned limestone hills curve round the lough basin prehistoric people settled on the well-drained sheltered soils. An early date of 2740 ± 40 bc (D-41), *c.* 3550–3450 BC, has come from the earlier of two superimposed homesteads. On the hillsides the black-budded ash and the hazel covered the slopes, overhanging the yellow celandine and the tall blue columbine. Red deer wandered in the trees alert for the wolf and the bear, for the barking of the hunters' dogs. At the forest edges, where the land had been cleared, whitebeam, hawthorn and cherry blossomed, white as quartz, in the Springtime. Overhead, reminding the villagers of the nearness of the Atlantic, they could see gulls and the soaring white-tailed eagle, flocks of cranes that flew slowly over the waters of the lough where mallards and little teals chuckled in the reeds.

For more than a thousand years timber houses, round and rectangular, cairns, standing stones and wedge-tombs were erected to the east of the mile-long lough, on Knockadoon peninsula, on the slopes of Knockfennel and Carrig Aille, and on Garrett or Geroid Island where charcoal from one hearth was as late as 1730 ± 140 bc (D-34), *c.* 2300–1950 BC. While men grazed their herds of oxen and a few pigs snuffled among the trees women worked in the settlements. They made pots in the Early Neolithic style of north-east Ireland, fine round-based ware with decorated T-shaped rims for suspending the vessels by thonging, pots that gradually during the third millennium became simpler in shape and ornament until in the Bronze Age flat-bottomed coarseware became common. Such pots could have been used to store the grain from the terraced patches by some huts. Through the misting rains, the sunshine and the winds of centuries the slow life continued like a stone at a stream's edge as the years drifted by.

Contacts with the north-east were kept up, for traders, perhaps travelling overland and long the Shannon, brought axes of porcellanite from Tievebulliagh mountain in Co. Antrim. And soon after 2300 BC the earliest British beaker-users came here at first maybe simply looking for farmland, but their descendants prospecting for the elusive copper sulphide ores that their smiths could transmute into the glowing daggers so favoured by their leaders. The wealthy aristocracy, with its ornate W/MR and N/MR beakers, established a community here, perhaps even a trading-post, whose occupants seem to have lived alongside the natives. Such contacts may have endured well into the Later Bronze Age.[24]

There are burial sites and stone circles all around the lough and in the surrounding country. Four miles south-east is a large boulder-ring at Ballynamona, now cut by a farm lane. On the north shore of the lough itself by Knockfennel is an oval, 13.4 × 9.1 m, also of low boulders. Just north-east of Lough Gur on Carrig Aille is a 55 m ritual earth circle with a 4.3 m thick bank lined inside and out with tall stones. There is an internal ring. Half a mile south is a stupendous standing stone. In 1909 Lewis wrote of how a local woman told him of a 'crock of gold under the stone which was guarded by a terrible ghost' that deterred nocturnal treasure-hunters. As the gold dematerialised during daylight hours the riches lay untouched.

On Knockadoon, as well as the huts, there is an enclosed sepulchral site, 31 m in diameter with an eastern entrance and a double kerb filled with rubble, with a small stone ring containing a cist with two skeletons, one a child. Such rings are not formally concentric stone circles inasmuch as they are free standing but are double walls to support a bank. In this they differ from rings like Machrie Moor V, Arran or Winterbourne Bassett, Wiltshire, in which each ring is independent of the other.

Half a mile across the water from Knockadoon in Grange townland is a complex of monuments that, although only two of them are true stone circles, deserves description. At the north-east is an oval, 22.9 × 16.2 m, of fifteen stones within a slight earth bank. There is a wide gap, apparently an entrance, on the south-west axis. Alongside are traces of a chambered tomb.

Hardly 30 m south is Grange henge sometimes known as the Lios or 'race-course', a massive bank of gravelly clay, 9 m wide, 1.2 m high, and 59 × 45.8 m from crest to crest, lined inside with stones that stand shoulder to shoulder around the wide interior. There is no ditch. Today trees grow on Grange and a field-wall brushes it. It was excavated in 1939.

In layout these three Grange rings have some likeness to other triple settings like Balnuaran of Clava, Inverness, whose central ring-cairn has been broadly compared with Grange;[25] like the Hurlers, Cornwall; and even more like Stanton Drew, Somerset, where, as at Grange, the alignment is not straight and where the north-east ring is the smallest. As there are constructional parallels between some Lough Gur monuments and the Priddy henges, Somerset only 7 miles south-west of Stanton Drew, such comparisons may contribute to an understanding of the somewhat puzzling associations of finds from Grange with others around the Bristol Channel in south-west Wales and Wessex. The ring is more than architecturally wondrous. If it can ever be interpreted it may one day reveal how much the large British open rings, stone or earth, are compositions of commerce and ceremony in which native and foreigner freely commingled.

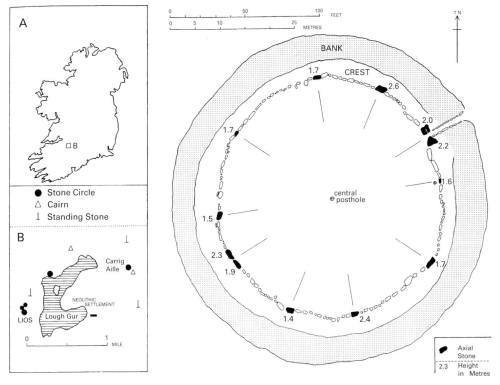

Fig. 33. Grange, Townland, Co. Limerick (after O'Riordain, 1951).

Grange is not an open stone circle nor a conventional circle-henge (Fig. 33). The stones that fringe its bank are contiguous, mostly local limestone but some of volcanic breccia from Grange Hill a mile away. Hiding their lumpy packing-stones is a thick layer of gravelly clay, now heavy with grass, over the 45.8 m wide interior. At the ENE, 78°, is a thin gravel-floored, stone-lined passage, 11.5 m long but only 1.1 m wide, which terminates in two gigantic inner portal stones. The site may stand on previously farmed land. What looks like the remnants of a field-wall pass under it.

Grange is instructive about prehistoric working methods. At the exact centre on the old land surface beneath the clay the excavators found a posthole 13 cm across, too slight for a totem pole but adequate for a focal post from which the 23 m radius of the inner bank could be marked out. This was done not by scribing an entire circle in the turf but by extending the rope to five roughly equidistant places on the eastern circumference and then to five others opposite. The ten spots were marked with poles. One socket survived by stone 17. In this way five diameters were fixed, the most important being that from the entrance to its opposing pair of stones for this was the major axis. If Somerville's calculations were correct[26] it was aligned to 258° on the moon's minimum midsummer setting about 2500 BC.

There is a crude east–west axis between stone 17, with its posthole, and 74, and, at right-angles, a meridional line between stones 41 and 106. The design looked like one of Thom's compound rings but more haphazardly achieved. The distances between the posts varied: 9.5 m, 17.1 m, 18.6 m, 14 m and 15.2 m, measuring clockwise from the entrance.

Meanwhile twelve monstrous stones were being dragged to the site. Holes were dug for them by each post, two at the entrance, two opposite where touching stones were set up, their tops making a V-notch ideal for sightings. The other eight stones replaced the circumferential posts and at this stage Grange looked like any large stone circle. But then, using the stones as end-markers, the first straightish section of the bank was piled up over the edges of the filled stone holes, 1.2 m high and flat-topped but with a vertical inner face that was supported by propping extra stones against it, their bases resting on the ground and held secure by heaped up cobbles. There was a squalid camp for the hundred or more workers on the west where fires burned and where refuse and filth gathered, occasionally strewn over with earth as the months of labour continued. People carried baskets of clay from the shores of the lough. Others dragged stones whose weight tore and gouged the interior of the circle. Packing-stones were manhandled to the pillars that were being pulled upright by gangs hauling heel-deep on the bank's top. And so, stretch by stretch, Grange was completed. Finally the level clay floor was laid.

Such a reconstruction is not fanciful. The average marking stone is 1.9 m high and stands in a prepared hole whereas the intermediate stones, 1 m tall, stand on the surface and can only have been erected by leaning them against the bank which, itself, is irregular with kinks where section joined section. Hearths, Late Neolithic pottery, and layers of turf were uncovered in its western sector.

The heaviest stone, at the north-east, 'Rannach Cruim Duibh', the prominent black stone, weighs over 60 tons and a hundred persons or more would have had to heave it over a mile from its hillside. It was set up in line with the midsummer sunrise. On 14 May 1785 the effort demanded to have built 'the large Druidical temple' amazed John Wesley. Comparing Grange with Stanton Drew and Stonehenge he wrote, 'How our ancestors could bring, or even heave these enormous stones what modern can comprehend.'[27]

The clay for the bank and floor came from a drift deposit to the south-east by the lough. With an average basketload of 30 lbs some 300,000 loads would have been needed, taking 100 workers sixty to seventy workdays from midsummer well into the Autumn.

The uneven heights of the lining stones makes it unlikely that the bank was intended as a viewing-platform for the uninitiated. Grange is more like a temenos in which many might participate. Its inner space, with an area of about 1,650 m^2, could accommodate three hundred or more dancers so that a population figure of up to 600 men, women and children is feasible. This would be sufficient to move the stones but too many for the adjacent Lough Gur occupation sites even if the nine or ten known houses were contemporary and had as many as eight people each. Nor would local people have required a camp. But within 12 miles are many other prehistoric sites: huts; ring-barrows at Ballingoola, Cahercorney, Lissard and Rathjordan with its early beakers; and the most south-westerly of all Irish passage-tombs at Duntryleague in whose chamber the side-slabs rise in steps like others in Brittany, so that, as with the open stone circles of west Britain, Grange could well have been a meeting-place for scattered groups.

The forgotten ceremonies included the deliberate breaking of pots. This practice was widespread. It has been seen at the RSCs of Loanhead of Daviot, Aberdeenshire, and Drombeg, Co. Cork. It occurred in chambered tombs like Audleystown, Down; in the stone circles of the Sanctuary, Wiltshire and Carneddau Hengwm, Merioneth; and in great earthwork enclosures like Durrington Walls, Wiltshire. At Grange many sherds were found under the bank and by the western stones near the lunar notch, and from them a date for the monument can be estimated.

There is a dichotomy. Whereas in the camp beneath the bank there was only early native pottery elsewhere later, coarse bucket-shaped pottery mingled in the interior with sherds of Ebbsfleet, beaker and grooved ware. This may mean that the ring is a native work that preceded the arrival of newcomers. The 'European' beaker and English Ebbsfleet fragments are probably no later than 2500 BC. This agrees well with the grooved ware and its characteristic accompaniment of lopsided arrowheads and end-scrapers which formed a large proportion of the flints near the stones. Such ware is of special relevance because it has been found not only in Wessex henges like Stonehenge, Maumbury Rings, Woodhenge, and the great enclosures of Durrington Walls, Marden and Mount Pleasant, but also in the circle-henge of Stenness in Orkney. If a date were hazarded for Grange within a century of 2500 BC this would accord with the evidence of the Irish pottery. Subsequent material, including food-vessels, a bronze awl and Class II coarseware of the Later Bronze Age may be accounted for as a sign of the monument's continuing use into the second millennium when a late, long-necked S3/W beaker was broken by the entrance. It would also agree with Somerville's hypothetical lunar date.

What impulses caused the building of Grange cannot yet be explained for it is not known which of the three Lough Gur rings is the earliest or if they were used simultaneously. What may be inferred is that it stemmed from the henge and circle tradition around the Irish Sea. In a time when prospectors from Wessex were reaching out to south-west Wales and to Co. Wicklow it may have been they who described the ceremonial rings they themselves had first seen in Ireland. Or the axe traders, for stone axes were discovered beneath the clay floor, could have been responsible. What part makers of grooved ware, perhaps related to the Boyne passage-tomb culture, played in the custom of henge building is uncertain. It may be noted that, early in its primary phase, the earthwork at Stonehenge with such pottery also seems to have been a lunar site like Grange.

'The precise relationship of Irish passage-tombs, Maes Howe-type tombs, Skara Brae, Rinyo, and the Grooved Ware cultures in general, may be obscure at present, but it would be hard to deny that it exists.'[28] In the flux of the late third and early second millennium BC when new routes were being opened many novel ideas tangled across the seaways, carried by trader, prospector, settler, by beaker, grooved-ware and native potter. Grange belongs to the tradition of open circles, not to the RSC culture of north-east Scotland or the MSCs of south-western Ireland. Its affinities lie to the east, in the Wicklows, in south-west Wales, in Wessex whence its newcomers travelled. It is more probable that they followed Irish rivers inland than that they sailed round the tempestuous peninsulas of Kerry. From Milford Haven across St George's Channel is only 80 miles of sea before the shelter of Waterford. From there they could follow the River Suir towards the landmark of Galtymore mountain then paddle westwards along the tree-darkened Aberlow between the towering Galtees and Slievenamuck and into the forested Golden Vale of Tipperary. A short portage would reach the headwaters of the Maigue flowing northwards past Ballynamona only a few miles from Lough Gur. Once explored, this Welsh-Irish route would soon become established.

The S3/W beaker at Grange is like others from the trading-post of Merthyr Mawr Warren on the south Welsh coast and from the Wick barrow, Somerset. The earlier combination of AOC, E and W/MR beakers at Grange is only matched in Ireland at Newgrange showing the attraction Lough Gur had for these immigrants.

One must travel 100 miles north-eastwards through passage-tomb country before coming to another small and scattered group. 'Allen Monlen M. D., R. S. S. saies that in Ireland are severall great Stones standing on end in a circular figure, like the stones at Biscawn but that there is no stone in the middle,' wrote John Aubrey but Mr Monlen was wrong. In Co. Cavan the ring of Crom Cruaich with a pillar standing inside it was destroyed by St Patrick because it was a monument of idolatry.[29] But this was an isolated exception. There were few stone circles in central, eastern Ireland. In the Boyne Valley of Co. Meath there were standing stones, henges and passage tombs including the gigantic mounds of Dowth, Knowth and Newgrange. Stone circles were almost absent although in the early eighteenth century John Anstis made sketches of cairns with apparent circles around them, perhaps their kerbs.[30] Only the tomb of Newgrange is surrounded by a ring of standing stones, incomplete. Thinking about the name Hicks speculated that etymologically it was 'An Uamh Greine', the 'Cave of the Sun', from grian, 'the sun'. Grange may have had a similar origin.[31]

Newgrange

Newgrange was seen by the Welsh antiquarian, Edward Lhuyd in the autumn of 1699. 'The most remarkable curiosity we saw by the way was a stately Mount at a place called New Grange near Drogheda, having a number of huge stones pitch't on end round about it.' This simple statement was the beginning of an unresolved argument. The ring is a tantalus. Nothing is certain about it, whether it was finished, its shape, its date and its relationship to the great passage-tomb. All that is definite is that twelve stones exist in a fragmented ring today. And some of them are broken.

So uncertain does archaeology remain about the ring's shape, whether it was completed and its chronological relationship to the tomb that in the attractive Newgrange Visitors' Centre not a single circle-stone is shown in any of the three reproduction models of the constructional stages of Newgrange.

O'Riordain's excavation of 1954 revealed that although cairn material had soon slipped down the monument's sides and had reached the east stone none of the slip was found beneath the stone or in its socket.[32] It has been argued that circle and tomb are of different periods because of the lack of Boyne art on the circle-stones, although the north-east stone did have a line of cupmarks along its base.

The decorated chambered tomb has a midwinter sunrise roofbox above the entrance. As a celestial grace-note it should be recognised that every nine years between its major and minor risings the moon also would have shone down the passage had the aperture been open. With known lunar calendars carved on the slabs of nearby passage-tombs[33] this was predictable. Lunar symbolism may have led to the choice of white quartz for the two blocking-stones in the roof-box.

Around the tomb is an incomplete ring of unshaped stones. They are massive, rough blocks, mainly of local Silurian grit. Four remain outside the entrance, the tallest about 2.5 m high. Virtually all the stones could have been collected within 10 miles but some of the circle-stones are syenite, the nearest source of which is close to Pomeroy 60 miles north.

Nine stones, averaging 2.1 m high, stand in a south-east to western arc outside the tomb. There is one more at the north-west and two at the north-east. With an assumed spacing of 8.5 m the ring would have contained some thirty-five to thirty-eight uprights and, if circular, had a diameter of 103.6 m. Excavations between 1962 and 1975 by Michael O'Kelly came upon no conclusive proof of 'missing' stoneholes and the original number of stones remains unknown. The excavator was explicit. 'If a regular spacing had been maintained there should have been two further sockets', and 'another socket might have been expected but none was found' and 'It will be appreciated that we were constantly on the alert for such traces'. Clare O'Kelly, archaeologist and wife of the excavator, added that 'Despite every care taken in the course of the excavations to establish the positions of the missing orthostats, the results were disappointing.'[34] She further commented that 'it may be that, apart from the run of consecutive stones 9 m apart in the south, the remainder were more widely spaced and that no more than about a dozen stones are missing'. Adding to perplexity, the ring is not concentric to the tomb. The north-west stone is about 8.5 m from the kerb and one at the north-east about 6.9 m. Those outside the entrance are only 6.2 m away.

Both the tomb and the ring are blunted ovoids, each with a flattened arc at the south-east. Alexander Thom concluded that the south-east was part of an ellipse, the north-west an egg designed from two circles drawn at the corners of right-angled triangles. The ring had diameters of 107.9 m sw–NE by 91.1 m, the tomb 86.3 × 59.7 m, dimensions that corresponded to multiples of his Megalithic Yard of 0.829 m: 130, 110, 104 and 72 respectively. Claire O'Kelly was unconvinced. There seemed too few points of contact between the layout and the plan to prove the geometry correct.[35]

Even its age is controversial. Three radiocarbon assays from burnt material in the tomb: 2475 ± 45 bc (GrN-5462); 2465 ± 40 bc (GrN-5463) and 2585 ± 105 bc (UB-361), calibrated to c. 3300–3150 BC. The ring may be much younger.

Excavations in 1982–3 by David Sweetman confirmed the suspected presence of a huge concentric ring of postholes just to the south of Newgrange. Some of the pits coincided with one of the three stones outside the entrance to the tomb and to a stonehole to the east. It is probable, though not positive, that the posts were earlier than the stones, the excavator believing 'that there were two distinct Beaker phases of activity, one associated with the large circle of pits' and a later which may have 'included the erection of the large stones of the so-called great stone circle'.

Eight dates obtained from the pits ranging from 2120 ± 60 bc (GrN-22801) down to 1935 ± 70 bc (GU-1619), averaged around 2028 ± 62 bc, c. 2600–2450 BC, several centuries after the construction of the chambered tomb.[36] Sadly, the stratigraphical relationship between the pit- and the stone-circle could not be proved beyond question. As the excavator regretted, 'It would therefore appear that the great stone circle is later than the pit circle, though from this evidence alone one cannot be certain.' He added, 'five stones of the great stone circle would have had to be removed or incorporated into the pit and post circle if the latter was constructed after the former . . . Since this is not the case, the great stone circle must be later than the pit and post monument.'[37] The stones remain a conundrum.

Hostility between the cults of chambered tombs with their burials and believers in open-air enclosures may be the explanation. Lying between the great open rings like Ballynoe to the north and others such as Athgreany to the south in the Wicklows there may have been an attempt to encircle the great cairn of Newgrange with an even greater, even larger ring of stones, imprisoning the tomb. If so, it failed. The antipathy of passage-tomb builders inhibited the building of further circles. Newgrange remains unique, isolated from the remainder of the stone circles of Britain and Ireland, one of the finest chambered tombs in western Europe and one of the most controversial of all stone circles.

Chapter Fifteen

The Stone Circles of Eastern Britain
From Fife to Oxfordshire

By my meanes many Antiquities have been reskued, and preserved (I myself now inclining to be Ancient) – or else utterly lost and forgotten.

John Aubrey, 1680, xci

Introduction

Here there were large open circles. In the centuries around 3000 BC when the chambered tomb of Newgrange was being built the first arm of the distributional 'X' (see chapter two) that had begun in Cumbria spread down from Scotland into England.

From the Ochil Hills of Fife, through the Southern Lowlands, into the Cheviots, along the eastern side of the Pennines into the Wolds and the Fens the region is a paradox. Covering nearly one-fifth of the 121,000 square miles of Britain and Ireland, much of it low-lying, fertile, patterned with slow, wide rivers, some of its territories were the most heavily populated in the country. Yet only 7 per cent of stone circles are located here. Whether as tiny as Mayshiel, East Lothian, in a rubble ring only 2.7 m across, high on a Lammermuir hillside, or as vast as the Devil's Quoits in Oxfordshire, so enormous that over 800 people could have assembled at ease inside it, these rings are rare and dispersed, fewer than ninety being known, some of them suspect, about one to every 250 square miles.

This is partly because much of this prehistoric landscape was avoided by man.

Southern Britain presented an illimitable forest of 'damp oakwood', ash and thorn and bramble, largely untrodden. This forest was in a sense unbroken, for without emerging from its canopy a squirrel could traverse the country from end to end; but in another sense it was limited, for the downs and heaths which here and there touched the sea or navigable rivers . . . were the terminals of far-reaching stretches of open and semi-open country, grassland and parkland . . . This open country was sometimes at valley level but more often consisted of low hills, plateaux, or ridges of moderate elevation but dominant; so that Man moved on his vocations above the environing forest, and his eye ranged over wide spaces.[1]

Although this panorama of a widely hostile land is being modified by discoveries of henge and settlement on the heavy clays of the Midlands it remains largely true.

But the major reason for the scarcity of stone circles in eastern Britain was the paucity of stone and the abundance of alternative forms of building material. Here there was timber in plenty and it is significant that, difficult though it is to rediscover such an ephemeral monument as a circle of posts, long rotted and overgrown, the majority of those known are in this area: Moncreiffe, Croft Moraig, Cairnpapple in Scotland; Arminghall in East Anglia; the Dorchester henges in Oxfordshire. It is noteworthy that in several of these rings the posts were replaced by standing stones, a reminder of the complexity of such multi-phase sites.[2]

The monuments men built were fashioned by custom and by the easiest material nearby. Stone is scarce in the earths and chalks of the east and south. Timber is plentiful. So is easily dug land. Hence the same area that contains only 7 per cent of the stone circles has well over 30 per cent of the henges, including most of the great enclosures whether the three Thornborough earthworks in Yorkshire, 244 m from outer ditch to outer ditch, or the Devil's Quoits, or Cairnpapple in West Lothian, 60 m from bank to bank, once thought to be a circle-henge but now known to be a henge enclosing a ring of posts.

These henges distort the picture of stone circles, being so much bigger that the megalithic rings are diminished by comparison with them, and it seems apparent that especially on the eastern side of the region people preferred to have ritual centres inside a ring of posts, almost undiscoverable today, or within earthen banks like the little-known henges of Coupland in Northumbria, Little Bromley, Essex, or Eggardon in Dorset. Stone circles are rare. It is only where rock appears, the millstone grit and limestone of the Pennines, sandstone sarsens of the Marlborough Downs, the granite of Cornwall, that megalithic rings were erected along this hard north–south spine with soils to its east and rock to the west, a geological juxtaposition that resulted in some of the most impressive megalithic monuments being built inside encircling banks: hybrids in which stone circle combined with surrounding earthwork, circle-henges like Balfarg, Arbor Low, Avebury and Stonehenge, the most spectacular prehistoric monuments in Britain and Ireland.

The Circle-Henges

Of these uncommon sites some like Brodgar and Stenness in the Orkneys are far to the north but, down the centre of Britain, along the 450 miles which separate Fife from Cornwall are eight circle-henges – nine if Long Meg is included – which share the characteristics of having large open rings within smallish henges, of being near trackways, in areas of Neolithic occupation, their builders displaying the same interest in north–south lines as those of western Britain.

In every case the megalithic ring is wrecked. At Avebury, the Devil's Quoits, at Balfarg, even the Stripple Stones, many of the stones have been smashed and removed, often by mediaeval Christians for piety or by predatory Tudor and Stuart robbers for profit. At Stonehenge the bluestones were uprooted. At the Devil's Quoits stones were removed for bridges. Not one stone is left at the Bull Ring. At Arbor Low the stones remain but all collapsed, slumping on the turf like cards blown over by a north wind.

From the size of the henges it seems they served large populations for the open interior is never less than 40 m across, 1,257 m^2. There was no burial mound to reduce such spaciousness, room enough for several hundred people, although Stenness, Cairnpapple, Arbor Low and Avebury did have Coves near their centres, symbolic burial-chambers that are also known in unenclosed stone circles like Stanton Drew and, just possibly, at Er-Lannic.

What is becoming clear is that these composite circle-henges were usually of several phases, often a ring of stones being added to an old henge, not unlikely if, as supposed, the earliest stone circles had henges as their prototypes. Such a sequence was almost certainly the case at Broomend of Crichie where an intrusive Perthshire six-stone ring of the Bronze Age was put inside the earthwork. At Stonehenge the blue-stones were added centuries after the construction of the earthwork. At Avebury the bank and the stones of the Outer Circle are considered coeval but successors to the inner rings. The great site of Balfarg in Fife encapsulates these questions.

It was part of a long-lasting but closely spaced ritual complex, which included two henges, two stone circles, a mortuary enclosure, cairns and cists that endured for almost two thousand years. Yet so savagely had weather and man treated the area that Balfarg, 90 m across from bank to bank of its earthwork, lay undiscovered until 1947 when an aerial photograph revealed the imperfect outlines of its ditch and bank. Before then only two isolated standing stones, 13 m apart, had been recorded by the Royal Commission.

Plans to have houses built on it caused Balfarg to be excavated in 1977–8. The work was challenging. Its eroded interior and the vestigial, almost non-existent post- and stoneholes in equally indeterminate layouts made interpretation difficult. Every one of the early conclusions had to be reconsidered. Yet there was a benefit. Because of its importance and with the delight of the Balbirnie stone circle close by Balfarg was reprieved. It has now been partly reconstructed.

It had a long life. Five thousand years ago on a level stretch of ground what may have been an inaugural feast was celebrated.

Wood and bones, perhaps of sheep, were consumed by fire. Grooved ware vessels were broken. Then a near-circle of sixteen posts was set up, all from trees at the edge of the nearby forest, oak, alder, hazel, willow, great posts up to 4 m high and anything from a half to five tons in weight. They rose in height towards the wsw where two taller stood outside as portals. Forty miles to the north-west by Loch Tay the circle of Croft Moraig had a similar entrance.

There is a hint of funerary activity. Almost 300 m to the east at the Balfarg Riding School there was a small henge. Inside it was a rectangular, wicker-walled mortuary enclosure with heavy scaffolds on which the bodies of the dead may have been exposed. A C-14 determination of 2475 ± 50 bc (GU-1670), offered a period of *c*. 3250–3150 BC for the age of the enclosure.

In it a sherd of grooved ware was encrusted with the residue of henbane, the powerful hallucinogenic described in chapter four. Mixed in a 'porridge' of meadowsweet, nightshade and hemlock it could have been smeared on the skin to produce trances and visions such as those induced by shamans. Mourners at Balfarg may have shared similar unworldly experiences.[3]

There were other arcane practices. Amongst the packing of the postholes at Balfarg were freshly smashed pieces of grooved ware, their mint condition suggesting that they had been deliberately shattered to be buried as deposits in the western, more vital side of the new ring 'as an isolated phenomenon'.[4] Four radiocarbon assays of 2085 ± 50 bc (GU-1161), 2230 ± 50 bc (GU-1160), 2320 ± 60 bc (GU-1162), 2365 ± 60 bc (GU-1163) averaged 2250 ± 55 bc or about 2950–2850 BC very roughly contemporary with the mortuary enclosure.

There were other, much slighter, almost undetectable post-rings, the outermost of which surrounded the circle and which may have been a fenced palisade to hide the interior from the profane world outside. A short stretch of hurdling was actually preserved under a stony layer.

That was the beginning but long years before the end. At some time all the rings, perhaps as many as six, were enclosed by a henge. The fact that no grooved ware was found in its deep ditch indicated that it was a secondary feature and the subsidiary fact that the rings stood eccentrically within the henge is a further indication that the structures were not of one period.

It was a large but not gigantic henge, 90 m across, whose inner ditch, apparently broken by a natural gully at the south, enclosed an internal arena 65 m across. At the WNW but not tidily aligned on the portals of the timber ring was an 8.5 m wide entrance.

More change followed. A stone circle of undressed sandstones replaced the posts. Its shape, size and nature have never been settled. From the aerial photograph Atkinson suggested a circle of ten or eleven stones in a ring with a diameter of 36.6 m. The excavator faced with exposed asymmetrical arcs of stoneholes thought that there might have been concentric rings graded to the WNW, the inner of twelve and the outer of twenty-four stones, twelve being a well-known number in north-east Scotland. Very approximately the diameters would have been c. 60 m and 50.3 m respectively. Both were sub-circular and both were problematical. If the diameter of the outer ring, calculated from the plan, were correct the circle would have passed through the centres of the ditch at both south and west.

Barnatt offered an alternative solution, wondering whether there had been a single, grossly non-circular ring. 'It is curious that neither ring is found together in any portion of the site. It is far more likely that both arcs form a singular non-circular ring displaced slightly from the henge centre to the north.'[5]

Reassessment of the 'natural gully' revealed that in part it was the final arc of the ditch, completing the circuit except for a constricted entrance, only 5 m wide, at the south. With two entrances so different in width and disposition, and not opposite each other, Balfarg has affinities with similar contradictions at Arbor Low, Stonehenge and elsewhere. Loveday has offered the plausible suggestion that often the two entrances of henges lay athwart an old path or trackway. At Balfarg the second, narrower non-axial entrance could have been an afterthought to an original single-entrance henge.[6]

What little certainty can be elicited from the meticulous excavation of a disastrous site is that of the two stones that remain the eastern was a circle-stone and the taller was the southern portal at the henge's WNW entrance. Unsurprisingly, beyond it, 3 miles away, the sun would have set at midsummer behind East Lomond Hill. Increasingly it is being shown that in these great rings seasonal rituals, death and the sun or moon form inseparable combinations.[7]

Three hundred metres to the ESE of Balfarg the stone circle of Balbridie has been dated to 1330 ± 90 bc, about 1700–1550 BC, and may have remained in use until as late as 1350 BC almost 2,000 years after the erection of Balfarg's first timber rings.

The stones of Balfarg have provided no date. Their story must end with the discovery of an untidy pit near but not at the centre of the ring. In it was a 1½ ton doleritic slab above the fragmentary remains of the skull, teeth and a tibia of the crouched inhumation of a twenty-year-old young man. With him was a handled beaker of about 1900 BC and a flint knife. With a capacity of two pints and probably filled with an alcoholic preparation it was presumably set there to make the 'journey to the afterworld a little less cold and cheerless'. He was the last prehistoric inhabitant of Balfarg.

It has been wondered whether the spacious circle-henge at Cairnpapple in West Lothian contained not a stone but timber ring. There is no certainty. Revisionism, the reassessment of published data, is admirable but revision does not have to follow. At Cairnpapple the excavator, Stuart Piggott, believed that an internal oval setting of pits, 35 × 28 m, were the holes for a stone circle. Because of the steep-sided nature of some of the cavities and a possible truncated ramp in one Mercer suggested that instead they could have been postholes. Barnatt disagreed. He pointed out that the pits of an internal cove were oval 'and hence are likely to have contained slabs rather than timber posts and hence this weakens Mercer's case for timber uprights in the circle'. With such ambiguity it is circumspect to retain the excavator's interpretation.[8]

Except that it is smaller Cairnpapple, excavated over two seasons in 1947 and 1948, closely resembles Arbor Low in the Peak District 200 miles to the south. Both sites are oval double-entranced henges with rock-cut ditches, stone rings, coves and entrances. There are more subtle similarities.

A grave dug in the rock at Cairnpapple is like that at Arbor Low and at Green Low nearby and 'is precisely the manner of digging Early Bronze Age graves in the chalk country of the south of England. . . . The technique may constitute another link with the south'.[9]

Cairnpapple stands on a basalt hill west of Edinburgh, and on a clear day one can see the Bass Rock to the east and the Arran mountains to the west, from coast to coast across southern Scotland. On such a propitious site a ritual centre was established in the Late Neolithic when seven pits, which may originally have held stones, were dug on three sides of a trapezoid open to the wsw. Like the Aubrey Holes at Stonehenge these pits were infilled and then redug to receive token cremations, one with a broken bone pin like those in four or five of the Aubrey Holes. On the old land surface were fragments of two stone axes, one from Great Langdale, the other from Graig Lwyd, tools that may have been broken during the clearance of the site in the late third millennium.

Years later people from the south built the henge above the oak and hazel woodlands, gangs digging rough sections of ditch into the basalt and heaping up superimposed layers of clay, turves, stones, earth and boulders onto the bank that was set back from the ditch like the bermed henges of southern and eastern England. Wide entrances were left at north and sse but, as at Arbor Low, on a line well away from the axis of the henge.

The Northumbrian henge of Coupland 50 miles east of Cairnpapple is asymmetrical in the same way.[10] On Cairnpapple's central area an egg-shaped ring, of twenty-four large stones, 1.2–1.5 m high, was erected, its apex at the ssw opposite that at Arbor Low. A 7.6 m gap here seems to be an entrance not quite in line with the henge causeway, again like Arbor Low in reverse and, rather unusually despite analogous pillars at rings like Pobull Fhinn, North Uist, two single stones stood just inside the perimeter at nnw and sse, making angled portals for henge and stone ring. It is either to this period or, less probably, to the first that a cove of three huge stones belonged, a construction well off-centre facing almost directly east.

Near the cove and also near the circumference of the stone ring were five burnt areas, one by a ditch terminal. In front of the cove were some mysterious rectangular pits, in places dug 0.8 m into the bedrock and which resemble quarry-pits. These might be the remains of a rectangular structure akin to those at Loanhead of Daviot. Two sherds of undecorated beaker in the north-west trench suggest these might be rock-cut graves like those noted in Derbyshire, the proportions being not dissimilar, disturbed at the time the cove was destroyed by a second group of beaker people intent on constructing a new burial place. How long this circle-henge was used before this destructive interference is hard to estimate. The burial by an eastern stone of a child with an N/NR beaker probably in the nineteenth century BC might be no more than a repetition of the well-known liking of beaker users for placing burials by megalithic pillars. The ring could be much earlier.

Quite different is the pit-burial by the cove whose stones must have been removed by that time because one of them seems to have been used as a marker or headstone for an oval setting of contiguous stones within which was an extended inhumation reminiscent of that by Arbor Low's cove. The body may have had a wooden mask placed over its face.[11] Such burials with large standing stones have affinities with the Clava kerb-cairns and the associated sites like Monzie in Perthshire,[12] a tradition that is known to be related to stone rings in Inverness but never with coves, and which may have caused its adherents to respect the ring at Cairnpapple but to adapt the cove for their own needs. With the body were two N2/L beakers of the eighteenth and seventeenth centuries BC, one with a base impressed with the bracken on which it stood before firing.

The little cairn over this burial could not have had a long life. Food-vessel users with no need for megalithic rings came to the site, ripped up the standing stones for use as kerbs for a new cairn, 15 m across, that overlay the former cove, beaker cairn and western stoneholes. There was a further enlargement effected by taking boulders from the henge bank to extend the food-vessel cairn to a diameter of 30 m, overlapping the silted ditch. Burials in inverted collared urns were placed in the extension. Cairnpapple was probably used for yet more burials in the Iron Age when four long graves were dug at the east, destroying one of the old stone-holes. Centuries later the Ravenna Geographer referred to a place, *Medio Nemeton*, somewhere near the Roman Antonine Wall from Forth to Clyde where Britain was at her narrowest. 'Nemeton . . . had the significance of an open sanctuary in the Celtic religious tradition',[13] and it is tempting to see in Cairnpapple direct evidence of that continuity of custom that is only hinted at elsewhere, the Middle Sanctuary on a hill in lowland Scotland where one could see from coast to coast, and where people had come to supplicate, to bury and to pray for over 2,000 years.

To the south of Cairnpapple there is a long geographical gap where henges took the place of large stone circles, no fewer than thirteen in Northumberland alone: among them Coupland, the segmented ditches of East Marleyknowe, the broken earthwork of Eswesley Station, cut through by an old railway line.

One hundred and fifty miles separate the Cheviots from the Derbyshire Peak District with its circle-henges of the Bull Ring and Arbor Low. The Bull Ring, a quarried site at the village of Doveholes near Buxton, stands at a height of 340 m on the limestone plateau above the wooded valley of the Dove. It is 10 miles NNW of Arbor Low on the same trackway that leads down to Whaley Bridge and the Mersey flowing out to the Irish Sea. Not one stone is left of the circle but the 79 × 75 m bank is upstanding and the ditch, from which some possible Neolithic coarseware came, can still be clearly seen with its exactly north and south entrances even though hacked and

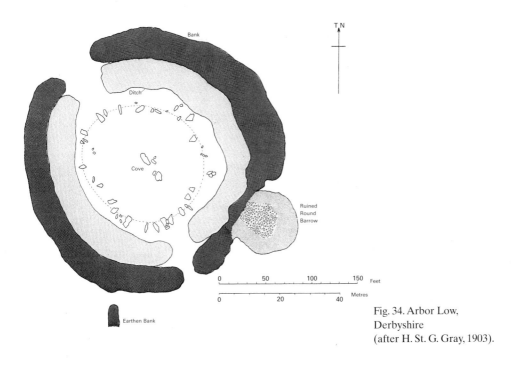

Bank

T N

Ditch

Cove

Ruined
Round
Barrow

0   50   100   150   Feet

0   20   40   Metres

Earthen Bank

Fig. 34. Arbor Low,
Derbyshire
(after H. St. G. Gray, 1903).

scarred by miners. This henge and Arbor Low occupy that limestone area of the Peak
District chosen by the builders of Neolithic chambered tombs like Green Low, Liffs
Low and Five Wells, quite distinct from the millstone grit moors east of the Derwent
where the majority of Bronze Age sites were built and where many of the food-vessels
and most of the collared urns have been discovered. The fact that two neatly cisted
Bronze Age food vessels were recovered from a round barrow imposed on Arbor
Low's bank suggests a much earlier date for the mutilated henge. Similar satellite
Late Neolithic and Early Bronze Age barrows have been noted elsewhere in
Derbyshire.

The highly situated site of Arbor Low (Fig. 34), Old English *eordburh-hlaw*, 'the
earthwork mound', at 370m O.D., is evocative to visit, walking up the slope from the
farm towards the green bank, the stones hidden, the mound of Gib Hill barrow, bro-
ken-topped from its many excavations, rising to view to the west.

The nineteenth-century antiquarian, Thomas Bateman, praised it. It was 'by far
the most important, as well as the most uninjured, remains of the religious edifices
of our barbarous forefathers that is to be found in the midland counties . . . [it is]
to be seen a short distance to the left hand of the turnpike road from Buxton to
Ashbourne'.[14]

Fifty years after Batemen the excavation of Arbor Low was part of a wider scheme.
In 1899 'the British Association set up a committee to enquire into the "Age of Stone
Circles", a project that I began with the digging of the Stripple Stones, Cornwall,'
wrote St George Gray, and it concluded with an investigation of Avebury, Wiltshire,
between 1908 and 1922. Funds were never plentiful: 'The two grants made by the
British Association for the work at Arbor Low amounted to £50.'[15]

Arbor Low's sub-circular bank, 79 × 75m across its crests, in places 2.1m high,
undulating, footworn, has entrances at the north-west, 9m wide, and SSE, only 6m
across but with a stone that may be the survivor of a portalled approach. Like Balfarg

and Cairnpapple the entrances are not opposite each other nor in line with the henge centre but are 5.5 m to its west. The food-vessel barrow, its top hollowed like a dented table-tennis ball, slumps by a terminal of the southern entrance. A long earthen row starts at the other terminal and curving south and west for a great distance towards Gib Hill with a heavy cist perched near its summit.

Inside Arbor Low's bank the ditch is now smoothed with turf but from which 1,415 m³ of solid limestone was gouged and manhandled up crude ramps and rock-cut steps onto the bank where boulders weighing up to a ton testify to the labour of the henge-builders. The ditch encloses an irregular 52 × 40 m area, 1,635 m², on which about fifty slabs and fragments of an original 41–43 limestone pillars lie white and carbuncled by millennia of weathering. It was not from the fresh ditch but from an exposed outcrop that the stones were obtained so that 'their pot-holes and crevices were worn away by Nature ages before the day on which they were set up'.

Whether the stones ever did stand has been questioned despite the unreliable eighteenth-century testimony of William Normanshaw who said that he had seen some erect as late as the 1740s. Certainly during his two excavations Gray found no stoneholes. Fortunately one large stone at the wsw is not totally prostrate and there are the erect stumps of seven others. It can be assumed that inadequate sockets in the hard bedrock left the stones, many 3 m to 3.7 m long, precariously and briefly balanced around an egg-shaped ring measuring approximately 41.5 × 37.2 m on a major ESE–WNW axis. A wider gap between the stones at the north-west near the henge's northerly causeway may be an entrance.

At the centre of the site are the remnants of a Cove that once faced north-eastwards. An extended male burial surrounded by stones was discovered just to its east. An area up to 4.9 m east had been dug out, in one place to a depth of 2.4 m and refilled with earth. Fragments of a human ulna were found in the infill but the excavation report does not give further details of what seems to be a rock-cut pit. 'It is possible that a skeleton or skeletons may have been removed from here.'

A pit dug 1.5 m into the bedrock was excavated under the multiple-burial cairn at Harland Edge 8½ miles east of Arbor Low.[16] In its filling was cremated bone and charcoal which provided a date of 1750 ± 150 bc (BM-210), c. 2350–1950 BC. Eight other rock-cut inhumation pits in Derbyshire, one at Shuttlestone being 2.4 m deep, four with bronze daggers, another at Smerrill Moor with a S2/W beaker make an Early Bronze Age horizon probable. If the cavity at Arbor Low is analogous and the result of secondary activity alongside the focal Cove, then the first phase of this circle-henge would appear to be in the early centuries of the third millennium BC when one of its functions may have been to act as an emporium for the distribution of stone axes from the Lake District,

The dating of Arbor Low presents the same problem as in other sites though the food-vessel burial does provide a *terminus ante quem* for the bank. In his excavations Gray made few finds. On the floor of the ditch-end of the henge's SSE entrance there was an antler pick and thirteen ox-teeth on the ditch floor. The north-western entrance was more productive. Six large flint flakes and scrapers had been deliberately set on a ledge low on the ditch wall 'perhaps purposely concealed; they could not have come by accident into the position in which they were found'. That they were a votive offering is indicated by their mint condition like the axes from other henges and the grooved ware sherds at Balfarg.[17] As well as flint implements in the opposite terminal there was a barbed-and-tanged arrowhead on the ditch bottom near a blackened hearth. It is reported that a magnificent flint knife, 'a beautifully formed blade', 15 cm long but no more than 1 cm thick, was found in June 1865 in the earthwork.[18] If this could be associated with the arrowhead and the other flints it would form a typical early southern beaker assemblage similar to that from the Green Low round barrow on the limestone of Alsop Moor 5 miles south of Arbor Low where a rock-cut pit held an inhumation with flints and an S1 beaker. Such southern beakers flourished in the early second millennium BC.[19] It is probable that Arbor Low was built centuries before then.

That the circle-henge was the Late Neolithic sub-tribal successor to earlier family groups is indicated by the fact that it occupies the centre of a 10-mile wide ring of megalithic chambered tombs with Five Wells to the north-west and Harborough Rocks to the south-east. Fittingly, in the ensuing Bronze Age, like Stonehenge, it became the focal point of a vast necropolis of round cairns.

Although the evidence is both scanty and frail there seems nothing to contradict the first structure at Arbor Low being the cove, standing exposed on its hillside, the centre of funerary rites during the transition between the abandonment of chambered tombs and the beginnings of open-air enclosures. Eventually it was enclosed in the henge, the focus of dispersed family groups, and subsequently the stone circle was built with the beginnings of a portalled avenue curving towards Gib Hill, 70 m across and 4.6 m high, conveniently conspicuous from the highway for the erection of a gallows in the eighteenth century.

Under that great round cairn with its Bronze Age cist there was an oval Neolithic long barrow in which 'a considerable quantity of charcoal and human bones' were found by William Bateman in 1824, yet another link between stone circles and death.[20] The final heaping of a round cairn onto the bank of Arbor Low itself may be a sign that even early in the Early Bronze Age the circle-henge was losing its power.

Almost 150 miles to the south of Arbor Low was another huge circle-henge, the Devil's Quoits in Oxfordshire, many days' travel along the River Derwent, through the forests of central England, across the headwaters of the Trent, onto the higher land of the hills of the southern Midlands. Like Balfarg and Arbor Low the ring had portals at its east and west entrances to an oval enclosure, 130 × 112 m, with over twenty-four big stones set in a circle 76 m. The site was partly excavated when it was being levelled for a wartime aerodrome and, because of an encroaching quarry, was further investigated when a slight central structure of timber was discovered. Seven assays ranging from 2215 ± 70 bc (OxA-3690) down to 1640 ± 70 bc (HAR-1888) imply long use for the site from c. 3000–1800 BC. Finds of beaker pottery and a Middle Bronze Age urn are in agreement with this. Another discovery of an Iron Age or early Roman brooch pin may be the result of curiosity of people in historic times about the worn down prehistoric structure.[21]

Typically the Devil's Quoits stood by an important trackway from the Midlands which avoided the forested clays near Wantage, passed the henge of Deadman's Burial, and stretched down to Uffington and the route into Wessex.[22] Most probably it was a trail used both by highland stone-axe merchants bringing their wares to Wessex and by north Wessex flint-traders travelling northwards from the Avebury district past the henges, the Rollright Stones circle, the cursuses in the Vale of Evesham, across Charnwood Forest and up into the Peak District where they would have come to the Derbyshire circle-henges of Arbor Low and the Bull Ring.

The cumulative impression from these circle-henges along the routes connecting northern and southern Britain is that of monumental sites being built in the early centuries of the third millennium BC for people gathering for trade and religion in the same manner as the great open circles of the west but much more susceptible to interference and destruction by makers of the native food-vessels.

The Smaller Rings of the North-East and the Midlands

Equally, the ring at Balbirnie, Fife, close to Balfarg, was subjected to food vessel interference. When the site, first dug into in 1883, was re-excavated in 1970 and 1971 and moved because of the widening of the Perth road a central rectangular setting of slabs was discovered within this 15 × 14 m ellipse whose ten stones, up to 1.8 m high, were graded to the south. Sherds of grooved ware were found by a stone in the north-east arc and suggest a date in the early years of the second millennium BC for the ring, a supposition supported by its elliptical shape and by a C-14 assay of 1330 ± 90 bc (Ga-K-3425), c. 1750–1550 BC, for later activity here.

The open rectangle, 3.3 × 2.8 m, was very like those at Stenness, Orkney, and at the earthwork enclosure of Mount Pleasant, Dorset, the latter aligned north–south with outlying stones at west, north and east and dated to 1680 ± 60 bc (BM-668), c. 2120–2000 BC. Such rectangular settings might be related to the 'hearth' at Lugg henge, Dublin, and to the timber mortuary houses known under some Neolithic long graves and beaker burials.[23]

At Balbirnie patches of cremated bone lay underneath some circle-stones. Whatever the ceremonies here they were interrupted when the site was converted into a cemetery. Four or five cists associated with a late beaker and a jet button were constructed within the ring. The date of about 1650 BC came from wood alongside the beaker. Stretches of low walling were put up between the stones forming a continuous barrier in much the same way as the prostrate connecting stones at Moncreiffe 13 miles north-west, and analogous to the embanked stone circles elsewhere in Britain that seem generally to belong to a period in the mid-second millennium. The artefacts at Balbirnie agree with such a horizon.

But the first cists did not long remain undisturbed and were seemingly rifled when later cists were built that contained the cremations of women and children like the pits of Weird Law enclosed cremation cemetery 45 miles to the south. One of these later cists held a food-vessel and a flint knife.

The stone circle was further abused. A low cairn was piled over all the cists. Sherds of deliberately broken urns, one with barley impressions, were scattered amongst the boulders, intermingled with small coagulations of burnt human bone. This last phase at Balbirnie occurred late in the second millennium BC, for a C-14 determination of 890 ± 80 bc (Ga-K-3426), a bracket of 1200 to 900 BC came from the land surface that had built up within the ring during the centuries while the stone circle remained open to the weather.

Although it should not be overstated it seems that the makers of food-vessels in particular regarded megalithic rings as little more than desirable locations for their cists, a duality in the people's attitudes permitting a recognition of the monument's sacred character whilst allowing them to transform its essential openness into a cairn-filled ring. Such cairns whether at Balbirnie or at Dun Ruadh or Gortcorbies in Northern Ireland tell the same story of the conversion of an ancient sanctuary into a later sepulchre. Food-vessel cists at rings like Machrie Moor, Arran, Cunninghar,

Clackmannan, or the small oval of Marchwell, Midlothian are chronological deceits. They cannot provide conclusive proof for the dating of these sites.

In the same way the bush-grown cairn at Newbridge outside Edinburgh may not be of the same date as its three surrounding stones. In it a fine rivetted bronze rapier of the Middle Bronze Age was discovered in 1830. Known also as Huly or Heelie Hill, even Old Liston, the mound, 30.8 m across and 3.4 m high, has a retaining wall around it. Around it the stones form an enormous, near-isosceles triangle, all that is left of an inchoate, geometrically protean orbicular setting: shape and date unknown.

'There may have been a twin circle encircling a barrow.' This suggestion of a huge concentric ring is debatable. In 1794 the site was described as 'a circular mound of earth, surrounded with large unpolished stones at a considerable distance from each other', their number and disposition being unspecified.

Because of the north-west, south-west and south-east situations of the trio of carboniferous boulders from Kaimes Hill several miles to the east Fred Coles thought they might be the remnants of two rings with diameters of 100 m and 60 m. His plan was quite accurate in its dimensions but not in directions. Alexander and Archie Thom made a detailed survey in 1965. Refining it in 1981 they recorded the stones, the north-west 2.3 m high, 30.8 m from the centre of the cairn; the ssw, almost directly to the south, 2.1 m high and 50.8 m away; and the ese, 1.4 m and 53.4 m distant from the cairn to its west.[24]

On the geometrical principle that a circle can always be fitted to three points although not always to four or more, it is possible that the stones were the remains of a true circle with a diameter of 89.6 m whose centre was 15.7 m south-east of that of the cairn. Alternatively the stones could be the remnants of a concentric circle, 60.1 m and 103.6 m across, that shared the cairn's centre. They could also be no more than unrelated monoliths. If the writer were compelled to make a choice between a concentric setting, a simple circle or independent pillars he would choose the second with the reservation that it could have been an ellipse with a long axis of about 112 m and a short of 96 m. Its later cairn was deliberately placed off-centre.

Such an arrangement would be reminiscent of Cairnpapple only 9 miles to the west where the ellipse surrounded an eccentrically set cairn of several phases from beaker to overhanging-rim urn. The reason for the asymmetrical siting there has not been explored although a wider gap at the south-east of the ring may have been aligned on the midsummer moon rising in a saddle of the far-off hills. At Newbridge the Thoms suggested that the cairn had been positioned so that from its high top an observer could look towards the big Lochend Stone 320 m to the east where, beyond it, the mid-year sun would have risen in a saddle on the Arthur's Seat some 10 miles away.

The three, thin writhing pillars at Lundin Links, Fife, are just as problematical. Ringed in battered iron railings on a golf-course, they huddle like captured triffids, more like standing stones than a ravaged circle. An obsequious eighteenth-century factor described them: 'some of them over 20 ft [6.1 m] in height, beneath which my ingenious and honoured patron, Baron Clark, having employed men to dig, several coffins were found, containing bones of men'. Their impressive heights persuaded Thom that the stones had been arranged for observations on the minimum moonrise and moonset. Whether they were ever part of a circle remains debatable although, if they were, an exaggerated form of Four-Poster is feasible.[25]

Indeed, whether in south-east Scotland or north-east England stone circles are uncommon, and great megalithic rings hardly exist. There are henges here: Coupland; Overhowden; Weston; Normangill and Rachan Slack as well as Balfarg and Cairnpapple, but only three large stone rings. Two are egg-shaped and lie on either side of the Merse-Teviot valley along which a traveller could cross the Cheviots, past the Burgh Hill oval and down Liddesdale to the Solway Firth. Both sites are close to a henge. Borrowston Rigg, north of the Teviot, 41.5 × 36.6 m on a WNW–ESE axis, lies overgrown on a moorland. Of its low stones none more than 60 cm high, one lying exactly at the north 3.1 m inside the circumference like an inlier at Cairnpapple. There are two stones 37 m to the north-west. Five miles WSW across the Leader Water is Overhowden henge, a large oval with a north-west entrance.

Thirty miles south-east of Borrowston Rigg is the second, more impressive ring of Threestone Burn at Ilderton, standing on a pronounced slope like Overhowden henge near which excavations unearthed many flints and a stone macehead. Overlooking the spacious valley to the ESE Threestone Burn, 36 × 29.3 m, stands on NW–SE axis with its biggest surviving stones, up to 1.7 m, high in its northern arc. Inside this open ring Victorian investigators uncovered spreads of burning like those in the southern rings of Fernworthy on Dartmoor, the traces of fire-rituals perhaps connected with seasonal sun festivals.

Eight miles north of Threestone Burn is the big Coupland henge in the archaeologically rich Milfield Basin of the Till valley. It is similar in size to Overhowden but with NNW and SSE entrances which may have been gated. Phosphate analyses have been seen as evidence for the 'ritual' henge being used as a cattle kraal with droveways leading to it from north and south.[26]

Other henges in the Basin, all small, had entrances facing a compass-range of directions. Rejecting astronomical explanations the excavator considered the wide gaps had permitted views to far-off hills, the Cheviots, the twin-peaked Yeavering Bell, spectacular uplands perhaps regarded as sacred places. Pits inside the henges, a group of 29–30, another of 12–14, seem to have been numerically significant but 'whether either of these sets of figures had any connexion with the counting of days or months must remain very questionable'.[27] If only enthusiasts for eclipse-predicting pits and nineteen lunar-month bluestones at Stonehenge would be as reticent.

In the same neighbourhood are the misleading Standing Stones of Hethpool. All are toppled on a level knoll between a steep-sided burn and a hillside. Heavy ploughing caused megalithic chaos. In the 1930s the wreckage was believed to have been a vast horseshoe or an oval of unshaped stones on a NW–SE axis. Current reconsideration of the scattered and broken layout has instead visualised an impossibly damaged northern ring and, 64 m away, a rather better preserved southern oval about 61 × 42.7 m, one of the largest rings in northern Britain.

Elsewhere there are no great circles. This was not a region of much Neolithic activity. Chambered tombs and long mounds are few. It is only around 2500 BC that settlement of land around the Forth estuary became widespread. 'The apparent sparseness of neolithic occupation in south-east Scotland may be contrasted with the increase in activity in the area in the 2nd and 1st millennia [bc].'[28]

In England, burial cairns like the round Copt Hill, Co. Durham, or the long Bellshiel Law, Northumberland, are singular Neolithic sites amongst the numerous Bronze Age monuments of this part of Britain: round barrows like Kirkhaugh with an A0C beaker and a gold earring; standing stones like the 3.7 m high cupmarked pillar at Swinburn Castle; stone rows like the Five Kings with two stones at right-angles to the alignment; and the hundreds of cup-and-ring marked rocks in Northumberland at one of which, Fowberry Moor, the retaining kerbs of a round burial mound included stones carved with the same symbols as those on the natural rock underneath.[29] Even the large henges with their two entrances and oval shapes are more probably of the early second than of the third millennium.

In the eastern Lammermuirs there are no large open rings, only little ring-cairns high in the hills, embanked ovals like Mayshiel or Spartleton Edge, 12.8 m across, with seven stones just showing above the peat and heather. This is the very fringe of stone-circle country. Forty miles south-west is the Burgh Hill group with their tall south-west stones. Thirty miles west is the once isolated six-stone ring of the Haerstones, or 'witch's stones' now hedged round in a cottage garden, intermediate between the small ovals of Perthshire and those of the Cheviots where the five disarranged slabs of the miscalculated Duddo Four Stones, starkly outlined on their ridge and once thought to be men turned to stone for winnowing on the Sabbath, the destroyed Fairnington, the Five Stanes and others hint at wide cultural connections between the lands to north and south of the Forth estuary. Embanked rings like Yadlee, only 8.2 m across, or Nether Dod, 12.2 m in diameter with a south-west entrance, are as much ring-cairns as stone circles. Kingside Hill 'represents a group of at least seventeen stone settings in south-east Scotland, unusual on account of the small size of their stones'.[30] The ring rests on an open moor, 300 m up, its thirty stones enclosing an 11.6 × 10.7 m space with a south-west entrance is very like the enclosed cremation cemetery of Weird Law 40 miles west. Both sites had central mounds. Charcoal from a crema-tion at Weird Law was dated to 1490 ± 90 bc (NPL-57) c. 1900–1700 BC. Such a period or even later is likely for many of these monuments with their mixture of stone circle and earthwork.

The Perthshire affinities are accentuated by the Four-Posters in Northumberland: the Goatstones with a cupmarked south-east stone, and the Three Kings in Redesdale which was shown to have a pillaged ring-cairn inside it when it was excavated in 1971. Neither site is likely to be earlier than the mid-second millennium and may be 'family' monuments built by small groups that had wandered southwards in search of good land. Fieldwork on the open, windblown moors of Northumberland is discovering sev-eral other modest examples of these remote Four-Posters like a trickling colony of emigrants from central Scotland in search of unclaimed land.

Farther south in Yorkshire the pattern is the same. There are great henges like the double-ditched trio at Thornborough, built on the gravel between the rivers Swale and Ure, their NW–SE entrances aligned quite neatly through the sites. Other henges: Cana, Nunwick, Hutton Moor crowd into the same few square miles between the rivers. There are standing stones such as the Devil's Arrows, Boroughbridge, monsters of millstone grit dragged 9 miles to a spot leading down to the best fording of the Ure. There is the tallest standing stone in Britain and Ireland at Rudston, in the churchyard, a moss-covered, monolithic grindstone, its tip broken but still standing 7.9 m above the ground. This 26-ton giant was hauled from Cayton Bay 10 miles away. An excavation by Sir William Strickland in 1776 was claimed to prove that 'its depth underground was equal to its height'.[31]

Significantly it rises at the eastern end of a chalk ridge near Bridlington where many stone axes have been found. The ridge begins at Rudston with its cursuses, its henge and long barrows, and bends down to Newbald by the Humber where there is another henge. At Rudston early beaker sherds came from one of several cursuses converging on the ridge.[32] The tall pillar, which stood in a rectangular ditched enclosure, once had a smaller stone to its east much like Maen Mawr in Wales and seems to have served the same directional purpose as a towering landmark on the trackway that led through one of the most densely populated areas of Neolithic Britain. Just as a pillar at St Asaph's church, Bernera, in the Hebrides is supposedly 'part of a small stone circle in which the Druids stood to observe the ravens and from their doings to draw auguries',[33] so the monolith at Rudston has been 'christianised' by enclosing it in the churchyard, another example of the persistence of paganism into mediaeval times.

But stone circles are rare. This is henge country and the very existence of the monstrous stones at Rudston and Boroughbridge is a contradiction as though to emphasise the scarcity of stone. Rings that have been called stone circles turn out not to be so. One in the east on the North Yorkshire Moors at Danby Rigg was actually a complex ring-cairn, its rubble bank worn down, one of its four tall stones remaining. Excavators found two late collared urns at its centre, upside down and holding cremated bone and charcoal.

Another so-called pair of circles at the High Bridestones is better interpreted as the wreckage of a stone row and a shattered Four-Poster across 137 m of heather-thick moor. Only Commondale on a gentle slope may be a genuine oval, 31.7 m across, the tallest of its stones a mere 61 cm high at the ESE and set radially like its neighbours. Digging here has resulted only in the discovery of a few, ill-recorded flint flakes. Another misnamed stone circle at Kirkmoor Beck Farm with ten stones just protruding through the turf around a 4.6 m space covered a few urn sherds, a flint and scraps of cremated bone. Such a site has more in common with ring-cairns than with the splendid open megalithic rings of western Britain.

If the North Yorkshire Moors are not fruitful territory for the seeker of stone circles the hills of western Yorkshire are only slightly more productive. The rings show the same mixture of mini-henge, stone circle and ring-cairn, two being adjacent at Dumpit Hill on Mossy Moor Ridge near Hebden, small and ravaged for wall-building. The Twelve Apostles on Ilkley Moor near the crest of a ridge is perhaps the best preserved of several such embanked rings in an area better known for its cup-and-ring-marked rocks. A slight earth bank surrounds a true circle, 15.9 m across, many of the stones fallen or missing. Of those still standing one over 1.2 m high leans at the northeast, its moorland setting contrasting against the cultivated hillsides of Wharfedale in the distance.

To find truly megalithic circles it is necessary to go deeper into the Pennines where 375 m up in the hills on a characteristic terrace is the Druids Altar, Grassington (Pl. 56), three standing stones remaining of a 'Scottish' Four-Poster, built like other Perthshire examples on a cairn, here badly disturbed at its south. The site has been misinterpreted as a ruined embanked circle, its name coming from a large, flat stone within, but this is the broken south-west pillar whose stump still survives at the corner of a 4 × 3.5 m rectangle, actually a true circle 5.3 m in diameter. Being seventy miles south of the nearest Four-Poster at the Goatstones, Northumberland, the Druids Altar is as isolated from its fellows as the Four Stones, Walton, in central Wales. Such is the ruinous state of this monument that it has also been visualised as the remains of a small chambered tomb with a crescentic façade. The embanked oval of Carperby, immediately below the towering Ivy Scar, with its likeness to the Welsh Druids' Circle, is 15 miles to the north.

Plate 56. The Druids Altar,
Grassington, Yorkshire.
A misunderstood Four-Poster
(Photograph: the author).

Of twenty or more rings in Yorkshire only three or four have stones more than
0.9 m high. Most stand in low, overgrown banks about 11 m across and enclose areas of
multiple burials like the enclosed cremation cemeteries to which they are related.
Four urns and a pygmy cup came from the 7.6 m Harden Moor.

To the south, despite the proud claim that no county has more stone circles than
Derbyshire where at least twenty can be visited, the same criticism can be made. Most
of them are simple or complex ring-cairns, not stone circles. Even though the county
can boast more general studies of its stone circles than any other – Lewis, 1903; J.
Ward, 1905; Andrews, 1907; Radley, 1966a; Barnatt, 1978, 1990 – there seem never to
have been more than five or six megalithic rings such as the Seven Stones in Hordron
in the Peak District against over a score of embanked rings.

This lovely and spectacular region rises at the south end of the Pennine Chain,
divided by the Derwent, rich in forested valleys pushing between the moors and worn
hills from Dovedale to High Peak and beyond. The stone rings demonstrate clearly
the development and change that occurred in these monuments during the second
millennium, starting as wide circles of heavy stones and concluding as tiny earthen
enclosures with slab-revetted interiors.

As long ago as 1787 the antiquarian, Major Hayman Rooke, who had already dug
into the barrow on Arbor Low, and been hoaxed with a spurious Roman urn, recognised how similar the rings on the moors of Derbyshire were to those in Yorkshire.
'About a quarter of a mile west [of Brimham Rocks near Ripley] is a Druid circle, with
a vallum of earth and stones, thirty feet diameter. It is exactly the same construction as
those on Stanton Moor.'[34]

Early settlement in the Peak concentrated on the rich soils of the western limestone
where Neolithic people built chambered tombs like Five Wells, its circular cairn overlying two earlier passage-tombs, and where many stone axes from the Lake District,
from north Wales and from the Group XX factory in Charnwood Forest just below
Derbyshire, indicate the distant contacts of this district in the third millennium BC.[35]
After 2500 BC people for a while occupied the same areas west of the Derwent with
increasing numbers of beaker burials often as contracted inhumations in deep, rock-
cut pits. At least thirty of their round cairns are known and 'there can be little doubt

Plate 57. Ninestone Close, Harthill, Peak District. Not a Four-Poster but a denuded stone circle (Photograph: the author).

that the new importance and prosperity of the Peak area depended on its strategic central position, linking the new North Welsh and North Irish expansion with Yorkshire to the north and the Fen Margin to the south. This network would seem the most likely for the growing trade in Irish gold and bronze equipment'.[36] Makers of food-vessels, their burials in ground-level cists twice as numerous as the beaker barrows, came in from Yorkshire and also from the west, but now, from about 2000 BC onwards, there was the first exploitation of the poorer millstone grit country east of the river, a colonisation increased by the settlement of other groups using collared urns for their cremated burials. These were the people mainly responsible for the widespread clearance of the mixed oak forest on the eastern uplands between 1800 and 1200 BC[37] and this was the time of the cremation cemeteries whose antecedents may be to the north-west of the Peak where the multiple cremations in the stone-lined enclosures of Todmorden and Mosley Height were accompanied by Pennine urns, pygmy cups, faience beads and fragments of bronze ware of what Bu'lock has called his late Peak II/III horizon from the early-second millennium onwards.[38]

In the Peak District the sequence of stone circles mirrors these chronological, environmental and cultural changes both from the limestone to the millstone grit, and from open megalithic rings to minute ring-banks around burial pits. Nine was frequently a preferred number for the stones. The farther to the east one travels the smaller the height of the stones until at the edge of districts like Big Moor the rings consist of low rubble banks with no standing stone anywhere in them. The only great Peak stone circles are on the limestone itself at the circle-henges of Arbor Low and the Bull Ring. The few other stone rings without banks, albeit much smaller, are very close to the limestone edge at the sites of Doll Tor and Ninestone Close (Pl. 57) where four enormous blocks, the largest stones in Derbyshire, remain of a 13.1 m ring at the side of a little terrace. It was dug into by Bateman in March 1847, when he found some badly fired sherds and a worked flint. The site is over-risen by the eroded crag of Robin Hood's Stride to the ssw like a horned devil rising from the hills. The major alignment of the ring was directed towards it. It was between the two horns that the major southern Moon would set at midsummer.[39]

Less than a mile to the east across a valley is the lonely plateau of Stanton Moor like a lost world, its top covered with a prehistoric necropolis of cairns, ring-cairns, standing stones and stone circles. Doll Tor at its west was another rare unbanked ring, 6.9 × 4.5 m in diameter, of six fair-sized stones. At some time the intervals between the stones were joined by drystone walling, and several urned cremations with pygmy cups were buried in the interior. Later the east stone was encapsulated in a ring-cairn like Gortcorbies, Co. Londonderry. Under a flat slab at the centre a female cremation lay in a pit with a segmented faience bead. Other cremations, three with collared urns, one with a star-shaped faience bead, had been placed around the inner edge of the stone bank which eventually was filled in to make a flat-topped platform cairn. The faience beads broadly indicate the date of Doll Tor's ring-cairn in a late relationship with other finds – at least twenty-five collared urns, seventeen early in the tradition; a food-vessel; four incense cups; fragments of bronze; a jet ring and late battle-axes, all of the Bronze Age – on Stanton Moor where 'on a rocky and uncultivated waste, about two miles in length and one-and-a-half in breadth, are numerous remains of antiquity, as rocking-stones, barrows, circles of erect stones etc., of undoubted British origin'.[40]

At the north is the embanked stone circle of the Nine Ladies (Pl. 58), small, its unremarkable stones, like so many of the later rings in Derbyshire, set in a low rubble bank. To the south-west is an outlier, the slab-like King Stone, 58 cm of millstone grit,

Plate 58. The embanked stone circle of the Nine Ladies, Stanton Moor, Peak District (Photograph: the author).

scratched with graffiti. Perhaps even later than the Nine Ladies is the line of three ring-cairns close by, from 12.2 m to 24.4 m in diameter, with north and south gaps in their banks, two with large tumbled stones along their inner edges. From the most northerly, half-hidden by trees, came four Pennine urns.

The juxtaposition of stone rings, complex ring-cairns and earth circles occur elsewhere. The flattened stone circle of the Seven Stones in Hordron, its stones entirely lost in towering summer bracken, is close to Moscar Moor ring-cairn which in turn is not far from the 30.5 m enclosed cremation cemetery of Bamford Moor whose bank is little more than 15 cm high. This is like another enclosed cremation cemetery at Wet Withens on Eyam Moor, 29.9 m across, enigmatically described by Thom as a 'Circle+'. A few stones lie on its thick and heathery bank. In the wide interior once supposedly supporting a nearly central stone, Bateman dug up a cist with an urn.

On Big Moor the typological sequence of Derbyshire rings is explicit. At the west a complex ring-cairn, Stoke Flat, stands by the steep Froggatt Edge. A conspicuously taller stone, 1.1 m high, marks a south-west entrance through the bracken-grown bank. Two miles to the east across the moor Barbrook sw, originally Barbrook I, an embanked stone circle, is a flattened ring 14.5 × 12.5 m across its bank with a taller stone at the south-west where the ground starts to fall from the vast, flat grassland. No finds are recorded from the two robbing-trenches dug by the Duke of Rutland's gamekeeper before 1939. A low, gnarled outlier pokes from the spiky grass and heather to the wsw.

The bank at Barbrook Centre (II) of small stones was retained by kerbs and, internally, by a drystone wall against which nine or ten stones stood. In the western half of the ring was a cairn over a pit in which there was a collared urn, two flint scrapers, a flint knife and a cremation from whose charcoal a date of 1500 ± 150 bc (BM-179), c. 2225–2650 bc, was obtained. There was evidence that a ritual fire had been lit after the cremation had been buried. To its east was a disturbed cist, its cover cupmarked. On the same moor, 2 miles NNE of Barbrook Centre, another ring-cairn at Brown Edge, Totley Moor, had no standing stones but within its stony bank was a foot-high cairn, cremations in pits with Pennine urns, and pygmy cups. The long-used site yielded a series of dates from three of its four pits; 1530 ± 150 bc (BM-212), 1250 ± 150 bc (BM-211) down to as late as 1050 ± 150 bc (BM-177) for the cremated burial of a youth with a Pennine urn, from as early as 2050 bc down to as late as 1000 bc, a time when the moorland was being abandoned. This 7.3 × 6.1 m, grass-high ring with its multiple burials is a long way in time from the awesome circle-henges of the limestone plateau.

On Brampton East Moor, 3 miles south of Barbrook sw, is the long-lost Four-Poster of Gibbet Moor at present the most southerly of those eastern refugees from the glens of Perthshire 300 tired miles to the north.

The Rollright Stones, Oxfordshire

South of Derbyshire there are no big groups of stone circles, only clusters in Dorset, Exmoor and north Wessex. There is also the remote Rollright Stones in Oxfordshire (Fig. 35), one of the most famous circles in Britain and Ireland. The name has nothing to do with any supernatural rotation of the stones but derives from *Hrolla-landriht* as the early spellings of *Rollindricht* and *Rollendri*, 'the estate with special local rights belonging to Hrolla' reveal.

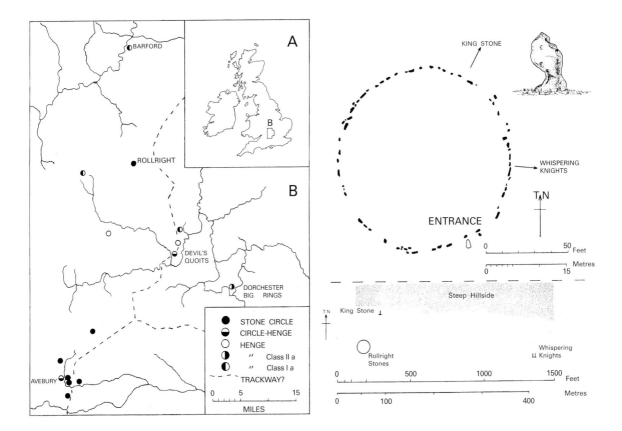

Fig. 35. The Rollright Stones, Oxfordshire.

The Oxford antiquarian Robert Plot told John Aubrey that it was

a great monument of Antiquity, a number of vastly great stones placed in a circular figure, which the Country-people call *Rolle-rich stones*, and have a fond tradition, that they were once men thus turn'd into stones. The highest of them all, which lyes out of the ring towards the east, they call *The King* because they fancy he should have been King of England, if he could have seen *Long-Compton*, a village within view at three or four steps farther . . . [By] the decays of time [the stones] are grown ragged and very much impaired.[41]

Centuries of weathering have eroded the friable stones into fragments that lie by or behind their rotting bases, creating the neat confusion of today's monument, described marvellously by Stukeley as 'the greatest Antiquity we have yet seen . . . corroded like worm-eaten wood by the harsh jaws of time'.[42]

The circle stands at the narrowest south-west point of a high limestone ridgeway with an outlier, the King Stone, at the top of the steep slope to the north-east. In the field to the ESE are the slumping, crumpled ruins of a portal dolmen called the Whispering Knights, 'a remarkable monument much taken notice of; 'tis what the old *Britons* call a *Kist vaen* or stone chest,' fantasised Stukeley.

To the east is the undulating landscape of Great Rollright, westwards the down-curving hillsides to the Evenlode plain. The chambered tomb of Ascott-under-

Wychwood and Neolithic axes from Enstone and Witney show the presence of Neolithic people in Oxfordshire. The association of an outlying portal dolmen and the occupation of the high country suggests that the Rollright Stones were put up in the early third millennium BC when the Midlands route was being increasingly used.

The geology is emphatic. Stone is scarce. Soils and clays predominate. So do henges. The Rollright Stones is isolated. It stands in an area of earthworks on the trackway leading south from the Midlands to the western Cotswolds and the basin of the Upper Thames. The possible henge, more probably ring-ditch, of Hampton Lucy is 16 miles NNW by the Avon. Beyond it was the hengiform Barford with a date of 2416 ± 64 bc (Birm-7), *c.* 3200–3000 BC. The double-entranced Westwell is 13 miles SSW of the Rollright Stones. The ovals of the Deadman's Burial mini-henge near a beaker cemetery, and the circle-henge of the Devil's Quoits are both about 16 miles SSE on the trackway. Condicote, double-ditched and with a south entrance, is 8 miles WSW at the start of the Cotswolds.[43]

In a landscape of shallow clay loams the atypical Rollright Stones was probably the assembly-place of people inhabiting a territory of some 20 square miles. It is at the very edge of stone-building country in company with chambered tombs like the Hoarstones or Adlestrop Hill at the outer limits of Neolithic megalithic barrows in the north Cotswolds. Builders of stone rarely settled farther east. Only at the Devil's Quoits is there a stone setting inside the henge, and there the stones were almost fanatically quarried from intractable gravel conglomerate.

The well-drained gravels of the Upper Thames supported a large and prosperous population in the Late Neolithic and Early Bronze Age along the land and river routes to Wessex and East Anglia. The Rollright Stones were erected on a high ridge above the forests, on ill-drained land always susceptible to summer drought and more suited to pastoralists than crop-growers. If the line of henges and the stone circle were at the edges of their 'territories' where the land merges into a fringe of forests, then each might have been the focus of inhabited land, separated from each other, and quite sufficient to support several hundred people in the richer, low-lying soils of the henges, perhaps little more than a hundred on the more exposed limestone upland.

The Rollright Stones was a true circle. The uprooting and replacing of many stones caused so much irregularity that it seemed its diameter could not be quoted accurately, but this was over-pessimistic. Using a combination of Barnatt's plan and Thom's method of planning to the middle of the stoneholes, not difficult with blocks averaging only 41 cm thick, a diameter of about 32.9 m is feasible.

With its portalled entrance at the south-east the ring was formed of over a hundred slabs standing shoulder to shoulder as continuous as a henge bank. They were crudely graded in height and weight, those at the north-west being taller and heavier than those opposite. They stood in a low broad bank with a 20 m wide gap at its south-east whose terminals were at the east and south. Central to the opening was the portalled entrance, 5 m wide, formed of four stones which had been selected for their opposing shapes. From inside the ring the circle-stone on the left was a flattish block but its partner was a thin pillar. Outside it the fallen stone was a thick slab that may have stood radially to the circle. Its companion opposite the flat-topped circle-stone was a slender pillar. Whether these combinations of 'female' flat-topped blocks and 'male' pointed pillars were chosen as forms of fertility symbolism remains debatable.

Plate 59. The outlier of the King Stone, Rollright Stones, Oxfordshire (Photograph: the author).

Seventy-six metres NNE of the perimeter, across the lane, is the King Stone (Pl. 59), a 2.4 m-high outlier, twisted and bent like a hunched hag. Despite Stukeley calling a long mound beyond it the 'Archdruid's Barrow' the rise is natural[44] and the King Stone may be taken as one more example of the outlying stones well known among the great open rings of western Britain. A few hundred metres down the sloping field to the north the hill's curvature hides the circle but the King Stone is clear against the skyline. From the King Stone the circle is visible. An outlier is not needed elsewhere here for the ground is quite level and the Rollright Stones may be seen from a long way away. It is another instance, like Long Meg and the Heel Stone of a sensible reason for these outlying stones.

Because of its NNE bearing from the circle Thom suggested that the stone had been put up in line with the rising of Capella in 1750 BC, a stellar alignment that is accurate but a date that is not. The King Stone was almost undoubtedly set up many centuries before that time.[45]

The Rollright Stones, the King Stone, the Whispering Knights presented few difficulties for their builders. Constructed of surface slabs lying conveniently close, none weighing more than six tons, the entire complex could have been dragged and erected by a work-gang of twenty in three weeks.

Local stories said the outlier was a king turned to stone, as were his men, by a witch who owned the land over which the ambitious conqueror marched. 'Go forward,' she cackled,

Seven long strides shalt thou take.
If Long Compton thou canst see
King of England thou shalt be.

But the unsuspected mound, Stukeley's 'long barrow', humped on the down-slope between his view and Long Compton and, malevolently triumphant, the witch cried,

As Long Compton thou canst not see,
King of England thou shalt not be,
Rise up! Stick! And stand still, Stone,
For King of England thou shalt be none;
Thou and thy men hoar stones shall be
And I myself an eldern tree.

The king became the King Stone, his warriors the circle, and some far-off muttering traitors the Whispering Knights.

One wonders what time-thin truths survive. 'The past has left marks deep in the human mind as real as the tangible marks which we search out among our fields and hills.'[46] At other stone circles, a hundred or more miles distant, there are legends to do with water, white blossoms, of midsummer, of sun, of fertility practices, all of which combine in the stories of the Rollright Stones to create a tantalus of shadows. It may be coincidental that the witch changed herself into an elder tree with its June clusters of creamy-white flowers, but 'on Midsummer Eve when the eldern tree was in blossom, it was the custom for people to come up to the King Stone and stand in a circle. Then the eldern was cut, and as it bled the king moved his head'.[47]

It is a pretty story. And the prettiness, though not the veracity, increased over the centuries. It began as a mediaeval belief in the petrifaction of sinners. There was no witch. She entered the fable with the witchcraft mania of the early seventeenth century. Then, some time after 1660, a hedge was planted between the circle and the lane alongside it. An elder tree grew in it. When cut resin, red as blood, oozed from it. Today the hedge, the tree, the witch have gone. The whimsy survives.[48]

In Tudor times there were reports of sabbaths being held there and rumours were muttered that Warwickshire witches went naked to the stones for their rites. The Rollright Stones are now supposedly free from such visitations. It is said that nocturnal practitioners at the stones were discouraged by cheerful calls from passing motorists of, 'Lovely night for the witches, then!' Modern suggestions that stone circles were meeting-places for the covens are probably no more than witchful thinking.

There were equally incredible notions. The stones of the circle went downhill at night to drink at a spring, especially at midnight on New Year's Day. If a young wife were infertile she would visit the circle at midnight and press the tips of her breasts against the stones just as barren women did in Brittany miles away across the English Channel. Stukeley wrote that the young people would meet at the Rollright Stones 'at a special time and make merry with cakes and ale'. The seasonal gatherings on winter nights and summer days, the processions from a source of water, the belief in the fecund power of the stones, the celebrations and merrymaking of young men and women, these are flashes of an ancient world glimpsed now through the frosted glass of time.

Expectedly in a ring where the activities were vital but left so little of substance behind, excavations have not been helpful. John Aubrey observed, 'Ralph Sheldon (my honoured Friend) of Beoley Esq, told me he was at some charge to digge within the Circle, to try if he could find any Bones: but he was sure that no body was buried there'.[49]

In 1982 and 1984 there were limited excavations in the circle and at the Whispering Knights where a flint plano-convex knife and scraper were found close to the tomb. Investigations near the King Stone raised the possibility that the pillar had been set up as a grave-marker for a round cairn that lay just NNW of the long, natural mound. Radiocarbon assays from secondary cremations of 1420 ± 40 bc (BM-2427) and 1540 ± 70 bc (BM-2430) with calibrated midpoints of c. 1734 BC and 1887 BC are of Early Bronze Age date. A tiny round cairn to the west of the King Stone covering an infant's cremation and a collared urn, yielded comparable dates of 1370 ± 90 bc (BM-2429) and 1530 ± 50 bc (BM-2428), the central equivalents of c. 1674 BC and 1874 BC.[50]

Insights by Lambrick proved the Rollright Stones to be a 'Cumbrian' stone circle. It was the correct size and shape, was of numerous, almost contiguous stones, was embanked, had cardinal and lunar orientations and a portalled entrance, all traits of the great rings of the Lake District. One of its functions may have been to act as an entrepôt on a ridgeway along which stone axes from the Langdale mountains were taken southwards to the rich settlements of Wessex.

It may even have been designed using a Cumbrian unit of measurement. The circle's hypothetical diameter of 32.9 m is one that is integral to a length of 0.794 m being almost exactly 42 of those units. This hypothetical 'Cumbrian Yard' fits other Lake District rings including Swinside, Brats Hill, Elva Plain and Castlerigg. The King Stone stands about 96 units outside the circle. If there is significance in this it does not follow that the distance was measured from the ring. Planners could have counted from the outlier when setting up the circle.

For astronomical enthusiasts the conjunction of Thom's Capella 'date' of 1750 BC, and the four unrelated C-14 assays averaging 1792 BC is evidence that the stone had been put up to commemorate the burials. To sceptics the stellar alignment is an illusion. There is little evidence of star-lines in any prehistoric monument of western Europe. It is arguable, indeed probable, that the burials were laid against a pillar venerated for its antiquity and already a thousand years old, maybe even older than the adjacent mound. The astronomical fact is that the difference of almost fifty years between the two sets of dates meant that by 1750 BC the swift-moving star would have been rising almost 2 m to the north of the King Stone.

In the beginning the King Stone may have been a single standing stone for a settlement near the trackway. Later the Rollright Stones were built alongside it and, finally the cairns in a protracted prehistoric sequence of: Early Neolithic ridgeway, King Stone, Whispering Knights, Late Neolithic Rollright Stones, Early Bronze Age disc- and saucer barrows, and Middle Bronze small cairn burials.

The ring had an astronomical refinement. Like other Cumbrian circles with external portals the builders neatly arranged the pair of stones on one side of the entrance, here the two on the north, to form an alignment. Standing in a 1.2 m long line the two were easy to sight along. The combination of the latitude, the azimuth, and horizon height, produced a declination of $-29°.3$, the rising of the southern moon.

At the Rollright Stones the juxtaposition of a portal dolmen, a type of chambered tomb well known in Wales, and a Cumbrian entrance circle, suggests that both the tomb and the ring were outliers of a tradition from the west. Portal dolmens like the Whispering Knights are known in western Wales and in Somerset. There are

Oxfordshire counterparts at Enstone, Langley and Spelsbury. The distribution implies an influx from the west onto the congenial Cotswold soils.

Entrance circles have a similar pattern. There may have been two at Ffridd Newydd, Dyfed, between a pair of portal dolmens at Carnedd Hengwm South and Cors y Gedol. South of the Lake District there are others at Gamelands, Westmorland, and at the portalled Druids' Circle, Penmaenmawr. The discovery in Oxfordshire of axes from both the Langdale mountains and from the Welsh axe factory of Graig Lwyd near the Druids' Circle indicates the exporting of those implements in the centuries around 3000 BC.

There is indirect support for the belief that the Rollright Stones had an early date. About 19 miles to the SSW seven assays were obtained from the ditch of the once-great circle-henge of the Devil's Quoits. Their dates, ranging from of 2215 ± 70 bc (OxA-3690) to 1640 ± 70 bc (HAR-1888), hint at occupation there from late in the Neolithic into the Early Bronze Age, perhaps from around 2850 BC down to 1900 BC. Discovery of Late Neolithic grooved ware in a posthole fits well with this time-span'.[51]

In the library of Corpus Christi College, Cambridge there is a fourteenth-century manuscript in which, added to a list of Wonders of Britain, there is a fascinating passage: 'In Oxenefordensi pago sunt magni lapides, hominum manu sub quadem quasi connexitate dispositi. Set a quo tempore; set a qua gente; set ad quid memorandum vel significandum fuerit factum hoc, nescitur. Ab incolis autem vocatur locus ille Rollendrith'.[52]

'In the Oxford country there are great stones, arranged as it were in some connection by the hand of man. But at what time this was done, or by what people, or for what memorial of significance is unknown. Though by the inhabitants that place is called Rollendrith.'

It is over 600 years since those words were written. Through the following centuries, truths have slowly been glimpsed. 'At what time?' Probably around 3000 BC. 'By what people?' By men and women of the Late Neolithic, pastoralists, members of loosely linked societies trading or bartering or presenting gifts of ritual objects such as stone axes, people of an open-air grooved ware cult.

'For what memorial?' Within this latticed panorama of emigration and traffic in which the Rollright Stones has to be envisaged as a staging-post between Yorkshire, Cumbria, Wales and Wessex there are intimacies for the ring itself. With an internal area of some 835 m² it could have accommodated an assembly of 150 participants without crowding. Its heaviest stone, no more than three tons, could have been set up by a dozen or so workers. Centuries earlier even the six-ton capstone of the Whispering Knights could have been manoeuvred into place by thirty labourers. There is no need to imagine a vast concourse. The congregation may have included men, women and children, even others from distant parts gathering at seasonal times of the year. 'Of what significance?' may ultimately be answered. At present it remains speculation.

Chapter Sixteen

The Stone Circles of Wessex

They told his Majestie, that they heard me say, concerning Aubury, that it did as much excell Stoneheng, as a Cathedral does a Parish church.

John Aubrey, 1691, 96

In September, following [1666] I survey'd that old Monument of Aubury with a plain-table . . . It is very strange that so eminent an Antiquitie [as Avebury] should lye so long unregarded by our Chorographers.

John Aubrey, 1693, 22, 33

Introduction

It is ironical that the two most famous stone circles of Britain and Ireland, Avebury and Stonehenge, are not at the centre of a megalithic region but at its edges.

Wessex, a region of southern England centred on the chalk uplands of Salisbury Plain in Wiltshire and of Cranbourne Chase in Dorset, is interesting geologically and archaeologically. In it there are all sorts of building materials: chalk at Maumbury Rings; timber at the early rings of the Sanctuary and Mount Pleasant; stone circles at Winterbourne Bassett; even an intermixing of all three at Stonehenge with its chalk bank, internal timber ring and sarsen circle.

As befits an area visited by people from all parts of Britain, bringing stone axes from Cornwall, Wales, Cumbria; copper and gold from Ireland; jet from Yorkshire, the stone rings have many different features: outliers, centre stones, concentric circles, avenues, sometimes blending together in unique forms of monument. The two greatest stand at the meeting points of natural ridgeways, the rivers, overland ridges that converge on Avebury, the central position of Stonehenge between the south coast and the Bristol Channel to the west, the Thames flowing eastwards towards the North Sea and the continent. But Avebury and Stonehenge differ in almost every respect. Because of the Breton style of architecture and art in its sarsen circle Stonehenge will be discussed separately, after the chapter on the cromlechs in Brittany.

The Stone Circles of Dorset

The stone circles of Wessex are characterised and distinguished by their avenues. Most are spoiled. Only a part of the Kennet avenue at Avebury is upstanding. Its western partner at Beckhampton is almost non-existent. Hardly a stone is left at the Sanctuary. Two avenues have collapsed at Stanton Drew. That at Stonehenge may have lost its stones. To the south in Dorset there is only a thin scatter of rings but amongst them there is a consistent report of former avenues.

Little Mayne was a site near the south coast. In April 1728 Roger Gale described it to Stukeley: 'A mile S.E. of Dorchester, at Priors Maen, was a circle of stones lateley broken to pieces by the owner of the ground, called Tallbot. The stones were very large and rude . . . There were two avenues pitcht of stones leading up to it, one from the South, the other from the East, as I could perceive from their remains, like those at Abury.'

The surveyors of the Royal Commission were entirely unconvinced. To them the stones were nothing more than a natural scatter of sarsens near the farm, and one of the 'avenues' was 'certainly a mediaeval road'. Stuart Piggott, however, who made notes on many of these Dorset rings commented that Gale was a reliable field-worker who had already seen Avebury and the fragmented avenues there.[1] Quite possibly in this part of Dorset there were megalithic features in common with north Wiltshire.

Two other Dorset rings are just as unsatisfactory. A few miles west of Little Mayne the small and much disturbed circle of Hampton Down had a 1.2 m wide track leading to it from the north but if this had been an avenue it was a very poor one.

Equally, the damaged and overgrown circle of Rempstone near Corfe Castle may have had an associated avenue but its credentials are suspect. Two parallel lines of buried stones on Rollington Hill half a mile west of the ring had been dug out by a farmer to avoid damage to his plough. 'At least 26 stones were seen "and they formed a double avenue at the east end."' The 'avenue' was 2.7 m wide, its pairs set 4.6 m apart. The direction seemed 'to be following the easiest gradient up a slight incline which if continued would pass just in front of Rempstone Hall'. The setting was destroyed in September 1957 with no excavation or detailed plan.[2]

The Dorset rings are strung along the coast from Rempstone to Kingston Russell, a distribution of over 20 miles with a mere seven sites in it, most at the west end, and all within 5 miles of the sea. Their comparatively small diameters are in noticeable contrast to the size of the huge earthworks of Mount Pleasant, Maumbury, Knowlton and Eggardon in this region.

The Dorset henges are on average four times the diameter of the megalithic rings which, characteristically, are oval, rather small, and stand at the edge of hillsides near but not in the cemeteries of round barrows along the Dorset Ridgeway for which this part of the country is famous. A majority of the rings are near Little Bredy where, at the foot of Crow Hill, is the Valley of Stones, a convenient source of sarsen and conglomerate slabs for the neighbouring megalithic tombs and stone circles. Two-thirds of the tombs and of the rings lie within 4 miles of this valley although the total distribution extends up to 16 miles away, clear indication that geological expediency underlay prehistoric man's choice of materials. It is probable therefore that timber rings await discovery farther east along the south Dorset Downs.

The most easterly of the rings, Rempstone with its questionable avenue, now lies wrecked at the margin of a wood amongst the bracken, quite close to the fine linear cemetery of the Nine Barrows. Typically, Rempstone is oval, 24.4 × 20.7 m.

Farther west near the Valley of Stones, Kingston Russell, a flattened circle about 27.7 × 20.6 m the longest stones at the north, is entirely fallen. So is the much smaller oval of Hampton Down to the east by the rim of Portesham Hill overlooking the coast 215 m below. Its history illuminates the perils of superficial fieldwork. In 1939 there were sixteen stones in a ring about 10.7 m across. Thom found it difficult to establish an accurate diameter, which is not surprising for when Wainwright examined it in 1964

Plate 60. The strangely graded pillars of the Nine Stones, Dorset (Photograph: the author).

there were twenty-eight stones. Even more disturbing than this evidence of modern interference was the discovery during excavation that not only was the number of stones wrong but the site also. The true prehistoric ring had stood to the west where there was now a hedge, and had consisted of an oval, about 7.6 × 6.1 m, of eight or nine stones. A track led to its north-east entrance marked by stakes and two sections of ditch. No finds came from this excavation. Like many other southern rings burials were not customary here.

In much better condition is the atypical Nine Stones, Winterbourne Abbas (Pl. 60), shaded by trees alongside a road, enclosed in iron railings. Unusually it is in a valley. Thom described it as a flattened circle of precisely the same proportions as Kingston Russell 2½ miles south-west, so identical that he was able to superimpose their plans although the Nine Stones was much smaller with axes of 9.1 × 7.6 m. Later he reinterpreted the ring as an ellipse 9.1 × 7.9 m.

There is, in fact, a resemblance to Kingston Russell for both sites were once graded to the north, the Nine Stones having two conspicuously taller stones, 1.2 m and 2.1 m high, on either side of a low block at the True North. In many ways the Nine Stones is like the group of rings in south-west Scotland with their pairs of oustandingly high pillars of which the flattened Loupin' Stanes is a good example. Those sites have their tallest stones at the south-west but the builders of the Nine Stones adopted the accepted north–south lines of southern England. There is some confirmation of its Scottish connection. Only 2½ miles to the south-west is the Clyde-Solway chambered tomb of the Grey Mare and Her Colts with a typical deeply concave forecourt, quite unlike the local Severn-Cotswold barrows.

These scattered Dorset ovals are probably of the Bronze Age. Although they cannot be directly associated with the barrow cemeteries neither can they be related to any distribution of Neolithic sites. At the Nine Stones the biggest of the stones, eight tons in weight, needed many people to move and erect it but the ring itself could accommodate only a few. This is even more true of the diminutive Hampton Down. Both these rings might more suitably be seen as focal points for one or two officiants, the remainder of the small community outside watching ceremonies that here, unlike the north of Britain, required no cremation deposits.

The Lesser Stone Rings of Wiltshire

Other than Stonehenge and Avebury there are not many stone circles in Wiltshire. Every one is ruined, in some cases not one stone remaining of what was an impressive site. The centre stone at Tisbury, the outlier at Winterbourne Bassett, the 'several great stones' at Clatford. These are all gone as is Falkner's Circle and the Sanctuary near Avebury, leaving only frustrating descriptions and vague positions behind. Yet they make a background for the two great rings, and their architecture reveals the influences to which stone-circle builders in Wessex were susceptible.

Most of the rings were low-lying. Tisbury, just north of the River Nadder 12 miles wsw of Stonehenge, appears to have been a circle-henge, 'a circular work with a vallum set round with stones, and a large stone set erect in the centre. On removing the stone, 3.7 × 1.2 m high, by Lord Arundel's order, to the old castle at Wardour, a skeleton was found at the depth of 46 cm under the surface, deposited close to the centre stone.[3] Such inhumations have been noticed by other centre stones like that at Longstone Rath henge, Co. Kildare.

Nothing is left of Tisbury. Nor is the small concentration of rings in Wiltshire, the group around Avebury, any more impressive. This district, at the meeting-point of the Kennet river and the Ridgeway, hard by the Marlborough Downs on which abundant sarsen stones lay, had long been an area of Neolithic occupation as the earthen long barrows and chambered tombs attest. Round barrows, mostly of the second millennium, line the Ridgeway itself, many of them heavy with trees planted by Gothick romanticists 200 years ago. But the stone rings have suffered.

Four miles east by the Kennet, probably in Broadstone West Meadows, eight huge stones stood in a wrecked circle that the author of *A Foole's Bolt Soon Shott at Stonage* called a 'pettie Stonage'. Stukeley saw it, 'over against Clatford at a flexure in the river, we met with several great stones', twelve sarsens 'flat upon the ground . . . 8 of them seem to lye in a circle & the other 4 may possibly have been the entrance or beginning of an Avenue' down to the river. None was left by 1890.[4]

Three miles sse of Avebury and just west of the Ridgeway the disturbed stones at Langdean Bottom are more probably the remains of a Dartmoor-type hut-circle like those at Grimspound. A few score metres to the south, in the same field, the vestiges of a double row crawl through the turf towards an overgrown cairn, another form of hybrid Dartmoor monument but not out of place amongst the Wessex avenues. Below the slope of the Ridgeway and very close to Avebury was Falkner's Circle, twelve stones set in a 36.6 m ring. Just one stone survived the intensive farming of the nineteenth and twentieth centuries.

Even the most problematical of the Wiltshire rings at Winterbourne Bassett is destroyed. In the early eighteenth century a large concentric stone circle stood here, everything questionable about it, its diameters of about 71 m and 45 m, confused as radii by Stukeley, its centre stone, and outlier/s. The stones were quite small but, according to Stukeley, at the centre was a higher pillar and to the west was 'a single broad flat and high stone standing by itself'. Other reports mention several outliers, perhaps the remains of an avenue. There is little left today, just a jumble of stones in a field at the corner of two lanes between the eastern downs and the lower land to the west.

Nine miles north-east of Avebury there used to be a tight group of stone circles. Little remains. By a little stream is the wreckage of the spacious Day House Lane ring at Coate, about 69 m across, first noticed by Richard Jefferies, its stones now fallen and almost overgrown. A mile to the west at Broome was another ring and avenue. John Aubrey wrote of 'a great stone 10 foot high (or better) standing upright, which I take to be the Remainder of these kind of Temples . . . in the ground below are many thus o o o o o in a right line'. The Longstone was finally destroyed in the mid-nineteenth century when the executors of a will 'purchased the remains of the Druidical temple at Broome, and after having them broken up they were conveyed to Cricklade' 8 miles to the north-west 'for the roads and footways of that town'.[5]

A mile south of Broome there has been a megalithic tragedy. In 1965 at Fir Clump, Burderop Wood, Richard Reiss noticed a fallen concentric ring of coarse sarsens. It was enormous, some 115 × 94 m. Thirty years later all the stones had gone, removed during the construction of the M4 motorway. One wonders why such large rings as this and Winterbourne Bassett were erected only a few miles north of Avebury.

The Sanctuary

The Sanctuary on Overton Hill is quite different. Its dull and stunted concrete reproduction lies at the point where the Ridgeway begins to drop from the Marlborough Downs to a ford across the Kennet before climbing Furze Hill past East Kennet long barrow on its way to central Wiltshire and Stonehenge. The Sanctuary does not excite the casual visitor. The A4 roars past it and the greying concrete blocks and cylinders marking the positions of former posts and stones do little for the uninstructed imagination. Yet this site is almost a chronicle of the history of stone rings in Wiltshire, their origin, their modifications, their destruction, their quiet mysteries.

From an imposing roofed timber building it was ultimately changed into a stone concentric ring linked to Avebury by a serpentine avenue of stones. John Aubrey saw it early in 1649 (Pl. 61), its sarsens quite big but 'most of them (now) are fallen downe'. He gave no name for it, simply calling it a 'British Trophie', but was told by a Dr Toope that the ring lay in Millfield. It was seen by Samuel Pepys in 1668, 'great high stones pitcht round'.

Within sixty years it was gone. Stukeley went to it in 1723 before a farmer, Griffin, smashed it up, 'the person that gain'd a little dirty profit'. 'This *Overton-hill*, from time immemorial, the country-people have a high notion of. It was (alas! it was!) a very few years ago, crown'd with a most beautiful temple of the Druids. They still call it the sanctuary.' In his field-notes he recorded the vandalism. '13. May 1724. This day I saw with grief several of the few stones left on overton hill carryed downward towards W. Kennet and two thirds of the temple plowd up this winter and the sods thrown into the cavitys so that next year it will be impossible ever more to take any measure of it'. The site was excavated in May and June 1930.[6]

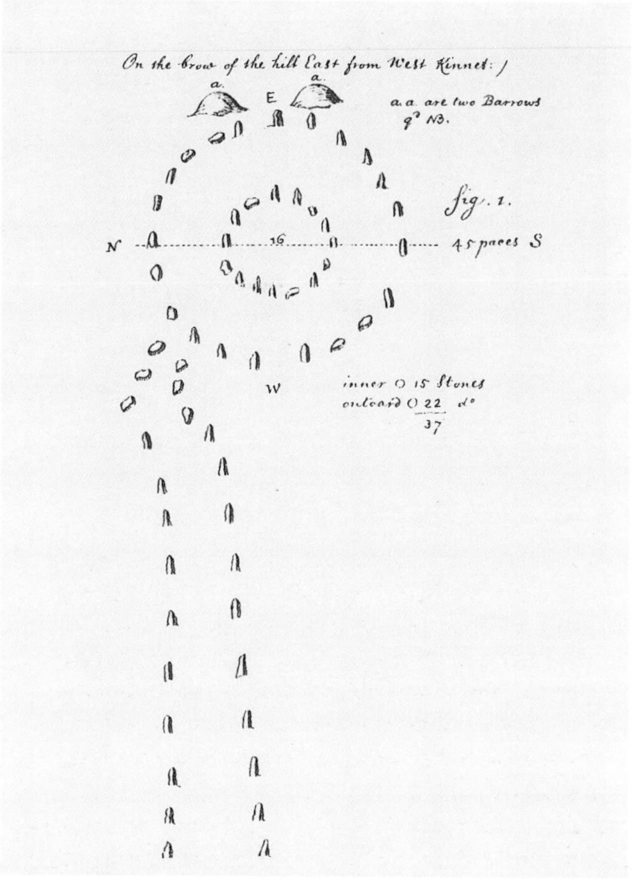

Plate 61. John Aubrey's plan of the Sanctuary before its destruction sixty years later. The avenue has been extended.

To claim to have disentangled a sequence for its eight rings, as early as 3600 BC, some of wood, some stone, would seem ingenuous but should be attempted. Studies by Piggott, Musson and Lees have offered varying possibilities based on detailed examinations of the excavation report.[7] It is reasonable to suppose that in such a prolific area of stone, timber was used for the first building because it was to be roofed, a conjecture improved by the discovery of tiny snail-shells, *Lymnaea peregra* and *Planorbis leucostoma* among others, in some postholes, water-loving molluscs which may have been carried uphill to the site on reeds and rushes intended for thatching. Many of these samples came from the innermost Circle G, the first to be erected, a 4 m ring of six tall posts set up on the hillside by Neolithic people whose rituals included the deposition of broken middle Neolithic Windmill Hill and Mortlake sherds.

The estimated diameters of the rings are of interest. Because different surveyors have measured either to the inside, centre or outside of posts, have used the original excavation plan or plotted the concrete stumps on the site itself, even the diameters are not certain. Maud Cunnington had the advantage of being able to measure to the centres of the exposed post- and stoneholes. Thirty years later Alexander Thom was able only to obtain the lengths 'by taking the mean of steel tape measurements to the centres of the [concrete duplicate] markers'. There are considerable discrepancies between the two sets of data (Table 15).

Ring	Cunnington m	Thom m	Material
A	39.6	39.5	Stone
B	19.8	19.8	Light timbers
C	13.7	14.3	Timber followed by stone
D1	10.5	10.5	Timber
D2	–	9.4	Timber
E	6.4	5.9	Timber
F	4.6	4.2	Timber
G	4.0	3.7	Timber

Table 15. Differing dimensions for the rings of the Sanctuary.

So few antlers and animal bones were found that it must be assumed that the Sanctuary was a place of ritual and not a domestic dwelling. Pollard's re-examination of the material discovered in the postholes supported this. 'The incorporation of funerary practices and ancestor rites into the construction of the monument is evident by the placing of a human lower mandible in stonehole 16 of Ring C and by the crouched burial of an adolescent placed in a shallow grave on the west side of stone C12. Strikingly, both were on the east side of Ring C'.

Lees has made a strong architectural case for all the posts of the Sanctuary belonging to a single roofed and galleried structure. Pointing out that Rings D, E and G had postholes of the same depth, 1.5 m to 1.6 m, he observed that 'in no respect could these be of identical depth if the construction were in different phases, and probably by different generations of people'.

His suggested and plausible solution was a building of which Circle C, 13.7 m across, provided the outer posts, the slighter stakeholes of the surrounding Ring B being the evidence of struts to support the walls. Inside, the holes of Rings D, E and F had held uprights supporting a thatched roof. Between C and D, perhaps 2 m above the ground, were galleries on which bodies of the dead were laid. At the heart of the building the six posts of Ring G rose to a towering height of 12.5 m. The central post was even higher, taking the load of a second, higher roof, a louvre or lantern open at the sides to admit light and give ventilation against the stench of corruption.

Pottery at the Sanctuary suggests that the activities were conducted by people contemporary, perhaps identical with those using the causewayed enclosure at Windmill Hill 3 miles north-west and the gigantic chambered tomb of West Kennet three-quarters of a mile west, places where human bones were vital to the rituals and where similar mixtures of Windmill Hill and Ebbsfleet pottery occur, Windmill Hill causewayed enclosure having no fewer than thirteen C-14 assays ranging from 2820 ± 70 bc (OxA-2421) to 2420 ± 50 bc (BM-2672), c. 3643–2918 BC.[8]

For centuries people went seasonally to such centres but, late in the third millennium BC, perhaps stimulated by the arrival of other groups, new monuments took the place of the causewayed enclosures, henges were built in the river valleys and consistently in them grooved ware has been found: at Stonehenge; at Avebury; at the earthwork enclosures of Marden; Durrington Walls; Mount Pleasant; and at Waulud's Bank, Bedfordshire, where the henge was 4 miles from a causewayed enclosure at

Maiden Bower. This pottery, made by people whose antecedents are still little understood, has also been discovered in timber structures of the period: the north and south rings at Durrington Walls and at Mount Pleasant, sometimes with a very few early beaker sherds. During the excavation of 1930 such sherds, were discovered in several postholes at the Sanctuary.

Inside there, at the ssw, four postholes flanked a recumbent stone. 'It is suggested,' wrote Cunnington, 'that this solitary stone on the south-western side of the Sanctuary is analogous to the solitary stone at Woodhenge, whatever the meaning or significance of that stone may have been'. Calculations show that from the centre of the Sanctuary the sarsen was in line with the major southern moonset. Just inside the inner ring two much heavier posts at the north-west marked an entrance whose sides were seemingly aligned on the settings of the midsummer sun at the north-west, and of the midwinter moon at the NNW.[9] Such solar and lunar associations strengthen the ritual interpretation of the site.

Around 2600 BC the mortuary house was replaced by two megalithic rings 13.7 m and 39.6 m across with Late Neolithic Ebbsfleet and early beaker sherds. The axis was realigned 10° to the west where three stone pillars, set radially on the outer circumference, formed an imposing entrance joined to a short stone avenue that would later be lengthened to lead down the hill towards a source of water. Ultimately the lines would be extended to link with Avebury's Kennet Avenue.

Against the eastern stone of the inner ring a burial, significantly of a young girl, lay half under a stone, head to the south, hands in front of her face looking towards the east and the mid-year sunrise. A B/W beaker by her legs shows this last phase had been completed by 2000 BC. Her bones, sent to the Royal College of Surgeon in London, were mislaid during the Blitz but have recently been rediscovered.

Whatever the ceremonies at the Sanctuary it is of interest to find a mathematical relationship between each of the postulated phases whereby either the number of posts or the diameter is approximately double that of its predecessor. Were other interpretations to be preferred there would still be 'a tendency towards recognisable patterns in the number of postholes'.[10]

As there was no structural necessity for such numerical elegance it is likely that the mathematical models were employed in the same ritualistic way as the standardised number of stones in other groups of stone rings. Close to the Sanctuary, the massive stone chambers at West Kennet, raised before 3600 BC from the evidence of four radiocarbon determinations, were laid out in an almost perfect isosceles triangle whose base was half its height. A comparable geometrical design has been proposed for Parc le Breos Cwm, Gwent. Ashbee was at pains to point out the mathematical properties of the Fussell's Lodge long barrow where the proportions of the trapezoidal mound were $1:2:3\frac{1}{2}$.

At West Kennet, finely reconstructed after the excavations of 1955 and 1956, it was evident that prehistoric people had taken away selected human skulls and long bones from the tomb, and 'It is possible . . . to compose the ghoulish picture of a visitor to the barrow picking up a partly decomposed arm, detaching the humerus, and flinging the other bones into a dark corner'. What was done with the chosen bones is unknown although finds of human bones, some already old and dry before being broken, in the ditches of Windmill Hill suggest that they too had been taken from an ossuary for use as fetishes or mementoes. Knowledge of this custom, as well as the recognition of a geometrical design at West Kennet, is relevant because similar practices have been detected at the circle-henge of Avebury a mile and a quarter north of the long mound.[11]

It is feasible that the stone circles of the Sanctuary that Stukeley watched being destroyed was an open-air symbol in stone of an uncovered symbol in wood of a roofed mortuary house. The concentric rings that resemble the inner and outer uprights of a roofed building may have been intended to reproduce such a building.

The Sanctuary has been described as a house or as an observatory for an astronomer-priest. It was more probably a temporary resting-place for the dead. The general lack of domestic rubbish, waste flints, hearths and middens suggest that this was never an ordinary dwelling place.

In the earlier Neolithic corpses were often buried to be disinterred only when the flesh had decayed or exposed in unroofed mortuary enclosures or laid on scaffolds before being taken away for burial. Such enclosures have been found at Normanton Down near Stonehenge and elsewhere. It is even possible that Stukeley had seen one when he sketched the ruins of the stone-lined rectangle outside the deep forecourt of the Old Chapel megalithic tomb on the high downs 3 miles north of the Sanctuary and alongside the same trackway. There may have been another half a mile south-west of West Kennet and described by Stukeley as 'a very large oblong work like a long barrow, made of stones pitch'd in the ground, no tumulus', an enclosure nearly 80 m long.[12] The suggested galleries inside the Sanctuary may well have performed a similar function.

With the growing Late Neolithic preference for round houses and for rituals associated with water the Sanctuary could have been erected as a circular mortuary house in which some dead were stored until their bones could be washed clean and taken away for funerary ceremonies and burial. Bodies certainly have been found nearby. Aubrey wrote, 'About 80 yards from this monument, in an exact plain here were some years ago great quantities of humane bones and skeletons'. They were extracted by Dr Toope of Bath to be ground into 'a noble medicine that relieved many of my distressed neighbours', who were probably unaware of the origins of the potions used in his lucrative practice.

There were dozens of bodies buried around the Sanctuary, 'soe close one by another that scul toucheth scul . . . I really believe the whole plaine, on that even ground is full of dead bodies,' wrote Toope, remarking on the 'Teeth wonderfully white, hard and sound. (No Tobaco taken in those daies)', a condition characteristic of Neolithic teeth. Hoare and Cunnington noticed how undecayed the teeth were in the excavations of prehistoric barrows. There was little sign of tooth loss and abscesses at West Kennet.[13]

Standing by the Ridgeway with West Kennet chambered tomb only three-quarters of a mile to the west, with East Kennet a mile and half to the south, the Devil's Den 2½ miles to the ENE and Adam's Grave a little farther to the south the Sanctuary was ideally situated as a central ossuary. Rituals connected with death seem likely there.

In the years around 3600 BC the dead may have been brought to the hill, commoners buried outside, others, the most important, laid inside the charnel-house, perhaps to be attended by a medicine-man or witch-doctor. On Malekula in the New Hebrides, on the opposite side of the world from Avebury, where stone circles were still being erected in the nineteenth century ordinary men were simply buried but chiefs were exposed on a scaffold, their bodies continually washed to hasten corruption. At a fixed time all the villagers bathed to prevent the sickness of death spreading amongst them, and a few days later there was a feast to celebrate the lower jaw dropping from the skull. Similar processes of decay may have been watched over at the Sanctuary by holy men.

If heated stones and charcoal were piled over the skeletons to hasten desiccation it would explain why lumps of scorched sarsen were discovered in the postholes. It is improbable that they came from the eighteenth-century stone-burning that Stukeley witnessed because by then these deep postholes had been earth-filled for thousands of years.

At West Kennet bones of the later bodies had quite often been charred but there was 'never any indication that burning had taken place in situ within the chambers or passage', and with the Sanctuary so close it may have been there that when the flesh had gone the last moisture in the bones was evaporated by heat. Scorched bones are known in many southern tombs: at Belas Knap, Tinkinswood, Nympsfield, Rodmarton, Stoney Littleton, at Temple Bottom just north-east of Avebury. At Tinkinswood the bones had been burned 'long after the flesh had perished from them'. It was a widespread Neolithic practice, perhaps, to remove all the liquid of life, possibly because in their metaphorical, analogistic thinking the people believed the spirit of the dead man might be preserved once it was released from the corruption of its body.

None of the early skeletons at West Kennet was burned and the introduction of scorched bones and two complete cremations may have coincided with the construction of the Sanctuary with its fire-crackled stones. If it were indeed a mortuary house from which disarticulated bones were removed it would explain the comparative scarcity of human bones there.

Concentric circles like the Sanctuary were never common, only about thirty being known in Britain and Ireland from Cnoc Fillibhir on Lewis in northern Scotland, down to Stonehenge, what concentrations there are being around the coasts of the Irish Sea and in Wiltshire. Half of them cluster around the North Channel. Most are unimpressively small, little ovals like Coolnasillagh, Co. Londonderry, or Castledamph, Co. Tyrone, with its small central cairn, a sepulchral feature which may reveal the origin of this group whose inner stone settings are basically surrounds for burials. This is true even for the big Druids Temple by Ulverston, with five central cremations and a primary urn, or Gunnerkeld near Shap some 30 miles to the north-east where the middle ring encloses a low mound with a cist. Oddendale concentric is a little way to the south.

The design of these rings is very like the chamber and kerbstones of a passage-tomb, an appearance which could account for the frequent scatters of stones or cobbles or 'paving' in the inner ring as figurative representations of the overlying cairn. As these northern double circles are most common at the fringes of passage-tombs their derivation may be sought in that tradition.

The Wiltshire concentrics did not have the same origin. An explanation for them as megalithic reproductions of timber settings is more probable. It is understandable that there are several on the Wiltshire chalklands whereas in regions of stone there are few: none in Cornwall, one, now destroyed, in the Lake District. 'On the Moor Green farm are 30 stones, called Kirkstones, forming part of two circles, similar in position to those at Stonehenge.' Such an explanation for the Sanctuary would add weight to the suggestion that this had been a roofed mortuary house whose upright rings of internal posts became symbolised in the permanence of an inner and outer stone circle.

Plate 62. The southern entrance slabs and south-west arc of stones, ditch and bank, Avebury (Photograph: the author).

Avebury

Stonehenge is often cited as the role-model for evidence of change and development in ritual monuments. Avebury is better (Pl. 62; fig. 36). Constantly added to, constantly adapting to social tensions it is a microcosm of a prehistoric world that was never still.

Avebury is the mightiest in size and grandeur of all megalithic rings. John Aubrey, who came upon it by accident while out hunting on Sunday, 7 January 1649, three weeks before the execution of Charles I, wrote that Avebury 'does as much exceed in greatness the so renowned Stoneheng as a Cathedral doeth a parish Church'. The comment is perceptive for whereas the early Stonehenge had a parochial plainness Avebury was a national monument whose magnificent complexity is now obscured by its size and the village, trees and roads inside it. 'I take this old, illshapen Monument,' added Aubrey, 'to be the greatest, most considerable and ye least ruined of any of this kind in our British Isles'.[14]

John Aubrey found Avebury hard to comprehend. 'By reason of the cross-streates, Houses, Gardens, orchards and severall small Closes; and the Fractures made in this Antiquity for the building of those Houses, it was no very easy Taske for me to trace out the Vestigia, and so to make this Survey'.[15]

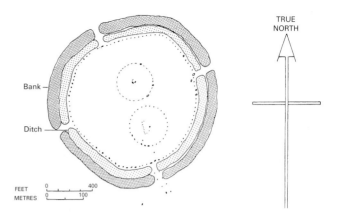

Bank —

Ditch —

FEET 0 400
METRES 0 100

TRUE
NORTH

Fig. 36. Avebury, Wiltshire.

Itemised it sounds ordinary. It consisted of: two avenues of standing stones leading to a chalk bank broken by four entrances whose causeways across the ditch provided access to a central plateau where the largest stone circle in Britain, Ireland and Brittany surrounded two smaller rings. One had a central stone and a rectangular setting. The other contained a circle or perhaps a horseshoe-shaped setting around a Cove. An intended third internal ring was left unfinished.

Even the most Gothick of poetry could not evoke the impact that this colossus has upon any mind sensitive to the lingerings of prehistory. An untidy ribbon-development of cottages, houses and shops crawl through it. A main road buckles through its anatomy. There is little peace here. Perhaps there never was. As long ago as 1289 the earthwork was called Waledich, Old English *weala-dic*, 'the dyke of the Britons', from the time of the Saxon penetration of Wessex when such embankments were helpful defences for either Briton or invader. It is not coincidence that the *here-path*, the Saxon army-road, marches over the downs straight through Avebury, perhaps 'the settlement of Afa the Saxon', perhaps 'the settlement by the afon or river', and westwards towards the Bristol Channel.[16]

Today Avebury is tidier, cleaner. With resolution one may dodge the cars and twist through the swing-gates to walk along the ditch where the bank engulfs the sky like a swelling wave. One may see stones as big as house-walls, stare between cottages across the earthwork to the farther bank a quarter of a mile of grass and stone away.

The site was little damaged until the early fourteenth century AD when many stones of the pagan place were fearfully buried by Christians, one an itinerant and gullible barber-surgeon who was trapped beneath a gigantic sarsen at the south-west. The Black Death of 1349 halted this pious vandalism. But between the mid-seventeenth and eighteenth centuries the economics of destruction smashed more stones for buildings. Some of the mediaeval buried stones were disinterred and re-erected by Keiller's workers of the Morven Institute of Archaeological Research in the late 1930s, Alexander Keiller being the landowner of the Morven estates in Aberdeenshire. Some of the reconstructed angular fragments were grotesquely reassembled.

In the seventeenth century Aubrey recorded how men would shatter a stone, heating it by fire, drenching it with cold water and immediately smashing with sledge-hammers so that 'it will break like the Collets [moulds] in a Glasse-House'. Stukeley saw the same destruction.

The barbarous massacre of a stone here with leavers and hammers, sledges and fire, is as terrible a sight as a Spanish *Atto de fe*. The vast cave they dig around it, the hollow under the stone like a glass-house furnace or a baker's oven, the huge chasms made through the body of the stone, the straw, the faggots, the smoak, the prongs, and the squallor of the fellows looks like a knot of devills grilling the soul of a sinner.[17]

By speaking with villagers he was able to compile a sad history of the vandalism and of the vandals responsible.

Aubrey had recorded seventy-eight stones. By 1724 Stukeley could only see thirty. It had been the smallest, most accessible stones that had gone first. In 1694 Walter Stretch demolished a stone from the northern ring to build the dining-room of the Catherine Wheel Inn nearby. By 1702 most of the Beckhampton Avenue extending from Avebury's west entrance had been removed for the houses that Aubrey saw. In the same year stones just outside the SSE entrance had been broken. Between 1694 and 1722 the inner north circle had been dismantled by 'Farmer Green' for his house and walls at Beckhampton. From 1700 to 1710 Richard Fowler attacked the south circle. The larger stones of Avebury's Outer Circle were not immune. Its northeastern quadrant was toppled around 1718. The south-western quarter was damaged in 1720.

The earthwork also suffered. Late in the seventeenth century part of the bank was levelled by the squire. The SSE entrance was widened to allow stage-coaches to pass. Since 1865 there have been intermittent excavations, the major investigations being by St G. Gray between 1908 and 1922, and by Keiller and Piggott, 1934–5 and 1939, the former doing much to restore Avebury and its Kennet avenue to something of their first splendour, his Hispano-Suiza roaring down the quiet lanes of the 1930s awak-ening the consciences of the archaeologically unaware.[18]

From the excavations and from the accumulated series of radiocarbon assays from the bank, ditch and stoneholes a prolonged sequence of developments at Avebury during the Late Neolithic period can be proposed:

a. First, in that vague time from about 3400 to 3200 BC between the blocking-up and abandonment of megalithic tombs and the innovation of open-air circles two, maybe three, Coves were set up, those unroofed imitations of burial-chambers;

b. around 3000 BC, an unenclosed settlement grew up around one of the Coves at its heart;

c. close to 2800 BC a stone circle was constructed at the centre of the occupied area. Another setting, perhaps a circle, perhaps a huge horseshoe-shaped setting around the Cove, was erected a few metres to the NNW and, later still, a third ring was begun but dismantled at a time of crisis in the centuries;

d. around 2600 BC, a great defensive ditch and bank were raised around the homesteads and ritual circles. The largest of all megalithic rings was set up around the inner lip of the ditch;

e. as many as two centuries later two avenues were laid out, short stretch by short stretch, to the west and south;

f. finally, at the beginning of the Early Bronze Age, Avebury was forsaken.

The site for the settlement had been chosen below Windmill Hill on a mild knoll in countryside once thickly wooded but for some centuries largely cleared of trees for grazing and agriculture. It lay at the heart of a penannular 2-mile-wide ring of deserted long barrows and chambered tombs, separated from them by half a mile of open countryside.[19]

Before this, in the vague centuries between the abandonment of chambered tombs and the construction of stone circles, two or three megalithic imitations of burial chambers, Coves, were erected, one later to be enclosed in the settlement, one to the west at Beckhampton and possibly one to the south towards West Kennet.

The Cove inside the northern ring of the settlement was a gigantic structure of huge slabs, two of whose tremendous stones still stand. Facing north-eastwards it may have been aligned on the midsummer sunrise but with two cumbersome sideslabs at least 10 m apart the 'sightline' would have been far from precise.

A second cove stood a mile wsw of Avebury at Beckhampton. Only one stone, a sideslab popularly known as 'Adam', survives. Originally, it and its partner, Eve 29 m to the east, a stone of the eradicated Beckhampton Avenue, were set not at right-angles but obliquely to the backstone rather like a folding hospital screen. As usual, their smoother faces were set inwards. It is probable that when the avenue was constructed its builders deliberately incorporated the cove, using the backstone as part of the avenue. In the same way the Heel Stone at Stonehenge was included in the later avenue there.

'Adam', a heavy sarsen, 4.9 m high and 3.3 m wide, weighs some 62 tons. It fell in 1911 and was re-erected in 1912. During the excavation the skeleton of a middle-aged man buried with Northern/Middle Rhine and other beaker sherds was discovered at its foot. Stukeley, in 1723, said that bones had been found there but later amended this to suggest that the 'bones' were fossils embedded in the stones. The cove faced a low rise, and was possibly aligned on the midwinter sunrise.

Half a mile south-east of Avebury's south entrance Stukeley believed there had been a third Cove where the Kennet lane crossed the avenue. Sixty years earlier John Aubrey wrote 'Southward from *Aubury*, in the ploughed field – neer *Kynnet* doe stand three huge upright stones perpendicularly, like the three stones at *Aubury* in Fig. •• they are called the Devill's Coytes'. Above the entry there is a sketch showing three tall, thin rectangular pillars with the sideslabs splaying outwards from the stone at the back.

Stukeley added to this, 'As soon as I saw longston cove and found it the interval of 50 stones from Aubury I conjecturd there must have been another such at Kennet avenue'. Counting the stones there, many more than are visible today, he came upon a gap in the avenue and surmised that a cove had stood there at the top of the rise south of where the avenue now ends and where two stones still straddle the road. From his sketch, Tab 22 in his *Abury*, the cove would have stood alongside the lane on a line between Silbury Hill and the disc barrow on Avebury Down.

Aubrey's words show that he was not describing the North Circle cove and, at first sight, his confident statement that the cove was south of Avebury and near the river Kennet does suggest that a cove-like structure had existed in the Kennet Avenue. The fact that he did not show it in his plan of the avenue is not proof of an error because he did not show any part of the Beckhampton Avenue either.

It has often been suggested, with good reason, that Aubrey writing years after his visits had confused the situation of the Beckhampton Cove, misplacing it, and his sketch of the three 'Devil's Coytes' with their out-turned sideslabs does resemble the setting at Beckhampton. It is strange, though, if it were the Beckhampton Cove he had seen so far outside Avebury that he failed to notice the stones of the avenue between it and the great stone circles.

The matter must be left unproven. Sadly, a resistivity survey in September 1989, was unable to determine the presence or absence of any stoneholes where the Kennet lane crossed the avenue because 'as much as 125 metres of this critical stretch of the Avenue may therefore have been interfered with' by the road and the adjoining fields.[20]

Not far from this protean enigma there was an even earlier site. Invisible today but lying between the sixth and tenth stones at the far end of the later Kennet Avenue there was a thick layer of Coombe Rock covering the chalk, a weird bedrock of pits, solution holes and clay-filled hollows, ideal for offerings to the fertile earth.

There were two big pits and ten smaller holes in a 68 m long line on the western side with two more pits and holes to the east. In those cavities 'dead' material was buried: flint flakes, weathered sherds of Ebbsfleet and Mortlake ware. The densest concentration was at the centre of this ritual area and when the avenue was constructed a gap was left respecting this magical shrine.

Rich soil for the healthy growth of crops was buried, sherds, animal bones, hazel and blackthorn charcoal, mostly hawthorn of bright spring blossom and autumn fruits, there were also hazel nuts. And 'foreign' stone: oolitic limestone, greensand, Forest Marble, Portland chert, slate, sandstone, even two pieces of Niedermendig lava from Germany. All were the relics that people had deposited, the 'ghosts' of things desired, fruit, meat, good flint and stone, broken Cornish and Welsh axes, vessels for food and drink, fertile soil. Five holes were clay-lined, probably for liquid. Three radiocarbon assays from bone in Pit 1 of 2330 ± 100 bc (HAR-1051); and charcoal from Holes 4 and 1 of 2310 ± 80 (HAR-9695) and 3830 ± 80 bc (HAR-9694), indicate a time around 3000 bc for the deposits.[21]

Decades later the first of the megalithic rings was erected on the crest of a knoll a quarter of a mile east of the Winterbourne stream. It was one of the biggest of stone circles, circular, 103.6 m in diameter and ideal for the ritual dancing of several hundred people, the remainder of the 26 acre-wide settlement being used for dwellings, cattle-stalls, barns, and the gathering of dispersed groups farming the land around, assembling for trade and engaging in systems of exchanged gifts with strangers from remote areas.

The circle probably had thirty high, broad sarsens in whose stoneholes were some weathered Late Neolithic sherds. Just off centre was a thick, 5.5 m-high pillar, that Stukeley called the Obelisk, 'of a vast bulk, 21 feet long and 8 feet 9 inches diameter' [6.4 × 2.7 m]. Smashed and removed it is now represented by an unappealing concrete pyramid. Four pits to its north were filled with dark brown earth, a practice reminiscent of other Neolithic soil-deposits such as those in the avenue. An urn full of bones was found near the Obelisk in 1880 when a flagstaff was erected but the 'fragments were carried off by the children'. Nothing is known of the burial.

Possibly matched to the east by a similar but unexcavated line of sarsens 15 m west of the Obelisk is a setting of twelve low stones. Nine of them stand in a straightish 31.2 m-long line. Other stones stood to the east at right-angles to the terminals. Isobel Smith speculated that the setting might symbolise the forecourt of a long barrow, the Obelisk occupying 'the place of the burials in an actual tomb'.[22] Acts of symbolism seem to have been performed inside megalithic rings including mimes of customs perpetuated from earlier burial and fertility practices so that a model of an orthostatic forecourt inside Avebury would not be inappropriate. Without complete excavation of the disturbed centre of the SSE circle only guesses may be made of its purpose.

Nearly 18 m to the SSE of the ring was another pillar, the Ring Stone, described by Stukeley as 'an odd stone standing, not of great bulk. It has a hole wrought in it and was probably design'd to fasten the victim, in order for slaying it'. In Cornwall the Reverend William Borlase had the same explanation for holed stones 'to which the Antients were wont to tye their Victims, whilst the Priests were going through their preparatory Ceremonies, and making Supplications to the Gods, to accept the ensuing Sacrifice'.[23]

From the size of its pit it appears to have been substituted for a former and larger outlier, possibly being preferred because of its natural perforation. Only the stump of the Ring Stone was left by its eighteenth-century breakers. Before the raising of Avebury's tall bank the outlier would have provided a clear view towards the height of Waden Hill but with an azimuth of about 165° the stone had no astronomical significance. Its battered stump rests unheeded and uninvitingly in the grass like a half-melted snowman.

A second ring was set up. Stukeley believed that its remains were those of a concentric circle. He was mistaken. A geophysical survey in 1989 made two important discoveries. The first was that there was no sign of a small concentric ring inside the North Circle.[24] The second was of an unexplained circular setting. The few surviving stones of the ring were either those of a 29–30 stone circle about 97.5 m across or of a megalithic horseshoe approximately 105 × 56.6 m with an open mouth towards the SSW. By an unwitting irony John Aubrey may have planned its remnants. The resistivity survey appears to confirm the former existence of a U-shaped setting rather than a stone circle, 'and it is therefore at least possible that Aubrey's . . . [1663] version in this area may yet turn out to be the most accurate of all'.[25]

At its centre was the north-east-facing Cove two of whose tremendous stones still stand. Possibly it had been aligned on the midsummer sunrise but with two short sideslabs at least 10 m apart the 'sightline' would have been far from precise.

At the north-east of this unresolved setting there was what seemed to be a genuine concentric circle, perhaps of postholes, the rings having approximate diameters of 30 m and 50 m. Such proportions are comparable to the hypothetical roofed structures inside Durrington Walls and may be the first physical indications of a supposed settlement inside the Avebury earthwork. It may have been very similar to the timber building at the Sanctuary.

It is odd that this structure, without question potentially the most important result of the survey, with its implications of early occupation, should be hardly mentioned in the book. Instead of an understandably triumphant announcement it is given no more than 'a tentative claim, qualified almost out of existence'.[26]

To the NNW of the circle/horseshoe was a third setting and it is puzzling that despite Keiller's specific field-notes it has been disregarded, even dismissed as non-existent. During the excavations of 1937 three stoneholes were found about 115 m NNW of the Cove. 'The excavation . . . situated between Stone 1, the colossal lozenge-shaped slab of the Diamond Stone standing at the northern entrance, and Stone-hole 2 disclosed the unsuspected existence of a definite stonehole' [Stone A]. Near it were its packing-stones and the stakeholes that had been used during its erection. 'So close was this stone-hole . . . to that of Stone 1 that it would not have been possible for a stone to have stood in each at the same time, and since Stone 1 has never fallen Stone A must have antedated it.' It must have been withdrawn for there were no sign of its destruction. Eleven metres to the NNW was a second stonehole [B]. A third [C] was a further 11 m away alongside the north-eastern edge of ditch that cut into it providing 'conclusive evidence that this stone-hole, and it is to be presumed Stone-holes A and B as well, antedated the bank and ditch and Outer Circle'.

The intended circle would have been practically the same diameter as the others to its SSE, about 105 m. With its stones spaced 11 m apart there would have been about thirty altogether. Sceptics should also consider Stukeley's plan of 1724 which shows a stone standing on the circle's northern arc *outside* the Outer Circle and against the ditch. Aubrey's 1666 plan may show the same stone as its place is shown immediately to the east of a stone about 30 m to the east of the NNE entrance.[27]

Such a line of three rings was not unique. With the three rings at Stanton Drew 30 miles to the west, with the three Hurlers on Bodmin Moor and possibly three rings at Tregeseal on Land's End, the three or four henges at Priddy in the Mendips, the planned complex at Avebury was not out of place in southern England.[28] The archaeological question is not whether a third ring had been intended but rather why the project was discontinued and why the three stones inside what was to be the great Outer Circle were uprooted.

It happened because of some threat or emergency that remains speculative but likely. At five sprawling settlements in Wessex deep ditches were dug and massive banks were heaped up in the decades around 2500 BC. There is a clear-cut correlation between a series of C-14 determinations obtained from organic material in the primary layers of the ditches, the only reliable source. Objects discovered under the banks may have lain there for a long time before being covered.

From Mount Pleasant in Dorset animal bone provided an assay of 2038 ± 84 bc (BM-667), an antler, 1991 ± 72 bc (BM-666) and charcoal, 1961 ± 89 bc (BM-663). At Marden in the Vale of Pewsey charcoal at the bottom of the ditch was dated to 1988 ± 48 bc (BM-557). Bone at Durrington Walls near Stonehenge gave a determination of 2015 ± 90 bc (BM-399) and charcoal, 1977 ± 90 bc (BM-398). Dates from Avebury are little different. There is one quite early from bone, 2350 ± 90 bc (HAR-10502) and two from stoneholes in the north-west quadrant of the Outer Circle, charcoal in Hole 41, 2180 ± 90 bc (HAR-10062), and from Hole 44, 1920 ± 90 bc (HAR-10327).

The median of these closely grouped assays is 2502 ± 82 BC, a bracket of 2600 to 2439 BC with a central period of 2500 BC. It is probable that it was in those years that the deep ditch was quarried around the settlement and inner stone circles at Avebury, the third being dismantled because it stood where the ditch would cross.

That the raising of the bank and digging of the ditch came after the construction of the inner rings can be seen today from the way that the NNW and SSE entrances although opposite each other are not connected by a straight road because it was necessary to avoid the internal settings. The path from the south leads northwards in a direction 115 m west of the NNW entrance, swings sharply eastwards for 60 m above the head of the south circle before turning north towards the farther entrance. This irregular prehistoric layout was perpetuated in historic times. Aubrey's plan of 1666 shows it, so does Stukeley's of 1723. And the modern Devizes–Swindon road twists like a chicane through the middle of the monument.

The flat-bottomed ditch, hacked from the chalk, measures 368 m, nearly a quarter of a mile, across its inner diameter and encloses 26 acres (10.5 ha). The ditch varies between 7 m and 10.1 m in depth and is 21.3 m wide at the top. From it was prised an almost unbelievable 111,850 m³ of chalk, about 200,000 tons to be broken, lifted and carried to the bank.

It may be assumed that at the crest of the dome a line from a focal peg was used to scratch a wavering circle, 173.7 m in radius, for the inner edge of the ditch, a NNW–SSE axis being set exactly at right-angles to another lying WSW–ENE to establish the positions of the four causeways. A massive post-socket in the SSE entrance may be all that remains of one of the markers.[29] Then with antler-picks, ox shoulder-blades, baskets, ropes of leather or animal hide or even grass, the ditches were quarried, quadrant by quadrant, in sections, gangs of workers driving the antler tines into fissures, levering, pushing, until the chalk broke, was shoved aside, dragged into a basket, hefted up ladders and chalk-cut terraces, hauled and dumped onto the bank where turf, cut from the virgin ground, formed a core for the rising layers of rubble, rock and soil. The more the work progressed the harder it became as the ditches delved into solid chalk, and the ragged white bank rose higher, until, when a ditch-section was finished, the jagged balk between it and its neighbour was hacked down and the antler picks flung away.

It is possible to calculate how long this took, using Atkinson's (1961) formula of:

$$\text{Man-Hours} = \frac{\text{Volume } (120+8L+2F)}{1,000}$$

where L = the mean vertical distance for material to be carried, and F = the mean horizontal distance. At Avebury this amounted to 1,560,000 man-hours of effort for the ditch and bank alone. On the much less certain hypothesis that 750 people laboured there, ten hours a day, for two months each year after the harvest was in, the enclosure would have taken about four years to complete.

There is an irregular berm, a narrow flat space, between the edge of the ditch and the outer bank which has an average circumference of 1,353 m. At its base it is 22.9 m to 30.5 m broad and was once about 6.7 m high. Four entrances, each 15.2 m wide, stand at NNW, ENE, SSE and WSW. Here the bank was higher and wider, its terminals revetted with timber grooved ware. The hypothetical date for the raising of Avebury's bank in the mid-third millennium BC, is supported by the presence of much native Mortlake pottery beneath the bank and on the ditch bottom, in both instances accompanied by a few sherds of Windmill Hill, Ebbsfleet and grooved ware, a ceramic mixture which together with typical Late Neolithic flintwork points to a time of building near 2500 BC before users of beakers came to the site, for their pottery is found only in later levels at Avebury.

Perhaps the work on Avebury's enclosure proceeded simultaneously with the erection of the gigantic Outer Circle, the more symmetrical south-east and north-west quadrants of the ditch and bank being put up while the stones were being dragged from the downs through the wide gaps at south and north-east. Certainly pottery from the stoneholes matches that from under the bank. About 100 unshaped sarsen slabs were sledded down the slopes. The heaviest weighed some 47 tons and as the strongest Neolithic rope had a breaking-strain of about a third of a ton skilled craftsmen were necessary to ensure the correct placement of the lines to avoid breakages and dangerous skewing once the stone was moving. The effort would have been less had a temporary track of logs been laid across soft patches of ground.[30] 6.7 m from the ditch edge stoneholes were dug, roughly a metre deep, one side sloped for a ramp down which the toe of the stone could be pushed up to the opposite vertical side where sap-greasy stakes had been rammed to ease the erection of the pillar. Slowly it was levered upwards until, at 70°, the levers were no longer effective and the stone had to be pulled upright with ropes.

Testimony to the care and expertise with which these monoliths were put up emerges from the presence of clay in the holes, useless as support but revealing any movement of the stone while it was still being held upright by timber props. Once it had settled the props were removed and sarsen packing-stones were jammed around its base, holding it securely.

Some of the gigantic blocks in the entrances demanded the strength of two hundred or more people. Even the smallest stone needed about fifty and, once the ditch was dug, there would hardly have been room for them on that side, which explains why of the eighteen stoneholes examined seventeen showed the stone to have been dragged upright from the interior of the ring.[31] The one exception stood by the NNW causeway. Furthermore, some eccentricities in the shape of the ring are explicable if the stones had to be kept well away from the ditch. Stone 50 at the NNW, for example, is over 12.2 m within the perimeter because here the ditch was crudely quarried and the stone had to avoid its inward bend.

When the task of completing this colossus of enclosures was finished the result was like a prehistoric version of a mediaeval fortified town with its protecting walls, its streets and houses, its temples and, as will be seen, its cemeteries.

The outer megalithic ring is by far the biggest in Britain, Ireland and Brittany with a calculated perimeter of 1078 ± 0.7 m mean radius of 172m, its centre about 11 m east of that of the earthwork. Many of the stones have been shattered, but the tallest seem to have stood at the NNW and SSE entrances, the smallest, 2.1–2.4 m high, at the others. From two of them avenues of standing stones led westwards towards Beckhampton and southwards towards the Kennet (Pl. 63). Somewhat surprisingly two early plans of Avebury, made before 1663 by John Aubrey and Walter Charleton do not show either avenue.[32] From one entrance an avenue of slighter stones led WSW towards the Winterbourne and beyond, past what may have been a Cove, the Longstones, of which two, Adam and Eve, still stand three-quarters of a mile from Avebury. This Beckhampton Avenue had been almost completely demolished by AD 1800.

Why neither of the early plans showed the Kennet Avenue is a mystery. Both men must have seen it. It has been supposed that a charter of AD 939 referred to this avenue but Brentnall disproved this over sixty years ago.[33]

The omission of the Beckhampton Avenue from the plans is simpler to explain. It was not until 1722 that Stukeley recognised it. 'Two stones lie by the parsonage-gate . . . Reuben Horsal remembers three stones standing in the pasture'. Others had been broken up in 1702 and 1714. Originally the avenue had extended from Avebury's western entrance but by the seventeenth century it was virtually unrecognisable. From mediaeval times villagers had been toppling its convenient stones for their cottages and only in the countryside, at the Longstones a mile WSW, were some erect. 'The Houses are built of the Frustrum's of those huge Stones'.[34]

Geo-physical examination in January 1989, of the avenue's course failed to produce incontrovertible proof of stoneholes but this may have been due to the unresponsive nature of the ground (Pl. 64). What is unappreciated is that there is impartial support for Stukeley's belief in the avenue.

The Reverend Thomas Twining, vicar of Wilsford and Charlton 8 miles south of Avebury, a contemporary of, but probable stranger to, Stukeley, made several visits to

Plate 63. The Kennet Avenue, Avebury (Photograph: the author).

Plate 64. The 1999 excavation of the Beckhampton Avenue, Avebury. Three pairs of stone holes can be seen (Photograph: Neil Mortimer).

Avebury in the early 1700s to prove it was Roman. Like Stukeley he also had seen the stones: 'Hence the large Stones to the West. The Remains of the Discus [part of the avenue] are still called the Devil's Quoits *as other Stones lying in the same field do show*' [my italics].[35] This statement owed nothing to Stukeley. Stukeley himself was hard-headed enough to question villagers about missing stones, 'Richard Fowler shew'd me the ground here, whence he took several stones and demolish'd them'; and 'Mr. Alexander told me he remember'd several stones standing by the parting of the roads under Bekhamton, demolish'd by Richard Fowler'.[36]

It has been argued that Stukeley uncritically accepted natural sarsens as toppled avenue stones because of his theory that the avenue formed the tail of a sacred 'serpent' of which the Kennet Avenue and the Sanctuary were the neck and head. The opposite was true. It was only after his recognition and planning of the genuine Beckhampton Avenue that he became aware of how snake-like it and the Kennet Avenue were. In 1722 he was not yet a biased convert to *dracontia*. He found no difficulty the next year in accepting the unsnaking Stonehenge avenue, 'Stonehenge strait avenue from the gate to the valley is 1400 cubits'. But by 1724 his head was full of serpents.

Because of that many sceptics claimed that "his" Beckhampton Avenue was an illusion. They were wrong. Geo-physical surveying in 1989 and limited excavation in 1999 led to the discovery of three pairs of stoneholes near Adam and Eve proving the sceptics mistaken. The avenue had been a reality.[37]

The Kennet Avenue still exists in part, 14.9 m wide, connecting Avebury with the Sanctuary 1½ miles to the south-east. It consisted of several changes of plan. At first a short stretch leading directly south was started and one stone just outside the entrance survives set at a distinct angle south-eastwards to the concrete substitutes for stones that skew away to the south. They too were added to.

The avenue was set out in a series of straightish lengths, each about 290 m long, threading between the oaks and hazels and shrubby blackthorns in the valley between Waden Hill and the Ridgeway, the stones increasing in height where the line kinked sharply at Avebury's SSE entrance to make a direct and dignified approach across the causeway. Both the avenues are connected with water, the Beckhampton stones crossing a stream, the other coming within 91.4 m of the Kennet although there is no proof that it ever went down to the riverside.

In 1666 John Aubrey began planning it 'but a showre of raine hindred me'. Both Keiller and Piggott in 1934–5 and Alexander and Archie Thom forty years later were luckier,[38] planning these twists and turns whose beginnings and ends were marked by deposits: a human legbone, a flint arrowhead, grooved ware, a pig's jawbone, ox bones, a crouched human burial, an intact grooved ware bowl, a skull fragment, Peterborough ware, a sarsen polissoir for sharpening stone axes, and halfway down, on the west side, the skeletons of three individuals and a broken beaker lay in part of a stonehole, the grave dug after the stone had been set up 'but while it was artificially supported'.[39]

There was more to this *via sacra*. Each pair of stones in this Kennet Avenue has a thin pillar opposite a squatter lozenge, and pillar and lozenge alternate along each of the two rows. The stones remain in their natural state and the differences in shape are not always remarkable but so regular is the phenomenon that it must have been deliberate, perhaps as male and female symbols to express the fertility beliefs with which the stone circles of Britain and Ireland are so intimately associated, all the more appropriate if related to the life-giving water nearby.

Only indirect dating is available for the Kennet Avenue but a B/W beaker at the Sanctuary shows the stone circle to be probably earlier than 2300 BC. Two other beakers buried by stones in the Kennet Avenue, an N2 in a grave dug after the erection of a stone, a European beaker alongside a flexed skeleton, as well as a carinated grooved-ware bowl in another grave, make a date much later than 2400 BC hard to accept.

That communal work continued for years around Avebury is proved by Silbury Hill a mile to the south, the primary mound of this 39.6 m high artificial mound having a date of 2145 ± 95 bc (1–4136) c. 2900–2500 BC. As Silbury Hill took about 18,000,000 man-hours to complete it can be reckoned that even with 500 labourers working through each autumn the project would have endured for well over fifty years, probably longer. Even with a year-long labour-force the earthwork would have taken fifteen years to build. There is no reason why the Kennet Avenue should not have been another undertaking, a double row of stones passing by the tree-darkened ground to the east, perhaps first intended as an approach from the Kennet, awkwardly linked to the short setting of portal stones at Avebury outside which may have been a great post or stone or cremation cemetery to be avoided but later adapted to link two precincts, the circle-henge and the long-known Sanctuary now newly translated into stone.

With a total population of 1500 in this region, an average 2½ acres of land per head under cultivation, as much lying fallow, and perhaps seven times this area unexploited because of rock, marsh, hillside, river and forest, this would give Avebury a 'territory' of roughly 53 square miles whose population density was twenty-eight people per square mile against the 576 of modern Britain.

Such estimates inevitably have broad parameters. With as little as 1 acre under cultivation for each person Avebury's territory might have been as small as 21 square miles; with as much as 5 acres, as large as 106 square miles. Forest clearance in the third millennium BC is well attested in the henge areas of Wessex the need for land becoming greater as the population increased.

The dominant people in Early Bronze Age Wessex may not have been agriculturalists but pastoralists engaged in dispersed transhumance and probably meeting in the Autumn and the Spring for stock adjustment. As cattle demand more space than crops, some 10–15 acres per beast, and as each person would have needed some five animals even if living off mixed farming then for 1,500 people the total grazing-land required would have been between 117 and 175 square miles. But because of transhumance these figures can be divided by at least two so that Avebury's territory would still be between 60 and 90 square miles even if occupied by early second-millennium pastoralists using the forest-lands cleared earlier by crop-growers. 'The grass-fallow stage is certainly an opportune moment for the development of pastoralist groups . . . and. . . the rise of the Wessex culture is synchronous with the scatter of later forms of southern beaker outside the central areas of Wessex, suggesting that one may have displaced the other.' The further suggestion that the round barrow cemeteries around the Marlborough Downs are relatively small because they may have 'been abandoned at one time, perhaps in favour of the larger, more central cemeteries of Salisbury Plain' is tempting when related to the construction of the sarsen Stonehenge as a monument intended to outdo Avebury.[40]

Territories of 30–90 square miles with radii of 3–5 miles would accord with the spacing of Marden 7 miles south of Avebury and 10 miles north of Durrington, and, if they were contemporary, may indicate that the population of Wessex around 2000 bc was approximately 6,000 to 12,000. Such numbers are sufficient for the building of the enclosures but not too many for their use nor for the provisioning of the workers. The manipulation of demographic figures, however, is a mathematical quicksand for there is no sure foundation for the calculations, and for the building of Avebury it is wisest to speak of a 'large number of people'.

As in other rings, whether the great circles of western Britain or the graded recumbents with their cremations in north-east Scotland, seasonal gatherings must be suspected at Avebury as the evidence of hazelnut shells at Windmill Hill or in the ritual pits of the Kennet Avenue imply, Autumn perhaps being the most convenient time for a concourse when the harvest was in, the beasts stalled, when the axe-traders might arrive with the stone tools that could be axe, hoe, plough-share or religious token. There are no axe-carvings at Avebury, or any other carvings on the stones, but scores of stone axes have been found in the district, axes from all parts of Britain: Cornwall, Cumberland, north and south Wales, Shropshire, and it is 'tempting to associate the trade in some measure with the magico-religious ceremonial connected with the great Avebury complex itself and with the well-known axe-cults of Neolithic and Early Bronze Age Europe'.[41]

People met at Avebury in part to order their lives, to make social agreements, partly simply for the pleasure of meeting again, partly to trade, partly to express ritually what their lives needed, creating no dichotomy between the natural and supernatural worlds although the latter had to be expressed symbolically through rites that embodied beliefs providing 'explanations for events which otherwise would be inexplicable'. This was their method of coping with what might ordinarily be disasters against which they had no power. In such terms the 'male' and 'female' stones of the Kennet Avenue become symbols of fecundity, an integral element of the beliefs and ceremonies within Avebury, for here was the essence of their dread, that life might cease or be threatened so fearsomely that only by invoking every possible force, totally and repeatedly, only then could they balance their precarious world, coming together at the time of warmth and light, of cold and darkness, making caricatures and carvings of sun and moon, lighting fires, offering good soil, calling upon their ancestors for protection, making sacrifices. Like Wagnerian music the primitive themes blend in a richness more emotional than scientific, all the more evocative and compelling to the group-mind.

The interior of Avebury itself was deliberately kept clean. A few pottery sherds in the ditch-bottom, some antler picks, are almost all the artefacts discovered during Gray's limited excavations. Like so many other southern British stone circles the activities did not include the deposition of oblations within the enclosure. There were, however, nineteen separate finds of human bones in the ditches: detached long bones, femurs, humeri, fibulae, radii, fragments of skulls, a tooth, and six mandibles, all reminiscent of the skeletal remains in the ditches of Windmill Hill where long bones also predominated.[42]

When it is realised that Gray dug much less than 4 per cent of Avebury's deep ditch it becomes likely that some 500 human remains rest there, not in the deepest part where antler picks and flints occupy the bottom in the first fast collapse of the chalk rims of the ditch but in the slower metre-thick silting of two or three centuries. Above them were Roman coins and artefacts.

The bones found by Gray, especially the tooth, the skull fragments, the jawbones, are most plausibly interpreted as parts of decaying skeletons exposed on scaffolds around the edge of the settlement, lying there until such time as the bones had lost all moisture and were free of any lingering and resentful spirit. Then they could be carried down the avenues to their burial in the round barrows, none of which was closer than half a mile from the earthwork enclosure. Nor were any farther than about 2 miles away. They peter out at Wansdyke to the west and Manton to the east.

There may have been a sacrifice at Avebury. A woman's body had been laid in the ditch-terminal by the southern entrance on the crumbling chalk. Women's remains have been found in similar locations: at Stonehenge, at Gorsey Bigbury henge in Somerset, at Marden only a few miles south of Avebury, all lying in the ditch alongside an entrance as though guarding the interior.

On a drizzling morning in 1922 while Gray was at breakfast the skeleton of a female dwarf was chanced upon but unnoticed. Her 'skull [had] apparently been trampled on before any part of it was actually recognised by the workmen engaged in this spot. Some of the bones had been thrown back.'

Around her body was an oval of small sarsen boulders, one of them the broken half of a ring-stone, maybe a fragment of the first one at Avebury. The woman lay in fine silt, her teeth worn, one missing. With her were flints, potsherds, a sheep's footbone and a small ball of chalk. Her head lay to the south like other female Beaker burials in Wessex, and all these 'sacrificial' burials seem to have been associated with beakers, that intrusive pottery whose users may have followed alien, possibly disliked cults by the natives of southern England.

'The ghosts of strangers, being unfamiliar with the country, are much less likely to stray away from their skulls', and so make better guardians observed Frazer when writing of the practice of sacrificing strangers at the time of harvest.[43]

Then, almost abruptly, Avebury was abandoned as though the power of the Marlborough Downs had been overwhelmed by that of Salisbury Plain and Stonehenge.[44] Of Middle or Late Bronze Age material or Iron Age very little has been found inside Avebury. And unlike Stonehenge with its numerous surrounding cemeteries there are few round barrows in the vicinity. Roman tourists visited the site as they did at Stonehenge and West Kennet. But there was no occupation there until Saxon times, and those superstitious invaders lived outside the enclosure. The neglect was fortunate for little serious damage was done until the eighteenth century.

Stukeley was not in error when he marvelled at 'those remarkable circles of stones which we find all over the kingdom' and exaggerated only a little when with the visionary's eye he called Avebury 'deservedly to be reckon'd among the greatest wonders on the face of the earth'.[45]

Chapter Seventeen

The Megalithic Enclosures of Brittany

It appeares ... that these kind of Temples were used in the Northern parts of Europe and I believe also in France, though no vestigia of them left: but (as I have shewed) sepulchres like those in Britain.

John Aubrey, 1693, 85

Introduction

Aubrey was right. In France there are many megalithic tombs similar to those in Britain and many of them are in good condition. But there were never many stone circles and not one of them survives in anything but a depressingly ruinous state. Trying to understand these megalithic wraiths is like shaking hands with a ghost, the rings mutilated almost beyond recognition, stones tumbled, wrongly re-erected, dragged away for roads and farmsteads, even for the Belle-Ile lighthouse in the Atlantic Ocean. To increase the challenge of discussing stone circles in western Europe, once outside Brittany there is a widespread near-emptiness.

Beyond France Neolithic and Bronze Age rings are rare, very scattered and often of very dubious status. At Odilienberg, Alsace, there was a circle which Kendrick likened to Stonehenge but which was in fact a folly of the fourth century AD. Perhaps akin to this was the Cuvelée du Diable at Forrières, Luxembourg, which even a century ago consisted of six small trilithons but which is now a ruin. Excavations early in this century produced no evidence of its date.[1]

Further north, in Denmark, single or multiple settings of stones may encircle the oak-coffin burials of the Early Bronze Age and boulder circles are fairly common in Scandinavia although belonging to periods as late as the Iron Age. Even later are the Viking dom-rings like that at Blomshülm, Bohüslan, where ten standing stones enclose a large area with a huge central stone. More impressive still are the scores of 'stone ships' at Lindholm Hoj near Aalborg in Jutland where low, shouldering uprights surround Viking cremations.[2] These are wonderful sites but they are not prehistoric stone circles.

It is noticeable that nearly all these monuments encircle burials and the concept of encompassing a grave mound with standing stones is so simple that it is not surprising to find it widespread. But with the exception of some French examples these continental circles are too far away or too late or too dissimilar to belong to the group of prehistoric rings formally known as stone circles.

Even in France there is only one concentration of rings and that is in Brittany. Beyond that province there is hardly a site. Four hundred miles south-east of Carnac and to the north-west of Montpellier in bleak countryside is the splendid ring of Le Planas in Gard, elliptical, 104×88 m, its thirty-nine tall stones having an even taller at the centre. Another huge oval is reported at Le Can de Ceyrac 20 miles to the ssw.[3]

Nearer to Brittany was the site of La Gorgue in the Pas de Calais 16 miles west of Lille, where ten large boulders were set in a circle 36.6 m in diameter. Just outside Paris at Nanterre was a small 'stone circle' of which the only record is a sixteenth century painting in the church of Saint-Merri, Paris. It consisted of thirty-eight small, closely set stones in a ring 6 m to 7 m across with Sainte Geneviève, the patron saint of Paris, sitting in the centre watching over her flock of sheep. The stones were dislodged and taken away in the early nineteenth century although some were still in the 'parc de Sainte Geneviève' as late as 1930. The ring was probably the kerbs of a denuded round cairn of which there is a surviving example at Saint-Maur-des-Fossés, a suburb to the south-east of Paris, the stones 'preserved in a garden of the museum of that town'.[4]

Other than these little-known and questionable rings only Brittany has a considerable number of stone circles. Not one is intact. Most are badly disturbed. They are called cromlechs, a term which in itself is confusing. The *Oxford English Dictionary* defines it as: 'A structure of prehistoric age consisting of a large flat, unhewn stone resting horizontally on three or more stones set upright, especially in Wales, Cornwall, Devonshire and Ireland . . . This is the application of the word in Welsh. In Brittany these structures are called *dolmens* (= tablestones) while *cromlech* is the name of a circle of standing stones.'

The word derives from *crom* meaning 'bowed or arched' and *llech*, 'a flat stone', which in Wales signifies a portal dolmen with its massive capstone resting on three pillars. In Brittany, paradoxically, it is a form of stone circle which, in respect of planning, listing, study and conservation, remains in much the same state as stone circles in Britain and Ireland thirty years ago, neglected and disregarded.

Because of these linguistic contradictions 'cromlech' becomes as structurally uninformative as 'henge' in Britain for a description of Late Neolithic earthwork enclosures. 'Henge' comes from the Anglo-Saxon *hengen*, 'hinged' or 'hanging' because the lintelled trilithons inside Stonehenge resembled gibbets for mass executions, hence Stonehenge, 'the stone gallows'. But Stonehenge is not typical of most 'henges' such as Castilly, Gorsey Bigbury or King Arthur's Round Table, which contained no trilithons. And perhaps the greatest linguistic irony of all is that Stonehenge is not a true henge with a smoothly continuous ditch except for entrances but a ditch of linked segments like those of the earlier causewayed enclosures. Both 'cromlech' and 'henge' are just as much megalithic shorthand for the convenience of archaeologists as 'stone circle', so many of which are not round but ovoid, egg-shaped or even subrectangular like the Four-Posters of central Scotland.

In the two major areas of distribution for 'cromlechs' in Brittany, Finistère in the north-west and Morbihan at the south-east, the 'rings' can be divided into three main types, none of them characteristic of those in Britain or Ireland: some rectangles known as *quadrilatérals*; a few ovals, cromlechs; and a multiplicity of horseshoes, *fer-aux-chevaux*. There are also some intrusive monuments from overseas.

Foreign Circles

The great settings of stones in Brittany are so different from those across the English Channel that it is unexpected to come upon a drawing of an 'English' stone circle with a possible avenue on the islet of Béniguet 3 miles out to sea in the Ushant archipelago. Like many other Breton rings it has been uprooted but an early nineteenth-century sketch shows it had up to twelve well-spaced stones in an oval about 25 × 15 m. In size, shape, spacing and pillar-like uprights it was quite unlike the usual Breton cromlech but very similar to oval rings in Cornwall such as Tregeseal East and Boscawen-Un with its central pillar.

Early contacts between Brittany, Britain and Ireland are firmly attested. The similarity of pottery, of Breton chambered tombs known as *dolmens-en-V* to Irish wedge-tombs, finds of Breton stone axes in Wessex, all reveal communication between the three countries. As the unknown writer of an old song wrote in *The Spanish Ladies*, 'From Ushant to Scilly is thirty-five leagues'. It is a reminder that prehistoric Britain and Ireland were not isolated from the European mainland.[5]

Sailing from the Pointe de Kermorvan in western Finistère, or from the Pointe du Raz to the south, a jutting peninsula 'against which the breakers foam, with high, over-hanging cliffs', within whose cavities, when the north wind blows, the waves resound like the hoarse roar of cannon-shots, merchants in their skin-sided, timber-framed boats passed along the scattered little islands of the archipelago where Ushant, the largest of the islands with its 60 m-high cliffs, was a summer haven.

In fair weather crews of ten men could reach the trading-post of St Michael's Mount in two days. 'The seaborne traders, in distrust of mainland native treachery, conducted their business on offshore islands where they would be safe from attack on their persons and from plundering of their cargoes.' The Cassiterides or Tin Islands of the Scillies or St Michael's Mount, 'accordingly, contained only the tin that was brought to them to be bartered on their neutral territory'.

This might explain the location of the megalithic ring on Ile Beniguet (Pl. 65), an island sanctuary for seamen from south-west England and a place where tin or other commodities could be safely exchanged. If it were tin the cromlech could be dated to the Early Bronze Age but this is speculation rather than supposition.

The same explanation could be applied to Ville-ès-Nouaux, a 'cist-in-circle' near St Helier on Jersey (Pl. 66). It is not large, about 6.4 × 5.8 m, of sixteen stones but the 1.8 m long slab at the wsw and its low flankers show that it is a typical south-west Irish recumbent stone circle with an equally typical internal boulder-burial. If it were to be transplanted to the Boggeragh mountains of Co. Cork it would fit snugly into the cultural landscape. Completing this cosmopolitan intrusion just to the south of this Hibernian emigré in First Tower park there is an *allée-couverte* from Brittany.[6]

Plate 65. Stone circle, now destroyed, on Ile Beniguet, Finistère. An early nineteenth-century sketch.

Plate 66. The 'cist-in-circle' Irish MSC with internal boulder-burial, Ville-ès-Nouaux, Jersey. An *allée-couverte* is in the background (Photograph: the author).

Both Ile Beniguet and Ville-ès-Nouaux are coastal sites and it is not difficult to recognise their foreign origins. Quite astonishing, however, is the existence of a Scottish stone circle a full 140 miles away from the Atlantic on the Grée de Cojoux at Saint-Just in Ille-et-Vilaine. Château-Bû is a variant Four-Poster from central Scotland built on top of a transepted passage-tomb that stands in an increasingly excavated and restored megalithic complex with two attractive stone rows of opposing quartz and schist, standing stones, a short Three-Stone row and a megalithic horseshoe. There is also a miniature horseshoe put up against the Four-Poster as though to announce, 'Breton is Best'. Why this Early Bronze Age ring should be found so far from its homeland is unknown. It has no counterpart anywhere in Brittany, 'a strange barrow . . . unique of its kind'.[7]

It has to be emphasised that these alien circles are not evidence of a one-way maritime traffic from Britain and Ireland. There is clear evidence of influences from Brittany affecting Britain, Ireland and Scotland.

Cromlechs in Brittany

Megalithic enclosures are not evenly distributed in Brittany. There are two remarkable but different concentrations: a collection of rectangles and horseshoes, fer-aux-chevaux, at the far west on the Crozon peninsula south of Brest; and an even larger group of cromlechs and horseshoes around Carnac on the south coast near the Gulf of Morbihan, 'little sea'. Horseshoes predominate.

It is noticeable that, like the conservatism of islands, only six miles ESE of Carnac on the Locmariaquer peninsula with its profusion of chambered tombs there is not a single cromlech, horseshoe or rectangle.

The area around the Gulf of Morbihan, 250 miles south-east of Land's End, contains megalithic works that demanded the efforts of hundreds of people (Fig. 37). Looking at the rows with their myriad stones, or the colossal standing stones, menhirs, or the half-submerged pair of horseshoes at Er-Lannic in the Gulf, one is aware of an obsessive fanaticism in the building of these monuments which are comparable in Europe only with the enormous sites around Avebury. But there is a difference.

Cromlechs in Brittany are not like the stone circles of Britain and Ireland. They are larger and of unusual designs, not only ovals and egg-shapes but also horse-shoes, rectangles and squares. Nor is there a true circle among them. They are also far less numerous. In the 121,400 square miles of Britain and Ireland there are about 1,250 rings. In the 10,500 square miles of Brittany, a twelfth the size of Britain and Ireland, proportionately there should be over a hundred cromlechs. There are forty-nine and six of these are doubtful.

There is a further difference. It is enlightening to compare the interiors of the cromlechs with those of the largest rings in Britain. Excluding the completely exceptional Outer Circle at Avebury, the areas of the biggest are: Stanton Drew, 9,887 m²; Brodgar, 8,430 m², Avebury South, 8,236 m²; Long Meg and Her Daughters, 7,991 m²; and the Twelve Apostles, 5,394 m², an average of 7,988 m². In Brittany, even omitting

Fig. 37. Cromlechs in Brittany.

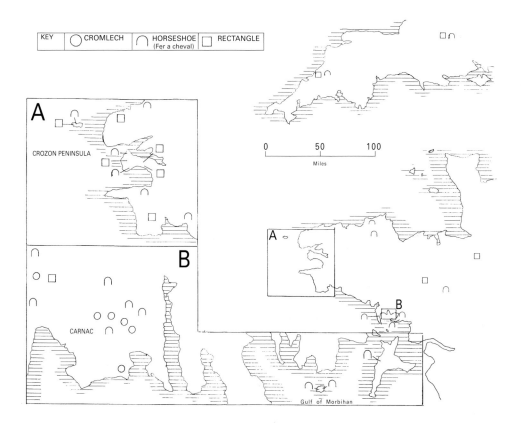

	Dimensions	Area m²
Cromlechs		
Kermorvan, Finistère	60 × 39	1,838
Ménec East, Morbihan	108 × 90	7,634
Ménec West, Morbihan	91 × 71	5,074
Horseshoes (Fer-aux-Chevaux)		
Er-Lannic North, Morbihan	72 × 54	3,287
Er-Lannic South, Morbihan	66.4 × 61	3,181
Grand Rohu, Morbihan	48 × 42	1,583
Kerbougnec, Morbihan	96 × 76	5,730
Kergonan, Morbihan	95 × 70	5,223
Kerlescan North, Morbihan	235 × 200	36,137
Kerlescan South, Morbihan	78 × 74	4,533

Table 16. Large Megalithic Enclosures in Brittany.

the overwhelming 36,137 m² of the afforested Kerlescan North horseshoe the great Breton cromlechs are of comparable size: Ménec East, 7,634 m², Kerbourgnec, 5,730 m²; Kergonan 5,223 m²; Ménec West, 5,074 m² and Kerlescan South, 4,533 m². They average 5,639 m², almost three-quarters the area of the giants in Britain and Ireland and manifestly were designed to accommodate a huge concourse of participants (Table 16). They are very nearly sixty times the size of the average British or Irish ring whose mean area is only 95 m².

Unlike the later Early and Middle Bronze Age 'family' rings of Britain and Ireland people in Brittany appear to have retained and used their great enclosures throughout the prehistoric period to the almost total rejection of smaller, more intimate kinship cromlechs, preferring to hold large, sub-tribal gatherings deep into the Bronze Age, maybe even into the Iron Age and later.

There is firm archaeological evidence of a wealthy, presumably chieftain class that may have determined the nature and the times of the assemblies. In the Morbihan region of south-eastern Brittany there are gigantic Carnac Mounds of the Middle Neolithic, incredible tumuli with an average bulk of 90 m long, 42 m wide and 5.5 m high, deliberately built over earlier passage-tombs. Imposing though they are even today like the Egyptian pyramids they had no accessible entrance, simply a closed internal cist with satellite cairns around it. In the cist were rich possessions for the dead man: fibrolite and jadeite axes, delicate and finely-shaped like the novelties of their bronze equivalents; rings of serpentine, opaquely green callais beads and pendants.[8]

The mounds have tell-tale locations. The Tumulus Saint-Michel overlooks the Ménec cromlechs and rows at Carnac. Two miles to the north Le Moustoir looms a mile from the rows of Petit-Ménec. It is a provoking possibility that the people buried in these monsters were the builders and officiants of the spacious cromlechs.

But even the splendid grave-goods of these powerful leaders were exceeded by the later luxuries of bronze and gold in the dagger-graves of the Armorican tumulus culture: honey-coloured barbed-and-tanged flint arrowheads, ceremonial bronze axes, bronze halberds, rivetted bronze daggers with gold-pinned pommels, the regalia and weaponry of a ruling warrior caste. These were rich burials like Rondossec near Carnac with its pair of intrusive gold bracelets. The metal objects of rivetted daggers, flat axes, gold plaques and amber pendants, dentated shaft-mountings, handled pots, artistically shaped flint arrowheads, such assemblages are comparable with others in the round barrow cemeteries of Wessex, the gold plaques in the Bush Barrow near Stonehenge matched by the 'box' of gold foil in the tumulus of La Motta, Lannion, a mound less than 150 miles of the easily crossed channel between northern Brittany and southern England.[9]

There is considerable support for the belief that the spacious cromlechs continued in use for centuries (Pl. 67). At Ménec West there had been a short avenue leading to the enclosure. Over the ensuing decades further extensions were added to it section by section like Avebury's Kennet Avenue whose stretches were ultimately linked to a second avenue leading to the Sanctuary. In the same manner Ménec West was finally joined to the even larger cromlech of Ménec East almost half a mile away. Yet, although the jerky avenue was now complete the custom of introducing still more stones continued over the centuries, erecting them in meaningless lines on either side of the avenue until there was today's chaos of eleven or more raggedly twisting rows that have bewildered visitors trying to understand the logic of their erectors.

There was no logic. Just habit. Two hundred years ago the antiquarian, Cambry, was told that even in the nineteenth century every year in June a further stone was put up. In 1825 the Abbé Mahé received confirmation of this with the embellishment that midsummer bonfires were lit near the new stones. A midsummer fire burnt on the Carnac Mound of the adjacent Tumulus Saint-Michel. When the Scotsman, James, Miln, was excavating at Kerlosquet, the 'place of burning' in the rows of Kermario during 1877 and 1888, the work was continually interrupted by cries of 'douar losquet', 'burnt earth'. Ten years or more earlier the Abbé Collet had dug at the foot of several stones, unearthing flints, undateable sherds, and the charcoal of fire-blackened soil.[10]

It is evidence of the continuity of a tradition whose original purpose had long been lost. Where once, centuries before, hundreds of men and women from miles around had solemnly approached the cromlech at midsummer, celebrating the height of the year, the June gatherings slowly deteriorated and shrivelled into parochial celebrations by villagers, the cromlech ignored, the reason for erecting a stone, lighting a bonfire, as forgotten as fireworks, Catherine Wheels and rockets on Guy Fawkes' Night or apple-tubs at Hallowe'en. It is today's irony that visitors wander wonderingly along those prehistoric and historic accretions of rows and overlook the spoiled but significant cromlech at their head.

The result of such prehistoric insistence on vast assemblies in Brittany is that there are few, if any, small family rings like those in the Irish counties of Cork and Kerry or Ynys-hir in Wales, or the little circles along the Dorset coast on the other side of the English Channel from Brittany. Possible exceptions to this lack of family shrines may have existed in the strange and limited number of rectangular settings.

Rectangles (Quadrilatérals)

There were never many of these well-designed but presumably late versions of megalithic enclosures, a few in the Morbihan, some questionable examples to the north in Côtes-du-Nord and Ille-et-Vilaine, others unrecorded, destroyed and forgotten. Even in Finistère, the *département* nearest to England, there were, for they have

Plate 67. The wandering rows of Kermario near Carnac, Brittany (Photograph: Alex Gibson).

all been removed, rectangles at Lanvéoc and Parc ar Varret, 'the field of the dead'. There was an enormous polygon, 60 × 30 m at Le Conquet, a fishing village from which travellers today embark for the islands of Moléne and Ushant. Only a few stones remain. On Ushant itself there was a rectangle, the Phare du Créach, with a line of stones dividing it in half.

In western Finistère several oblongs stood on the Crozon peninsula, Lanvéoc 3½ miles NNE of Crozon itself, the rough, unimpressive blocks of Ty ar c'Huré, 'the curate's house', near Morgat, its rectangle linked with wandering lines of slabs that Devoir considered to be aligned on both the midsummer and midwinter sunrises. A related architectural feature of these sites is of interest when considering cross-channel associations.

The closest part of Britain to the Crozon peninsula is Cornwall and it is unlikely to be coincidental that one of the exceedingly rare rectangles in England is to be found there on Bodmin Moor at King Arthur's Hall. Like Lanvéoc it also was cardinally arranged, its longer sides lying north–south. Lanvéoc's were east–west and it may be that one purpose of these small settings was to record astronomical and polar or equinoctial orientations. This was certainly true of the most famous of all Breton rectangles, the quadrilateral of Crucuno a few miles to the west of Carnac.[11]

Two miles NNW of Plouharnel Crucuno, also known as Park-er-Vinglas or Champs de l'Ardoise, 'the field of slate', is an especial example of the megalithic amazements in Brittany. In the corner of a field often bright with buttercups its head-high stones are technically awesome in their exact positioning. As a spectacle the site can be a disaster, reached by a long, often deeply muddy and befouled track, and frequently overgrown in a density of yellow-flowering but spiky gorse and broom.

The twenty-two almost touching pillars form a well-designed quadrilateral, 33.2 m long, precisely east–west, by 24.9 m north–south, a ratio of 4:3, with a slightly convex southern side. The NE–SW diagonal is 41.5 m long, subtending an angle of 54°–234°.

In 1882 only nine of the stones stood. In that year, F. Gaillard, a hotelier of Plouharnel, was empowered to restore monuments that had been acquired by the State and he re-erected the fallen pillars, the tallest at the south-east corner. The perfection of his oblong and its tantalising sightlines so intrigued him that he later wrote about orientations in megalithic monuments.[12]

So elegant was his restoration that it provoked controversy, some suspecting that the site was an eighteenth-century folly, others doubting that such regularity could have been achieved in prehistory. 'The quadrilateral of Crucuno, Erdeven – unfortunately we do not know what it was like before its restoration – is a rectangle with an exact east-west orientation; its dimensions are such that the diagonals lie in the direction of the rising sun at the solstices'.[13]

The reservations were unnecessary. Fifteen years before Gaillard Sir Henry Dryden and W. C. Lukis had made a plan of the site at a scale of 1:240, one of a 'seriés de [90] plans des plus précieux par leur extrême précision'[14] and this nicety of surveying confirmed the accuracy of Gaillard's work.

In July 1970, while Alexander Thom and a team were undertaking the immensity of plotting the hundreds of stones in the Carnac rows his son, Archie, and two colleagues made their own plan of Crucuno, examining the setting for possible sightlines. From east to west the long sides, particularly the northernmost, were directed towards a gently rising skyline and the western sunset. From north-east to south-west along the diagonal there was an orientation towards the midwinter sunset. The short sides were in line with True North. Tentatively it was suggested that the solar alignments provided a date around 1,800 BC, not impossible if the Breton rectangles were the very latest of the megalithic enclosures.[15] There was a difficulty. There were no foresights and therefore Crucuno, like Castlerigg in the English Lake District, could never have been more than 'a symbolic observatory'.[16]

Dissatisfied with this conclusion the three surveyors returned in 1972 and discovered some likely menhirs. To the west lay La Chaise du Pape, 'the Pope's chair'. To the south were three other prostrate pillars, 2.7 m to 3.7 m long, the fallen remains of a short row known as Er Men Cam. With these hypothetical foresights it was concluded that Crucuno was not only a solar monument of considerable accuracy but also contained sightlines to eight lunar extremes.

Yet the site they had surveyed may not have been complete. In 1926 Brigadier-General William Sitwell recorded an internal inverted equilateral triangle of stones with 5.5 m long sides set centrally north–south but off-centre to the east. Only its stoneholes remain. Although not making any astronomical claims for Crucuno Sitwell did suggest possible alignments that used the triangle, one north-westwards to a standing stone that has since disappeared, another westwards to a large menhir that was 'now hidden in trees'.

He was enthusiastic about the potential of the rectangle. 'Even as it stands there are so many remarkable combinations between its sides and the triangle within, that possibly the whole was prepared by ancient craftsmen as a tracing board, whence lines could be drawn to fix and limit the curves of the great serpent in its long and tortuous windings', referring to the lines of Ménec 3 miles to the south-east.[17]

An important comparison should be made about Crucuno. With its neat rectangularity, and the use of its sides and diagonal to define celestial events it has a uniquely compelling parallel with the quadrilateral of the Four Stations at Stonehenge.

Stone Circles (Cromlechs)

No date has been obtained from either the cromlechs or their avenues and rows but two widely spread assays from the Tumulus Saint-Michel may provide a clue. Two samples of charcoal provided determinations of 3770 ± 300 bc (Sa-96) and 3030 ± 150 bc (Gsy-89). With a broad range from 4070 bc to 2880 bc little reliance can be placed on its centred equivalent of *c.* 4300 BC but this could be some indication that the large Breton cromlechs near Carnac were erected many centuries before their counterparts in Britain or Ireland.

It comes as a surprise to discover that amongst the twenty sites listed as cromlechs, omitting Ile Beniguet as an interloper, only three are certain to be settings of standing stones that completely surrounded their interior: Kercado, and Ménec East and West. The remainder, from Beg Rouz Vorc'h in Finistère to Kerzerho in the Morbihan, all of them damaged, despoiled or destroyed, may be the ruins of megalithic horseshoes, *fer-aux-chevaux*, with open mouths and, normally, with spaced stones, although Tossen-Keler in Côtes-du-Nord is an exception to this. The confirmed cromlechs have an almost continuous run of stones around their circumference.

Of the three cromlechs Kercado near the eastern end of the lines of Kermario at Carnac is an irregular and broken ring enclosing a well-preserved passage-tomb from which an assay of 3890 ± 300 bc (Sa-95) was obtained, a bracket of *c.* 5050 to 4450 BC. The ring is later. It is a broad oval about 19 × 18 m, has a long gap from WSW to ESE where its tallest stone stands outside the tomb's entrance and another space from there to the south.

The stones are almost contiguous but they are not placed symmetrically around the perfectly circular tomb as though they had been rather casually set up with little attention to neatness. In this indifference, in the possibly unfinished cromlech and in the stone on top of the Kercado cairn there are unanticipated likenesses to the interrupted, loosely arranged ring around the Irish passage-tomb of Newgrange which also had an overlying stone. In 1699 Edward Lhuyd saw the block, 'a stately Mount . . . having a number of huge stones pitch'd on end round about it, and a single one on the top'.

The parallels are surely coincidental. Yet during Lhuyd's visit what may have been a perforated Breton artefact was found in Newgrange's eastern chamber. It has been 'suggested that it was an axe similar in type to the polished greenstone ones found in large numbers in the tumuli of the Morbihan'.[18] As there is a difference of over a thousand years between the radiocarbon assays from the two tombs these observations must be taken as one more example of the unhelpful coincidences that prehistory has left for today's bewildered archaeologist.

The other true cromlechs at Carnac, Ménec East and West are of interest for quite different reasons. The eastern, now reduced to a mere twenty-two stones on its western arc was a vast egg-shaped enclosure 108 m NW–SE by 90 m. It stood at the head of level ground towards which twelve haphazard rows straggled up a slope. The western cromlech is smaller but in much better condition despite the plundering houses and walls in and around it. It also is egg-shaped, though inverted, but only 91 m NE–SW by 71 m. Seventy stones survive with good runs at the north-west and from east to south-west, standing shoulder to shoulder unlike the well-separated pillars of the rows that approach them. A space in the eastern perimeter of the cromlech was probably the entrance at the end of an original avenue that was absorbed and obscured by the gradual additions of five more rows on either side of it. It is possible to be so precise about these features because of the excellent plans made by Alexander and Archie Thom between 1970 and 1974.[19]

The reason for the ovoid shape of these cromlechs was probably astronomical with the long and short axes, unavailable in a circle, being used to indicate solar events. The long axis of the eastern cromlech, lying 304°–124° seems to have been aligned on the midwinter sunrise and the short axis of its western partner, 232°–52°, towards the midsummer sunrise. Speculation that these enclosures were intended for large gatherings, perhaps assembling at midwinter and midsummer for their rituals, is seemingly supported by lingering memories of these events. 'In connection with the subject of orientation in the Morbihan, it is interesting to note that at Kerlescant [sic] the winter solstice is celebrated by a holiday, whilst Ménec greets the summer solstice and Kermario the equinoxes with festival days'.[20] This is a long way from proof.

These few cromlechs are surrounded, or were because many of them are almost unrecognisable today, by many of their probable successors, the megalithic horseshoes or *fer-aux-chevaux*. Hardly 500 m west of Ménec West there was a probable horseshoe at the west end of the Kermario rows. 'There is no terminating circle,' wrote Lukis, 'but it is conjectured that one formerly existed'. There are hints. Examination of James Miln's detailed plan does show a good southern arc of a much disturbed semi-circle at the head of the rows. At the other end of the lines a mile from Ménec there are 'some remains of a semi-circle, because of the embankments, which seem to correspond with a structure visible in aerial photographs'.

Less than half a mile farther east is the well preserved horseshoe of Kerlescan South with an even larger one lurking in the thick woods to its north. Such an associated pair of *fer-aux-chevaux* is matched by another couple, side by side, at Er-Lannic in the Gulf of Morbihan 8½ miles ESE of Ménec. Four miles to their east was Kergonan on the Ile-aux-Moines, also in the Gulf, the undisturbed and most complete horseshoe of all.

One and a half miles north of the Ménec cromlech is yet another arc of a horseshoe at the Champ de la Croix. A seventh stands in disarray, '6 blocks belonging to a semi-circle', at the Vieux-Moulin near Plouharnel not 3 miles WNW of Ménec. Half a mile beyond is the site but only three or four massive stones of Sainte-Barbe once 'arranged in the form of a segment of a circle'. Uncertainty must remain about the cromlech or horseshoe at Kerzerho some 5 miles north-west of Ménec, its drunken rows of titanic blocks stumbling like ossified giants but, across the road from them, alongside a house, Mein Glaz, 'blue-green stone', rearranged and undecipherable are standing stones, one with cupmarks, in no recoverable order. And to complete this impressive spread of horseshoes, one to every 8 square miles around Carnac, there is the spacious site of Kerbourgnec on the Quiberon peninsula 6 miles SSW of Ménec East across the bay.[21]

Horseshoes (Fer-aux-chevaux)

The most numerous of the three types of Breton enclosure is the horseshoe (Pl. 68), large and plentiful in the Morbihan, uncommon in the north where Tossen-Keler in the Côtes-du-Nord is a visually rewarding monument, small infrequent and often mingling in a confusion of lines and rectangles in Finistère where there is also a reconstructed site at Pen-ar-Land on Ushant. Usually standing in isolation there are two

Plate 68. The Tribunal fer-à-cheval (horseshoe), St Just, Brittany (Photograph: the author).

instances, at Kerlescan and Er-Lannic, where a pair of horseshoes stand side by side.

There has been little or no speculation as to the cause of these emergent shapes but, like the cromlechs, the need for clear-cut alignments may have provided the motive. It is arguable that a horseshoe was simply a truncated cromlech, an oval cut in half to create an open mouth and an apex towards which an observer would look. The provision of taller stones there, as at Kergonan, would act as a foresight.

Chronologically there seem to be two designs, one with straightish sides like an upside-down U or croquet hoop, the other more curvilinear, widening out to resemble the outline of a monk's tonsure. The first is likely to have been the earlier. Some clues to support this belief come from the linked horseshoes at Er-Lannic.

Across the Gulf of Morbihan east of Carnac on an islet hardly 90m across are the two stone settings of Er-Lannic North and South, the northern once believed to be a sub-rectangular cromlech with a horseshoe alongside it. Lying at a slight angle to each other their terminals touch in an arrangement like a distorted ∪∪. The ornately decorated passage-tomb of Gavr'inis, 'the island of goats', is 550m to the north. Other island-bound tombs in the Gulf such as Ile Longue and Penhape on the Ile aux Moines suggest that before the region was inundated in post-Roman times it had been a plain crossed by sluggish rivers, a fertile sandy district whose hills provided well-drained sites for occupation and for the burial places of Neolithic settlers. Since the rising of the sea, however, the area has become an archipelago of wooded islands hemmed at low tide by wide mudbanks and trapped by heavy currents when the sea is full.

The northern site of Er-Lannic on its tiny island where tidal underflows make landing a cautious venture was first noticed from Gavr'inis by the antiquarian, Dr G. Closmadeuc in August 1866, when only four or five standing stones were visible. Eleven years later, going to the site, to his amazement he detected some huge slabs of the southern setting under the swirling waters.

At high tide all the southern horseshoe and a third of the northern are submerged beneath strong races that have not only forced tall stones over but have shifted them from their proper positions so that it is almost impossible to be certain of the original plan despite the re-erection of some stones after the excavations of 1923–6. In any case, what is probably the poorest plan of a megalithic ring ever published, almost indecipherable, made the interpretation of the shape and size of this unique site extremely difficult. Fortunately the plan has been superseded by further research in 1991–2 when the northern horseshoe was replanned and when underwater archaeology achieved the first detailed survey of its submerged partner.[22]

The northern horseshoe, restored by Zacharie le Rouzic and Saint-Just Péquart, was 72m long and 54m wide, lying approximately 127°–307°, its mouth open to the south-east. Its north-eastern side was sharply flattened, its northern corners were rounded, its south-western side was convex just as the *fer-à-cheval* of Kerlescan South had one straight and one curved side, a trait also known at Lagatjar in Finistère.

The almost contiguous stones are between 1.2m to 1.8m in height and are set in a low bank of earth and stones. One singularly high pillar stands at the north-west, 4.4m tall, rising high above its neighbours. Another gigantic stone, La Roche du Forgeron, 'the blacksmith's stone', stood where the rings touch. There also appears to be a north-west facing Cove at the centre of the mouth possibly looking towards three decorated pillars at the peak of the horseshoe and, beyond them, to the midsummer sunset. A Cove in the Morbihan with its profusion of megalithic tombs would not be surprising.

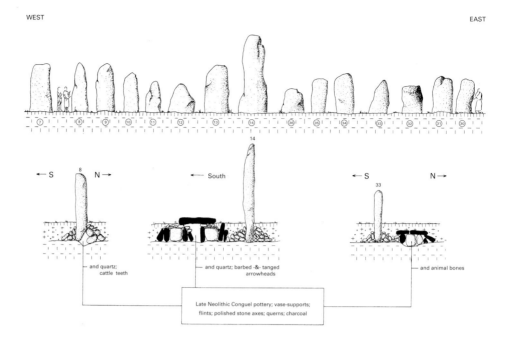

Fig. 38. Er-Lannic. Elevations of stones on the north-west arc, and sections through some cists.

Outside the cromlech are two outliers, the first, prostrate, 7m long, about 110m WNW of the centre of the horseshoe, the other 3m high, 60m from the centre on a line that precisely bisects the long, straight north-east chord of the ring. There are other signs of planning. The huge water-covered stone, Le Men er Gou or Carek er Goh, 'the old stone', at the south of the semi-oval and the large pillar at the intersection of the rings lay on a north–south line, one more indication of the interest prehistoric people had in these cardinal positions.

It is in the profusion of its finds that the northern horseshoe at Er-Lannic differs from the majority of stone circles in Britain and Ireland (Fig. 38). Excavation revealed that beneath the encircling bank each pillar stood in a neat setting of packing-stones within which were scatters of bone, teeth of oxen, flint flakes, quartz implements, mauls, granite grinders and polishers, whole and broken stone axes, and masses of Castellic and Chassean sherds of the Middle Neolithic period between 4500 and 4000 BC.

The reason for such profusion was that the *fer-à-cheval* had been built on a previously occupied hillside. Both inside and outside the bank were many rough cists or 'ritual hearths', the stones fire-reddened, holding charcoal and over three-quarters of a ton of pottery sherds as well as polished axes, polissoirs and querns, the relics of centuries of recurring ceremonies. Domestic débris, huts, traces of cultivated ground found to the north belonged to this period, later people erecting the horseshoe on land that had already been cleared.

Some of the stone of which the Er-Lannic axes were made was dolerite whose axe factory source was Séledin 48 miles north of Carnac near Plusselien in central Brittany. First exploited near 4000 BC the industrial site had a developed phase around 2700 BC when fire was used to extract the stone. Several products of this Group X factory have been found in southern England as far away as Worcestershire demonstrating the wide scope of the axe trade 5,000 years ago.[23] But many of the smaller fibrolite axes at Er-Lannic came from a local outcrop at Port Navalo 2 miles south, and the hillside may once have been a working area, an atelier where the roughed-out axes were polished before being bartered.

Of the sherds on the island many were from little vase-supports often decorated with *pointillé* triangles derived from the early Neolithic Chassey cultures of south and east France. At Er-Lannic, however, they were constantly associated with coarse, round-based Conguel ware of the Late Neolithic. Vase-supports are rare elsewhere in the Morbihan. At Er-Lannic their juxtaposition with the other material, and the absence of contemporary metalware, suggests a broad date around 3500 BC to 3000 BC for the construction and use of the megalithic setting.

From the number and size of the stones and the area of the enclosure it is probable that a large population of five or six hundred people used Er-Lannic for their midsummer and midwinter ceremonies. It seems that the north-east outlier was aligned on the maximum midwinter moon rise from the centre of the northern ring. There is a wide gap between the stones at this point. To the north-west the tall stone may have marked the midsummer sunset which, perhaps, was observed from the 'Cove' which apparently faced that direction. One of the packing-stones had nine cup-marks on it, small artificial depressions.

What ceremonies were enacted in the ring cannot be told. Some evidence for a solar axe-cult comes from the carvings of stone axes on stones. There is a motif of a simple axehead on a 1.5 m high pillar on the eastern side. At the centre of the western side one stone has cupmarks, another has a simple axe and two shafted axes ground out on it and a third stone has an enigmatic symbol of four close-set, vertical, parallel lines, the two outer having out-turned tops like a glass jar holding sticks of celery. The motif has been seen as a yoke, a form of carving not found outside Brittany and an interpretation not favoured by Shee Twohig. Rollando thought it might be an 'état très évolué et simplifié des réprésentations de la déesse', a very simplified depiction of the female guardian of the dead showing only her shoulders.[24] Almost to the point of annihilation.

Immediately to the south of the horseshoe was the associated setting of Er-Lannic South. Once a good plan had been made of its stones it became apparent that the second *fer-à-cheval* was not only of a different shape from its northern partner but had been much more imposing and elegant. Whereas the northern horseshoe was built of local granite this was composed of coarse-grained, quartz-mottled gneiss from a mile or two away. It was more regularly curved as though more care had been taken in its construction, a good semi-circle 61 m across with stones of similar heights around 4 m when standing, bigger and heavier than those to the north with two monstrous terminals once towering as dominant portals to the interior. The excavators considered that the superiority of the layout was a sign that the *fer-à-cheval* was a monument later than the less well-fashioned setting to the north.[25]

With a major axis of about 115°–295° the site may have been arranged to be in line with the May Day, Beltane, sunset at the WNW. It is noticeable how constantly these horseshoes were laid out with entrances open to the eastern side of the horizon: north-east at Pen-ar-Land; east at Grand Rohu, Kerbourgnec and Tossen-Keler; south-east at Crucuny, both sites at Er-Lannic, Graniol, Kergonan and Kerlescan North. Kerlescan South was an exception, open to the north. People entered the horseshoes from the east but they looked towards the west.

At Er-Lannic the probable associations with water, the fierce fires, the outliers, the suggestion of an axe-cult, the north–south axial lines, all these serve to evoke impressions of seasonal meetings for people from miles away. The exact nature of the rites at Er-Lannic as the midsummer sun set or the moon rose in the midwinter night sky above the fire-sparkling river or, centuries later, as the May sun set cannot be recaptured.

Any account of the megalithic enclosures of Brittany must be handicapped by the sad state of ruin amongst so many of them. It is trebly fortunate, therefore, that as well as the excellently restored quadrilateral of Crucuno there are three fine *fer-aux-chevaux*: Tossen-Keler, Pen-ar-Land and Kergonan. Only the last has not been disturbed.

On the north coast near Tréguier in Côtes-du-Nord is Tossen-Keler, 'the mound with chestnut trees'. It is a site of three distinct phases that the excavations of 1963 and 1964 were able to clarify: 'la succession chronologique foyers, hémi-cycle, tumulus', a developing sequence of hearths, horseshoe and mound over several centuries.[26] It had been set up in a region once rich in megaliths: *allées-couvertes*, passage-tombs, menhirs but agriculture has demolished them, making room for the cultivation of cauliflowers and artichokes. At the beginning of the century Tossen-Keler had been a great mound, 50 m across, 12 m high, covered in ferns and gorse but in 1960 the farmer began levelling it and it was decided that the site should be excavated.

It proved a mystery. The tumulus covered no burial-chamber or cist, contained some Late Neolithic sherds and it did not consist of one compact pile of stones but was composed of a group of rough cairns separated by tortuous channels very similar to the Early Neolithic Scottish mound of Fochabers excavated by the writer in 1972 and 1974.[27] Tossen-Keler was at least a thousand years later.

On the old land surface at its centre were two large hearths, charcoal from one providing an assay of 2550 ± 260 bc (Gif-280), a span of 3550 to 2950 BC. The later date is more likely. In the excavators' opinion the hearths were the first features and the mound was the last. The most intriguing outcome of the investigation was the uncovering of a spacious horseshoe of touching rough blocks, mostly local granite, that had been used as a kerb by the builders of the mound.

Open to the east it was oval in shape, 25 m wide and 33 m long. Amongst its fifty-eight stones was a very big quernstone. Also found were three carved slabs which, from their haphazard positioning, had very probably been taken from a dismantled *allée-couverte* nearby. On the southern side of the horseshoe was a stone set at right-angles to the circumference. A deeply engraved chevron pattern and a 'T' were carved on it. Nearby a second stone, upside down, had a hafted axe almost identical to another in the *allée-couverte* of Mougau-Bihan 40 miles to the south-west in Finistère. At the western head of the *fer-à-cheval* was the third block, also inverted, with a stylised figurine, termed a *déesse-mère* or 'mother-goddess' in the excavation report,[28] the female protectress of the dead known in many Breton megalithic tombs, often accompanied by the weapon of an axe or a dagger. At Tossen-Keler 'she' was depicted very simply as a four-sided near-rectangle. At the end of the excavation the three decorated stones were removed for safe-keeping and the stones of the horseshoe were taken to Tréguier where they were re-erected by the riverside with shrubs and bushes planted inside them.

Tossen-Keler was complicated in its history. Pen-ar-Land, 'the heath on the headland' on Ushant, may have been complicated in its alignments. It is also an uncommon exception to the rule that stone circles and associated monuments are not found on islands. Placed near the edge of a steep cliff overlooking the sea and in a considerable state of dilapidation it was excavated and repaired in 1988. Little was recovered, some unhelpful flints and some Bronze Age sherds that may be the only signs of a time when the conveniently shaped enclosure was used as a sheep-fold.

At the extreme east of the island the site was a little *fer-à-cheval* only 13 m long and 10 m wide, its head to the north-east around 52°. With a wandering perimeter of stones no more than 60 cm to 80 cm high there were two rather taller at the centre. Near the monument was a Four-Stone row arranged north–south and a pair of stones oriented east–west. Such obvious alignments intrigued the investigators who suggested that the horseshoe and the rows 'at the extremity of the known world' had been an important element 'dans le culte astronomique préhistorique', claiming that the long axis of the horseshoe pointed toward the midsummer sun rising over the sea, that other stones marked the equinoxes, the Spring, the Autumn and that there were even some better-dressed slabs recording positions of the moon.[29]

It is possible that the astronomical theory is overstated for those jaggedly low slabs, blocks and boulders in such a restricted setting but it may be significant that both Pen-ar-Land, and Tossen-Keler 85 miles to the ENE, were both close to the sea, the Atlantic seaways and to southern England.

This was certainly not true of Kergonan on the Ile-aux-Moines, far to the south of Brittany in the Gulf of Morbihan. What should be an almost undamaged monument is a spacious U-shaped *fer-à-cheval*, open to the south-east, 70 m deep, 95 m wide at its mouth. It would have been capable of holding a thousand people at a time when the island was not cut off from the mainland but was one of the greater ridges on the plain.

The pity is that this promising horseshoe of great stones, preserved on a patch of land between encircling houses is a mess. There are not only stones but an interfering line of trees, shabby buildings, little wild flowers entangled in barbed-wire and a wilderness of weeds and undergrowth. One yearns for scythes, a skip, saws and secateurs.

No more than five or six stones are missing, some removed when a footpath was trampled out from the road to the little estate. Of its thirty-one remaining stones, twenty-four stand. They are thin flat-topped slabs 1 m to 3 m high, almost contiguous, their smoother sides facing inwards. The majority are linked by a low drystone wall. There are reports that the mouth of the cromlech, now open, was once lined with small stones side by side with a tall terminal menhir at each end, 2.5 m to 3 m high. That at the north-east is known as the Pierre de Moine because in outline it resembles a cloaked monk. Other stones are much lower except those at the north-western head of the horseshoe where they stand 3 m to 5 m high in a predictable grading upwards.

There have been no organised excavations but in 1864 W. C. Lukis found two quartz strike-a-lights that are now in the British Museum. In 1877 a Dr Mauricet picked up some flint wasters at the foot of some of the lower stones.[30]

The astronomy of the design is controversial. Merlet deduced that to the south-east end of the axis, 127°, the featureless midpoint of the mouth was in line with the mid-winter sunrise.[31] But there was no foresight. More probably it was the opposite end to the north-west that was the target where the tallest stones stood in line with the mid-summer sunset, one of them known ominously as the 'Pierre de Sacrifice'.

An avenue of small stones may have led to the site from the south. In the early nineteenth century the English antiquarian, the Reverend Bathurst Deane, wrote that its course from Penab 'was formerly traceable in the direction of the island from south to north; but when we saw it there were very few stones remaining; sufficient, however, to convince me of the nature of the temple'.

An axe-carving on one of the stones reported but un-numbered by Le Rouzic is almost impossible to find because of the weatherworn condition of the uprights and the engulfing vegetation. Recently a rectangle, probably anthropomorphic, has been noticed on another stone.

About 30 m to the wsw of the horseshoe there had been a tall pillar, Pierre Colas, 4.8 m long. When the foundations of a house were being dug close to it in 1810 some of its packing-stones were removed and shortly afterwards the menhir fell. Unable to re-erect it the workers built the house over it leaving a little of its base exposed in the garden. René Merlet saw it in September 1916, a piece of fine-grained, blue granite. Interested in the possibility of dating megalithic monuments by solar extrapolation he took meticulous observations from Er-Lannic 2½ miles away and calculated that from there Pierre Colas would have stood to the north-east at 52°.7 where the midsummer sun would have risen in about 3000 BC, a time when Er-Lannic was already old. Although his methodology is suspect the 'date' may be close to the truth for the menhir and for Kergonan.[32]

The horseshoe's associations with funerary rites are attested by its art, its solar alignment and its other names of 'Le Cercle de la Mort' and of Er Anké, 'Er Ankeu, the notorious harbinger of death who usually appears as a skeleton in a white shroud, driving a cart with squeaky wheels'.

At the end of this discussion about the megalithic enclosures of Brittany there is an important cultural connection to be made. There are hundreds of stone circles in Britain and Ireland but horseshoes are rare.

Three horseshoes of timber are recorded in Britain and Ireland: inside the Arminghall henge, Norfolk, in the ring of posts at Lugg in Co. Dublin, and in the Machrie Moor I stone circle, on the island of Arran. In the north of Scotland there is an earthen example at Cowiemuir, Moray, and there are, or were, megalithic sites at Haerstanes, also in Moray, and at Achavanich and Broubster in Caithness, maybe also at Latheronwheel in the same county. On Bodmin Moor in Cornwall there is an immense D-shaped horseshoe on East Moor. The ambiguous 'ruinous Remains of a Temple' at Ballynahattin, Co. Louth, may also be a horseshoe, 'being open to the East'. It is within 3 miles of Dundalk Bay.[33]

With the single exception of Croft Moraig in the centre of Perthshire all these settings are close to the coast as though they were the ritual centres of people from overseas. There are, of course, two more megalithic horseshoes inside Stonehenge.

Chapter Eighteen

Stonehenge

I am now come to Stoneheng, one of our English Wonders, that hath been the Subject of so much Discourse.

John Aubrey, 1693, 74

Introduction

To end a book about stone circles with a chapter on Stonehenge is like ending a book about the Hundred Years War with a chapter on Joan of Arc. Both are late in the story, both are of misleading appearance and both are of somewhat dubious parentage. Both are also of considerably elevated status.

Stonehenge mystifies (Pl. 69). Over the past twenty-five years there has been almost a score of scholarly books dedicated to its problems: its age, the source of its stones, how they reached Salisbury Plain, whether there were sacrifices, whether the ring was an observatory, if its builders were numerate, how the stones were erected, what the sequence of construction was, whether it was ruined, more than a literary £300's worth of claim and contradiction without consensus. There has even been a learned paper entitled, 'Stonehenge: its possible noncompletion, slighting and dilapidation'.[1]

In summary the history of the monument is simple (Fig. 39). At some time around 3100 BC on the chalk downs west of the Christchurch Avon people began building what was to become the most famous of Britain's prehistoric monuments, first named and described in the early twelfth century by Henry, Archdeacon of Huntingdon, as one of the four wonders of the island, *Stanenges*, the place of the stone gallows or hanging-stones because the trilithons resembled mediaeval gibbets. Starting as a well-built timber structure with an ordinary henge around it Stonehenge may have had unfinished concentric arcs of Welsh bluestones added to it when Beaker people were in Wessex, a feature which in turn was superseded in the mid-third millennium BC by a lintelled sarsen circle around a horseshoe-shaped setting of trilithons whose huge boulders were dragged eighteen back-breaking miles from the Marlborough Downs many centuries after the first digging of the ditch.

Wrecked in antiquity, chipped for mementoes in the eighteenth and nineteenth centuries, threatened with demolition in the 1914–18 war, sold at auction in 1915 for £6,600, given to the nation in 1918, it was dug into by the Duke of Buckingham in 1620, by Stukeley in 1723, partly excavated by Cunnington in 1801, by Gowland in 1901, widely by Hawley, 1919–26, and amongst others by Atkinson, Piggott and Stone

Plate 69. The 'male' and 'female' bluestones astride the axis inside Stonehenge. The Heel Stone is outside (Photograph: the author).

from 1950, by Atkinson and Evans in 1978 when the skeleton of a young man killed by arrows was found, then by Pitts when signs of a partner to the Heel Stone were discovered, this ravaged colossus rests like a cage of sand-scoured ribs on the shores of eternity, its flesh forever lost. Stonehenge grudges its secrets. Each one explained – the date, the source of the stones, the builders – leads to greater amazements, a spiralling complexity that even now eludes our understanding so that our studies remain two-dimensional and incomplete.

The Henge

That was a simple statement of the history. The reality is far from simple. The interlocking, indistinct phases are as intricate as a Scottish square dance with patterns shifting, partners changing, nothing still. Seeking stability in these uncertainties is as frustrating as watching a damaged, black-and-white silent film through dark sun-glasses.

In 1956, having excavated at Stonehenge, Atkinson put forward what remains the most probable order of development: a. in the Late Neolithic an earthwork enclosure with a possible internal timber building was constructed; b. a ring of fifty-six pits, the

Aubrey Holes with human cremations in them, was laid out inside the bank. During a period of Beaker domination; c. bluestones from south-west Wales were brought to the site and erected in the Q and R Holes. At the beginning of the Early Bronze Age powerful chieftains of the Wessex Culture had the bluestones removed; d. and the monstrous sarsen circle and trilithons set up their place. Later; e. the bluestones were returned, some in a circle, others in a horseshoe-setting. Finally; f. in the Middle Bronze Age two rings of pits, the Y and Z Holes, were dug around the sarsen circle in a project that appeared to be unfinished.[2]

In 1982 Pitts offered modifications, a primary phase of the ditch and bank, the Aubrey Holes and questionable timber structure; an early megalithic phase when the Heel Stone received a partner, Stone 97, and when cremations were placed in the Aubrey Holes. This was followed by a later megalithic phase when the first straight section of the avenue was built, and when the bluestone settings were succeeded by the sarsens; and lastly, a post-megalithic phase in which the avenue was extended towards Amesbury, and the Y and Z Holes were dug.[3]

Thirteen years later came the magisterial and monumental *Stonehenge In Its Landscape*, 1995, 618 pages of dispassionate analysis of the evidence, an indispensable archive for any student of Stonehenge. In it Rosamund Cleal, her co-editors and colleagues collated unpublished data, evaluated them, provided a critical list of radiocarbon assays that unexpectedly put the sarsen circle in the Late Neolithic and offered a cautiously scholarly succession of events for the monument: I, 2950–2900 BC, a henge with three entrances at a time when the ring of Aubrey Holes held posts; II, 2900–2400

Fig. 39. Stonehenge.

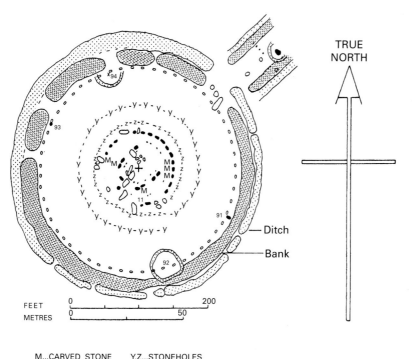

TRUE NORTH

Ditch

Bank

FEET 0 _____ 200
METRES 0 _____ 50

M...CARVED STONE   Y.Z...STONEHOLES
11...SOUTH SARSEN   91-94...FOUR STATIONS

BC, the ditch silted, and inside the earthwork were posts of a south avenue, of a putative central timber structure and posts across the north-eastern causeway were designed to create a controlled entrance to the site. Cremations were placed in the partly filled Aubrey Holes. 'Bluestones' from south-west Wales were erected in an uncompleted concentric horseshoe setting. The Heel Stone had Stone 97 set up alongside it. In phase III of 2550–1600 BC, there was an involved series of minor phases: the bluestones were dismantled; the sarsen circle and trilithons were constructed, perhaps never completed at their south-west; a ring of bluestones was set up in a circle inside the sarsens; then rearranged in a circle and oval; then in an internal horseshoe; and, in conclusion the Y and Z Holes were laid out around the possibly unfinished site.[4] Amidst these evaluations it is noteworthy that Atkinson's sequence for the bluestones and sarsens remained unchallenged.

There are questions to be asked, the first being why its builders chose an awkward site for Stonehenge. There were three imperatives: earlier Neolithic occupation; a preceding cursus; and the ancient Heel Stone.

Like several great stone circles, Avebury, Stanton Drew, Arbor Low, Stonehenge was built at the heart of a ring of Early Neolithic long barrows, at least sixteen of them within 3 miles. If each of the territories supported fifty to sixty men, women and children there may have been a local population of a thousand or so people, numerous enough to construct the earthwork but not too many to be accommodated inside it.[5]

None of these barrows in the vicinity of Stonehenge had a megalithic chamber. Obtainable stones of the right size and shape were never abundant on Salisbury Plain where the local materials were flint, clay and wood from the thick oak forests of the Neolithic. It was malleable wood that was used in the construction of the barrows' flint-covered, ridge-roofed mortuary cell in which the dead were laid. And it was skilled carpenters rather than masons that erected the timber building at Stonehenge.

A second consideration in respect of the henge's situation was the presence of a centuries-old ritual enclosure, the cursus. Stonehenge stands on a slope that falls steadily to the north and also declines towards the east even though there was level ground within a few hundred paces. Whoever agreed on the place deliberately rejected the flatter ground despite the difficulties that would be involved in constructing a roofed building on such distorted terrain, rejecting it because of the cursus half a mile to the north, an almost 2-mile long rectangular enclosure first noticed by Stukeley on 6 August 1723. He believed it to be a race-course but the ditched-and-banked earthwork was more probably an assembly-place for people engaged in funerary rituals.[6]

It is impossible to enter the minds and understand the motives of a society of 5,000 years ago whose only surviving message exists in a half-destroyed pattern of holes on a hillside, but two hypotheses about the location of Stonehenge can be tested. The people who dug the holes for the timber building and erected the shaped posts may have wanted their building to be conspicuous from all directions and also to overlook the cursus. For those conditions to be fulfilled there was only one place for the structure.

Although the posts vanished long ago, the sarsens of Stonehenge show how visible the wooden building would have been. The stones can be seen from quite long distances from the east, west and north, but from the south their position is critical. Were the ring to stand farther down its north-facing slope it would have been concealed from the Lake long barrow a mile and half to the south. Conversely, were it to be higher up the slope much of the cursus would have been obscured. Its entire line can be seen from Stonehenge but if an observer moves back only to the southern entrance of the henge much of the cursus's western sector is hidden by the curve of the hillside. It is likely, therefore, that the building was situated as high on the slope as possible in order to be observable from all the surrounding countryside without losing the prospect of the cursus to its north. It might be asked why it was not constructed a few hundred yards to the west where the land was level, where the cursus was still in full view and where the site was still visible from all around. The answer may rest with another of the builders' requirements.

The Heel Stone was the third problem. Sometimes thought to belong to a later phase[7] the outlier had never been shaped and its roughness is in contrast to the sarsens of the great circle which were pounded and ground into smoothness. It is arguable, although unproveable, that the stone had stood, solitary but conspicuous, on the false crest above the cursus, a territorial marker and guide to wayfarers on the Plain. Its existence made the positioning of Stonehenge a matter of fine judgement. With the construction of the timber building and the henge the pillar's function was to be transformed.

Hints of an enormous timber building were found during Hawley's excavations in the 1920s when postholes implied that it had two doorways, one at the north-east looking towards the Heel Stone, a second at the south towards which an avenue of upright timbers led from the earthwork and its southern entrance. It was a circular structure of almost exactly the same diameter, 29.6 m, as the famous, much later sarsen circle. There were two concentric rings of sturdy timber uprights, held firmly by ring-beams across their tops, supporting a pitched and thatched roof.

In *Stonehenge In Its Landscape* this tenuous structure is included in the second phase some time after the ditch and bank had been laid out. There is no archaeological evidence either for or against this judgement. 'There were few stratigraphic relationships . . . but where such relationships are recorded the posthole is almost always the earlier feature. This and the fact that there [sic] were almost all devoid of finds, led Hawley to the conclusion that they were dug early in the history of the monument'. Here in this book the opposite view is taken, that the wooden edifice came before the henge, an interpretation in accord with the writer's analysis of the purpose of the causeway postholes. It is a balance of probabilities.[8]

The purpose of the building is debatable. The flimsiest of clues comes from the Elizabethan, William Camden who claimed that 'men's bones are frequently here dug up' adding 'ashes and pieces of burnt bone frequently found' but it is little more than guesswork to think of the structure as a mortuary-house where the dead lay until their flesh had rotted.[9] It is feasible, however, that in the beginning it stood alone like others near it, Woodhenge, or the Sanctuary at Avebury, with a lightweight, theoretically roofed avenue leading to it from the south. In his excavations Hawley stated that he believed that it 'was contemporary with the causeway at the main entrance and places where similar post-holes have occurred, as they are all identical in method of making and appearance'.[10]

He was referring to a discovery of 1922. Like the great stone circles of the Lake District the early phase of Stonehenge had two alignments built into it, one astronomical at the north-east entrance towards the extreme rising of the northern moon, the other to the cardinal point of south at the other causeway. It is argued that these sight-lines were established before the digging of the henge but then incorporated into it. A

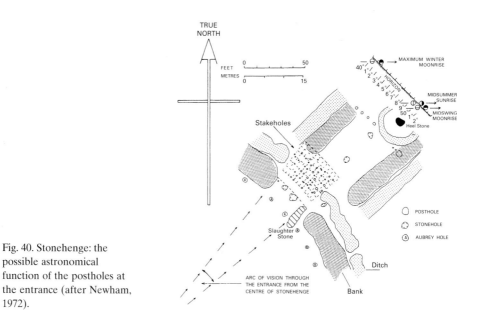

TRUE NORTH

FEET
METRES

MAXIMUM WINTER MOONRISE

MIDSUMMER SUNRISE

MIDSWING MOONRISE

Heel Stone

Stakeholes

○ POSTHOLE
⬠ STONEHOLE
Ⓐ AUBREY HOLE

Slaughter Ⓐ
Stone

Ditch

ARC OF VISION THROUGH
THE ENTRANCE FROM THE
CENTRE OF STONEHENGE

Bank

Fig. 40. Stonehenge: the possible astronomical function of the postholes at the entrance (after Newham, 1972).

midsummer sunrise alignment from the henge centre to the Heel Stone has been claimed since the eighteenth century but it is imprecise.

The north-east entrance is now about 10.7 m wide but it was broader before the ditch-ends weathered and crumbled and the bank slipped and spread. Across it Hawley discovered fifty-six seemingly inexplicable postholes straggling in six incomplete rows.[11] Arguments persist. It has been theorised that they formed a restricted entrance with two narrow passages, 'a fine double-passage timber entrance' observed Fleming.[12] A different interpretation was proposed by Newham who suggested that the holes had held sighting-posts put up one by one, year by year to mark the changing positions of the northern moon as it moved from its minor rising at 61°, NNE, to its major rising nine years later at 41°.7.[13] The henge had been carefully positioned so that the Heel Stone stood midway between these events at 51°.4, an emphatic full degree and more from the midsummer sunrise at 50°. At the latitude of 51°.2 and with the surrounding skyline a fairly constant 0°.5 the most westerly posts at the edge of the bank and ditch stood close to a declination of 28°.3, that of the midwinter full moon's most northerly rising. As there are several other circles in which a side of an entrance was used as a sighting-device, The Rollright Stones amongst them, Newham's theory is plausible (Fig. 40).

Observers must have recorded the moon's movements for over fifty years, watching it over three complete lunar cycles of 18.61 years until they were certain of the time to hold their midwinter nocturnal ceremonies. If this interpretation is correct then the henge was laid out after these sightings because the causeway postholes had to be removed. They were replaced by a single line of six heavier posts standing SE–NW well away from the entrance. Year by year the moon would rise behind each one. Such observations had been a part of Neolithic religious practices and had a long history amongst the prehistoric inhabitants of Britain, Ireland and Brittany for many centuries.

Then the henge, 110 m across, was begun, a ditch, a low outer bank and a broader, higher one inside. Diggers with antler picks hacked out pits deep enough to stand in and then levered away the jagged lumps of chalk to make elongated hollows like wartime foxholes, steep-sided, flat-bottomed and man-high. Pit after pit was quarried and from the air the site looked like a child's model railway to which more and more trucks were added. A couple of men, used to digging on their homesteads, could have shifted half a ton in an hour, the rubble shouldered in wickerwork panniers and leather sacks by labourers onto the bank along the inner edge of the ditch. When finished it was broken by causewayed entrances, a wide one at the north-east, the other, narrower at the south. The bank was a considerable barrier and may have supported a stockade that prevented outsiders from seeing into the enclosure. The spacious interior must have been for a community from miles around.

Toiling eight hours a day four men could complete a section in a fortnight before smashing down the crude ends between it and its neighbours and moving on to the next part. From the ditch about 6,000 tons of turf, soil and chalk was removed. Even allowing for bad weather and weariness, a workforce of two hundred could have finished in two months, about 11,000 man-hours,[14] perhaps after the harvest. The remains of flying ants, insects that flourish only in the autumn, have been recovered from another late Neolithic project, Silbury Hill, and Stonehenge may similarly have been begun around September.

Radiocarbon assays suggest that the henge was built around 3100 BC. From the south entrance came four determinations of 2600 ± 60 bc (OxA-4833); 2505 ± 40 bc (OxA-4835), 2510 ± 45 bc (OxA-4834), 2570 ± 100 bc (OxA-4842). From the ditch came nine more, 2431 ± 18 bc (UB-3788), 2425 ± 19 bc (UB-3787), 2480 ± 18 bc (UB-3789), 2417 ± 18 bc (UB-3790), 2415 ± 18 bc (UB-3792), 2443 ± 18 bc (UB-3793), 2482 ± 22 bc (UB-3794), 2460 ± 60 bc (BM-1583), 2440 ± 60 bc (BM-1617), a narrow span from about 3200 to 3100 BC.[15]

The inner edge of the ditch is so perfect a circle with a radius of some 55 m that it could not have been shaped had the central building been standing. It is arguable, therefore, that the outline of the earthwork had been scribed out before the erection of the timber structure. This might explain why the four radiocarbon determinations from the south entrance were on average a hundred years earlier than others from the ditch, 2546 ± 62 bc against 2443 ± 28 bc, about 3200 BC and 3100 BC, the two entrances marking the south and the northerly moonrise, the circuit of the ditch only dug when those positions had been settled after years of observations.

There is some evidence for a third entrance at the south-west, or more precisely ssw, 196°, a direction without astronomical significance. A disturbed cattle-skull was found there. Hawley also discovered cattle jawbones, a skull and a red deer tibia in the ditch-ends on either side of the south causeway giving 'strength' to that entrance. Dates from the bones of 2600 ± 60 bc (OxA-4833), 2505 ± 40 bc (OxA-4835), 2510 ± 45 bc (OxA-4834) and 2570 ± 100 bc (OxA-4842), c. 3400–3200 BC, are much older than assays from antlers lying in other parts of the ditch and makes it likely that these were 'curated' bones, perhaps tokens of a cattle-cult.

'If these bones really had been kept for several generations prior to their deposition, perhaps for up to two hundred years before the Ditch was dug, this reinforces the impression that early Stonehenge owed more to the traditions of the preceding centuries than to a new and innovative "henge" tradition'. As cattle-bones have been found in prominent positions in Early Neolithic long barrows such as Fussell's Lodge near Stonehenge and as the henge contained a moonrise alignment akin to those known in the easterly-facing barrows such continuity is entirely plausible.[16] The Stonehenge skulls may have come from the earlier building, lying there alongside the dead.

The Aubrey Holes

There was change and from it comes clear evidence of the arcane nature of the rites during this contentious phase. The timber building decayed or was dismantled and around 2900 BC; fifty-six pits were dug in a great ring just inside the bank. Containing no physical remains they were backfilled, dug again, many to receive human cremations with long bone pins. The pits were the handiwork of a cult associated with grooved ware.

In the summer heatwave of 1666, the year of the Great Fire of London, John Aubrey noticed five 'little cavities in the ground', where thicker grass was growing in the earth-filled holes. He thought they were places where 'one may well conjecture the stones c. c. were taken and that they did stand round within the Trench (ornamentally) as at Avebury'.[17]

There was little geometrical about them. On the circumference of a ring with a diameter of 86.6m they varied in width and depth, sub-circular and misshapen. Nor were they evenly spaced, the average 4.9m between their centres varying by as much as 43cm.[18] Their diggers had not bothered with symmetry.

Nine radiocarbon determinations, one from Aubrey Hole 32, and eight from secondary silting in the ditch, ranging from 2447 ± 18 bc (UB-3791) to 1848 ± 275 (C-602) suggest a period around 2950 to 2800 BC.[19]

Since Aubrey's time the pits named after him have been contradictorily interpreted as stoneholes for a great circle, as holes for high posts forming a large ring; as ritual pits for the deposition of offerings of soil and water in rites of sympathetic magic. Bender wondered whether upright posts in the holes had been replaced by cremations and Stonehenge 'seems to have become a cemetery'.

Most controversially, they have been claimed to be markers for the prediction of eclipses. 'There can be no doubt that Stonehenge was an observatory; the impartial mathematics of probability and the celestial sphere are on my side,' stated Gerald Hawkins with remarkable confidence.[20]

If the Aubrey Holes were laid out for purposes of scientific curiosity proof must come from the holes themselves. There are other henges with 'Aubrey Holes' but never with fifty-six (Table 17), a figure that is critical for Hawkins' eclipse theory. It is a number found at Stonehenge alone. In similar henges of the same period with similar pits containing similar material there is nothing to confirm that their makers had anything but an animistic interest in the sun or moon. Cairnpapple had 7 pits, both Maxeys had 10, at the five Oxfordshire Dorchester mini-henges the number varied from 8 to 14, Maumbury Rings had 44 to 45.[21]

Thom concluded that the diggers had respected the cardinal positions of their forebears. 'Since the position of the first Aubrey Hole is 3° 7′ from geographical north and the mean spacing is 6°.429 the north point is very nearly midway between two holes, and since there are 8×7 holes then all the cardinal points and the four intermediate points lie midway between holes.'[22]

This explains the layout. Pairs of holes were dug astride the north, east, south and west points. Then the four intervening arcs were filled with twelve more holes, the total of fifty-six being fortuitous, no more than $(4 \times 2) + (4 \times 12)$, a chance combination made by semi-numerate people with no thought of eclipse prediction.

In recent years Aubrey's idea has been modified with some of the holes having held stones while the majority had supported posts. Against this Atkinson, who with

No.	Site	No of Pits	Diameter Metres	Spacing Metres	Miles from Stonehenge	Contents
1	CAIRNPAPPLE West Lothian	7	17.1	7.6	330	Bone pins, cremations
2	LLANDEGAI Caernarvon	5	7.6	4.9	170	Cremations
3	MAXEY A, Northamptonshire	10	13.4	4.3	125	Cremation
4	MAXEY B	10	9.5	3.1	125	Cremations
5	DORCHESTER I, Oxfordshire	13	6.4	1.5	45	Bone pins, flints, antlers
6	DORCHESTER IV	8	6.1	2.4	45	Cremations
7	DORCHESTER V	13	10.4	2.4	45	Cremations, antler picks, Peterborough ware
8	DORCHESTER VI	12	11.9	3.1	45	Cremations, flints, Late Neolithic ware
9	DORCHESTER XI	14	12.2 × 11.0	2.7	45	Animal bones, antler picks, cremations
10	MAUMBURY RINGS, Dorset	44 or 45	51.5	3.7	45	Antlers, carved bone, animal bones
11	STONEHENGE, Wiltshire	56	86.8	4.9	–	Bone pins, flints, cremations

Table 17. Henges in Britain with 'Aubrey Holes'.

Piggott and Stone, excavated two pits, stated that in Hole 32 'there was no evidence of an original timber post or of packing-stones suggesting a stone upright', later insisting that 'they were never intended to hold any kind of upright, either the bluestones, as was supposed soon after their discovery, or wooden posts', a view that he restated more than twenty years later. The evidence is so flimsy and equivocal that we may never be sure even of the physical properties of these pits let alone of their intended function.[23]

In 1920 Hawley searched for the 'cavities' with a steel bar, excavating thirty-two in all, 1–30 clockwise and 55 and 56 at the west of the main entrance. In 1950 Atkinson and colleagues excavated two more, 31 and 32, from the latter of which charcoal supplied a radiocarbon date of 1848 ± 275 bc. The excavations showed that almost as soon as these rough-sided basins were dug in the early third millennium BC they were backfilled with their own chalk rubble, some of which had been scorched. The pits were respected. Later generations reopened them.

The majority contained burnt human bone. The first cremations were messy, with splinters of charred bone and lumps of wood-ash bundled and packed into hollows at the bottom of the holes. Little was found with these interments, but many of the holes were redug to receive not a crude mass but a neater, more ritualised offering of tiny bone fragments from which all ash had been washed. With some of these cremations there were characteristic grooved ware objects: long bone pins; flints; a chalk ball in a pit by the south entrance.

Followers of the cult paired items together in ceremonies of fetishism, believing that the combined objects would animate the magical powers of the Other-World, the evocation of supernatural spirits by association and exclusion. A chalk ball could be placed with antler and animal bone; flint flakes could not be grouped with anything; bone pins could lie with antler, with animal bone and with finely made flint fabricators.

Only in one pit was anything discovered with a primary cremation. In Aubrey Hole 55, two antlers rested under a thick layer of ash and bone and it is notable that these exceptional offerings were in the pit alongside the north-east axis of the earthwork, perhaps deposited there to add vitality to the entrance. Two Aubrey Holes at the east and south of the henge each had a rich assortment of articles, both containing antler, animal bones and long bone pins as though to enhance two of the cardinal points.

In the grooved-ware cult positioning was important. The NE–SW axis was stressed by the antlers in Aubrey Hole 55 at the north-east and by the unusual presence of pottery in Aubrey Hole 29 at the south-west. Here there was the base of a small grooved ware vessel very like a Breton vase-support, resembling an enlarged napkin ring. Hawley thought it might have been a 'lamp, as the surface of the upper part is blackened as if greasy matter had been burned upon it'. Originally this small pot had four protruding lugs, each pierced for suspension from a house-beam where it may have given dim light.[24]

The entrances were emphasised. The only other grooved ware sherds were discovered in the ditch by the south entrance, and the absence of cremations in the Aubrey Holes immediately to the east of both entrances suggests a refusal to have human bones there. When Hawley was excavating in the ditch close to the south causeway he unearthed half a dozen sherds. Two could be joined together and on them was a typical grooved ware chevron pattern.

Everything had purpose. Every offering, every action was conditioned by the demands of the cult, everything was ordered. The Aubrey Holes have frequently been described as a cemetery but to deem them no more than that is to misunderstand the reasons for the cremations. These were ritual offerings.

There were others at Stonehenge, in the ditch and along the inner edge of the bank, cremations different from those in the Aubrey Holes but just as punctiliously positioned. Whether in the grass-covered ditch or just under the turf of the henge itself, the majority of these pockets of bone were so small that Hawley believed them to be the remains of children. Hardly any ash or anything else lay with them, just one or two bone pins and some blackened antlers. They seemed so insignificant that they have generally been disregarded. Yet in some respects they are more informative than the famous cremations in the Aubrey Holes. It is possible that it was the bones of men that were buried in the holes. Women and children might have merited less prestigious parts of the enclosure. But the location of their interments was no less carefully planned.

At the exact east two cremations lay side by side in the ditch. Also in the ditch, alongside both entrances, there were arrangements of an adult, a child and animal bones, one group just west of the north-east causeway, another by the south entrance where two adult cremations were accompanied by the smaller limbs and teeth of a

Plate 70. The macehead from Stonehenge (Photograph: Mick Aston).

child with a long bone pin. Another adult, probably a woman and a child, were buried in the ditch at the south-east close to where Station Stone 91 would stand. One wonders whether these remains were those of sacrifices.

If the cremations in the ditch were small, those along the inner edge of the bank were mere handfuls of bone set in hollows no deeper than a saucer. Yet with the people's obsession for arrangement they concentrated no fewer than nine of these cremations together at the ESE.

The position must have been important and it was here that Hawley came upon the loveliest object ever found at Stonehenge. It was a beautifully polished macehead of hornblendic gneiss, shaped like a doll's cushion and hardly bigger, with a shafthole drilled through it (Pl. 70). 'The trueness of the boring is quite wonderful when it is remembered that there was only sand and a revolving cutter of wood or bone held in a bow-drill for making it.'[25]

Maceheads were vital to the cult. They were often made of attractive stone or gleaming antler. There is even one of red pottery from Longtown in Cumbria. The excellent quality of many of them suggests that they were made by a specialised craftsman or a small number of skilled workers. One of Cornish greenstone tumbled from a round barrow that Cunnington and Hoare were digging at Winterbourne Stoke barely a mile from Stonehenge.

The Stonehenge specimen, coming from either Scotland or, more probably Brittany, was delightful, striped in thin wandering ribbons of beige and brown, as smoothly hard as planed teak. Such lovely artefacts were not for mundane use but were fetishes or talismen, literally charming.

One might wonder why such a precious and potent object was left at the south-eastern circumference of the ring, lying amongst a group of children's cremations in scoops not 'deep enough in the more solid ground to cover all the bones'. The cult is the connection. From its fixation on position and pattern only an important location could justify such a luxurious offering being left there.

The macehead and the cremations marked an important lunar event. They were on the line between the centre of Stonehenge and the point on the horizon where the midsummer moon rose at its most southerly near 142°. It was a crucial orientation.[26] It continued and elaborated a lunar tradition established centuries before with the mid-winter postholes of the north-east causeway. The children, like a girl at Woodhenge, may have been sacrificed to sanctify the ground.

The alignment was marked by a heavy post. In 1924 Hawley recorded the largest posthole some 30 m south-east of the centre of the henge and a little to the right of the major southern moonrise. Two smaller postholes were found near it.

It was the old creed in a new form. The charnel-house had gone but there were still human bones. The lines to the moon were made stronger. Precious objects were buried in secret rites understood by only a few. Rough stone balls were buried in the ditch, even in the Aubrey Holes, like others in the passage-tombs of the Boyne Valley. There they were often found in pairs, presumably to represent testicles. In the flint-mine of Grimes Graves comparable objects were associated with a phallus carved out of chalk. At Tara in Ireland thirty such balls had been left in a tomb by whose mound a phallic granite pillar stood. Balls like these, often found with the dead alongside carvings of male organs can plausibly be interpreted as symbols of rebirth, of an awakening from the dead. Their presence at Stonehenge reveals something of the monument's purpose.

Such speculation is unverifiable. More certain is that at some time after 2800 BC the interior of Stonehenge was transformed.

The Bluestones

> Mr . . . Gethin of the Middle Temple London, told me, that at Killian-hill (or a name like it) in Ireland, is a monument of Stones like that at Stoneheng; and from whence the old Tradition is that Merlin brought them to Stonehenge by Conjuration.
>
> John Aubrey, 1693, 126

In prehistory there were not only Dark Ages but dark ages within Dark Ages. The earliest bluestone phase at Stonehenge is just such a period, lacking dates and artefacts. Worse, it may not even be a phase at all. Case wondered whether the bluestones were not the very last of all the stones at Stonehenge, arriving at the sarsen ring some time between 2250 and 2000 BC.[27]

In this blurred time of flux little is certain. For his second stage Atkinson proposed that there had been a concentric circle of bluestones, a sarsen rectangle, the Four Stations, and an earthen banked avenue. The first is questionable. The avenue is now known to be later. But undoubtedly the henge was altered.

There was a spectacular change. People of different beliefs from the grooved ware adherents, probably users of the fine beaker vessels of whose sherds there are twice as many as grooved ware at Stonehenge[28] changed the earthwork from a lunar to a solar monument by the most economical of transformations. They shifted the axis over 3° eastwards simply by widening the north-east entrance. The causeway had been about 11 m across but now its south-eastern terminal was backfilled with 'clean white chalk which had been brought from elsewhere and cast into the ditch', material perhaps dug out of the Q and R Holes which had been prepared to receive the blue-stones and which set so hard that it 'gave the idea of the chalk being wet when cast into the ditch'.[29] It was a dramatic alteration. Whereas the former axis had been 46°.6 the new one was close to 49°.9, almost in line with the Heel Stone 'and very close to coinciding with the rising midsummer sun when half its disc was above the horizon'.[30]

Traces of a Beaker cult of the sun emerge from burials and possessions. From a round barrow in the Lake cemetery 2 miles south of Stonehenge came six barbed-and-tanged arrowheads. In the same grave was a bronze dagger and three broken beakers, a 'European' (E), an 'All-Over-Corded' (AOC) and, informatively, a lovely 'Wessex/Middle Rhine' (W/MR), the most elegant and attractive of all beaker forms. There was also a heavy dolerite battle-axe from the Preseli mountains of south-west Wales, the presumed source of Stonehenge's bluestones. No fewer than six W/MR vessels lay in a nearby barrow. In the grave 'was a fragment of slate, perhaps a copy of an early Irish flat bronze axe'.[31]

Strict laws of the cult determined the disposition of a corpse. On Salisbury Plain the practice for W/MR burials was for the body to be laid in a crouched position, as though asleep, with its head to the north. In 1803 Cunnington wrote that 'the head to the north is the most ancient position', and in 1804, 'in primary interments at a great depth the head generally lies to the north, or nearly so'.

Under another barrow at Lake the long grave-pit was aligned north–south, a custom that became prevalent with the development of W/MR beakers. Interest in the cardinal points occurred in the orientations of the final long barrows, in the southern entrance to Stonehenge and in the layout of the Aubrey Holes. By early Beaker times north was the customary place for the skull.

Such an orientation may have been solar symbolism in a society in which the fires of metal-smiths, the rippling gold of molten copper and the eye-blinding brilliance of the sun may have mingled in a rich, solar cosmology unlike the cold, lunar mysticism of Neolithic people. Such opposing creeds could explain why the axis of Stonehenge was changed.

With Beaker people it is not only the alignment of their burials that suggests the sun was important to them. There is also the material and decoration of their little discs of' gold. The colour was reminiscent of the sun and the discs were embossed with circular patterns around a central cross like solar rays (Pl. 71). A miniature from Farleigh Wick in Wiltshire, was made of two pieces of gold foil beaten together. 'These discs are believed to be connected with Sun-worship – a cross within a cross being a well-known solar symbol.'[32]

Almost a score of these delightful objects are known in Britain and Ireland. Gold and copper were the first metals to be worked in these islands, the ores almost certainly being Irish, possibly brought into Wessex by Beaker prospectors. A gold disc from Kilmuckridge on the coast of south-east Ireland is similar to the one from Farleigh Wick, 'providing an interesting link between northwest Wessex, only 18 miles from the Bristol Channel, and the extreme south-eastern corner of Ireland'.[33]

From the Preselis across the Irish Sea to Wexford was only 50 miles and this probably was the way chosen by men searching for gold and copper. Gold was elusive. Copper was easier to trace. Rich deposits existed in south-western Ireland and experienced miners could recognise likely sources from the plants that flourished in copper-rich soils, the pinks, mints, mosses, oaks with dead lower leaves and purple stems, trees and bushes with stunted roots.

Plate 71. Gold 'solar' button cap found with a W/MR beaker at Mere, 20 miles west of Stonehenge.

Returning homewards the expedition steered their wooden-framed, leather-lined boats towards the landmark of the Preselis, the source of the dolerite axe-factories, some of whose perforated maceheads, battle-axes and axe-hammers have been found on Salisbury Plain.

Having changed the entrance the newcomers dug a ditch around the Heel Stone. In his excavations of 1979 Pitts discovered a stonehole near the outlier. Now known as Stone 97 it was at 48°.4 about 3 m north-west of the Heel at 51°.3 and if the two stones had stood together they would have formed a narrow setting through which the mid-summer sunrise at 50°.4 would shine into the centre of Stonehenge and the Altar Stone. From parallels with other pairs of stones Stone 97 was probably lower, and flat-topped unlike the peaked Heel. It may have been another example of the 'male and female' symbolism known elsewhere in Britain, Ireland and Brittany. There were comparable groupings of opposites at Stonehenge, the tall Slaughter Stone at the entrance accompanied by the lower Stone E, and two bluestones straddling the axis just inside the sarsen ring, the graceful Stone 49 10cm higher than the stocky, broad Stone 31 to its east.[34]

When the conversion was finished four rough sarsens were set up at the corners of a long SE–NW oblong inside the bank of the henge. Clockwise from the south-east they were numbered by Petrie 91–94. Stone 91 has fallen, 92 has gone but its hole was located by Hawley in 1921. Stone 93 is a stump. The hole of the missing Stone 94 was found by Richard Atkinson and Alexander Thom in April 1978. Following its discovery it was possible to cite the exact dimensions and angles of the rectangle.

The oblong was almost perfect and had been laid out with great care. Its long SE–NW sides measured about 80m, the short from 32.7m to 34.2m. The corners were very close to right-angles, forming a regular parallelogram.[35]

This almost unique arrangement has attracted little attention or curiosity and most books have been content to mention the stones without comment. Atkinson wondered whether the diagonals had been used to fix the centre of the stone circle as 'permanent and symbolic memorials of an operation of field geometry which . . . [today]

would tax the skill of many a professional surveyor' or even if the rectangle had been 'part of an earlier circle of widely spaced sarsens'.[36]

The unshaped sarsens are a cipher whose three arcane constituents have only quite recently been decoded over some sixty-year intervals. Stone 92 at the south-east and 94 opposite were removed in antiquity, their positions recorded by irregularly oval mounds in whose ditch bluestone fragments were found in the southern mound or 'barrow'. The two stones had been aligned 140°–320°.

'Aligned' is intentionally chosen. In 1846 the short sides were recognised to point to the midsummer sunrise. In that year, unaware that the mounds marked the places of former stones, the Reverend Edward Duke claimed that they had been observation 'stations' towards the foresights of stones 91 and 94 that acted as gnomons like the pins of sun-dials. 'The astronomer,' wrote Duke, 'taking his station [at Stone 92] . . . at the summer solstice, and turning to the north-east, would see that majestic luminary in all his splendour mounting in the horizon, and making his first appearance over the gnomon [Stone 91]'.[37]

The top of Station Stone 91, 2.7 m long, if erect and observed from Station 92 to the south-west would have been level with the horizon. To the south-west, Station Stone 93, only 1.2 m tall, still just touched the southern horizon when seen from Station 94. 'This plainly tells the fact that these differing heights of the . . . gnomons is for the purpose of accommodating the eye of the astronomic observer to the horizon over its apex'. It also tells that it was the first appearance of a heavenly body that interested prehistoric people rather than when it was fully risen.

Over a century later in 1961 Hawkins demonstrated that the long SE–NW sides of the rectangle were virtually in line with the most northerly setting of the moon. Neither his lunar nor Duke's solar orientations were accurate to more than about half a degree but quite good enough for observers uninterested in celestial minutiae.

Until the twentieth century it was never asked why the builders had chosen to set out a rectangle rather than an easier square but in 1906 Lockyer offered an explanation. From the middle of the sarsen circle where the diagonals of the rectangle intersected a line 'over the N.W. stone [Stone 93, not 94 at the NNW] would mark the sunset place in the first week in May'. He was correct.

The SE–NW diagonal from Stone 91 to Stone 93 has a bearing of 297° ± 30′ towards the May Day or Beltane sunset, the very limited declinations of the 'window' from +16°.65 to +17°.2 neatly straddling the 16°.72 declination of the May Day sunset. In 1976 Thatcher in a study of the Four Stations emphasised that 'many of the megalithic alignments in Brittany and in Great Britain point to the sunrise and sunset at those four dates' of early February: the 'Celtic' festival of Imbolc; early May or Beltane; August or Lughnasa; and the beginning of November, Samain.[38]

Logic insists that the Four Stations belonged to a phase before the sarsen circle whose thick and tall slabs would have blocked the diagonal sightline. The subsequent erection of the circle implies a rejection of the Beltane alignment and it may have been at that time that the rectangle was despoiled, Stone 91 toppled, Stone 93 truncated and Stones 92 and 94 removed and replaced by mounds.

There are two enduring myths about Stonehenge. Both are popular. Both are wrong and it is encouraging that neither is mentioned in *Stonehenge In Its Landscape*. The first is almost a fairy story that the bluestones were brought to Salisbury Plain from Wales by human beings. This is romance rather than realism and the thinking is as wishful as the second illusion that the fourth-century BC Greek historian,

Plate 72. The Preselis, Pembrokeshire (Photograph: the author).

Hecataeus of Abdera, was referring to Stonehenge when he wrote of a 'spherical temple' on an island beyond Gaul 'no smaller than Sicily'. As was shown in chapter eleven Callanish in the Outer Hebrides is a more likely candidate.

Human transportation is an equal fantasy. It came about because Geoffrey of Monmouth stated that Merlin had brought the stones from Ireland and put them 'up in a circle in exactly the same way as they had been arranged on Mount Killaurus in Ireland'. It was a legend that appealed to modern archaeologists because the bluestones had come from the Preseli range of south-west Wales (Pl. 72) midway on the route that seafarers would have taken on their way from the precious copper-lodes of the Wicklow mountains to Wessex.

Once H. H. Thomas identified the source of stones in 1923 the apparent connection between Wales and Wessex led E. H. Stone the very next year to suggest that there had been a magical, megalithic ring in the Preselis 'and that on the occasion of a tribal war in which the Salisbury Plain people were the victors, the stones of the sacred circle were carried off as a trophy to be re-erected at Stonehenge' because the spotted dolerite possessed therapeutic properties.[39]

The theoretical Welsh ring is very dubious. Nevertheless, many people, including the present writer, accepted that the Preseli slabs had reached Salisbury Plain through human muscle-power and fanaticism. There are, however, several facts that argue compellingly against this.

No other circle in Britain, Ireland or Brittany contains stones that were brought more than a few miles at the most. Secondly, Geoffrey of Monmouth, no geologist, referred to the Irish ring as Chorea Gigantum, 'the giants' dance' and obviously was referring to the bulky sarsens of Stonehenge rather than the unobtrusive bluestones. There are other objections. Not one ritual monument near the Preselis such as the Gors Fawr circle was built solely of the 'magical' spotted dolerite. Some like Dyffryn Synfynwy contained none.[40] Logistically, the hypothetical sea, river and overland journey would have been almost impossibly difficult and dangerous, especially in craft lacking sails.[41] The 'bluestones', moreover, are not a cohesive group of fastidiously selected spotted dolerites but a riff-raff of hard, friable and soft minerals. The seventon Altar Stone, a heavy sandstone block always described as coming from the Cosheston Beds near Milford Haven, a minute area of Old Red Sandstone but lying conveniently between the Preselis and the sea may, instead, have derived from the Senni Beds, a region twenty times bigger, of which the nearest part is around Kidwelly 30 miles east of Milford Haven and the farthest around Ross-on-Wye a further 70 miles to the east. If so, then movement of the stones by men becomes unbelievable. Finally, and very tellingly, there was at least one bluestone on Salisbury Plain long before Stonehenge, found by William Cunnington in 1801 in the mound of Boles or Bowls long barrow only 11½ miles to the WNW of Stonehenge.[42]

Whether these stones were transported by men along the 200 miles of water and land between Carn Meini and Salisbury Plain or whether they were moved at least part of the way by glaciation is unproven. Even the glaciation is disputed. The more recent Pleistocene, ending around 8000 BC is the one favoured by a majority of geologists but there is increasing evidence that the bluestones could have been carried some two and half million years ago during the Pliocene, since when the collapse and dispersal of the cover would explain the scarcity of bluestone material on Salisbury Plain.[43]

Experienced prospectors in the Preselis preferred spotted dolerite for the axes they made and bartered, ignoring other coarser-textured slabs and blocks. No such discrimination exists in the motley of Welsh stones at Stonehenge. Those so-called 'bluestones' are not homogeneous. They are a rag-bag. Of the soft, erodible, altered volcanic ash, rhyolitic tuff and calcareous ash some were so friable that they survived only under ground. Two-thirds of the stones were of the hard spotted dolerite, but a tenth were of softer altered volcanic ash all of which were rapidly reduced to stumps. There was also plain dolerite, rhyolite, rhyolitic tuffs and sandstone. In addition to this mineralogical farrago there were individual blocks of calcareous ash, a stump, and the greenish sandstone of the Altar Stone.[44] Such a mixture at Stonehenge may reflect the natural ratios of the different types of outcropping stones at the Preselis. Should this prove to be true it would make the likelihood of glaciation all the more probable. It should, moreover, be pointed out that the Altar Stone is not a blue stone and did not come from the Preselis. There was no reason for men to choose it.

Atkinson believed that the Q and R Holes had been dug to receive stones standing in two concentric circles of 26.2 m and 22.6 m diameters. Such rings may have been visualised as truncated but symbolic representations in enduring stone of the tall double rings of impermanent posts that had been the framework of the dismantled timber building, change and continuity combined.

Reassessment suggests that the project may never have been completed and that it is arguable that rather than circles a semi-circle, or a 'rectangle' with rather rounded sides, even a horseshoe-shaped setting may have been intended, an entrance-gap at the north-east corresponding to a similar gap between the Heel Stone and Stone 97.[45]

Whatever its intended shape to its south-west was the so-called Altar Stone, about 3.8 m high, 1 m wide and 0.5 m thick, over six tons of smooth sandstone, standing on the axis and facing the midsummer sunrise. Its probable stonehole, deeper and wider than those for other bluestones, was found by Hawley in 1924, having been cut through by seventeenth-century treasure-seekers who left a broken glass flagon behind. Also in it, but probably as a deliberate deposit rather than as discarded rubbish, was a fragment of a Cornish greenstone axe.

It seems that the Altar Stone was still standing when the sarsen circle of Stonehenge was being erected.

The likelihood of a stone standing in this position is strongly suggested by the unusual direction of the erection ramp of Sarsen Stone 56 of the great (third) Trilithon. The ramp for this stone approaches the standing stone 56 on its short, north-western side. To have erected this very large stone from the side and probably, judging from ramp extending in front of it, to have had to manipulate it from the interior, seems such a complicated undertaking that only the presence of something standing close behind it seems likely to have made such a course of action necessary.[46]

There is a final observation about the question of the bluestones. Niel was puzzled. 'One thing about "glacial solutions" has always puzzled me: The glaciers seem to have brought just enough stones to make the monument. If one asks what happened to the others, large and small, the answer given is that they disappeared long ago.'[47] There is another explanation. They may never have existed. If the solution lies with glaciation then a miscellany of stones from the Preselis, some half- or almost completely buried, lay within a few miles of Stonehenge. Their discoverers may have planned an ambitious concentric megalithic setting. But when the last bluestone was unearthed and the countryside scoured no more were to be found. The stones were removed. Centuries later they were returned inside the sarsen circle, modified into a less impressive single circle of about fifty-seven stones enclosing an elegant horseshoe of nineteen pillars. Even in the golden age of prehistory there could be blunders. Stonehenge was no exception.

> All our Druid temples are built, where these sort of stones from the surface can be had at reasonable distances . . . It was a matter of much labour to draw them hither, 16 miles.
>
> William Stukeley, 1740, 6

The Sarsen Circle

Around 2400 BC the most impressive ring of standing stones in Britain, Ireland or Brittany was put up at Stonehenge, a circle of thirty 5 m-high sarsens, numbered 1–30 by Petrie, capped by thirty lintels, 100–130. Inside it was a grandiose horseshoe-shaped setting of even taller stones, five lintelled archways that rose in height towards the south-west, the trilithons, 51–52, 53–54, 55–56, 57–58 and 59–60, their lintels being 152, 154, 156, 158 and 160.[48] The centre of the circle was about 30 cm to the north-east of that for the Aubrey Hole circle and for the Four Stations.

Two, perhaps four, pillars flanked the north-east entrance, the Slaughter Stone and its companion, Stone E. On either side of them may have been Stones D and F. The processional way of an earth-banked avenue led uphill towards them from the direction of the Cursus.

It was the most optimistic undertaking of megalithic Britain and may never have been completed. All the stones had come from the Marlborough Downs 18 miles to the north and if a genuine feat of strength and determination were needed to replace the fictitious story of the bluestone epic it would surely be this, the transportation of blocks with an average weight of 26 tons over miles of rough country with only man's will, his ingenuity and the possible use of oxen to achieve the task. The building of a pyramid has been described as the obsession of a single-minded megalomaniac. Stonehenge merits the same respect.

Until recently the earliest assays from Stonehenge III of 1620 ± 110 bc (I-2384) and 1720 ± 150 bc (BM-46) suggested that the sarsen circle had been erected around 1670 bc, *c.* 2050 BC. This has been disproved. The 'date' of 1620 ± 110 bc (I-2384) obtained from an antler in an unfinished R Hole has been rejected on the grounds of humic acid contamination. The other date of 1720 bc is now only one of a group of much earlier determinations: 2073 ± 21 bc (UB-3821) from the hole of Stone 1 at the north-east of the ring; and from the horseshoe of trilithons: Stone 53 or 54, 2035 ± 45 bc (OxA-4840); Stone 56, 1720 ± 150 bc (BM-46); Stone 57, 1910 ± 40 bc (OxA-4839); and from Stonehole E alongside the fallen Slaughter Stone 1935 ± 40 bc (OxA-4838) and 2045 ± 60 bc (OxA-4837).[49]

It has become an article of faith that these determinations show that the sarsen ring was erected around 2600 BC in the Late Neolithic period. There is a rider. 'The Sarsen Circle, for instance, seems very likely to be the first dated event (over 95% confidence) but as this relies on only one sample [UB-3821] which could be residual our confidence may be misplaced'.[50] Examination of the five other assays from Stone E at the north-east entrance and from the trilithons which must have preceded the erection of the circle a period closer to 2400 BC is statistically better.

Unexpectedly, assays from bone and antler in the ditch of the avenue produced later dates: 1985 ± 50 bc (OxA-4884), 1728 ± 68 bc (BM-1164), 1915 ± 50 bc (OxA-4905) and 1770 ± 70 bc (HAR-2013), a range of 2400–2150 BC indicating that the approach had been an addition to the sarsen monument and clearly not laid out to commemorate the way along which men had dragged the bluestones from the River Avon $1\frac{1}{4}$ miles to the south-east.[51] It was not unusual. Other stone circles such as Avebury and Callanish had later avenues.

These newly acquired assays indicate that this phase of Stonehenge began around 2400 BC, a few generations before the rise of the Wessex Culture whose rich leaders used but did not build Stonehenge. They inherited the monument from ancestors who generations before had been in contact with chieftains in Brittany.

The reasons for such change are unknown. For centuries, while Stonehenge had remained a provincial henge to which some rather ordinary bluestones were added, only 18 miles to the north the great circle-henge of Avebury had been a brilliant and stupendous monument amid such wonders as the West Kennet long barrow, the Sanctuary, the manmade mountain of Silbury Hill, a complex of enormous megalithic works that could well have been the envy of the inhabitants of Salisbury Plain.

The incredible sarsens of Stonehenge may have been a response to this. They were the products of woodworkers accustomed to shaping timber but also people who had resources of manpower and food-supply and organisation. Their monument was different from the spaciousness of Avebury. It was for only a few élite.

This Stonehenge was an illusion. Built in unyielding sandstone it was a replica in size and appearance of the early ring-beamed timber building. It was carpentry in stone.

With the expansion of the trade in copper, bronze and gold there arose in the Early Bronze Age a splendid Wessex culture represented by chieftains whose rich dagger-burials adorn the bell-barrow cemeteries like Normanton, Lake and Wilsford around Stonehenge. It was not these warrior-chieftains of the Early Bronze Age who inaugurated the final and most glorious phase of Stonehenge but earlier groups such as the S2/W Beaker users, people akin to others in Brittany where contacts with southern Britain had been established for years. 'In conclusion, while we can say that there is an undeniable relationship between Wessex and Brittany, study of the details of the burials reveals the care taken on both sides of the Channel to preserve regional identity.'[52] Which may explain why although a megalithic horseshoe, Breton in style, was set up at Stonehenge it was surrounded by a native stone circle hardly known in Brittany.

Whoever they were, whoever the genius who planned it, Stonehenge was a marvel of design and administration that demanded the labours of hundreds over many years. From the Marlborough Downs scores of sarsens were achingly hauled, each an average of twenty-six dragging tons, over grass, stream, downslope, long pulls around the Pewsey marshes, up the inch-inch-inch back-straining steepness of Redhorn Hill, more miles across the West Down, ropes greasy-black with sweat, day by day, to the last exhausted exultant sight of the Heel Stone, two months of strain for the labourers, fed by others, the settlements for miles empty of all but the old. One stone a year may have been all.

First to be erected were the uprights of the trilithons, 'three-stones', their lintel-pegs bashed from their tops, then their lintels levered upwards on heavy hardwood cribs, then the outer circle of uprights, 29.6 m across, 4.7 m high, the outer rough and inner smoothed faces contained within perfect circles, and finally, their lintels placed on top, curved to the line of the circle (Pl. 73). Unlike the circle the tops of the trilithons were not level. At the mouth of the horseshoe Trilithons 51–53 and 59–60 were 6.1 m tall, the central trilithons, 53–54 and 57–58 higher by 40 cm, the Great Trilithon, 55–60 at the south-west, a towering 7.3 m above the ground. Somewhere lay the discarded bluestones, rejected.

The heavy stones were dressed, pounded with mauls, sides ground into shallow flutings, rubbed smooth, more months of work, heaved erect into their holes. The modern technological age reveres Stonehenge for the engineering of its stones, just as, at Knossos in Crete, the cunning parabolas of the drains from the Queen's lavatory distract attention from the vitality of the frescoes. Yet the people who struggled to shape, to create the sarsens were building a monument for their lives.

Decades later the bluestones were replaced, first in a circle, then in an oval, finally where many of them stand now, about sixty in an irregular circle around the trilithons, nineteen others, tooled and shaped, in a horseshoe setting within the sarsen horseshoe, the Altar Stone replaced, perhaps standing, perhaps prone, near the centre of the completed monument.

There is something else. The axis was unchanged but reversed, away from the northeast towards the south-west and the midwinter sunset as the rising heights of the trilithons and the bluestone horseshoe show.

It was with rounded sarsen mauls, some no bigger than a tennis-ball but others as large as a pumpkin and weighing up to 64 lbs, that people shaped the stones. Jagged projections had probably been heated and then suddenly chilled with cold water before the largest mauls, encased in a network of leather and perhaps fitted with long straps 'in order that they might be used by two or more men', were swung crashingly down on the sarsen time after time, pulverising away uneven lumps, slowly evening the surface.

With the worst bits removed, gangs of workers lined up, four or five on either side of the stone, and with smaller mauls rubbed backwards and forwards on it as though it were a prehistoric washboard, sandy dust trickling away, scraping and scouring the surface into fluted ridges that would later be polished flat by a similar process. The

Plate 73. The magnificently engineered curve of the lintels, Stonehenge (Photograph: the author).

effect of this broad tooling can still be seen on the fallen Stone 59 whose ripples were left untouched.

It was tiring, it was boring and it must have seemed everlasting. In an hour of continuous rubbing no more than 98 cm^3 of dust would be removed. If some 5 cm of stone had to be levelled from the face of an average upright, 4.1 m long by 2.1 m wide by 1.1 m deep the task would have taken 378 man-hours. If eight people worked ten hours daily on the stone, they would have spent four or five tediously long days before the sarsen could be turned over for its side to be dressed, then over again and its outer face smoothed, then over again for its second side to be polished, a fortnight or more of aching, day-long toil.

In the turmoil of those years Stonehenge must have been a bustling, dirty, rowdy place with the smashes of the hammerstones, the rhythmical scrape and screech of the grinding mauls, the chatter, the bellowing of orders over the noise as the stones were levered upright, cries of warning, the distant shouting of a team dragging yet another sarsen across the last mile of the Plain. It has been estimated that one and three-quarter million working-hours were needed to build this sarsen phase of Stonehenge. Around 2400 BC the entire population of Wessex, from north Wiltshire to the south coast of Dorset, may have been about 50,000 men, women and children.

With 200 able-bodied labourers working ten hours every day, hauling, shaping and erecting the stones, the project, theoretically, could have been completed in three years. It is most unlikely that any prehistoric community would have persisted so unceasingly and the work of preparing the stones alone is quite likely to have taken far longer. Years, and quite probably generations, are more convincing.[53] When one realises that there were to be massive sarsens for the circle and trilithons, forty pillars, thirty-five lintels, three or more portal stones the mere slog and drive required for the smoothing of the stones amazes the modern reader. And this was the beginning.

Woodworking techniques demanded more than planed surfaces. The stones had to be connected together as though dowelled by a megalithic carpenter. The tops of the uprights had to be bashed and scoured into two or more bulbous pegs to hold the lintels securely. The circle-lintels had to be delicately curved to follow the long line of the ring. They had to be chamfered with bevelled edges to fit firmly on their uprights. Two deep mortise-holes were pounded and pestled out of their undersides, the spacing neatly measured so that they could receive the tenons of the two pillars across which they would lie. The ends of these incredible lintels were also beaten into toggle-joints, with the V-shaped 'beak' of one end to be inserted into the V-shaped groove of the adjoining lintel like pieces of a geometrical jigsaw, socketed together, stone by stone, in a huge, immovable ring high above the ground. In a timber building the result would have been an achievement for any prehistoric architect. In sarsen it was a miracle.

The workers had to be fed and they had to be sheltered if they came from far away. There is the chance that the base of a skin-covered hut 'for at least one skilled stone-worker' was discovered in 1980. A stone 'floor' was found in a shallow dip just outside Stonehenge to the west of the Heel Stone. In the debris were the signs of occupation, flint implements, knapped stones, animal bones and what may have been a hearth whose charcoal provided a date of 1450 ± 150 bc (HAR-4878), c. 2140–1410 BC, late but not entirely impossible to reconcile with the time when the sarsen ring or later alterations were undertaken. Men who could fashion the almost intractable sarsen were essential if the stones were to be turned into replicas of wooden beams. As rather similar floors were noticed by Hawley, there may have been a temporary camp of masons on site during the warmer months. It may have been these men who supervised the order by which the uprights and the lintels were set in place.[54]

For a megalithic ring that was constructed four thousand years ago with only the simplest of tools, the layout is surprisingly symmetrical. Thirty stones, on average 26 tons in weight and measuring 4.1 m high by 2.1 m wide and 1.1 m thick, were surmounted by thirty 6–7 ton lintels whose tops were never more than 10 cm from the horizontal, despite the skewed nature of the site. Petrie, in his precise survey of 1877, calculated that the mean error from the level was only 48 mm, an astonishing accuracy attained by pre-planning, so that Stone 30 by the entrance was nearly a foot shorter than Stone 10 at the south where the land was lower.[55]

The regularity of the spacing is also remarkable. The builders chose to have the stones twice as broad as the gaps alongside them so that the 2.1 m wide sarsens had 1.1 m spaces on either side. How well the planners succeeded can be demonstrated by simple arithmetic. One stone plus one gap, 2.1 + 1.1 m = 3.2 m. Thirty such combinations would produce a circumference of 96 m. The actual perimeter is 93.3 m, a deviation of no more than 10 cm for each stone and the gap by it.

On particular sarsens were carvings of bronze axes. Their positions demonstrate not only the continuation of a solar axe-cult but also carry on the tradition of cardinal lines in stone circles. Four carvings, one of a dagger, are at the south on the inner face of Trilithon 53. There are others on the outer faces of eastern circle-stones. Sub-rectangular carvings were ground out on the inner side of Trilithon 57 and lintel 120 at the west. It is revealing that the carvings occur on the outsides of stones of the circle, to be seen as people approached, but on the inner surfaces of the trilithons at the heart of the ring where they would be seen by only a privileged few.

Stonehenge and Brittany

Stonehenge is a mongrel. The ring is a half-caste of two excellent pedigrees but of distinctly mixed parentage unlike the majority of stone circles. Most are of pure-bred lineage and characteristic of their country: Swinside in England; the embanked circle of Meini-gwyr in Wales; Loanhead of Daviot in Scotland; the parochial rings of Beaghmore in Northern Ireland; Carrowmore in Co. Sligo and the typical Five-Stone circle of Kealkil in Co. Cork. All these are of almost unblemished national architecture. Stonehenge is not. It is an imitation of a timber ring. And it contains incontestable Breton traits.

The shape of the Four Stations has few counterparts in Britain or Ireland but is closely matched by the layout of rectangles in Brittany where at Crucuno, like Stonehenge, both the sides and the diagonal are in line with astronomical events.

The sarsen and bluestone horseshoes at Stonehenge have only dispersed relatives in these islands, two in England, one or two in Ireland, five or six distantly in Scotland, and all but one are close to the coast as though the alien monuments of people from overseas. The horseshoe of posts at Arminghall in Norfolk was surrounded by a henge but, like Stonehenge, had preceded it as the direction of the posts' ramps showed, away from the south-west entrance. 'It is likely that the timber horseshoe here predates the henge monument . . . perhaps by a considerable degree.'[56]

It has been claimed that the eight oak posts had been four lintelled archways like the trilithons at Stonehenge but the excavator thought this improbable. 'The spacing of the posts is rather irregular [from 2.0 m to 2.9 m] and there is certainly no trace of pairing . . . One may feel inclined to doubt rather strongly that they ever formed parts of trilithons.'[57] Charcoal from the southern post provided an assay of 2490 ± 150 bc (BM-129) which is similar to that from Tossen-Keler in Côtes-du-Nord, 2550 ± 260 bc (Gif-260), both in the midspan of *c.* 3300–3250 BC.

The rarity of horseshoe arrangements outside Brittany, the numerous examples there, graded in height and astronomically aligned like the Stonehenge trilithons makes influence from Brittany plausible, particularly given the existence on Salisbury Plain of Breton artefacts, the handled pot from the Winterbourne Stoke bell-barrow to the west of Stonehenge, the macehead of gneiss and the little handled vessel that Hawley found at Stonehenge and the cultural similarities between the weaponry and goldwork of the rich warrior graves of the Wessex culture and the Armorican dagger-graves.

It can be argued that the rectangle is a geographical coincidence although it would be difficult to claim this for the horseshoes. The megalithic art is indisputable. There is nothing like it on any other stone circle in Britain or Ireland except for one axe at Drombeg a mile from Glandore harbour and the Celtic Sea.

Megalithic art in these islands was abstract and unrealistic, cupmarks, cup-and-ring marks, occasional spirals at Long Meg, grooves and arcs. The symbolism of these patterns, possibly solar or lunar, remains elusive.

The repertoire at Stonehenge is different, a dagger, metal and stone axes, rectangles assumed to be anthropomorphic in origin, these are Breton motifs in early passage-tombs, the *dolmens à couloir* and the later *allées-couvertes*, on menhirs and on cromlechs. They are recognisable representations of weapons and are frequently associated with what is clearly a female from the breasts carved on her, placed at the junction of a tomb's passage and burial-chamber.

'She' is often portrayed as a rectangle with a domed 'head' or indented 'necklace' and sometimes as an unadorned oblong at sites such as Tossen-Keler, Mané Bras, Penhape, Goërem, Gâvres and Les Pierres-Plates. With an armoury of a bow at Barnenez or more usually a stone axe at early tombs like the Table des Marchands, Mané Ruthuel or Penhape she has been termed 'la déesse en écusson', the protectress of the dead.

Her axe can be shown as an outline of the blade, as blade and thonged haft together, even as the shaft alone with a curved top like a shepherd's crook.[58] Such economical shorthand is known in many tombs. On three of the four sides of the Kermarquer menhir are at least eight of these abbreviated axe-shafts as icons of the 'goddess'.[59]

'Her' figure can also be shown as a stone pillar in the tomb with head and shoulders crudely hacked out of the granite at Ile Guennoc off the coast at Ploudalmézeau or more finely shaped with breasts and necklace at Crech-Quillé near Lannion.[60]

It is in the later *allées-couvertes* that the rectangle gave way to carvings of pairs of breast in high relief. The stone axe was replaced by a metal dagger or axe. Clear examples of these juxtapositions exist at the northern tombs of Kergüntuil, Prajou-Menhir and Mougau-Bihan.[61] Unnoticed by tens of thousands of visitors from Roman times until 1953 every aspect of Breton art with the exception of the breasts has been recorded at Stonehenge, not scattered indiscriminately but fashioned on particular sarsens in particular places.

At Stonehenge there were carvings only on stones at the cardinal points of east, south and west. On the outer faces of three circle-stones at the east Stone 3 has motifs of three axes. Exact east was emphasised by about a dozen axes on Stone 4. The adjacent Stone 5 has one axe. Some of these carvings are so close to the ground that they may have been made before the stones' erection.[62]

At the south of the trilithon horseshoe the innermost side of Stone 53 bears the image of the famous dagger and fourteen or more axes, again some very low down . Opposite it, at the west and also facing inwards, Stone 57 carries a heavily-worn oblong likened by Atkinson to 'a cult figure, possibly a mother-goddess' (Pl. 74).[63] There is a smaller replica below it. A very weathered third rectangle was recognised in 1958 on the underside of the fallen Stone 120, the lintel of Stones 19–20.

Such 'rectangles', once termed *boucliers*, 'shields', or *marmites*, 'cooking-pots', are now accepted as anthropomorphic symbols. They, the axes and the daggers duplicate the art at Stonehenge with only the English Channel and a few land-miles between them. The authenticity of the 'rectangle' on Stone 57 as an anthropomorph is confirmed by the proximity of a 'crook', the shaft of a stone axe just above it. Not being metal this may have been one of the earliest carvings at Stonehenge, made before the stone was put up.

It is the cumulative effect of the 'package': the rectangle, the horseshoes, the variety

Plate 74.
The anthropomorphic
rectangle on the now erect
Stone 57. Above, just to its
right, can be seen an inverted
axe-carving (Photograph:
Richard Atkinson)

of art, the central pillar that makes Breton influence convincing. In isolation each one of the links could be contested. As a closely woven combination they persuade. One does not have to visualise boatloads of invading warriors imposing their will on the natives of Salisbury Plain. The appeal of elegant architecture and arcane symbolism from one powerful society to another will suffice.

The trilithon carvings at Stonehenge were planned as a composition. For a devotee inside the horseshoe, facing the south-west, the weapons of a dagger and axes on Stone 53 were to his left. To the right were the anthropomorphs and it is not sacrilegious to regard them in the same way as the crucifix is visualised by Christians today, as personified symbols of holiness. Enhancing this impression of sacred space, redolent of life, death, fertility and sunset, chalk 'axes' and a 'fine stag horn' were recovered from the ramps of Stones 56 and 57 alongside the rectangle. A chalk phallus was found close to Stone 57 itself.[64]

With carvings of weapons and figurines on either side of him a suppliant would have faced what today is an almost unremarked, unconsidered Breton connection at Stonehenge, the Altar Stone. This 5 m-long sandstone pillar now lies half-buried beneath the fallen Trilithon 55 but originally it may have stood erect near the centre of the circle. The pillar could have been regarded as the embodiment of the guardian of the dead. Such internal stones are rare elsewhere in these islands but are well-known in the north and west of Brittany where they stand inside the chambers of passage-tombs such as Ile Guennoc, Barnenez and Ty-ar-Boudiquet.

In Britain 'protectresses' also occur in yet another maritime context, on Anglesey where the chamber of the Bryn Celli Ddu passage-tomb contains an isolated pillar described as 'unique in the British Isles. It might perhaps be compared to some of the decorated menhirs in Brittany'. In the passage of the nearby Barclodiad y Gawres, 'the apronful of the goddess', 'is a tall stone with the entire front surface decorated with a well-organised design which could be interpreted anthropologically'. The carving is so striking that it has been termed a representation 'of the Mother Goddess herself watching over the dead'.

Such sea-linked stones create a persuasive Breton origin and sepulchral function for the Altar Stone at Stonehenge, an awesome personification of the power of death, the centre-piece of a sanctum where deposits of axes, a phallus, antlers, objects of fertility, lay buried but potent, hidden within the sacred horseshoe of colossal sarsens upon whose sides images of the protectress of the dead merged with her embodiment and with the setting of the midwinter sun at the dark dying of the year.

The Final Years

However modified they were the customs at Stonehenge were the elemental ones of supplication for the continuance of life. At first in the midwinter darkness of a tree-scattered landscape, paths marked by animal tracks, nights disturbed by the baying of wolves, everyone performed the rituals in an open enclosure. In later centuries perhaps only a few priests enacted more formalised rites within a monument planned in accordance with their more codified cosmogony. But still the sun and moon were paramount and the symbolism of fire and axe and water survived, the stones acquiring by association properties not only of averting ill but, more positively, of possessing curative powers. Geoffrey of Monmouth wrote that people would pour water over the stones to cure the sick. 'There is not a single stone among them which hasn't some medicinal virtue'.

There are heretical suggestions that the sarsen structure was never finished, that the south-west sector had been left incomplete. Or it may have been the continuing use of Stonehenge by Celtic priests of the Iron Age, the Druids, with their opposition to foreign authority that caused Romans to wreck it. Although they normally endeavoured to incorporate native cults within their own pliant pantheon the Romans did not tolerate subversion of their rule, and destroyed places they suspected of being centres of hostility. When the Druids incited a rebellion on their sacred island of Anglesey the Britons were slaughtered 'and the groves sacred to their savage rites were cut down'. The same may have happened at Stonehenge. Tacitus does not tell us. Toppled, robbed, chipped, fallen stones worn by two thousand years of visitors' feet, Stonehenge retains its solemnity, an awesome stone circle.

It lingered in use like many of the stone circles into the first millennium BC when with new customs and sometimes new people coming into the country such rings were less favoured. But still folk came to them.

What remains for the archaeologist are the tangible relics of stone circles, the twigs of the first-fruits, the charcoal in the rings, the human bones, 'the accumulation of factual detail' that so far from distracting attention from any vision of the past serves to give this vision shape and substance even though it is realised that the matter which most concerns us, the mind of man, is the least likely of all the mysteries of stone circles to be revealed. Where the stone came from, how the pillars were erected, and when, these problems may be answered by scientific deduction. Geometrical designs can be examined. Burials and offerings, carvings, may with difficulty and diffidence be interpreted. Future work may be concerned with accurate planning, and with geographical analysis of territorial patterns, the relationship of stone circles to other monuments in their locality. But the sounds and the colours are gone forever.

Now only the stones remain, bleak, leaning against the winds that blow across their silence. The fires are out. The midsummer sun has for years risen above empty, fallen rings. The people and their fears are gone. There are only the stones but they hold messages for those not hard of hearing.

Stonehenge is a compilation. As well as its sarsens from the Marlborough Downs of England and its bluestones from the Preseli mountains of Wales it had other cosmopolitan associations. Geoffrey of Monmouth believed that Merlin had brought the stones from Mount Killaurus in Ireland. The lovely macehead of gneiss that Hawley discovered may have come from Scotland. The trilithon horseshoe, the carvings of weapons and figurines were Breton in origin. In such widespread connections, all brought together in one great monument, Stonehenge was the epitome of the stone circles of Britain, Ireland and Brittany.

> What is Stonehenge? It is the roofless past;
> Man's ruinous myth; his uninterred adoring
> Of the unknown in sunrise cold and red;
> His quest of stars that arch his doomed exploring.
>
> And what is Time but shadows that were cast
> By these storm-sculptured stones while centuries fled?
> The stones remain; their stillness can outlast
> The skies of history hurrying overhead.
>
> Siegfried Sassoon, 'The heart's journey'

Appendix

C-14 Assays from Stone Circles

AVEBURY

Under bank

2690 ± 70	(HAR-10325)
2240 ± 90	(HAR-10500)
2430 ± 80	(HAR-10063)

In bank and ditch

2210 ± 90	(HAR-10326)
2350 ± 90	(HAR-10502)
1740 ± 80	(HAR-10064)

Outer stone circle

2180 ± 90	(HAR-10062)
1920 ± 190	(HAR-10327)
130 ± 110	(HAR-9696)
510 ± 70	(HAR-10061)

West Kennet avenue

2330 ± 100	(HAR-10501)
2310 ± 80	(HAR-9695)
3830 ± 80	(HAR-9694)

BALBIRNIE

89 ± 80	(GaK-3426)
1330 ± 90	(GaK-3425)

BALFARG

2230 ± 50	(GU-1160)
2085 ± 50	(GU-1161)
2320 ± 60	(GU-1162)
2365 ± 60	(GU-1163)

BALFARG RIDING SCHOOL

2470 ± 50	(GU-1670)

BALNUARAN OF CLAVA
NORTH-EAST

3585 ± 55	(AA-25230)
1585 ± 45	(AA-25231)
1645 ± 60	(AA-25232)
1580 ± 45	(AA-25233)
1525 ± 45	(AA-25234)
1650 ± 50	(AA-25255)
1195 ± 55	(AA-25256)
995 ± 50	(AA-25257)

BALNUARAN OF CLAVA
SOUTH-WEST

790 ± 55	(AA-21251)
820 ± 55	(AA-21252)
840 ± 60	(AA-21253)
815 ± 60	(AA-21254)
905 ± 70	(AA-21261)

BALNUARAN OF CLAVA
RING-CAIRN

4460 ± 80	(AA-21255)
1655 ± 75	(AA-21256)
1040 ± 70	(AA-21257)
505 ± 130 AD	(AA-21258)
660 ± 95 AD	(AA-21259)
4720 ± 85	(AA-21260)

BALNUARAN OF CLAVA SOUTH
RING-CAIRN

730 ± 45	(AA-25226)
795 ± 45	(AA-25227)
820 ± 45	(AA-25228)
171 ± 45 AD	(AA-25229)

BARBROOK II

1500 ± 150	(BM-197)

BEAGHMORE

1605 ± 45	(UB-23)
1535 ± 55	(UB-11)

BERRYBRAE

1500 ± 80	(HAR-1849)
1360 ± 90	(HAR-1893)

CAIRNWELL

2730 ± 80	(GU-4402)
1150 ± 50	(GU-4397)
1120 ± 60	(GU-4399)
1070 ± 50	(GU-4396)
1070 ± 70	(GU-4400)
1020 ± 50	(GU-4398)
1020 ± 50	(GU-4401)

CALLANISH [CALANAIS]

2260 ± 50	(AA-24966)
2235 ± 45	(AA-24964)
2190 ± 45	(AA-24959)
2145 ± 45	(AA-24969)
2250 ± 50	(AA-24960)
2165 ± 45	(AA-24963)
2105 ± 50	(AA-24961)
1630 ± 45	(AA-24956)
1625 ± 45	(AA-24968)
1605 ± 50	(AA-24962)

CARROWMORE 4

3800 ± 85	(LU-1840)
2370 ± 75	(LU-1750)

CASHELKEELTY

945 ± 35	(GrN-17510)
715 ± 50	(GrN-9172)

CULTOON

765 ± 40	(SRR-500)

DEVIL'S QUOITS

2060 ± 120	(HAR-1887)
1640 ± 70	(HAR-1888)

DROMBEG

790 ± 80	(OxA-2683)

LOCHMABEN STONE

2525 ± 85	(GU-1591)

MACHRIE MOOR I

2520 ± 50	(GU-2316)
2130 ± 90	(GU-2324)
2030 ± 180	(GU-2325)

MACHRIE MOOR XI

1740 ± 50	(GU-2323)

NEWGRANGE

Pre-tomb
2585 ± 105	(UB-361)
2530 ± 60	(GrN-9057)

Tomb
2475 ± 45	(GrN-5462)
2465 ± 40	(GrN-5463)

Pit-circle
2040 ± 40	(GrN-6343)
1935 ± 35	(GrN-6342)
2100 ± 40	(GrN-6344)
2035 ± 55	(UB-2392)
2035 ± 45	(UB-2393)
1925 ± 90	(UB-2394)

NEWTON OF PETTY

675 ± 45	(AA-25216)
800 ± 45	(AA-25217)
895 ± 45	(AA-25218)
1630 ± 50	(AA-25219)
940 ± 45	(AA-25220)
735 ± 45	(AA-25221)
835 ± 45	(AA-25222)
815 ± 45	(AA-25223)
670 ± 45	(AA-25224)
1805 ± 50	(AA-25225)

REANASCREENA

830 ± 35	(GrN-17509)

SANDY ROAD

1200 ± 150	(GaK-787)

STENNESS

2356 ± 65	(SRR-350)
2238 ± 70	(SRR-351)

STONEHENGE

Pre-Stonehenge. Mesolithic
6450 ± 100	(OxA-4920)
6570 ± 80	(OxA-4919)
6930 ± 120	(GU-5109)
7180 ± 180	(HAR-455)
6140 ± 40	(HAR-456)

Phase 1a. Ditch. Structured deposit
2600 ± 60	(OxA-4833)
2505 ± 40	(OxA-4835)
2570 ± 100	(OxA-4842)
2510 ± 45	(OxA-4834)
2431 ± 18	(Ub-3788)

Ditch. Primary.1b
2480 ± 18	(UB-3789)
2431 ± 18	(UB-3788)
2425 ± 19	(UB-3787)
2417 ± 18	(UB-3790)
2415 ± 18	(UB-3792)
2443 ± 18	(UB-3793)
2482 ± 22	(UB-3794)
2460 ± 60	(BM-1583)
2440 ± 60	(BM-1617)

Phase 2
1848 ± 275	(C-602)
2447 ± 18	(UB-3791)
2415 ± 55	(OxA-4904)
2350 ± 60	(OxA-4881)
2345 ± 60	(OxA-4841)
2320 ± 65	(OxA-4882)
1925 ± 55	(OxA-4880)
2365 ± 60	(OxA-4843)
2350 ± 70	(OxA-4883)

Phase 3. Sarsen circle
2073 ± 21	(UB-3821)
2035 ± 45	(OxA-1840)
1910 ± 40	(OxA-4837)
1720 ± 150	(BM-46)

Bluestone circle
1915 ± 50	(OxA-4900)
1790 ± 40	(OxA-4878)

Bluestone horseshoe
1745 ± 55	(OxA-4877)

Entrance
1935 ± 40	(OxA-4838)
2045 ± 60	(OxA-4837)

Y & Z holes
1391 ± 22	(UB-3822). Y 30
1350 ± 90	(UB-3823). Y 30
1499 ± 24	(UB-3824). Y 30
1590 ± 45	(OxA-4836). Z 29

Beaker burial
2010 ± 60	(OxA-4866)
1835 ± 70	(OxA-5044)
1875 ± 60	(OxA-5045)
1825 ± 55	(OxA-5046)
1765 ± 70	(BM-1582)

Avenue
1985 ± 50	(OxA-4884)
1728 ± 68	(BM-1164)
1915 ± 40	(OxA-4905)
1770 ± 70	(HAR-2013)

STRICHEN

200 ± 60	(BM-2315)
100 ± 80	(BM-2317)
1140 ± 60	(BM-2316)

TEMPLE WOOD NORTH

3075 ± 190	(GU-1296)

TEMPLE WOOD SOUTH

1090 ± 55	(GU-1297)
857 ± 50	(SRR-530)
1275 ± 105	(GU-1300)
1120 ± 80	(GU-1529)
1105 ± 110	(GU-1527)
1030 ± 100	(GU-1045)
1020 ± 230	(GU-1299)
995 ± 215	(GU-1298)
975 ± 65	(GU-1528)
928 ± 45	(SRR-531)
1745 ± 80 AD	(GU-1530)

TOSSEN-KELER

2550 ± 250	(GiF-280)

Bibliographical Abbreviations

Am Sci	*American Scientist*
Ann Exc Rep	*Annual Excavation Report (HMSO)*
Ant	*Antiquity*
Ant J	*Antiquaries Journal*
Arch Ael	*Archaeologia Aeliana*
Arch-Astr	*Archaeoastronomy*
Arch Camb	*Archaeologia Cambrensis*
Arch Ire	*Archaeology Ireland*
Arch J	*Archaeological Journal*
Arch Scot	*Archaeologia Scotica*
Archs Inst Hist Sci	*Archives Internationales d'Histoire des Sciences*
AW	*Archaeology in Wales*
BBCS	*Bulletin of the Board of Celtic Studies*
CA	*Cornish Archaeology*
Caithness F S	*Caithness Field Club*
CBA	*Council for British Archaeology*
Curr Anth	*Current Anthropology*
Curr Arch	*Current Archaeology*
DAJ	*Derbyshire Archaeological Journal*
D & E	*Discovery & Excavation, Scotland*
ECA	*Early Celtic Art (Arts Council)*
GAJ	*Glasgow Archaeological Journal*
Gents Mag	*Gentleman's Magazine*
IARF	*Irish Archaeological Research Forum*
J Anth Inst	*Journal of the Anthropological Institute*
JBAA	*Journal of the British Archaeological Association*
J B Astr Ass	*Journal of the British Astronomical Association*
JCHAS	*Journal of the Cork Historical & Archaeological Society*
JDANHAS	*Journal of the Derbyshire Archaeological & Natural History Society*
JGHAS	*Journal of Galway Historical & Archaeological Society*
JHA	*Journal for the History of Astronomy*
JIA	*Journal of Irish Archaeology*
JKAS	*Journal of the Kerry Archaeological Society*
J Inst Navig	*Journal of the Institute of Navigation*
JRAI	*Journal of the Royal Archaeological Institute*
JRSAI	*Journal of the Royal Society of Antiquaries of Ireland*
JRIC	*Journal of the Royal Institute of Cornwall*
JRSS	*Journal of the Royal Statistical Society*
Math Gaz	*Mathematical Gazette*
MM	*Meyn Mamvro*
NCH	*Northumberland County History*
New Sci	*New Scientist*

NMAJ	*North Munster Archaeological Society*
NMI	*National Monuments of Ireland*
NSA	*New Statistical Account of Scotland*
OJA	*Oxford Journal of Archaeology*
ONB	*Object Name Book*
OSA	*Old Statistical Account of Scotland*
Oxon	*Oxoniensia*
PBNHPS	*Proceedings of the Belfast Natural History & Philosophical Society*
PDAS	*Proceedings of the Devon Archaeological Society*
PDAES	*Proceedings of the Devon Archaeological Exploration Society*
PDNHAS	*Proceedings of the Dorset Natural History & Archaeological Society*
Phil Trans Roy Soc	*Philosophical Transactions of the Royal Society*
PPS	*Proceedings of the Prehistoric Society*
PRIA	*Proceedings of the Royal Irish Academy*
PRS	*Proceedings of the Royal Society*
PSAL	*Proceedings of the Society of Antiquaries of London*
PSAN	*Proceedings of the Society of Antiquaries of Newcastle*
PSAS	*Proceedings of the Society of Antiquaries of Scotland*
PUBSS	*Proceedings of the University of Bristol Spelaeological Society*
PWCFC	*Proceedings of the West Cornwall Field Club*
RCAHM-E	*Royal Commission for Ancient & Historic Monuments – England*
RCAHM-S	*Royal Commission for Ancient & Historic Monuments – Scotland*
RCAHM-W	*Royal Commission for Ancient & Historic Monuments – Wales*
SAF	*Scottish Archaeological Forum*
Sci	*Science*
Sci Am	*Scientific American*
TAASFC	*Transactions of the Anglesey Antiquarian Society Field Club*
TAMS	*Transactions of the Ancient Monuments Society*
TBFC	*Transactions of the Berwick Field Club*
TCNS	*Transactions of the Cardiff Naturalists' Society*
TCWAAS	*Transactions of the Cumberland & Westmorland Antiquarian & Archaeological Society*
TDA	*Transactions of the Devon Association*
TDGNHAS	*Transactions of the Dumfriesshire & Galloway Natural History & Archaeological Society*
TGAS	*Transactions of the Glasgow Archaeological Society*
THAS	*Transactions of the Hunter Archaeological Society*
TISS	*Transactions of the Inverness Scientific Society*
TLCAS	*Transactions of the Lancashire & Cheshire Archaeological Society*
TPPSNS	*Transactions & Proceedings of the Perthshire Society of Science*
TSANHS	*Transactions of the Shropshire Archaeological & Natural History Society*
TTB	*Thom, Thom & Burl*
UJA	*Ulster Journal of Archaeology*
VA	*Vistas in Astronomy*
VCH	*Victoria County History*
WAM	*Wiltshire Archaeological Magazine*
YAJ	*Yorkshire Archaeological Journal*

Notes

INTRODUCTION

1 Rogers, P. *Johnson & Boswell in Scotland*, 1993, 72, 53.
2 Chapman, R. W. (ed.) *The Letters of Samuel Johnson, III*, 1952, 86.
3 Stevens, F. *Stonehenge Today & Yesterday*, 1938, 4, 56–8.
4 Mee, A. *The King's England. Oxfordshire*, 1942, 154–5.
5 Lambrick, G., 1988.
6 Thom, Thom & Burl, 1980, 277.
7 Wheeler, Sir M. *Archaeology From the Earth*, 1954, v; *ibid.*, *Alms for Oblivion: an Antiquary's Scrapbook*, 1966, 49.
8 Michell, J. *The View over Atlantis*, 1973, 22.
9 Fojut, N., Pringle, D. & Walker, B. *The Ancient Monuments of the Western Isles*, 1994, 12.
10 Dames, M. *The Avebury Cycle*, 1977, 190.
11 Francis, G. *The First Stonehenge*, 1986, 99–100.
12 Meaden, G. T. *The Stonehenge Solution*, 1992, 159–62.
13 Aubrey, 1695, 67.
14 Auchterhouse: *PSAS 39*, 1904–5, 294–5; Laggangarn: *PSAS 10*, 1972–4; 58.
15 Hoare, 1812, 239; Long Meg: Sullivan, J. *Cumberland & Westmorland, Ancient & Modern*, 1857, 128.
16 *Gent's Magazine. Archaeology, II*, 1865, 31.
17 Strichen: *PSAS 38*, 1903–4, 279–80; *Curr Arch 84*, 1982, 16–19; Burl, 1995, 107–9, no. 116.
18 Merlet, M., 1974, 5.
19 Smiles, S. *The Image of Antiquity*, New Haven & London 1994, 197–217.
20 *WAM 39*, 1915, 132.
21 *TCWAAS 36*, 1936, 69–70.
22 Swire, 1966, 4.
23 Scouëzec, 1979, 382–4; Giot et al., 1979, 405.

CHAPTER ONE

1 There is an interesting account of the development of county archaeological societies in: Simmons, J. (ed.) *English County Historians*, East Ardsley, 1978.
2 The stones of Stonehenge: Atkinson, R. J. C., 1979, 185. For Geoffrey of Monmouth, see Hanning, R. W. *The Vision of History in Early Britain*, New York & London, 1966.
3 The Stonehenge bluestones: Burl, 1984. For the mediaeval belief in giants, see 'A digression on giants' in, Ferguson, A. B. *Utter Antiquity. Perceptions of Prehistory in Renaissance England*, Durham & London, 1993, 106–13.
4 Judicial courts: Coles, F. R., 1902, 529; Allcroft, 1927, 278; Crone, A., 1983. Farmland: Stout, 1961.
5 Norden, 1607, 48, 65. For Tudor and Stuart antiquarian fieldwork, see: Mendyk, S. A. E. *Speculum Britanniae*, Toronto, 1989; also, Fox, L. (ed.) *English Historical Scholarship in the 16th and 17th centuries*, London, 1956.
6 Antiquaries: Aubrey, 1670, 4; pagan temples: Aubrey, 1693, I, 24. James Garden: Aubrey, 1693, I, 185.
7 Toland on Aubrey, 146; on druids, 120.
8 Toland on Callanish, 122–3.
9 Stonehenge and the midsummer sunrise: Smith, J., 1771, 63–4; Stukeley, 1740, 35, 56. For William Stukeley, see Piggott, 1985; for eighteenth-century scholarship, see Piggott, 1989.
10 Bonney, T. G., 1866, in: *Gentleman's Magazine. Archaeology, II*, 1886, 6.
11 Maclagan and brochs: Maclagan, 1875, vi; Lewis, A. L., 1888, 46. Pradenne and Stonehenge: *Ant 11*, 1937, 87–92.
12 Astronomy and astrology: Allcroft, 1927, 264.
13 Astronomical criticisms: Atkinson, R. J. C., 1956, 86; Engleheart *Antiquity 4*, 1930, 346.
14 Radiocarbon and dendrochronological dating: Renfrew, 1976b, 70–83.
15 Assessments of Thom's arithmetical, geometrical and astronomical theories: Heggie, 1981; Ruggles, 1984a; Wood, J. E., 1978.
16 Druids and the moon: Green, M. *A Dictionary of Celtic Myth and Legend*, London, 1992, 153–4.
17 Practical fieldwork: Aubrey, 1693, 25; Aubrey on horseback: from John Aubrey's own life, 'To be interponed as a sheet of wast paper in the binding of a book'. Powell, A., 1949, 21.

CHAPTER TWO

1 Briard & Giot, 27.
2 Neolithic burial practices, see Thomas, J., 1991, 104–28; also: Huntingdon, R. & Metcalf, P., *Celebrations of Death. The Anthropology of Mortuary Ritual*, 1979; Chapman, R., Kinnes, I. & Randsborg, K. (eds) *The Archaeology of Death*, 1981.
3 Somerville, 1923, 193; also, Burl, 1988d.
4 Orientations of Neolithic burial mounds: earthen long barrows: Ashbee, P. *The Earthen Long Barrow in Britain*, 1984, 28–30; on Salisbury Plain: Burl, 1987, 96. Megalithic tombs, Scotland: Henshall, I, II; Brittany: Burl, 1985, 23–5; *dolmens à couloir* and *allées-couvertes*: l'Helgouach, 1966, 78, 82, 283; Severn-Cotswold tombs: Daniel, 1950, 80; Irish wedge-tombs: de Valera & O'Nuallain, 1982, fig. 36, *ibid.*, 1989, fig. 80; Loughcrew cemetery: Patrick, J. *Arch Irish Research Forum 2 (2)*, 1975, 12; Carrowkeel cemetery: *ibid.*, 13. Lunar orientations of passage-tombs have been recorded in Denmark and Sweden, see Hårdh, B. & Roslund, C. 'Passage graves and the passage of the moon', in *Acta Archaeologica Lundensia 8 (20)*, 1991, 35–43.
5 Causewayed enclosures: Smith, I. F., 'Causewayed enclosures', in Simpson, D. D. A. (ed) 1971, 89–112; Palmer, R. *PPS 42*, 1976, 161–86; Mercer, R. *Causewayed Enclosures*, 1990; Bewley, R. *Prehistoric Settlements*, 1994, 49–57.
6 Mercer, 1981, 63.
7 Parallelithons: Burl, 1993, 86. Proto-archaeologue: Hawkins, 1966a, 12, 54.
8 Ballymacdermot: *UJA 27*, 1964, 3–22; de Valera, 1960, 124, plate xxvi.

9 Scott, J., 1969, 190–1.
10 Court-cairns: de Valera, 1960; Twohig, E. S., *Irish Megalithic Tombs*, 1990, 21.
11 Cairnholy: *PSAS 83*, 1949, 115. Rites in forecourts: Henshall, II, 77–8, 165.
12 Burl, 1979, 113.
13 Disruption and attacks: Burgess, 1980, 234–7; Bradley, 1984, 34–5; Darvill, 1987, 75–7.
14 Volcanoes and climate: *Arch Ireland 2 (2)*, 1988, 71–4; *Nature 332*, 1988, 344–6; *Curr Arch 117*, 1989, 310–13. In Ireland: O'Kelly, M., 1989, 65–7; Mitchell, F., 1990, 134–5. In Scotland: *Holocene 2 (3)*, 1992, 260–5. See also Smith, C. D. & Parry, M. (eds) *Consequences of Climatic Change*, 1981; Baillie, M. G. L. *A Slice Through Time: Dendro-Chronology and Precision Dating*, 1995; Dalfes, N. H., Kukla, & Weiss, H. (eds) *Third Millennium BC Climate Change and Old World Collapse*, 1997; ibid. *Exodus to Arthur. Catastrophic Encounters with Comets*, 1999. For arguments against volcanic disasters, see 'Bronze Age myths? Volcanic activity and human response', *Ant 71*, 1997, 581–93; Reply: *Ant 72*, 1998, 425–7, 427–33.
15 5–9 January 1362: Langland, W. *The Vision of Piers Plowman*, Passus V, 15–20. Peru: *Daily Telegraph*, 23 May 1997. Eruption of the Laki volcano, 1783: *Geographical Journal 161 (2)*, 1995, 125–34.
16 Comets: *British Archaeology 30*, 1997, 6–7; Peiser, B. J., Bailey, M. & Palmer, T. (eds) *Natural Catastrophes during Bronze Age Civilisations*, BAR, Oxford, 1998.
17 Burl, 1988c.
18 Stukeley, 1743, 32–4.
19 Yr Allor and Meini-gwyr: Stukeley, 1776, II, Tab. 83; Lhuyd, *RCAHM-Pembrokeshire*, 1925, fig. 14; Camden *Britannia*, 1695, 628; *Archaeology in Wales 27*, 1987, 11–12. For doubts of the status of Yr Allor as a cove, see Barker, C. T. *The Chambered Tombs of South-West Wales*, 1992, 55. For nearby tombs, *ibid.*, 28–32.
20 Street House long cairn: *PPS 50*, 1984, 151–95. 'Wossit': *Curr Arch 111*, 1988, 124–7; *PPS 54*, 1988, 173–202.
21 Burl, 1976, 40.
22 Burl, 1991, 13–20.
23 Burl, 1976, 17; Burl, 1993, 31. Dates for timber rings: Gibson, A., 1998, 45–61, particularly 48–9.
24 For 'late' Irish rings such as Drombeg: Twohig and Ronayne, 74.
25 Harding with Lee, 362–72.
26 Burl, 1993, 28–9.
27 Aubrey, 1693, 125, 127.
28 Eogan, 1994.
29 Straffon, C., priv. comm. 25 May 1995; Ashbee, P. *Ancient Scilly*, 1974, 300.
30 The Boyne Valley and the Orkneys: Cooney & Grogan, 1994, 79, 92; *JRSAI 118*, 1988, 35; Bradley, R., 1984, 58–69. 'Argonauts': Childe, V. G. *Scotland before the Scots*, 1946, 36.
31 Tombs in the Outer Hebrides: Henshall, II, 117, 119; Muller, J. *The Chambered Cairns of the Northern and Western Isles*, 1988, 26, 35.
32 Druim Dubh: Curtis & Curtis, 1994b, 2.
33 Cultoon: MacKie, E. *The Megalith Builders*, 1977, 102–4.
34 Rosdoagh: Killanin, Lord & Duignan, M. W. *The Shell Guide to Ireland*, 1967, 291; de Valera, R. & O'Nuallain, S., 1964, 3. For the slighting of megalithic tombs in Ireland: Cooney & Grogan, 1994, 79.
35 Stonehenge and Brittany: Burl, 1997.
36 Lichfield cathedral: Stukeley, 1776, I, 61.
37 Megalithic missionaries: Childe, V. G. *The Dawn . . .*, 6th

ed., 1976, 325–6. Opposition to: *ibid. The Prehistory of European Society*, 1958, 129.

CHAPTER THREE

1 Fergusson, 2.
2 Er-Lannic: le Rouzic, 1930; Stenness: Caseldine & Whittington in Ritchie, J. N. G., 1976, 40.
3 Jackson, J. in Ryan, 1991, 34.
4 Mohen, 1989, 176–7; Joussaume R. *Dolmens for the Dead*, 1988, 102–3.
5 Ropes: Atkinson, R. J. C., 1961, 293; Burl, 1979a, 144–7; Mohen, 1989, 168.
6 Oxen: Atkinson, R. J. C., 1961, 292; *The Countryman 101 (2)*, 1996, 83; *Daily Telegraph*, 30 June 1995 (Letters).
7 Thom, 1961a et seq.
8 Cowan, 1969; 'Megalithic compound ring geometry' in Ruggles, C. L. N. (ed.) 1988a, 378–91.
9 Barnatt and Moir, 1984, 210. The possibility of rings being set out by eye alone is also discussed with diagnostic histograms in Barnatt, 1989, I, 24–8. For other evaluation of the Pythagorean geometry of megalithic rings, see: Angell, 1976; 1977; Heggie, D. C., 1981, 60–82.
10 Patrick & Wallace, 231.
11 Fleming, 1972, 59.
12 Moel-ty-Uchaf: Thom, 1967, 84.
13 Robin Hood's Ball: Thomas, N. *WAM 59*, 1964, 1–27.
14 Barrow 41: Waddell, J. *Denbigh Historical Trans 23*, 1974, 17.
15 Machrie Moor I: Roy et al., 64.
16 Excavation of Machrie Moor I: Burl, 1983c.
17 Marker-points at Temple Wood: Thom, Thom & Burl, 1980, 145. Unmentioned in excavation report: Orkney, J. C. in Scott, J., 1989, 98, 120–1.
18 Stukeley, 1740, 21; 1743, 20.
19 Moel-ty-Uchaf: Thom, 1967, 43.
20 Druid's Cubit: Stukeley, 1723, 16; 1740, 15.
21 Inigo Jones, 1655, 7, 55, 64, 66. Roman foot (*pes*): Berriman, 126; Petrie, 1880, 23.
22 'Hestingsgarth Foot'; Nelson, E. M. *The Cult of the Circle-Builders*, London, 1911, 12–14; alpha and beta measures: Mann, L. McK. *Craftsmen's Measures in Prehistoric Times*, 1930. Maria Reiche: obituary, *Daily Telegraph*, 16 June 1998, 28. Criticism of her 'yardsticks': Hadingham, E. *Lines to the Mountain Gods*, London, 1987, 138.
23 Borrum Eshoj: Glob, P. V., 38.
24 Body-measurements: Hicks, R., 1977; Leonardo da Vinci: Popham, A. E. *Drawings of Leonardo da Vinci*, London, 1946, fig. 215. 71, 137.
25 Stukeley at Avebury: 1743, 19; Deacon, B. *Malekula. A Vanishing People in the New Hebrides*, 1934, 31.
26 Woodhenge: Cunnington, M., 1929, 7–8. 'Beaker Yard': Burl, 1987, 124–5. Thom, 1967, 74–5, also calculated the perimeters of the rings and redefined the diameters in M.Y. as: 9.8, 16.2, 22.6, 28.9, 41.7 and 48.0.
27 'Perth Yard': Burl, 1988a, 7–8; 'Cork Yard': Burl, 1995, 227.
28 Newgrange: Powell, A. B., 1994, 86–90.
29 Counting-systems: Burl, 1976b.
30 Stone circle construction: Peet, 1912, 9; Fergusson, 95, 99.
31 Balance: Smith, I. F., 1965, equilibrium: *BBCS 21*, 1965, 262.
32 Goggleby Stone: *RCAHM-Westmorland*, 1936, 206, no. 85. Excavation: Clare, 1978.
33 Kilbride-Jones, 1934, 83–90; Stewart, M. E. C., 1966a, 14.
34 Engineering: Atkinson, R. J. C., 1961, 298.
35 Andrew Marvell: *The First Anniversary of the Government under Oliver Cromwell*, 1, 245.
36 Hampton Down: *PDNHAS 88*, 1967, 122–7.

37 Stone numbers in the Hebrides and Cumbria: Burl, 1976b; in south-west Ireland: O'Nuallain, 1984a, 3; in Devon and Cornwall Burl, 1976a, 123; Barnatt, 1982, 67.

38 Scottish recumbent stone circles: Burl, 1976b, 18, 32.

39 Twelve-Stone rings: *ibid.*, 28.

40 Aubrey Holes at Stonehenge: Burl, 1987, 89–90.

41 Archaeo-astronomical studies: Lockyer, 1906, 1909; alignments from circle-centres: Hyslop & Hyslop, 17–46; circle to circle: Somerville, 1923; Thom, 1967, 97–101, Type CC; to outlier: Smith, J., 1771, 63–4, Wilson & Garfitt, 120; to peaks and hill-notches, Lewis, A. L., 1883, Thom, op. cit. For a general assessment, see: Heggie, 1981, 1982. No reference to current research would be complete without citing the crucial fieldwork undertaken by Ruggles, 1999. Groups of similar sites in a restricted area: Burl, 1969b.

42 Sighting-devices: Hawkins, G. S., 1966, 6, 7.

43 Grey Croft: Thom, 1967, 99, L1/10, 'Seascale', declination +36°.3, Deneb, 'Good outlier'. Excavation details: Fletcher, 1958.

44 Earthen long barrows: Ashbee, 1984, 26–30; chambered tombs, Burl 1983, 21–9.

45 Sixteen month calendar: Thom, 1967, 107–17. In phase: *ibid.*, 109.

46 Stone circle declinations: Thom, 1967, Table 8.1, 97–101.

47 Beltane rituals: Ross, 1967, 83; Hutton, 1996, 218–25. Poem; *ibid.*, 228.

48 St Walburga: Farmer, D. H. *The Oxford Dictionary of Saints*, 1987, 428–9; Walpurgisnacht and witches: Guiley, R. E. *The Encyclopaedia of Witches and Witchcraft*, 1989, 354; Frazer, 1913a, 159–64, 238.

49 Toland, 1726, 120–1; Fergusson, 1872, 125. Symmetrical rings: Wernick, R., *The Monument Builders*, London, 1975, 110.

50 Sir Thomas Browne, *Hydriotaphia*, 1658, in: *Religio Medici and Other Writings*, Everyman, 1906, 132.

CHAPTER FOUR

1 Fleming, A., 1973a, 177.

2 Orme, B. *Anthropology for Archaeologists*, London, 1981, 218.

3 Thomas, J., 1991, 73, 105.

4 Firth, R. *Elements of Social Organisation*, London, 1961, 229; Evans-Pritchard, E. E. *Theories of Primitive Religion*, London, 1965, 112.

5 Calendars: Coligny: King, J. *The Celtic Druids' Year*, London, 1994, 141–5; Hutton, 1996, 410–11. Movements of the moon: Guiley, R. E. *The Lunar Almanac*, London, 1991, 9. Irish 'moon' calendar: Roberts, J. *The Stone Circles of Cork & Kerry. An Astronomical Guide*, Skibbereen, 1996, 5. Gods and goddesses: Green, M. *Dictionary of Celtic Myth and Legend*, London, 1992; Stewart, R. J. *Celtic Gods, Celtic Goddesses*, London, 1990.

6 Caesar: Edwards, H. J. (trans.) *The Gallic War*, London, 1979, 337. Ancestry of druids: Piggott, 1968, 235.

7 Hillforts: Cunliffe, 1974, 248. Continuity: Chadwick, 1970, 164. Cairnpapple: Woodward, A. *Shrines and Sacrifice*, 1992, 53. Swanwick shaft: Fox, C. *Ant J 8*, 1928, 331–6; Wilsford Shaft: *Ant 37*, 1963, 120; as a well: Bradley, R., 1978, 50. Excavation report: Ashbee, P., Bell, M., & Proudfoot, E. *Wilsford Shaft: Excavations 1960–2*, London, 1989; *Ant 64*, 1990, 191.

8 Neolithic origins of Celtic festivals: Burl, 1983a, 33–5.

9 May fires: Frazer, 1919, 150; *ibid.*, 1922, 609; Long, G. *The Folklore Calendar*, 1996, 69–74; Neolithic tool-kit: Baity, 1973, 416.

10 Axe-cults. Double-axes: Hawkes, C., 1974, 211; fertility: Kühn, H. *The Rock Pictures of Europe*, 1966, 185; Woodeaton: Ross, A., 1967, 48.

11 Axe-pendants in Brittany: Riskine, 1992, 91, 94. Non-functional axes: Roe, 1968, 168.

12 Grey Croft: Fletcher, 1958, 3, 6.

13 Thunderbolts: Evans, J., 1872, 51.

14 Mother-goddess: Cles-Reden, 1961, 58; Crawford, O.G.S. *The Eye Goddess*, 1957; Childe, 1940, 67; Graves, R., 1961, 102; Graves, R. P. *Robert Graves and the White Goddess, 1940–85*, 1995, 103ff.

15 Sun and megalithic art: Brennan, M. *The Stars and the Stones*, London, 1983, 32–66. Newgrange: Patrick, 1974; Ray, T. P., 1989. Brittany and Ireland: Powell, T.G.E. *Prehistoric Art*, London, 1966, 114.

16 Dancing: Frazer, 1922, 122, 610, 537. Dancing and petrifaction in England and Brittany: Menefee, 1974, 33.

17 Dancing around barrows: Grinsell, 1959, 157; Fox, C., 1959, 98.

18 Swan's leg-bone: Hoare, 1812, 199–200. European musical instruments: *Ant 34*, 1960, 6–13; Megaw, J. V. S. 'Problems and non-problems in palaeo-organology: a musical miscellany' in Coles, J. M., & Simpson, D. D. A. (eds) 1968, 333–58. Resonance in tombs and circles: *British Archaeology*, 1997.

19 Isobel Gowdie: Radford, K. *Fire Burn*, London, 1989, 82–6.

20 Axe-cult and dancing: Gelling & Davidson, 22–6.

21 Skara Brae: MacKie, E. W., 1977b, 193–4, 202.

22 Animal cults: Ross, A., 1967, 127ff; Coles, J. M., 1971b.

23 Bestiality: Ross, A., 1972, 159; Gelling & Davidson, 68. 'Nothing could be more explicit than Fig. 30e, and the same thing is indicated very clearly in Fig. 30f.' see also fig. 31, 60; Taylor, T., 1996, 173, 248–9; James, E. O. *Prehistoric Religion. A Study in Prehistoric Archaeology*, London, 1959, 224.

24 Taylor, T. 'Uncovering the prehistory of sex', *British Archaeology 15*, 1996, 8–9; *ibid.*, 1996, 187–92 where the identification of standing stones as phallic images is enthusiastic.

25 Shamans and dancing: Lissner, I. *Man, God and Magic*, London, 1961, 274.

26 Spring festival: Gelling & Davidson, 56.

27 Standing stones as phallic symbols: Daniel, G., 1950, 120; Cutner, H. *A Short History of Sex Worship*, London, 1940, 170–327. Condry, W. *Woodlands*, London, 1974, 150.

28 John Gerarde *The Herball or Generall Historie of Plantes*, London, 1597.

29 Mead: Dickson, J. H. 'Bronze Age mead', *Ant 52*, 1978, 108–12; Dineley, M. 'Finding magic in Stone Age ale', *British Archaeology 19*, 1996, 6.

30 Egtved: Glob, P. V., 1974, 51–64.

31 Ashgrove: *PSAS 97*, 1964, 166–79. Balfarg beaker: Mercer, R., 1981, 72–9; *Balfarg henge*, Glenrothes Development Corporation (n.d.), 4–5. Neolithic brewers: M. Dineley, *British Archaeology 27*, 1997, 4.

32 Hemp: Pearson, M. P. *Bronze Age Britain*, London, 1993, 85.

33 Drugs: Sherratt, A. 'Flying up with the souls of the dead', *British Archaeology 15*, 1996, 14.

34 Balfarg Riding School. Barclay & Russell-White, 1993, 43–210. Moffat, B., 109, 185. Henbane: Potterton, D. (ed) *Culpeper's Colour Herbal*, London, 1983, 95.

35 'Flying ointment': Guiley, R. E. *The Encyclopaedia of Witches and Witchcraft*, Oxford, 1989; Woodruff, U. & Wilson, C. *Witches*, Limpsfield, 1981, 104. Also for the effects of henbane: Schultes, R. & Hoffman, A. *Plants of the Gods. Their Sacred Healing and Hallucinogenic Powers*, Rochester, Vermont, 1992, 70–1, 86–91.

CHAPTER FIVE

1 Megalithic tombs in Ireland: Twohig, 1990, 8. Boyne-type tombs: *ibid.*, 45.
2 Early dates for Boyne-type tombs: Eogan, 1986, 225–6.
3 Davies, O., 1938, 112.
4 Kitchen, F. T., 1983, 153–5.
5 Boulder circles as stone circles: *ibid.*, 153.
6 Fergusson, 1872, 181, Twohig, 1990.
7 Carvings on Listoghil: *Arch Ire 8 (1)*, 1994, 14–15.
8 Carrowmore excavations: Burenhult, G. *The Archaeology of Carrowmore*, Stockholm, 1984.
9 Inishowen, Co. Mayo: Stukeley, 1776b, fig. 80; Killanin & Duignan, 1969, 86.
10 Inishowen, Co. Donegal: Toland, 1726, 60–1. Carrowreagh tomb and circle: Lacy, 1983, no. 99, p. 41; no. 325, p. 69.
11 Bocan: Lacy, 1983, 71.
12 Oliver Davies at Beltany: *UJA 2*, 1939, 293.
13 Art at Beltany: van Hoek, M. A. M. 'The prehistoric rock art of Co. Donegal, Pt.II', *UJA 51*, 1988, 21–47; 'Tops', 25–6.
14 Astronomical alignments at Beltany: Somerville, 1923, 212–14. Burl, A., 1985, 'The sun, the moon and megaliths', *UJA 50*, 1987, 7–21.
15 The sun rising: *Arch Ire 2 (2)*, 1988, 50.
16 Winter solstice at Beltany: *UJA 2*, 1939, 214.
17 Bealltaine: *ibid.*, 212.
18 Cupmarked stones in Scottish recumbent stone circles: Ruggles & Burl 1985, S54–S57.
19 The declination of early May: Thom 1967, 110; Burl 1983, 34.
20 Court-cairns in northern Ireland: Twohig, 1990, 17–26; O'Kelly, M., 1989, 85–92.

CHAPTER SIX

1 Carnac cromlechs: Worsfold; Riskine, A.-E., 1992, 57–96.
2 Brodgar and Stenness: James Garden in Aubrey, 1693, I, 218; Martin, 1716, 365; Toland, 1726, 124.
3 Stanton Drew as a calendar site: Stukeley, 1776b, 174; Sibree, E. *Stanton Drew Stones*, Bristol, 1919.
4 Prehistoric epochs in the year: Thom, 1967, 107–17; Burl, 1983, 34.
5 Neolithic tombs on Arran: Henshall, II, 1972, 22–3. Carmahome, *ibid.*, 393–4; *PSAS 59*, 1925, 252–3.
6 Group IX porcellanite axes from Tievebulliagh: Ritchie, P. R. in Coles, J. M. & Simpson D. D. A., 1968, 124; Clough & Cummins, 1988, 57.
7 Irish halberds in Scotland: Burgess, 1980, 75; food-vessel bowls: Harbison, 1988, 105; Irish lunulae: Taylor, J., 1980, 132; Clarke, D.V. *et al.*, 1985, 261; Irish Bronze material on Arran: McLellan, R. *The Isle of Arran*, 1976, 74, 76.
8 Bronze dagger and Wessex contacts: *ibid.*, 65–9.
9 Pitchstone: Macgregor, M., Herriot, A. & King, B. C. *Excursion Guide to the Geology of Arran*, Glasgow, 1965, 44–5; *PSAS 52*, 1918, 140–9.
10 Ritchie, P. R., 1968, 121–3; Clough & Cummins, 1988, 233.
11 Midsummer sunrise: Barnatt & Pierpoint, 110–12.
12 Aboriginal stone axe trade: Bunch & Fell, 15.
13 Boats: Lethbridge, T. *Boats and Boatmen*, London, 1952, 68, 119–20; Bowen, E. G. *Britain and the Western Seaways*, 1972, 36–41.
14 Bradley, R., 1984, 58.
15 Tidal races: Scott, Sir L., 1951, 32.
16 Alexander Thom and Callanish: Thom, A. S., 1995, 175.
17 Diodorus Siculus and Callanish: Oldfather, C. H. (trans.) *Diodorus of Sicily, Bks II, 35-IV, 58*, London, 1979, 37–41; Burl, 1993, 64–5.

18 Dating of the Group XII axe-factory: Smith, I. F. in Clough & Cummins (eds), 1972, 14. Distribution of its products: Clough & Cummins, 1988, 8, 134, Map 11, 275.
19 Shapes of rings in Wales: Burl, 1985b, 79–81.
20 Dimensions of Mitchell's Fold: Hartshorne, 1841, 35; Grimes, 1963, 125; Lewis, A. L., 1882a, 4; Stukeley in Lukis, 1887, III, 178; Thom in Thom, Thom & Burl, 1980, 25.
21 Ducarel: Nicols, J. B. *Illustrations of Literary History, IV*, London, 1822. Letters from James Ducarel to his brother, 11 May and 8 June, 1752.
22 Dating of Four-Posters: Burl, 1988a, 31–2. See also the recent C-14 assays from Park of Tongland, Kirkcudbright: *PPS 58*, 1992, 314–15.
23 Group XIII, Preseli products: Clough & Cummins, 1988. Distribution map, 276; implements in Wales, 204; in Wessex at Stonehenge, 157–8.
24 Standing stones as trackway markers: Bird, 1977, 111–15.
25 Flint cores in Shropshire: Bird, 1977, 93–133; Jones, H. C. 'Flints in the Clun Valley', *Shrewsbury Chronicle*, 8 March 1934; Chitty, L. F. *Arch Camb 104*, 1955, 193–5; *ibid.*, *TSNHAS 10*, 1926, 233–46.
26 Lake District grinding and polishing sites: Bradley & Edmonds, 144; Manby, T. G. 'The distribution of roughout "Cumbrian" and related axes of Lake District origin in northern England', *TCWAAS 65*, 1–37. Penrith assembly-places: *Ant 62*, 1988, 555–7.
27 Destruction of a stone circle: Heelis, A. J. *TCWAAS 12*, 1912, 153. Mayburgh, King Arthur's Round Table and the Little Round Table: Dymond, C. W., 1891.
28 Flu cremation barrows in Yorkshire: *TCWAAS 38*, 1938, 1–31; *ibid. 40*, 1940, 169–206; Bradley & Edmonds, 158–60.
29 Bradley & Edmonds, 150, 153.
30 Giant's Ring: *UJA 20*, 1957, 44–50; *Arch Ire 5 (4)*, 1991, 12–15.
31 Cornish axe-sources: Fox, A., 1973, 40.
32 Causewayed enclosures as dépôts: Edmonds, M. 'Towards a context for production and exchange; the polished axe in earlier Neolithic Britain' in Scarre & Healy (eds), 69–86.
33 Inferential dating of axe-factories: Smith, I. F. 'The chronology of British stone implements' in Clough & Cummins (eds), 1979, 14. For Group XIII, see, p. 20.
34 Sources of tuff in the Langdales: Bradley & Edmonds, 71–81.
35 *PPS 46*, 1980, 57, 59.
36 *Ant 48*, 1974, 201–5.
37 Copper mines in Britain and Ireland: O'Brien, 1994; *ibid.*, 1996; *Early Metallurgical Sites in Great Britain, BC 2000 to AD 1500*, Blick, C. R. (ed.) London, 1991. For tin in Cornwall: Fox, A., 1973, 94, 96.

CHAPTER SEVEN

1 Stone & Wallis, 1951, 118.
2 Pennington, 1970, 68.
3 Entrances, portals and short avenues: Burl, 1993, 31–9, 41–7.
4 Shapes of flattened rings: Brats Hill, Waterhouse, 56; Castlerigg, *ibid.*, 95. Location of Sprinkling Tarn and other Langdale sources: Bradley & Edmonds, 1993, 71. Superimposition of Brats Hill and Castlerigg plans: *TTB*, 1980, 29–31. Brats Hill rectangle: Williams, B., 1856b, 225–6.
5 Finds of stone axes: Williams, B., 1856a; Fell, 1964b. For Grey Croft: Fletcher, 1957. Broomrigg C: Waterhouse, 110.
6 Kemp Howe's avenue: Burl, 1993, 47–9. Gamelands: *TCWAAS 6 (O.S.)* 1881–2, 183–5.
7 Enclosed cremation cemeteries: Ritchie, J.N.G. & MacLaren, A., 1972; Banniside Moor: Collingwood, W. G.,

1910; Blackheath: Bu'lock, 1961; Mosley Height: Bennett, W. 1951.

8 Barrows and settlement: *TLCHAS 12*, 1912, 262; Skelmore Heads: *TCWAAS 63*, 1963, 1–30; *ibid.*, *72*, 1972, 53–6.

9 Access routes: *Ant J 68 (2)*, 1988, 206. 'Cache' of axes: *TCWAAS 90*, 1990, 99–103.

10 References to stone axes and circles: Vale of St John: *TCWAAS 3 (O.S.)*, 1877, 247; 'manufactory': Cowper, 1934; 'brass celt': Stukeley, 1776, II, 44; Hird Wood: Waterhouse, 145; Castlerigg: Williams, B., 1856b, 225–6, and Cowper, *TCSAAS 34*, 1934, 95; Grey Croft: Fletcher, 1958, 6.

11 Beakers: Clarke, D. L., 1970; food-vessels: Simpson, D.D.A., 1968; collared urns: Longworth, 1984, 30–2, fig. 23. Recent finds: beakers: *TCWAAS 96*, 1996, 13–26; food vessel sherds: *TCWAAS 85*, 1985, 11–17; collared urn: *TCWAAS 90*, 1990, 22; cordoned urn: *TCWAAS 95*, 1995, 35–54.

12 Distribution of Lake District circles: Collingwood, R. G., 1933, 173.

13 Dating of Group VI factories: Cummins & Clough, 1988, 74–5. Lochmaben Stone: Crone, 1983. Group VI axes in Scotland: Williams, J. 'Neolithic axes in Dumfriess and Galloway', *TDGNHAS 47*, 1970, 111–22; Burl, 1988b,183–4. See also Ritchie, P. R. & Scott, J. G. in Clough & Cummins, 1988, 88.

14 Astronomy in Cumbria: Thom, 1967, 99, table 8.1, L1/1–L1/10.

15 Beaker burials: Lanting & van der Waals, 37, 40; and food vessel burials: Tuckwell, 1972, 99–101.

16 Castlerigg outlier: Anderson, W. D., 1923. Thomas Gray: Dymond, C. W., 1881, 51. Portalled entrances: Burl, 1993, 29–40.

17 Enclosure at Long Meg: Soffe, G. & Clare, T. 'New evidence of ritual monuments at Long Meg & Her Daughters, Cumbria', *Ant 62*, 1988, 552–7.

18 Legends: Grinsell, 1976, 164–5; Burl, 1994a, 1–4.

19 Population densities and stone circles: Burl, 1988b, 189.

20 Anti-clockwise spirals: Brennan, *The Stars and the Stone*, 1983, 189–203. Spirals on Long Meg: Beckensall, 1992a, 8–13. Spiral at Castlerigg: Frodsham, 1996, fig 6a, 112, 113. Eastern horizon heights: Thom, 1966a, 56, fig. 39.

21 March, H. C. 'A new theory of "stone circles" ', *TLCHAS VI*, 1888, 98–111.

22 Cairns inside Long Meg: Camden, *Britain*, 1637 edition, 777; Aubrey, 1693, 115–16.

23 Excavations. At Castlerigg, *TCWAAS VI (O.S.)*, 1883, 505. At Studfold: Mason & Valentine, 1925.

24 Circles on Burn Moor: Dymond, C. W., 1881, 55–7; Brats Hill: Waterhouse, 1985, 56. Castlerigg, *ibid.*, 95; Thom, *TTB*, 1980, 36–41, L1/6A–L1/6E.

25 Bronze Age climate: Simmons & Tooley, 1981, 231ff; Heeley, H.C.M. 'Pedogenesis in Britain' in Harding, A. F. (ed). *Climatic Change in Later Prehistory*, 1982, 114–26.

26 Cairnfields: Northumberland: Jobey, 1968, 146; Yorkshire Moors: Fleming, 1971a, 22. See also Ward, J. E. 'Cairns on Corney Fell, West Cumberland', *TCWAAS 77*, 1977, 1–5.

27 Oddendale: Turnbull, P. 'Excavations at Oddendale, 1990. Interim report', Cumbrian County Council. Twelve-stone rings around the North Channel: Burl, 1976b, 22.

28 Group VI axes and perforated objects in Britain: Clough & Cummins, 1988, 17, 25, 34, 36, 43, 46, 50, 57, 62, 67, 72, 78, 87, 134.

CHAPTER EIGHT

1 Boats: Case, H. 'Settlement patterns in the north Irish Neolithic', *UJA 32*, 1969, 3–27.

2 Tides and the Irish Sea: Waddell, J. 'The Irish Sea in pre-history', *JAI 6*, 1991/2, 29–40.

3 Random choice of stones: *Arch Irel 10 (4)*, 35.

4 Distribution of Irish tombs: Twohig, E. S. *Irish Megalithic Tombs*, 1990, 22, 34, 46, 57. Passage-tomb colonisation: Evans, E., 1966, 47.

5 Exchange and trading networks: Case *UJA 32*, 1969.

6 Slough Na More: Tizard, 1909, 227.

7 Manufacture of Group IX axes: *UJA 49*, 1986, 19–32. Arran pitchstone: Mallory & McNeill, 49.

8 Group IX axes in England: Clough & Cummins, 1982, 4. In Scotland: *ibid.*, 87.

9 Ballygalley house: *UJA 53*, 1990, 40–9. Group VI axes in Ireland: Mandal & Cooney, *JAI 7*, 1996, 55. Antrim, 2; Armagh, 1; Fermanagh, 1; Galway, 1; Limerick, 1.

10 Finn McCool: Mallory & McNeill, 47.

11 Vicar's Cairn: Chart et al, 1940, 70.

12 Mullaghmore Four-Poster: Burl, 1988a, 76–8. Glentirrow: *ibid.*, 200–1.

13 Sequence of events at Ballynoe: Mallory & McNeill, 73.

14 Baetyls: Burl, 1981a, 45; Macalister, 1921, 354–5.

15 Commentators about Ballynoe: concentric circles: Maca-lister, 1928, 107; beakers: Herity, 1974, 151, 187; primary passage-tomb: Herity & Eogan, 1977, 127; small passage-tomb: Eogan, 1986, 212–13; final stage: Harbison, 1988, 98; from overseas: Evans, 1966, 95.

16 Baetyls at Ballynoe: Groenman-van-Waateringe & Butler, 78, fig. 2.

17 Bronze Age kerbed round cairns in Northern Ireland: Chart, 1940, 70, 83, 95.

18 Castle Mahon excavations: Collins, 1956.

19 Millin Bay excavations: Collins & Waterman, 1955.

20 Old Parks: Ferguson, 1895. Balnabraid: Ritchie, J.N.G., 1967.

21 Settlement in the Sperrins: Case *UJA 32*, 18. Scottish beakers: Clarke, 1970, 75, Welsh: *ibid.*, 228. English food vessels: ApSimon (in Case *UJA 32*), 38. Collared urns: *ibid.*, 57.

22 Cuilbane: *UJA 48*, 1985, 41–50. Dun Ruadh: *UJA 54–5*, 1991–2, 36–47.

23 'High-and-low' double rows in the Sperrins: Burl, 1993, 78. Shapes of pairs of standing stones: *ibid.*, 192–3.

24 The Corick complex: Davies, O., 1939a, 10, no. 28; Chart, 1940, 211; Evans, E., 1966, 151; McConkey, 53.

25 Excavation at Beaghmore: May, 1953.

26 Pollen analysis: Pilcher, 1969.

27 Goodland excavation: Case, *UJA 32*, 1969, 12–15. Further details: Cooney & Grogan, 51; Harbison, 1988, 38; O'Kelly, M., 1989, 136–7.

28 Winterbourne Steepleton 4a: Grinsell, 1959, 155. Sutton 268: Fox, C., 1959, 100.

29 Beaghmore C-14 assays: Pilcher, 1969, 80; Pilcher, 1975, 83–4.

30 Beaghmore astronomy: Thom, A. S. 'The stone rings of Beaghmore: geometry and astronomy', *UJA 43*, 1980, 15–19.

31 Horizon heights and trees at Beaghmore: Burl, 1987b, 11–12; *ibid.*, 1993, 105.

32 Excavation at Drumskinny: Waterman, 1964.

33 Wind Hill: Tyson, *Bury Arch Grp*, 1972. Brenig 51; Lynch, F. & Allen, D. 'Brenig Valley excavations' 1974. Interim report, *Trans Denbighshire Hist Soc 23* 1–25, 1975, 8.

34 Gortcorbies circle and cairn: May, 1947.

35 Clogherny Meenerriggal: Davies, O., 1939b, 36. Clogherny West: *ibid.*, 40.

36 Dun Ruadh excavations: Davies, O., 1936; *UJA 54–5*, 1991–2, 36–47; *Arch Ire 7(2)*, 1993, 14–15.

37 Castledamph: Davies, O., 1938. Alignements du Moulin: *Gallia Préhistoire 22*, 1979, 526–9; Burl, 1993, 107–9.

38 Wood-Martin, W. G. *Pagan Ireland. An Archaeological Sketch*, London, 1895, 264.

CHAPTER NINE

1 Petrified wedding: Stukeley, 1776, II, 174. Other legends attached to Stanton Drew: Grinsell, 1973.

2 Uncountable stones and storm: Wood, J., 1747, 148.

3 Burying of stones: Stukeley, 1776, II, 170.

4 Estimates of the central circle's diameter: Stukeley, 1776, II, 91.4 m; Wood, J., 1747, 115.2 m, Crocker, in Hoare, Sir R. C. *The History of Modern Wiltshire*, II, 1826, 52–3, 115.2 m; Wilkinson, Sir J. G., *JBAA 16*, 1860, 114, 115.8 × 105.2 m; Kains-Jackson, *Our Ancient Monuments...*, 1880, 34, 115.2 × 105.2 m; Dymond, C. W., 1894, 112.2 m; Prain & Prain in Thom, 1967, 35, 80, 111.3 m; Thom, 1967, 113.5 m; Barnatt, II, 1989, 114.6 × 112.8 m.

5 Hautville's Quoit: Aubrey, 1693, 68; Stukeley, 1776, II, 169.

6 Alignments between the three circles to the cove: Wood, J., 1747, 151; and the outlying stone: *ibid.*, 149.

7 Finds at Stanton Drew: Gay, J. *A Fool's Bolt soon Shott at Stonage*, 1725, 27, in: Legg, R. (ed.) *Stonehenge Antiquaries*, Milborne Port, 1986. 121–6.

8 The chambered tombs within seven miles of Stanton Drew: Brays Down; Chewton Mendip II; Chewton Mendip III; Dundry; Dundry Hill; Fairy's Toot; 'The Mountains', Felton; 'Mountain Ground', Chewton Mendip I; Red Hill, Wrington; Tunley Farm, Camerton; Water Stone: Grinsell, 1971, 83–4, 93–4; 1994, 8.

9 Long and round barrows around Stanton Drew: Grinsell, 1971, 56, 83–4, 92–4; Stukeley, 1776, II, 170.

10 Battle Gore and the Devil: Grinsell, 1976, 98.

11 Similarity between the Withypool, Stannon and Fernacre stone circles: Gray, H. St G., 1907, 42.

12 Almsworthy: Gray, H. St G., 1931. Way's reinterpretation in 1939: Grinsell, 1970, 39–40; Burl, 1993, 121.

13 Camden, 1610 (1637 edition, 203). For a detailed corpus of the Exmoor monuments, see Quinnell & Dunn, 1992.

14 White Ladder double row: Eardley-Wilmot, 24–5, 32. For the distribution of short settings of standing stones: Burl, 1993, 245, 250, 259

15 Changing climate on Dartmoor: Simmons, 1969, 207; Simmons & Tooley, 1981, 243–5, 268; Castledine, C. J. & Maguire, D. C. *South-Western England J. Biogeography 13*, 1986, 225–64.

16 Territories of the great rings: Butler, J., 1991b, 91–2. Population and land-use: Burl, 1976, 324.

17 Shovel Down and sexual symbolism: Burl, 1993, 52.

18 Siting of the large Dartmoor circles: Turner, J. R., 1990, 55–6.

19 Fernworthy beaker and finds: *TDA 30*, 1898, 107 f; Clarke, D. L., 1970, I, 224; II, 479, no. 158.

20 Dartmoor hut-circles: Worth, 1967, 99–132; Fox, A., 1973, 100–13; Greeves, T., *The Archaeology of Dartmoor from the Air*, 1985, plates 2–8; Gerrard, 1997, 37–61.

21 Foales Arrishes: 'Squaw': Baring-Gould, 1907, 177. Settlement: Butler, 1991a, 57–9.

22 Legis Tor: Worth, 1967, 144–7; Butler, 1994, 111–14. Trevisker pottery: Gibson, A. & Woods, A., 1990, 260–1.

23 Exe Head: Chanter & Worth, 1906, 544; Quinnell & Dunn, 1992, 40.

24 Dartmoor rows: Burl, 1993, 50–4, 81–4, 93–6, 112–23. Exmoor: *ibid.*, 234–5, 237, 241.

25 Dartmoor stellar astronomy: North, J., 1996, 242–8. Dartmoor chronology: Burl, 1993, 23. Cholwichtown: Eogan, 1964.

26 Merrivale and the 'Plague Market': Breton, H. H., 1931 (2), 70.

27 Shaugh Moor excavations: *PPS 45*, 1979, 1–34. C-14 assays: 24.

28 William Borlase to Stukeley in Lukis, 1883, II, 57.

29 The Hurlers: Camden, *Britain*, 1610, 192, and slightly different in *Britannia*, 1695, 9; Norden, 1597–1604?, 23, 66.

30 Grading: Barnatt, 1982, 69–71, 184–5.

31 Multiple sites: Burl, 1976, 117–19.

32 Leskernick circles: Barnatt, 1989, 412–13.

33 Claverdon Down, Bathampton circles: Quinn, P. *3ʳᵈ Stone 27*, 1997, 11–12.

34 Circle to circle astronomy: Thom, 1967, 100.

35 Thornborough: *PPS 2(2)*, 1936, 51. Priddy: Tratman, 1967.

36 For a list of Welsh gorsedds, eisteddfods and their dates, see: Miles, D. *The Secret of the Bards of the Isle of Britain*, 1992, 236–40.

37 Alignments to tors on Bodmin Moor: Lewis, A. L., 1892, 147; *ibid.*, 1896, 5; Lockyer, 1909, 419–20; Tilley, 25–8.

38 For Anasazi kivas such as Casa Rinconada, see: Williamson, R. A. *Living in the Sky*, Boston, Massachusetts, 1984, 112–13.

39 Numbers of stones in large Cornish circles: Burl, 1976, 119–20. Criticism of over-precision: Barnatt, 1982, 26–8. Nineteen: Straffon, C. *Pagan Cornwall. Land of the Goddess*, 1993, 26.

40 Naked dancers at Boscawen-Un: Editorial, *Cornwall Archaeological Society Newsletter 82*, September, 1996.

41 Meaning of the Stripple Stones name. I am most grateful to Dr Oliver Padel of Cambridge University for this interpretation. A very informative booklet about the ancient Cornish language is Weatherhill, C. *Cornish Place Names and Language*, Sigma, Wilmslow, 1995.

42 Excavations at the Stripple Stones: Gray, H. St G., 1908. Apses like those at the Stripple Stones: Wainwright with Longworth, 1971, 194.

43 Stukeley to Borlase: Lukis, 1883, 56.

44 Alignment of the King Arthur's Down rings: Barnatt, 1982, 20. King Arthur's Hall: Norden, 1597–1604?, 49–50. Swimming-pool: Johnson & Rose, 29. Construction of Irish henges: Burl, 1983, 15–16.

45 Welsh comparisons with King Arthur's Hall: Fynnonbrodyr and Dan-y-coed: Grimes, 1963, 141–5, nos 29, 31; Harding with Lee, 323–4, 430. Fynnon-newydd: *BBCS 31*, 1984, 177–90. Elsewhere there have been almost as many interpretations as there have been writers: 'while it may be prehistoric, it may also be a reservoir of much later date', Ashe, G. *A Guide to Arthurian Britain*, 1980, 16; 'the fort of Arthur's Hall', Chambers, E. J. *Arthur of Britain*, 1927, 186; 'a cattle pound . . . a place of assembly, a cockfighting pit, or a [Roman] earthwork . . . we think . . . a monument with ritualistic or burial undertones', Duxbury, B. & Williams, M. *King Arthur Country in Cornwall*, 1979, 53; 'a medieval date seems more likely', Johnson & Rose, 29; 'this curious earthwork . . . neolithic?'; '*might* be neolithic and for which *comparanda* can certainly be found (distantly) in the neolithic record', Mercer, R., *CA 25*, 1986, 67; Weatherhill, C., 1985, 73; 'mysterious prehistoric monument', Westwood, J. *Gothick Cornwall*, 1992, 32; 'some primitive temple', Williams, M. *Cornish Mysteries*, 1980, 42–4. The best objective accounts of the site are: Lewis, A. L., 1896, 5; Barnatt, J., 1982, 196–7; and Johnson & Rose, 28–9. East Moor: Johnson & Rose, 29.

46 Cornwall, Ireland and Brittany: Christie, P. M. *CA 25*, 1986, 104. Rectangles in Brittany: Burl, 1985, 175; Burl, 1993, 54–5. Breton stone axe: *CA 33*, 1994, 225–6. Ile Béniguet stone circle: Burl, 1993, 54–5.

47 Caerloggas: Miles H. 'Barrows on the St Austell granite', *Cornish Archaeology 14*, 1975, 5–81; the timber ring, 24–58.

48 Pendulum at the Merry Maidens: Lethbridge, T. *The Legend of the Sons of God*, 1973, 21. Tom Lethbridge: Daniel, G. *Ant 46*, 1972, 5–6.

49 Centre stones of Cornish circles: Barnatt, 1982, 67–8; Mercer, R., *CA 25*, 1986, 69.

50 Boskednan and Carn Galva: Barnatt, 1982, 70, fig. 3.4, 165.

51 Trethevy Quoit: Norden, 1597–1604?, 60–1, sketch.

52 Standing stones as landscape markers: Peters, F., *CA 29*, 1990, 33–42.

53 Botallack, St Just: Thom, A., 1967, 65–6; Borlase, W., 1769, 199, plate XVI; Russell, 'Parochial check-list of antiquities. St Just in Penwith', *PCWFC 2*, 1959, 100.

54 Men an Tol. Porthole entrances: Corcoran, 1969, 34; Daniel, 1950, 43–6. Fifth stone: Lukis, 1885a, 17, plate xxxiv. Curative legends: Borlase, W., 1769, 177–8; Michell, 1974, 82–5. Probing: Preston-Jones, A. 'The Men an Tol reconsidered', *CA 32*, 1993, 5–16. Southern moonset: *Meyn Mamvro 26*, 1995, 6–8; *ibid. 29*, 1995–6, 5–7. Natural perforation: Cooke, I. *Mermaid to Merry Maid: a Journey to the Stones*, 1987, 48. Napalm: *Meyn Mamvro 41*, 2000, 3.

55 Graded stones at Land's End. Barnatt, 1982: Boscawen-Un, w, 161; Boskednan, NNW, 165; Merry Maidens, SSW, 156.

56 Two halves of the Celtic year: Frazer, 1922, 33, 634.

57 Pre-Celtic festivals: Ross, 1967, 57,145; Ross, 1972, 181, 200; Burl, 1983, 34–5; Hutton, R., 1991, 176–8; Green, M., 1992, 42, 125, 136, 185–6; King, J. *The Celtic Druids' Year*, 1994, 123–33, 136–40, 169–90, 216–17.

58 Polaris and other stars near the North Pole: Jones, Sir H. S. *General Astronomy*, 1961, 57; Pickering, J. *1001 Questions Answered about Astronomy*, 1960, 178, 296; Thom, A. S., 1995, 175.

CHAPTER TEN

1 Grey Hill circle and cemetery: Bagnall-Oakley, M. E. & W., 16–17; TTB, 1980, 398; Children, G. & Nash, G. *A Guide to Prehistoric Sites in Monmouthshire*, Little Logaston, 1996, 61–3.

2 Excavation of Meini-gwyr: Grimes, 1938.

3 Meini-gwyr: Camden, 1695, 628; Stukeley, 1776b, plate 83, 2nd. Yr Allor: *Archaeology in Wales 27*, 1987, 10–12; *ibid. 32*, 1992, 67, PRN 1000; Barker, C. T. *The Chambered Tombs of South-West Wales*, 1992, 55; *Arch Camb*, 1893, 186–7.

4 Welsh beaker groups and stone circles: Clarke, 1970, 224.

5 Gors Fawr: Grimes, 1963, 145–6; TTB, 396. Astronomy: Bushell, 1911, 319; Thom, A., 1967, W9/2, 101. The outliers: Burl, 1993, 188–9. Fernworthy: Worth, 1967, 222–4; Butler, 1991b, 162–5. Brisworthy, TTB, 108; Butler, 1994, 133–4. The Preselis: Briggs, S., 1986, 9.

6 Preseli 'bluestones' and Stonehenge: Burl, 1984: Thorpe, R. S. et al., 1991, 115–16. Destruction of other circles: *Ant 30*, 1956, 34–6.

7 Prehistoric trackways: Bowen & Gresham, 1967, 56–63; Barber C. & Williams J. G., 143.

8 Fridd Newydd excavations: Crawford, 1920. Beakers: Clarke, 1970, II, 525, 1871F, 1872F.

9 Moel Goedog: Lynch, F. 'Moel Goedog circle 1, a complex ring-cairn near Harlech', *Arch Camb 133*, 1984, 8–50; Barnatt, 1989, II, 387–8.

10 Embanked stone circles and circle-henges: Roese, 1980b, 167.

11 Llandysiliogogo: Bowen, E. G. 'A stone in Llandysiliogogo church, Cards', *Ant 45*, 1971, 213–15. Ysbyty Cynfyn: Grimes, 1963, 127–8. As a fake: Briggs, S., 1979.

12 Nant Tarw's astronomy: Thom, 1967, 101, W11/4.

13 Cerrig Duon. Geometry: Thom, 1966a, fig. 34 'Maen Mawr'. Criticism: Barnatt & Moir, 1984, 209.

14 Avenue at Rhos y Beddau: Burl, 1993, 77; Burl, 1995, 183.

15 Ynys-hir excavation: Dunning, 1943. Leskernick: *PPS 63*, 1997, 157. Banniside Moor: *TCWAAS 10*, 1910, 342–53.

16 Ring-cairns in Wales: Lynch, F., 1972, 64. In Britain and Ireland: Lynch, 1979.

17 Danby Rigg: Elgee, F., 1930, 134.

18 Clun-Clee trackway: Chitty, 1963, 191.

19 Kerry Hill as a compound ring: Thom, A., 1967, 87–8. 'Kerry Pole', W6/1.

20 Cefn Coch as an ellipse: The Rev. Richard Farringdon, 'Snowdonia Druidica', 1769, National Library of Wales, MS 4988; Burl, 1987b, 80–1, frontispiece.

21 The geometrical design of ellipses and the Druids' Circle: Thom, 1967, 78–9.

22 Woodhenge: Cunnington, 1929, 11, 13. Cultoon: MacKie, 1977, 94, 102–4. Nabta: *Nature*, 392, 1998, 488–91.

23 Bryn Gwyn circle: Edward Lhuyd: Camden, 1695, 676; Rowlands, *Mona Antiqua Restaurate*, 1766, 89. The Four-Posters, *ibid.*, 92, fig. 4. The drawing shows the henge of Castell Bryn Gwyn, a cairn, the Bryn Gwyn circle and two Four-Posters, 'four of them standing as I described them, but of the other four . . . there is but one now standing'. Each ring seems to have had either a central stone or pit. Castell Bryn Gwyn henge: Lynch, F., 1991, 102.

24 Bryn Celli Ddu. Excavation of the tomb: Hemp, W. J. 'The chambered cairn of Bryn Celli Ddu', *Arch 80*, 1930, 179–214. Discussion: Lynch, F., 1991, 94–101. Astronomy: Lockyer, 1909, 430–1; Burl, 1985b, 80.

25 Shape of henges: Burl, 1991, 15–16; O'Kelly, M., 1989, 132–7. Stout, G. 'Embanked enclosures of the Boyne region', *PRIA C, 91 (9)*, 1991, 245–84.

26 Penbedw Park: *RCAHM-Flintshire, II*, 1912, 12–13; Davies, E., *The Prehistoric and Roman Remains of Flintshire*, 1949, 89–91; Grimes, 1963, 118–19; TTB, 1980, 374–5, W4/1, 'Penbedw Hall'. Pennant, T., 1784, I, 441.

27 Circle 275 excavation: Griffiths, W., 1960, 317–18.

28 Circle 278 excavation: Griffiths, 1960, 318–22. Urn: Longworth, 1984, 323, no. 2102.

29 Halliwell, J. (ed.) Gwynn, Sir. J. *An Ancient Survey of Pen Marn Mawr*. London, 1859, 24.

30 Druids' Circle excavation: Griffiths, 1960, 31–22, 327–9. Design: Thom, A., 1967, 77, W2/1, 'Penmaen-mawr', 100, May sunrise, Deneb rising. Contrast in plans: Burl, 1976, 270.

31 Perforated whetstones: Davies, E. *The Prehistoric and Roman Remains of Flintshire*, 1949, 124, 450, 452.

32 Bryn Cader Faner: Lynch, 1979, 2, 5.

33 Child-burials and sacrifices: Lynch, F., 1972, 72. On Anglesey, *ibid.*, 1991, In Bronze Age Ireland: Waddell, 1970, 98; *ibid.*, 1990, 20.

CHAPTER ELEVEN

1 Entrance alignment at the Girdle Stanes: Burl, 1995, 121–3.

2 The Girdle Stanes: Burl, 1995, 121–3; Hyslop, J. & Hyslop, R. *Langholm As It Was*, Sunderland, 1912, 26–38.

3 Group VI axes in south-west Scotland: Ritchie, R. & Scott, J. G. in Clough & Cummins, 1988, 87, table 32. In vicinity of the Twelve Apostles: Williams, J., 1970.

4 Destruction of the Carasalloch ring: *NSA Dumfriess*, 1845, 559.

5 Maponus and the Lochmaban Stane: Ross, 1967, 458, 463.

6 Whitestanes Muir: Scott-Elliott, J. & Rae, I., 'The small cairn fields of Dumfriesshire', *TGDNHAS 44*, 1967, 108–11.

7   Wildshaw Burn: *CA 124*, 1991, 149; *D & E Scotland*, 1993, 89; *ibid.*, 1995, 87.

8   Cultoon: MacKie, 1977, 44–5, 92–5. Chambered tombs: Henshall, 1972, 431–6.

9   Temple Wood: Scott, J. G., 1989.

10 Distribution of Group VI and IX axes: Ritchie, P. R. & Scott, J. G. in Clough and Cummins, 1988, 85–91. On the mainland: Group VI – Argyll, 5; Ayr, 18; Dumfriess, 25; Kirkcudbright, 19; Wigtownshire, 67 (total, 134). Group IX – 7, 2, 0, 3 (12). On islands: Group VI – Arran, 8; Islay, 0; Inverness/Skye, 1; Uist/Lewis, 0; Orkney/Shetland, (total, 10). Group IX – 6, 4, 5, 3, 2 (total, 20).

11 Sea-route: Scott, Sir L., 1951, 22.

12 Corryvrechan. Orwell; Somerville, C. *The Other British Isles*, London, 1990. Winter gales: Tizard, 1909, 254, 262ff. Small craft: Thom, 1971, 10.

13 Alcohol on Rum: *Soc. Botan. Edinburgh Newsletter 49*, 1989.

14 Long distance travel: Scott, L., 1951, 32; Müller, J., *The Chambered Cairns of the Northern and Western Isles*, Edinburgh, 1988, 35.

15 Parish boundaries on South Uist: Pearson, M. P. *British Archaeology 12*, 1996, 7.

16 Early settlement: Piggott, 1956, 231. Fertile soils: Henshall, 1972, 117.

17 Pottery sequence: Müller, J. *The Chambered Tombs of the Northern and Western Isles*, Edinburgh, 1988, 24. Eilean Domhnuill: Armit, 1996, 43–52; Eilean an Tighe: Scott, L., *PSAS 85*, 1951, 1–37. Shulishader: Armit, 1996, 61, 238; as a votive deposit: Sheridan, A., in: Sharples & Sheridan, 1992, 198–201.

18 Group IX axes on Lewis: Armit, 1996, 61.

19 Calanais: Burl, A. 'Calanais meets the old tea-shoppe', *British Archaeology 17*, 1996, 14.

20 Astronomers and Callanish: Martin, 1716, 9; wrecked observatory, Somerville, 1913, 93; computer, Hawkins, 1966a, 186; burial, Daniel, 1962, 72; lunar and stellar site, Thom, 1967, 122, with refined alignments, *ibid.*, 1971, 68. Chambered tomb, Henshall, 1972, 138. Documentation: Ponting, G. & M., 1979. Excavation: Ashmore, 1995.

21 Source of the stones: Ashmore, 1995, 18.

22 Orkney-Cromarty type tomb: Davidson, J. L. & Henshall, A. S., *The Chambered Cairns of Orkney*, Edinburgh, 1989, 177–80.

23 'High-and-low' double rows in Ireland: Burl, 1993, 61.

24 Astronomical deductions: Toland, 1726, 122–3; Somerville, 1912, 24–37; Hawkins, 1966a, 185; Thom, 1966, 48; 1967, 122; 1971, 68.

25 Toland, Diodorus Siculus and Callanish: Toland, 1726, 188–91.

26 Pytheas of Marseilles, Greek navigator and explorer. Was commissioned to establish a sea-route to tin and amber supplies of northern Europe. Sailed past Spain, Gaul and to Britain. First to use that name. Circumnavigated the island, recording its sides in the correct proportions of 3, 6, 8. He may also have reached Norway. The date of his voyage is variously quoted as *c.* 330 BC, 310–16 BC and 240–38 BC. Carpenter, R. *Beyond the Pillars of Hercules*, 1973, 205; Cary, M. & Warmington, E. H. *The Ancient Explorers*, 1963, 48; Casson, L. *The Ancient Mariners*, Princeton, 124–6.

27 Stonehenge as a solar temple: Burl, 1987a, 140.

28 Alexander Thom and Callanish: Thom, A. S. *Walking in All The Squares. A Biography of Alexander Thom*, Glendaruel, 1995, 175.

29 The Pleiades: Frazer, Sir J. G. *Spirits of the Corn and Wild, V, I*, 1912, 122.

30 Assays for Callanish: Ashmore, 1999. Short stone chronology: Burl, 1993, 23, 152–80. Peat forming at Callanish: Bohncke, S. J. P. in Birks, H. H. (eds) *The Cultural Landscape – Past, Present and Future*, 1988, 460–1.

31 Legends at Callanish: Swire, 1966, 20.

32 Henges and water: Atkinson, Piggott & Sandars, 1951, 84.

33 Maltese temple-builders: Cles-Reden, 1961, 74.

34 Caithness chambered tombs: Davidson, J. L. & Henshall, A. S. *The Chambered Cairns of Caithness*, Edinburgh, 1991.

35 Clachtoll: Welsh, 1971.

36 Learable Hill: Myatt, 1988a, 301–3; Burl, 1993, 129–31.

37 Rows in Caithness and Sutherland: Myatt, 1988a, 277–318. In sets of three: Burl, 1993, 123–31.

38 Latheronwheel: Gunn, 1915, 343.

39 Breton *fer-aux-chevaux*: Burl, 1993, 153; Burl, 1995, 297–9.

40 The Camster cairns: Davidson & Henshall, *The Chambered Cairns of Caithness*, 89. Achavanich: Thom, Thom & Burl, 1990, 288–9.

41 Freswick Bay: *AA Book of the Seaside*, 1972, 284–5. St John's Point: Tizard, 1909, 321–9.

42 Chambered tombs on Orkney and the surrounding islands: Davidson, J. L. & Henshall, A. S. *The Chambered Cairns of Orkney*, 1989.

43 Stenness as an ellipse: Curtis, G. R. 'Geometry and astronomy of the Stones of Stenness, Orkney' in Ritchie, J. N. G., 1976, 48–9.

44 Stones of Brodgar and Stenness: Ritchie, J. N. G., 1976.

45 Alignments at Brodgar: Thom & Thom, 1973.

46 Calculations of work-forces: Ralston, I. B. M., 'Estimate of the effort involved in the construction of the Stones of Stenness, Orkney' in Ritchie, 1976, 50–2.

47 Radiocarbon assays from Stenness: Ritchie, 1976, 21.

48 The Barnhouse pillar: Spence, M. *Standing Stones and Maeshowe of Stenness*, Paisley, 1894, 12.

49 Dogs, Lascaux: Daniel, G. *Lascaux and Carnac*, London, 1955, 70. Thame: Jessup, R. *Curiosities of British Archaeology*, London, 1961, 145. Barnhouse settlement: Pearson, M. P., 1993, 55.9.

50 An élite at Skara Brae: MacKie, 1977b, 202.

51 Claims that the hearth-sides were aligned on the mid-summer and midwinter sunrises and sunsets because 'Orkney is the only place in the British Isles where these four directions are perpendicular to each other', Pearson, M. P., 1993, 59, are mistaken. Latitude 55°, 300 miles to the south, on a line from Newcastle at the east to the Aran Islands on the west is the correct candidate with risings and settings of about 45°, 135°, 225° and 315°.

52 Temples of the sun, moon, and the Comet Stone: Toland, 1726, 124; Marwick, E. *The Folklore of Orkney and Shetland*, 1975, 61–2.

53 Odin's Stone: Marwick, E., 1976, 34; Pearson M. P., 1993, 59. Dancing by moonlight: *RCAHM-Orkney, II*, 1946, 50–1.

54 The axe as a cult object: Stone and Wallis, 1951, 135.

CHAPTER TWELVE

1   Hector Boece, *History of Scotland*, 1527. Quoted in Allcroft, 1927, 146–7.

2   *NSA 12, Aberdeen*, 1845, 115.

3   Neil Sharples, priv. comm., 22 June 1996.

4   Newgrange: O'Kelly, M., 1982. Knowth and its satellites: Eogan, 1986.

5   Group IX axes from Loch Lomond to Banff: Dumbarton and Stirling, 5 axes; Perthshire, 5 axes; Grampians, 16 in Aberdeen, 4 in Banff and Moray, 1 in Angus; Ritchie, P. R. & Scott, J. G. in Clough & Cummins, 1988, table 32, 87.

6 Neolithic presence: Shepherd, 1987, 123–5.
7 Coles, F., 1903, 123.
8 Berrybrae: Burl, 1976b, 25–31. N3 beaker: Clarke, D. L., I, 196.
9 Well-drained soils: Glentworth and Muir, 1963, 142. For the situations of RSCs in relation to the soils see O'Dell, A. C. & Walton, K. *The Highlands and Islands of Scotland*, London, 1962, 53–4, fig. 20. Auchqhorthies: Aubrey, 1665, 183. Hut-circles: *D & E*, 1989, 20–1.
10 Horizontal recumbent stones: Burl, 1976b, 31–2.
11 'Keeling': Kilbride-Jones, 1934.
12 Aikey Brae: Stuart, 1856, xxii. 'Fun': *Curr Arch 125*, 1991, 238.
13 Nether Balfour: Wilson, D., 1863, 160.
14 RSCs and the megalithic yard: Thom, 1967, 136–7, B1/1–B4/4. The formula for calculating the perimeter of an ellipse: *ibid.*, 31.
15 Cork-Kerry RSCs: Fahy, 1962, 67.
16 Easter Aquorthies: Lynch, F. 'Colour in prehistoric architecture' in Gibson & Simpson (eds), 1998, 62–7. Red stones in the Clava passage-tombs: *Curr Arch 148*, 1996, 142. Quartz and the moon: Burl, 1976b, 37.
17 Early astronomical investigators: Lewis, A. L., 1888; Lockyer, 1909, 378–411; Browne, G. F., 1921, chapters 4, 13; Thom, 1967, 98, B1/8–B2/5.
18 RSCs and the moon: Burl, 1980a. Azimuths: Ruggles, 1984, S68, table 3. To the midpoint of the recumbent from a line perpendicular to it.
19 Boece and the moon: Allcroft, 1927, 147.
20 Perpendicular line to the recumbent: Ruggles, 1984, S64.
21 Cupmarked stones and astronomy: Ruggles and Burl, 1985, S54–S56. Hill of Avochie: *PSAS 37*, 1903, 228; *ibid. 40*, 1906, 318–20.
22 Rectangles at: Stenness, Ritchie, J. N. G., 1974a; at the Sands of Forvie, Aberdeenshire, Kirk, 1953, 158; at Mount Pleasant, Dorset, Wainwright, 1970c; and at Balbirnie, Fife, Ritchie, J. N. G., 1974b, 9.
23 Letter from James Garden to John Aubrey, 15 June 1692: Aubrey, 1693, 187. Cothiemuir Muir and Keig church: information Lord Forbes, 15 May 1984.
24 Cullerlie: Kilbride-Jones, 1935, 219.
25 Four-Posters: Burl, 1998a.
26 Broomend of Crichie. Excavation: Dalrymple, 1884. Battle-axe: Roe, 1966, 241.
27 Possible RSC at Broomend: Maitland, 1757, 154; Burl, 1981a, 183. James Garden's letter to John Aubrey, 6 March 1693: Aubrey, 1693, 208.
28 Old Parks, Kirkoswald: Ferguson, 1895.
29 Innesmill. The minister: *NSA XIII*, 1845. Coles, 1906, 198–201.
30 Inverness ring-cairns: Henshall, I, 358–86.
31 Kincardineshire ring-cairns: Henshall, I, 400–2.
32 Raigmore: Simpson, D. D. A., 1996, 82. Boghead: *PSAS 114*, 1984, 35–73.
33 Henshall, I, 120.
34 Ring-cairns in northern Britain: Henshall, II, 270; Kenworthy, 1972; Ritchie & MacLaren, 1972; Burl, 1972.
35 Excavations of Clava cairns: Piggott, 1956.
36 Beauly tombs: Childe, V. G., 1940, 74–5; Henshall, II, 271. Dates for Clava cairns: *Curr Arch 161*, 1999, 184.
37 Samuel Johnson: Rogers, P. (ed.) *Johnson and Boswell in Scotland*, London, 1993, 70–2. Kinchyle of Dores' cremation: Henshall, I, 381.
38 Culdoich: *D & E Scotland*, 1982, 14. Frenish: Swire, 1963, 29–31.
39 Delfour and midwinter sunset: Thom, 1967, 87, fig. 7.4, 98, B7/10.

40 Shapes of Clava ring-cairns: Thom, 1967, 137, B6/1–B7/19; Thom, Thom & Burl, 1980, 242–73.
41 Corrimony excavation section: Piggott, 1956, 178, A–B. Balnuaran of Clava: Bradley, 1996. Avielochan: Henshall, I, 360.
42 Cupmarks at Balnuaran and Tordarroch: Henshall, I, 364, 385.
43 Clava astronomy: Burl, 1981d, 257–65; Scott, D., 'An astronomical assessment of the Clava cairns', unpublished report, 1980?
44 Orkney-Cromarty azimuths: Burl, 1981d, 266.
45 Thom and Clava passage-tombs: Thom, 1966a, 18. Alignments for the dead: Burl, 1981d, 262.
46 Corrimony: Piggott, 1956, 174–84. Kerveresse: *Locmariaquer: Aperçu de la Pensée Mégalithique dans le Golfe du Morbihan*, Fontenay-le-Fleury, 1981, 74, no. 19.
47 Balnuaran of Clava sw: Henshall, I, 364–6; Bradley, 1996; Somerville, 1923, 217–22.
48 Sir Thomas Browne *Hydriotaphia or Urn-Burial*, 1658; Everyman, London, 1937, 92.
49 Clava kerb-cairn: Piggott, 1956, 192.
50 Carmahome: *PSAS 59*, 1924–5, 253–4; Henshall, II, 393–4.

CHAPTER THIRTEEN

1 Four-Posters: Burl, 1988a, 10.
2 Coles, F., 1908, 107.
3 Lundin Farm: Stewart, M.E.C., 1966b. Glenballoch: ApSimon, 1969, 40. Lyles Hill: Evans, E., 1953, 18, 48.
4 Fortingall: Coles, F., 1908, 121–5; Burl, 1988a, 166–75.
5 Moncreiffe: Stewart, M.E.C., 1985.
6 Shian Bank astronomy: Thom, 1966a, 15, fig. 26.
7 Sandy Road, Scone: Stewart, M.E.C., 1966a. Multiple rings: Burl, 1998.
8 Fowlis Wester: Young, Lacaille et al., 177; Thom, 1971, 54.
9 Monzie: excavation, Mitchell and Young, 1939; art: Allen, J. R., 1882, 89–92; Galician art: Simpson, D.D.A. & Thawley, J., 1972, 86.
10 Ruggles, 1988b, 243.
11 Croft Moraig: excavation, Piggott & Simpson, 1971. Breton 'horseshoes': Burl, 1997.
12 Glen Lyon and Brittany: Ross, A., 1970, 66.
13 Bleasdale: Dawkins, 1900; Varley, 1938. For a review of timber circles, see Gibson, A., 1994.
14 Prehistoric routeways: Scott, Sir L., 1951, 35; Stewart, M.E.C., 1959.
15 Bargrennan and Clyde chambered tombs: Henshall, 1972.
16 Bloak Moss: Turner, J., 1965, 1970; Simmons & Dooley, 1981, 234. The Four Stones, Dunlop: Burl, 1988a, 122.
17 Longstone Rath: *PRIA 30*, 1913, 351–60.
18 Non-central stones: Thom, 1967, 62.
19 Cauldside Burn carving: Morris, R.W.B., 1979, 79, 'Cambret Moor', GAL32. Pass through the hills: Bradley, 1997, 100.
20 Galician art: Morris, R.W.B., 1989, 45–80.
21 Carved stones and proximity to copper sources: Morris, R.W.B., 1979, 16–17.
22 The Thieves: Thom, 1967, 68, 124, fig. 6.12. Embanked stone circle: Barnatt, 1989, II, 339.
23 Pairs of standing stones: Burl, 1993, 181–202.
24 Park of Tongland: Coles, F., 1905, 305–6; Burl, 1988a, 136–7; McCullagh, R.P.J. *PPS 58*, 1992, 312–21.
25 Torhousekie: Burl, 1974b.
26 Settlement sites: Barnatt & Pierpoint, 1983, 102.
27 Machrie Moor excavations: Bryce, J., 1862.
28 Shapes of rings on Machrie Moor: Roy, McGrail and Carmichael, 1963.

29 Haggarty, 1991.
30 Arran tombs: Henshall, II, 368–96. Monamore, *PSAS 97*, 1963–4, 1–34.
31 Excavation of Site I: Haggarty, 1991, 60–4, 70–3.
32 Site XI: MacKie, 1975, 127. Excavation: Haggarty, 1991, 64–5, 73–6.
33 Five-Stone circles: O'Nuallain, 1984a, 30–45; 1995, 36.
34 Colours in cairns: Charlton Marshall: Grinsell, 1959, 99. Huish Champflower, Grinsell *Somerset Barrows*, *I*, 1969, 34. Saintoft: Atkinson, J. C. *Forty Years in a Moorland Parish*, 1891, 148. Wapley Moor: Elgee, F., 1930, 91. Arran: Jones, A. 'On the earth-colours of Neolithic death', *British Archaeology 22*, 1997, 6.
35 Auchagallon: Bryce, T. H., 1910, 119.
36 Midsummer sunrise: Barnatt & Pierpoint, 111–12.
37 Clyde tombs and territories on Arran: Renfrew, 1973b, 134.
38 Blackwaterfoot cairn: *PSAS 36*, 1901–2, 117–20. Collessie cairn: *PSAS 12*, 1876–7, 439–47. Goldwork: Taylor, J., 1980, 23.

CHAPTER FOURTEEN

1 Copper resources: Herity, 1970.
2 Copper mines: O'Brien in Twohig & Ronayne, 85–92. Also O'Brien, W., 1994; 1996. Ross Island: *British Archaeology 36*, 1998, 8–9. Dates for Mount Gabriel: Burl, 1993, 166–7.
3 British axes in Ireland: Mandal and Cooney, *JAI 7*, 1996, 43, 51, 53. A network of contacts: O'Brien, W., 1994, 229–51. See also Waddell, J. 'The Irish Sea in prehistory', *JAI 6*, 1991–2, 35.
4 *Sépultures en V*: Helgouac'h, 1966, 189–95. Dates for Liscuis: Hibbs, 1984, 322–3. Dates for Labbacallee and Toormore: Twohig & Ronayne, 72, 74.
5 Somerville, 1909, 105, wrote of recumbent stone circles in Ireland. O'Nuallain, 1975, rejected the term in favour of 'multiple-stone circles'.
6 Numbers of stone circles: Walsh, P. *Arch Irel 11(3)*, 1997, 11.
7 Shapes of Irish stone circles: Patrick and Wallace, 1982, 250, 259.
8 Fertility symbolism at Avebury: Smith, I. F., 1965, 197. In Ireland: Hicks, R., 'The year at Drombeg', 2nd Oxford Archaeoastronomical Conference, Merida, Yucatan, Mexico, 16 January 1986.
9 Case, *Ant 44*, 1970, 105–14. 109.
10 Quartz at Knocknakilla: Gogan, 1931.
11 Cashelkeelty circles: Lynch, A., 1982a, 65–9.
12 Dates for Cork and Kerry stone circles: Twohig & Ronayne, 72, 74.
13 Paired stones outside Irish stone circles: Burl, 1993, 260–2.
14 Irish Four-Posters: O'Nuallain, 1984b, 63–71. Barratrough: Gosling, 1991, 18, no. 63.
15 Kealkil: O'Riordain, S., 1939. The axial stone: O'Nuallain, 1984a, 41–2, no. 81.
16 Declinations of Cork-Kerry circles: Barber, J., 1973. Criticisms: Freeman, P. R. & Elmore, W. 'A test for the significance of astronomical alignments', *Archaeoastronomy 1*, 1979, S90–S93. Patrick, J. & Freeman, P. R. 'Revised surveys of Cork-Kerry stone circles', *Archaeoastronomy 5*, 1983, S50–S56.
17 Orientations of wedge-tombs: de Valera & O'Nuallain, 1982, fig. 36.
18 Barber, 1972, 67.
19 Boulder-cists: O'Nuallain, 1978; Walsh, P., 'In circle and row: Bronze Age ceremonial monuments', in Twohig & Ronayne, 112–13.
20 Masonbrook: Macalister, 1917. Meenanare: Cuppage, 1986, 36, no. 46; Toal, 1995, 50, no. 32.

21 Cong: Lohan, M., 1993; Fahy, J. A. *The Glory of Cong*, Cong, 1986; Wilde, W. 'On the Battle of Moytura', *PRIA 9*, 1866, 546–50.
22 Timoney: *PPS 3*, 1937, 363; Stout, G. T. *Archaeological Survey of the Barony of Ikerrin*, 1984, 17–19 'Cullaun 4'.
23 O'Kelly, M. J. & C. *Illustrated Guide to Lough Gur, Co. Limerick*, Ardnaire, 1978.
24 Beakers: Clarke, D. L. 1970, 569, 94. Later Bronze Age ware: Cleary, R. in Twohig & Ronayne, 114–20; Cooney & Grogan, 1994, 49–50, 168–70.
25 Grange and Balnuaran of Clava: Henshall, 1972, 275.
26 Somerville and astronomy: Windle, 1912, 287.
27 John Wesley: *Gent's Mag. Archaeology, II*, 1886, 119.
28 Grooved ware relationships: Henshall, 1972, 286.
29 Monlen: Aubrey, 1693, 226. Crom Cruaich: Burl, 1995, 211.
30 Newgrange, Grange and the sun: Hicks, R. E., 1975, 195.
31 Lunar calendars: Brennan, 1983, 135–57.
32 Anstis: O'Riordain & Daniel, 1964, 37, 78–9. The sketches are in the British Museum, Stowe MS 1024.
33 1954 excavation: O'Riordain & O'Leochaidhe, 1956.
34 Search for stoneholes: O'Kelly, M., 1982, 80–2; O'Kelly, C., 1982, 96.
35 Geometrical shape of the ring: Thom in MacKie, 1977a, 72. Doubts: O'Kelly, C., 1978, 97–8.
36 Dates for the pit-circle: Sweetman, 1985, 218.
37 Relationship between the pit- and stone circle: Sweetman, 1985, 208, 216.

CHAPTER FIFTEEN

1 C. Fox, 1933, 82.
2 A corpus of known timber circles is given in Gibson, 1998, 123–44.
3 Shamans, drugs and trances. Devereux, P. *Shamanism and the Mystery Lines*, Slough, 1992. In particular, see Pt II (6), 'Trance, dance and magic plants', 136–70.
4 Deposition of grooved ware sherds: Mercer, 1981, 96.
5 Diameters of Balfarg's stone circles: Atkinson, 1952, 58; Mercer, 1981, 70–2, 114–15; Barnatt, 1989, II, 311.
6 Loveday, R., 'Double entrance henges – routes to the past?' Unpublished paper, 1996.
7 Midsummer sunset at Balfarg: latitude, 56°.2; azimuth, 310°; horizon 3°.8; declination, +24°.3.
8 Cairnpapple. Stone- or postholes? Piggott, 1948, 83–6; Mercer, 1981, 155; Barnatt, 1989, II, 329.
9 The grave: Piggott, 1948, 115.
10 Coupland: Atkinson, R.J.C., 1952, 64.
11 Wooden mask: Piggott, 1948, 115.
12 Burials and Clava cairns: Ritchie & MacLaren, 10.
13 Nemeton: Piggott, 1948, 118.
14 Bateman, T., 1848, 109.
15 Excavation of the Stripple Stones: St G. Gray, 1908; of Avebury: St G. Gray, 1935. Limited funds: *ibid.*, 105.
16 Cove and burial at Arbor Low: St G. Gray, 1903, 480.
17 Ritual deposit: Gray, 1903, 470.
18 Flint knife: Jewitt, 1870, 117–18; Evans, J., 1897, 352.
19 Dates for beaker pottery: Burgess, 1980, 62–76.
20 Gib Hill: Bateman, 1848, 31.
21 Dating the Devil's Quoits: Barclay, A., Gray, M. and Lambrick, G., 1995, 45–6.
22 *Oxon 29–30*, 1964–5, 'Discussion'.
23 Mount Pleasant's rectangle: Wainwright, 1970c, 323.
24 Newbridge: Daniel, G., in: Piggott, 1962a, 69; *OSA Midlothian*, 1794, 69; Coles, F. R., 1903, 201–4; Baldwin, J. R., 161, no. 97. The Thoms kindly sent the author a copy of their surveys and the amended dimensions are calculated from it. Their site G9/14.

25 Lundin Links: Thom, A., 1971, 55–6, 76, P4/1. As a Four-Poster: Burl, 1988a, 126–7.
26 Coupland as a cattle compound: *Nature 387*, 1997, 553–4; Waddington, C. *Land of Legend*, 1997.
27 Milfield henges: Harding, A., 1981, 131.
28 The Neolithic in south-eastern Scotland: Ritchie, J. N. G. and A., 1972, 19.
29 Beckensall, 1983, 131–46; 1986, 10.
30 Kingside Hill: Baldwin, J. R., 1985, 163.
31 The length of the Rudston pillar: *Arch 5*, 1779, 95–7.
32 Rudston, cursuses and beakers: D. P. Dymond, 1966, 92.
33 St Asaph's standing stone: Swire, 1966, 205.
34 Hayman Rooke: Marsden, B. M. *The Early Barrow Diggers*, Princes Risborough, 1974, 33–4; Marsden, B. M. *Pioneers of Prehistory*, Ormskirk, 1984, 13. Stanton Moor: *Arch 8*, 1787, 209–17.
35 Stone axes: Moore & Cummins, 1974, 74.
36 The Peak District as a central region: Clarke, D. L., 1970, 216.
37 Forest clearance: Hicks, S. P., 1972, 17.
38 Cremation cemeteries: Bu'lock, 1961, 3; Varley, *Cheshire before the Romans*, 1964, 53; Burgess, 1974, 189.
39 Ninestone Close and the moon: Barnatt, 1978, 157–8.
40 Urns in Derbyshire: Longworth, 1984, 171–80. Battle-axes: Roe, F. E. S. in Clough & Cummins, 1979, 41–2. Stanton Moor: Bateman, T., 1848, 116.
41 Camden, 1695, 254.
42 Stukeley, 1743, 10.
43 Harding and Lee, 1987: Barford, 287; Condicote, 154; Deadman's Burial, 238; Devil's Quoits, 239; Hampton Lucy, 426; Westwell, 259.
44 Archdruid's barrow: Stukeley, 1743, 12. Natural mound: Ravenhill, 1932, 17.
45 Capella: Thom, 1967, 100, S6/1.
46 J. Hawkes, *A Guide to the Prehistoric and Roman Monuments in England and Wales*, London, 1973, 186.
47 Folk-stories: A. J. Evans, 1895; Grinsell, 1977.
48 The Rollright witch: Burl, 1999, 12–23.
49 Aubrey, 1693, 72.
50 Excavations and C-14 assays: Lambrick, 1988, 72, 75, 79, 110.
51 Radiocarbon dates from the Devil's Quoits: Barclay, A. et al., 46.
52 Corpus Christi College: Ravenhill, 1932, 2–3.

CHAPTER SIXTEEN

1 Little Mayne: Lukis, 1883, 28. Piggott on Gale: Piggott, S. and C. M., 1939, 140, 148–50.
2 Rempstone's 'avenue': *PDNHAS 81*, 1959, 114–16; Knight, P., 1996, 94.
3 Tisbury: Hoare, 1812, 251.
4 Broadstones, Clatford. Aubrey, 1693, 50. Rev. Robert Gay, author of *A Foole's Bolt*, c. 1665, in Legg, R., 1986, 26. Stukeley, 1776a, 140, *WAM 52*, 1948, 390.
5 Broome: Aubrey, 1693, 106–7; *WAM 23*, 1887, 115–16.
6 The Sanctuary: Aubrey, 1665, 50, 55; Stukeley, 1743, 31; Piggott, 1985, 32, plate 12. Its excavation: Cunnington, 1931.
7 The sequence of construction at the Sanctuary: Piggott, 1940; Musson, 1971; Lees 1999. Measurements at the Sanctuary: Cunnington, 1931, 304; Thom, Thom & Burl, 1980, 125. Rebuilding: Musson, 1971, 368. Finds: Pollard, *PPS 58*, 1992, 221–2.
8 Radiocarbon assays from Windmill Hill: *OJA 12 (1)*, 1993, 333. Windmill Hill: human bones, Smith, I. F., 1965, 100.
9 Archaeoastronomy at the Sanctuary: south-west stone, azimuth 215°, latitude 51°.4, declination −30°7.
10 Sanctuary skeleton: *British Archaeology 48*, 1999, 4. Numbers of postholes: Musson, 1971, 375.
11 West Kennet triangle: Atkinson, in, Piggott, 1962b, 15. Parc le Breos: Atkinson, R. J. C., 1961, 296. Fussell's Lodge: Ashbee, 1966, 36. Removal of bones from West Kennet: Wells, in Piggott, 1962b, 81. Bones at Windmill Hill: Smith, I. F., 1965, 137.
12 Mortuary enclosures: Stukeley, 1723. Bodleian Library, Oxford, Gough Maps, 231, f.10ʳ.
13 Dr Toope: Aubrey, 1693, 52–4.
14 'Ill-shapen' Avebury: Aubrey, 1670, 319.
15 Aubrey, 1693, 39. See also Camden, 1695, 111.
16 'Herepath': Burl, 1979, 31.
17 Destruction: Aubrey, 1693, 38; Stukeley, Bodleian Library, Oxford, Gough Maps, 231, f.25ᵛ; Stukeley, 1743, 15–16, 31, 36.
18 Excavations at Avebury: St G. Gray, 1935; Keiller and Piggott, 1939: Smith, I. F., 1965.
19 Open settlement: Burl, 1979, 114, 143; Evans, J. G., 1971, 268. Ring of tombs: Burl, 1979, 76; Woodward and Woodward, 279–81.
20 Coves: Avebury: Burl, 1988c, 12; Beckhampton: *ibid.*, 14; Kennet: Aubrey, 1693, II, 822–3; Stukeley, Bodleian Library, Oxford, Gough Maps, 231, 236, cf. 5; Stukeley, 1743, 36, Tab. XIX, 42, Tab. XXII. Resistivity survey: Ucko et al., 1991, 193.
21 Occupation/ritual area: Smith, I. F., 1965, 210–16. Radiocarbon assays: Whittle, 1993, 33. Clay-lined holes: Burl, 1979, 189–90.
22 Symbolic forecourt: Smith, I. F., 1965, 250.
23 Holed stones and sacrifices: Stukeley, 1743, 25; Borlase, W., 1769, 179.
24 No inner concentric circle: Ucko et al., 1991, 222–6.
25 Megalithic horseshoe: Aubrey, 1693, 44; Ucko et al., 227; Burl, 1992.
26 Roofed timber building: Ucko et al., 1991, 227, Plate 69A; Burl, 1979a, 179; Bradley, *Times Higher Education Supplement*, 15 June 1991, 22.
27 Third circle at Avebury: Keiller, A. 'Avebury. Summary of excavations, 1937 and 1938', *Ant 13*, 1939, 227.
28 Multiple stone circles in south-western England: Burl, 1998.
29 Smith, I. F., 1965, 204.
30 Transportation of sarsens: Browne, B. S. 'Neolithic engineering', *Ant 37*, 1963, 140–4. See also Mohen, J. *The World of Megaliths*, 1989, 168–82.
31 Smith, I. F., 1965, 221; Clay: Clare, T., 1978, 10–13.
32 Burl, 1992.
33 Brentnall, H. C. 'The Saxon bounds of Overton', *Marlborough College NHS*, 1938, 116–36.
34 Beckhampton Avenue: Aubrey, 1693, 38; Stukeley, 1743, 23.
35 Twining, Rev. T. *Avebury in Wiltshire, a Roman Work . . .*, 1723.
36 Stukeley's questions: Stukeley, 1743, 36, 43.
37 Beckhampton: Stukeley, 1723, 97; Ucko et al., 195–9; *3ʳᵈ Stone 36*, 1999, 4. *WAM 93*, 2000, 1–8.
38 The Kennet Avenue: Aubrey, 1693, 37; Keiller & Piggott, *Ant 10*, 1939, 417–27; Thom & Thom, *JHA 7*, 1976, 193–7.
39 Deposits in the avenue: Burl, 1993, 45–7.
40 Fleming, A. 'Territorial patterns in Bronze Age Wessex', *PPS 37*, 1971, 138–66 Smith, R. W. 'The ecology of Neolithic farming systems as exemplified by the Avebury region of Wiltshire', *PPS 50*, 1984, 99–120.
41 Axe-cults: Stone & Wallis, *PPS 17*, 1951, 99–188. 134; Burl, 1979a, 100.
42 Human bones in Avebury's ditch: Gray, 1935, 148.
43 The female dwarf: Gray, 1935, 145–7; Burl, 1979a, 226–7; Frazer, Sir J. G. *Spirits of the Corn and Wild, I*, 1912, 242.

44 Abandonment of Avebury: Burl, 1979a, 242–4. Contrasts between cemeteries on the Marlborough Downs and Salisbury Plain: Woodward & Woodward, 1996 – Avebury, 279–81; Stonehenge, 281–7.
45 Stukeley, 1743, 101.

CHAPTER SEVENTEEN

1 Odilienberg: Kendrick, 1927; Piggott, 1968,71. La Cuvelée du Diable: de Laet, 1958, 111.
2 Lindholm Hoj: Munksgard, E. *Denmark: an Archaeological Guide*, London, 1970, 79–80; Dyer, J. *Discovering Archaeology in Denmark*, Princes Risborough, 1972, 50; Balfour, M. *Megalithic Mysteries*, London, 1992, 7, 'Norresundby'.
3 Le Planas: Burl, 1995, 262.
4 Sainte Geneviève: *Ant 47*, 1973, 292–3; *Ant 48*, 1974, 134–6.
5 Ile Beniguet. Pontois, 1929, 126. 'The Spanish Ladies': *Early Ballads Illustrative of History, Traditions and Customs and Ballads and Songs of the Peasantry of England*, London, 1877, 454–5. Of unknown date. In his novel, *Poor Jack*, of 1840 Marryat speaks of the song being very old.
6 Ville-ès-Nouaux. Burl, 1995, 187, 189; Johnston, D. E. *The Channel Islands. An Archaeological Guide*, Chichester, 1981, 75–7.
7 Château-Bû. Burl, 1988a, 39–40. Unknown elsewhere: Giot, 1960, 37.
8 Carnac Mounds. Giot, 1960, 109–14; Giot et al., 1979a, 218–25; Patton, M., 1993, 106–13.
9 Dagger-graves and artefacts: Burl, 1999, 156–8.
10 Extensions to avenues: Burl, 1993, 134–42. Burning: Burl, 1993, 136, 138, 143–4.
11 Crucuno: Thom, Merritt & Merritt, 1973.
12 Gaillard: Giot et al., 1979a, 19. Prehistoric astronomy: Gaillard, F. 'L'astronomie préhistorique', *Les Sciences Populaires*, 1890.
13 Doubts: eighteenth-century folly: Daniel, G. *Ant 49*, 1975, 81. Pre-restoration: Giot, 1960, 120.
14 Dryden & Lukis. Plans: Giot et al., 1979a, 19.
15 Crucuno, 1800 BC: Thom, Merritt & Merritt, 1973, 450.
16 Symbolic observatories: Crucuno: *ibid.*, 451; Castlerigg, Thom, A., 1971, 12.
17 Sitwell, W., 1930, 96–7.
18 Lhuyd's recognition of a stone on Newgrange: O'Riordain & Daniel, 1964, 31; O'Kelly, M., 1972, 26, 27. Plan of Kercado: l'Helgouach, 1964, 28.
19 Ménec avenue and rows: Burl, 1993, 134–40. Plans: Thom & Thom, 1977. East, 14, West, 11.
20 Festivals: Worsfold, 21–2.
21 Horseshoes around Ménec East: Kermario West, Lukis, 1875, 19, Miln, 1881, 3; Kermario East, Giot, 1960, 123; Kerlescan South, Burl, 1993, 140–3; Kerlescan North, Thom & Thom, 1978, 96; Er-Lannic, Gouezin, P. *Le Site Mégalithique d'Er Lannic*, 1998; Champ de la Croix, Thom & Thom, 1978, 119; Vieux-Moulin, Giot, 1960, 123–4; Sainte-Barbe, Lukis, 1875, 26; Kerzerho, Burl, 1995, 259–60; Saint-Pierre-Quiberon, Thom & Thom 1977, 7; Kergonan, Minot, 26–8.
22 Plan of Er-Lannic: le Rouzic, 1930, 4; Gouezin, *Le Site Mégalithique d'Er Lannic*, 6–7.
23 Group X products in England: Clough & Cummins, 1988, 17, 19, 25, 50–1.
24 Art at Er-Lannic: Péquart & Le Rouzic, 1927, plates 7–9; Gouezin, *Le Site Mégalithique d'Er Lannic*, 13. Twohig, E. S. *The Megalithic Art of Western Europe*, 1981, 123. Rejection of the 'yoke', *ibid.*, 54–8. 'Déesse: Rollando, Y., *La Préhistoire du Morbihan*, 1971, 46, 49.

25 Er-Lannic South. Gouezin, *Le Site Mégalithique d'Er Lannic*, 7–8.
26 Phases at Tossen-Keler: Giot et al., 1979a, 275.
27 Rough cairns at Tossen-Keler: Briard & Giot, 1968, 8–17. At Fochabers: Burl, A., *PSAS 114*, 1984, 35–73. 43.
28 La Déesse-mère: Briard & Giot, 1968, 30.
29 Astronomy and architecture at Pen-ar-Land: Briard, 1990, 50–1; priv. comm., Briard, J. & Goffic, M. le, 'Un observatoire préhistorique à Ouessant', July 1988.
30 Discoveries at Kergonan: Minot, n.d., 26–8.
31 Astronomy: Merlet, R., 1974, 7–10.
32 Pierre Colas: Merlet, M. 1929, 13–26.
33 Horseshoes in Britain and Ireland: Burl, 1999, 152–3.

CHAPTER EIGHTEEN

1 Recent books about Stonehenge: F. Niel *The Mysteries of Stonehenge*, London, 1975; F. Hoyle *On Stonehenge*, London, 1977; L. E. Stover & E. Kraig *Stonehenge and the Origins of Western Culture*, London, 1979; M. Balfour *Stonehenge and its Mysteries*, London, 1979; J. Fowles & B. Brukoff *The Enigma of Stonehenge*, London, 1980; R. Legg *Stonehenge Antiquaries*, Milborne Port, 1986; A. Burl *The Stonehenge People*, London, 1987; R. Castleden *The Stonehenge People*, London, 1987; W. M. F. Petrie *Stonehenge: Plans, Description, and Theories*, London, 1989; C. Chippindale *Who Owns Stonehenge?*, London, 1990; J. Richards *Stonehenge*, London, 1991; R. Castleden *The Making of Stonehenge*, London, 1993; C. Chippindale *Stonehenge Complete*, London, 1994; R. Cleal et al. *Stonehenge In Its Landscape*, London, 1995; J. North *Stonehenge, Neolithic Man and the Cosmos*, London, 1996; D. Souden *Stonehenge. Mysteries of the Stones and Landscape*, London, 1997; B. Cunliffe & C. Renfrew (eds) *Science and Stonehenge*, London, 1997; B. Bender *Stonehenge. Making Space*, Oxford, 1998. Non-completion: Paul Ashbee *WAM 91*, 1998, 139–43.
2 Sequence of construction: Atkinson, 1956, 58–94.
3 Revised sequence: Pitts, 1982, 128–9.
4 Revised sequence: Cleal et al., 1995.
5 Earthen long barrows: Burl, 1987a, 18–19, 50.
6 Stukeley, 1723, 75; 1740, 4.
7 Date of the Heel Stone as a later feature: Cleal et al., 272–6.
8 Timber building: Hawley, 1926, 8; 1928, 172; Burl, 1987a, 52–6. Stratigraphy: Cleal et al., 147–8.
9 Men's bones at Stonehenge: Camden, 1695, 96.
10 Avenue, timber building and causeway postholes all contemporary: Hawley, 1926, 3.
11 Hawley's discovery of the causeway postholes: 1924, 35; 1925, 31.
12 The postholes as an entrance barrier: Cleal et al., 142–7; Fleming, A. *PPS 62*, 1996, 444.
13 Astronomy of the postholes: Newham, 1972, 15–17.
14 Startin & Bradley, 'Some notes of work organisation and society in prehistoric Wessex' in Ruggles & Whittle (eds), 1981, 289–96. 293.
15 Radiocarbon determinations: Cleal et al., 522.
16 SSW entrance: Cleal et al., 70–1, 113. Dates: *ibid.*, 522. Fussell's Lodge: Burl, 1987a, 16. Astronomy: *ibid.*, 26–8.
17 Discovery of the Aubrey Holes: Aubrey, 1693, 76.
18 Dimensions of the Aubrey Hole ring: Atkinson, 1967, 93.
19 Radiocarbon assays for Stonehenge I: Cleal et al., 522–5.
20 Theories about the Aubrey Holes: a great stone circle, Hawley, 1921, 30–1; a large timber ring, Cunnington, R. H., 1935, 25–8; as ritual pits, Atkinson, 1956, 169–71; posts followed by cremations, Bender, *Stonehenge. Making Space*, 1998, 56; the zodiac, Postins M. W. Stonehenge. *Sun, Moon*

and *Wandering Stars*, 1982, 9–14; a female deity, Meaden, T., *Stonehenge. The Secret of the Solstice* 1987, 112–13. Eclipse prediction: Hawkins, G. S., 1966a, vi. see also: Hoyle, F., *On Stonehenge*, 1977.

21 Henges with 'Aubrey Holes': Burl, 1981b; *ibid.*, 1987a, 88.
22 The layout of the Aubrey Holes: Thom, Thom & Thom, 'Stonehenge', *JHA 5 (2)*, 1974, 83.
23 Stones and posts, Cleal et al., 1995, 107. No stones or posts, Atkinson et al., 1952, 18; Atkinson, 1956, 106; 1979, 28.
24 'Vase-support': Hawley, 1923, 17.
25 The macehead: Hawley, 1925, 34.
26 Midwinter moonrise: Burl, 1987a, 103.
27 Bluestones last to arrive: Case, *WAM 90*, 1997, 165.
28 Proportions of beaker to grooved ware sherds: Case, H., *WAM 90*, 1997, 165.
29 The widened entrance: Hawley, 1924, 30.
30 Midsummer sunrise: Thom, Thom & Thom, *JHA 5 (2)*, 1974, 84.
31 Finds from Lake barrows: Grinsell, 1978c, 37–40.
32 Gold discs: *WAM 52*, 1948, 270–1; Taylor, J., 1980, 131.
33 Wessex and Ireland: Clarke, D., 1970, I, 95.
34 Stone 97: Stone 97, Pitts, 1982, 83–7. 'Male and female' pairings of stones: Burl, 1987a, 202; *ibid.*, 1993, 26 and with other references.
35 Dimensions of the Four Stations: Atkinson, R. J. C., 1978, 50–2.
36 Possible functions of the Four Stations: Atkinson, 1979, 33, 79, 130.
37 Duke, 1846, 142–6.
38 Astronomy of the diagonal: Lockyer, 1906, 93; Thatcher, 'The Station Stones at Stonehenge', *Ant 50*, 1976, 144–5. A minimalist view of Stonehenge astronomy is expressed by Ruggles in Cunliffe & Renfrew (eds), *Science and Stonehenge*, 1997, 203–29. A completely negative opinion is given in *Stonehenge and Neighbouring Monuments*, 2nd ed., K. Osbourne, 1995, 20, where 'the claim is not supported by the archaeological record'.
39 Source of the bluestones: Thomas, H. H., *Ant J 23*, 1923, 236–60. A magical stone circle: Stone, E. H., 1924, 65.
40 Stones of monuments around the Preselis: Thorpe et al., 1991, 115–16.
41 Dangers of the bluestone journey: Burl, 1999, 113–15. No sails: McGrail in Scarre & Healy (eds), 1993, 203.

42 Belief in human transportation: Burl, 1976, 308–9. Objections to human transportation: Kellaway, *Nature 233*, 1971, 30–5; Thorpe et al., 1991; Burl, 1984; 1987a, 131–5; 1999, 107–23. Boles Barrow: Burl, 1999, 118–21.
43 Pliocene glaciation: Kellaway, G. *Hot Springs of Bath*, 1991, 243–8, 260–73.
44 Mineralogical farrago: Thorpe et al., 1991, 106.
45 Possible intended shape of the Q & R setting: Cleal et al., 188.
46 The putative hole for the Altar Stone, WA3639: Hawley, 1926, 11; Cleal et al., 179, 181, 187–8.
47 Problem of glaciation: Niel, F., *The Mysteries of Stonehenge*, 1975, 136.
48 Numbering of the stones: Petrie, W.M.F., *Stonehenge: Plans, Descriptions, and Theories*, 1880, 9.
49 Accepted radiocarbon dates for the circle: Cleal et al., 524.
50 Doubts over the stone circle assay for Stone 1 (UB-3821): Cleal et al., 533.
51 Assays for the avenue: Cleal et al., 526. Later avenues: Burl, 1993, 29–74.
52 Briard, J., 186, in Scarre & Healy (eds), 1993.
53 Work-forces: Richards, J. and Whitby, M. in Cunliffe & Renfrew (eds), *Science and Stonehenge*, 1997, 233, 249–52.
54 Worker's hut: Pitts, M., 1982, 99–104. Charcoal assay: *ibid.*, 128; Cleal et al., 511, 519.
55 Level tops of the lintels: Petrie, 1880, 13.
56 Arminghall horseshoe: Gibson, 1998, 36, 47.
57 Arminghall post settings: Clark, J. G., 1936, 14.
58 Breton motifs: Twohig, 1981: Mané Bras, figure 84; Penhape, F123; Goërem, F134; Les Pierres-Plates, F147; Barnenez, F77; Table des Marchands, F102; Mané Ruthuel, F164. See also: 'L'art dans les premiers dolmens à couloir', in, Giot et al., 1979, 177–88.
59 Kermarquer: l'Helgouac'h, J. & Lecornec, J. 'Le menhir de Kermarquer à Moistoirac (Morbihan)', *Bull. De la Soc. Polym. Du Morbihan*, 1969, 1–7.
60 Ile Guennoc: Twohig, 1981, figure 178, Ile Gaignog; Burl, 1985, 58. Crech-Quillé: Burl, 1999, 166.
61 Kergüntuil: Twohig, 1981, figure 151; Prajou-Menhir, F153; Mougau-Bihan, F156.
62 Carvings close to the ground: Cleal et al., 31–2, figs 18–20.
63 Atkinson, 1956, 32, 178.
64 Chalk axes and phallus: Cleal et al., 201, 204. 'Stag horn': Hawley, 1926, 12.

County Gazetteer of the Stone Circles in Britain, Ireland and Brittany

Sites are arranged alphabetically under old county or Breton *département* names for Brittany; the Republic of Ireland; and the United Kingdom: Channel Isles; England; Northern Ireland; Scotland and Wales.

Because the regional distribution of stone circle architectural styles was affected and often confined by natural barriers such as rivers and mountains sites in the Gazetteer for Scotland and Wales are listed under the pre-1974 names for counties whose boundaries were usually determined by the same barriers. To overcome any confusion names of the 1974 larger conglomerations, regrouped for bureaucratic convenience, are cited in brackets after the former name: e.g. Pembrokeshire (Dyfed) and Roxburghshire (Borders).

The most important details are given for each site in the following order.

1. The customary name for the ring
2. The condition of the site:
   1 Good; worth visiting
   2 Restored
   3 Ruined but recognisable
   4 Destroyed or unrecognisable
   5 Uncertain status, including misidentified sites and hybrid rings such as complex ring-cairns (Lynch, 1972)
   6 Possibly a fake
3. Grid reference
4. Diameter (where known) in metres. Two diameters are given if the ring is non-circular. Where available Thom's (1967) classification is given:
   CA, CB, CD = Flattened circles CE = Ellipses
   CI, CII = Egg-shaped rings; Complex Sites
5. Architectural details, using the following abbreviations:

A	Avenue	PgT	Passage-tomb
Adj	Adjacent	Pl	Plain
a/h	arrowhead	Pol	Polished
B	Bank	Pros	Prostrate
BD	Boulder-dolmen	Pt	Portals or entrance
bkr	beaker	Q	Quartz
C	Concentric circle	R	Single stone row
CH	Circle-henge	2R	Double stone row
Cn	Cairn	RC	Ring-cairn
Cr	Cup-and-rings	Rect	Rectangle
Crem	Cremation/s	Rest	Restored
Ct	Cist	RPt	Radial portals
Dest	Destroyed	RSC	Recumbent stone circle
Em	Embanked	S	Centre stone
Ent	Entrance	St	Stone
Exc	Excavated	StC	Stone circle
fl	flint/s	Tang	Tangential
f/v	food vessel	V	Cove
Gr	Graded in height	WgT	Wedge-tomb
HS	Horseshoe		
Indet	Indeterminate	4P	Four-Poster
MC	Multiple circle (RSC)	5	5-Stone ring
Neo	Neolithic	6	6-stone ring
O	Outlier/s	8	8-stone ring
Pair	Two standing stones		

6. Other details:
   i. Where applicable, date of excavation; finds; and C-14 determinations with laboratory numbers.
   ii. References. These are given by author's name if the work is cited in the Bibliography, adding a date only if the author appears more than once; or by volume, number, date and page. All Thom's (1967) catalogue numbers are given followed by his name for the ring if this differs from the customary one.
   iii. Astronomical details are abstracted from Thom's 'A' lines (1967, 97ff) and, selectively, from other sources. The following abbreviations are employed:

   MR Moonrise   SR Sunrise
   MS Moonset   SS Sunset
   Stars are given by name.

County Statistics

	1	2	3	4	5	6	Total
BRITTANY							
Côtes-du-Nord	–	1	–	1	–	–	2
Finistère	–	2	1	13	2	–	18
Ille-et-Vilaine	2	–	1	–	2	–	5
Morbihan	2	2	6	12	2	–	24
	4	5	8	26	6	–	49
REPUBLIC OF IRELAND							
Cavan	–	–	3	1	3	–	7
Clare	–	–	–	–	1	–	1
Cork	18	–	57	19	9	–	103
Donegal	1	–	2	–	2	–	5
Dublin	–	–	2	1	–	–	3
Galway	–	–	1	–	–	1	2
Kerry	6	1	9	4	–	–	20
Kildare	–	–	1	2	–	–	3
Laois	–	–	1	–	–	–	1
Limerick	–	1	2	1	–	–	4
Longford	–	–	1	–	–	–	1
Louth	–	–	–	2	–	1	3
Mayo	2	–	4	3	2	–	11
Meath	–	–	1	2	1	–	4
Sligo	–	–	4	1	–	–	5
Tipperary	–	–	1	2	2	–	5
Wexford	–	–	1	–	1	–	2
Wicklow	1	–	2	2	2	–	7
	28	2	92	40	23	2	187
UNITED KINGDOM							
Channel Isles							
Guernsey	–	–	1	3	–	–	4
Jersey	–	1	–	1	–	–	2
	1	1	4	–	–		6
England							
Cheshire	–	–	–	1	1	–	2
Cornwall	0	6	13	11	8	–	38
Cumberland	3	2	13	15	5	–	38
Derbyshire	3	1	13	9	5	–	31
Devon	2	11	33	16	11	–	73
Dorset	1	–	2	3	–	1	7
Co. Durham	–	–	–	1	–	–	1
Isle of Man	–	–	–	–	–	1	1
Lancashire	–	–	4	5	4	–	13
Northumberland	2	1	10	1	5	–	19
Oxfordshire	–	1	–	1	1	–	3
Shropshire	–	–	2	2	2	–	6
Somerset	–	–	5	4	5	–	14
Westmorland	–	1	9	4	8	–	22
Wiltshire	–	–	3	7	5	1	16
Yorkshire	1	–	12	8	11	–	32
	12	23	120	87	71	3	316

	1	2	3	4	5	6	Total
Northern Ireland							
Antrim	–	–	1	1	3	–	5
Armagh	–	–	–	2	1	–	3
Down	1	–	2	–	2	–	5
Fermanagh	–	1	3	9	5	–	18
Londonderry	–	1	17	14	4	–	36
Tyrone	–	7	36	42	4	–	89
	1	9	59	68	19	–	156
Scotland							
Aberdeen	8	3	41	67	11	–	130
Angus	–	–	7	6	1	–	14
Argyllshire	1	2	2	1	2	–	8
Arran	5	–	7	4	3	–	19
Ayrshire	–	–	2	2	3	–	7
Banffshire	–	–	7	6	5	–	18
Berwickshire	–	–	–	1	1	–	2
Bute	–	–	2	2	–	–	4
Caithness	–	–	9	2	4	–	15
Clackmannan	–	–	–	1	2	–	3
Colonsay	–	–	–	–	1	–	1
Dumfriesshire	1	–	6	6	2	–	15
East Lothian	–	–	7	3	–	–	10
Fife	–	2	1	4	–	–	7
Hebrides	–	1	16	3	6	–	26
Inverness	3	5	12	10	2	–	32
Islay	–	–	1	1	1	–	3
Kincardine	2	1	9	8	1	–	21
Kirkcudbright	1	–	10	3	5	–	19
Lanarkshire	–	–	–	–	2	–	2
Moray	1	–	4	6	2	–	13
Mull	–	–	2	–	1	–	3
Nairn	–	–	2	2	–	–	4
Orkney	–	1	1	–	–	–	2
Peebles	–	–	2	–	–	–	2
Perthshire	5	5	41	18	9	–	78
Renfrewshire	–	–	–	–	1	–	1
Ross & Cromarty	1	–	2	1	–	–	4
Roxburgh	1	–	4	4	1	–	10
Selkirk	–	–	1	1	–	–	2
Shetland	–	–	2	–	5	–	7
Sutherland	–	–	9	2	3	–	14
Tiree	–	–	2	–	–	–	2
West Lothian	–	–	–	1	–	–	1
Wigtown	1	–	1	3	4	–	9
	30	20	212	168	78	–	508

	1	2	3	4	5	6	Total
Wales							
Anglesey	–	–	–	4	–	–	4
Brecks	1	–	8	2	1	–	12
Caernarvon	3	–	2	5	2	–	12
Cardigan	–	–	–	1	1	1	3
Carmarthen	–	–	2	3	–	–	5
Denbigh	–	–	1	1	4	–	6
Flints	–	–	–	–	–	1	1
Glamorgan	1	–	–	–	–	–	1
Merioneth	–	–	4	4	2	–	10
Monmouth	–	–	–	2	1	–	3
Montgomery	1	–	3	5	1	–	10
Pembroke	1	–	1	3	2	–	7
Radnor	1	–	2	3	1	–	7
	8	–	23	33	15	2	81

	1	2	3	4	5	6	Total
BRITTANY	4	5	8	26	6	–	49
IRELAND	28	2	92	40	23	2	187
CHANNEL ISLES	–	1	1	4	–		6
ENGLAND	12	23	120	87	71	3	316
NORTHERN IRELAND	1	9	59	68	19	–	156
SCOTLAND	30	20	212	168	78	–	508
WALES	8	–	23	33	15	2	81
GRAND TOTALS	83	60	515	426	212	7	1,303

BRITTANY

Cromlechs

FINISTÉRE

1   *Beg Rouz Vorc'h, Trégunc* (5) $5\frac{1}{2}$ km ESE of Concarneau/ *c.* 28/ Pl?, adj 7.4 h St/ Gilbert, 1962, 227–8, no. 22.

2   *Ile Beniguet* (4) $4\frac{1}{2}$ km W of Le Conquet, Ushant archipelago/ *c.* 25 × 15/ Destr. A?/ Pontois, 1929, 124, 126 ['Sanctuaire druidique']; Burl, 1993, 55, 230.

3   *Kerhoué, Plouhinec* (5) 14 km WSW of Douarnenez/ ?/ Pl?/ Scouëzec, 537.

4   *Kerlouan* (4) 9 km N of Lesneven/ ?/ Destr. Pl?/ *Bull. Soc. Arch. Finistère*, 1890; Pontois, 91, 92; Eudes, 47.

5   *Landaoudec* (4) 2 km N of Crozon/ ?/ Destr. Pl, HS, A/ exc. Pol st axe, du Chatellier, 32; Pontois, 115–16; Giot et al., 417; Scouëzec & Masson, 120–2; Burl, 1993, 95–6, 230.

6   *Madeleine, La, Lestriguiou* (4) $1\frac{3}{4}$ km NE of Penmarc'h/ ?/ Destr. Cromlech, 4 × R/ du Chatellier, 28; Burl, 1985, 70, no. 80; *ibid.*, 1993, 241.

7   *St Eden* (4) $2\frac{1}{2}$ km N of Plouescat/ ?/ Destr. Pl?/

Eudes, 72; Scouëzec, 515–16; Burl, 1985, 75, no. 92c; Scouëzec & Masson, 100.

8   *Trémazan* (4) 5 km WNW of Ploudamalmèzeau/ ?/ StC?/ Pontois, 1929, 124.

ILLE-ET-VILAINE

9   *Château-Bû* (1) $1\frac{1}{2}$ km W of Saint-Just/ 7 × 6/ 4P?, on oval mound 35 × 26, PT, ext 3-st R/ Exc. 1991: Burl, 1993, 250; Giot, 1960, 37; Burl, 1988a, 56–7.

10   *Demoiselles, Les* (5) 200 m W of Langon/ 10 × 6/ Cromlech?, 6 × R/ Gilbert, 1964, 122–3, no. 443; Scouëzec, 305; Eudes, 48–9; Burl, 1985, 82, no. 100; Burl, 1993, 133, 242.

MORBIHAN

11   *Grah-Niohl* (4) 1 km N of Arzon/ *c.* 50/ Destr cromlech/ Merlet, 1974, 19–21, 31, 35; Kergal, 1981, 134, no. 264; Burl, 1985, 113, no. 134b.

12   *Kercado* (3) $2\frac{1}{2}$ km NE of Carnac-Ville/ *c.* 19 × 18/ Cromlech, int Pgt, Exc. 1863, 1924. Bones, Neo sherds, Grand Pressigny fl, crems. C-14, 3890 ± 300 bc (Sa 95): P. R. Giot, *PPS 37 (2),*

1971, 209/ l'Helgouac'h, 1966, 107, 111, 113/1926. Burl, 1985, 137, no. 176; Scouëzec & Masson, 174–6.

13 *Kercado W* (4) 1(r) km NE of Carnac-Ville/ ?/ Destr. Cromlech?/ Giot, 1983, 21.

14 *Kerpenhir* (5) 1(r) km SSE of Locmariaquer/ ?/ Site of a former cromlech, A?/ Kergal, 1981, 55–7, 72, no. 13; Burl, 1993, 231, 238.

15 *Kerzerho* (4) (r) km SE of Erdeven/? Destr. Cromlech, Ext. 10 × R, cms/ Lukis, 1875, 27–8; Giot, 1960, 124; Gilbert, 1962, 228–30, no. 23; Burl, 1985, 145–6, no. 187a; Giot, 1983, 20; Scouëzec & Masson, 178–80; Burl, 1993, 111–12, 239, 242.

16 *Ménec E* (4) 1(c) km N of Carnac-Ville/ 108 × 90/ Cromlech/ Thom & Thom, 1977, 1B, 14; Thom & Thom, 1978, 64, 70 (plan, 64); Kergal, 1978, 43; Burl, 1993, 139–40/ Astron: MdW SR, MdS SS, Burl, 1985, 158, no. 203c.

17 *Ménec W* (3) 1 km NNW of Carnac-Ville/ 91 × 71/ Cromlech, A?, ext 12 × R/Thom & Thom, 1978, 62–77 (plan, 63); Kergal, 1978, 43; Burl, 1993, 136–7/Astron: MdW SS, MdS SR, Burl, 1985, 155–7, no. 203a.

Horseshoes

CÔTES-DU-NORD

18 *Pédernec* (4) 12 km WSW of Guingamp/ ?/ Destr. HS, Adj 8.5 h menhir/ Gilbert, 1962, 201–3; Burl, 1985, 40. no. 19b.

19 *Tossen-Keler* (2) Originally just w of the Château d'Eau, 13 km NE of Lannion. Now at Tréguier, 18 km ENE of Lannion/ 33 × 25/ HS, Ent?, Cn, art/ Exc. 1963–4. Multi-phase. (a) Hearths, 2550 ± 250 bc (Gif-280. (b) HS. (c) Cn: Briard & Giot, 1968, 5–40/ Burl, 1985, 45–6, no. 33; Patton, 155–6; Burl, 1993, 143.

FINISTÈRE

20 *Lagatjar* (3) 9 km WNW Crozon/ 57 × 55/ Pontois, 110, plan.

21 *Landaoudec* (4) 2 km N of Crozon/ ?/ Destr. Pl, HS, A/ Exc. Pol. st axe: Du Chatellier, 32/ Pontois, 115–16; Giot et al., 417; Scouëzec & Masson, 120–2; Burl, 1993, 55–6, 230.

22 *Pen-ar-Land, Isle of Ushant* (2) 3 km ENE of Lampaul/ 13 × 10/ HS, 2 × R/ Rest, 1988; Briard, 1990, 50–1/ Burl, 1993, 245/ Astron: MdS and equin SR, Briard, 1990, 51.

23 *Ty ar c'Huré N* (4) 3 km SSW Crozon/ ?/ Pontois, 115.

ILLE-ET-VILAINE

24 *Château-Bû* (3) 15 km NE of Redon/ on mound of PgT/ Burl, 1995, 252, no. 359.

25 *Tribunal, Le, Saint-Just* (1) 100 m w of the Château-Bû/ 16/ HS, O/ Gilbert, 1962, 238, no. 33; Gilbert, 1964, 156–7, no. 472; Scouëzec, 628, 633–6; Burl, 1985, 92–3, no. 110h; Briard, 1987, 64, 70; Briard, 1990, 57; Scouëzec & Masson, 60.

MORBIHAN

26 *Champ de la Croix, Crucuny* (2) 4 km N of Carnac-Ville/ 40 × 32?/ Rest. 1926–7, HS, art, O, [Parc-er-Groez, 'field of the cross']/ Gilbert, 1962, 232, no. 28; Thom & Thom, 1978, 119–20 (plan); Burl, 1985, 131, no. 167a.

27 *Er-Lannic N, Gulf of Morbihan* (3) 2 km s of Larmor-Baden/ 72 × 54/ Em, cms, art, V? 2 × O./ Exc. 1923–6. Chassey and Conguel ware, animal bones, fl, Q: Z. le Rouzic, 1930/ Bull Soc. *Polymathique du Morbihan*, 1882, 8–24; Le Rouzic & Péquart, 42, 76, figs 7–9; Shee, 1981, fig. 181; *Bull Soc. Polym du Morb*, 1971, 5–14; Merlet, 1974, 3–7, 32–4; Burl, 1976, 130–6 (plan); Giot et al., 411–13; Burl, 1985, 111, no. 132b; le Roux, 1985, 31–4; Giot, 1988, 13; Patton, 1993, 23–5, 121–3; Gouezin, 1998. Astron: Maj N MR, Maj N MS, Burl, 1976a, 135.

28 *Er-Lannic S* (4) 3b S, Gulf of Morbihan (4) Immed s of 27/ 61/ Z. le Rouzic, 1930; Gouezin, 1998.

29 *Grand Rohu, Arzon* (4) 6 km w of Sarzeau/ *c.* 48 × 42/ Destr. HS?/ Merlet, 1974, 26–9, 31; Kergal, 1980c, 37; Burl, 1985, 113–14, no. 136a.

30 *Graniol, Pen Hap* (4) 9.5 km WNW Sarzeau/ 53 × 44/ Merlet, 1974, 19–20, plan.

31 *Kerbourgnec, Saint-Pierre-Quiberon* (3) 4 km N of Quiberon/ 96 × 76/ HS or cromlech?, ext. 5 × R/ Lukis, 1875, 29, 35; Thom & Thom, 1977, 7, 22; Thom & Thom, 1978, 20–1 (plan); Burl, 1985, 158–9, no. 204b; Giot, 1988, 12.

32 *Kergonan* (1) 1³/₄ km of landing-stage, Ile-aux-Moines/ 70 × 95/ HS, art, A?, [Cercle de la Mort, 'circle of death', 'Er Anké', 'the goddess of death']/ Exc. 1864. Q. 1877 fl flakes: Minot, 26–7; Deane, 212; Merlet, 1974, 7–19, 34; 1865. Giot et al., 411; Burl, 1985, 114, no. 139a; le Roux, 1985, 16–7; Astron: 1866. MdS SS?, Burl, 1995, 258.

33 *Kerlescan N* (4) 3(c) km NE of Carnac-Ville/ 235 × 200/ HS/ Thom & Thom, 1978, 92–6 (plan, 96). Burl, 1985, 141, no. 180c.

34 *Kerlescan S* (1) 100 m s of Kerlescan N/ 78 × 74/ HS?, ext. 13 × R with int A?/ Thom & Thom, 1978, 92–7 (Plans 93, 94); Burl, 1985, 139–41, no. 180a; Burl, 1993, 140–3.

35 *Kermario E* (4) 2(r) km NE of Carnac-Ville/ ?/ 'Some remains of the arc of a semi-circle': Giot, 1960, 123.

36 *Kermario W* (4) 1.5 km N of Carnac-Ville/ ?/ Miln, 1881, 3.

37   *Llan-er-Groëz* (3) 400 m N of Mané Kerioned/ 300/ Kergal, 1980, 70.

38   *Sainte-Barbe* (4) 1.7 km WNW of Plouharnel/? HS, ext. 8 × R/ Lukis, 1875, 26; Burl, 1985, 164, no. 213; *ibid.*, 1993, 243.

39   *Vieux Moulin, Le, N* (5) 1 km NW of Plouharnel/? HS or 2 4-St R?/ Deane, 210; Giot et al., 410; Burl, 1985, 166, no. 216; Scouëzec & Masson, 176–7; Burl, 1993, 1–2, 153–4, 246.

Rectangles

FINISTÈRE

40   *Kermorvan* (4) 1 km NW of Le Conquet/ *c.* 60 × 39/ Polygon/ Pontois, 31, 124; Niel, 114; Giot et al., 409.

41   *Landaoudec* (4) 2 km N of Crozon/ ?/ Pontois, 115–16. Sketchplan.

42   *Lanvéoc* (4) 5 km NNE of Crozon/ ?/ Destr. Rect cromlech/ du Chatellier, 32; Giot, 1960, 120; Burl, 1993, 54.

43   *Parc-ar-Varret* (3) 1 km NNW of Porspoder/ 40 × 15/ Rect. cromlech [Champ des Morts], int st, ext Pair/ Gilbert, 1962, 224, no. 15.

44   *Phare du Créach, Isle of Ushant* (4) 2.5 km W of Lampaul/ ?/ Destr. Rect. cromlech/ Giot, 1960, 120; Giot et al.

45   *Ty-ar-c'Huré* S, *Crozon* (4) 1 km SE of Morgat/ *c.* 70 × 20/ Destr. Rect cromlech, A/du Chatellier, 31, 124; Pontois, 1929, 98, 115, 117; Giot, 1960, 120; Gilbert, 1962, 225; Burl, 1993, 55–6 [house of the curate], 230/ Astron: MdW SR?, Lockyer, 1909, 486.

ILLE-ET-VILAINE

46   *Cordon des Druides* (5) 5 km NNE of Fougères/ ?/ Cromlech?, R/ Gilbert, 1962, 220–1, no. 6; Burl, 1985, 85–6, no. 103; Scouëzec, 238.

MORBIHAN

47   *Crucuno* (2) 3 km NNW of Plouharnel/ 33.2 × 24.9/ Rest. 1882, Rect cromlech [Parc Vein Glass, 'field of the blue stone']/ Gaillard, 1892; Burl, 1985, 133, no. 171b; Burl, 1987, 141–9; Scouëzec & Masson, 183–5/ Astron: MdS SR, MdW and equin SS, Thom, A. & A. S., and Merritt, R. L. & A., 450–4.

48   *Jardin aux Moines, Brocéliande Forest* (2, 5) 2(r) km ENE of Néant-sur-Yvel/ 25 × 6/ Rect. PgT?/ Exc. 1983. Neo sherds: J. Briard, 1989, 41–56/ J. Briard, 1987, 76–8; J. Briard, 1990, 12–13; Mohen, 121–2.

49   *Narbon, Le, Morbihan* (4) 1.5 km SSW of Erdeven/ ?/ ?/ Sherratt, 1998, 132.

REPUBLIC OF IRELAND

CAVAN

1   *Banagher A* (3) H 466 997/ *c.* 16/ Em/ O'Donovan, 13.

2   *Banagher B* (3) H 466 997/ 40 × 35/ int PgT?/ O'Donovan, 13.

3   *Crom Cruaich* (4) *c.* H25. 15./ ?/ S/ Aubrey, I, 123; *PRIA 36*, 1924, 23; Ross, A., 1986, 117–18, 142–3; Burl, 1995, 211.

4   *Killycluggin* (3) H 240 157/ 22 × 18.6/ Ent?, O/ *JRSAI 52*, 1922, 113–16; *ibid.* 82, 1954, 68; *UJA 41*, 1978, 49–54; O'Nuallain, 1995, 9 [Ballyconnell]; O'Donovan, 13.

5a   *Kilnavert A* (5) H 235 156/ 11.8 × 10.9/ Adj, Cn?/ *JRSAI 68*, 1938, 112; Paterson et al., 1938, 148; O'Donovan, 13.

5b   *Kilnavert B* (5) *c.* H 235 156/ ?/ Adj/ Killanin & Duignan, 1969, 94 [Ballyconnell].

6   *Lissanover* (5) H 229 158 /?/ ?/ Evans, E., 1966, 67; Burl, 1995, 212; O'Donovan, 13.

CLARE

1   *Ballyallia Lake* (5) *c.* R 345 810/ ?/ StC?/ *JRSAI 46*, 1916, 99.

CORK

MC = multiple ring, the Irish equivalent of the Scottish recumbent stone circle. Names in square brackets [Loughatooma] are those cited in Burl, 1976. Ck = the Cork reference number given there.

1   *Ahagilla* (3) W 333 435/ *c.* 7/ MC?, Ent/ priv. comm., O'Nuallain, 19.10.90; *Arch Irel 11 (3)*, 1997, 11.

2a   *Annagannihy NW* (5) W 386 850/ 6.0/ MC?, ext Pair/ Conlon, 1916, 161–2; Barber, J., 1972, I, 50, C48; Burl, 1976, 336, Ck2a; O'Nuallain, 1984a, 47, no. 9; Burl, 1993, 260.

2b   *Annagannihy SE* (5) W 401 836/ 7.5 × 4.5/ MC?/ Conlon, 1916, 156–7; Barber, J., 1972, I, 50–1, C49; Burl, 1976, 338, Ck58, [Loughatooma]; O'Nuallain, 1984a, 47, no. 10.

3a *Ardgroom Outward NE* (4) V 728 563/ ?/ 5s?/
O'Nuallain, 1984a, 18, no. 20.

3b *Ardgroom SW* (1) V 707 553/ 7.3/ MC, Gr, cm?,
O/ Barber, J., 1972, I, 24, 87. C2; Burl, 1976, 336,
Ck3; O'Nuallain, 1984a, 18, no. 21/ Astron: Maj S
MS, Barber, J., 1973, 32.

4 *Ballyvackey* (3) W 344 426/ 8.5/ MC, RPt, O, ext
BD?/ Burl, 1976, 336, Ck4; O'Nuallain, 1984a,
23–4, no. 35; Roberts, J., 1985, 46.

5 *Ballyvouskill* (3) W 254 849/ *c.* 3.5/ 5, Pf, 75 ×
6.5, B/ O'Nuallain, priv. comm. 2.11.87.

6a *Baurgorm NE* (3) W 023 469/ 2.6/ 5, Pt, ext Pair/
O'Nuallain, 1984a, 42–3, no. 85; Burl, 1993, 260.

6b *Baurgorm SW* (3) W 014 460/ 2.6 × 2.5/ 5, O/
Burl, 1976, 336, Ck5; O'Nuallain, 1984a, 43, no.
86.

7a *Bellmount Upper NE* (4) W 429 642/ *c.* 4/ 51,
Ent/ Barber, J., 1972, I, 41–2, C26; Burl, 1976,
336, Ck6 [Bellmount Lower]; O'Nuallain, 1984a,
38, no. 73.

7b *Bellmount Upper SW* (3) W 427 641/ 3.9 × 3.6/ 5,
Gr/ Barber, J., 1972, I, 42 C27; Burl, 1976, 336,
Ck7; O'Nuallain, 1984a, 38–9, no. 74/ Astron:
Equin SS, Barber, J., 1973, 32.

8 *Bohonagh* (1) W 308 368/ 9.9/ MC, Gr, RPt, Q,
ext BD, cms/ Exc, 1959. Central pit, crem, flints:
Fahy, 1961; Somerville, 1930, 75–7; Barber, J.,
1972, I, 10–11, C22; Burl, 1976, 222, 336, Ck8;
O'Nuallain, 1984a, 24, no. 36; Burl, 1995, 213,
213–14; Roberts, J., 1985, 29–31/ Astron: Equin
SS, Somerville, 1930, 76; Fahy, 1961, 99–100.

9 *Breeny More* (4) W 050 552/ *c.* 14/ MC, Pt, 4 ×
int BD/ O'Nuallain, 1984a, 19, no. 24.

10 *Brookpark* (5) W 325 876/ ?/ 4P?/ Barber, J.,
1972, I, 52; Burl, 1976, 337, Ck10; O'Nuallain,
1984a, 46, no. 7; Burl, 1988a, 79.

11 *Cabragh* (3) W 278 798/ 3.2/ 5, ext 4-st R/
Conlon, 1918, 134–6; O'Nuallain, 1984a, 35–6,
no. 63; Burl, 1993, 246 [Cabragh N].

12 *Canrooska* (3) V 936 583/ 2.4/ 5, ext Cn, ext 3-st
R/ O'Nuallain, 1984a, 39, no. 76.

13a *Cappaboy Beg NW* (3) W 082 612/ 2.3 × 1.8/ 5/
Barber, J., 1972, I, 32, C12; Burl, 1976, 337, Ck11;
O'Nuallain, 1984a, 39, no. 77.

13b *Cappaboy Beg SE* (3) W 097 604/ 4.5 × 2.9 × 2.2
× 2.4/ 4P, ext Pair/ O'Nuallain, 1984b, 69, no. 1,
78, no. 19; Burl, 1988a, 79; Burl, 1993, 260.

14 *Cappanaboul* (3) W 033 533/ 10.5/ MC, int BD/
Barber, J., 1972, I, 28, C4; Burl, 1976, 336, Ck9
[Brinny More]; O'Nuallain, 1984a, 18–19, no. 22.

15a *Carrigagrenane NE* (3) W 258 438/ ?/ 5, Q/
Barber, J., 1972, I, 39, C25; Burl, 1976, 337, Ck13;
O'Nuallain, 1984a, 44–5, no. 91.

15b *Carrigagrenane SW* (3) W 254 432/ 8.5/ MC, Pt,
S/ Somerville, 1930, 81–3; Barber, J., 1972, I, 38,
C23; Burl, 1976, 337, Ck12; O'Nuallain, 1984a,
22–3, no. 33.

16a *Carrigagulla NE* (3) W 371 838/ 3/ 5, RPt, Gr/
Conlon, 1917, 157; Barber, J., 1972, I, 46, C36;
Burl, 1976, 337, Ck14; O'Nuallain, 1984a, 32–3,
no. 56.

16b *Carrigagulla SW* (3) W 370 834/ 9/ MC, S Pt/
Conlon, 1917, 156; Barber, J., 1972, I, 46–6, C37;
O'Nuallain, 1984a, 12, no. 4; Burl, 1995, 215, 215.

17 *Carriganimmy* (1) W 293 827/ 3.3/ 5, O/
O'Nuallain, 1984a, 32, no. 55.

18 *Carriganine* (5) W 325 719/ ?/ 5?/ O'Nuallain,
1984a, 37, no. 69.

19 *Carrigaphooca* (4) W 293 735/ 5.5?/ MC, Q, S/
Conlon, 1918, 139; Barber, J., 1972, I, 47, C39;
Burl, 1976, 337, Ck16; O'Nuallain, 1984a, 15, no.
11.

20 *Carrigonirtane* (3) W 285 807/ *c.* 2.8/ 5, Ent, O?/
O'Nuallain, priv. comm. 2.11.87.

21 *Clodagh* (1) W 152 499/ 2.7/ 5, Gr, ext Pair/
O'Nuallain, 1984a, 43–4, no. 88; Burl, 1993, 260;
Burl, 1995, 216; Roberts, J., 1985, 55/ Astron:
MdW SS? Roberts, J., 1985, 55.

22 *Cloghboola Beg* (3) W 305 853/ 3.9 × 2.8/ 5, RPt,
Gr, O × 2, ext radial-cn, R?/Barber, J., 1972, I,
51, C50, C55; Burl, 1976, 337, Ck18; O'Nuallain,
1984a, 31, no. 53; O'Nuallain, 1984b, 78, no. 20;
Burl, 1993, 252.

23 *Cloghboola More* (3) W 274 867/ 3.1/ 5/ Barber,
J., 1972, I, 48, C41; Burl, 1976, 337, Ck17
[Cloghbolla]; O'Nuallain, 1984a, 31, no. 52.

24 *Coolaclevane* (3) W 288 638/ 7.5/ MC, Pt/
Barber, J., 1972, I, 30, C11; Burl, 1976, 337, Ck20
[Coolclevane]; O'Nuallain, 1984a, 15, no. 13.

25 *Coolmountain* (4) W 190 608/ 9.2/ MC?/ Barber,
J., 1972, I, 32, C10; Burl, 1976, 337, Ck21;
O'Nuallain, 1984a, 17, no. 17.

26 *Coulagh* (4) V 631 492/ 8.5/ MC/ O'Nuallain,
1984a, 20, no. 25.

27 *Cousane* (1) W 113 568/ 3.2 × 2.4/ 5/ Barber, J.,
1972, I, 29, C8; Burl, 1976, 337, Ck22;
O'Nuallain, 1984a, 40, no. 79.

28 *Cullenagh* (3) W 150 519/ ?/ 5?/ Power et al.,
1992, 24, no. 71.

29 *Cullomane* (1) W 035 455/ 3.9 × 3.4/ 5, Ent, O/
O'Nuallain, 1984a, 42, no. 84.

30 *Cuppage* (5) R 777 041/ 20/ Pl?/ *JRSAI 62*, 1932,
115; Burl, 1976, 337, Ck23 [Cuppoge];
O'Nuallain, 1984a, 46, no. 4.

31a *Currabeha N* (4) W 411 644/ *c.* 7/ MC, Ent?/
O'Nuallain, 1984a, 16, no. 14.

31b *Currabeha S* (3) W 411 639/ 8.5/ MC, Q, S/
Barber, J., 1972, I, 41, C28; Burl, 1976, 337, Ck25;
O'Nuallain, 1984a, 16, no. 15.

32 *Derreenataggart* (3) V 665 464/ 7.7/ MC, Ent, Gr/
Somerville, 1928, 63; Fahy, 1959, 24; Barber, J.,
1972, I, 23–4, C1; Burl, 1976, 337, Ck26;
O'Nuallain, 1984a, 20, no. 26; Burl, 1995, 217.

33　*Derrynafinchin* (3) W 048 621/ *c*. 8/ MC, int BD, Q/ Barber, J., 1972, I, 30–1. C13; Burl, 1976, 337, Ck27; O'Nuallain, 1984a, 16, no. 16.

34　*Derryarkane* (1) W 052 537/ *c*. 3/ 5, Ent/ O'Nuallain, priv. comm. 12.10.89. Power et al., 1992, 24, no. 72.

35　*Dooneens* (5). W 382 815/ ?/ 5?/ O'Nuallain, 1984a, 48, no. 18.

36　*Drombeg* (1) W 247 352/ 9.3/ MC, Pt, cm, Gr/ Exc. 1957–8. Urn, crem. C-14: 13 ± 140 bc (TCD-38), recalculated as: AD 600 ± 120 (D-62): Fahy, 1959. Further recalculated as 790 ± 80 bc (OxA-2683). Twohig & Ronayne, 74/ Somerville, 1909; Fahy, 1959; Fahy, 1960; Barber, J., 1972, I, 2–3, 9–10; Burl, 1976, 217–18, 221, 222, 337, Ck30; O'Nuallain, 1984a, 24–5, no. 37; Burl, 1993, 217–18; Burl, 1995, 218–19, 219; Roberts, J., 1985, 21–4 [Drumbeag]/ O'Nuallain, 1995, 43/ Astron: MdW SS, Somerville, 1909, 108; near MdW SS, Fahy, 1959, 14–15, MdW SS, Barber, J., 1973, 32.

37　*Dromgarriff* (4) W 622 821/ 3?/ 5/ broken 'earthen vessel'/ O'Nuallain, 1984a, 34, no. 60.

38　*Dromgarvan* (3) V 808 502/ 3 × 2.4/ 5/ Burl, 1976, 336, Ck1 [Adrigole]; O'Nuallain, 1984a, 42, no. 83.

39　*Dromkeal* (3) W 003 544/ *c*. 9/ MC, int BD?/ Power et al., 1992, 22, no. 53.

40　*Dunbeacon* (3) V 927 392/ 8/ MC, S/ Barber, J., 1972, I, 31, C14; Burl, 1976, 337, Ck31; O'Nuallain, 1984a, 22, no. 32.

41　*Garryglass* (4) W 223 451/ ?/ MC?, S/ Burl, 1976, 337, Ck32 [Durraghalicky]; O'Nuallain, 1984a, 20, no. 27.

42　*Glanbrack* (3) W 271 444/ 2.8/ 5, ext Pair/ O'Nuallain, 1984a, 44, no. 90.

43a　*Glantane NE* (4) W 281 839/ 4.5/ MC, B, ext Pair?/ Burl, 1976, 337, Ck37 [Glentane E]; O'Nuallain, 1984a, 11, no. 2.

43b　*Glantane SW* (3) W 280 833/ 5/ MC, Gr/ O'Nuallain, 1984a, 12, no. 3.

44　*Glanycarney* (4) W 146 575/ ?/ 5? 4P?/ Barber, J., 1972, I, 32, C9; O'Nuallain, 1984a, 48, no. 23; Burl, 1988a, 79.

45　*Glenleigh* (3) W 318 903/ 3.4/ 5, Ent/ Barber, J., 1972, I, 44–5, C33; Burl, 1976, 337, Ck36; O'Nuallain, 1984a, 30, no. 50.

46　*Glenreagh* (3) R 189 035/ 3.5/ 5, O?/ O'Nuallain, 1984a, 30, no. 49.

47　*Gortanacra* (3) W 203 755/ 8/ MC/ O'Nuallain, 1984a, 14, no. 9.

48　*Gortanimill* (1) W 208 741/ 7.8/ MC, S, Q/ Conlon, 1918, 125–6; Barber, J., 1972, I, 45, C34; Burl, 1976, 337, Ck38; O'Nuallain, 1984a, 14, no. 10; Burl, 1995, 221.

49　*Gorteanish* (4) V 860 396/ 8/ MC, int BD? ext BD/ inf: Archaeological Branch, Ordnance Survey, Dublin; Power et al., 1992, 43, no. 215.

O'Nuallain, 1984b, 69, no. 2; Burl, 1988a, 80–1; Burl, 1995, 220–1.

51　*Gortnatubbrid* (3) W 193 758/ 2.4/ 5, Ent/ O'Nuallain, 1984a, 34, no. 61.

52　*Gortroe* (5) W 259 605/ 8.5/ MC, B, ext Q, O/ Burl, 1976, 337, Ck34, [Gertroe]; O'Nuallain, 1984a, 17, no. 18.

53　*Gowlane* (3) W 483 857/ 6.5/ MC, Pt/ Barber, J., 1972, I, 49, C47; Burl, 1976, 337, Ck39; O'Nuallain, 1984a, 12, no. 5.

54　*Grenagh* (4) W 568 841/ 5/ 5?/ Conlon, 1916, 70–1; O'Nuallain, 1984a, 33–4, no. 59.

55　*Illane* (3) W 047 596/ 2.7 × 2.3/ 5, ext Cn/ O'Nuallain, 1984a, 39–40, no. 78.

56　*Inchireagh* (3) W 190 565/ 3 × 2.4/ 5/ O'Nuallain, 1984a, 42, no. 82.

57　*Inchybegga* (3) W 048 462/ 3 × 2.7/ 5/ O'Nuallain, 1984a, 43, no. 87.

58　*Kealagowlane* (3) V 876 523/ c8/ MC, int BD/ P. Walsh, priv. inf. 29.6.98.

59　*Kealkil* (1) W 055 555/ 2.8 × 2.5/ 5, Gr, ext Pair, ext radial-Cn/ Exc 1938. Central cross-trench. O'Riordain, 1939/ Barber, J., 1972, I, 7–8, 28–9, C5; Burl, 1976, 221–2, 337, Ck41; O'Nuallain, 1984a, 41–2, no. 81; O'Nuallain, 1984b, 75, no. 13; Power et al., 1992, 25, no. 78 [Kealkill]; Burl, 1993, 192, 261; Burl, 1995, 222–3.

60　*Kilboultragh* (4) W 319 756/ 9/ MC, S, Gr?/ Exc. *c*. 1922/ Burl, 1976, 338, Ck43; O'Nuallain, 1984a, 13–14, no. 7.

61　*Kilmartin Lower* (3) W 452 824/ 3.4/ MC, O/ Exc. *c*. 1925/ O'Nuallain, 1984a, 13, no. 6.

62　*Kilmeedy W* (3) W 238 881/ *c*. 3.5/ 5/ O'Nuallain, priv. comm. 2.11.87.

63　*Knockantota* (4) W 558 877/ ?/ 5?/ O'Nuallain, 1984a, 48, no. 15.

64　*Knockaunvaddreen* (5) R 512 048/ *c*. 12/ ?/ Burl, 1976, 338, [Knockane, Ck45]; O'Nuallain, 1984a, 46, no. 3.

65a　*Knockavullig NE* (4) W 430 704/ 2.4 × 2.3/ 5/ Conlon, 1917, 161; Barber, 1972, I, 48, C43; Burl, 1976, 338, Ck48; O'Nuallain, 1984a, 38, no. 71.

65b　*Knockavullig SW* (3) W 428 702/ 3.2/ 5, Ent/ Conlon, 1917, 161–2; Barber, J., 1972, I, 48, C44; Burl, 1976, 338, Ck49; O'Nuallain, 1984a, 38, no. 72.

66　*Knocknakilla* (1) W 297 841/ 2.7/ 5, Ent, Q, ext Pair, radial-Cn/ Exc. 1930. No finds: Gogan, 1931/ Barber, J., 1972, I, 6–7, 44, C32; Burl, 1976, 221, 383, Ck63 [Mushera Beg]; O'Nuallain, 1984a, 32, no. 54, O'Nuallain, 1984b, 75, no. 14; Burl, 1993, 190, 192, 261; Burl, 1995, 223, 223.

67a　*Knocknaneirk NE* (1) W 372 633/ 3.9 × 3.1/ 5/ Barber, J., 1972, I, 40, C29; Burl, 1976, 338, Ck47 [Knockaneirk B]; O'Nuallain, 1984a, 39, no. 75.

67b　*Knocknaneirk SW* (3) W 371 626/ 9.5/ MC/ Barber, J., 1972, I, 40–1, C29; Burl, 1976, 338,

Ck46 [Knocknaneirk A]; O'Nuallain, 1984a, 17–18, no. 19/ Astron: Min S MS, Barber, J., 1973, 32.

68 *Knockraheen* (1) W 303 802/ 4.1 × 3.6/ 5, ext Q Pair, O, ext radial-Cn/ Conlon, 1918, 137–8; Barber, J., 1972, I, 49, C45; Burl, 1976, 338, Ck54 [Lackaduv]; O'Nuallain, 1984a, 34–5, no. 62; O'Nuallain, 1984b, 75, no. 15; Burl, 1993, 261.

69a *Knocks NW* (3) W 299 457/ 9/ MC, Pt/ Exc. post-1984 bank and ditch covering w part of ring removed. Site now entire. O'Nuallain, priv. comm. 12.10.89/ Barber, J., 1972, I, 36–7, C21; Burl, 1976, 338, Ck53; O'Nuallain, 1984a, 20–1, no. 28.

69b *Knocks SE* (4) W 302 443/ 8.5/ MC, Ent, S/ Barber, J., 1972, I, 38, C16; Burl, 1976, 338, Ck52; O'Nuallain, 1984a, 21, no. 29/ Astron: Maj S MS, Barber, J., 1973, 32.

70 *Labbamolaga Middle* (5) R 765 176/ 7.5 × 1.8/ 4P?, orig. 5?/ O'Nuallain, 1984b, 71, no. 7.

71 *Laharankeal* (3) W394 771/ *c.* 1.5/ 5, Gr, Ent/ Barber, J., 1972, I, 47, C40; Burl, 1976, 338, Ck55; O'Nuallain, 1984a, 36, no. 64/ Astron: Maj S MS, Barber, J., 1973, 32.

72 *Leckaneen* (3) W 439 768/ *c.* 3.5/ 5, Ent, ext pros st/ O'Nuallain, 1984a, 36, no. 66.

73a *Lettergorman NE* (3) W 267 473/ 6.8 × 2.9/ 4P, O/ Barber, J., 1972, I, 39, C24; Burl, 1976, 338, Ck56; O'Nuallain, 1984b, 70, no. 4; Burl, 1988a, 82–3; Power et al., 1992, 26, no. 85.

73b *Lettergorman SW* (3) W 262 456/ 3.1 × 2.8/ 5, Ent, Q/ Barber, J., 1972, I, 37, C17, [Knockawadra]; Burl, 1976, 338, Ck50 [Knockawadra]; O'Nuallain, 1984a, 44, no. 89.

74 *Lissacresig* (1) W 269 753/ 3.6 × 3/ 5/ Burl, 1976, 338, Ck69, [Scrongare]; O'Nuallain, 1984a, 37, no. 68.

75 *Lissard* (4) W 582 902/ *c.* 8/ MC, S/ Conlon, 1916, 69–70; Burl, 1976, 338, Ck66, [Reim na Gaoithe]; O'Nuallain, 1984a, 11, no. 1.

76a *Maughanaclea Centre* (1) W 089 563/ 2.6 × 2.2/ 5, O/ O'Nuallain, priv. comm. 2.11.87.

76b *Maughanaclea NE* (3) W 104 565/ 11.5/ MC, 2 × int BD/ Barber, J., 1972, I, 29, C6; Burl, 1976, 338, Ck59; O'Nuallain, 1984a, 19, no. 23/ Astron: Min S MS, Barber, J., 1973, 32.

76c *Maughanaclea SW* (3) W 080 556/ 3.9 × 2.8/ 4P/ Barber, J., 1972, I, 31, C7; O'Nuallain, 1984b, 69–70, no. 3, 78, no. 21; Burl, 1988a, 84–5.

77 *Maulatanvally* (3) W 264 442/ 9.5/ MC, Q, S/ Somerville, 1930, 79–81; Barber, J., 1972, I, 36, C15 [Mauletanvalley]; O'Nuallain, 1984a, 21, no. 30; Roberts, J., 1985, 41.

78 *Mill Little* (3) V 989 565/ 3.1 × 2.4/ 5, RPt, ext BD + 2 × BD?, ext Pair/ Barber, J., 1972, I, 24–5, C3 [Faranadadda]; Burl, 1976, 337, Ck33, [Faranfada]; O'Nuallain, 1984a, 40, no. 80; Burl, 1993, 261.

79a *Oughtihery SE* (3) W 413 801/ 2.9/ MC/ Conlon, 1916, 152; Barber, J., 1972, I, 47, C38; Burl, 1976, 337, [Keel Cross, Ck42]; O'Nuallain, 1984a, 8, no. 14/ Astron: Min S MS, Barber, J., 1973, 32.

79b *Oughtihery NW* (3) W 390 820/ 2.9 × 2.7/ 5, Ent/ Conlon, 1916, 160–1; Barber, J., 1972, I, 49, C46; Burl, 1976, 338, Ck64; O'Nuallain, 1984a, 33, no. 57.

80 *Pluckanes* (4) W 536 846/ 3.7 × 3.2?/ 5?, sherds?, ext 3-st R/ Conlon, 1916, 139; O'Nuallain, 1984a, 33, no. 58; Burl, 1993, 253; *JCHAS 103*, 1998, 141–7.

81 *Reananerre* (1) W 203 729/ 2.6 × 1.9/ 5/ O'Nuallain, 1984a, 37, no. 67.

82 *Reanascreena* (1) W 265 410/ 9.8 × 9.3/ MC, B, RPt, Gr/ Exc 1961. Crem: Fahy, 1962. C-14, 945 ± 35 bc (GrN-17510), 830 ± 35 bc (GrN-17509), AD 255 ± 30 bc, 1963. 'peat' (GrN-17511), Twohig & Ronayne, 74/ Somerville, 1930, 77–9; Barber, J., 1972, I, 11–12, C20; Burl, 1976, 218, 222, 338, Ck65; 1965. O'Nuallain, 1984a, 23, no. 34; Burl, 1995, 227–8, 227; Roberts, J., 1985, 38–9.

83 *Rosnacalp* (3) W 380 708/ 3/ 5, Ent/ Conlon, 1917, 157–8; Burl, 1976, 338, Ck67 [Rosnascalp]; O'Nuallain, 1984a, 37, no. 70.

84 *Rylane* (1) W 438 813/ 3.7 × 2.9/ 5, Ent/ Conlon, 1916, 152; Barber, J., 1972, I, 48, C42; Burl, 1976, 338, Ck68; O'Nuallain, 1984a, 36, no. 65/ Astron: Maj S MS, Barber, J., 1973, 32.

85 *Teergay* (3) W 291 694/ 7.5/ MC?/ Barber, J., 1972, I, 45–6, C35; Burl, 1976, 338, Ck71; O'Nuallain, 1984a, 15, no. 12.

86 *Templebryan* (3) W 389 437/ 9.5/ MC, Q, S, Ent?/ Barber, J., 1972, I, 37–8, C18; Burl, 1976, 338, Ck72; O'Nuallain, 1984a, 22, no. 31.

87 *Trawebane* (3) W 042 477/ 2.4/ 5, Ent/ Power et al., 1992, 25, no. 82.

88 *Tullig* (4) W 310 876/ ?/ 5?/ Barber, J., 1972, I, 52, C52; O'Nuallain, 1984a, 31, no. 51.

DONEGAL

1 *Ballykenny* (5) C 257 240/ ?/ Circle or oval?/ Somerville, 1909, 226–7; Lacy, 1983, 74; McConkey, 41.

2 *Beltany, Tops* (1) C 255 005/ 44.2/ Pf, cms, O/ Somerville, 1923, 212–14; Ross, 1967, 115; Lacy, 1983, 72–3 [Tops]; O'Nuallain, 1995, 15/ Astron: Beltane SR, Somerville, 1923, 214; Burl, 1987b, 12–14; Burl, 1995, 230–1.

3 *Bocan* (3) C 544 475/ *c.* 18.3/ O?/ Exc. nineteenth century. 'earthen urns': H. P. Swan, *Twixt Foyle and Swilly*, 1949, 113/ Burl, 1976a, 339 [Culdaff]; Lacy, 1983, 70–1; McConkey, 41 [Glackadrumman]; O'Nuallain, 1995, 15/ Astron: MdW SS?, *JRSAI 59*, 1929, 152.

4 *Cashelenny* (5) H 172 745/ *c.* 15/ Ent?/ Lacy, 1983, 71; McConkey, 41.

5 *Lettermore* (3) G 84. 84. / ?/ Pl?/ Lacy, 1983, 71, 72; McConkey, 42.

DUBLIN

1 *Ballyedmundaff* (4) O 18. 21. / *c*. 12/ Pl?/ Churcher, 1985, 16.

2 *Knockanvinidee* (3) O 06. 23. /9.8 × 9.1/ C?/ *JRSAI 55*, 1925, 126; Churcher, 1985, 117.

3 *Piperstown K* (3) *c*. O 115 217/ 2.9/ Cn, O?/ Exc. 1962. Pit, crem: Rynne & O'hEailidhe/ Churcher, 1985, 17.

GALWAY

1 *Masonbrook* (6?) M 658 147/ 21.3/ Em, int Cn?/ Exc. 1916. No finds: *JRSAI 44*, 1914, 352; *JRSAI 45*, 1915, 310; *PRIA 33*, 1916–17, 505 [The Ring; Seven Monuments]; Harbison, 1970, 98 [Moanmore East]; Burl, 1995, 232.

2 *Streamstown* (3) L 647 535/ 1.8 × 1.8?/ 4P?/ Gosling, 1991, 32.

KERRY

1a *Cashelkeelty W* (4) V 747 575/ 17/ MC/ Exc. 1977. flint scraper. C-14: 970 ± 60 bc (GrN-9173), 715 ± 50 bc (GrN-9172), Twohig & Ronayne, 74/ Lynch, A., 1981a, 64–9, 76–84. [Cashelkeelty I]/ O'Nuallain, 1984a, 29–30, no. 47.

1b *Cashelkeelty E* (3) V 748 575/ 1.5/ 5, ext 4-st R/ Exc. 1977. No finds: Lynch, A., 1981a, 84–5 [Cashelkeelty II]/ O'Nuallain, 1984a, 45, no. 93; Burl, 1993, 166, 169, 192; Burl, 1995, 232–3.

2 *Doughill* (4) V 962 696/ 9/ MC, Ent?/ Burl, 1976, 339, Ky 1; O'Nuallain, 1984a, 27, no. 42.

3 *Dromagorteen* (3) V 958 653/ *c*. 10/ MC, int BD/ *Arch Ire 11 (3)*, 1997, 11.

4 *Dromatouk* (1) V 953 714/ 2.7/ 5/ O'Nuallain, 1984a, 45, no. 92.

5 *Drombohilly* (3) V 790 607/ 8.5/ MC, RPt/ Barber, J., 1972, I, 20, K1; Burl, 1976, 339, Ky3; O'Nuallain, 1984a, 30, no. 48; Burl, 1995, 233/ Astron: Maj S MS, Barber, J., 1973, 32.

6 *Dromod* (3) V 545 694/ 4/ MC, O/ Burl, 1976, 339, KY4; O'Nuallain, 1984a, 26, no. 39.

7 *Dromroe* (3) V 880 657/ 9.5/ MC, Ent, int BD, S/ Barber, J., 1972, I, 21–2, K3; Burl, 1976, 339, Ky5; MC. O'Nuallain, 1984a, 28–9, no. 45/ Astron: Equi SS, Barber, J., 1973, 32.

8 *Grousemount* (3) W 098 702/ 3.2 × 2.8/ 4P/ *Arch Ire 11 (3)*, 1997, 11.

9 *Gurteen* (1) W 006 698/ 10.5/ MC, RPt, Gr, int BD, Cms?/ Barber, J., 1972, I, 22–3, K5 [Gorteen]; Burl, 1976, 339, Ky7; O'Nuallain, 1984a, 27–8, no. 43; Burl, 1995, 234/ Astron: Maj S MS, Barber, J., 1973, 32.

10 *Kenmare* (1) V 907 707/ 17 × 15/ MC? int BD, Cm/ Barber, J., 1972, I, 23, K6; Burl, 1976, 339, KY9; O'Nuallain, 1984a, 26–7, no. 41; Burl, 1995, 234; O'Nuallain, 1995, 36.

11 *Killowen* (4) V 924 716/ ?/ MC, S or BD?, Cm?, Ent?/ Burl, 1976, 339, Ky10; O'Nuallain, 1984a, 26, no. 40.

12 *Lackeroe* (3) *c*. V 960 689/ 8/ MC, int BD in HS?/ P. Walsh, priv. inf.

13 *Lissyviggeen* (1) V 998 906/ 4, bank 21.3/ MC?, Gr, Em, 2 × O/ *JRSAI 16*, 1883–4, 306–7; Burl, 1976, 220, 339, Ky12; O'Nuallain, 1984a, 25, no. 38; Burl, 1993, 191; Burl, 1995, 234–5.

14 *Lohart* (2, badly) V 824 663/ *c*. 11/ Pl?, int BD?/ Barber, J., 1972, I, 21, K2; Burl, 1976, 339, Ky16 [Tuosist]; O'Nuallain, 1984a, 28, no. 44.

15 *Meenanare* (4) Q 479 162/ ?/ ?/ C/ *North Kerry Arch Survey*, Dingle, 1995, 31, no. 32.

16 *Reenkilla* (1) V 768 577/ 3.5 × 2.5 × 2.7 × 1.9/ 4P, O/ O'Nuallain, 1984b, 71, no. 5; Burl, 1988a, 86–7.

17 *Scartaglin* (3) R 050 048/ 3+/ 5, O/ O'Nuallain, 1984a, 2.11.87.

18 *Shronebirrane* (3) V 735 554/ 7.5/ MC, Gr/ Barber, J., 1972, I, 22, K4; Burl, 1976, 339, Ky6 [Drumminboy]; O'Nuallain, 1984a, 29, no. 46.

19a *Uragh NE* (1) V 832 635/ 2.5 × 2.4/ 5, Ent, O/ *J. Kerry Arch. Hist. Soc 20*, 1987, 112–13; Roberts, J., *Antiquities of the Beara Peninsula*, n.d., 45.

19b *Uragh SW* (3) V 825 628/ 9.5 × 7.5/ MS, int BD, ext 3 × BD?/ *J. Kerry Arch. Hist. Soc 20*, 1987, 112, 114–16. (Site possibly confused with Lohart [Tuosist], ibid, 115–16).

KILDARE

1 *Brewel Hill* (4) N 833 013/ Em 67, StC 17/ CH?/ *JRSAI 61*, 1931, 126–7 [Piper's Chair]; Churcher, 1985, 24; Burl, 1995, 236.

2 *Broadleas* (3) N 928 075/ 32 × 28/ Pl/ *JRSAI 61*, 1931, 130–1 [Piper's Stones]; Churcher, 1985, 15–16.

3 *Whiteleas* (4) N 926 065/ 23.8/ Pl?/ *JRSAI 61*, 1931, 127 [Bracked Stones]; Churcher, 1985, 116.

LAOIS

1 *Slatt Lower* (3) S 568 827/ *c*. 14/ Em, Ent?, int Cn?, O?/ *Arch Inventory of Co. Laois*, 1995, 4, no. 18.

LIMERICK

1 *Ballynamona* (3) R 696 384/ ?/ Pl/ Evans, E., 1966, 143.

2 *Grange* (2) R 640 410/ 59 × 45.8/ Em, Pt/ Exc. 1939. Knockadoon I, II ware (Case, 1961, 224,

227, 228), E and S3/W bkrs (Clarke, 1970, II, 526, 1901F, 1903F), bronze: O'Riordain, 1951/ *PRIA 30C*, 1912, 283; Burl, 1976a, 226–31 [Lios]; Cowan, 1988, 387–8; R. M. Cleary, 'The Later Bronze Age at Lough Gur: filling in the blanks', in Twohig & Ronayne (eds), 114–20. Astron: Nov (Samain) SS, MS SR, Windle, 1912, 287.

3   *Lough Gur C* (3) R 641 411/ 22.9 × 16.2/ Em, int Cn?/ Windle, 1912, 292–3; O'Nuallain, 1995, 16, 35.

4   *Lough Gur D* (4) R 640 411/ 52?/ A?/ O'Riordain, 1951, 38.9.

LONGFORD

1   *Cartronbore, Granard* (3) *c.* N 16. 55. / *c.* 20/ Pl?/ O'Nuallain, 1995, 9.

LOUTH

1   *Ballynahattin* (4) J 041 099/ *c.* 130/ CH?, HS?, Bank 130, int C StCs, 70? 40?, Ent/T. Wright, *Louthiana III*, 1748, 9–10 [Ballynahatne]; Borlase, W. C., 1897, I, 308; Buckley, 1986, 18 [Carn Beg]; *Arch Ire 2, (2)*, 1988, 53–5.

2   *Killin* (5, 4) J 009 101/ ?/ Int PgT?, art/ Destr. 1826: *Co. Louth Arch & Hist J*, 1907, 60/ Buckley, 1986, 6, no. 48; O'Nuallain, 1995, 8.

3   *Ravensdale Park* (6) J 083 156/ 7 × 4/ StC?, ext 4-st R?/ Borlase, W. C., 1897, II, 421; Buckley, 1986, 18.

MAYO

1   *Ardcorkey* (4) M 17. 41. / *c.* 28/ Ent?/ *JGAHS 31*, 1964–5, 15.

2   *Carrowreagh* (3) M 26. 65. / 17/ int PgT/ *JGAHS 31*, 1964–5, 14.

3a *Cong E* (3) M 164 558/ 13.2 × 12.6/ Pf or int Cn?/ Stukeley, 1776, II, 80a, 84 (1); *RCAHM-S*, 1925, xxxv (plans by Edward Lhuyd); Evans, 1966, 162; Lohan, 1993, 23, 27 [Tonaleeaun 1]; Burl, 1995, 239–41.

3b *Cong N* (1) M 163 553/ 16.2 × 15.9/ Variant MSC, int Cn, Ent/ Lohan, 1993, 22, 23, [Glebe 1]; Burl, 1995, 241; O'Nuallain, 1995, 32.

3c *Cong S* (3) M 163 557/ 33/ Em/ Lohan, 1993, 23, 25 [Nymphsfield 2]; Burl, 1995, 241; O'Nuallain, 1995, 33–5.

3d *Cong W* (1) M 162 558/ 16.5 × 16.2/ Pl/ W. Wilde, *Lough Corrib*, 1872, 234; Lohan, 1993, 23, 24 [Nymphsfield 1]; Burl, 1995, 241; O'Nuallain, 1995, 32–3.

4   *Inishowen* (5) M 128 615/ 20?/ Em, Pf, StC?/ Stukeley, 1776, II, 84 (2nd); W. Wilde, *Lough Corrib*, 1872, 227–8.

5   *Killadangan* (4) L 942 825/ ?/ Destr./ de Valera & O'Nuallain, 1964, 98.

6   *Rathfran* (3) G 192 334/ 18/ Em/ *JRSAI 81*, 1951, 180 [Summerhouse Hill]; de Valera & O'Nuallain, 1964, 95; O'Nuallain, 1995, 35.

7   *Rathfranpark* (4) G 184 333/ ?/ Destr. post-1951/ *JRSAI 81*, 1951, 180 [Mullaghmore]; de Valera & O'Nuallain, 1964, 95.

8   *Rosdoagh* (5) F 827 383/ 16.5 × 9.1/ C/ de Valera & O'Nuallain, 1964, 1–4; Harbison, 1992, 252; Burl, 1995, 242.

MEATH

1   *Ballinvalley* (3) N 581 785/ 29 × 27/ Ent, int PgT?, ext R?/ Moore, 1987, 40; O'Nuallain, 1995, 8; *Arch Ire 9 (4)*, 1995, 28–9.

2   *Donaghmore* (5, 4) N 86. 68. / ?/ ?/ *JRSAI 22*, 1892–3, 126.

3   *Dowth* (4) O 035 744/ 6.4?/ Destr. by quarrying: Moore, 1987, 40.

4   *Newgrange* (4?) O 007 726/ *c.* 107.9 × 91.1/ Int. PgT, art/ Exc. 1962–75. Finds from PgT. Pendants, balls, beads, fl, pins. Bones, crem. C-14, Pre-tomb, 2585 ± 105 (UB-361), 2530 ± 60 bc (GrN-9057). From tomb, 2475 ± 45 bc (GrN-5462), 2465 ± 40 bc (GrN-5463): O'Kelly, 1982. Post-tomb, pre-StC? 2040 ± 40 bc (GrN-6343), 1935 ± 35 bc (GrN-6342), 2100 ± 40 bc (GrN-6344), 2035 ± 55 bc (UB-2392), 2035 ± 45 bc (UB-2393), 1925 ± 90 bc (UB-2394): P. D. Sweetman, *PRIA 85*, 1985, 195–20, 208–9/ G. Coffey, *New Grange and other Incised Tumuli*, 1912; O'Kelly, C., 1978; O'Kelly, M., 1987, 41; Cowan, 1988, 387–8, 391; O'Nuallain, 1995, 6–8; Burl, 1995, 242–3/ Astron, MdW SR, Patrick, 1974; Nature 337, 1989, 343–5.

SLIGO

1   *Carrowmore 9* (3) *c.* G 663 335/ 13.7 × 12.5/ Pl Kitchin, 1983, 160; Burl, 1995, 246.

2   *Carrowmore 11* (3) 21.3 × 19.2/ Pl Kitchin, 1983, 161; Burl, 1995, 246.

3   *Carrowmore 26* (3) 16.2 × 14.6/ Pl Kitchin, 1983, 163, boulder-circle; Burl, 1995, 245.

4   *Carrowmore 57* (3) 16.2 × 15.1/ Kitchin, 1983, 166, boulder-circle; Burl, 1995, 245 (There are boulder-circles at Sites 1, 2, 4, 5, 7, 10, 15, 16?, 17, 18, 19, 22, 27, 36, 37, 38, 48, 56, 62). Kitchen, *PPS 49*, 1983, 151–75; Burenhult, 1984; Burl, 1995, 243–6.

5   *Tanrego Bay* (4) *c.* G 62. 30. / *c.* 8/ Pf. Destr. 1858/ Herity, 1974, 17 [Cuchallin's Tomb].

TIPPERARY

1   *Bauraglanna* (3) R 837 677/ 17 × 14.8?, 15 × 12.8/ Pl/ Killanin & Duignan, 1967, 387 [Fir Bréaga]; *JRSAI 117*, 1987, 142–4.

2 *Borrisnoe* (5) S 078 783/ 17/ Int mound, Ct, O/ Stout, G., 1984, 22.

3 *Coumroe* (4) R 773 763/ *c.* 8.3/ Pl/ inf: S.O'Nuallain.

4 *Rearnogy More* (4) R 84. 59. / 4.5/ O, ext R/ *N. Munster A.J. 12*, 1969, 90.

5 *Timoney Hills* (5) S 194 837/ 61/ V?, Ct?/ *PPS 3*, 1937, 363; Stout, G., 1984, 17–19.

WEXFORD

1 *Carrickbyrne* (5) S 82. 24. / 6.1 × 4.9/ 8/ *JRSAI 16*, 1883–4, 41.

2 *Robinstown Great* (3) S 811 291/ *c.* 4.9 × 3.4/ 4P, ext Pair?, Q/ O'Nuallain, 1984b, 17, no. 6; Burl, 1988a, 788–9.

WICKLOW

1 *Athgreany* (1) N 930 032/ 23/ O? cms?/ *JRSAI 61*, 1931, 128 [Pipers' Stones]; Churcher, 1985, 8; O'Nuallain, 1995, 10–11.

2 *Ballyfolan* (5) O 04. 18. / 16/ Cn/ *JRSAI 63*, 1933, 47–8; Churcher, 1985, 9.

3 *Ballyfoyle* (4, 5) O 03. 15. / *c.* 4.5/ 5?/ Churcher, 1985, 10.

4 *Blessington Desmesne* (4) N 97. 13. / ?/ Pl?/ Churcher, 1985, 10 [Piper's Stones].

5 *Boleycarrigeen* (3) S 938 892/ 14/ Em, Ent, Gr/ *PRIA 42*, 1934, 39; Churcher, 1985, 10–11; O'Nuallain, 1995, 11–13.

6 *Castleruddery* (3) S 916 942/ 29.3/ C, Em, Q Ent, ext. R/ Resistivity survey, 1984. Double-ditch around StC. Churcher, 1985, 27–33/ *JRSAI 75*, 1945, 266–7; O'Nuallain, 1995, 12.

7 *Tournant* (5) N 87. 00. / 13.4+ / Pf, S?, O?/ *PRIA 42*, 1934, 38; Churcher, 1985, 14.

UNITED KINGDOM

Channel Isles

These monuments, known as Cists-in-Circles, may be a variant form of stone circle but strongly influenced by chambered tomb design. Because of the unclear nature of their architecture the status of each is preceded by '5'.

GUERNSEY

1 *Mare és Mauves* (5, 4) WV 346 834/ 15/ Int Cts/ Exc. 1837, 1844. Sherds, fl: Cox, 1976, 35–6/ Kinnes & Grant, 1983, 60; Bender, 232.

2 *Martello 7* (5, 4) WV 341 835/ ?/ ?/ Bender, 232–3.

3 *Plate Mare, La* (5, 4) WV 336 831/ 4.6?/ Ct, cms/ Exc. 1837, 1840. Bkrs, late Neo sherds, 2 pol st axes, fl a/h. 1981. Bkr. Kinnes & Grant, 1983, 58/ Cox, 1976, 33–4.

4 *Sandy Hook, l'Islet* (5, 3) WV 331 822/ D-shaped, 9 × 7.2/ Cts, 2 ancillary rings to N and S/ Exc. 1912. Sherds, fl: *Guernsey Soc Nat Hist 6*, 1913, 400–14/ Cox, 1976, 17–20; Kinnes & Grant, 1983, 46–7.

JERSEY

5 *Hougue des Platons* (5, 4) 656 556/ 9 × 8.2/ Ct/ Exc. 1914, 1936. Crems: Kinnes & Hibbs, 1988, 74–5; Burl, 1995, 187.

6 *Ville-ès-Nouaux* (2) 635 499/ 6.4 × 5.8/ Variant MSC, int BD, adj allée-couverte/ Exc. 1883. No finds: *Bull Assoc de la Soc Jersiaise 1*, 1884, 422–35; Burl, 1995, 187.

England

CHESHIRE

1   *Church Lawton South* (4) SJ 808 557/ 23 × 21/ Pl, int mortuary house. Covered by sand. Cn/ priv. comm. R. McNeil, 16.6.83.

2   *New Farm, Henbury* (5) SJ 887 728/*c.* 7.3 6.1/ Pl, ext pit/ Exc. 1970. Ext pit, fire, char and ash. *TLChS 78*, 1975, 79–80. Astron: MdW SR. *ibid.*

CORNWALL

1   *Altarnun* (2) SX 236 781/ 15.2 × 13.7/ Pl, R?, S?/ Rest. 1889/ Tregelles, 396–7; Thom, 1967, S1/2 [Nine Stones]; Barnatt, 1982, 190–2./ Astron: Min N MR. Thom, 1967, 100.

2   *Boscawen-Un* (2) SW 412 273/ 24.9 × 21.9 CB/ Pl, Gr, Q, Ent, S, 19 st/ Rest. 1862/ Aubrey, I, 70, 104–5, 226; Stukeley, 1740, 54; Dunkin, 1870, 97–9, 101–2; Lukis, 1885, 1, 23 Pl. 2; Tregelles, 379; Thom, 1967, CB, S1/13; Weatherhill, 20; Barnatt, 1982, 159–62; *CA 25*, 1986, 69; Straffon, 1992, 6–7; Burl, 1999, 78–83.

3   *Boskednan* (3) SW 434 351/ 21.9/ Pl, 22–23 st, ext Cn/ Lewis, A. L. 1905, 433; Dunkin, 1870, 99–100; Lukis, 1885, 2, 24, Pl. 4; Tregelles, 386–8; Thom, 1967, S1/11 [Nine Maidens, Ding Dong]; Weatherhill, 1981, 21; Barnatt, 1982, 165–7; Straffon, 1992, 9; Burl, 1999, 73–5.

4   *Candra Hill* (4) SX 132 794/ 44/ Pl/ O.S. SX 17 NW 50.21.

5   *Craddock Moor* (3) SX 248 183/ *c.* 39.3/ Pl, 27–8 st/ *JRIC 25*, 1938, 61–2; Barnatt, 1980, 21–2; Barnatt, 1982, 198; *CA 25*, 1986, 65.

6   *Crowan Ridge* (3) SW 664 348/ *c.* 25.5/ Pl/ Barnatt, 1989, II, 402.

7   *Duloe* (2) SX 235 583/ 11.9 × 11.3 CA/ Pl, Q/ Rest, Exc. *c.* 1863. Trevisker urn/ Borlase, W. C., 1872, 247–52; *JBAA 38*, 1882, 149; Lukis, 1885, 14, 30, pl. 13; Thom, 1967, S1/3 [Duloo].

8   *Fernacre* (3) SX 144 799/ 46 × 43 CD/ Pl, O?, 77–95 st/ Lukis, 1885, 3, 30, Pl. 6; Tregelles, 394–5; Thom, 1967, S1/7 [Rough Tor], 57; Barnatt, 1982, 170–2; Cowan, 1988, 386–7 [Rough Tor]; *CA 25*, 1986, 63./ Astron: equin SR, Barnatt, 1982, 171; Barnatt, 1989, II, 404–5.

9   *Goodaver* (2) SX 208 751/ 32.7 × 31.5/ Pl, 30–2 st/ Barnatt, 1980, 23–4. TTB, 1980, 102–3 [Trezibbet]; Barnatt, 1982, 187–90, Burl, 1995, 33.

10a   *Hurlers NNE* (3) SX 258 713/ 34.7/ Pl, 26–8 st/.

10b   *Hurlers Centre* (3)/ 41.7 × 40.5, CII/ S, art? 26–8 st/ Exc. 1936. Flints. Radford, 1938, 319.

10c   *Hurlers SSW* (4) 31.9/ Pl, 26–8 st, ext Pair/ Norden, J. *Description of Cornwall*, 1603–7,

65–6; Camden, 1695, 9; Aubrey, I, 104; Dymond, C. W., 1879a; Lukis, 1885, 4, 31, pls. 10, 11, 12; *PPS 1*, 1935, 134; *PPS 4 (2)*, 1938, 319; Thom, 1967, S1/1; TTB, 1980, 74–5; *CA 25*, 1986, 63–5, 69; Barnatt, 1989, II, 408–10; Burl, 1995, 3–4.

11a   *King Arthur's Down NW* (3) SX 134 775/ 23.5 × 23/ Adj, Pl, 16–23 st.

11b   *King Arthur's Down SE* (4) SX 134 775/ *c.* 23.3/ Adj, Pl?, / Barnatt, 1980, 19–20; *CA 25*, 1986, 67.

12   *King Arthur's Hall* (5) SX 129 776/ 47 × 20/ Rect/ *J.Anthr. Inst 25*, 1896, 5, Pl. I; Johnson & Rose, 1994, 28–9; Burl, 1995, 34.

13a   *Leaze SE* (3) SX 136 772/ 24.8/ Pl, 22 st/ Tregelles, 392–3; Thom, 1967, S1/6; TTB, 1980, 84–5; Barnatt, 1982, 172–4.

13b   *Leaze NW* (4) SX 134 775/ 23/ Pl; N. Johnson, priv. comm., 16.8.78; TTB, 1980, 85; Ord. Surv. 17 NW 49.93.

14a   *Leskernick NW* (4) SX 186 799/ 30.4/ Pl, 20–2 st/ Johnson & Rose, 1994, 31 [Leskernick II]; Barnatt, 1989, II, 413; *PPS 63*, 1997, 157.

14b   *Leskernick SE* (3) SX 188 796/ 30.6/ Pl, Gr, 31 st/ Barnatt, 1980, 17–18; Johnson & Rose, 1994, 31 [Leskernick I]; Barnatt, 1989, II, 412; *PPS 63*, 1997, 157.

15   *Louden Hill* (3) SX 132 794/ 45.5 × 43/ Pl, 33–9 st/ Barnatt, 1980, 20–1; *CA 25*, 1986, 63; Barnatt, 1989, II, 413; Johnson & Rose, 1994, 31.

16   *Men-an-Tol* (5) SW 426 349/ 17–18/ Pl?, 20–2 st, ext Cn/ Exc. 1885. 1 flint; probing, 1992/ Lukis, 1885, 17, 25, pl. 34; / Barnatt, 1982, 223–6; *CA 33*, 1993, 5–16; Preston-Jones, A. *The Men-an-Tol. Management and Survey*, 1993, Truro. Damage: *Meyn Mamvro 41*, 2000, 2.

17a   *Merry Maidens NE* (2) SW 432 245/ 23.8/ Pl, Ent, 19 st/ Rest. 1862–9/ Lukis, 1885, 1, 21, pl. 1; Tregelles, 382; Thom, 1967, S1/14; Weatherhill, 1981, 25; Barnatt, 1982, 154–9; *CA 25*, 1986, 69–71; Barnatt, 1989, II, 414; Straffon, 1992, 4–5; Burl, 1999, 67–73.

17b   *Merry Maidens SW* (4) SW 431 244/ *c.* 27/ Pl/ Lockyer, 1909, 268; Barnatt, 1982, 157–8; Barnatt, 1989, II, 395 [Boleigh].

18   *New Downs* (5) SW 701 507/ ?/ Pl?/ *CA 1*, 1962, 114; Burl, 1976, 341; Barnatt, 1980, 24.

Nine Stones, see Altarnun.

19   *Porthmeor* (5) SW 444 366/ *c.* 34.4 × 29.6 CB/ Em, Ent/ Lukis, 1885, 28; *CA 6*, 1967, 86; Thom, 1967, S1/12; TTB, 1980, 94–5; *Meyn Mamvro 12*, 1990, 7, 13.

20   *St Breocks Down* (5) Norden, J. *Description of Cornwall*, 1603–7, 48 [Nine Sisters]; *Meyn Mamvro 26*, 1995, 3; *Meyn Mamvro 27*, 1995, 4.

21 *Stannon* (3) SX 126 800/ 42.7 × 40.5 CA/ Pl,
Gr?, 71–82 st, S?, O?, ext 4-st row/ Tregelles,
395–6; Thom, 1967, S1/8 [Dinnever Hill], 58,
TTB, 1980, 88–9; Barnatt, 1982, 167–70; Barnatt,
1989, II, 420./ Astron: Beltane SR. Barnatt, 1982,
169; *CA 25*, 1986, 63.

22 *Stripple Stones* (4) SX 143 752/ 44.8/ CH, S, B,
Ent, V?, *c*. 28 st/ Exc. 1905. Flints. Gray, 1908/
Lukis, 1885, 3, 21, pls 8, 9; Thom, 1967, S1/4; *CA
25*, 1986, 65–7; Barnatt, 1989, II, 420–1; Johnson
& Rose, 1994, 33; Burl, 1995, 36–7.

23 *Treddinick* (5) SW 442 349/ 9.1?/ Pl?/ Borlase,
W., 1769, 198, 206; *CA 4*, 1965, 71; Barnatt, 1980,
24; Barnatt, 1990, 10.

24 *Treen* (5) SW 444 366/ *c*. 33 × 28/ Em, Iron Age
enclosure?/ *PWCFC 2*, 1957–8, 183; Weatherhill,
1985, 109, no. 40.

25a *Tregeseal E* (2) SW 387 324/ 21.8 × 21 CA/ Adj,
Pl, *c*. 21 st/ Rest. 1932/ Lukis, 1885, 2, 27, Pl. 3;
Tregelles, 385; Thom, 1967, S1/15 [Botallack];
TTB, 1980, 100–1; Barnatt, 1982, 162–5; *CA 25*,
1986, 69; Straffon, 1992, 8; Burl, 1999, 75–8.

25b *Tregeseal Centre* (4) SW 386 323/ ?/ Adj, 18–19
st/ Destr. pre-1905/ *Meyn Mamvro 2*, 1986, 2–3.

25c *Tregeseal W* (4) SW 385 323/ 23.2?/ Adj, Pl?,
18–19 st/ Barnatt, 1982, 164; *Meyn Mamvro 2*,
1986, 2–3.

26 *Tregurnow* (5) SW 437 245?/ ?/ ?/ *West Penwith
Survey*, 1971, 36.

27 *Trehudreth Down* (4) SX 126 727/ *c*. 8/ Em?/
Barnatt, 1989, II, 422.

28 *Trippet Stones* (3) SX 131 750/ 33/ Pl, 26 st?/
Lukis, 1885, 3, 21, pl. 7; Tregelles, 389; Thom,
1967, S1/5 [Treswigger].

29a *Wendron N* (4) SW 683 365/ *c*. 18/ Adj, Pl/
Lukis, 1885a, 2, 29 [Nine Maidens, The Virgin
Sisters].

29b *Wendron S* (3) SW 683 365/ 16.3/ Adj, Pl, 14–15
st/ Tregelles, 388; Thom, 1967, S1/10 [Nine
Maidens].

CUMBERLAND (CUMBRIA)

1 *Annaside* (4) SD 099 853/ *c*. 18/ Pl?/ Parker &
Collingwood, 18; Waterhouse, 1985, 90.

2 *Ash-House Wood* (4) SD 192 873/ 30.5/ Pl, Pf/
TCWAAS 29, 1929, 257; Waterhouse, 1985, 91,
93.

3 *Blakeley Raise* (2) NY 060 140/ 16.6/ Pl, int Cn?/
Rest. 1925/ Quine, 22–5; *TCWAAS 28*, 1928, 410;
Clare, 1975, 7–8 [Kinniside]; Waterhouse, 1985,
68–70; Barnatt, 1989, II, 341/ Astron: Maj N MS.
Thom, 1971, 71–3, L1/16 [Blakeley Moss].

4 *Brats Hill* (3) NY 173 023/ 32 × 29.5 CA/ Pl, 5
int Cns, O?/ Exc. 1827. Antlers: Williams, B.,
1856b/ Dymond, C. W., 1881, 55–7; Thom, 1967,
60, L1/6e [Burnmoor E]; Clare, 1975, 9–11;
Waterhouse, 1985, 55–6; Barnatt, 1989, II, 342.

5 *Broad Field* (4) NY 425 445/ on mound 19.2/ Pl,
3 int Cts, A?/ Exc. 1789. 'Pieces of skull and
bones': *Arch 10*, 1792, 105–9/ Waterhouse, 1985,
153; Barnatt, 1989, II, 467–8.

6a *Broomrigg N* (3) NY 548 467/ 50.9 × 50 CE/
CH?, O or A/ Exc. 1934, 1950, no finds:
TCWAAS 35, 1935, 77; *TCWAAS 53*, 1953, 5–8/
Waterhouse, 1985, 107–9 [Broomrigg A].

6b *Broomrigg Centre E* (5) NY 550 466/ 5.5 × 4.5/
Pl/ Exc. 1960. Sherds, flint: *TCWAAS 75*, 1975,
17/ Waterhouse, 1985, 113 [Broomrigg D].

6c *Broomrigg Centre W* (5) NY 548 466/ 3.4/ Pl,
Cn/ Exc. 1950. Flint: Hodgson, 1952, 1–8/
Waterhouse, 1985, 107, 110 [Broomrigg B].

6d *Broomrigg S* (5, 2?) NY 548 465/ 15.6/ Pl, Cn, 2
× Ct, O?/ Exc. 1948–9, crems, urn, jet beads,
bronze. Recon?: *TCWAAS 50*, 1950, 30;
Longworth, 1984, 166, no. 190/ Waterhouse, 1985,
110 [Broomrigg C].

7 *Brougham Hall* (4, 5) *c*. NY 52. 28/ 18.3?/ int
Cn?/ Pennant, 1774, 257; Waterhouse, 1985, 153.

8a *Castlerigg E* (1) NY 292 236/ 32.9 × 29.9 CA/
CH?, Ent, 3 int Cns, spiral, V?/ Exc. 1882, no
finds: *TCWAAS VI (O.S.)*, 1883, 505/ Nicolson &
Burn, II, 80; Dymond, 1881, 50–5; Thom, 1966,
fig. 39; Clare, 1975, 2, 11, 12; Waterhouse, 1985,
95–8; Barnatt, 1989, II, 343–4; Bradley, 1997,
111./ Astron: Samain (Nov) SR. Thom, 1967, 99,
L1/1.

8b *Castlerigg W* (4) NY 293? 236/ 33+?/ ?/ Stukeley,
1776, II, 48.

9 *Chapel Flat* (4) NY 37. 50./ *c*. 27/ Cn?, V?/
Nicolson & Burn, 477; Waterhouse, 1985, 153.

10 *Elva Plain* (3) NY 176 317/ 33.5/ Pl, O?/
TCWAAS 23, 1923, 29–32; Waterhouse, 1985,
74–6.

11a *Gretigate NE* (3) (3) NY 057 037/ 7.3/ Adj, Cn? /
Exc. 1960. Flints, haematite: Stout, 1961/
Waterhouse, 1985, 67 [Gretigate C].

11b *Gretigate NW* (3) NY 057 037/ 22.9 × 18.9 CE/
Adj, Pl, Cn?/ Exc. 1960. Crem? Stout, 1961/
Waterhouse, 1985, 67 [Gretigate B]; Barnatt,
1989, II, 468.

11c *Gretigate SE* (4) NY 058 036/ NY 057 036/ *c*.
31.7/ Adj, Pl/ Stout, 1961; Waterhouse, 1985,
66–7 [Gretigate A].

12 *Grey Croft* (2) NY 034 024/ 27.1 × 24.4 CD/ Cn,
O/ Exc. 1949. Gp VI axe, jet ring, hawthorn
berries: Fletcher, 1957/ Thom, 1967, L1/10
[Seascale]; Waterhouse, 1985, 62–5.

13 *Grey Yauds* (4) NY 544 486/ 47.5/ Pl, O/
Nicolson & Burn, II, 495; Hutchinson, W., I, 175;
Dymond, 1881, 47; *TCWAAS 7*, 1907, 67–71;
TCWAAS 35, 1935, 171; Waterhouse, 1985, 151.

14 *Hall Foss* (4) SD 112 857/ *c*. 23/ Pl/ Hutchinson,
W., I, 553 [Standing Stones]; *TCWAAS 1 (O.S.)*,
1874, 278; Waterhouse, 1985, 90.

15 *Kirkstones* (4) SD 106 843/ ?/ C, ext Cn/ Hutchinson, W., I, 554; *TCWAAS 1, (O.S.)*, 1874, 278; Waterhouse, 1985, 90.

16a *Lacra NE* (4) SD 151 813/ 18.3 × 15.6 CE/ Pl, A or R?/ Exc. 1947. OHR urn: Dixon & Fell, 5–13. Longworth, 1984, 168, no. 213/ Waterhouse, 1985, 49–52 [Lacra D].

16b *Lacra NW* (3) SD 150 813/ 16.2/ Pl/ TTB, 1980, 48–9 L1/12 [Lacra E]; Waterhouse, 1985, 46 [Lacra A].

16c *Lacra S* (1) SD 149 810/ *c*. 15.2/ int Cn, S?/ Exc. 1947. Crem: Dixon & Fell,13–20/ TTB, 1980, 48–9, [Lacra S]; Waterhouse, 1985, 46–9 [Lacra B]. Lacra C 100 m to the E is a 3-st row: Burl, 1993, 157, 250.

17 *Lamplugh* (4) NY 065 177/ *c*. 31/ Pl/ Nicolson & Burn, 477; Waterhouse, 1985, 93.

18 *Le Wheles* (5) NX 989 180/ ?/ ?/ *TCWAAS 33*, 1933, 174 [Corcickle], destr. 1628; *TCWAAS 58*, 1958, 4; Waterhouse, 1985, 89, 93.

19a *Long Meg and Her Daughters NE* (3) NY 571 373/ 109.4 × 93 CB/ CH?, Pt, O, Crs, spirals: Beckensall, 1992, 6–13/ Nicolson & Burn, II, 448–9; Dymond, 1881, 43–7; *Ant 62*, 1988, 552–7; Burl, 1994a; Burl, 1999, 33–5/ Astron: MdW SS. Thom, 1967, 99, L1/7.

19b *Long Meg and Her Daughters SW* (4) *c*. NY 570 372/ *c*. 15/ Pl?, O/ Stukeley, 1776b, 47; Ant 8, 1934, 328–9.

20a *Low Longrigg NE* (3) NY 172 028/ 21.6 × 15.2 CE/ Adj, int Cns/ Dymond, 1881, 55; TTB, 1980, 36–7 [Burn Moor A]; Waterhouse, 1985, 61.

20b *Low Longrigg SW* (3) NY 172 027/ 15.2/ Adj, int Cn/ Dymond, 1881, 55; TTB, 1980, 36–7 [Burn Moor B]; Waterhouse, 1985, 61.

21 *Lowhouse* (5) NY 496 343/ ?/ st 2.4 m h, Cn?/ O.S., 13.12.1966.

Motherby, see Penruddock.

22 *Penruddock* (4) NY 419 282/ 15.6?/ Pl?/ 'an excellent peristalith', blown up, *c*. 1850, *PSAL 3*, 1856, 224; by orders of Duke of Norfolk's steward, *VCH Cumberland, I*, 248; Ferguson, 1906, 248; *TCWAAS 23*, 1923, 256; Waterhouse, 1985, 154.

23 *Ringlen Stones* (4) NX 995 107/ *c*. 55/ Pl?/ Hutchinson, 1794, II, 25; Parker & Collingwood, 8; Burl, 1976, 342 [Egremont]; Waterhouse, 1985, 93.

24 *Shapbeck Plantation* (3) NY 552 188/ 22 × 20.5, ?, ?/ 3C, int Cn/ *TCWAAS VI (O.S.)*, 1882, 176; *TCWAAS 86*, 1986, 248–50; Barnatt, 1989, II, 352–3.

25 *Studfold* (3) NY 040 224/ 32.8 × 25.9 CE/ Pl/ Exc pre-1924, no finds: Mason & Valentine, 269/ *TCWAAS 23*, 1923, 34; Thom, 1967, L1/14 [Dean Moor]; Waterhouse, 1985, 71–3 [Studfold Gate].

26 *Swinside* (1) SD 172 883/ 28.7/ Pt/ Exc. 1901, no finds: Dymond, 1902/ Gough, III, 432; Hutchinson, 1794, 554–5; Dymond, 1881, 47–50; TTB, 1980, 34–5; Waterhouse, 1985, 42–4; Burl, 1999, 173–85/ Astron: MdW SR: Burl, 1995, 49.

27a *White Moss NE* (3) NY 172 024/ 15.9/ Adj, int Cn/ Dymond, 1881, 55; Thom, 1967, l1/6 [Burnmoor D]; TTB, 1980, 38–9; Waterhouse, 1985, 56–61.

27b *White Moss SW* (3) NY 172 023/ 16.6/ Adj, int Cn/ Dymond, 1881, 55; Thom, 1967, L1/6 [Burnmoor C]; TTB, 1980, 38–9; Waterhouse, 1985, 56–61.

DERBYSHIRE

Abney Moor, see Smelting Hill.

1 *Abney Ridge* (4) SK 202 803/ *c*. 15/ adj, Em, int Cn/ Radley, 18; J. Barnatt, priv. comm. 7.1.86.

2 *Arbor Low* (3) SK 160 636/ bank 79 × 75, st 'circle' 41.5 × 37.2 CII/ CH, R, V, Pt, Cn on bank/ Exc. 1901–2, flints, skeleton: Gray, H. St G. 1903. Cairn: Bateman, T. *Vestiges of the Antiquities of Derbyshire*, 1848, 64–5: ct, 2 f/vs; Howarth, 1899, 114–15, 129–30/ *Arch 7*, 1785, 131–48; Barnatt, 1990, 31–9; Burl, 1995, 49–51/ Astron: MdS SR, MdW SS, Maj N MR. Barnatt, 1978, 84–7.

3 *Ash Cabin Flat* (3) SK 269 862/ 5.5 × 4.5/ Em/ Barnatt, 1989, II, 365.

4 *Bamford Moor SE* (1) SK 221 845/ 7.9 × 6.8/ Em, Pf, Gr? O/ Barnatt, 1978, 162–7; Barnatt, 1990, 47; Barnatt, 1995, 46.

5a *Barbrook Centre* (2) SK 277 758/ 13.4/ Em, int Cns/ Exc. 1966, OHR urn, crems, flints, shale ring. C-14: 1500 ± 150 bc (BM-197): *JDANHS 86*, 1966, 115–17; Rest. 1989, char under bank, 1585 ± 70 bc (OxA-2440): Barnatt, 1995, 27–38/ Longworth, 1984, 173, no. 276/ Barnatt, 1978, 110–11; Barnatt, 1990, 55–7 [Barbrook II].

5b *Barbrook NE* (3) SK 283 772/ 26.2 × 23.4 CB/ Em/ Barnatt, 1978, 114–15; TTB, 1980, 20–1; Barnatt, 1989, II, 366–7 [Barbrook III, Owler Bar]; Barnatt, 1995, 43.

5c *Barbrook SW* (3) SK 278 755/ 14.5 × 12.5 CB/ Em, Pf, cm?, O/ Barnatt, 1978, 100–1; TTB, 1980, 18–19; Barnatt, 1990, 57–9 [Barbrook I]; Barnatt, 1995, 46.

Broomhead I, see Ewden Beck.

6 *Brown Edge* (4) SK 288 789/ 7.3 × 6.1/ Em, int Cn/ Exc. 1963. In pit, crem, C-14: 1050 ± 150 bc (BM-177), OHR urn, flints; 2nd pit, crem, urn, C-14: 1250 ± 150 bc (BM-211); 3rd pit, crem, urn, pygmy cup, C-14: 1530 ± 150 bc (BM-212); 4th pit, urn?: *Arch J 123*, 1966, 1–26. Longworth, 1984, 174, nos 276–8/ Barnatt, 1990, 52–5.

7 *Bull Ring* (4) SK 078 783/ *c.* 53 × 46/ CH?, R?/ Exc. 1902, 'Neolithic or Bronze Age' sherds lost: *VCH Derbyshire I*, 1905, 182/ 1949, 2 sherds, Alcock, 1950; Barnatt, 1988/ J. Pilkington, *The Present State of Derbyshire, II*, 1789, 462; *JDANHS 37*, 1915, 77–86; Atkinson, R. J. C. et al., 1951, 100–1; Barnatt, 1978, 88–90; Barnatt, 1990, 39–41.

8 *Doll Tor* (3) SK 238 628/ 6.9 × 4.5/ Pl? int Cn? + secondary Cn/ Exc. 1852, sherds, urns, incense cups: T. Bateman, 1861, 84; J. P. Heathcote, 1931–3, crems, urns, faience, *DAJ 60*, 1939, 116–25/ Barnatt, 1990, 79–82.

9 *Ewden Beck* (3) SK 238 966/ 15.9 × 14.7/ Em, 2 Ents, 2 int Cns/ Burl, 1976, 343 [Broomhead I]; Barnatt, 1989, II, 368; Barnatt, 1990, 42.

Eyam Moor I, see Wet Withens.

10a *Eyam Moor NW* (3) SK 231 789/ 8 × 7.7/ Em, int Cn, Ent?/ Barnatt, 1990, 3–5 [Eyam Moor II].

10b *Eyam Moor SE* (3) SK 232 787/ 13 × 12.3/ Pl, int Cn/ Barnatt, 1989, II, 368–9 [Eyam Moor III].

Froggatt Edge, see Stoke Flat.

11a *Gibbet Moor N* (3) SK 282 708/ *c.* 4 × 4 (5.7)/ 4P/ Barnatt, 1986, *DAJ 106*, 18–101; Burl, 1988a, 73; Barnatt, 1989, II, 369.

11b *Gibbet Moor S* (5) SK 281 702/ 13 × 10.5/ 4P? Em?/ Barnatt, 1990, 64. Domestic? Agricultural?

12 *Handsome Cross* (4) SK 26. 94./ *c.* 7.5 × 6.5/Em?, int Cn/ Barnatt, 1989, II, 369.

Hordron Edge, see Seven Stones in Hordron.

13 *Nine Ladies* (1) SK 247 634/ 11.5 × 10.5/ Em, int Cn, O/ Exc. eighteenth century. Finds?: *Arch 6*, 1782, 112/ *DAJ 100*, 1980, 15–16; TTB, 1980, 16–17; Cowan, 1988, 386–7, 391; Barnatt, 1990, 76–7; Barnatt, 1995, 44, 46.

14 *Ninestone Close* (3) SK 225 625/ 13.1/ Pl?, 2 cms? on south st/ Exc. 1847: sherds, flints: T. Bateman, *Vestiges . . .* , 1848, 102, 111; 1877: no finds: L. Jewitt, *Grave Mounds and their Contents*, 1870, 74 [Nine Ladies, Grey Ladies, Hartle Moor]/ Thom, 1967, D1/4; Barnatt, 1990, 82–3; Burl, 1995, 53–5/ Astron: Maj S MS behind Robin Hood's Stride, Barnatt, 1978, 157.

15 *Offerton Moor* (5) SK 212 806/ 23 × 18.5/ Em, C?/ *Arch 7*, 1785, 177; Ward, J., 1905, 183; *Trans Hunter Index*, 1956, D86, 87; Barnatt, 1990, 69.

16 *Park Gate* (5) SK 280 685/ 12.4 × 11.8/ Em, Gr? cm S st, int Cn, ext Cn/ Andrew, 1907, 74; Barnatt, 1990, 64–6; Barnatt, 1995, 43.

17 *Ringstones* (4, 5) SK 006 896/ ?/ ?/ Barnatt, 1990, 84.

18 *Seven Brethren* (4) SK 309 639 or SK 307 642/ 8 × 6.5/ Em?. [Also known as Seven Bridiron]/ Barnatt, 1990, 68; Barnatt, 1995, 44–5.

19 *Seven Stones in Hordron* (1) SK 215 868/ 15.9 × 15.2/ Pl, O?/ Exc. 1992. Pf? orig 16 st?: Barnatt,

1995, 38–41/ Ward, J., 1905, 183; Thom, 1967, 137, CA [Moscar Moor]; TTB, 1980, 22–3; Barnatt, 1990, 45–7.

20 *Smelting Hill* (4) SK 202 803/ 7.5/ Em/ Radley, 18; Barnatt, 1990, 69. [Abney Moor I].

21a *Stanton Moor Central* (5) SK 248 632/ 19.5/ Em, ents, StC or RC/ Barnatt, 1990, 77–9 [Stanton Moor III].

21b *Stanton Moor N* (3) SK 249 636/ 10 × 9/ Em, Ent/ Barnatt, 1990, 75 [Stanton Moor I].

21c *Stanton Moor S* (3) SK 247 629/ 13.5 × 12.5/ Em, ent/ Exc. 1930s or 1940s, finds?: Barnatt, 1990, 79 [Stanton Moor IV].

Stanton Moor II, see Nine Ladies.

22 *Stoke Flat* (3) SK 249 767/ 11/ Em, 1 Ent at SW, int cn, Pf/ Exc. pre-1939. urn, crem: *Arch J 123*, 1966, 17/ Barnatt, 1989, II, 372–3 [Froggatt Edge]; Barnatt, 1990,49, 50; Barnatt, 1995, 46.

23 *Top of Riley* (4) SK 226 768/ ?/ Em, 1+ Ents?/ Wood, W., *History of Eyam*, 1842, 30; Barnatt, 1989, II, 472.

24 *Tunstead* (4) SK 026 792/ *c.* 12.2 × 10.7/ Em, 2 Ents, O?/ Exc. *c.* 1905, inv urn: Andrew, 82–4/ Allcroft, 1927, 228; Barnatt, 1978, 187 [Cadster].

25 *Wet Withens* (5) SK 225 790/ 29.9/ Em, Ct, S?/ Exc. 1840? no finds: T. Bateman, *Vestiges . . .* , 1848, 113/ Ward, J., 1905, 158; Thom, 1967, D1/2 [Wet Withers]; Barnatt, 1990, 71–2; Burl, 1995, 55; Barnatt, 1995, 44.

26 *Woodbrook Quarry* (4, 5) SK 285 657/ *c.* 11/ RC?/ Barnatt, 1990, 66.

D E V O N

1 *Assacombe* (3) SX 661 826/ 8.5/ Int Cn, A/ Worth, 1967, 224; Grinsell, 1978, [Lydford 6]; Barnatt, 1989, II, 394 [Assycombe Hill]; Burl, 1993, 80–1; Turner, 1990, 79 [Assicombe Hill].

2 *Bellever Tor SW* (4) SX 641 762/ 7/ Cn/ Turner, 1990, 79.

Belstone, see Nine Maidens.

3 *Brent Fore Hill* (5) SX 668 613/ *c.* 13/ C?, int Cn, A/ Worth, 1967, 234–5; Barnatt, 1989, II, 396; Turner, 1990, 79.

4 *Brisworthy* (2) SX 565 655/ 24.8/ Em, Gr, Ent?/ Exc. 1909, charcoal: *TDA 48*, 1916, 99–100/ Rest. 1909. Breton, 1932, 23–4/ Thom, 1967, S2/3; TTB, 1980, 108–9; Barnatt, 1989, II, 396–7; Turner, 1990, 80; Butler, J., 1994, 133–4.

5a *Broad Down Centre* (5) SY 174 944/ *c.* 25/ int Cn, Ct/ Exc. 1868. crems, bone bead: *TDA 4*, 1870, 295–304/ Fox, A., 1948, 1–16 [E]; Barnatt, 1989, II, 397.

5b *Broad Down N* (4) SY 174 945/ 16/ int Cn/ Fox, A., 1948, 1–16; Barnatt, 1989, II, 397.

5c *Broad Down S* (5) SY 174 944/ *c.* 36/ int Cn, Ct/ Exc. 1868. Crem, shale cup, bronze dagger: *TDA*

4, 1870, 295–304/ Fox, A., 1948, 1–16 [D]
Barnatt, 1989, II, 397.

6 *Brown Heath* (5) SX 641 653/ 10.1 × 9.2 CA/ Cn,
Ct, A/ Worth, 1967, 203; Davidson & Seabrook,
28; Barnatt, 1989, II, 398.

7 *Buckland Ford* (5) SX 657 660/ 9.6 × 8.2 CII/
Cn/ Worth, 1967, 458; Davidson & Seabrook, 26;
Barnatt, 1989, II, 503; Turner, 1990, 81.

8 *Burford Down* (5) SX 637 601/ 9.7/ Cn, R/
Breton, 1932, 10 [Yadsworthy]; Davidson &
Seabrook, 25; Barnatt, 1989, II, 398; Turner,
1990, 78.

9 *Butterdon Hill* (3) SX 656 588/ 11.1/ Cn, R/
Worth, 1967, 203; 204–5; Barnatt, 1989, II, 398–9;
Turner, 1990, 78.

10a *Buttern ESE* (4) SX 649 884/ 24.5/ Adj, Pl/
Worth, 1967, 253; Barnatt, 1989, II, 399; Turner,
1990, 78; Butler, J., 1991b, 194.

10b *Buttern WNW* (4) SX 643 886/ *c.* 28/ Adj, S?/
TDA 26, 1894, 304.

11 *Cator Common* (4) SX 674 780/ 13.8/ Em/
Turner, 1990, 70.

12 *Challacombe Down* (2) SX 689 808/ 8/ 3 × R/
Brailsford, 1938, 463–4; Turner, 1990, 81.

13 *Cholwichtown* (4) SX 584 622/ 5.8 × 4.8 CE/ Pit,
R/ Exc. 1961, no finds: Eogan, 1964/ Thom, 1967,
72, S2/7 [Lee Moor]; *PPS 35*, 1969, 203–19; TTB,
1980, 112–13; Barnatt, 1989, II, 399
[Cholwichtown Waste]; Turner, 1990, 82; Butler,
J., 1994, 109–10.

14 *Collard Tor* (5) SX 558 620/ 8.1/ Cn, R/ Worth,
1967, 208; Barnatt, 1989, II, 400. Turner, 1990, 79.

15a *Cornridge NW* (4) SX 547 896/ 33.5 × 31.5/ Pl/
Barnatt, 1989, II, 400.

15b *Cornridge SE* (3) SX 551 891/ 20/ Cn/ Turner,
1990, 77.

16a *Corringdon Ball NW* (3) SX 666 612/ 8.7/ Cn, R/
Barnatt, 1989, II, 400.

16b *Corringdon Ball SE* (4) SX 666 611/ 14.5/ 9 × R,
Cn/ Worth, 1967, 231; Davidson & Seabrook, 25;
Barnatt, 1989, II, 401; Butler, 1993, 91–3.

17 *Cosdon Beacon* (2) SX 643 915/ 7 × 6.5/ Cn, 2 ×
Ct, 3 × R/ Rest. Exc. 1896. Finds?: *TDA 30*, 1898,
90–115/ Worth, 1967, 218; Grinsell, 1976, 95;
Burl, 1993, 121–2; Butler, J., 1991b, 204–6.

18 *Deadman's Bottom* (3) SX 607 670/ 16/ Em/
Turner, 1990, 70.

19 *Down Ridge* (3) SX 655 720/ *c.* 25/ Pl/ Exc. 1904,
charcoal: *TDA 23*, 1905,/ *TDA 71*, 1939, 322–3/
Worth, 1967, 256–8; Pettit, 139; Turner, 1990, 80;
Butler, J., 1993, 201–2.

20 *Down Tor* (2) SX 586 692/ 11/ Cn, R/ Rest. 1894:
Breton, 1932, 51–3/ Crossing, 101; Worth, 1967,
212; Barnatt, 1989, II, 402–3; Turner, 1990, 78;
Butler, J., 1994, 71–4 [Hingston].

21a *Drizzlecombe Centre* (3) SX 592 670/ 8.4 × 7.9 /

Cn, R/ Worth, 1967, 210; Barnatt, 1989, II, 403;
Burl, 1993, 113–16; Butler, J., 1994, 139; Leger-
Gordon, 1994, 65; Burl, 1995, 58–9.

21b *Drizzlecombe NNW* (3) SX 592 671/ 9 × 8.5/ Cn/
Barnatt, 1989, II, 403; Butler, J., 1994, 140.

22c *Drizzlecombe SSE* (3) SX 592 670/ 11.3 × 10/
Cn, R/ Worth, 1967, 210; Barnatt, 1989, II, 403–4;
Turner, 1990, 78; Butler, J., 1994, 138/ Astron:
Maj N MR: Burl, 1993, 115.

23 *Eight Rocks* (4) *c.* SX 645 925/ ?/ R?/ Crossing,
213; Grinsell, 1976, 95.

24a *Fernworthy N* (1) SX 658 841/ 18.3/ Gr, D, R/
Exc. 1897. Charcoal: *TDA 30*, 1898, 97–115/
VCH Devon, I, 1906, 356–60; Worth, 1967, 222–4;
Barnatt, 1989, II, 405; Turner, 1990, 80; Butler, J.,
1991b, 162–5; Burl, 1995, 59–60.

24b *Fernworthy W* (4) SX 654 841/ *c.* 9.5/ int Cn, D/
Worth, 1967, 222–4; Grinsell, 1978, 145 [Lydford
21]; Barnatt, 1989, II, 406; Turner, 1990, 81.

25 *Glasscombe Corner* (3) SX 660 608/ 3.5/ Pl, R/
Turner, 1990, 82.

26a *Grey Wethers N* (2) SX 638 831/ 31.6/ Adj, Pl/
Exc. 1891, 1898. Rest. 1909: *TDA 31*, 1899,
146–55/ TTB, 1980, 104–5; Barnatt, 1989, II,
406–7; Turner, 1990, 81; Butler, 1991b, 165–6;
Leger-Gordon, 1994, 60, 70–2; Burl, 1995, 60–1.

26b *Grey Wethers S* (2) SX 638 831/ 35.5/ Adj, Pl,
Rest. 1909/ Barnatt, 1989, II, 407; Turner, 1990,
80.

27 *Harbourne Head* (3) SX 691 649/ 15/ Em, Cn/
Turner, 1990, 70.

28 *Harford Moor* (4) SX 645 596/ *c.* 14.5/ Cn/
Grinsell, 1978, 141 [Harford 26]; Barnatt, 1989,
II, 408; Turner, 1990, 77.

29 *Hartor* (5) SX 577 717/ 8.8/ Cn, D/ Worth, 1967,
213; Barnatt, 1989, II, 408.

30a *Joan Ford Newtake E* (3) SX 631 721/ 8.2/ Em,
Ct/ Turner, 1990, 70.

30b *Joan Ford Newtake W* (4) SX 630 721/ *c.* 7.6/ R?/
Grinsell, 1978, 153 [Lydford 91]; Barnatt, 1989,
II, 410; Turner, 1990, 81.

31 *Lakehead Hill* (2) SX 645 776/ 8 × 6.7/ Ct, R/
Rest. pre-1895: *TDA 28*, 1896, 174–9/ Worth,
1967, 239; Barnatt, 1989, II, 411.

32 *Lakehead Newtake* (3) SX 644 778/ 5.8/ Int Cn/
Worth, 1967, 182.

33 *Langstone Moor* (2) SX 556 782/ 20.4/ C, R?/
Rest. 1894: Breton, 1932, 73/ Worth, 1967, 217;
Barnatt, 1989, II, 411–12; Turner, 1990, 81
[Longstone Moor]; Butler, J., 1991b, 75–6.

34 *Mardle* (4) SX 675 693/ 6.5/ Em/ Turner, 1990, 70.

35a *Mardon Down N* (3) SX 767 876/ 8.3/ Em/
Rowe, 1876, 120–1; Turner, 1990, 70.

35b *Mardon Down S* (3) SX 767 871/ 38.5/ Pl, orig
70 st, now 23/ *PDAS 32*, 1974, 164–6; Barnatt,
1989, II, 413; Turner, 1990, 80.

36a *Merrivale SE* (3) SX 553 746/ 20.3 × 18.7/ C?, Gr/ Exc. 1871, no finds: *TDA 4*, 1871, 491–516/ Crossing, 94; Barnatt, 1989, II, 414; Turner, 1990, 81; Butler, J., 1994, 23–32; Leger-Gordon, 1994, 68; Burl, 1995, 61–2.

36b *Merrivale N* (4) SX 553 748/ 8/ Em/ Turner, 1990, 70.

36c *Merrivale Centre N* (3) SX 554 744/ 4.4 × 3.7/ Cn, 2 × A/ Barnatt, 1989, II, 414; Turner, 1990, 79.

36d *Merrivale Centre S* (3) SX 555 744/ 20.5 CB/ Pl, O/ TTB, 1980, 106–7; Barnatt, 1989, II, 415; Burl, 1995, 62.

36e *Merrivale NW* (3) SX 553 747/ 15/ Em, Ct?/ Turner, 1990, 70.

37 *Nine Maidens, Belstone* (3) SX 612 928/ *c.* 7/ Pl, int Cn/ Crossing, 209; [Nine Stones], 222 [Seventeen Brothers]; Worth, 1967, 43, 190; Turner, 1990, 81; Butler, 1991b, 208–9; Leger-Gordon, 1994, 69–70.

38 *Ringmoor Down* (2) SX 563 658/ 12.5/ Cn, A or R?/ Rest. 1911. Breton, 1932, 26/ *TDA 73*, 1941, 234–5; Worth, 1967, 209; Thom, 1967, S2/4; TTB, 1980, 110–11; Barnatt, 1989, II, 416; Turner, 1990, 77; Butler, J., 1994, 142–3.

39 *Rock Tor* (3) SX 612 614/ 7.5/ Pl/ Turner, 1990, 81.

40 *Scorhill* (1) SX 654 873/ 26.2/ Pl/ Worth, 1967, 249; Barnatt, 1989, II, 417; Turner, 1990, 80; Butler, J., 1991b, 192–3; Leger-Gordon, 1994, 59–60, 70.

41 *Seven Lords' Land* (3) SX 741 762/ 8.5/ Cn/ Turner, 1990, 77.

42a *Shaugh Moor N* (3) SX 554 623/ 9.7/ S/ Turner, 1990, 81.

42b *Shaugh Moor S* (5) SX 554 634/ 15.2/ Cn, R/ Worth, 1967, 208; Barnatt, 1989, II, 417. Turner, 1990, 81.

43 *Shell Top* (5) SX 598 638/ 20/ Pl/ *DAS 31*, 1973, 20.

44 *Sherberton* (3) SX 639 731/ 30/ Pl/ Worth, 1967, 254–6; Barnatt, 1989, II, 417–18; Turner, 1990, 80; Butler, J., 1993, 217–18.

45a *Shovel Down NW* (3) SX 658 861/ *c.* 17.5/ Pl/ Worth, 1967, 219–22 (Shuggledown); Barnatt, 1989, II, 418; Turner, 1990, 81; Butler, 1991b, 178, 180.

45b *Shovel Down SE* (3) SX 659 860/ 9 × 8.6, 6.6, 4.9 × 4.6/ 3 × C, Pt, Cn, A/ Pettit, 149–54; Barnatt, 1989, II, 418–19; Turner, 1990, 82; Butler, J., 1991b, 178–84.

46 *Skerraton Head* (3) SX 701 650/ 13/ Em/ Turner, 1990, 70.

47 *Sourton Tors* (4) SX 547 896/ *c.* 33.5/ Pl/ Pettit, 138–9 [Sowton Tors]; Turner, 1990, 80; Butler, J., 1991b, 219.

48 *Spurrells Cross* (3) SX 658 598/ 11/ Cn, R/ Davidson & Seabrook, 25; Turner, 1990, 78.

49a *Stall Moor NE* (3) SX 635 644/ 16.6/ Cn, R/ Crossing, 403; Worth, 1967, 182, 204; Davidson & Seabrook, 25 [Erme Row]; Barnatt, 1989, II, 419–20; Turner, 1990, 81; Leger-Gordon, 1994, 64; Burl, 1995, 64–5.

49b *Stall Moor SW* (5) SX 632 624/ 6.5 × 6.1 CI/ int Ct/ Davidson & Seabrook, 28; Barnatt, 1989, II, 419; Turner, 1990, 79/ Astron: MdW SR, 1800 BC. Davidson & Seabrook, 33.

50 *Stonetor Hill* (4) SX 652 854/ *c.* 20/ ?/ Turner, 1990, 81.

51a *Trowlesworthy E* (3) SX 576 639/ 6.7/ Cn, A/ Crossing, 430 [the Pulpit]; Worth, 1967, 209; TTB, 1980, 112–13; *TDA 18*, 1976, 147–57; Barnatt, 1989, II, 422–3; Turner, 1990, 82; Butler, J., 1994, 169–72; Burl, 1995, 65.

51b *Trowlesworthy W* (3) SX 575 639/ 6.1/ Cn, R/ Worth, 1967, 209; Barnatt, 1989, II, 423; Turner, 1990, 82.

52 *Whitchurch Common* (3) SX 530 749/ 6.5/ Em/ Turner, 1990, 70.

53 *White Moor Down* (2) SX 632 896/ 20/ Pl, Ent?, O?/ Rest. 1896: *TDA 29*, 1897, 148/ *TDA 28*, 1896, 181–2; Worth, 1967, 248; Barnatt, 1989, II, 424; Turner, 1990, 81 [Whitemoor]; Butler, J., 1991b, 203–4 [Little Hound Tor]; Leger-Gordon, 1994, 65, 68; Burl, 1995, 65–6.

54 *Wigford Down* (3) SX 547 649/ 7.2/ Em/ Turner, 1990, 70.

55 *Yar Tor* (5) SX 681 738/ 11/ Cn, 3 × R/ Worth, 1967, 188; Barnatt, 1989, II, 425; Butler, J., 1991a, 126–7.

56 *Yellowmead* (2) SX 574 678/ 20.7 × 19.3, 15.4 × 14.1, 12 × 11.3, 6.5/ 4 × C, A or Rs?/ Rest. 1921: Breton, 1932, 55–60/ *TDA 54*, 1922, 70–2; Worth, 1967, 188–91; Barnatt, 1989, II, 425–6; Turner, 1990, 82; Butler, J., 1994, 74–6; Burl, 1995, 66–7.

DORSET

1 *Broad Stone* (4) SY 596 904/ *c.* 7.3/ Pl/ Aubrey, I, 106–7; Warne, 1872, 117, 119; Piggott S. & C. M., 150; Dunkin, 1871, 148; Knight, 1996, 108–10.

2 *Hampton Down* (6) SY 596 865/ 7.6 × 6.1/ A?/ Exc. 1965, no finds. Wainwright, 1967/ Piggott S. & C. M., 142; Thom, 1967, S4/3; TTB, 1980, 120–1; Barnatt, 1989, II, 434–5; Burl, 1995, 67–8.

3 *Kingston Russell* (3) SY 577 878/ 27.7 × 20.6 CB/ Pl/ Warne, 1872, 116; *PDNHFC 29*, 1908, lxxix; Piggott S. & C. M., 142; Thom, 1967, S4/2; TTB, 1980, 118–19; Barnatt, 1989, II, 435.

4 *Little Mayne* (4) SY 723 870/ *c.* 9/ 2 × A?/ R. Gale, 1728, in: Lukis, 1883, 128 [Priors Maen]; Dunkin, 1871, 156–7; Warne, 1872, 120–3; *PDFC 30*, 1909, xlv; Piggott S. & C. M., 148–50; *RCAHM-Dorset, II*, 1970, 513; Knight, 1996, 130–3.

5	*Lulworth* (4, 5) SY 87. 81. /?/ Pl?, destr. *c.* 1870/
Warne, 1872, 136; Piggott S. & C. M., 150.;
Knight, 1996, 87–8.

6	*Nine Stones* (1) SY 611 904/ 9.1 × 7.9 CE/ Ent/
Aubrey, I, 106–7; Anbrey, II, 720–1; Stukeley,
1776, II, Tab 92; Dunkin, 1871, 146–8; Warne,
1872, 117–18; Piggott S. & C. M., 146–8; Thom,
1967, S4/1; TTB, 1980, 118–19; Barnatt, 1989, II,
435; Burl, 1995, 68.

7	*Rempstone* (3) SY 994 821/ 24.4 × 20.7/ Pl, A?/
Piggott S. & C. M., 146; *PDNHAS 81*, 1959,
114–23; Barnatt, 1989, II, 436.

DURHAM

1	*Eggleston* (4) NY 982 252/ ?/ Em?, Cn?/
Hutchinson, W. *The History & Antiquities of the
County of Durham, III*, 1796, 277; Barnatt, 1989,
II, 358.

ISLE OF MAN

1	*Billowen* (5) SC 267 701/ 10.6 × 6/ Ent?, C?, Q, /
Exc. 1929, *Proc I .O. Man, 4 (4)*, 1945, 506–16/
*Billowen Neolithic Landscape Project, Isle of
Man, 1995*, 1996, 44–7, University of
Bournemouth.

LANCASHIRE

1	*The Beacon* (5) SD 280 842/ 29.9 × 27.4/ Em,
Ent, RC?/ *Arch 53*, 1889, 418; Waterhouse, 1985,
82; Barnatt, 1989, II, 493.

2	*Bleaberry Haws* (3) SD 264 946/ 5.2 × 4/ Paved,
Cn?/ Exc. 1886. flints: *TCWAAS (O.S) 9*, 1888,
499/ *Arch 53*, 1893, 419; Waterhouse, 1985,
39–41; Barnatt, 1989, II, 42.

3	*Burwain's Farm* (5) SD 888 358/ ?/ Em/ *TCLAS
11*, 1894, 158–9; *Arch J 123*, 1966, 20, 26.

4	*Cheetham Close* (3) SD 716 158/ 15.5/ O/
TCLAS 12, 1894, 42; Barnatt, 1989, II, 356; Burl,
1995, 68–9.

5	*Delf Hill* (3) SD 914 331/ *c.* 4.6/ Em?/ Exc. 1982.
Urns, crems: *Gent's Mag*, 1842, 413/ priv. comm.,
F. Lynch, 19.10.82; Barnatt, 1989, II, 356.

6	*Druids' Temple* (3) SD 292 739/ 26.5, 8.4/ C, Gr,
paved, Ent?/ Exc. 1911. Pennine urn
(Longworth, 166, no. 194): Gelderd & Dobson
[Sunbrick]; 1921: Atkinson, W. G./ Thom, 1967,
L5/1 [Birkrigg Common]; TTB, 1980, 70–1;
Waterhouse, 1985, 35–8 [Druids' Circle];
Barnatt, 1989, II, 344–5; Burl, 1995, 69.

7	*Extwistle Moor* (5) SD 903 343/ ?/ Cn/ Exc.
1887? Urn (Longworth, 217, no. 805), flint
battle-axe: *TCLAS 11*, 1893, 158/ *Ant J 18*, 1938,
170; Barnatt, 1989, II, 498 [Hellclough II].

8	*Hellclough* (4) SD 903 343/ *c.* 17.5 × 17/ Em, Ct,
RC?/ Exc. 1886. urn (Longworth, 217, no. 806),

crems, bronze pin: *TCLAS 5*, 1888, 272–86/
TLCAS 11, 1893, 159; Barnatt, 1989, II, 498–9.

9	*The Kirk* (5) SD 251 827/ 22.9/ Em, A?/ *Arch
53*, 1893, 417; Waterhouse, 1985, 83–5; Barnatt,
1989, II, 495, RC?

10	*Mosley Height* (4) SD 881 302/ 12.8/ Em, paved,
Pt?/ Exc. 1950. Pennine urns (Longworth, 218,
nos 811–13. [Cliviger]), pygmy cups, faience,
bronze, crems: Bennett, 1951/ Radley, 1966a,
20–6; Waterhouse, 1985, 38; Barnatt, 1989, II,
499; Burl, 1995, 69–70.

11	*Ring Stones Hill* (4) SD 892 367/ ?/ ?/ *TLCAS 9*,
1856, 33; Barnatt, 1989, II, 499.

12	*Worsthorne Moor* (4) SD 885 329/ ?/ ?/ Exc.
1887. Crem: *TLCAS 11*, 1893, 158. Bu'lock, 39.

Not a stone circle, Summerhouse Hill, SD 501 744.
Collapsed stones of a tor mistaken for a circle. North &
Spence.

NORTHUMBERLAND

1	*Biddlestone* (5) NT 954 074/ 33.5 × 21.5/ ?/ O.S.
Southampton, NT 90 NE. Barnatt, 1989, II, 497
[Biddlestones].

2	*Cartington* (3) NU 056 046/ 4.4/ Pl/ Greenwell,
W. *British Barrows*, 1877, 429, no. CCVII; *Hist of
Northumberland 14*, 59; Barnatt, 1989, II, 498.

3	*Crawberry Hill* (1) NY 880 563/ 8.5 × 7.8 CA?/
Pl, O/ priv. comm., D. M. Taylor, 2.3.89.

4	*Doddington Moor* (3) NU 012 317/ 12.2/ Pl/ *Hist
of Northumberland 14*, 21; *Arch Ael 34*, 1956,
142–9; Barnatt, 1989, II, 356.

5	*Duddo Four Stones* (2) NT 931 437/ 9.8/ Pl, 6–7
cms, SW st/ Exc. *c.* 1890. Crem: *TBFC 10*,
1879–80, 542–4/ Sitwell, 6–7; *TBFC 28*, 1932, 84;
TTB, 1980, 66–7 [Felkington]; Barnatt, 1989, II,
357; Burl, 1995, 70–1.

6	*Early Knowe* (5) NU 083 336/ ?/ ?/ Barnatt,
1989, II, 470.

7	*Elsdon* (3) NT 70. 06./? ?/ *Hist of
Northumberland 15*, 60; J. L. Mack, *The Border
Line*, 1924, 221; Barnatt, 1989, II, 470.

8	*Fontburn Reservoir* (3) NZ 032 936/ ?/ 4P, cm,
crs/ Beckensall, 1992b, 60, 61.

9	*Goatstones* (1) NY 829 748/ 4.9 × 4.9 (6.9)/ 4P,
cms, int Cn?/ *PSAN 5*, 1931–2, 304–6; Burl, 1971;
Burl, 1988a, 66–7; Barnatt, 1989, II, 358.

10	*Hart Heugh* (3) NT 968 260/ *c.* 42.9 × 26.2, E-W/
Pl/ priv. comm., P. Deakin, 14.7.97.

11a	*Hethpool N* (5) NT 892 278/ ?/ Adj, Pl/ *PSAN 6*,
1935, 116; P. Topping, 'Hethpool stone circle',
Northern Archaeology 2 (2), 1981, 3–10; Barnatt,
1989, II, 359.

11b	*Hethpool S* (3) NT 892 278/ 61 × 42.7/ Adj, Pl/
Topping, ibid; Barnatt, ibid.

12	*Ilderton* (3) NT 971 205/ 36 × 29.3 CB/ Pl/ Exc.

pre-1862. Charcoal: *TBFC 4*, 1856–62, 450 [Threestone Burn]; Thom, 1967, L3/4 [Lilburn]; TTB, 1980, 68–9; Barnatt, 1989, II, 359.

13 *Nunwick Park* (4) NY 885 741/ 8.7?/ Pl?/ *Hist of Northumberland 15*, 60; Barnatt, 1989, II, 360.

14 *Ridley Common* (3) NY 778 698/ ?/ Int Cn?/ O.S. Southampton, NY 76 NE 44; Barnatt, 1989, II, 470.

15 *Simonburn* (5) NY 802 712/ 9/ Gr?, Pf?, Pt?, int Cn/ O.S. Southampton, NY 87 SW 18; Barnatt, 1989, II, 360.

16 *Three Kings* (3) NT 774 009/ 4.3 × 4.3 (6.1)/ 4P, RC/ Exc. 1971. fl, crem?: Burl & Jones/ *PSAN 5*, 1911–12, 234; Burl, 1988a, 68–9; Barnatt, 1989, II, 360.

17 *Whinny Hill* (3) NO 093 276/ *c.* 6.7 × 4.8, N–S/ Pl, crs?/ priv. comm., P. Deakin, 14.7.97.

18 *Yeavering Bell* (5) NT 918 270/ 12.2?/ C?/ *TBFC 19*, 161; Sitwell, 4; B. Hope-Taylor, *Yeavering*, HMSO, 1977, 108, 335; Barnatt, 1989, II, 471.

OXFORDSHIRE

1 *Devil's Quoits* (4) SP 411 048/ Bank 130 × 112, circle 76/ CH, 2 Ents/ Excs: 1940, Grimes, 1960; 1972, 1973; Gray, M., 1975; 1988; Barclay, A., Gray, M. & Lambrick, G., 1995. Neo, MBA, IA, R-B, med sherds; animal and human bone; flints. C-14: 2215 ± 70 bc (OxA-3690), 2060 ± 120 bc (HAR-1887), 2045 ± 60 bc (Ox-3687), 2005 ± 65 bc (OxA-3689), 1895 ± 65 bc (OxA-3688), 1795 ± 60 bc (OxA-3686), 1640 ± 70 bc (HAR-1888)/ Aubrey, I, 106–7; *ANL 4*, (3), 1951, 41; *ANL 4 (5)*, 1952, 70; Harding with Lee, 239–42; Barnatt, 1989, II, 433–4.

2 *Rollright Stones* (2) SP 296 308/ 32.9/ Em, ent, Gr, O/ Excs: 1670s. No finds: Aubrey, I, 72; 1986, no finds: Lambrick, 1988, 43–6/ Aubrey, I, 70–3; Stukeley, 1743, 10–14; Evans, A. J., 1895; Ravenhill, 1932; TTB, 1980, 136–7, S6/1; Lambrick, 1983; Lambrick, 1988; Barnatt, 1989, II, 436–7; Burl, 1999, 9–31/ Astron: Maj S MR, Burl, 1995, 73.

3 *Stonor Park* (2, 5) *c.* SP 741 892/ *c.* 24 × 17/ Pl? / *VCH Oxford*, VIII; Plot, *The Naturall Historie of Oxfordshire*, 1677.

SCILLY ISLES

English Island Point, St Martin's, SV 939 153. On the O.S. 2″ 'Isles of Scilly' map the site is mistakenly called 'stone circle'. The stones are the kerbs of a denuded chambered tomb listed as Gun Hill in P. Ashbee, *Ancient Scilly*, 1974, 300. Priv. comm., C. Straffon, 12.5.95.

SHROPSHIRE

1 *Druid's Castle* (4) SO 351 981/ *c.* 6 × 6 (8.5)?/ 4P? / *Arch Camb 10 (Suppl. II)*, 1910, 88 ; E. Lhuyd, 1698 [Medgels Fold], in: *TSANHS 46*, 1932, 200–3 [also known as Mitchell's Fold Tenement]; Burl, 1988a, 70–2.

2 *Hoarstones* (3) SO 324 999/ 23.2 × 19.8 CA/ S/ Exc. 1924, no finds: Chitty, 1926, 248/ Hartshorne, 1841, 39–40 [Marsh Pool]; A. L. Lewis, 1882a, 3–4; Chitty, 1926; Grimes, 1963, 127; Thom, 1967, 65, D2/2 [Black Marsh]; TTB, 1980, 26–7; Cowan, 1988, 379; Barnatt, 1989, II, 383–4; *AW 38*, 1998, 108/ Astron: N, E, and to hills, Chitty, 1926, 248–9.

3 *Mitchell's Fold* (3) SO 304 983/ 28.4 × 25. CA/ S?, Pt?, O/ J. Nichols, *Literary Anecdotes, IV*, 1822, 621–3; Hartshorne, 1841, 35–7; A. L. Lewis, 1882a, 4–7; Lukis, 1887, 178–9; Grimes, 1963, 125–7; Thom, 1967, D2/1; Grinsell, 1981; TTB, 1980, 24–5; Barnatt, 1989, II, 386–7; Burl, 1995, 74–6; *AW 38*, 1998, 108.

4 *Pen-y-Wern* (5) SO 313 788/ *c.* 27.4/ O?/ Chitty, 1963, 178; Barnatt, 1989, II, 502.

5 *Robin Hood's Chair* (4) SJ 34. 25./ ?/ ?/Hartshorne, 1841, 276; C. S. Burne, *Shropshire Folklore*, 1883, 638; Grinsell, 1976, 157.

6 *Shelve* (5) SO 335 992/ ?/ ?/ O.S. Southampton SO 39 NW 13; Barnatt, 1989, II, 502.

7 *Whetstones* (4) 50 305 976/ / Pl. Dest. *c.* 1860/ Hartshorne, 33; Grimes, 1963, 124–5.

SOMERSET (AVON.)

1 *Almsworthy* (5) SS 844 417/ 34.1 × 28.7?/ R × 6?/ Gray, St G., 1931; Grinsell, 1970, 41; Barnatt, 1989, II, 503; Burl, 1993, 121.

2a *Bathampton A* (4)/ ST 775 653/ Adj?, A *c.* ST 816 643/ *JBAA 13*, 1857, 98–113; Tratman, 1958, 110–11; O. G. S. Crawford & A. Keiller *Wessex from the Air*, 1928, 144–7; Dobson, 1931, 62; Barnatt, 1989, II, 505; P. Quinn *3rd Stone 27*, 1997, 11–12.

2b *Bathampton B* (5) ST 775 653/ Adj?, A/ references as for 2a.

3 *Cheddar Head* 950 ST 509 525/ ?/ ?/ *Banwell Arch Soc*, 1985–6, 4–7.

4 *Chew Stoke* (4) ST 560 616/ ?/ ?/ Tratman, 1958, 112; Barnatt, 1989, II, 505; *The Ley Hunter 126*, 1996, 30–1.

5 *Crapnell* 950 ST 596 455/ ?/ A?/ *Wells N. H. & A. Soc 45*, 1933, 42–6.

6 *Dun's Stone* (5) ST 018 331/ ?/ St st 2.1 m h, adj 'circle of smaller stones'. Destr. nineteenth century/ *PSANHS 74*, 1928, 137–8; Whybrow, 1970, 11; Eardley-Wilmot, 28.

7 *Leigh Down* (4) ST 542 639/ *c.* 18.3/ ?/ Tratman, 1958, 112; Barnatt, 1989, II, 505.

8 *Mattocks Down* (4) SS 602 439/ 45 × 20?/ Rect or 2 R. Westcote, 1630, in: Chanter & Worth, 1905, 378–80; Grinsell, 1970, 45–6; Barnatt, 1989, II, 473; Burl, 1995, 89–90.

9 *Porlock* (3) SS 844 447/ 24.4/ O?/ Gray, St G., 1929; Gray, St G., 1950; Barnatt, 1989, II, 415–16.

10a *Stanton Drew Centre* (3) SS 603 630/ 112.2/ Adj, A, ext V, O/ Aubrey, I, 46–7, 65–9; Stukeley, 1776, II, 269–77 [Weddings]; J. Wood *A Description of Bath, I*, 1765, 147–58; Dymond, 1896; Tratman, 1966; Grinsell, 1973; Burl, 1993, 41–4; Barnatt, 1989, II, 441–2; Burl, 1995, 76–9; Burl, 1999, 47–63/ Astron: Maj S MS, Thom, 1967, 100, S3/1.

10b *Stanton Drew NE* (3) SS 604 631/ 29.6 CE/ Adj, A/ references as for 8a.

10c *Stanton Drew SSW* (3) SS 603 629/ 44.2 CE/ Adj/ references as for 8a.

11 *Twinhoe* (5) ST 74. 59./ ?/ ?/ *PSNHAS 108*, 1963–4, 16; *Bath & Cambourne Arch Soc*, 1966, 7–12; Barnatt, 1989, II, 506.

12 *Whit Stones* (5) *c.* SS 853 462/ ?/ Pl or R?/ Grinsell, 'Somerset barrows. Pt 1: west and south', *PSANHS 113*, 1969, 4 [Porlock 1].

13 *Withypool Hill* (3) SS 836 343/ 36.4/ Pl/ Gray, St G, 1907; Barnatt, 1989, II, 242.

WESTMORLAND (CUMBRIA)

1 *Casterton* (5) SD 640 799/ 18/ Em, Pf?/ *RCAHM-Westmorland*, 1936, 66–7; *TCWAAS 53*, 1953, 3; *TCWAAS 63*, 1963, 85; Waterhouse, 87–8; Barnatt, 1989, II, 355.

2 *Castlehowe Scar* (3) NY 587 154/ 7 × 6/ Pl/ *RCAHM-Westmorland*, 1936, 90; Thom, 1967, L2/11; Waterhouse, 1985, 132; Barnatt, 1989, II, 494, kerb-cairn?

3 *Crosby Ravensworth* (5) NY 64. 11./ *c.* 18/ C + A *c.* 100 × 1/ *TCWAAS 27 (O.S.)* 1870, 200–3.

4 *Gamelands* (3) NY 640 082/ 42.1 × 35.1 CA/ Em, Ct?/ Ploughed *c.* 1862, flints: C. Fell, 1964a/ *PSAS 4*, 1860–2, 444; *TCWAAS (O.S.) 6*, 1882, 183–5; *TCWAAS (O.S.) 32*, 1932, 173–7; Thom, 1967, L2/14 [Orton]; TTB, 1980, 64–5; Waterhouse, 1985, 141–2; Barnatt, 1989, II, 345–6.

5 *Gunnerkeld* (3) NY 568 178/ 32 × 29/ C, Cn, Ct, Ent?/ Dymond, 1979b; Clare, 1975, 4–5; TTB, 1980, 56–7, L2/10; Waterhouse, 1985, 127–9; Barnatt, 1989, II, 347.

6 *Hird Wood* (5) NY 417 059/ 19.8?/ C?, Cn?/ *TCWAAS 34*, 1934, 92; Waterhouse, 1985, 143–5 [Hird Wood]; Barnatt, 1989, II, 468–9.

7 *Howes Well* (3) NY 640 081/ *c.* 5/ C?, int Cn?/ O.S. 1″ Sheet, no. 83.

8a *Iron Hill N* (5) NY 596 148/ 14.5 × 11.5 CD/ Cn/ *RCAHM-Westmorland*, 1936, 90; Waterhouse,

1985, 133–6; Barnatt, 1989, II, 495, a robbed cairn.

8b *Iron Hill S* (5) NY 596 147/ 7.1 × 6.2 CE?/ Cn/ Exc. pre-1861, antler, animal bone: *Arch J 18*, 1861, 36/ Thom, 1967, L2/12 [Harberwain]; other references as for 7a.

9 *Kemp Howe* (3) NY 567 133/ *c.* 24.4/ Pl, A?/ Camden, 1695, 808; Stukeley, 1776, II, 42–3; *Arch J 18*, 1861, 26–32; Lukis, 1885, 313–20; *TCWAAS (O.S.) 15*, 1898, 27–34; *RCAHM-Westmorland*, 1936, 206; T. Clare, 1978; Waterhouse, 1985, 125–6; Barnatt, 1989, II, 347–8; Burl, 1993, 100–1.

10 *Knipe Scar* (5) NY 552 188 / *c.* 15/ C?, S, Ent/ Exc. *c.* 1880. charcoal: *TCWAAS (O.S.) 6*, 178/ *TCWAAS 7*, 1907, 211–14 [Druids' Circle']; Waterhouse, 1985, 154; Barnatt, 1989, II, 495.

11 *Kopstone* (5) NY 496 216/ 23.2, 17.5, / Em, C?/ Taylor, M. W., 326; Waterhouse, 1985, 117–18; Barnatt, 1989, II, 34.

12 *Leacet Hill* (5) NY 563 263/ *c.* 11.5 × 9.8 CII/ Int Cn/ Exc. 1880. Crems, urns (Longworth, 167, no. 195 [Brougham]), f/v, pygmy cup, pyre?: *TCWAAS V (O.S.)*, 1881, 76–8, 96; Thom, 1967, 69; Waterhouse, 1985, 114–15; Barnatt, 1989, II, 349.

13 *Mayburgh* (4) NY 519 285/ bank 117, 'circle' *c.* 24?/ CH, 4P?/ Aubrey, I, 113–14; Stukeley, 1776, II, 43–4, 46; Nicolson & Burn, I, 414, II, 404; Dymond, 1891, 191–200; Clare, 1975, 11–12; Burl, 1988a, 58–9; Waterhouse, 1985, 146–9; Barnatt, 1989, II, 469; *PPS 58*, 1992, 249–53.

14a *Moor Divock NW* (4) NY 491 227/ *c.* 7.5/ Pl/ Taylor, M. W., 333 [Moor Divock 6]; Barnatt, 1989, II, 496.

14b *Moor Divock Centre* (3) NY 493 222/ *c.* 14/ Cn, A/ Exc. *c.* 1860, crem, urn (no catalogue): *PSAS 4*, 1860–2, 446 [Standing Stones]/ Taylor, M. W., 332–3 [Moor Divock 5]; Waterhouse, 1985, 120; Barnatt, 1989, II, 496.

14c *Moor Divock SE* (3) NY 494 220/ 5.8/ Cn, A/ Exc. 1866, crem, f/v (Kinnes & Longworth, 99, no. 183 [Askham]): Greenwell, W. *British Barrows*, 1877, 400/ Taylor, M. W., 328–30 [Moor Divock 4]; Waterhouse, 1985, 118–20; Barnatt, 1989, II, 351–2.

15 *Oddendale* (2) NY 593 129/ 26.2/ C, Cn, S, Ent?/ Exc. pre-1879, crem: *JBAA 35*, 1879, 369/ TTB, 1980, 62–3, L2/13; Waterhouse, 1985, 136–8; Barnatt, 1989, II, 352.

16 *Rawthey Bridge* (4) SD 71. 97. / ?/ ?/ *TCWAAS 26*, 1926, 5; Waterhouse, 1985, 154; Barnatt, 1989, II, 470.

17 *Swarth Fell* (3) NY 457 192/ 16/ Em?/ *TCWAAS 21*, 1921, 273; *RCAHM-Westmorland*, 1936, 40 [Barton Fell]; Waterhouse, 1985, 123–4; Barnatt, 1989, II, 497.

18 *White Hag* (3) NY 607 116/ *c.* 5.7 × 4.5/ Pl, O?/

RCAHM-Westmorland, 1936, 89; Waterhouse, 1985, 138–9.

19 *Wilson Scar* (4) NY 549 182/ 18.3/ Pf/ Exc. 1952, crems, inhum, flints: *TCWAAS 84*, 1984, 31–40/ *TCWAAS 35*, 1935, 69; Barnatt, 1989, II, 497, denuded cairn?

WILTSHIRE

1a *Avebury Inner Centre* (4) SU 103 700/ If C, 97.5, 51.8 (Smith, I. F., 1965, 201), if horseshoe (Aubrey, I, 44–5), 105 × 56.6 (Ucko et al., 223)/ Adj, C?, V.

1b *Avebury Inner S* (3) SU 103 700/ 103.6/ Adj, S, O/ Smith, I. F., 1965, 198–201.

1c *Avebury Inner N* (5) SU 103 700/ c. 105/ Burl, 1979a, 163–4.

1d *Avebury Outer* (3) SU 103 700/ 384 × 364 × 356 (TTB, 1980, 126–7, S5/3)/ Adj, 2 × A/ Exc. 1865, sherds: *WAM 10*, 1867, 209–16; 1881, sherds, animal bones: Smith, A. C., 1885, 139–45; 1894, antlers, flints: Gray, St G., 1935, 103–4; 1908–22, sherds, antlers, human bone: Gray, St G., 1935; 1934–9, E, N2, bkrs (Clarke, 1970, II, 501, 1070–2), grooved ware, Ebbsfleet ware: Smith, I. F., 1965, 224–43. C-14: Outer Circle, 2180 ± 90 bc (HAR-10062), 1920 ± 90 bc (HAR-10327), 480 ± 70 bc (HAR-10061), 130 ± 110 bc (HAR-9696); under bank, 2240 ± 90 bc (HAR-10500), 2430 ± 80 bc HAR-10063); old land surface, 2690 ± 70 bc (HAR-10325); bank, 2210 ± 90 bc (HAR-10326); ditch, 2350 ± 90 bc (HAR-10502), 1730 ± 80 bc (HAR-10064); Kennet Avenue, occupation area, 2330 ± 100 bc (HAR-10501), 2310 ± 80 bc (HAR-995), 3830 ± 80 bc (HAR-9694): *PPS 58*, 1992, 205/ Aubrey, I, 33–45; Stukeley, 1743; Gray, St G., 1935; Smith, I. F., 1965, 175–254; Thom, Thom & Foord, 1976; Freeman, 1977; Burl, 1979a; Cowan, 1988, 388–90; Ucko et al.; Burl, 1992a; A. Whittle, *Oxford J. A. 12 (1)*, 1993, 29–53. Skeleton of the barber-surgeon: *Past 32*, 1999, 1–2.

2 *Avebury Down* (5) c. SU 131 709/ c. 5.5/ S?/ Exc. 1849. Samian sherd, Coarse sherds, ox bones, flints etc: *Proc. Arch. Inst.* Salisbury, 1851, 105–6/ *WAM 42*, 1921, 54–6.

3 *Broadstones* (4) SU 163 690/ c. 5/ Pl, A?/ Aubrey, I, 50–1; R. Gay, c. 1660, [broad Stones], in, Legg, 1986, 26; Stukeley, 1776, I, 140; *WAM 52*, 1947–8, 390–2; *WAM 56*, 1955, 192–3.

4 *Broome* (5) SU 167 825/ ?/ A?/ Aubrey, I, 106, 107; *WAM 23*, 1887, 115–16.

Clatford, see Broadstones.

Coate, see Day House Lane.

5 *Conkwell* (5) ST 794 628/ c. 30/ S?/ *WAM 51*, 1945, 230–1; *VCH Wilts I, 1*, 124.

6 *Day House Lane* (4) SU 181 824/ c. 69/ Pl, A?/ *WAM 27*, 1894, 171–4; *VCH-Wiltshire, I (1)*,

1957, 56; TTB, 1980, 134–5, S5/6. Not to be confused with the Long Stone, Broome. Aubrey, I, 107; *VCH-Wiltshire, I, (1)*, 1957, 111–12; Burl, 1979a, 237.

7 *Falkner's Circle* (4) SU 109 693/ 36.6/ Pl?/ *WAM 19*, 1881, 55–8; Smith, A. C., 1885, 147; *VCH-Wiltshire, I (1)*, 1957, 33.

8 *Fir Clump, Burderop Wood* (4) SU 161 814/ 115 × 94/ C/ priv. inf: R. H. Reiss, 23. 1. 96; *Nat Mons Record*, Swindon, 13. 2. 96; *WAM 27*, 1894, 174.

9 *Harestone Down* (5) SU 113 664/ 10?/ S?, ext V? / Meaden, T., *Secrets of the Avebury Stones*, 1999, 109–12.

10 *Langdean Bottom* (5) SU 118 657/ 10.1/ A? / *WAM 42*, 1923, 364–6; *VCH-Wiltshire, I (1)*, 1957, 67. 'Dartmoor' hut-circle? *3rd Stone 26*, 1997, 24–6.

11 *Sanctuary* (4) SU 118 679/ timber rings: 19.8, 10.5, 9.4 (Thom, D2), 4.6, 4; stone circles: 39.6, 13.7: Cunnington, 1931, 304/ C, A, O?/ Exc. 1930, Ebbsfleet, BW, AOC bkrs (Clarke, D, 1970, II, 501, nos 1063, 1064F), human burial: Cunnington, M., 1931/ R. Gay, c. 1660, in, Legg, 1986, 26 [Sevenburrowes hill]; Aubrey, I, 56 [Millfield]; Stukeley, 1743, 31–2 [Sanctuary]; Musson, 1971, 368; Burl, 1979a, 124–8, 193–8; Thom, Thom & Burl, 1980, 124–5, S5/2; *PPS 58*, 1992, 13–26.; Lees, D., 1999. Discovery of the skeleton: *Past 32*, 1999, 1–2.

12 *Stonehenge* (3) SU 122 422/ 29.6/ CH, HS, S, A, O/ Exc. 1901: Sarsen mauls and hammerstones, fl and st axes, antlers, animal bones, coins: *WAM 33*, 1903, 20–8. 1919–26: grooved ware, S2/W, W/MR bkrs (Clarke, 1970, II, 501, nos 1047F, 1048F): Hawley, W., 1921–8. 1950: *Ant J 32*, 1952, 14–20; 1968, 1979, 1980: *PPS 48*, 1982, 75–132. C-14: *Mesolithic*: 7180 ± 180 bc (HAR-455); 6930 ± 120 bc (GU-5109); 6570 ± 80 bc (OxA-4919); 6450 ± 100 bc (OxA-4920); 6140 ± 140 bc (HAR-456). Animal bone: *pre-circle*, 3400 ± 80 bc (OxA 4902);

Phase 1 Henge: 2600 ± 60 bc (OxA4833), 2570 ± 100 bc; (OxA-4842), 2510 ± 45 bc (OxA-4834), 2505 ± 40 bc (OxA-4835), 2482 ± 22 bc (UB-3794), 2480 ± 18 bc (UB-3789), 2460 ± 60 bc (BM-1583), 2443 ± 18 bc (UB-3793), 2440 ± 60 bc (BM-1617), 2431 ± 18 bc (UB-3788), 2425 ± 19 bc (UB-3787), 2417 ± 18 bc (UB-3790), 2415 ± 18 bc (UB-3792);

Phase 2 Aubrey Hole 32; 1848 ± 275 BC (c-602); Secondary ditch: 2447 ± 18 bc (UB-3791); 2415 ± 55 bc (OxA-4094); 2365 ± 60 bc (OxA-4843); 2350 ± 70 bc (OxA-4883); 2350 ± 60 bc (OxA-4881); 2345 ± 60 bc (OxA-4841); 2320 ± 65 bc (OxA-4882); 1925 ± 55 bc (OxA-4880);

Phase 3

Sarsen circle: 2073 ± 21 bc (UB-3821), 2045 ± 60 bc (OxA-4837), 2035 ± 45 bc (OxA-4840), 2010 ± 0

bc (OxA-4886), 1935 ± 40 bc (OxA-4838), 1915 ± 50 bc (OxA-4900), 1910 ± 40 bc (OxA-4839), 1875 ± 60 bc (OxA-5045), 1835 ± 70 bc (OxA-5044), 1825 ± 55 bc (OxA-5046), 1790 ± 740 bc (OxA-4878), 1745 ± 55 bc (OxA-4877), 1765 ± 70 bc (BM-1582), 1720 ± 150 bc (BM-46);

Bluestone circles: 2447 ± 18 bc (UB-3791), 2415 ± 55 bc; (OxA-4904), 2365 ± 60 bc (OxA-4843), 2350 ± 60 bc (OxA-4881), 2350 ± 70 bc (OxA-4883), 2345 ± 60 bc (OxA-4841), 2320 ± 65 bc (OxA-4882), 1925 ± 55 bc (OxA-4880), 1848 ± 275 bc (C-602);

Beaker burial: 2010 ± 60 bc (OxA-4886), 1875 ± 60 bc (OxA-5045), 1835 ± 70 bc (OxA-5044), 1825 ± 55 bc (OxA-5046), 1765 ± 70 bc (BM-1582);

Avenue 1985 ± 50 bc (OxA-4884), 1915 ± 40 bc (OxA-4905), 1770 ± 70 bc (HAR-2013), 1728 ± 68 bc (BM-1164), 1499 ± 24 bc (UB-3824), 1391 ± 22 bc (UB-3822), 1350 ± 19 bc (UB-3823);

Y & Z Holes: 159 ± 45 bc (UB-4836), 1499 ± 24 bc (UB-3824), 1391 ± 22 bc (UB-3822), 1350 ± 19 bc (UB-3823). Bayliss, A., & Housley, R. & McCormac, G., in Cleal et al., 521–6./ Aubrey, I, 74–102; Jones, I, 1665; Stukeley, 1740; Wood, J. 1747; Smith, J., 1771; Harrison, W. J., 1901; Stone, E. H., 1924; Thom & Thom, 1974; Grinsell, 1975; Grinsell, 1978b; Atkinson, R. J. C., 1979; Burl, 1981b; Burl, 1987a; Petrie & Hawkins, 1989; Castleden, R., 1993; Cleal et al., 1995; Burl, 1999, 101–67./ Astron: MdS SR, Stukeley, 1740, 35, 56; Smith, J., 1771; Lockyer, 1909, 62–8; MdS SR, MdW SS, Maj N MR, Maj S MR, Pleiades rising, Newham, 1964, 20–2; MR SR, Maj S MR, Maj N MS, Hawkins, G. E., 1966a, 170; Newham, 1972; Thom, Thom & Thom, 1975; Burl, 1987a, 60–1, 67–70, 76–9./ Geology: *Ant J 23*, 1923, 236–60; Burl, 1984; *PPS 57 (2)*, 1991, 103–57; *3rd Stone 37*, 6–9.

13 *Tisbury* (4) *c.* ST 951 299/ ?/ Pl? S?/ Hoare, 1812, 251; *WAM 51*, 1946, 423; *VCH-Wiltshire, I*, 1957, 114; *Old Wardour Castle*, HMSO, 1968.

14 *Winterbourne Bassett* (4) SU 094 755/ 71?, 45?/ C, S?, O?, A?/ Stukeley, 1743, 45; *PSAL 9 (III)*, 1883, 344–51; TTB, 1980, 132–3; Smith, A. C., 1885, 76–8/ Astron: equi SR? TTB, 1990, 76.

YORKSHIRE

1 *Appletreewick* (1) SE 065 632/ 8.5 × 7.5/ Pl/ *YAJ 41*, 1965, 317; priv. comm. J. Barnatt, 7.1.86; Barnatt, 1985, II, 355.

2 *Blakey Topping* (5) SE 873 934/ 16.5?/ Pl/ Elgee, 1930, 105; Barnatt, 1985, II, 362.

3 *Brackenhall Green* (5) SE 130 390/ *c.* 46 × 9/ C, Em/ *YAJ 29*, 1929, 358; Cowling, 1946, 71; Bennett, P., 1995, 17–18. Enclosure?

4 *Bradup* (4) SE 089 439/ 9.1/ Em/ Raistrick, 1929, 356; Cowling, 1946, 71 [Kirkstones; Brass

Castle]; Barnatt, 1985, II, 498, ruined cairn?; Bennett, P., 1995, 19–20.

5 *Carperby* (3) SD 990 904/ 28 × 23.8/ Em, Cn/ Raistrick, 1929, 354–5; Barnatt, 1985, II, 355.

6 *Cloughton Moor* (5) TA 003 959/ 9.5/ Cn?, Ct?/ *Man 14*, 1914, 164 [Druid Stones] R. Knox, *Descriptions of East Yorkshire*, 1885.

7 *Commondale* (3) NZ 637 108/ 31.7/ C?, O?/ Exc. *c.* 1968, flints: *YAJ 42*, 1969, 240./ Elgee, 1930, 104 [Sleddale]; Barnatt, 1985, II, 362 [Sleddale].

8 *Danby Rigg* (4) NZ 708 065/ 12.8/ Em, RC?/ Exc. pre-1860, 2 urns (Longworth, 241, no. 1115): *Gents' Mag. 14*, 1863, 440–4/ Elgee, 1930, 104; Barnatt, 1985, II, 362.

9 *Druid's Altar* (3) SD 949 652/ 4 × 3.5 (5.3)/ 4P, Pf/ Lewis, A. L., 1914, 163 [Druids' Temple]; Raistrick, 1929, 356 [Bordley]; Allcroft, 225–6 [Grassington]; Burl, 1988a, 72–3; Barnatt, 1985, II, 356–7.

10a *Dumpit Hill NE* (3) SE 029 639/ 10.8/ Adj, Cn/ *YAJ 41*, 1963–6, 325; Barnatt, 1989, II, 357.10b *Dumpit Hill SW* (3) SE 029 639 10.5/ Pl, Adj, int Cn/ *YAJ 41*, 1963–6, 325; priv. comm. J. Barnatt, 7.1.86; Barnatt, 1985, II, 357.

10b *Dumpit Hill SW* (3) SE 029 639 10.5/ Pl, Adj, int Cn/ *YAJ 41*, 1963–6, 325; priv. comm. J. Barnatt, 7.1.86; Barnatt, 1985, II, 357.

11 *Dunsley Moor* (5) NZ 842 089/ 100 × 14/ 4P?/ R. Knox, *Early Yorkshire . . .*, 1855, 81–2; *PSAL 3*, 1853–6, 58; Elgee, 1930, 106; Burl, 1988a, 72.

12 *Fearby, Masham* (5) *c.* SE 188 798/ ?/ Pl?/ S. Cunliffe-Lister, *Days of Yore. A History of Masham and District*, 1978, 1,3.

13 *Grubstones* (5) SE 136 447/ 10.7 × 9.6/ Em, Cn?/ Raistrick, 1929, 357–8; Cowling, 1946, 70; Barnatt, 1989, II, 358–9; Bennett, P., 1995, 33–4.

14 *Harden Moor* (5) SE 073 388/ 7.6/ Em/ Exc. *c.* 1959, 4 urns (Longworth, 278, nos 1587–90 [Bingley], pygmy cup: *Arch J 123*, 1966/ Barnatt, 1985, II, 498, ring-cairn; Bennett, P., 1995, 35.

15 *Harland Moor* (3) SE 675 926/ *c.* 20 × 19/ Em/ priv. comm. R. H. Hayes, 23.9.71; Barnatt, 1989, II, 362.

16a *High Bridestones NW* (3) NZ 850 046/ 7.6 × 5.1/ Adj, 4P?, O?/ Elgee, 1930, 105; Burl, 1988a, 74–5; 1995, 91.

16b *High Bridestones SE* (4) NZ 850 046/ 4.6 × 4/ Adj, 4P?, 2 × O?/ references as for 13a.

17 *Horncliffe* (5) SE 131 435/ *c.* 9.8 × 7.6/ C, Cn, cm/ Exc. pre-1869, no finds: Raistrick, 1929, 358/ Lewis, A. L., 1914, 163–4; / Cowling, 1946, 71; Longworth, I, *Yorkshire*, 1965, 86; Barnatt, 1985, II, 499; Bennett, P., 1995, 37–9.

18 *How Tallon* (3) NZ 052 072/ 14.5 × 11.6/ Pl/ *Arch Newsbulletin, CBA 3, 3 (2)*, 1977, 11; TTB, 1980, 72–3; Barnatt, 1985, II, 499, prehistoric?

19 *Kilnsey* (3) SD 951 680/ 5.5/ Em/ *YAJ 41*, 1963–6, 326; Barnatt, 1985, II, 499.

20 *Kirkmoor Beck Farm* (5) NZ 924 030/ 4.6/ int Cn/ Exc. 1968, urn (no entry in Longworth): *YAJ 42*, 1969, 250–1/ Barnatt, 1985, II, 500, cairn kerb.

21 *Mudbeck* (3) NY 954 077/ *c.* 18.6/ Pl, O/ Curtis, in: Ruggles, 1988a, 375–6; Barnatt, 1989, II, 359–60, [Mudbeckside].

22 *Nettlehole Ridge* (3) SD 979 563/ 7.9/ Em?, C?/ *YAJ 41*, 1965, 322.

23 *Pennythorne Hill* (4) SE 140 408/ *c.* 15/ Em?/ Exc. 1843, 2 urns. *Arch*, 1846/ Bennett, P., 1995, 45–6.

24 *Ringstone Edge* (4) SE 044 182/ 12.2/ Pl/ Exc. pre-1905, urn; 1905, 5 × crems: *Trans Halifax Ant. Soc*, 1932, 153; G. G. Watson, *Early Man in the Halifax District*, 1952, 94; *Arch J 123*, 1966, 26; Bennett, P., 1995, 48–9.

25 *Todmorden* (5) SD 943 252/ 27.4/ Em/ Exc. 1898, Pennine urns (Longworth, 280, nos 1607–1619),

pygmy cup, faience, jet, amber, flints: L. Roth, *The Yorkshire Coiners*, 1906, 307–22/ Lewis, A. L., 1914, 163–4; Raistrick, 1929, 357; Barnatt, 1985, II, 499–500, ring-cairn.

26 *Twelve Apostles* (3) SE 126 450/ 15.9/ Em/ Raistrick, 1929, 357; Barnatt, 1985, II, 360–1; Bennett, P., 1995, 56–7.

27 *Walshaw Dean Reservoir* (4) SD 967 342/ 11/ Pl/ L. Roth, *The Yorkshire Coiners*, 1906, 304–5; G. G. Watson, *Early Man in the Halifax District*, 1952, 89; Barnatt, 1985, II, 361; Bennett, P., 1995, 58.

28 *Weecher Reservoir* (4) SE 137 418 / *c.* 25/ Pl?/ Raistrick, 1929, 358; Cowling, 1946, 71; Barnatt, 1985, II, 471; Bennett, P., 1995, 58–9.

29 *Windy Hill* (4) SE 138 403/ *c.* 15/ Em?/ ashes, crem?, broken urn/ Bennett, P., 1995, 60.

30 *Yockenthwaite* (5) SD 899 794/ 7.6/ C?, int Cn?/ Raistrick, 1929, 355–6; Longworth, I, *Yorkshire*, 1965, 43–4; 86; priv. comm. J. Barnatt, 7.1.86; Barnatt, 1985, II, 500, a kerb-cairn?

Northern Ireland

ANTRIM

1 *Ballycraigy* (4) D 384 039/ ?/ (i) ring-ditch; (ii) StC?/ McConkey, 36.

2 *Ballrickard More* (5) J 362 981/ 45.7/ C, S/ McConkey, 37.

3 *Cushleake Mountain* (5) D 223 345/ 15 × 14/ Pl?/ McConkey, 36.

4 *Slievenagh* (5) H 991 028/ ?/ 'Druidical circle'/ *UJA 8*, 1945, 103; McConkey, 36.

5 *Tobergill* (3) J 208 905/ 14/ Pl/ Chart, 37; McConkey, 37.

ARMAGH

1 *Armagh* (4) H 872 450/ ?/ StC?/ McConkey, 39.

2 *Ballybrolly* (5) H 845 462/ 21/ Int PgT/ Chart, 64; Herity, 1974, 225; McConkey, 39, kerb of a cairn?.

3 *Vicar's Cairn* (4) H 91. 39./ 40.2/ Int Cn, art/ Destr. pre-1868. Exc. *c.* 1785, 1815: Chart, 70/ Borlase, W. C., 1897, I, 297–9.

DOWN

1 *Ballynoe* (1) J 481 404/ 29.9/ Int Cn, Ct, Ent, 4 × O?/ Exc. 1937–8. Crems, Carrowkeel ware: *Palaeohistoria 18*, 1976, 73–110/ Chart, 120–1;

McConkey, 43–4; Burl, 1995, 191–2; O'Nuallain, 1995, 15.

2 *Castle Mahon* (3) J 552 470/ 21.3 × 19.8/ Ct/ Exc. 1953. Crems, fl, Neo sherds: *UJA 19*, 1956, 1–10/ McConkey, 43; O'Nuallain, 1995, 15.

3 *Millin Bay* (5) J 629 495/ 22.9 × 15.2/ 9 × Cts, art/ Exc. 1953. Inhums, crem, Carrowkeel ware: Collins & Waterman, 1955/ Evans, E. E., 1966, 103–5; McConkey, 43; O'Nuallain, 1995, 15.

4 *Mullaghmore* (3) J 191 272/ 2.7 × 2.7 (3.8)/ 4P, O, adj 2 RC/ Exc. 1948–9. Int pit, crem, bucket-shaped pot: *UJA 12*, 1949, 82–8; *UJA 19*, 1956, 11–28; Burl, 1988a, 76–7.

5 *Newcastle* (5 or 6) J 374 300/ 45.1 × 42.7/ Ent?/ Chart, 135; Evans, E. & O'Nuallain, S., *Arch. Survey of Co. Down*, 1966, 93; McConkey, 44.

FERMANAGH

1 *Aghatirourke* (4) H 169 320/ 2.4/ Em, 5?/ Chart, 177; Burl, 1995, 194–5.

2 *Annaghmore Glebe* (4) H 427 201/ 38.4/ Int Cn/ Destr. 1712. Int Cts: *JRSAI 15*, 1881, 538 [Druid's Temple]/ Chart, 184; McConkey, 49.

3 *Brougher* (3) H 359 529/ ?/ Tang R, O/ Chart, 156; McConkey, 46.

4 *Cavancarragh* (4) H 299 449/ 6/ Tang R/ *JRSAI 14*, 1876–8, 499–510; McConkey, 47; Burl, 1995, 195.

5   *Cleffany* (5) H 398 468/ ?/ ?/ McConkey, 47.

6   *Cloghor* (5) H 295 405/ 18.1/ Pl/ Exc. 1852. Ct?, bones. 1981. Pits: *UJA 44–5*, 1981–2, 47–51.

7   *Corraderrybrock* (3) H 031 437/ 14.5, 6.5/ C, S?/ Chart, 158; McConkey, 46.

8   *Drumskinny* (2) H 201 707/ 14 × 13/ Ent?, Int Cn, ext R/ Exc. 1962. Neo sherds, fl: *UJA 27*, 1964, 30–2/ O'Nuallain, 1995, 14.

9   *Eshbrally* (5) H 413 340/ ?/ StC?/ Chart, 181; McConkey, 48.

10   *Formil* (4) H 159 676/ ?/ Tang A/ Chart, 145; McConkey, 45; Burl, 1995, 196.

11   *Killee* (5) H 314 455/ ?/ Pl?/ Chart, 167; McConkey, 46.

12   *Kiltierney* (4) H 218 625/ 11.1 × 10.2/ (i) Pf, variant RSC? (ii) enclosed crem cemetery/ Destr. and Exc. 1974. 7 × inhums, beads, urn: *UJA 40*, 1977, 32–41/ *JRSAI 13*, 1874–5, 467; Chart, 146; McConkey, 46; Burl, 1995, 196–7.

13a   *Montiaghroe Centre* (3) H 194 693/ 15/ 2 × tang R, O, adj/ Chart, 144; McConkey, 45 [Montiaghroe A].

13b   *Montiaghroe SE* (4) H 191 692/ ?/ Pl, adj / Chart, 144; McConkey, 45 [Montiaghroe B].

13c   *Montiaghroe SW* (4) H 197 691/ 15/ 2 ext tang Rs, O, adj / Chart, 144; McConkey, 45 [Montiaghroe C].

14   *Mullyknock* (4) *c.* H 31. 46. / ?/ ?/ *JRSAI 3*, 1874–5, 534; McConkey, 47.

15   *Tattenbuddagh* (5) H 460 429/ ?/ ?/ McConkey, 47.

16   *Toppan* (4) H 060 415/ *c.* 4 × 3.7/ Ext Pair/ Chart, 169; Evans, E., 1966, 114 [Cloghastuckane]; McConkey, 47.

LONDONDERRY

1   *Altaghoney* (3) C 515 013/ 16.6 × 16.1/ Tang A/ Davies, O., 1939a, 11; Evans. E., 1966, 204; McConkey, 53.

2a   *Aughlish NE* (3) C 662 043/ 6/ Pl/ Chart, 205, no. 5; McConkey, 52, no. 5.

2b   *Aughlish N* (3) C 662 043/ 9.4 × 8.5/ Pl/ Chart, 205, no. 4; McConkey, 52, no. 4.

2c   *Aughlish Centre N* (3) C 662 043/ 9.2 × 8/ Tang A/ Chart, 205, no. 3; McConkey, 52, no. 3.

2d   *Aughlish Centre S* (5) C 662 043/ 10.3 × 7.8/ C?/ Chart, 204, no. 2; McConkey, 52, no. 2.

2e   *Aughlish S* (3) C 662 043/ 12.6 × 12.1/ C/, 2 × O, Tang R/ Borlase, W. C., 1879, II, 419 [Caughill]; Chart, 204, no. 1; McConkey, 52, no. 1.

3a   *Ballybriest NE* (4) H 766 887/ ?/ Adj/ Chart, 212/ McConkey, 54.

3b   *Ballybriest NW* (4) H 765 887/ 3.4/ Adj/ Chart, 212 [Carnanvane]; Davies, O., 1939a, 14; McConkey, 54.

3c   *Ballybriest SE* (5) *c.* C 772 852/ *c.* 10/ destr./ McConkey, 54.

3d   *Ballybriest SW* (3) H 760 880/ 6.4/ Int Cn?/ Chart, 212; Evans, E., 1966, 149; McConkey, 54.

4a   *Ballygroll ENE* (3) C 533 137/ *c.* 15 × 10/ Adj, Ent?, Tang R?/ *UJA 44–5*, 1981–2, 29; McConkey, 51; Harbison, 1992, 88.

4b   *Ballygroll N* (4) C 533 137/ ?/ Ext R/ McConkey, 51.

4c   *Ballygroll WSW* (3) C 533 137/ 10.8/ Adj, C?/ Chart, 198, Davies, O., 1939a, 14; *UJA 44–5*, 1981–2, 29; McConkey, 51.

5a   *Ballyhacket A* (4) C 756 338/ ?/ Adj., Destr./ Davies, O., 1939a, 10; McConkey, 50.

5b   *Ballybriest B* (4) C 756 338/ ?/ Adj, Destr/ Davies, O., 1939a, 10.

6a   *Ballyhacket E* (3) C 580 115/ 12.8/ Tang R?/ Davies, O., 1939a, 9, no. 26; Chart, 199–200; McConkey, 51.

6b   *Ballyholly NE* (3) C 577 118/ 7.6 × 7.3/ Adj, Tang R, ext 3-st R/ Davies, O., 1939a, 9; Chart, 199–200; McConkey, 50.

6c   *Ballyholly SW* (4) C 577 118/ 7.1/ Int Cn?, S?/ McConkey, 50.

7   *Carbalintober* (4) C 83. 11. / ?/ ?/ Destr. 1833: Davies, O., 1939a, 14/ McConkey, 51.

8   *Coolnasillagh* (3) C 785 003/ 14.4 × 12.4/ C, Ct, O, ext Pair?/ Chart, 208; Davies, O., 1939a, 9; McConkey, 53.

9a   *Corick* (4) H 779 896/ *c.* 6.7/ S, 6 × ext R/ Adj. 3 × StC, destr/ Chart, 211; Davies, O., 1939a, 10; McConkey, 53; Burl, 1995, 198–9.

9b, c, d(4) H 779 896/ ?/ Adj/ References as for 9a.

10   *Cuilbane* (2) C 830 122/ 12.8/ Pl, int Ct?/ Rest. 1985. Neo fl cache: *UJA 48*, 1985, 41–50/ McConkey, 51; O'Nuallain, 1995, 14.

11   *Ervey* (5) C 517 126/ *c.* 9/ Int PgT/ Chart, 199; McConkey, 50.

12a   *Gortcorbies NE* (3) C 739 254/ 13.5, 4.6/ C, Ct/ Exc. 1945. Fl, charcoal, animal bones, 'ceremony of consecration': May, 1945, 5–22/ *JRSAI 99*, 1969, 63ff.

12b   *Gortcorbies SW* (5) C 739 254/ 21.9/ Int Cn, Ct/ Exc. 1945. Urn, f/v: May, 1945, 9–22/ McConkey, 50.

13   *Lackagh* (3) C 47. 08. ?/ 11.3/ Pl/ Davies, O., 1939a, 12; McConkey, 52.

14   *Letteran* (4) H 794 890/ ?/ Int Cn/ Davies, O., 1939a, 10 [The Moat]; McConkey, 54.

15   *Magheramore* (4) C 831 135/ ?/ ?/ Davies, O., 1939a, 14; McConkey, 51.

16   *Mobuy* (4) H 783 859/ ?/ Pl?/ McConkey, 54 [Druid's Circle].

17a   *Owenreagh NW [NE]* (3) H 740 904/ 9.5 × 8.6/ Adj/ McConkey, 53.

17b Owenreagh NW [SW] (3) H 740 904/ ?/ Adj/ McConkey, 53.

17c Owenreagh SE (3) H 741 903/ 8.2/ C?, int Cn?, O, ext Pair/ Chart, 210–11 [Druid's Circle]; Davies, O., 1939a, 11; McConkey, 53.

18 Templemoyle Caugh (3) C 663 054/ 9.2/ O, ext Pair, adj PgT?/ Chart, 203; McConkey, 52.

TYRONE

1a Aghalane A (3) H 495 925/ 35.1 × 28.7/ S, O, ext 3-st R/ Chart, 218; Davies, 1939a, 11; McConkey, 57; Burl, 1995, 201.

1b Aghalane B (4) H 495 925/ ?/ Ct/ Chart, 218.

1c Aghalane C (4) H 495 925/ ?/ ?/ Chart, 218.

2 Aghascrebagh (5) H 616 838/ 7.5/ C, Ct?/ Davies, 1939a, 7; McConkey, 59.

3a Beaghmore SE [A] (2) H 685 842/ 11.9 × 9.6/ Adj, 2 × Tang R/ Exc. 1945–9. Adj Cn. Porcellanite axe: May, 1953/ Evans, E, 1966, 198–9; McConkey, 59–60; O'Nuallain, 1995, 13–14; Burl, 1995, 201–2.

3b Beaghmore NW [B] (2) H 685 842/ 10 × 9.8/ Adj, Pt?, 2 × Tang R/ Exc. 1945–9. No finds: May, 1953/ Evans, E., 1966, 198; Burl, 1995, 201–2.

3c Beaghmore NE [C] (2) H 685 842/ 17.1 × 15.9/ Adj, 2 × Tang R/ Exc. Pits, char, fls, Neo bowls: May, 1953/ Burl, 1995, 202.

3d Beaghmore SW [D] (2) H 685 842/ 16.8 × 16.2/ Adj, Ext adj Cn/ Exc. 1945–9.

3e Beaghmore E (2) H 685 842/ 20.7 × 16.8/ Adj. many int st, Cn, R/ Exc. 1945–9, Cn. Crem, Ct: May, 1953/ Evans, E., 1966, 198–9; Burl, 1995, 202; Arch Ire 12(2), 1998, 8, 'Dragon's Teeth'.

3f Beaghmore ESE [F] (2) H 685 842/ 10/ Adj/ Exc. 1945–9, May, 1953, Burl, 1995, 202.

3g Beaghmore WNW [G] (2) H 685 842/ 9.8/ Adj, Ent, Tang R/ Exc. 1945–9, May, 1953, Burl, 1995, 202. Dating for complex: 1605 ± 45 bc (UB-23), 1535 ± 55 bc (UB-11), 775 ± 55 bc (UB-163): UJA 38, 1975, 83–4/ Astron. for complex: MdS SR?, Maj N MR?, UJA 43, 1980, 17–18. MdW SS, early Dec SS, Burl, 1993, 105.6.

4a Beleevnabeg NW (4) H 691 833/ ?/ Pl?, O/ McConkey, 60.

4b Beleevnabeg SE (4) H 693 828/ ?/ Gr, C?/ Chart, 233; Davies, 1939a, 8; McConkey, 63.

5a Broughderg Centre N (3) H 653 843/ ?/ Adj, Ent, O/ McConkey, 61.

5b Broughderg Centre S (3) H 653 843/ 9 × 8/ Adj, Ent/ McConkey, 61; Burl, 1995, 203.

5c Broughderg NE (3) H 661 873/ 13.8 × 12.2/ Tang A/ McConkey, 60; Burl, 1993, 78; Burl, 1995, 203.

5d Broughderg SW N (3) H 650 861/ 15.6 × 15.1/ adj, C, Ent/ McConkey, 61; Burl, 1995, 203.

5e Broughderg SW S (4) H 650 861/ ?/ Adj, Ent?, int Cn, Tang R/ McConkey, 61.

6a Castledamph NW (3) H 522 925/ 13/ Adj/ Davies, 1938; McConkey, 57.

6b Castledamph SE (3) H 522 925/ 11.6 × 11.2/ Adj/ McConkey, 57.

6c Castledamph S (3) H 522 924/ 18.3, 9.1/ C, Cn, R/ Exc. 1937. Ct, cm, crem: Davies, 1938/ Chart, 217–18; Evans, E, 1966, 199; McConkey, 57, Burl, 1995, 203–4.

7 Castlemervyn Demesne (4) H 336 573/ c. 12/ S/ Chart, 246; Davies, 1939a, 9; McConkey, 66.

8a Clogherny Butterlope E (4) H 493 947/ ?/ Adj, Pl?/ Chart, 217; McConkey, 58.

8b Clogherny Butterlope W (3) H 493 947/ 12.2/ Adj, O?/ Exc. 1937. Pits. 'At least four other ruined circles besides the one excavated'. Davies, 1939b, 40/ Evans, E, 1966, 200; McConkey, 58; Burl, 1995, 204.

9 Clogherny Meenerriggal (3) H 488 945/ 16.2/ Int WgT/ Exc. 1937. Crem. fl a/h: Davies, 1939b, 36/ Evans, E, 1966, 200; McConkey, 57; Burl, 1995, 204–5; O'Nuallain, 1995, 14.

10a Copney East Group NE (3) H 599 770/ 9/ Adj/ UJA 46, 1983, 148 [Circle F]; Burl, 1995, 205.

10b Copney East Group SW (3) H 599 770/ 9/ Adj/ UJA 46, 1983, 148 [Circle G]; Burl, 1995, 205.

10c Copney East Group W (4) H 599 770/ ?/ Pl?/ UJA 46, 1983, 148 [Circle H].

10d Copney East Group Centre (4) H 599 770/ ?/ Pl?/ UJA 46, 1983, 148 [Circle I].

10e Copney East Group S (4) H 599770/ ?/ Pl?/ UJA 46, 1983, 148 [Circle J].

10f Copney East Group Central Group. (3) H 599 770/ 10 × 8/ Cn?/ UJA 46, 1983, 148 [Circle E].

10g Copney East Group West Group. NE (3) H 599 770/ 24 × 22/ Adj, Cn, O/ UJA 46, 1983, 148 [Circle C]; Arch Ire 12(1), 1998, 24–8.

10h Copney East Group Centre. (3) H 599 770/ 17/ Adj, Cn, R/ UJA 46, 1983, 148 [Circle B; Arch Ire 12 (1), 1998, 24–8.

10i Copney East Group SW (3) H 599 770/ 15.6/ Adj, Cn/ UJA 46, 1983, 148 [Circle A]; Arch Ire 12(1), 1998, 24–8.

11a Cornamaddy A (4) H 686 697/ 9/ Adj, Tang R/ Chart, 244; Davies, 1939a, 10; McConkey, 66.

11b Cornamaddy B (4) H 686 697/ 9/ Adj, Tang R/ Chart, 244; Davies, 1939a, 10; McConkey, 66.

12 Cregganconroe (4) H 663 758/ c. 12/ Pl?/ Chart, 237; McConkey, 64.

13a Cregganconroe NE (3) H 648 752/ 11.3 × 9.5/ Adj, Tang R?/ McConkey, 64; Burl, 1995, 205–6.

13b Cregganconroe SW (4) H 648 752/ c. 8/ Adj/ McConkey, 66.

14 Creggandevesky (4) H 636 740/ 10.7/ Ext Pair/ Chart, 238; McConkey, 65.

15a Culvacullion Centre N (3) H 495 889/ 9.5/ Adj/ McConkey, 58; Burl, 1995, 206.

15b *Culvacullion Centre S* (3) H 495 889/ 10.1/ Adj/ McConkey, 58; Burl, 1995, 206.

15c *Culvacullion N* (3) H 495 889/ 10.1 × 9.8/ Gr, Adj R/ McConkey, 58; Burl, 1995, 206.

15d *Culvacullion S* (3) H 495 889/ 18.6 × 1.2/ C × 4, Tang R/ McConkey, 58; Burl, 1995, 206.

16a *Davagh Lower N* (4) H 706 867/ 10 × 9/ HS?, Adj 3-st R/ McConkey, 60.

16b *Davagh Lower S* (3) H 706 867/ 16.2/ Em?, Tang R/ McConkey, 60; Burl, 1993, 78; Burl, 1995, 206, RC?

17 *Dooish* (4) H 318 698/ 4.6?/ R?/ Chart, 243; Davies, 1939a, 9; McConkey, 66.

18a *Doorat NW, E* (4) H 493 968/ 12 × 11.2/ Adj, R?/ McConkey, 56.

18b *Doorat NW, W* (4) H 493 968/ 9.5 × 7.4/ Adj, R?/ McConkey, 56.

18c *Doorat SE, NE* (3) H 495 966/ 10.8 × 9.7/ Adj, Gr?, McConkey, 56.

18d *Doorat SE, SW* (3) H 495 966/ 6.2 × 5.5/ Adj, O, adj R/ McConkey, 56; Burl, 1995, 206.

19 *Dun Ruadh* (5) H 624 844/ RC, 11.3 × 8.8, HS, 9/ CH, Ct, RC/ Exc. 1909, 1935–6. Multi-phase (i) Neo, Grimston/Lyles Hill ware; (ii) RC, HS, Em; (iii) Cn, Cts, f/vs (Waddell, 1970, 131): *PBNHPS I (1)*, 1935–6, 50–75. 1987. Ad fem and child crems. 2137–1940 BC (UB-3047), 1877–1702 BC (UB-3048): *UJA 54–5*, 1991–2, 36–47/ Evans, E, 1966, 201; McConkey, 59.

20a *Dunbunrawer A* (4) H 465 851/ ?/ Tang R/ Davies, 1939a, 7.

20b *Dunbunrawer B* (4) H 465 851/ ?/ Adj/ Davies, 1939a, 7.

20c *Dunbunrawer C* (4) H 465851/ ?/ Adj/ Davies, 1939a, 7.

21a *Glassmullagh NNE* (4) H 387 804/ ?/ R?/McConkey, 61 [Ring 3].

21b *Glassmullagh NNW* (3) H 387 804/ 9.1 × 7.4/ Ent?, ext Pair/ McConkey, 61 [Ring 4].

21c *Glassmullagh SE* (3) H 387 804/ 7.6 × 7.5/ Adj/ McConkey, 61 [Ring 2]; Burl, 1995, 206.

21d *Glassmullagh SW* (3) H 387 804/ 7.8 × 7.4/ Adj/ McConkey, 61 [Ring 1].

22 *Glengeen* (5) H 380 561/ 12.5/ Tang R/ Davies, 1939a, 22; McConkey, 67.

23 *Golan* (3) H 440 819/ 8.1 × 8/ Adj 3-st R?/ Chart, 231; McConkey, 62.

24 *Knocknahorna* (4) H 410 989/ 16.4 × 13.1/ Ent/ Chart, 215; Davies, 1939a, 7; *UJA 42*, 1979, 17; McConkey, 56; Burl, 1993, 47.

25 *Loughmacrory* (4) H 582 776/ 12.2/ C?/ Chart, 232; McConkey, 62.

26a *Meendamph A* (3) H 458 976/ 16.5 × 16.4/ Adj, int Cn?, Tang R?/ Chart, 216; Davies, 1939a, 11; McConkey, 56.

26b *Meendamph B* (4) H 458 976/ ?/ Adj/ McConkey, 56.

27a *Moymore* (4) H 710 745/ 6.8/ Adj/ McConkey, 64 [Ring 1]; Burl, 1993, 78; Burl, 1995, 206–7.

27b *Moymore* (4) H 710 745/ 7.1 × 6.1/ Adj, Tang R/ McConkey, 64 [Ring 2].

27c *Moymore* (3) H 710 745/ 11.6 × 10.9/ Adj, int Cn?/ McConkey, 64 [Ring 3].

27d *Moymore* (3) H 710 745/ 6 × 5.4/ Adj, ext A/ McConkey, 64 [Ring 4].

27e *Moymore* (3) H 710 745/ 5.2 × 4.9/ Adj, Tang 3-st R/ McConkey, 64 [Ring 5].

27f *Moymore* (3) H 710 745/ 6.7 × 5.7/ Adj/ McConkey, 64 [Ring 6].

27g *Moymore* (3) H 710 745/ 7.5 × 6.8/ Adj/ McConkey, 64 [Ring 7].

27h *Moymore* (4) H 710 745/ 13.1 × 12/ Adj, int Cn?/ McConkey, 64 [Ring 8].

27i *Moymore* (3) H 710 745/ 7.3 × 6.5/ Adj/ McConkey, 64 [Ring 9].

28 *Mullanmore* (4) H 588 747/ *c*. 15/ Pl/ Davies, 1939a, 10; McConkey, 64.

29a *Oughtboy A* (4) H 586 937/ *c*. 5/ Adj/ Chart, 218; Davies, 1939a, 11; McConkey, 58.

29b *Oughtboy B* (4) H 586 937/ *c*. 5/ Adj/ McConkey, 58.

30a *Reaghan N* (4) H 441 819/ 11.3 × 11.2/ Adj/ McConkey, 62.

30b *Reaghan S* (4) H 441 819/ 9.3 × 7.7/ Adj, O, adj R?/ McConkey, 62.

31a *Scraghy NW* (3) H 208 743/ *c*. 18/ Pl/ Chart, 234 [Druid's Circle]; Davies, 1939a, 7; McConkey, 63; Burl, 1995, 208–9.

31b *Scraghy SE* (4) H 211 730/ 11.2?/ C?/ Chart, 234; Davies, 1939a, 7; McConkey, 63–4.

32a *Tremoge Centre E* (4) H 664 736/ 18.2 × 11/ Pl, O/ McConkey, 65; Burl, 1995, 209.

32b *Tremoge Centre W. E* (4) H 657 736/ ?/ Adj/ McConkey, 65.

32c *Tremoge Centre W. W* (4) H 657 736/ ?/ Adj, R/ McConkey, 65.

32d *Tremoge N* (4) H 662 738/ ?/ ?/ McConkey, 65.

32e *Tremoge SW* (3) H 654 733/ 10.5/ Adj, Tang A/ McConkey, 65; Burl, 1995, 209.

33 *Tulnacross* (5) H 719 795/ ?/ ?, Pf/ Davies, 1939a, 8; McConkey, 63, natural?

34a *Turnabarson NW* (4) H 685 699/ ?/ StC?, R/ Chart, 244; McConkey, 66.

34b *Turnabarson SE* (4) H 689 698/ ?/ ?/ McConkey, 66.

Scotland

ABERDEENSHIRE (GRAMPIAN)

1 *Aikey Brae* (3) NJ 959 471/ 16.6 × 12.8/ RSC, Em, Gr/ Exc. pre-1881, no finds: *Great North of Scotland Railway Guide*, 1881, 105/ Coles, F. R., 1903–4, 266–7; Barnatt, 1989, II, 268; Clark, M. G., 10.

2 *Ardlair* (3) NJ 552 279/ 11.6/ RSC, Pf, RC/ Exc. *c.* 1821; 1857, crem: Stuart, 1856, xxii/ Maclagan, C, 1875, 74; Coles, F. R., 1901–2, 557–9; Thom, 1967, B1/18 [Holywell]; TTB, 1980, 182–3; Barnatt, 1989, II, 268/Astron: Maj S MR, Ruggles, 1984b, S74, no. 37.

3 *Arnhill* (4) NJ 531 456/ *c.* 18.3/ RSC, Pf, cm/ Coles, F. R., 1901–2, 571–4; *PSAS 37*, 1903, 227; Barnatt, 1989, II, 268–9/ Astron: Maj S MS, Ruggles, 1984b, S74, no. 49; Ruggles & Burl, 1985, S57.

4 *Auchmachar* (4) NJ 948 503/ *c.* 15.2/ RSC, Em/ *PSAS 19*, 1885, 373–4; Coles, F. R., 1903–4, 273–5; Barnatt, 1989, II, 269.

5 *Auchmaliddie* (4) NJ 881 448/ ?/ RSC/ Coles, F. R., 1903–4, 262–4; Barnatt, 1989, II, 269.

6 *Auld Kirk o'Tough* (3) NJ 625 092/ 31.3/ RSC, cm, crs/ Coles, F. R., 1899–1900, 171–3; Ritchie, J., 1918, 90; Barnatt, 1989, II, 269.

7a *Backhill of Drachlaw E* (1) NJ 672 463/ 8.5 × 7.4/ Adj, 6/ Coles, F. R., 1903, 118–21; Thom, 1967, B1/24 [Blackhill]; TTB, 1980, 186–7; 70–1.

7b *Backhill of Drachlaw W* (4) NJ 672 463/ ?/ 6?/ Coles, F. R., 1902–3, 121; Barnatt, 1989, II, 271.

8 *Balnacraig* (4) NJ 603 035/ 13.7/ RSC, RC, cms/ Coles, F. R., 1899–1900, 171; Ritchie, J., 1918, 87; *PSAS 53*, 1919, 68–9; Barnatt, 1989, II, 271.

9 *Balquhain* (3) NJ 735 241/ *c.* 20.4/ RSC, cms, O, Q/ Exc., 1900, paving: Coles, F. R., 1900–1, 235–6/ *ibid.*, 230–7; Logan, 1829, 200; Ritchie, J., 1918, 91–4; Thom, 1967, B1/11; TTB, 1980, 172–3; Barnatt, 1989, II, 271/ Astron: Min S MS, Burl, 1981a, 195; Maj S MR, Maj S MS, Min S MS, Ruggles & Burl, 1985, S57, no. 62.

10 *Berrybrae* (3) NK 028 572/ 13 × 10.7/ RSC, Gr, Em, Q/ Exc. 1975–8, crems, fl, N3 bkr (Clarke, 1970, 191–3, 196); C-14: 1500 ± 80 bc (HAR-1849), 1360 ± 90 bc (HAR-1893), recalculated as 1190 ± 90 bc: Harwell, 21.8.81: Burl, 1979b, 25–32, 124–5/ Coles, F. R., 1903–4, 288–91; Barnatt, 1989, II, 272; Clark, M. G., 10–11/ Astron: Min S MS, Burl, 1979b, 125; Ruggles, 1984b, S74, no. 24.

11 *Binghill* (4) NJ 855 023/ 10.4/ RSC/ Aubrey, I, 182–3 [Old Chapel]; Coles, F. R., 1899–1900, 187–8; *PSAS 60*, 1926, 309; Barnatt, 1989, II, 272.

12 *Blue Cairn* (3) NJ 411 063/ 23.2/ RSC, Cn/ Exc. 1875, urn sherds, animal bones: Ogston, 1931, 109/ Ogston, 108–9, 122 [Ladieswell]; *Aberdeen Univ. Rev. 33*, 1950, 428/ Astron: MdW SS, Ruggles, 1984b, S74, no. 78.

13 *Bowman Hillock* (4) NJ 40 398/ 20.4?/ Pl/ *D & E*, 1973, 60.

14 *Braehead* (4) NJ 592 255/ ?/ RSC, Pf, cm/ Coles, F. R., 1902, 549–52; Ritchie, 1918, 99/ Astron: Maj S MS, Ruggles & Burl, 1985, S57.

15 *Brandsbutt* (4) NJ 760 223/ 25/ Pl?/ Coles, F. R., 1901, 229–30; *PSAS 113*, 1983, 630–4.

16 *Broomend* (4) NJ 62. 25. / ?/ RSC?/ 'cists and urns', Coles, F. R., 1901, 241 [Husband Hillock]/ Keiller, 1934, 20; Barnatt, 1989, II, 483.

17a *Broomend of Crichie N* (4) NJ 779 197/ 14+/ RSC?, A?/ W. Maitland, 1757, 154; *PSAS 54*, 1920, 167–71.

17b *Broomend of Crichie S* (4) NJ 779 196/ *c.* 13.7/ CH, 6, A/ Exc. 1855, urns (Cowie, 103; *Edinburgh Museum Catalogue*, 1892, 183, E1–4), axe-hammer (Roe, 1966, no. 350, IV EN): *PSAS 18*, 1884, 319–25; 1858, 1866, Cts, N2, N3 Indet. bkrs (Clarke, II, 510, nos 1433–1437F): *PSAS 7*, 1868, 110–15/ Aubrey, I, 208; Maitland, 1757, 154; Ritchie, J., 1920; TTB, 1980, 216–17; Barnatt, 1989, II, 273–4.

18 *Burreldales* (5) NJ 739 396/ *c.* 40?/ ?/ Coles, F. R., 1903, 102.

19 *Cairn Ennit* (3) NJ 678 504/ *c.* 26/ variant RSC, Adj/ Coles, F. R., 1903, 137–40; Barnatt, 1989, II, 307 [Whitehill Wood – South].

20 *Cairn Riv* (4) NJ 674 466/ *c.* 33/ RSC, Cn/ Exc. 1862, axe-hammer, bronze, V-perforated jet button (*PSAS 37*, 1902–3, 178): Coles, F. R., 1903, 122–4.

21 *Cairnhall* (5) NJ 785 175/ ?/ Em/ Coles, F. R., 1901, 217–18; priv. comm. A. Harding, 16.6.85; *D & E*, 1993, 34.

22 *Cairnton* (4) NJ 58. 44. /?/ RSC/ Coles, F. R., 1903, 131–2.

23 *Candle Hill* (3) NJ 599 299/ 13.1/ RSC, Cn, Gr?/ Part-exc.1996. Postholes, char. *D & E*, 1996, 8/ Coles, F. R., 1902, 540–5; Keiller, 1934, 14; Barnatt, 1989, II, 276/ Astron: Maj S MS, Ruggles, 1984b, S74, no. 39.

24 *Candy* (4) NJ 533 303/ ?/ ?/ Coles, F. R., 1902, 566–8.

25 *Castle Fraser* (1) NJ 715 125/ 20.4/ RSC, Em, Pf, RC, Gr, ext Pair/ Exc. 1856, urns: Coles, F. R., 1901, 197–201/ Logan, 1829, 200 [Balgorkar]; *PSAS 60*, 1926, 307; *PSAS 109*, 1978, 269–77;

TTB, 1980, 198–9, B2/3; Barnatt, 1989, II, 276–7/
Astron: Maj S MS, Ruggles, 1984b, S75, no. 66.

26 *Chapel o'Sink* (4) NJ 706 189/ 14.9/ RSC?, RC?/
Coles, F. R., 1901, 217; *PSAS 51*, 1917, 40–1;
PSAS 60, 1925–6, 306, 307; Thom, 1967, B1/16
[Westerton]; Grinsell, 1976, 208; TTB, 1980,
180–1.

27a *Clatt NE, Bankhead* (4) NJ 529 270/ *c.* 14/ Adj,
RSC, A?/ Coles, F. R., 1902, 554–5; *PSAS 60*,
1925–6, 306; Ruggles, 1984b, S56.

27b *Clatt SW, Hillhead* (4) NJ 528 265/ *c.* 23/ Adj,
RSC, RC?, A?/ *NSA 12, Aberdeen* 1845, 851–2;
Coles, F. R., 1902, 553–4;

28 *Clochforbie* (4) NJ 80.58. / ?/ RSC/ Aubrey, I,
183? [Chapelden]; Coles, F. R., 1904, 291–3;
PSAS 60, 1925–6, 309; Keiller, 1934, 21 [Gray
Stone].

29a *Colpy A* (4) NJ 63. 32. / ?/ Adj?/ 'several urns':
NSA 12, Aberdeen 1845, 732/ Coles, F. R., 1902,
577; *PSAS 51*, 1917, 126–7; Barnatt 1989, II, 459.

29b *Colpy B* (4) NJ 63. 32. / ?/ Adj/ *NSA 12,
Aberdeen* 1845, 732.

30 *Corrie Cairn* (5) NJ 552 205/ 18.9?/ RSC?, Cts,
Q/ Exc. 1864, urn, f/v? (Cowie, 104), bkr?
(*Edinburgh Museum Catalogue*, 1892, 163,
EA21, 172, EE23): *PSAS 7*, 1867, 24–5 [Cairn
Curr]/ J. Stuart, II, 1867, lix–lx.

31 *Corrstone Wood* (4) NJ 510 271/ ?/ RSC/ Coles,
F. R., 1902, 560–1; Thom, 1967, B1/21 [Mains of
Dumminor].

32 *Corrydown* (3) NJ 707 445/ *c.* 23/ RSC, Cn/
Coles, F. R., 1903, 109–12; *PSAS 60*, 1925–6, 306.

33 *Cortes* (5) NJ 99. 58. /?/ RSC?/ *NSA 12,
Aberdeen* 1845, 293 [Druid Temple].

34 *Cothiemuir Wood* (3) NJ 617 198/ 22.4 × 19.7/
RSC, Cn, Ct, cms/ Exc. *c.* 1650, 'ashes of some
burnt matter': Aubrey, I, 187/ *NSA 12, Aberdeen*,
1845, 946; Maclagan, C, 1875, 74; Coles, F. R.,
1901, 214–17; *PSAS 60*, 1926, 306 [Devil's
Hoofmarks]; Grinsell, 1976, 209/ Astron: Maj S
MS, Burl, 1981a, 196; Maj S MS, Ruggles & Burl,
1985, S57, no. 48.

35 *Crookmore* (4) *c.* NJ 588 184/ 'large'/ RSC, A?/
Exc. 1828, 2 stone vessels 'paterae' (*Edinburgh
Museum Catalogue*, 1892, 59, nos 10, 11): *PSAS,
I*, 1854, 116–17; W. D. Simpson, *The Province of
Mar*, 1943, 51/ Coles, F. R. 1901, 211; Keiller,
1934, 18, 19.

36 *Cullerlie* (2) NJ 785 043/ 10.1/ 8, 8 × int kerb-
Cns, Gr/ Exc. 1934, crems, sherd, fl: Kilbride-
Jones, 1935, 215–22/ Coles, F. R., 1901, 187–9
[Echt]; Thom, 1967, B2/7; TTB, 1980, 206–7;
Barnatt, 1989, II, 279–80.

37 *Culsalmond* (4) NJ 64. 32. / ?/ RSC?/ *NSA 12,
Aberdeen* 1845, 732; Coles, F. R., 1902, 577.

38 *Culsh* (4) NJ 87. 48. / 9.1?/ RSC?, Q/ *NSA 12,
Aberdeen* 1845, 177; Coles, F. R., 1904, 264
[Standing Stones Farm].

39 *Deer Park* (3) NJ 684 156/ 3.7 × 3.7 (5.2)/ 4P/
NSA 12, Aberdeen 1845, 463; Coles, F. R., 1901,
201–3; Thom, 1967, B2/10; Burl, 1988a, 92–3.

40 *Doune Hill* (4) NJ 48. 06. / ?/ Pl?/ *PSAS, I*, 1854,
260.

41 *Druidsfield* (4) NJ 578 177/ 15.2/ RSC, A?/ Exc.
1828. 2 stone ladles, 'paterae': Wilson, 1863, I,
159–60/ *NSA 12, Aberdeen* 1845, 449; Coles, F.
R., 1901, 209–10/ Astron: Maj S MR, Ruggles,
1984b, S75, no. 52.

42 *Druidstone* (3) NJ 616 222/ 16.8?/ RSC, O?/
Keiller, 1934, 17. Astron: Maj MS, Ruggles,
1984b, S74, no. 47.

43 *Drumfours* (4) NJ 561 110/ ?/ Pl?, cms?, O?/
Coles, F. R., 1902, 490–1; Ritchie, J., 1918, 89–90;
Keiller, 1934, 6, 20.

44 *Dunnideer* (4) NJ 608 284/ ?/ RSC/ Coles, F. R.,
1902, 537–8; Barnatt, 1989, II, 281.

45 *Dyce* (1) NJ 860 133/ 18/ RSC, RC, Gr/ *NSA 12,
Aberdeen* 1845, 122; Maclagan, C, 1875, 77;
Lukis, 1885, 308–9; Coles, F. R., 1900, 188–91;
Keiller, 1934, 9, 13, 15; Thom, 1967, B2/1
[Tyrebagger]; TTB, 1980, 194–5.

46 *Easter Aquorthies* (1) NJ 732 208/ 19.2 × 16.8/
RSC, Pf, Ct, Gr/ Coles, F. R., 1901, 225–9; Thom,
1967, B1/6; TTB, 1980, 162–3/ Astron: Maj S MS,
Ruggles, 1984b, S70.

47 *East Crichie* (4) *c.* NJ 98. 45. /?/ ?/ *PSAS 19*,
1885, 376.

48 *Ellon* (5) NJ 954 302/ 6.1/ Pl/ Aubrey, I, 183
[Fochell, 'below the chapel']; *PSAS 51*, 1917, 34;
O. S. Edinburgh, NJ 93 SE 8.

49 *Forvie* (5) NK 011 260/ 19.9/ RSC?/ Exc., 1951:
C-14, 652 ± 115 bc (Q-761), *Radiocarbon 17*,
1975, 47. *Aberdeen Univ Rev 35*, 1953, 150, [Site
D]/ Thom, 1967, 72, 79, 136, B1/27; TTB, 1980,
192–3 [Sands of Forvie]; Barnatt, 1989, II, 485.
Ring-cairn?

50 *Frendraught* (4) NJ 62. 41. / 26?/ RSC/ *PSAS 51*,
1917, 30.

51 *Fullerton* (3) NJ 783 179/ 25.9/ Em/ Exc. *c.* 1850,
grave, flat-rimmed ware?: Anderson, J., 108/
Coles, F. R., 1901, 218–19 [Fularton]; *PSAS 69*,
1935, 445–8 [Foularton].

52 *Gask* (4) NJ 802 064/ *c.* 15/ Pl?, cms, cr/ *PSAS
52*, 1918, 86–7; *PSAS 53*, 1919, 65–6 [Springhill].

53 *Gaval* (4) NJ 981 515/ ?/ RSC, Em?/ *PSAS 19*,
1885, 376; Coles, F. R., 1904, 280–1.

54 *Gingomyres* (4) NJ 46. 42. / *c.* 18.3/ RSC/ Exc.
pre-1853, charcoal, animal bones: *PSAS 1*, 1854,
141/ Coles, F. R., 1906, 185–6.

55 *Glenkindie* (3) NJ 414 147/ 6/ 8?/ *D & E*, 1993,
36.

56 *Greenhill* (5) NK 097 401/ ?/ ?/ Coles, F. R.,
1904, 258.

57 *Greymuir Cairn* (5) NJ 675 452/ *c.* 16.8/ Ct?/
Coles, F. R., 1903, 124–5.

58 *Hatton* (4) NK 050 364/ ?/ RSC?/ Destr. 1831, 2 urns, fl knives, bracer. 1862, 1863, st axes: O.S. Edinburgh/ Coles, F. R., 1904, 257–8.

59 *Hatton of Ardoyne* (1) NJ 659 268/ 24.4/ RSC, Pf, RC/ Exc. pre-1856, urn, bkr, crem (no catalogue): Stuart, J., 1856, xxii/ Coles, F. R., 1901, 241–6/ Astron: MdW SS, Ruggles, 1984b, S74, no. 56.

60 *Hill of Bucharn* (4) NJ 518 360/ c. 8 × 8 (11.3)/ 4P/ Destr. *c.* 1810, bones: Burl, 1988a, 95.

61 *Hill of Fiddes* (4) NJ 934 243/ 14?/ RSC, Pf, Em/ *Arch 5*, 1777, 246; Fergusson, J., 264; Coles, F. R., 1902, 509–12.

62 *Holywell* (4) NJ 552 279/ c. 24.4/ Cts, cm/ *c.* 1861, urn (no catalogue): Coles, F. R., 1902, 555–6/ *PSAS 44*, 1910, 212–13; *PSAS 52*, 1918, 99–102.

63 *Howemill* (4) NJ 580 107/ 8.5 × 8.5 (12)/ 4P, cms, O/ Coles, F. R., 1902, 491–3; Burl, 1988a, 95.

64 *Huntly* (4) 529 399/ c. 13.7/ RSC?, cms?/ Coles, F. R., 1902, 568–70.

65 *Image Wood* (3) NJ 524 990/ 4 × 3.1/ 6/ Exc. pre-1904, no finds: Coles, F. R., 1905, 206–8/ Ogston, 1931, 87–8; Keiller, 1934, 4.

66 *Inchbaire* (4) NJ 61. 96. /?/ ?/ *PSAS 53*, 1919, 69 [The Worship Stones].

67 *Inschfield* (4) NJ 624 294/ 27.4/ RSC/ Coles, F. R., 1902, 547–9 [Nether Boddam]; Thom, 1967, B1/14; TTB, 1980, 178–9/ Astron: Maj S MS, Ruggles, 1984b, S75, no. 40.

68 *Kirkton of Bourtie* (3) NJ 801 250/ 21.6?/ RSC/ Coles, F. R., 1902, 513–16; Thom, 1967, B1/7; TTB, 1980, 164–5/ Astron: Maj S MS, Ruggles, 1984b, S75, no. 61.

69 *Leslie* (4) NJ 59. 24. / ?/ ?/ *NSA 12. Aberdeen*, 1845, 1022 [Druid temple].

70 *Loanend* (4) NJ 604 242/ c. 17?/ RSC, cms/ 'urn found': *PSAS 41*, 1907, 116/ Coles, F. R., 1901, 239–41/ Astron: Min S MS, Ruggles, 1984b, S74, no. 46.

71a *Loanhead of Daviot N* (1) NJ 747 288/ 20.5/ RSC, RC, Pf, Gr, cms/ Exc. 1932, crems, Neo sherds, flat-rimmed ware, AOC, Indet. bkrs (Clarke, II, 511, nos 1467F–1469F): Kilbride-Jones, 1935/ *NSA 12. Aberdeen*, 1845, 822; Coles, F. R., 1902, 517–21; *PSAS 52*, 1918, 96–8; Thom, 1967, B1/26; TTB, 1980, 190–1; Barnatt, 1989, II, 289–91/ Astron: MdW SR, Thom, 1967, 98; Maj S MS, Ruggles & Burl, 1985, S57, no. 59.

71b *Loanhead of Daviot S* (4) NJ 750 282 /?/ ?/ Destr. *c.* 1820. *NSA 12, Aberdeen*, 1845, 822; *PSAS 69*, 1934–5, 169.

72 *Logie Coldstone* (4) 459 055/ ?/ 4P?/ Destr. *c.* 1847, human bones, ashes, sherds: *PSAS 1*, 1854, 260 [Doune]/ O.S. Edinburgh, NJ 40 NE 4; Burl, 1988a. 95–6.

73a *Logie Newton Centre* (3) NJ 657 392/ 7/ Adj, Pl, Q/ *NSA 12. Aberdeen*, 1845, 287; Coles, F. R., 1903, 97–101.

73b *Logie Newton E* (3) NJ 657 392/ 6.4/ Adj, Pl, Q/ references as for 72a.

73c *Logie Newton W* (3) NJ 657 392/ 6.4/ Adj, Pl, Q/ references as for 72a.

74 *Loudon Wood* (3) NJ 962 497/ 18.5/ RSC, Em/ *PSAS 19*, 1885, 374–5 [Pitfour]; Coles, F. R., 1904–5, 270–2; Clark, M. G., 11.

75 *Mains of Hatton* (3) NJ 699 425/ 20.4/ RSC/ Coles, F. R., 1903, 112–15; *PSAS 60*, 1925–6, 305; Thom, 1967, B1/25 [Charlesfield]; TTB, 1980, 188–9; Grinsell, 1976, 210–11.

76 *Marnoch* (4) NJ 597 502/ ?/ RSC?/ Coles, 1906, 179–81.

77a *Melgum Centre* (5) NJ 472 052/ Bank, 28 × 26; stone circle, 22/ Adj, Pl/ *PSAS 61*, 1926, 265; Ogston, 95–6; Thom, 1967, B2/8; TTB, 1980, 208–9/ Astron: MdW SR over Tomnaverie hill, Ogston, 96.

77b *Melgum E* (3) NJ 473 052/ 22.6/ Adj, Cn/ PSAS 61, 1926, 265; Ogston, 95–6.

77c *Melgum NW* (3) NJ 471 053/ 29/ Adj, Pl/ references as for 76c.

78a *Midmar Kirk N* (5) NJ 699 065/ ?/ ?/ *PSAS 53*, 1919, 64–5 [Balblair]; Burl, 1995, 102.

78b *Midmar Kirk S* (2) NJ 699 064/ 17.4/ RSC, Gr, O?/ *NSA 12. Aberdeen*, 1845, 115; Coles, F. R., 1900, 179–80; Browne, G. F., 60–3; Thom, 1967, B2/17/ TTB, 1980, 222–3/ Astron: Min S MS, Ruggles, 1984b, S74, no. 71.

79 *Mill of Carden* (4) NJ 69. 25./ ?/ RSC?/ Coles, F. R., 1902, 531; Keiller, 1934, 12, 20 [Carden Stone; Candle Hill, Oyne].

80 *Mill of Kelly* (5) NJ 890 353/ ?/ St C?/ *D & E*, 1992, 37.

81 *Mundurno* (4) NJ 940 131/ ?/ RSC?/ Coles, F. R., 1904, 303; Keiller, 1934, 20.

82 *Nether Balfour* (4) NJ 539 172/ ?/ RSC, Pf, A?/ Pf: priv. comm. T. Hutchinson, 24.10.81/ Destr. *c.* 1847, st cup: *PSAS 10*, 1873, 196/ *NSA 12. Aberdeen*, 1845, 449; Wilson, D, 1851, 159–60; Maclagan, C., 1875, 97–8.

83 *Nether Corskie* (4) NJ 749 096/ ?/ RSC, cms/ Coles, F. R., 1903, 83–4; Ritchie, J., 1918, 87; Barnatt, 1989, II, 463. RSC, 4P or P?

84 *Nether Coullie* (4) NJ 709 156/ c. 24/ RSC/ Coles, F. R., 1901, 203; Keiller, 1934, 21.

85 *Nether Dumeath* (4) NJ 425 378/ c. 12/ RSC?/ Coles, F. R., 1906, 184–5.

86 *Netherton* (3) NK 043 573/ 17.4/ RSC, RC/ *NSA 12. Aberdeen*, 1845, 709; Coles, F. R., 1904, 284–8.

87 *New Craig* (4) NJ 745 296/ ?/ RSC, Pf, cms?/ Coles, F. R., 1902, 521–4; Ritchie, J., 1918, 94–6/ Astron: Maj S MS, Ruggles, 1984b, S75, no. 58.

88 *North Strone* (1) NJ 584 138/ 19.8 × 19.1/ RSC, RC?, B, Q/ Exc. pre-1902, urn sherd: *Scottish N & Q*, 1897, 178/ Coles, F. R., 1902, 493–6; *Arch J 78*, 1921, 364.

89   *Old Keig* (3) NJ 597 194/ 25.6?/ RSC, Em/ Exc. 1932–3. flat-rimmed ware, Indet. bkr (Clarke, 1970, II, 512, 1479F): Childe, 1934/ Logan, 1829, 200, 201; *PSAS 67*, 1933, 37–53; *PSAS 68*, 1933–4, 372–93.

90   *Old Rayne* (3) NJ 679 280/ 26.2?/ RSC/ Exc. 1856–7, urn, crem, charcoal, (*Edinburgh Museum Catalogue*, 1892, 184, EP23, 24), B3 bracer (Clarke, I, 261; II, 447): Stuart, J., I, xxi/ *PSAS 2*, 1857, 429; Coles, F. R., 1902, 527–31; Thom, 1967, B1/13; TTB, 1980, 176–7; Grinsell, 1976, 211.

91   *Pitglassie* (3) NJ 686 434/ 18.3/ RSC, cms/ Coles, F. R., 1903, 109; Ritchie, J., 1918, 99.

92   *Potterton* (4) NJ 952 163/ ?/ RSC, cms, Pf?/ *NSA 12, Aberdeen*, 1845, 244; *PSAS 41*, 1917, 36–8 [Temple Stones]; Ritchie, J., 1918, 91.

93   *Raich* (3) NJ 618 436/ 4.4 × 4.4 (6.2)/ transitional 4P, Pf/ Coles, F. R., 1903, 126–7; Keiller, 1934, 4; Burl, 1988a, 96–7; Burl, 1995, 299.

94   *Rappla Wood* (3) NJ 736 402/ *c.* 15.2/ RSC?, Pf, Cn/ Exc. 1860. Crem: *PSAS 4*, 1862, 429; 1862, urn (Cowie, 107), bronze razor (*Edinburgh Museum Catalogue*, 1892, 166): *PSAS 10*, 1874, 434–6/ Coles, F. R., 1903, 102–6 [Burreldales].

95   *Schivas* (4) NJ 902 352/ 27.4/ ?/ Coles, F. R., 1903, 93–4 [Mill of Schivas].

96   *Sheldon* (3) NJ 823 249/ 32.9/ RSC?, Gr, O/ *NSA 12, Aberdeen* 1845, 622; Coles, F. R., 1902, 512–13; Thom, 1967, B1/8; TTB, 1980, 166–7.

97   *Shethin* (3) NJ 882 328/ 3.8 (5.4)/ transitional 4P, Cn, Q/ Coles, F. R., 1902, 526–7; Keiller, 1934, 4 [Fountain Hill]; TTB, 1980, 170–1, B1/10; Burl, 1988a, 98–9; Barnatt, 1989, II, 301.

98   *Shielburn* (4) NJ 675 463/ ?/ ?/ Coles, F. R., 1903, 117–18.

99d *Skelmuir Hill* (4) NJ 984 416/ ?/ ?/ *PSAS 19*, 1885, 376 [Standing Stones].

100 *South Fornet* (3) NJ 782 109/ 26.8/ RSC/ Coles, F. R., 1902, 496–7.

101 *South Ley Lodge* (4) NJ 767 132/ 29.6?/ RSC/ Coles, F. R., 1902, 500–1; Thom, 1967, B2/14; TTB, 1980, 218–19 [Ley Lodge]/ Astron: Maj S MS, Ruggles, 1984b, S75, no. 67.

102 *South Ythsie* (3) NJ 885 304/ 5.8 × 3.4 (6.7)/ transitional 4P, Pf, RC?, O?/ Coles, F. R., 1902, 524–6; Keiller, 1934, 6, 7; Thom, 1967, B1/9, 8.5 × 7.9, CB; TTB, 1980, 168–9; Burl, 1988a, 100–1; Barnatt, 1989, II, 302.

103 *Stonehead* (3) NJ 601 287/ *c.* 19 × 16?/ RSC/ Coles, F. R., 1902, 538–40 P. Donaldson, priv. comm. 3.10.99/ Astron: MdW SS, Ruggles, 1984b, S74, no. 41.

104 *Stonyfield* (3) NJ 589 376/ *c.* 13.7/ ?/ Coles, F. R., 1902, 575–7.

105 *Strichen* (2) NJ 936 544/ 12.1 × 11/ RSC, Em, Q, Cn?, Ct, cm/ Exc. 1978–82, crem, sherds. C-14,

secondary burial, 1140 ± 60 bc (BM-2316). *D & E*, 1979, 77; *D & E*, 1980, 9; *D & E*, 1981, 12–13; *Curr Arch 84*, 1982, 16–19/ *PSAS 19*, 1885, 372; Coles, F. R., 1904, 279–80; Thom, 1967, B1/1; TTB, 1980, 156–7; Clark, M. G., 11–13; Barnatt, 1989, II, 302–3/ Astron: Maj S MR, Ruggles, 1984b, S74, no. 7.

106 *Sunhoney* (1) NJ 716 058/ 25.3/ RSC, Em, RC, cms/ Exc. 1855, crem, urn: Stuart, J., I, xxi. 1868: *PSAS 14*, 1879–80, 308/ Logan, 1829, 202; Coles, F. R., 1900, 181–7 [SeanHinny]; Browne, G. F. 56–60; Thom, 1967, B2/2; TTB, 1980, 196–7; Barnatt, 1989, II, 303/ Astron: Min S MS, Burl, 1981a, 195; Min S MS, Ruggles & Burl, 1985, S57, no. 72.

107 *Tofthills, Clatt* (5)/ NJ 55. 26.?/ ?/ Pl?/ Ritchie, J., 1926, 306 [Sunken Kirk].

108 *Tomnagorn* (3) NJ 651 077/ 22.3/ RSC, RC, Pf/ Coles, F. R., 1900, 173–9; Thom, 1967, B2/16 [Tannagorn]; TTB, 1980, 220–1.

109 *Tomnaverie* (3) NJ 486 034/ 17.1/ RSC, RC, Pf?/ *NSA 12, Aberdeen* 1845, 842; Coles, F. R., 1905, 208–13; Ogston, 93–5; Thom, 1967, B2/9; TTB, 1980, 210–11; Barnatt, 1989, II, 304.

110 *Tuack* (4) NJ 795 154/ 7.3/ Em/ Exc. pre-1855, crems, bronze, 2 urns (*Edinburgh Museum Catalogue*, 1892, EP5, 6): Stuart, J., I, xx–xxi; Stuart, J., II, xxii/ Coles, F. R., 1901, 192.

111 *Upper Auchnagorth* (3) NJ 839 563/ 13.7/ Pl?/ Coles, F. R., 1904, 281–4; Thom, 1967, B1/5; TTB, 1980, 160–1.

112 *Upper Ord* (4) NJ 484 269/ 22.6?/ RSC?, O?/ Coles, F. R., 1902, 563–5.

113 *Upper Crichie* (4) *c.* NJ 956 443/ ?/ ?/ *PSAS 19*, 1885, 375–6.

114 *Upper Third* (4) NJ 677 394/ ?/ RSC?/ Coles, F. R., 1903, 101–2.

115 *Wantonwells* (4) NJ 619 273/ ?/ RSC, Pf/ Coles, F. R., 1902, 535–6; Keiller, 1934, 15; Thom, 1967, B1/2; TTB, 1980, 174–5.

116 *Waulkmill* (4) NJ 473 052/ ?/ ?/ Coles, F. R., 1905, 213–17; Ogston, 96.

117 *West Haughs* (4) NJ 68. 38. /23.2?/ 6?/ Coles, F. R., 1903, 102.

118 *Wester Echt* (3) NJ 739 084/ 29.3?/ RSC/ *NSA 12, Aberdeen* 1845, 738; Coles, F. R., 1900, 187; *PSAS 53*, 1919, 64–5.

119 *Wheedlemont* (4) NJ 480 265/ 26.5+/ RSC?/ Coles, F. R., 1902, 561–3; Keiller, 1934, 4.

120 *Whitehill* (3) NJ 643 135/ 22?/ RSC, RC, Ct, A?/ *NSA 12, Aberdeen* 1845, 613; *PSAS 19*, 1885, 372–3; Coles, F. R., 1901, 203–8; Keiller, 1934, 8, 16, 17, 19 [Tillyfourie]; Thom, 1967, B2/18; TTB, 1980, 224–5; *D & E*, 1989, 19.

121 *Whitehill Wood* (3) NJ 678 505/ 8.2/ Adj, 6?/ Coles, F. R., 1903, 137–40; Thom, 1967, B4/1

[Carnousie House]; Thom, 1967, 234–5; Barnatt, 1989, II, 307 [Whitehill Wood – North].

122 *Yonder Bognie* (3) NJ 601 458/ 24.4/ RSC, Gr, RC?/ Exc. 1856, crem, urn: Stuart, J., II, xxii [Wardend]; f/v urn (Cowie, 113; Longworth, 303, no. 1878). Food-vessel urn wrongly attributed to Newton of Montblairy, Banff? Barnatt, 1989, II, 487/ Anderson, 1886, fig. 128; *Ant J 7*, 1927, 115/ *PSAS 4*, 1862, 448; Coles, F. R., 1903, 127–31; Thom, 1967, B1/23; TTB, 1980, 184–5; Barnatt, 1989, II, 308.

ANGUS (TAYSIDE)

1 *Auchterhouse* (4) NO 346 392/ 4.7 × 1.9 [5.1]?/ 4P, cms, ext Pair/ *ONB 9*, 1860. 13 [The Witches Stone]; / *JBAA 37*, 1881, 260–2; *PSAS 39*, 1905, 393–6 [Spittal Stones]; Burl, 1988a, 102–3.

2 *Balgarthno* (3) NO 353 316/ 6.1/ Pl/ Exc. 1856: jet ring, flint. (*Edinburgh Museum catalogue*: EP 188–9): *PSAS 2*, 1854–7, 443; Stuart, J., I, xxiii, [Nine Stanes of Invergowrie]/ Coutts, 1970, 18; Grinsell, 1976, 214, [Deil's Cradle].

3 *Balkemback* (3) NO 382 384/ 11 × 11 (15.6)/ 4P, cms, crs/ *JBAA 37*, 1881, 259–61; Warden, A. J., 228; Burl, 1988a, 102–3.

4 *Blackgate of Pitscandlie* (3) NO 484 528/ 15.2/ Cn, Cr/ Exc. pre-1850. Urn, incised sandstone: Warden, A. J., 98/ Simpson, J. Y., 68; Thom, 1967, P3/2; Burl, 1976a, 192 [Pitscandlie]; TTB, 1980, 346–7.

5a *Brankam Hill NW* (3) NO 300 559/ 1.5 × 1.5 [2.1]/ Adj, 4P/ Burl, 1988a, 106.

5b *Brankam Hill SE* (3) NO 301 557/ 1 × 1 [1.4]/ Adj, 4P/ Burl, 1988a, 106.

6 *Carse Gray* (3) NO 462 538/ 5.1 × 5.1 (7.2)/ 4P?/ Burl, 1988a, 107.

7 *Colmeallie* (4) NO 565 781/ 13.7 × 11/ RSC, Gr, RC/ Jervise, 104–6, [kil-meallie ='kirk on small eminence']/ Astron: MdW SS, Ruggles, 1984b, S74, no. 96.

8 *Corogle Burn* (3) NO 348 601/ 3.5/ 4P. ext Pair/ Thom, 1967, P3/1 [Glen Prosen]; Burl, 1988a, 108–9/ Astron: Maj S MS, Thom, 1966a, 34.

9 *Dalbog* (4) NO 587 719/ ?/ int Ct?/ Destr. 1840. Jervise, 25. [Tornacloch, 'knoll of stones'].

10 *Easter Pitforthie* (4) NO 619 614/ ?/ ?/ Burl, 1976a, 354.

11 *Mylnefield* (4) NO 334 301/ Ellipse?/ 6?/ Elliot, A. *Lochee As It Was*, 1911, 203–4.

12 *Newbigging* (4) NO 541 693/ *c*. 17/ RSC?, C, RC?/ *ONB Angus*, 1858–65, 61; Destr. *c*. 1830, 'black, clammy earth, mixed with pieces of charcoal', Jervise, 152–3.

Pitscandlie, see Blackgate.

13 *Westerton* (5) NO 536 521/ ?/ Pl?, cms/ Simpson, J. Y., 1867, 17–18 [Turin]; *PSAS 112*, 1982, 561–3.

ARGYLLSHIRE (STRATHCLYDE)

1 *Bealoch Mor* (5) NM 83. 04. /4?/ S?/ priv. comm. A. Thom, 20.5.77.

2 *Benderloch* (5) NM 906 386/ ?/ ?/ Destr. *c*. 1871. *PSAS 9*, 1872, 88–9. Ruggles, 1984a, 141.

3 *Glebe Cairn* (3) NR 833 989/ 10.7, 8.2/ C, int Ct. Beneath Cn, 33.5 diam. Exc. 1864: *PSAS 6*, 1864–6, 339/ Scott, 1989, 79.

4 *Nether Largie* (3) NR 828 976/ / 4P/ *RCAHM-Argyll*, 6, 1988, 136; *D & E*, 1993, 75.

5 *Pobull Burn* (4) NR 709 270/ 46?/ Pl/ *c*. 1820, 'urn, coin found'. *PSAS 64*, 1929–30, 317; *D & E*, 1960, 12–13; Ruggles, 1984a, 189, KT28.

6 *Strontoiller* (1) NM 906 292/ 19.8/ O/ *PSAS 9*, 1870–2, 89, 104; Thom, 1967, A1/2 [Loch Nell]; TTB, 1980, 140–1; Ruggles, 1984a, 143, LN17; Barnatt, 1989, II, 250–1.

7a *Temple Wood N* (2) NR 826 979/ 10.5 × 10/ Pl. Adj./ After earlier timber structure, circle? Exc. 1979–80. C-14, 3075 ± 190 bc (GU-1296): Scott, 1989, 115.

7b *Temple Wood S* (2) NR 826 979/ 13.5 × 12.5/ Adj. Em, Ent, S, 2 int Cts, crems, spirals, RC. Multi-phase. 2 ext Cts./ Exc. 1928, 1929–30, 1974–80: N3, 3 b/t a/hs, fl scraper. 11 late C-14: 1275 ± 105 bc (GU-1300), 1120 ± 80 bc (GU-1529), 1105 ± 110 bc (GU-1527), 1090 ± 55 bc (GU-1297), 1030 ± 100 bc (GU-1045), 1020 ± 230 bc (GU-1299), 995 ± 215 bc (GU-1298), 975 ± 65 bc (GU-1528), 928 ± 45 bc (SRR-531), 857 ± 50 bc (SRR-530), AD 1745 ± 80 (GU-1530): Scott, 1989, 116–17/ Craw, 1929, [Half Moon Wood]; Craw, 1930; Thom, 1966, 21, A2/8; TTB,1980, 144–7; Barnatt, 1989, II, 251–2; Scott, 1989/ Astron: Maj N MS, Thom, 1971, 45–8.

ARRAN (STRATHCLYDE)

1 *Auchagallon* (1) NR 893 346/ 14.9 × 14.1/ Variant RSC?, Ct?/ Exc. pre-1910. No finds: Bryce, 1910, 119/ *PSAS 4*, 1860–2, 501; Thom, 1967, 72, [Auchengallon]; McLellan, 31–2.

2 *Aucheleffan* (1) NR 978 251/ 4.9 × 4.9 (6.7)/ 4P/ Exc. 1902. No finds: *PSAS 37*, 1902–3, 66/ Bryce, T. H., 1910, 123–4; Burl, 1988a, 110–11.

3 *Ballymichael Bridge* (3) NR 924 322/ 3.5 × 2.9 (4.6)/ 4P/ Bryce, 1910, 150; *D & E*, 1977, 9; Burl, 1988a, 12–13.

4 *Drumadoon* (5) *c*. NR 891 288/ 5?/ Ct/ Exc. pre-1845. Urn; *c*. 1901, charcoal: Bryce, T. H., 1901–2, 18–30/ McLellan, 48. 'Denuded round cairn?

5 *Glen Shirag* (4) NS 00. 37./ 'Large'/ Destr. 1813/ Bryce, J., 1862, 505/ Bryce, T. H., 1910, 149.

6a,b,c *Glenree* (3) NR 948 269/ 3.5/ 4P + 2 4P to E/ *D & E*, 1996, 78.

7 *Kildonan* (5) NS 031 208/ ?/ ?/ Bryce, T. H., 1910, 125.

8   *Lamlash* (3) NS 018 336/ 6.4/ 4P? or 6?, int Ct, O/ Exc. 1861, flint: Bryce, J., 1862, 513–14/ *PSAS 40*, 1905–6, 296–9; Burl, 1988a, 114–15/ Astron. SE to NW indicates Ben Nuish; circle to outlier to Goat Fell. Coles, F. R., 1906, 296.

9   *Largybeg Point* (5) NS 053 233/ 7.5 × 2.9 [8]/ Bryce, 1910, 152; Burl, 1988a, 116–17.

10 *Machrie Burn* (1) NR 908 351/ 3.4 × 2.7 (4.3)/ 4P/ Exc. 1909, no finds: Bryce, J., 1910, 154/ D & E Scotland, 1977, 9; Burl, 1988a, 118–19.

11a *Machrie Moor I* (3) NS 912 324/ 14.6 × 12.2 CE/ Pl/ Exc. 1861, no finds: Bryce, J., 1862, 502; 1978–9, 1985–6. Phases: (a) agriculture; (b) timber rings, C. *c.* 19.5 C-14s, 2130 ± 90 bc (GU-2324), 2520 ± 50 bc (GU-2316), 2030 ± 180 bc (GU-2325), O, grooved ware; (c) agriculture; (d) st C, granite and sandstones; (e) pit with bipartite urn, fls, crem: Haggarty, 1991/ Roy et al., 64; Thom, 1967, 72 [Tormore]; Barnatt, 1989, II, 247/ Astron: MdS SR, Barnatt & Pierpoint, 111.

11b *Machrie Moor II* (3) NS 911 324/ 12.8/ 2 Cts/ Exc. 1861. f/v, 4 fl a/hs (*Edinburgh Museum Catalogue*, 1892, 183, EP 7–11): Bryce, J., 1862, 502/ Thom, 1967, 72, [Tormore]; TTB, 1980, 152–3; Barnatt, 1989, II, 248/ Astron: MdS SR, Barnatt & Pierpoint, 111.

11c *Machrie Moor III* (4) NS 910 325/ *c.* 16.3 × 15.4 CI/ 2 Cts/ Exc. 1861. F/v, 2 fl a/hs, human skull, bones: Bryce, J., 1862, 502–3/ Roy et al., 62–4; Barnatt, 1989, II, 248/ Astron: Min N MR, Barnatt & Pierpoint, 111.

11d *Machrie Moor IV* (3) NS 910 324/ *c.* 6.4/ 5-St, 7m? or 4P 7.8 × 5.5, Ct/ Exc. 1861, f/v (Abercromby, I, 118, no. 67), 3 fl a/hs, bronze pin (*Edinburgh Museum Catalogue*, 1892, 183, EP 12–16: Bryce, 1862, 503/ Burl, 1988a, 120–1; Barnatt, 1989, II, 248/ Astron: MdS SR, Barnatt & Pierpoint, 111.

11e *Machrie Moor V* (1) NS 908 323/ 18.1, 11.6 CI/ C, Pf/ Exc. 1858, no finds. J. MacArthur, *The Antiquities of Arran . . .* , 1861, 51–2; 1861, no finds: Bryce, J., 1862, 504/ Roy et al., 60–2, [Suidhe Choir Fhion, 'Fingal's Cauldron Seat']; Barnatt, 1989, II, 249/ Astron: Min S MR, Barnatt & Pierpoint, 111.

11f *Machrie Moor X* (4) NS 900 327/ *c.* 21.7/ (a) Pl?, Pf? (b) RC 19.2/ Exc. pre-1861? no finds: Bryce, J., 1862, 505; 1979, no finds. Burl, *The Arran Naturalist 4*, 1980, 26/ McLellan, 28–30; Barnatt, 1989, II, 249.

11g *Machrie Moor XI* (1) NS 912 324/ *c.* 13.6 × 12.2/ Pl/ Exc. 1978–9, 1985–6. Phases: (a) Agriculture; (b) timber ring, 14.7 × 12.9/ Pl, O?, grooved ware, flints, (c) agriculture; (d) stone circle, 13.6 × 12.2, C-14 1740 ± 50 bc (GU-2323); (e) empty pit, adj pit, crem; (f) agriculture: Haggarty, 1991/ MacKie, 1975, 127 (Circle 1a); Barnatt, 1989, II, 260/ Astron: MdS SR, Barnatt & Pierpoint, 111.

12 *Shiskine* (3) NR 924 322/ 3.5 × 3.5 (5)/ 4P/ *D & E*, 1977, 9.

13 *South Sannox* (4) NS 014 457/ ?/ C/ Bryce, J., 1862, 505; Barnatt, 1989, II, 454.

AYRSHIRE (STRATHCLYDE)

1   *Beoch* (3) NS 53. 09. / 11.3/ Em?, Cn, Cr/ Exc. 1937. 3 urns (Morrison, no. 48), Indet. bkr (Clarke, 1970, II, 514, no. 1557F [Dalmellington], indet): *PSAS 72*, 1937–8, 235.

2   *Blackshaw Moor* (5) NS 25. 47. /?/ C?/ Smith, J., 1895, 12; Barnatt, 1989, II, 479. RC?

3   *Four Stones* (4) NS 379 550/ 4.4 × 4.4 (5.7)/ 4P, crem/ Exc. *c.* 1816. *PSAS 11*, 1874–6, 291/ Burl, 1988a, 122.

4   *Gray Stanes* (5) NX 087 816/ 180?!/ '233 paces'/ Pl?/ Smith, J. 1895, 222–3; Barnatt, 1989, II, 334. [Gray Stanes o'Garleffan].

5   *Haggstone Moor* (5) NX 06. 72./ 13.4?/ Pl?/ Smith, J. 1895, 223; Barnatt, II, 1989, 491, kerbstones?

6   *Nith Lodge* (3) NS 54. 10. /9.1 × 4.6/ Em/ Exc. 1937. Urn (Morrison, no. 450, pygmy cups (Morrison, nos 46, 47), battle-axe (Roe, 1966, no. 371, IVD N): *PSAS 72*, 1937–8, 241; Barnatt, 1989, II, 492, kerbed cairn?

7   *Molmont* (4) NS 514 371/ 18.3/ Pl?/ Smith, J. 1895, 101; Barnatt, 1989, II, 454.

BANFFSHIRE (GRAMPIAN)

1   *Bellman's Wood* (4) NJ 605 505/ *c.* 6.9/ RSC?/ Coles, F. R., 1905–6, 181–2.

2   *Doune of Dalmore* (3) NJ 185 308/ 15.9/ RC/ Coles, F. R., 106–7, 136–9.

3a *Gaul Cross N* (5) NJ 535 639/ *c.* 18/ Adj/ Coles, F. R., 1905–6, 187–9; Barnatt, 1989, II, 461.

3b *Gaul Cross S* (5) (5) NJ 535 639/ *c.* 18/ Adj, 6?/ *c.* 1830, 'several articles of silver': Stuart, J., 1867, lxxxii/ *T. Banff FC 2*, 1883–7, 92; *PSAS 38*, 1903–4, 437–8; Coles, F. R., 1905–6, 187–9; Barnatt, 1989, II, 284–5, RSC?

4   *Harestane* (4) NJ 664 438/*c.* 18/ RSC?, cm, int Cts?/ Coles, F. R., 1903, 116–17; *PSAS 52*, 1917–18, 108.

5   *Hatton* (4) NJ 270 418/ 11/ Pl?/ Aubrey, I, 183, [Leachell Beandich, 'the blessed chapel']; Coles, F. R, 1906, 194–7.

6   *Kimmonity* (4) NJ 54. 47./ *c.* 15/ ?/ Coles, F. R., 1903, 132; Barnatt, 1989, II, [Redhill?]

7   *Lower Lagmore* (3) NJ 180 359/ 19.8/ Destr. int PgT?, cm/ Coles, F. R., 1907, 139–41; Henshall, 1963, 390.

8   *Marionburgh* (3) NJ 183 364/ 22.6/ RC?/ Coles, F. R., 1907, 151–4; Henshall, 1963, 391.

9 *Nether Cluny* (4) NJ 315 381/ ?/ ?/ Destr. *c.* 1840. 'all the cattle died'/ Coles, F. R., 1907, 158–60; Grinsell, 1976, 212.

10 *Nethertown* (3) NT 185 291/ ?/ RSC?/ *D & E*, 1993, 41.

11 *Newton of Montblairy* (5) NJ 68. 55. /?/ ?/ Exc. pre-1886, f/v urn (Cowie, 113; Longworth, 303, no. 1878)/ Anderson, 1886, fig. 128; *Ant J 7*, 1927, 115; *PSAS 69*, 1934–5, 195; Barnatt, 1989, II, 487, Yonder Bognie?

12 *North Burreldales* (3) NJ 676 549/ 6.5 × 6.1 (8.9)/ 4P?/ Stuart, J., 1857, 370; Coles, F. R., 1906, 165–7; TTB, 1980, 236–7, B4/2; Burl, 1988a, 123.

13 *Rothiemay* (3) NJ 550 487/ 28/ RSC, cms, crs/ Coles, F. R., 1903, 133–7; Ritchie, J., 1918, 104; Thom, 1967, B4/4 [Millton]; TTB, 1980, 238–9; *D & E*, 1998, 66–7/Astron: Maj S MS, Burl, 1981a, 195; Maj S MR, Maj S MS, MW SS, Ruggles & Burl, 1985, S57, no. 23.

14 *St Brandan's Stanes* (4) NJ 608 611/ ?/ RSC?, cms/ Coles, F. R., 1906, 172–5; Ritchie, J., 1918, 104.

15a *Sandend Bay A* (5) NJ 560 658/ 18?/ Adj, int Ct?/ Coles, F. R., 1906, 171.

15b *Sandend Bay B* (5) NJ 560 658/ ?/ Adj, Pl?/ same ref as 14a.

16 *Thorax* (3) NJ 582 549/ 6.8 × 5.4 CE/ 6, cms/ *PSAS 6*, 1864–6, Appendix, 14; Coles, F. R., 1906, 175–8; Ritchie, J., 1918, 102–4.

17 *Upper Lagmore* (3) NJ 176 358/ *c.* 18/ Gr, Pf?, int PgT/ Coles, F. R., 1907, 141–9; Henshall, 1963, 389–90.

Benbecula, Outer Hebrides, see HEBRIDES
Berneray, Outer Hebrides, see HEBRIDES

BERWICK

1 *Borrowston Rigg* (5) NT 558 523/ 41.5 × 36.6/ WNW-ESE CII/ Pl? or Cn?/ *RCAHM-S*, 1915, xxxi, no. 226; TTB, 1980, 304–5, G9/10; Barnatt, 1989, II, 329.

2 *Kirktonhill* (4) NT 47. 54. / ?/ ? Destr. *c.* 1864/ Burl, 1976a, 355; Barnatt, 1989, II, 491, [Kirkton Hill].

BUTE (BORDERS)

1 *Ettrick Bay* (3) NS 044 667/ 15.3 × 12 CE/ Pl, O/ J. K. Hewison, *Bute in the Olden Times, I*, 81–3, [Kilmachalmaig]; TTB, 1980, 154–5.

2 *Kingarth* (3) NS 093 555/ 26.2/ Pl, Q, Os/ J. K. Hewison, *Bute in the Olden Times, I*, 78–80; *Trans Bute NHS 15*, 1963, 61–2; *D & E*, 1975, 17.

3a *St Colmac's A* (4) NS 04. 66. /?/ ?, Adj/ *Agricultural Survey of Buteshire*, 1816, 118–19.

3b *St Colmac's B* (4) NS 04. 66. / ?/ ?, Adj/ reference as for 3a.

CAITHNESS (HIGHLAND)

1 *Achnagoul* (3) ND 160 325/ 88 × 63/ *D & E*, 1989, 27; Myatt, 1989.

2 *Achanarras Hill* (5) ND 145 552/ 18.3/ Pl?/ *RCAHM-S*, 1911a, no. 141; Barnatt, 1989, II, 234, Cn?

3 *Achavanich* (3) ND 188 417/ 68.6 × 26/ HS, Ct/ *RCAHM-S*, 1911a, no. 293; Thom, 1967, N1/2; Barnatt, 1989, II, 234; Burl, 1995, 120–1/ Astron: Maj S MR, Dryden, in: Fergusson, 1872, 530–1.

4 *Acherole* (4) ND 22. 51. ? ?/ ?/ *RCAHM-S*, 1911a, no. 484; Barnatt, 1989, II, 476.

5 *Aultan Broubster* (3) ND 045 599/ 62.5 × 53/ Pl/ *RCAHM-S*, 1911a, no. 402; Myatt, 1973, 9; Barnatt, 1989, II, 235.

6 *Backlass* (3) NO 079 423/ 7.5/ Pl, O/ *RCAHM-S*, 1911a, no. 142; *D & E*, 1989, 27; priv. comm. L. Myatt, 14.9.89.

7 *Bouilag* (3) ND 091 330/ 1.8 × 1.2 (2.1)/ 4P/ *D & E*, 1983, 54; priv.comm. L. Myatt, 27.1.89.

8 *Broubster* (3) ND 048 608/ 42.7 × 27.4/ HS/ *RCAHM-S*, 1911a, no. 163; Barnatt, 1989, II, 235–6; Burl, 1995, 121.

9 *Dorrery* (3) ND 069 557/ 73/ Pl/ Myatt, 1988b/ Astron: MdW SS, *ibid.*, 67–68.

10 *Forse* (3) ND 208 363/ 48/ Pl/ Thom, 1967, N1/5; TTB, 1980, 322–3.

11 *Guidebest* (3) ND 181 351/ 57.3 × 52/ Pl, int Cn?/ Fergusson, 1872, 531–2; *RCAHM-S*, 1911a, no. 279; Thom, 1967, N1/13; TTB, 1980, 324–5.

12 *Latheronwheel* (4) *c.* ND 186 332/ ?/ C?/ Gunn, 1915, 343; priv comm. L. Myatt, 12.3.94.

13 *Old Hall of Dunn* (5) ND 204 564/ ?/ ?/ *RCAHM-S*, 1911a, no. 483.

14 *Shurrery* (5) ND 04. 57. /?/ ?/ *RCAHM-S*, 1911a, no. 381.

15 *Warth Hill* (5) ND 371 698/ 16?/ C?, int Cn, 2 Cts/ *RCAHM-S*, 1911a, no. 41; Barnatt, 1989, II, 476.

CLACKMANNAN (CENTRAL)

1 *Beinn an Tuirc* (5) NR 753 362/ 15/ Ct?/ *D & E*, 1998, 24.

2 *Cunninghar, Tillicoultry* (5) NS 925 971 / Bank, 32.3 × 29.3, St C, *c.* 18/ Ct, art/ Exc. 1894. Inhum. F/v (Cowie, 1978, 119), urn (Longworth, 295, no. 1783): *PSAS 29*, 1894–5, 190–3; *PSAS 33*, 1898–9, 358–65; Morris, R., 1981, 82; Barnatt, 1989, II, 318–19.

3 *Hawk Hill* (4) NS 92. 92. /?/ ?/ Dest. *c.* 1917/ *RCAHM-S*, 1933, no. 601.

COLONSAY (STRATHCLYDE)

1 *Scalasaig* (5) NR 386 937/ ?/ O?/ *D & E*, 1970, 5; priv. comm. I. F. MacLeod, 30.4.71; Barnatt, 1989, II, 480.

DUMFRIESSHIRE (DUMFRIES & GALLOWAY)

1 *Girdle Stanes* (3) NY 254 961/ *c.* 39/ CH, Pt, R?/ *PSAS 31*, 1896–7, 281–9; Hyslop & Hyslop, 21–2, 25–36, 41–3, 48; TTB, 1980, 298–9.

2 *Greystone, The* (5) NX 98. 76. / ?/ ?/ Exc. pre-1886. Pygmy cup (Morrison, no. 94): *TDGNHAS 5*, 1886–7, 38–41; *PPS 17*, 1951, 80.

3 *Kirkbog* (4) NX 877 939/ ?/ ?/ *RCAHM-S*, 1920, no. 81.

4 *Kirkhill* (3) NY 140 960/ 11.6?/ Pl/ *RCAHM-S*, 1920, no. 625; *TDGNHAS 11*, 1923–4, 106; Thom, 1967, G7/3 [Wamphray]; TTB, 1980, 294–5.

5 *Kirkslight Rig* (3) NY 223 885/ *c.* 16/ 2 int Cts?/ *D & E*, 1973, 23.

6 *Lochmaben Stane* (4) NY 311 660/ *c.* 55 × 46/ Pl/ Exc. 1982. No finds. C-14, 2525 ± 85 bc: Crone, 1983 [Clochmabenstane]/ *OSA Dumfriess*, 1841, 266; Hyslop & Hyslop, 54; Burl, 1985, 123.

7a *Loupin' Stanes Centre* (1) NY 257 966/ 13.8 × 12.1 CA/ Gr, Pf/ *PSAS 31*, 1896–7, 281–5; *RCAHM-S*, 1920, no. 199; Hyslop & Hyslop,19–21, 41–3; Thom, 1967, G7/4; TTB, 1980, 296–7/ Astron: MdS SS, Thom, 1967, 98.

7b *Loupin' Stanes NW* (4) NY 256 966/ *c.* 13/ Pl?/ Burl, 1995, 124.

7c *Loupin' Stanes SE* (4) NY 258 965/ *c.* 23 × 18/ Pl?/ Burl, 1995, 124.

8 *Twelve Apostles* (3) NX 947 794/ 86.6 × 79.3 CI/ Pl, Q, adj. cursuses/ *PSAL 10*, 1883–5, 303–4; *PSAS 28*, 1893–4, 84–90; TTB, 1980, 288–9, G6/1; Burl, 1995, 124/ Astron: MdW SS, Burl, 1995, 124.

9 *Westerkirk* (4) *c.* NY 31. 90/ ?/ Pl? Dest. post-1841?/ Hyslop & Hyslop, 17.

10 *Whitcastles* (3) NY 224 881/ 54.9 × 43.1 CE/ Pl/ Hyslop & Hyslop, 20; *RCAHM-S*, 1920, no. 307; Thom, 1967, G7/6; TTB, 1980, 300–1.

11 *Whiteholm Rigg* (3) NY 217 827/ 20.1 × 18.9 CA/ Pl, O/ *RCAHM-S*, 1920, no. 603; Thom, 1967, G7/2 [Seven Brethren]; TTB, 1980, 292–3.

12 *Windy Edge* (4) NY 430 838/ *c.* 42 × 39/ Pl?/ *OSA_16. Dumfriess*, 1795, 85; *RCAHM-S*, 1924, 28, no. 47.

13 *Woodhead* (5) NY 21. 66. / ?/ ?/ *RCAHM-S*, 1920, no. 5.

EAST LOTHIAN (LOTHIAN)

1 *Crow Stones* (3) NT 618 652/ 1.8 × 1.8 (2.6)/ 4P/ *RCAHM-S*, 1924, no. 245; TTB, 1980, 306; Burl, 1988a, 124.

2 *Kell Burn* (3) NT 645 641/ 3.1 × 2.1 (3.7)/ 4P?/ *RCAHM-S*, 1924, no. 143; Thom, 1967, G9/13/ Astron: MdS SS, MacKie, 1975, 94.

3 *Kingside Hill* (3) NT 627 650/ 11.6 × 10.7/ Cn, S?/ *RCAHM-S*, 1924, no. 240; *D & E*, 1987, 30–1; Baldwin, 1985, 162–3.

4 *Mayshiel* (3) NT 617 646/ 2.7/ Em/ *RCAHM-S*, 1924, no. 238; Baldwin, 1985, 16 163.

5 *Nine Stones* (3) NT 626 654/ 6.4/ Pl?/ *RCAHM-S*, 1924, no. 239; Thom, 1967, G9/11 [Ninestone Rig]; TTB, 1980, 306–7.

6 *Penshiel* (4) NT 641 631/ ?/ ?/ *RCAHM-S*, 1924, no. 243.

7 *Penshiel Grange* (4) NT 641 632/ 8.2 × 4.6 (9.6)/ 4P/ *RCAHM-S*, 1924, no. 242; Barnatt, 1989, II, 338–9.

8 *Penshiel Hill* (4) NT 632 642/ ?/ S?/ *RCAHM-S*, 1924, no. 241.

9 *Spartleton Edge* (3) NT 64. 67. /12.8/ Em?, S?/ *RCAHM-S*, 1924, no. 185; Barnatt, 1989, II, 493. Cn?, RC?

10 *Yadlee* (3) NT 654 673/ 8.2/ Pl/ *RCAHM-S*, 1924, no. 172; Baldwin, 1985, 163.

FIFE (FIFE)

1 *Balbirnie* (2) NO 285 030/ 15 × 14 CE/ Cn, Cts × 4, cms, crs/ Exc. 1883. urns (*Edinburgh Museum Catalogue*, 1892, EP26, SF31). 1970–1. Crems, grooved ware, S4 bkr, f/v, urns, jet button. C-14, 1330 ± 90 bc (GaK-3425), 890 ± 80 bc (GaK-3426): Ritchie, J.N.G., 1974/ *RCAHM-S*, 1933, no. 418; Morris, R.W.B., 1981, 72; Barnatt, 1989, II, 309–10/ Astron: MdS SR? *Balbirnie stone circle*, Glenrothes Development Corporation leaflet.

2 *Balfarg* (2) NO 281 032/ Multi-phase: (a) henge 64.9, (b) timber ring 25, (c) St c 60. 50.3/ CH, C, Gr, Ent, Pt/ Exc. 1977–8. Phase (b), grooved ware. C-14, 2365 ± 60 bc (GU-1163), 2320 ± 60 bc (GU-1162), 2230 ± 50 bc (GU-1160), 2085 ± 50 bc (GU-1161): Phase (d) central pit, crem, handled bkr: *PSAS 111*, 1980–1, 63–171; *PSAS 118*, 1988, 61–7; Barnatt, II, 1989, 310–12; Burl, 1995, 126–7.

3 *Dunino* (4) NO 53. 11. /?/ ?/ *RCAHM-S*, 1933, no. 221.

4 *Kirkhall, Lochore* (4) NT 177 958/ ?/ ?/ *D & E*, 1993, 27.

5 *Lundin Links* (3) NO 404 026/ 31 × 9.1 (32.3)/ 4P?/ Exc. pre-1790. V-shaped jet button?/ *Arch J 6*, 1849, 258–9; *PSAS 37*, 1902–3, 212–15; Burl, 1988a,126–7/ Astron: Min S MS, Thom, 1971, 55–6, P4/1.

6 *Strathendry* (4) NO 228 014/ ?/ 4P?, int ct?/ *OSA 6, Fife*, 1793, 52; *RCAHM-S*, 1933, 189, no. 390.

7 *Torryburn* (4) *c.* NT 035 870/ *c.* 4.9 × 3.7 [6.1]/ 4P?, O + cms/ *RCAHM-S*, 1933, 273, no. 526; Walker & Ritchie, 1987, 178 [Tuilyies].

Harris, Outer Hebrides, see HEBRIDES

HEBRIDES (WESTERN ISLES)

Benbecula
1 *Gramisdale* (5) NF 825 561/ *c.* 31/ S?/ *RCAHM-S*, 1928, no. 353; Thom, 1967, H4/1 [North Ford]; TTB, 1980, 314–15; Barnatt, 1989, II, 478. PT?

2 *Suidheachadh Sealg* (3) NF 825 552/ 26/ Cn?, Ct?/ *RCAHM-S*, 1928, no. 352; Thom, 1967, H4/2 [Gramisdale South]; TTB, 1980, 316–17; Barnatt, 1989, II, 478. PT?; TTB, 1990, I, 256.

Berneray
3 *Barra* (5) NL 564 803/ *c.* 10/ C, O?/ Thom, 1967, H6/5; Ruggles, 1984a, 57, UI61 [Leac a'Langich]; TTB, 1990, I, 264.

4 *Bhruist* (3) NF 924 828 /?/ ?/ *RCAHM-S*, 1928, no. 132; Barnatt, 1989, II, 477.

Harris
5 *Borvemore* (5) NG 020 939/ ?/ Pl/ Exc. 1864. Inhum? *RCAHM-S*, 1928, no. 136; Ruggles, 1984a, 84, LH37 [Scarista].

Lewis
6 *Achmore* (3) NB 317 292/ 41/ Pl/ Ponting, G. & M., 1981b; *D & E*, 1983, 39; Curtis, 1988, 362–3; *D & E*, 1989, 72.

7 *Aird Sleitenish* (3) NB 031 199/ 6.6/ C?, Cn?/ *D & E*, 1973, 48; Ruggles, 1984a, 28, LH32.

8 *Callanish* (2) NB 213 330/ 13.4 × 11.8 CA/ S, A, 3 × R, int PgT/ Exc. 1857. Crem: *PSAS 3*, 1857–60, 110. Exc. 1980–1. Hebridean sherds, AOC, N4 bkrs, grooved ware; 7 × C-14: 2260 ± 50 (AA-24966) to 2105 ± 50 (AA-24961), *c.* 2825 BC. Ponting, G. & M., 1984a, 19–21; P. Ashmore, 1995 [Calanais]/ Toland, 122, 188–9; Henshall, 1972, 461–2; Thom, 1967, 96, 123, H1/1; Ruggles, 1984a, 80, LH16; Ponting, G. & M., 1984a; Curtis, 1988, 354–6, [Callanish I]; *D & E*, 1993, 111–12; *ibid.*, 1994, 96; Burl, 1993, 14–16, 59–61, 63–5, 178–80; Burl, 1995, 148–51; / Astron: Maj S MS, Hawkins, G. S., 1966a, 189; MdW SS, Maj N MR, Maj N MS, Maj S MS, Ponting, 1988, 427–31.

9 *Cean Hulavig* (3) NB 230 304/ 13.3 × 9.5 CE/ S, Cn/ *PSAS 38*, 1903–4, 189; *RCAHM-S*, 1928, no. 93; Burl, 1976, 358 [Garynahine]; Ponting, G. & M., 1984b, 19–20; Ruggles, 1984a, 80, LH21; Curtis, 1988, 358–62 [Callanish IV]; Ashmore, 1995 [Ceann Thulabhaig].

10 *Cnoc Ceann a'Gharaidh* (3) NB 222 325/ 21.6 × 18.9/ Cn, S?, earlier timber ring?/ *PSAS 3*,

1857–60, 116; *RCAHM-S*, 1928, no. 353; Thom, 1967, H1/2 [Callanish II]; Burl, 1976, 358 [Loch Roag]; Ponting, G. & M., 12–15; 1984b, Curtis, 1988, 356–8 [Callanish II]; Burl, 1995, 151.

11 *Cnoc Fillibhir* (3) NB 225 325/ 13.7 × 13.1 CE/ C/ *RCAHM-S*, 1928, no. 91; Thom, 1967, H1/3 [Callanish III]; Curtis, 1988, 358 16 × 10 [Callanish III]; Burl, 1995, 152.

12 *Cul a Chleit* (5) NB 247 303/ ?/ Pl/ *RCAHM-S*, 1928, no. 95; Ruggles, 1984a, 80–1, LH22. An unlikely St C.

13 *Druim Dubh (black ridge)* (4) NB 382 305/ 28 × 21/ Pl, toppled in antiquity?/ priv. comm., M. R. & G. R. Curtis, 1992; *Curr Arch 147*, 1996, 98–9.

14 *Loch Raoinavat* (3) NB 233 461/ 28.6/ Pl?/ Ponting, M., MacRae R. & Ponting, R. *A mini-Guide to Shawbost stone circle*, 1983; *D & E*, 1983, 39, [South Shawbost]; Curtis, 1988, 364–5.

15 *Na Drommanan* (4) NB 230 336/ 21.6 × 19.8 CA/ C?/ Ponting, G. & M., 1984b, 30–1, [Callanish X]; Curtis, 1988, 361–2; Barnatt, 1989, II, 478 [Druim Nam Eun], rock outcrop?; Ashmore, 1995, 13.

16 *Priest's Glen* (5) NB 409 354/ *c.* 47/ Pl?/ *RCAHM-S*, 1928, no. 56; *D & E*, 1981, 51; Ruggles, 1984a, 84, LH2; Barnatt, 1989, II, 241.

North Uist
17 *Beinn a Chaolais* (5) NF 90. 77. /18/ ?/ RCAHM-S, 1928, no. 241.

18 *Carinish* (3) NF 832 603/ 43.1 × 39.8/ Pl/ Beveridge, 1911, 260; *RCAHM-S*, 1928, no. 248; Ruggles, 1984a, 106, UI40; Curtis, 1988, 370–2.

19 *Cringraval* (4) NF 811 644/ 36.6/ Pl/ *RCAHM-S*, 1928, no. 251; Ruggles, 1984a, 102, UI35.

20 *Loch a Phobuill* (3) NF 829 630/ 39.6 × 35.1/ Em/ Beveridge, 1911, 260; *RCAHM-S*, 1928, no. 249; Thom, 1967, H3/18 [Sornach Coir Fhinn]; TTB, 1980, 312–13.

21 *Pobull Fhinn* (3) NF 844 650/ 37.8 × 28/ Em, Pts, Pf, O?/ Beveridge, 1911, 259; *RCAHM-S*, 1928, no. 250; Thom, 1967, H3/17; TTB, 1980, 310–11; Ruggles, 1984a, 102, UI33 [Ben Langass]; Curtis, 1988, 368–70 [Sornach Coir Fhinn].

Raasay
22 *Storab Burn* (3) NG 557 410/ 5.2/ Pl/ *D & E*, 1996, 73; *Assoc of Certificated Archaeologists, Occ Paper 18*, Glasgow University, 1996, 24.

Skye
23 *Kilbride* (4) NG 590 203/ ?/ ?, O? 'Clach na H'Annait' (stone of the church)/ *RCAHM-S*, 1928, 215, no. 676; *Prehistoric Skye*, 1995, 52.

24 *Kilchrist, Glebe* (3) NG 619 202/ ?/ ?/ *D & E*, 1990, 28.

25 *Meal-da-Bheinn* (3) NG 629 121/ ?/ ?/ *D & E*, 1991, 45.

26 *Na Clachan Bhreige* (3) NG 543 177/ 3.7 × 3.2 (4.9)/ 4P?/ Exc. *c.* 1860. Black polished stone:

PSAS 5, 1863–4, 14/ RCAHM-S, 1928, no. 667; Thom, 1967, H7/9 [Strathaird]; TTB, 1980, 318–19; Burl, 1988a, 196–7; *Prehistoric Skye*, 1995, 53–4.

27 *Snizert* (3) NG 386 596/ 3.4 × 3.2/ Pl?/ *D & E*, 1989, 44.

INVERNESS (HIGHLAND)

1 *Aviemore* (2) NH 896 134/ 23.2/ RC, Gr/ Henshall, 1963, 360–1; Thom, 1967, 81, B7/12; TTB, 1980, 258–9.

2a *Balnuaran of Clava Centre* (2) NH 757 444/ 31.6/ RC, cm?/ Exc. 1953. Flints: Piggott, 1956, 188–90/ Henshall, 1963, 361–2; Thom, 1967, B7/1 (1); TTB, 1980, 246–7.

2b *Balnuaran of Clava NE* (2) NH 757 444/ 34.8 × 31.5 Cl/ PgT, Gr, P9f, cms/ Exc. *c.* 1854. Bones: *PSAS 18*, 1883–4, 345: exc. 1995, single-phase: *D & E*, 1995, 39/ Henshall, 1963, 362–4; Thom, 1967, B7/1 (3); TTB, 1980, 246–7/ Astron: MdW SS, Somerville, 1923, 217–22.

2c *Balnuaran of Clava SW* (2) NH 756 443/ 31.7/ PgT, Pf, Gr, cms/ Exc. *c.* 1828. Flat-rimmed ware: Lauder, T. D. *An Account of the Great Floods of August, 1829 . . .* , 1830, 418–19; exc. 1995, single-phase: *D & E*, 1995, 39/ Henshall, 1963, 364–5; Thom, 1967, B7/1 (2); TTB, 1980, 246–7/ Astron: MdW SS, Somerville, 923, 217–22.

3 *Boblainy* (4) NH 493 396/ 13.7/ PgT or RC?/ *PSAS 20*, 1885–6, 350–1; Henshall, 1963, 366.

4 *Bruiach* (1) NH 499 414/ 22.3/ RC, cms/ Henshall, 1963, 366–7.

5 *Carn Daley* (3) NH 494 314/ 18.3?/ PtG Exc. *c.* 1900. No details/ Henshall, 1963, 367–8; Barnatt, 1989, II, 256.

6 *Clava* (3) NH 757 444/ Kerb-circle, Q, cms/ Exc. 1953. Crem: Piggott, 1956, 192.

7 *Corrimony* (2) NH 383 303/ 21.3/ PgT, Q, cms/ Exc. 1952. Bone pin, inhum?: Piggott, 1956, 175–84/ Henshall, 1963, 368–70; Barnatt, 1989, II, 256–7.

8 *Croftcroy* (4) NH 682 332/ 9.8+/ PgT/ Henshall, 1963, 370; Thom, 1967, B7/17 [Farr P. O.]; TTB, 1980, 268–9.

9 *Culburnie* (1) NH 491 418/ *c.* 20.5 × 22/ RC, cms/ Henshall, 1963, 370–1.

10 *Culchunaig* (4) NH 742 442/ 32?/ PgT or RC/ Henshall, 1963, 371.

11 *Culdoich N* (3) NH 751 437/ *c.* 35/ RC, cms/ Exc. 1953. Crems of 1 male, 1 female, charcoal: Piggott, 1956, 190–2; *PSAS 89*, 1955–6, 85–8, 89. Postholes, ard-marks, cm st. Only one stone of 'circle': *GAJ 9*, 1982, 31–7/ Henshall, 1963, 371–2;Thom, 1967, B7/2 [Miltown of Clava] mistaken for the nearby Clava Cairn, no. 24, at NH 752 439]; TTB, 1980, 248–9.

12 *Culdoich S* (5) NH 755 428/ *c.* 10/ PgT?, O?/ *D & E*, 1998, 49–50.

13a *Cullearnie N* (3) NH 725 476/ 20 × 18?/ PgT or RC?, Adj/ Henshall, 1963, 372–3.

13b *Cullearnie S* (5) NH 725 475/ ?/ Adj. PgT, St C/ Crem, urn. *D & E*, 1991, 41 [Upper Cullernie].

14 *Dalcross Mains* (3) NH 779 484/ *c.* 21.3/ PgT/ Piggott, 1956, 194; Henshall, 1963, 374; Thom, 1967, B7/6 [Castle Dalcross]; TTB, 1980, 254–5; MacCarthy, C., 1996, 92–4.

15 *Daviot* (3) NH 727 411/ *c.* 27/ RC. Ct/ Exc. *c.* 1820. Skull: *PSAS 16*, 1881–2, 293/ Henshall, 1963, 374; Thom, 1967, B7/5; TTB, 1980, 252–3.

16 *Delfour* (3) NH 844 085/ 34.1?/ RC/ Henshall, 1963, 374–5; Thom, 1967, B7/10 [Easter Delfour]; TTB, 1980, 256–7/ Astron: MdW SS, Thom, 1967, 98.

17 *Druidtemple, Leys* (3) NH 685 420/ 22.9 × 20.7/ PgT, Ct, Q/ Exc. 1824? Gold rod found: Wilson, 1863, I, 164 [Leys]. *c.* 1882: *PSAS 16*, 1881–2, 293. 1952. Crem, young adult: Piggott, 1956, 185; *PSAS 89*, 1955–6, 88, 89/ Henshall, 1963, 375–6; Thom, 1967, B7/18; TTB, 1980, 270–1.

18 *Gask* (3) NH 679 358/ 36.6/ RC, cms/ Henshall, 1963, 378; Thom, 1967, B7/15 [Mains of Gask]; TTB, 1980, 264–5; MacCarthy, C., 1996, 92.

19 *Grenish* (4) NH 907 154/ 31.4?/ RC/ Henshall, 1963, 378–80; Thom, 1967, B7/13 [Loch na Carraigean]; TTB, 1980, 260–1.

20 *Kinchyle of Dores* (3) NH 621 388/ 21.1/ PgT/ Exc. 1952. Crem of 1 individ: Piggott, 1956, 185–6; *PSAS 89*, 1955–6, 88–9/ James Boswell, 30 August 1773; Henshall, 1963, 380–1; Thom, 1967, B7/19 [River Ness]; TTB, 1980, 272–3; Cowan, 1988, 384, 391 [River Ness].

21 *Leanach* (4) NH 732 444/ 29.3/ PgT or RC?/ Henshall, 1963, 382.

22a *Mains of Clava NW* (4) NH 759 446/ ?/ Adj, PgT or RC?/ Henshall, 1963, 382.

22b *Mains of Clava SE* (4) NH 760 445/ ?/ St C?, Adj/ Henshall, 1963, 382.

23 *Midlairgs* (4) NH 714 368/ *c.* 14/ PgT or RC/ Henshall, 1963, 382–3.

24 *Milltown of Clava* (4) NH 752 439/ Henshall, 1963, 383.

25 *Newton of Petty* (3) NH 734 485/ 24.4/ PgT or RC?/ Henshall, 1963, 383.

26 *Torbreck* (1) NH 644 404/ 5.2/ Gr/ *PSAS 16*, 1881–2, 355; Henshall, 1963, 385.

27 *Tordarroch* (3) NH 680 335/ 35.4/ RC, cms/ Henshall, 1963, 385–6; TTB, 1980, 266–7, B7/16 [Farr West]; *D & E*, 1989, 29.

28 *Tullochgorm* (4) NH 965 214/ *c.* 20 × 14 CE/ RC/ Aubrey, I, 177–81 [Chapel Piklag]; Henshall, 1963, 385–6; Thom, 1967, B7/4 [Boat of Garten]; TTB, 1980, 250–1; MacCarthy, C., 1996, 94.

ISLAY (STRATHCLYDE)

1 *Ardilstry* (3) NR 442 492/ 2.9 × 2.8 (4.0)/ 4P/ *RCAHM-S*, 1984, no. 76; Ruggles, 1984, 180, IS37; Burl, 1988a, 128–9.

2 *Cultoon* (4) NR 196 570/ 41 × 33.5 CE/ Pt?/ Exc. 1974. Flint. C-14, pre-1765 ± 40 bc (SRR-500): MacKie, 1977b, 44–5, 92–5/ *RCAHM-S*, 1984, no. 94; Barnatt, 1989, II, 244/ Astron: MdW SS, MacKie 1977a, 103–4.

3 *Lossit Burn* (5) NR 202 560/ 12.8/ Em?/ *D & E*, 1961, 19; Barnatt, 1989, II, 480. Domestic?

KINCARDINESHIRE (GRAMPIAN)

1 *Auchlee* (3) NO 890 969/ 17.2 × 16.2/ RSC, gr, em, RC?, Ct, Pf/ Exc. *c.* 1800? No finds: *NSA Kincardine, 11*, 1845/ priv. comm. J. Chisholm, 7.5.77; *D & E*, 1977, 19.

2 *Auchquhorthies* (1) NO 901 963/ 23.7 × 22/ RSC, RC/ Exc. 1858? Urn?: Stuart, J., 1856, xix/ Aubrey, I, 177 [Auchincorthie]; *PSAS 14*, 1879–80, 305–7; Coles, F. R., 1900, 145; Keiller, 1934, 3, 8ff; Thom, 1967, B3/1 [Aquorthies N]/ Astron: Maj S MR, Ruggles, 1984b, S74, no. 86.

3 *Cairnfauld* (3) NO 754 941/ 22.9/ RSC?, Gr/ Exc. pre-1900. Bones: Coles, F. R., 1900, 155–7/ *PSAS 14*, 1879–80, 304; Thom, 1967, B2/11; TTB, 1980, 256–7. Stones removed, cattle diseased, *PSAS 60*, 1925–6, 306.

4 *Cairnwell* (3) Was NO 907 973/ 9.1/ RSC?, RC/ Exc. 1858. Urns; *PSAS 5*, 1862–4, 131/ *JRAI 17*, 1888, 47; Henshall, 1963, 400/ 1995, moved 175 m to NW. Now NO 906 974. *D & E*, 1995, 33/ Exc. multi-phase (a) timber structure, crems; (b) RC; (c) StC, 8 st? C-14: 2730 ± 80 (GU-4402); 1150 ± 50 (GU-4397); 1120 ± 60 (GU-4399); 1070 ± 50 (GU-4396); 1070 ± 70 (GU-4400); 1020 ± 50 (GU-4398); 1020 ± 50 (GU-4401). *c.* 3062–2774 BC. *PSAS 127*, 1997, 255–79.

5 *Camp, The* (4) NO 816 772/ 24.4/ RSC?, RC?/ Coles, F. R., 1902–3, 193.

6 *Cloch* (5) NO 781 679/ ?/ RSC, cms/ priv. comm. J. Chisholm, 7.5.77.

7 *Cotbank of Barras* (4) NO 827 791/ 18.3/ RSC?/ Coles, F. R., 1902–3, 198–9.

8 *Craighead* (2) NO 912 977/ 8.5 × 7.3/ 4P?/ Exc. 1858. Bones. *PSAS 5*, 1962–4, 130–1/ Lukis, 1885, 305; Coles, F. R., 1900, 152–3; Burl, 1988a, 130–1.

9 *Dunnotar* (4) NO 836 833/ ?/ ?/ Destr. *c.* 1840. *ONB Kincardine 6*, 1865, 71.

10 *East Mulloch* (4) *c.* NO 734 923/ *c.* 11/ Pl/ *PSAS 14*, 1879–80, 304–5.

11 *Esslie the Greater* (3) NO 717 916/ 25 × 23.3/ RSC, RC/ Exc. 1873. Bone: *PSAS 14*, 1879–80, 301–2/ Aubrey, I, 182–3 [Templeton]; Coles, F. R., 1900, 162–6; Thom, 1967, B2/4 [Esslie South]; TTB, 1980, 200–1/ Astron: MdS SR, Min N MS,

Thom, 1967, 98; Maj S MR, Ruggles, 1984b, S74, no. 90.

12 *Esslie the Lesser* (3) NO 722 921/ 13.4/ RSC/, RC?, Ct?/ Exc. 1873. No finds: *PSAS 14*, 1879–80, 303 [Mulloch West]/ Coles, F. R., 1900, 166–7; Thom, 1967, B2/5 [Esslie N]; TTB, 1980, 202–3.

13 *Garrol Wood* (3) NO 725 912/ 18 × 14.6 CB/ RSC, RC, Pf/ Exc. 1904. Urn: Coles, F. R., 1904, 190–203/ Aubrey, I, 182–3 [Templeton]; *PSAS 14*, 1879–80, 300–1; Coles, F. R., 1900, 157–62; Thom, 1967, B2/6; TTB, 1980, 204–5.

14 *Glassel* (1) NO 649 997/ 5.9 × 3.3 (6.8)/ 4P, O/ Exc. 1879. No finds. 1904. Fl: Coles, F. R., 1905, 203–5/ *PSAS 14*, 1879–80, 308–9; Coles, F. R., 1900, 168–71; Thom, 1967, B3/6 [Kynoch Plantation]; TTB, 1980, 212–13; Burl, 1988a, 132–3.

15 *Millplough* (4) NO 819 754/ ?/ RSC?/ Coles, F. R., 1902–3, 196–8.

16 *Old Bourtreebush* (4) NO 903 961/ 30.5 × 22.6?/ RSC?/ Exc. 1863. No finds: *PSAS 5*, 1862–4, 34/ Aubrey, I, 178; *PSAS 14*, 1879–80, 306–7; Coles, F. R., 1900, 141–6; Thom, 1967, B3/2; TTB, 1980, 228–9; Barnatt, 1989, II, 295–6.

17a *Raedykes NW* (3) NO 832 906/ 14.3/ RC, Gr/ *PSAS 57*, 1922–3, 20–8, 25–6; Henshall, 1963, 401–2; Thom, 1967, B3/4; TTB, 1980, 230–1.

17b *Raedykes SE* (3) NO 833 905/ 17.4/ RC/ Exc. 1964–5. No finds: *D & E*, 1965, 24/ *PSAS 23*, 1922–3, 23; Henshall, 1963, 402; Thom, 1967, B3/3; Barnatt, 1989, II, 298. Variant RSC?

18 *Raes o'Clune* (3) NO 795 949/ 17.1/ RSC/ *PSAS 14*, 1879–80, 295–6, 299–300; Coles, F. R., 1900, 153–5; *PSAS 53*, 1918–19, 71–3; Thom, 1967, B3/7 [Clune Wood]; TTB, 1980, 232–3.

19 *Tilquillie* (4) NO 724 940/ ?/ RSC, O?/ *PSAS 53*, 1918–19, 71; Barnatt, 1989, II, 304.

KIRKCUDBRIGHTSHIRE (DUMFRIES & GALLOWAY)

1 *Bagbie* (3) NX 498 564/ 2.6 × 1.7 (3.1)/ 4P, ext Pair, ext Cn/ *RCAHM-S*, 1914, 157; Thom, 1967, G4/13 [Kirkmabreck]; Burl, 1998a, 134–5.

2 *Cauldside Burn* (3) NX 529 571/ 25/ Pl/ Coles, F. R., 1895, 311–12; *RCAHM-S*, 1914, no. 16; Thom, 1967, G4/14; TTB, 1980, 286–7/ Astron: MdW MR, Thom, 1967, 98.

3 *Claughreid* (3) NX 517 560/ 10.7 × 8.8 CE/ S/ *RCAHM-S*, 1914, no. 293; Thom, 1967, 72.

4 *Drannandow* (3) NX 401 711/ 27.2/ Pl/ *RCAHM-S*, 1914, no. 366; Thom, 1967, G4/3; TTB, 1980, 280–1.

5 *Drummore* (3) NX 688 459/ *c.* 25.9/ ?/ *T. Hawick A. S.*, 1908, 20–8; *RCAHM-S*, 1914, no. 237; Grinsell, 1976, 239–40.

6   *Easthill* (3) NX 919 739/ 24.7 × 23.8 CE/ Pf?, cms?, O?/ Coles, F. R., 1895, 309–10; *RCAHM-S*, 1914, no. 332; Thom, 1967, G5/9 [Maxwellton]; TTB, 1980, 276–7/ Astron: MdS SR, TTB, 1980, 277.

7   *Ernespie* (4) NX 774 632/ ?/ 4P?/ *RCAHM-S*, 1914, no. 202; Coles, F. R., 1895, 306 [Torrs, Kelton].

8a *Glenquickan N* (1) NX 509 582/ 16.8 × 14.6 CA/ S, cobbled, Gr?/ Coles, F. R., 1895, 307–9; *RCAHM-S*, 1914, no. 292; Thom, 1967, G4/12 [Cambret Moor]; TTB, 1980, 284–5.

8b *Glenquickan S* (4) NX 508 581/ ?/ ?/ Thom, 1967, 64. 2nd circle, removed by 1955.

9   *High Auchenlarie* (3) NX 539 534/ 13.7?/ Cn/ Coles, F. R., 1895, 306–7; *RCAHM-S*, 1914, no. 18.

10 *Holm of Daltallochan* (5) NX 554 942/ 24.9 × 18.5 CE/ cms?/ *PSAS 14*, 1879–80, 284; Coles, F. R., 1895, 310–11; *RCAHM-S*, 1914, no. 97; Thom, 1967, G4/1 [Carsphairn]; Burl, 1976, 206. Field-clearance around a drumlin.

11 *Kirkgunzeon* (4) NX 865 666/ 9/ Cn?/ Destr. 1790–1870. Coles, F. R., 1895, 302.

12 *Knockshinnie* (5) NX 681 450/ *c.* 22/ O?/ Coles, F. R., 1895, 304.

13 *Lairdmannoch* (3) NX 662 614/ 6.4/ S/ Wilson, D, 1863, I, 169; Coles, F. R., 1895, 312; *RCAHM-S*, 1914, no. 446.

14 *Little Balmae* (5) NX 68. 44. /27.4?/ ?/ Coles, F. R., 1895, 304; Barnatt, 1989, II, 466.

15 *Loch Stroan* (3) NX 640 709/ 21 × 18 CE/ S/ *TDGNHAS 22*, 1938–40, 164; Burl, 1976, 208 [Loch Roan]; Barnatt, 1989, II, 337.

16 *Park of Tongland* (5) NX 699 560/ 5.7 × 5.1 (7.7)/ 4P or 2 × Pairs?, Cn/ Exc. 1987. Multi-phase. (a) cultivation; (b) 13 pits with 2 urns, accessory cup, bone button, crems. C-14, 1610 ± 50 bc (GU-2382), 1610 ± 50 bc (GU-2378), 1530 ± 50 bc (GU-2379), 1510 ± 60 bc (GU-2380), 1480 ± 50 bc (GU-2377), 1460 ± 50 bc (GU-2374), 1090 ± 50 bc (GU-2381); (c?) Pair + pair/ (d) Cn. C-14, 1440 ± 50 bc (GU-2376), 1430 ± 60 bc (GU-2375): *PPS 58*, 1992, 312–21/Coles, F. R., 1895, 305–6; *RCAHM-S*, 1914, no. 445; Burl, 1988a, 136–7; Barnatt, 1989, II, 338.

17 *Stroangassel* (3) NX 589 869/ 22/ S, C?/ priv. comm., M. L. Ansell, 20.2.73.

18 *Thieves* (5, 4) NX 404 716/ 8.5 × 7?/ Em/ *RCAHM-S*, 1914, no. 367; Thom, 1967, 67, 68, 124, G4/2; R. J. C. Atkinson, in Ruggles & Whittle, 1981, 208; Barnatt, 1989, II, 339.

LANARKSHIRE (STRATHCLYDE)

1   *Annathill Farm* (5) NS 720 710/ 32/ Emb, 2 ents, 3 ext R?/ *D & E*, 1990, 38.

2   *Wildshaw Burn* (3) NS 882 271/ 50 × 40/ Pl, unfinished?/ *D & E*, 1990, 37–8; *Curr Arch 124*, 1991, 149/ Astron: MdW SR, *D & E*, 1993, 89; MdW SS, MdS SR, *D & E, Scotland*, 1995, 87.

Lewis, Outer Hebrides, see HEBRIDES

MIDLOTHIAN (LOTHIAN)

1   *Marchwell* (5) NT 22. 61./ 12?/ Cn?/ Exc. No date. f/v: *RCAHM-S*, 1929, no. 105; *PSAS 75*, 1940–1, 220; V. G. Childe, *Scotland Before the Scots*, 1946, 115, no. 243.

2   *Newbridge* (5) NT 123 726/ 112 × 96?/ Cn, St C, C, or Os?/ Exc. 1830. Middle Bronze Age bronze rapier, bones: Wilson, 1863, 1, 81 [Old Huly]; *PSAS 12*, 1876–8, 449–50/ *PSAS 10*, 1872–4, 151; *PSAS 38*, 1902–3, 201–4 [Heelie Hill]; *RCAHM-S*, 1929, no. 131; Barnatt, 1989, II, 492.

MORAY (GRAMPIAN)

1   *Alves* (3) NJ 162 628/ 6.7 × 6?/ 6, Gr?, O/ *D & E*, 1970, 33; priv. comm., I. Keillar, 23.3.71.

2   *Bogton Mill* (4) NJ 274 608/ 32/ Pl?/ Coles, F. R., 1906, 201–4.

3   *Browland* (3) NJ 338 647/ 3.3 × 2.6 (4.2)/ 4P/ Coles, F. R., 1907, 160–2; Burl, 1988a, 138–9.

4   *Chapel Hill* (5) NJ 03. 46. / 10.7/ Pl?/ Coles, F. R., 1907, 170–1.

5   *Cowiemuir* (5) NJ 371 631/ 16.8 × 12.2/ Em?, Gr?, HS/ Coles, F. R., 1906, 192–4.

6   *Drum Divan* (4) NJ 192 431/ ?/ ?/ Coles, F. R., 1907, 155–8.

7   *Edinkillie* (3) NJ 048 414/ *c.* 58/ Pl/ *D & E*, 1972, 30.

8   *Haerstanes* (4) *c.* NJ 27. 60. / ?/ HS?/ *PSAS 9*, 1870–2, 256.

9   *Innesmill* (3) NJ 289 641/ 33.5/ RSC?, cms?/ Exc. pre-1870. No finds: *T. Inverness Sci. Soc, II*, 44/ *PSAS 9*, 1870–2, 256 [Nine Stanes]; Coles, F. R., 1906, 198–201; Thom, 1967, B5/1 [Urquhart]; Grinsell, 1976, 213; TTB, 1980, 241–2.

10 *Llanbryde* (4) *c.* NJ 270 612/ ?/ ?/ Destr. 1810. *PSAS 9*, 1870–2, 256.

11 *Loch-hill* (4) *c.* NJ 288 688/ ?/ ?/ Destr. *c.* 1840. *PSAS 9*, 1870–2, 256.

12 *Nether Cluny* (4) *c.* NJ 316 381/ ?/ ?/ Destr. *c.* 1840. Coles, F. R., 1907, 158–60; Grinsell, 1976, 212.

13 *Templestone* (1) NJ 068 568/ 3.4 × 2.7 (4.3)/ 4P, Gr, RC?/ Coles, F. R., 1907, 167–9; Burl, 1988a, 140–1.

MULL (STRATHCLYDE)

1   *Loch Buie* (3) NM 618 251/ 13.4/ O × 3/ *Arch J* 5, 1848, 217; Thom, 1967, M2/14; TTB, 1980, 318, 320–1; Ruggles, 1984a, 139 ML28.

2   *Tenga* (3) NM 502 462/ *c.* 35?/ Pl/ *RCAHM-S*, 1946c, no. 1358; Ruggles, 1984a, 127 ML13 [Loch Frisa].

3   *Torr Aint* (5) NM 444 498/ 6/ St C?/ *D & E*, 1993, 70.

Balliscate NM 499 541, Burl, 1976a, 361 (Mull 1) is not a stone circle but a 3-Stone row. TTB, 1990, II, 272, M1/8 [Tobermory]; Ruggles, 1984a, 243, ML4 [Sgriob-ruadh]; Burl, 1993, 255.

Dervaig NM 439 520, Burl, 1976a, 361 (Mull 2) is not a stone circle but a 4-Stone row. TTB, 1990, II, 269. M1/6 [Dervaig C]; Burl, 1993, 248.

Maol Mor NM 435 531, Burl, 1976a, 361 (Mull 4) is not a stone circle but a 4-Stone row. TTB, 1990, II, 267, M1/4 [Dervaig A]; Burl, 1993, 248 [Dervaig NNW].

NAIRN (HIGHLANDS)

1   *Auldearn* (3) NH 924 553/ 16.8/ PgT or RC?/ Henshall, 1963, 387; Grinsell, 1976, 202; Bord & Bord, 1990, 180–1.

2a *Little Urchany W* (3) NH 866 485/ *c.* 19.5/ Adj, PgT or RC?/ Henshall, 1963, 388; Thom, 1967, B6/1; TTB, 1980, 242–3.

2b *Little Urchany W* (4) NH 866 485/ ?/ PgT or RC?/ Destr. *c.* 1840. *PSAS 16*, 1881–2, 328.

3   *Moyness* (4) NH 952 536/ *c.* 28/ RC/ Exc. 1856. 'Clay urn'. Stuart, 1867, xxii/ Henshall, 1963, 388; Thom, 1967, B6/2; TTB, 1980, 244–5.

North Uist, Outer Hebrides, see HEBRIDES

ORKNEYS (ORKNEY)

1   *Ring of Brodgar* (2) HY 294 132/ Ditch, 123, st c103.6/ CH, O/ Exc. 1973. C-14, 375 ± 45 bc (SRR-503), 255 ± 60 bc (SRR-502): Renfrew, 1979, 39–43/ Aubrey, I, 218–19; Toland, 124; *RCAHM-S*, 1946, no. 875; Thom & Thom, 1973; TTB, 1980, 328–9; Ritchie, J. N. G., 1988; Barnatt, 1989, II, 231.

2   *Stenness* (3) HY 306 125/ 32.3 × 30.6/ CH, V, O/ Exc. 1973–4. Grooved ware. C-14, 2356 ± 65 bc (SRR-350), 2238 ± 70 bc (SRR-3510, 1730–270 bc (SRR-592): Ritchie, J. N. G., 1976/ Aubrey, I, 218–20; Toland, 124–5; *RCAHM-S*, 1946, no. 876; Curtis, R. 1988, 372–4; Barnatt, 1989, II, 232–3.

PEEBLES-SHIRE (BORDERS)

1   *Harestanes* (3) NT 124 443/ 4.6/ 6?/ Coles, F. R., 1903, 199–201; *RCAHM-S*, 1967, no. 107.

2   *Nether Dod* (3) NT 080 228/ 12.2/ Em/ *RCAHM-S*, 1967, no. 108.

PERTHSHIRE (TAYSIDE)

1   *Airlich* (3) NN 959 386/ 7.9 × 6.7 CB/ Em, C, RC?/ Coles, F. R., 1910, 159–63; Thom, 1967, P1/16 [Meikle Findowie]; TTB, 1980, 344–5.

2   *Ardblair* (2) NO 159 438/ 16 × 11.5/ 6, Gr/ Stewart, 1966a, 20; Coles, F. R., 1909, 115–20; TTB, 1980, 330–1 [Leys of Marlee]; Barnatt, 1989, II, 309.

3   *Bachilton* (4) NO 005 241/ ?/ ?/ Coles, F. R., 1911, 103–4.

4   *Balmuick* (3) NN 785 247/ 2.7 × 2.7? (3.8)/ 4P?/ *PSAS 18*, 1883–4, 306–8; Coles, F. R., 1911, 51–3; Burl, 1988a, 144–5.

5   *Balnabroich* (3) NO 102 569/ 7.7 × 5.6/ Pl, O?/ Exc. 1865, crem?: *North-east Perth: an Archaeological Landscape*, 1990, 22.

6a *Bandirran W* (3) NO 209 309/ 8.5 × 7.6/ Pl? Gr?, S?/ *PSAS 98*, 1964–6, 142–3; Stewart, 1966a, 20; Barnatt, 1989, II, 313.

6b *Bandirran E* (4) NO 210 309/ *c.* 14.5/ S?, 2O?, emb?/ *D & E*, 1997, 62–3.

7a *Blackfaulds N* (3) NO 141 316/ 9.9 × 7/ Adj, S, cms?/ *PSAS 26*, 1890–1, 223–4; Stewart, 1966a, 20; Thom, 1967, P2/9 [Guildtown]; Barnatt, 1989, II, 313; *South-East Perth: an Archaeological Landscape*, 1994, 33.

7b *Blackfaulds S* (5) NO 145 316/ ?/ Adj, ?/ *PSAS 26*, 1890–1, 224 [Brownie's Knowe].

8a *Blair Atholl E* (3) NN 888 629/ 4.2 × 3.1 (5.2) 4P, int Cn?/ *D & E*, 1975, 65; Burl, 1988a, 146–7.

8b *Blair Atholl W* (5) NN 873 627/ 2.7 × 2.7? (3.8)/ 4P or Pair?/ *PSAS 98*, 1964–6, 142–3; Burl, 1988a, 147.

9a *Broad Moss NE* (5) NO 198 488/ 6.7/ Adj/ Coles, F. R., 1909, 107–9; *North-east Perth: an Archaeological Landscape*, 1990, 23. Hut-circle?

9b *Broad Moss SW* (5) NO 198 488/ 6.7/ Adj/ *North-east Perth: an Archaeological Landscape*, 1990, 23; priv. comm., A. A. Thorman, 22.7.96.

10 *Broughdarg* (3) NO 137 670/ *c.* 3 × 3 (4.2)/ 4P?/ *PSAS 29*, 1894–5, 99; Burl, 1988a, 189.

11a *Carse Farm N* (3) NN 802 488/ 3.7 × 2.4 (4.4)/ 4P, cms/ Exc. 1964. Urn: *D & E*, 1964, 39–40/ Coles, F. R., 1908, 125–8; TTB, 1980, 332–3, P1/4 [Weem]; Burl, 1988a, 148–9.

11b *Carse Farm S* (5) NO 802 485/ 9.8 × 9.8? (13.9?)/ 4P?, cms/ Exc. 1964. Crem: *D & E*, 1964, 40/ Coles, F. R., 1908, 128; *PSAS 45*, 1910–11, 386–8; Burl, 1988a, 150–1.

12 *Clach na Tiompan* (4) NN 831 329/ 3.1 × 2.5 (4.1)/ 4P, int Cn, Q/ Exc. 1954, charcoal: Henshall & Stewart, 1956, 122–4/ Coles, F. R., 1911, 96–100; Burl, 1988a, 152–3.

13 *Clachan an Diridh* (3) NN 925 553/ 4.4 × 4.2 (6.1)/ 4P/ Wilson, 1863, I, 165–6; Coles, F. R., 1908, 108–12; Thom, 1967, P1/18; Burl, 1988a, 154–5/ Astron: Maj S MS, Thom, 1967, 158–9.

14 *Coilleaichur* (3) NN 845 466/ *c.* 49/ RSC?, Cr?/ Coles, F. R., 1910, 147–9; Barnatt, 1989, II, 314–15.

15 *Colen* (4) NO 110 311/ 6.4/ 8, Gr, cms/ *PSAS 26*, 1891–2, 222–3; TTB, 1980, 354–5, P2/6; Barnatt, 1989, II, 315.

16a *Commonbank NW* (3) NO 175 248/ *c.* 3 × 3 (4.2)/ Adj, 4P?, Adj Pair/ *D & E*, 1973, 44; Burl, 1988a, 156; *South-East Perth: an Archaeological Landscape*, 1994, 33.

16b *Commonbank SE* (3) NO 177 247/ 11.5 × 6.2 (13)/ Adj, 4P, cms/ *D & E*, 1973, 44; Burl, 1988a, 156.

17 *Comrie Bridge* (4) NN 786 468/ *c.* 4.1 × 3.5 (5.4)/ 4P, ext Pair/ Coles, F. R., 1910, 136–8 [Taymouth]; Barnatt, 1989, II, 316.

18 *Craighall Mill* (3) NO 184 480/ 5 × 3.4 (6.1)/ 4P, O, cms/ *PSAS 15*, 1880–1, 89–92 [Glenballoch]; Coles, F. R., 1909, 104–6; Burl, 1988a, 158–9.

19 *Cramrar* (3) NN 723 454/ 7.6?/ 4P?/ Coles, F. R., 1910, 124–6 [Cromraor]; *D & E*, 1967, 40; *ibid.*, 1968, 33; Burl, 1988a, 160–1.

20 *Croft Moraig* (3) NN 797 472/ 12.2/ Multi-phase: (a) timber ring; (b) st horseshoe, 7.9 × 6.4 m; (c) Em st circle 12m. Variant RSC, Gr, Em, Ent, cms/ Exc. 1965. Neo sherds, flat-rimmed ware: Piggott & Simpson/ Coles, F. R., 1910, 139–47; Thom, 1967, P1/19; TTB, 1980, 348–9; Barnatt, 1989, II, 316–18.

21 *Culhawk Hill* (5) NO 353 562/ *c.* 10/ Pl?/ *D & E*, 1985, 58.

22 *Druid's Seat Wood* (3) NO 124 313/ 8.5/ Pl/ *PSAS 26*, 1891–2, 223; Thom, 1967, P2/3 [Blindwells]; TTB, 1980, 354–5.

23 *Dunmoid* (2) NN 780 212/ 2.9 × 2.7 (4)/ 4P, Ct?/ Exc. *c.* 1840. Urn: Coles, F. R., 1911, 56–9; Burl, 1988a, 162–3.

24 *Faire na Paitig* (3) NO 074 660/ 2.8 × 2.8 (4)/ 4P/ *North-east Perth: an Archaeological Landscape*, 1990, 24.

Fonab Moor, see Clach an Diridh.

25 *Faskally Cottages* (3) NN 930 589/ *c.* 6.4/ Pl/ Coles, F. R., 1908, 113–16.

26 *Ferntower* (1) NN 874 226/ 3.1 × 2.7 × 7.3 × 4.2 (7.7?)/ 4P, cm, ext Pair/ Coles, F. R., 1911, 75–8; Burl, 1988a, 164–5.

27a *Fortingall NE* (3) NN 747 470/ 6.3 × 5 (8)/ Adj, variant 4P/ Exc. 1970. Crem?: Burl, 1988a, 169/ Coles, F. R., 1908, 121–2; TTB, 1980, 336–7, P1/6.

27b *Fortingall SW* (3) NN 747 470/ 7.7 × 5.9 (9.7)/ Adj, variant 4P/ Exc. 1970. Iron Age jet ring: Burl, 1988a, 169, 175/ Coles, F. R., 1908, 121.

27c *Fortingall SE* (4) NN 746 469/ 23?/ RSC?/ Part-exc. 1970. No finds: Burl, 1988a, 175/ Coles, F. R., 1908, 122–4; TTB, 1980, 336–7, P1/6; Barnatt, 1989, II, 320–1. 4P?

28a *Fowlis Wester E* (3) NN 923 249/ 5.9/ Int RC, cms/ Exc. 1939. Int pits, crems, Q: Young et al., 1943/ Coles, F. R., 1911, 89–93; Thom, 1967, P1/10.

28b *Fowlis Wester W* (3) NN 922 249/ 7.3/ Adj, Q, O/ Exc. 1939. Pit, crem: Young et al./ Coles, F. R., 1911, 89–93; Thom, 1967, P1/10; Burl, 1976a, 196–7/ Astron: E = Maj N MR, W = Maj N MS, Thom, 1971, 53–6.

29 *Gallowhill* (4, 5) NO 168 360/ ?/ 4P?/ *South-East Perth: an Archaeological Landscape*, 1994, 33. 34, no. 152.

30 *Glenballoch Farm* (4) *c.* NO 182 482 / ?/? Exc. pre-1880, fv urn (Cowie, 132; (*Edinburgh Museum Catalogue*, 1892, 161, EA2): *PSAS 15*, 1880–1, 88–92/ Coles, F. R., 1909, 102–3; Burl, 1988a, 176–7, 178; *North-east Perth: an Archaeological Landscape*, 1990, 25 [Kynballoch].

31 *Glenkilrie* (3) NO 123 624/ *c.* 6.3 × 6.3 [8.8]/ 4P?, Pf/ *North-east Perth: an Archaeological Landscape*, 1990, 24.5.

32 *Glenshervie Burn* (4) NN 826 330/ *c.* 3 × 3 (4.2)/ 4P, int Cn?/ *PSAS 88*, 1954–6, 124; Burl, 1988a, 179.

33 *Greenland* (3) NN 767 427/ 8.3/ Gr/ Exc. 1924. Crem: *PSAS 59*, 1924–5, 77–8/ *PSAS 43*, 1908–9, 271–4; Coles, F. R., 1910, 132–6.

34 *Inverarnon* (3) NN 316 185/ 31.1, 21.6/ C, 2 × O or R?/ *PSAS 63*, 1928–9, 339–41.

35 *Killin* (1) NN 577 328/ 9.5 × 8.5 CE/ 6, Gr, cms/ Coles, F. R., 1910, 130–2, [Kinnell]; Thom, 1967, P1/3; TTB, 1980, 331–2; Stevenson, 1985, 150.

36 *Kinloch* (3) NO 117 475/ 3.5 × 3 (4.6)/ 4P/ *D & E*, 1975, 66; Burl, 1988a, 179.

37 *Kirriemuir* (4) NO 392 546/ ?/ ?/ *D & E*, 1981, 45.

38a *Lundin Farm NW* (4) NN 880 506/ 5.8 × 5.3? (7.9?)/ 4P?, int Ct?, cms/ Coles, F. R., 1908, 132; Stewart, 1966b, 127, 144–5; Burl, 1988a, 180–1.

38b *Lundin Farm SE* (1) NN 882 505/ 4 × 3.4 (5.3)/ 4P, Cn, Q/ Exc. 1962. Crems, AOC bkr (Clarke, 1970, II, 520, no. 1737.1), urn (Longworth, 312, no. 1986 [Aberfeldy]), coarse ware: Stewart, 1966b/ Coles, F. R., 1908, 133–5; Burl, 1988a, 182–3.

39 *Machuinn* (3) NN 882 401/ 6.7 × 5.8/ 6/ Coles, F. R., 1910, 126–30.

40 *Moncreiffe* (2) NO 132 193 [now NO 136 193]/ 9.1/ Multi-phase. (a) Henge 11.3 × 10, Ent. (b) St C 8.8, RC, Q, S? (c) Larger RC, Q, RSC?, 9, O?, cms (d) Destr. in Late Bronze Age/ Exc. *c.* 1830. Bones: *PSAS 6*, 1864–6, Appendix, p. 15. 1974. Bkr, flat-rimmed ware, cordoned urn, crem: *PSAS 115*, 1985, 125–50/ 1975. *PSAS 16*, 1881–2, 92–5; TTB, 1980, 350–1, P1/20; Cowan, 1988, 384, 391; Burl, 1995, 162–3.

41   *Moneydie* (4) NO 059 288/ *c.* 27.4/ ?/ Coles, F. R., 1911, 104–5.

42   *Monzie* (3) NN 882 243/ 4.9/ Int Ct, Q, cms, O + cms etc/ Exc. 1938. Flat-rimmed ware, crems: Mitchell & Young, 1939/ *PSAS 16*, 1881–2, 89; Coles, F. R., 1911, 82–4; *PPS 4*, 1938, 323; TTB, 1980, 340–1, P1/13.

43   *Muir of Gormach* (3) NO 117 475/ 3.8 × 3.5 [5]/ 4P/ *North-east Perth: an Archaeological Landscape*, 1990, 25.

44   *Murthly* (2?) NO 103 386/ 10.1/ Em, 6?/ Exc? 1863, 1870. Urns adj to St C: (*Edinburgh Museum Catalogue*, 1892, 184, EQ1–4): *PSAS 9*, 1870–2, 268–9/ Coles, F. R., 1908, 158–61.

45   *Na Carraigean Edintian* (1) NN 839 620/ 3 × 3 (4.2)/ 4P, Gr, RC?/ Coles, F. R., 1908, 105–9; *PSAS 49*, 1914–15, 19–20; Burl, 1988a, 186–7.

46   *Parkneuk* (3) NO 195 514/ 4.5 × 3.5 (5.9)/ 4P, Gr/ Coles, F. R., 1909, 95–7; *D & E*, 1982, 34; Burl, 1988a, 188–9.

47   *Pitsundry* (4) NO 056 345/ *c.* 12.2/ S/ Coles, F. R., 1908, 154–7 [Blelock].

48   *St Martins* (3) NO 160 312/ 7.5/ 4P?, Gr/ Stewart, 1966a, 21; Burl, 1988a, 191; Barnatt, 1989, II, 326.

49a   *Sandy Road E* (4) NO 131 265/ ?/ Adj/ Stewart, 1966a, 11.

49b   *Sandy Road W* (2) NO 132 265/ 7.5 × 6.2 CE/ Adj, Gr/ Exc. 1961. Flat-rimmed ware. C-14, 1200 ± 150 bc (GaK-787): Stewart, 1966a/ Coles, F. R., 1909, 126–30; Thom, 1967, P2/11 [Scone]; TTB, 1980, 360–1; Barnatt, 1989, II, 326–7.

50   *Shealwalls* (3) NO 239 514/ 1.5 × 1.5 [2.1]/ 4P/ *D & E*, 1986, 42.

51   *Shian* (5) NN 847 414/ *c.* 32 × 24/ ?, Q/ *PSAS 45*, 1910–11, 395; priv. comm. P. Crew, 14.2.79.

52a   *Shianbank NW* (3) NO 156 273/ 8.4/ Adj/ Stewart, 1966a, 21; Thom, 1967, P2/8/ TTB, 1980, 358–9; Barnatt, 1989, II, 327/ Astron: MdS SS, Thom, 1967, 100.

52b   *Shianbank SE* (3) NO 156 273/ 8.4/ Adj/ Stewart, 1966a, 21; Thom, 1967, P2/8; TTB, 1980, 358–9; Barnatt, 1989, II, 327.

53   *Spittal of Glenshee* (1) NO 117 475/ 3.5 × 3 (4.6)/ 4P/ Exc. 1894, no finds: *PSAS 29*, 1894–5, 96–9/ *PSAS 39*, 1904–5, 395–6; Thom, 1967, P2/14, [Glenshee]; Burl, 1988a, 190–1; *North-east Perth: an Archaeological Landscape*, 1990, 25 [Grave of Diarmid].

54   *Stockmuir* (4) NO 242 328/ ?/ ?, 9st/ *South-East Perth: an Archaeological Landscape*, 1994, 33. 152.

55   *Strone Hill* (3) NO 288 567/ 2.5 × 2.5 (3.5)/ 4P/ *D & E*, 1985, 60; Burl, 1988a, 107.

56   *Tegarmuchd* (3) NN 803 486/ *c.* 16?/ ?/ Coles, F. R., 1910, 149–53.

57   *Tigh na Ruaich* (3) NN 976 534/ 7.9 × 6.4 CE/ Exc. 1855. 4 urns: Stuart, 1856, xix/ Coles, F. R., 1908, 116–21; Thom, 1967, P2/2 [Ballinluig]; TTB, 1980, 352–3.

58   *Tirinie Farm* (5) NN 798 484/ *c.* 8.5 × 6.7 [10.8]/ 4P?/ Exc. 1974, no finds: *D & E*, 1974, 59; Burl, 1988a, 192.

59   *Tom-na-Chessaig* (5) NN 770 220/ ?/ ?/ Coles, F. R., 1910, 55.

60   *Tullybannocher* (4) NN 755 225/ 8.3? [11.7]/ 4P?, cms/ Coles, F. R., 1911, 50–1; Stewart, M. E. C., 1966a, 144–5; Thom, 1967, P1/8 [Comrie]; Burl, 1988a, 193.

61a   *Tullybeagles E* (3) NO 013 362/ 7?/ Adj/ Coles, F. R., 1911, 102–3; Thom, 1967, P1/14; TTB, 1980, 331–2; *D & E*, 1989, 64.

61b   *Tullybeagles W* (4) NO 012 362/ 9.8/ Adj, Gr/ Coles, F. R., 1911, 102–3.

62   *Tullymurdoch* (3) NO 194 514/ 13.7/ Pl?/ Coles, F. R., 1909, 97–9.

63   *Wester Torrie* (4) NN 646 045/ 6.7 × 5.5?/ 6?/ *PSAS 36*, 1901–2, 618–20; *D & E*, 1982, 6.

64   *Williamston* (3) NO 138 310/ ?/ ?/ *South-East Perth: an Archaeological Landscape*, 1994, 33. 152.

65   *Woodside* (3) NO 184 500/ *c.* 4 × 4 (5.7)/ 4P?/ Coles, F. R., 1909, 99–102; TTB, 1980, 356–7, P2/5 [Hill of Drimmie]; Burl, 1988a, 194–5; *North-east Perth: an Archaeological Landscape*, 1990, 26.

RENFREWSHIRE (STRATHCLYDE)

1   *Covenanter's Stone* (5) NS 477 532/ 7.6/ Pl/ *D & E*, 1963, 45.

ROSS & CROMARTY (HIGHLAND)

1   *Applecross* (4) NG 71. 44. / ?/ S holed/ Wilson, 1863, *Prehistoric Annals, I*, 142; *T. Hawick Arch Soc*, 1911, 57–9; A. MacBain, *Celtic Mythology and Religion*, 1917, 171–2; Grinsell, 1976, 205.

2   *Carn Urnan* (3) NH 566 523/ 22.3/ PgT/ *PSAS 16*, 1881–2, 477–9; Henshall, 1963, 343.

3   *Edderton* (3) NT 709 851/ ?/ Em, Ct, O/ Exc. 1866. F/v, crem: *PSAS 5*, 1862–4, 311–15/ E. MacKie, 1975, 212–13/ Astron: Oimelg and Samain (Feb and Nov) SS, D. Scott, *The Solar Stones of Edderton*.

4   *Lochalsh* (1) NG 831 174/ ?/ ?/ O. S. Edinburgh NG82 NW5; priv. comm., J. H. Fidler, 1.5.77; Barnatt, 1989, II, 480. Stone circle?

ROXBURGHSHIRE (BORDERS)

1   *Burgh Hill* (3) NT 470 062/ 16.3 × 13.4 CI/ Pl/ Exc. pre-1873. No finds: G. Watson, 1908, 25 [Brugh Hill]; *RCAHM-S*, 1956, II, no. 1011; Thom, 1967, G9/15 [Allan Water]; TTB, 1980, 308–9.

2 *Fairnington* (4) NT 667 285/ ?/ ?/ *RCAHM-S*, 1956, II, no. 911; Barnatt, 1989, II, 498. Kerbed barrow?

3a *Five Stanes A* (3) NT 752 168/ *c*. 15/ Adj, C?/ *NSA, Roxburgh*, III, 1845, 258–9; Watson, 1908, 21; *RCAHM-S*, 1956, I, no. 349; Thom, 1967, G8/7 [Dere Street III]; TTB, 1980, 332–3.

3b *Five Stanes B* (4) NT 75. 16. / ?/ Adj/ *NSA, Roxburgh, II*, 1845, 258–9.

4 *Frogden* (4) NT 772 298/ ?/ ?/ Destr. pre-1881 by gunpowder: G. Watson, 1908, 27 [Trysting Stones]; *RCAHM-S*, 1956, I, no. 549.

5 *Harestanes* (4) NT 640 243/ ?/ ?/ G. Watson, 1908, 26; *RCAHM-S*, 1956, I, no. 22.

6 *Ninestane Rigg* (1) NY 518 973/ 7× 6.5/ Pl/ G. Watson, 1908, 23–5; *RCAHM-S*, 1956, I, no. 113; Thom, 1967, G8/2; Grinsell, 1976, 239; TTB, 1980, 294–5.

7 *Stonedge* (3) *c*. NT 536 077/ 7.3 × 4.9/S, ct?/ G. Watson, 1908, 25.

8 *Tinnis Hill* (5) NY 430 838/ *c*. 40/ Pl?/ G. Watson, 1908, 23.

9 *Trestle Cairn* (3) NT 751 161/ *c*. 14.6/ Pl?/ G. Watson, 1908, 26–7; Thom, 1967, G8/6 [Dere Street II]; TTB, 1980, 303.

SELKIRK (STRATHCLYDE)

1a *Douglas Water NW* (4) *c*. NT 273 288/ *c*. 15/ Pl, cms?/ Exc. *c*. 1880. No finds: *History and Poetry of the Scottish Borders*, 1893, 2nd ed/ *PSAS 47*, 1912–13, 381–3.

1b *Douglas Water SE* (3) *c*. NT 274 287/ 13.4 × 6/ Int Ct?, cms?/ *PSAS 47*, 1912–13, 383–4.

SHETLANDS (SHETLAND)

1 *Fidlers Crus* (5) *c*. HU 620 927/ ?/ Cns? RCs?/ *RCAHM-S*, 1946c, no. 1226; Feachem, 86.

2 *Giant's Stones* (5) HU 243 805/ 18.2/ R?/ Thom, A. S. & Merritt, 1978, 54–6; Turner, V. *Ancient Shetland*, 1998, 47–8..

3a *Gletna E* (5) HU 592 021/ 33/ Pl?/ priv. comm. P. Grant, 1.12.77.

3b *Gletna W* (5) HU 591 021/ 20/ A?/ reference as for 2a.

4 *Hjaltadans* (5) HU 623 924/ 11.3/ Ent, ct?/ Grinsell, 1976, 183; Fojut, 56; Westwood, 505–7; Burl, 1995, 167–8; Laing, L., *Orkney & Shetland. An Archaeological Guide*, 1974, 249.

5 *Loch of Strum* (3) HU 405 501/ 5 × 4/ Pl/ Thom, A. S. & Merritt, 1978, 59–60; TTB, 1980, 368–9.

6 *Westings Hill* (3) HU 406 460/ ?/ Pl?/ Fojut, 26, 56.

Skye, Inner Hebrides, see HEBRIDES.

SUTHERLAND (HIGHLAND)

1 *Aberscross* (3) NH 771 990/ 7.3/ Ct/ Exc. 1867. Crem: *PSAS 7*, 1886–8, 473–5/ *RCAHM-S*, 1911b, no. 291; Thom, 1967, N2/2 [The Mound]; TTB, 1980, 326–7.

2 *Achany* (3) NC 560 029/ 26.8/ Pl/ *RCAHM-S*, 1911b, no. 461 [Druim Baile Fiur].

3 *Auchinduich* (3) NC 584 002/ 8.5/ C?/ *RCAHM-S*, 1911b, no. 91.

4 *Balnakeil* (3) NC 392 673/ 2.5 × 1.4 (2.9)/ 4P?, Pf/ *D & E*, 1972, 44; Burl, 1988a, 198–9.

5 *Clachtoll* (3) NC 037 278/ *c*. 12/ S/ *D & E*, 1971, 45.

6 *Cnoc an Liath Bhaid* (3) NC 728 102/ 9.1 × 7.1 CE/ C, Cn?/ Exc. Finds? *RCAHM-S*, 1911b, no. 518; Barnatt, 1989, II, 236.

7 *Dailharraild* (3) NC 678 390/ 6.7/ Cn/ *PSAS 7*, 1862–4, 358; *RCAHM-S*, 1911b, no. 247.

8a *Learable Hill NE* (4) NC 895 241/ 17.1/ Cms/ *RCAHM-S*, 1911b, no. 375.

8b *Learable SW* (3) NC 893 235/ 21.6 × 17 CE/ Int Cn/ *RCAHM-S*, 1911b, no. 374; Thom, 1967, N2/1; Thom A. & A. S., 1978, 25.

9 *Lindsidemore* (5) NH 545 992/ 16.8 × 15.9, 13.1 × 12.2/ C?, int Cn?/ *RCAHM-S*, 1911b, no. 92; Barnatt, 1989, II, 476.

10a *River Shin NW* (3) NC 582 049/ 4/ Adj, Pl/ *RCAHM-S*, 1911b, no. 462; Thom, 1967, N2/3; TTB, 1980, 326–7.

10b *River Shin SE* (4) NC 583 049/ 6.3/ Adj, Pl/ *RCAHM-S*, 1911b, no. 463; Thom, 1967, N2/3/ Astron: MdW SR? Thom A. & A. S., 1978, 28.

11a *Syre A* (5) *c*. NC 68. 43. / *c*. 9/ Adj, ent?, ct?/ *PSAS 5*, 1862–4, 359.

11b *Syre B* (5) *c*. 68. 43. / *c*. 9/ Adj, ent?/ *PSAS 5*, 1862–4, 359.

TIREE

1a *Hough E* (3) NL 959 451/ 39.6 × 32.9/ Adj, ct?/ E. Beveridge, Coll & Tiree, 1903, 130 [Moss A]; *RCAHM-Argyll, 3*, 1980, 68, no. 107; Ruggles, 1984, 123; Burl, 1995, 170–1.

1b *Hough W* (3) NL 958 451/ *c*. 40/ Adj/ E. Beveridge, *Coll & Tiree*, 1903, 130 [Moss B]; *RCAHM-Argyll, 3*, 1980, 68, no. 107; Ruggles, 1984, 123; Burl, 1995, 170–1.

WEST LOTHIAN (LOTHIAN)

1 *Cairnpapple* (4) NT 987 717/ 35.1 × 28 CI/ CH, Pt, V/ Exc. 1947–8. Neo sherds, bone pins, Gp VI, VII st axes, N/NR, N2/L bkrs (Clarke, 1970, II, 522, nos 1790–1793F): Piggott, 1948/ Ross, 1967, 63; Thom, 1967, P7/1; R. Mercer, *PSAS 111*, 1981, 155 (timber, not stone uprights?), 164; Burl, 1988c, 14; Barnatt, 1989, II, 329–31.

WIGTOWNSHIRE
(DUMFRIES & GALLOWAY)

1 *Balmannoch* (5) NX 0. 57. /?/ 6?/ Murray, 1981, 29.

2 *Eldrig Loch* (4) NX 326 497/ *c.* 4/ S?/ *RCAHM-S, 1912*, no. 230 [Carlin Stone]; Murray, 1981, 21; *D & E*, 1985, 11, diameter, 24 m?

3 *Glentirrow* (3) NX 145 625/ 2.7 × 2.4 (3.6)/ 4P, O/ *RCAHM-S*, 1912, no. 48; Murray, 1981, 24–7; Burl, 1988a, 200–1.

4 *Laggangarn* (5) NX 210 723/ 12.8 × 10.1?/ StC?, R?/ *PSAS 10*, 1872–4, 56–8; Murray, 1981, 221–3; TTB, 1990, I, 204.

5 *Longcastle* (5) NX 382 581/ 12?/ ?/ Murray, 1981, 23–4.

6 *Miltonish* (5) NX 192 740/ 0.9 × 0.6 (1.1)/ 4P?, RC, ct/ *PSAS 33*, 1898–9, 184; Murray, 1981, 27–8; Burl, 1988a, 201.

7 *Steeps Park* (4) NX 245 527/ ?/ ?/ *PSAS 33*, 1898–9, 170; Murray, 1981, 28.

8a *Torhousekie E* (1) NX 383 565/ 21.4 × 20 CA/ Variant RSC, RC/ *PSAS 31*, 1896–7, 90–4; *RCAHM-S*, 1912, no. 531; Thom, 1967, G3/7; Burl, 1974b; TTB, 1980, 274–5; Murray, 1981, 19–21.

8b *Torhousekie W* (4) NX 381 565/ 9?/ ?/ *PSAS 31*, 1896–7, 91; *RCAHM-S*, 1912, no. 532; Murray, 1981, 21–2.

Wren's Egg NX 361 420. *RCAHM-S*, 1912, no. 12. Omitted. A pair of stones and a glacial erratic. Masters, 1977; Murray, 1981, 218–19; Burl, 1993, 194, 195.

Wales

ANGLESEY (GWYNEDD)

1 *Bryn Celli Ddu* (4) SH 508 702/ 19.2 × 17.4/ Destr. in antiquity, S?, PgT/ Exc. 1865, 1927–8. StC, Q, crems: *Arch 80*, 1930, 179–214; Lynch, F., 1991, 93–101; Burl, 'Stone circles: the Welsh problem', *CBA Report 35*, 1985, 72–82, 80; Burl, 1995, 184–6/ Astron: MdS SR, Lockyer, 1909, 427; MW SS, Burl, 1995, 185.

2 *Bryngwyn Stones* (4) SH 462 669/ *c.* 12/ S?/ Camden, 1695, 676; H. Rowlands, *Mona Antiqua Restaurata*, 1766, 89, Pl. 4; Stukeley, 1776, II, Pl 91, 2nd; Burl, 1995, 186.

3a *Tre'r Dryw Bach E* (4) SH 468 668/ ?/ Adj, 4P?, S?/ H. Rowlands, *Mona Antiqua Restaurata*, 1766, 92, Pl. 4.

3b *Tre'r Dryw Bach W* (4) SH 468 668/ ?/ Adj, 4P?, S?/ *ibid*.

BRECKNOCKSHIRE (POWYS)

1 *Banc y Celyn* (3) SO 052 463/ 19 × 16/ Ent?/ *AW 33*, 1993, 45.

2 *Cerrig Duon* (1) SN 852 206/ 18.8 × 17.6 CI/ Pl. O, A/ Grimes, 1963, 138–9; Thom, 1967, W11/3 [Maen Mawr]; TTB, 1980, 392–3; Burl, 1993, 78 *AW 38*, 1998, 63.

3 *Craig y Fan Ddu* (5) SO 056 180/ ?/ R?/ *AW 15*, 1975, 25.

4 *Cwmdu* (3) SO 166 239/ 2.5 × 2.5 (3.5) 4P, adj Pair/ priv. comm., P. M. Jones, 12.12.76.

5 *Darren Esgob* (4) SO 242 315/ *c.* 15/ Pl?, ext 3-st R/ *AW 16*, 1976, 17.

6a *Nant Tarw ESE* (3) SN 819 258/ 20.7 × 19 CE/ Adj, O/ Grimes, 1963, 136–7; Thom, 1967, W11/4 [Usk River]; TTB, 1980, 394–5.

6b *Nant Tarw WNW* (3) SN 819 258/ *c.* 20.7 × 17.8/ Adj, ext R O?/ Grimes, 1963, 136–7; Thom, 1967, W11/4 [Usk River]; TTB, 1980, 394–5 *AW 38*, 1998, 63.

7 *Odyn-fach* (3) SO 090 122/ 15/ Pl/ *AW 15*, 1975, 26.

8 *Pen y Beacon* (4) SO 239 373/ 29.5/ Pl/ *AW 13*, 1973, 62; Briggs, 1986, 8.

9a *Trecastle Mountain ENE* (3) SN 833 311/ 23.2/ Adj/ Grimes, 1963, 135–6; Thom, 1967, W11/2 [Y Pigwyn]; TTB, 1980, 390–1.

9b *Trecastle Mountain WSW* (3) SN 833 311/ 7.3/ Adj/ Grimes, 1963, 135–6; Thom, 1967, W11/2; TTB, 1980, 390–1.

10 *Ynys-Hir* (3) SN 921 383/ 18/ Gr?/ Exc. 1940. No finds: Dunning, 1943/ Grimes, 1963, 134–5; Thom, 1967, W11/5; TTB, 1980, 396–7.

CAERNARVONSHIRE (GWYNEDD)

1a *Bwylch y Ddeuffan NE* (5) SH 715 717/ 6/ Adj, StC?, 2 × R/ *AW 16*, 1976, 20–1; Barber & Williams, 137.

1b *Bwylch y Ddeuffan SW* (5) SH 715 717/ 1 × 0.5/ Adj, 4P?/ *AW 16*, 1976, 21.

2 *Cefn Coch* (4) SH 548 427/ *c.* 21 × 19/ O?/ R. Farrington, *Snowdonia Druidica*, 1769; *Arch Camb*, 1868, 479; Grimes, 1963, 113–14; Burl, *CBA Report 35*, 1985, 80–1.

3 *Cefn Maen Amor* (3) SH 738 735/ 8.5/ Pl?/ *AW 26*, 1986, 27.

4 *Cerrig Pryfaid* (1) SH 724 713/ 21.3 × 19.8/ O/ *RCAHM-W*, 1956, no. 177; Grimes, 1963, 115; Barber & Williams, 138.

5 *Circle 275* (1) SH 725 747/ 3.1/ 5/ Exc. 1958. Q: Griffiths, 1960, 317–18/ Thom, 1967, W2/1b; TTB, 1980, 372–3; Burl, 1995, 177.

6 *Cors y Carneddau* (3) SH 718 746/ 16.5/ Pl?/ Grimes, 1963, 118.

7 *Cwm Mawr* (4) SH 553 414/ 20.1 × 16.5?/ ?/ *Arch Camb*, 1868, 479; Grimes, 1963, 113–14.

8 *Druids' Circle* (1) SH 723 746/ 25.7 × 24.5 CE/ Em, Pt, Q/ Exc. 1958. Enlarged f/v, f/v, 3 whetstones, bronze knife: Griffiths, 1960, 305–17, 322–7/ Camden, 1695, 673–4; Grimes, 1963, 116; Thom, 1967, W2/1 [Penmaenmawr]; TTB 1980, 380–1; Burl, 1995, 176–8/ Astron: Beltane SS, Burl, 1995, 177.

9 *Hafoty* (4) SH 747 752/ *c*. 12/ Pl. O/ *Arch Camb*, 1912, 55; Grimes, 1963, 118.

10 *Red Farm* (4) SH 732 750/ 30.5?/ *RCAHM-W*, 1956, no. 276; Grimes, 1963, 117.

11 *Tal y Braich* (4) SH 705 608/ *c*. 37/ Pl, Em?/ *AW 26*, 1986, 27.

CARDIGAN (DYFED)

1 *Bryn y Gorlan* (4) SN 749 547/ *c*. 18/ Pl?, O/ *Arch Camb 129*, 1980, 154–7.

2 *Hirnant* (5) SN 753 839/ 6.1 × 5.8/ Int Cn?/ Field visit, 5.4.71.

3 *Ysbyty Cynfyn* (6?) SN 752 791/ ?/ CH?, Em?, nineteenth-century folly?/ Grimes, 1963, 127–8; S. Briggs, *Arch Camb 128*, 1979, 138–46; Barber & Williams, 112 [Ysptty Cynfyn].

CARMARTHENSHIRE (DYFED)

1 *Bannau Sir Gaer* (4) SN 809 244/ *c*. 18/ Pl/ *AW 17*, 1977, 17.

2 *Cerrig Cynant* (3) SN 801 441/ 20+/ Pl/ Briggs, 1986, 8.

3 *Cefn Gwernffrwd* (3) SN 737 493/ *c*. 24/ S?/ *Arch Camb 124*, 1975, 111–13.

4 *Meini-gwyr* (4) SN 142 267/ Bank, 36, StC *c*. 18/ Em, Pt/ Exc. 1938. F/v: *PPS 4*, 1938, 324. 1985. Pits: *AW 25*, 1985, 19/ Aubrey, I, 122; Grimes, 1963, 141–3; *AW 27*, 1987, 11; Thorpe et al., 1991, 116, no. 14.

5 *Y Naw Carreg* (4) SN 561 099/ 18.3?/ Pl?/ Grimes, 1963, 139–41; Grinsell, 1976, 249.

DENBIGHSHIRE (CLWYD)

1 *Capel Hiraethog III* (5) SJ 032 545/ *c*. 18.3/ Int Cn/ E. Davies *Prehistoric & Roman Remains in Denbighshire*, 1929, 101–2.

2 *Cerrig y Drudion* (4) SJ 943 533/ ?/ Pl/ *Arch Camb*, 1855, 268; Barber & Williams, 102, no. 2.

3 *Cwm Rhiwiau* (3) SJ 059 305/ 11.5 × 10.5/ Pl, 2 × O/ *AW 26*, 1986, 26.

4 *Pen-y-Gaer* (5) *c*. SH 964 473/ ?/ Em. C?/ Aubrey, I, 119.

5 *Preseb y Fawch Frech* (5) SJ 023 509/ ?/ Pl?/ E. Davies *Prehistoric & Roman Remains in Denbighshire*, 1929, 91–2.

6 *Y Foel Frech* (5) SJ 012 539/ ?/ ?/ Barnatt, 1989, II, 392.

FLINTSHIRE (CLWYD)

1 *Penbedw Park* (6?) SJ 171 679/ 29.9/ O/ *RCAHM-W*, 1912, no. 47; E. Davies, 1949, 89–91; Grimes, 1963, 118–19; Thom, 1967, W4/1; TTB 1980, 374–5; Burl, 1995, 172.

GLAMORGAN (WEST GLAMORGAN)

1 *Mynydd y Gelli* (1) SS 975 942/ 9.1/ Ct/ *Arch Camb*, 1906, 282, 286–92; *AW 6*, 1966, 30.

MERIONETH (GWYNEDD)

1 *Bryn Cader Faner* (3) SH 648 353/ 6.7/ StC in Cn, Ct/ Bowen & Gresham, 86–8.

2 *Cerrig Arthur* (3) SH 631 188/ 15.9 × 12.8/ Em?, Pf/ *RCAHM-W*, 1921, no. 116; Bowen & Gresham, 38; Barber & Williams, 141.

3a *Ffridd Newydd N* (4) SH 616 213/ 32.9/ Adj, Em or CH/ Exc. 1919. FP Bkr (Clarke, 1970, II, 525, 1871F [Carneddau Hengwm]): Crawford, 1920/ *Arch Camb, 1*, 1920, 99–128; Grimes, 1963, 119–20.

3b *Ffridd Newydd S* (4) SH 616 213/ 50.6/ Adj, Em or CH/ Exc. 1919. FP bkr. (Clarke, 1970, II, 525, 1872F [Carneddau Hengwm]): Crawford, 1920/ Bowen & Gresham, 35–7.

4 *Llecheiddior* (4) SH 611 217/ 19.8 × 15.2/ Em?, cm/ Bowen & Gresham, 37–8; *AW 20*, 1980, 28.

5 *Llyn Eiddew Bach III* (3) SH 642 346/ *c*. 12.8/ Pl/ Burl, 1995, 179.

6 *Moel Goedog W* (5) SH 610 324/ 7.6/ Pl/ Exc. 1978. 10 pits, urn: *AW 18*, 1978, 37–9/ Bowen & Gresham, 88.

7 *Moel-ty-uchaf* (5) SJ 057 371/ 11.5 × 11.2 × 10.8 Compound/ Cn?, Ent?, Ct, O/ Bowen & Gresham, 80–2; Thom, 1967, 84–6; Barber & Williams, 103 [Cadair Bronwen]; Cowan, 1988, 384–5, 391; Burl, 1995, 179.

8 *Pabell Llywarch Hen* (4) SH 940 366/ ?/ Ent?, destr. pre-1746/ Bowen & Gresham, 283.

9 *Pen y Stryd* (3) SH 725 312/ 17.1/ Pl/ Bowen & Gresham, 39.

MONMOUTH (GWENT)

1 *Ctfn-Carnau* (5) ST 360 455/ ?/ St C?/*AW 38*, 1998, 99.

2 *Grey Hill* (4) ST 438 935/ 10/ Em? Ct?, O/ M. E. & W. Bagnall-Oakeley, *Account of Rude Stone Monuments in Monmouthshire*, 1889, 16–17; Thom, 1967, W13/1 [Grey Hill]; TTB, 1980, 398–9, cairn-circle; *3rd Stone 24*, 1996, 18–20. *AW 38*, 1998, 99.

3 *Trostrey* (4) SO 359 043/ *c.* 20/ St *AW 36*, 1996, 65; *AW 37*, 1997, 59–60; *AW 38*, 1998, 99, 100–1, 164–5.

MONTGOMERYSHIRE (MONMOUTH)

1 *Bryn yr Aran* (3, 5) SN 935 953/ 9?/ 4P?, O?/ priv. comm., A. Gibson, 27.3.98

2 *Cerrig Gaerau* (3) SH 904 005/ 21/ Pl/ *Arch Camb*, 1866, 540; Grimes, 1963, 122.

3 *Dyffryn Lane, Berriew* (4) SJ 204 014/ Bank 85, St C, 10–11 St, CH, int Cn/ Exc. *c.* 1857. No finds: *Arch Camb 3*, 1857, 296–9/ Harding & Lee, 1987, 339–40; A. Gibson, *Montgomery Collections 83*, 1995, 41–58.

4 *Kerry Hill* (1, 5) SO 158 860/ 26.5 × 25.1 × 24.8 Compound/ S/ Grimes, 1963, 123–4; Thom, 1967, 87–8, W6/1 [Kerry Pole]; Bird, 1977, 22.

5 *Lled-croen-yr-ych* (4) SH 903 005/ 24.7 × 22.9/ O/ Grimes, 1963, 122–3.

6 *Llyn-y-Tarw* (4) SO 025 976/ 20 × 19/ Pl?/ *Arch Camb 131*, 1982, 136–8; Barber & Williams, 163.

7a *Rhos y Beddau N* (5) SJ 057 302/ 11.4 × 10.5/ Pl?/ *AW 26*, 1986, 38.

7b *Rhos y Beddau S* (3) SJ 058 303/ 12.8/ A/ *Arch Camb*, 1868, 176; Grimes, 1963, 120–2; Thom, 1967, W6/2; Burl, 1993, 77–8 *AW 38*, 1998, 63.

8 *Whetstones* (4) SO 303 976/ *c.* 30/ Pl?/ Destr. *c.* 1870. Human bones: *TSANHS 4*, 1892, 272/ Hartshorne, 1841, 33–4; *RCAHM-W*, 1911, 23, no. 116; *Arch Camb*, 1926, 412; Grimes, 1963, 124–5; Barnatt, 1989, II, 473.

9 *Y Capel* (4) SH 999 000/ 26 × 23/ Pl?/ *AW 17*, 1977, 23; *Arch Camb 127*, 1978, 122–3.

PEMBROKESHIRE (DYFED)

1 *Beddarthur* (5) SN 130 324/ *c.* 22 × 8/ S?/ Barber & Williams, 122–3 [Meline].

2 *Dyffryn Synfynwy* (3) SN 059 284/ 22 × 18.9/ Cn/ *Arch Camb 11*, 1911, 296f; *RCAHM-W*, 1925, no. 313; Thorpe et al., 1991, 115.

3 *Gors Fawr* (1) SN 134 294/ 22.3/ Gr, O, ext Pair/ *RCAHM-W*, 1925, no. 731; Grimes, 1963, 145–6; Thom, 1967, W9/2; TTB 1980, 386–7; Thorpe et al., 1991, 116.

4 *Letterston III* (4) SM 937 294/ *c.* 12.2/ Em, Pt/ Exc. 1961. Urn: Savory, 1964/ Lynch, F., 1972, 75; Thorpe et al., 1991, 115.

5 *Pennybridge* (4) SM 953 001/ *c.* 9/ Pl/ Destr. 1918: *RCAHM-W*, 1925, no. 1065; Grimes, 1963, 146–7; Thorpe et al., 1991, 116.

6 *Rhos y Clegyrn* (5) SM 913 354/ 24.7 × 20.1 × 7.3/ Em, ext P/ *RCAHM-W*, 1925, no. 1065; Thom, 1967, W9/5 [St. Nicholas]; TTB, 1980, 384–5; Williams, G., 1988, 89–91; Burl, 1993, 268; John, T., *Sacred Stones*, 1994, 37–40. Probably kerbing of a barrow.

7 *Waun Maun* (4) SN 084 341/ 45.7?/ Pl?/ *RCAHM-W*, 1925, no. 768; Grimes, 1963, 149–50; Thorpe et al., 1991, 115.

RADNORSHIRE (POWYS)

1 *Banc Du* (5) SO 042 792/ 12.8?/ S/ Grimes, 1963, 128–30; Bird, 1977, 78.

2 *Cwm Saesan* (4) SN 964 776/ ?/ 4P?, R/ *RCAHM-W*, 1913, 142, no. 586; Burl, 1988a, 203.

3 *Four Stones* (1) SO 245 607/ *c.* 2.2 × 1.7 (2.9)/ 4P cms/ *Arch Camb 6*, 1911, 103; *RCAHM-W*, 1913, no. 615b; Thom, 1967, W8/3; TTB 1980, 384–5; Burl, 1988a, 202–3.

4 *Gelli Hill* (3) SO 095 583/ 21.3 × 19.5/ O?/ *RCAHM-W*, 1913, no. 41b; Grimes, 1963, 130–1.

5 *Rhos Maen* (4) SO 143 579/ 24.1/ ?/ Grimes, 1963, 131–2; Thom, 1967, W8/2.

6 *Six Stones* (3) SO 162 516/ 27 × 24/ *RCAHM-W*, 1913, no. 65; Grimes, 1963, 133–4; *AW 26*, 1986, 41.

7 *Temple, The, Llandridnod* (4) SO 058 612/ ?/ Destr/ Barber & Williams, 170.

Bibliography

ALCOCK, L. (1950). 'The henge monument of the Bull Ring, Dove Holes, Derbyshire', *PPS 16*, 81–6.

ALDRIDGE, MAJOR R. B. (1964–5). 'Some megalithic and other sites in Counties Mayo and Sligo', *JGAHS 31*, 11–15.

ALLCROFT, A. H. (1927). *The Circle and the Cross, I. The Circle*, London.

ALLEN, J. R. (1882). 'Notes on some undescribed stones with cup-markings in Scotland', *PSAS 16*, 1881–2, 79–143.

—— (1904). *Celtic Art in Pagan and Christian Times*, London.

ANDERSON, J. (1886). *Scotland in Pagan Times. The Bronze and Stone Ages*, Edinburgh.

ANDERSON, W. D. (1915). 'Some recent observations at the Keswick stone circle', *TCWAAS 15*, 98–112.

—— (1923). 'Plough-markings on stones', *TCWAAS 23*, 109–12.

ANDREW, W. D. (1907). 'The prehistoric stone circles', in Cox, Rev. J. C. (ed) *Memorials of Old Derbyshire*, London. 70–88.

ANGELL, I. O. (1976). 'Stone circles: megalithic mathematics or Neolithic nonsense?' *Math Gaz 60*, 188–93.

—— (1977). 'Are stone circles circles?', *Science & Archaeology 19*, 16–19.

APSIMON, A. M. (1969). 'The earlier Bronze Age in the north of Ireland', *UJA 32*, 28–72.

—— & GREENFIELD, E. (1972). 'The excavation of Bronze Age and Iron Age settlements at Trevisker Round, St. Eval, Cornwall', *PPS 38*, 302–81.

ARMIT, I. (1996). *The Archaeology of Skye and the Western Isles*, Edinburgh.

ASHBEE, P. (1960). *The Bronze Age Round Barrow in Britain*, London.

—— (1966). 'The Fussell's Lodge long barrow excavations, 1957', *Arch 100*, 1–100.

—— (1972). 'Field archaeology; its origins and development', in Fowler, P. (ed), 38–74.

—— & CORNWELL, I. W. (1961). 'An experiment in field archaeology', *Ant 35*, 129–34.

ASHMORE, P. (1995). *Calanais. The Standing Stones*, Stornoway.

—— (1996). *Neolithic and Bronze Age Scotland*, London.

—— (1999). 'Dating the ring of stones and chambered cairn at Calanais', *Ant 73*, 128–30.

ATKINSON, R.J.C. (1952). 'Four new "henge" monuments in Scotland and Northumberland', *PSAS 84*, 1949–50, 57–66.

—— (1961). 'Neolithic engineering', *Ant 35*, 292–9.

—— (1962). 'Fishermen and farmers', in Piggott, S. (ed), 1–38.

—— (1965). 'Waylands Smithy', *Ant 39*, 126–33.

—— (1966). 'Moonshine on Stonehenge', *Ant 40*, 212–16.

—— (1967) 'Further radiocarbon dates for Stonehenge', *Ant 61*, 63–4.

—— (1968). 'Old mortality: some aspects of burial and population in Neolithic Europe', in Coles, J. M. & Simpson, D.D.A. (eds), 83–93.

—— (1972). 'Burial and population in the British Bronze Age', in Lynch, F. & Burgess, C. (eds), 107–16.

—— (1974). 'Ancient astronomy: unwritten evidence', in Hodson, F. R. (ed), 123–31.

—— (1978) 'Some new measurements at Stonehenge', *Nature 275*, 50–2.

—— (1979). *Stonehenge*. Revised edition, Harmondsworth.

ATKINSON, R.J.C., PIGGOTT, S. & SANDARS, N. (1951). *Excavations at Dorchester, Oxon, 1*, Oxford.

ATKINSON, W. G. (1922). 'Report on the further excavations carried out at the "Druid's Circles" on Birkrigg', *TCWAAS 22*, 246–52.

AUBREY, J. (1670). *Wiltshire. The Topographical Collections of John Aubrey [1659–70]*, Jackson, J. E. (ed), Devizes, 1862.

—— (1680). *Brief Lives* [1679–80], Dick, O. L. (ed), London, 1949.

—— (1691). *The Natural History of Wiltshire* [1656–91], Britton, J. (ed), 1857. Reprint, Newton Abbot, 1969.

—— (1693). *Monumenta Britannica, Parts I and II. 1–600* [1665–93]. Fowles, J. (ed), Milborne Port, 1980.

MONUMENTA BRITANNICA *Part III. 601–1143* Fowles, J. (ed), Milborne Port, 1982.

—— (1696). *Miscellanies upon Various Subjects*, in *Three Prose Works. John Aubrey*, Buchanan-Brown, J. (ed), Fontwell, 1972, 5–125.

BAGNALL-OAKLEY, REV. W. & M. E. (1889). *An account of the Rude Stone Monuments and Ancient Burial Mounds in Monmouthshire*, Newport.

BAHN, P. see Hawkes, J.

BAILLIE, M.G.L. see Pearson, G. W.

BAITTY, E. C. (1973). 'Archaeoastronomy and ethnoastronomy so far', *Curr Anth 14*, 389–449.

BAKKER, J. A. (1999). 'Two drawings of Stonehenge from 1662 by Willem Schellinks', *In Discussion with the Past*, Sarfarij, H., Verwers, W.J.H. and Woltering, P. J., eds., Zwolle.

BALDWIN, J. R. (1985). *Exploring Scotland's Heritage. Lothian and the Borders*, Edinburgh.

BARBER, C. (1982). *Mysterious Wales*, London.

—— (1986). *More Mysterious Wales*, Newton Abbot.

BARBER, C. & WILLIAMS, J. G. (1989). *The Ancient Stones of Wales*, Abergavenny.

BARBER, J. (1972). 'The stone circles of Counties Cork & Kerry, I, II', unpublished M.A. thesis, University College, Cork.

—— (1973). 'The orientation of the recumbent-stone circles of the south-west of Ireland', *JKAHS 6*, 26–39.

BARBER, R. (1988) (ed). *The Worlds of John Aubrey. Being a Further Selection from his Writings on Antiquities, Science and Folklore*, London.

BARCLAY, A., GRAY, M. & LAMBRICK, G. (1995). *Excavations at the Devil's Quoits, Stanton Harcourt, Oxfordshire, 1972–3 and 1988*, Oxford.

BARCLAY, G. (1989). 'Henge monuments: reappraisal or reductionism?', *PPS 55*, 260–2.

—— (1992). 'Are the Clava "passage-graves" really passage-graves?', in Sharples & Sheridan, 77–82.

BARCLAY, G. & RUSSELL-WHITE, C. J. (1993) (eds). 'Excavations at the ceremonial complex of the 4th to 2nd millennium BC at Balfarg/Balbirnie, Glenrothes, Fife', *PSAS 123*, 32–210.

BARCLAY, G. J. & RUGGLES, C.L.N.. (1999) 'On the frontier? Recumbent stone circles in Kincardineshire and Angus', *Tayside and Fife Arch J 5*, 12–22.

BARING-GOULD, S. (1907). *A Book of Dartmoor*, 2nd ed., London.

BARNATT, J. (1978). *Stone Circles of the Peak*, London.

—— (1980). '*Lesser known stone circles in Cornwall*', *CA 19*, 17–29.

—— (1982). *Prehistoric Cornwall. The Ceremonial Monuments*, Wellingborough.

—— (1989). *Stone Circles of Britain, I, II*, Oxford.

—— (1990). *The Henges, Stone Circles and Ringcairns of the Peak District*, Sheffield.

—— (1998). 'Monuments in the landscape: thoughts from the Peak', in Gibson, A. & Simpson, D.D.A. (eds), 92–105.

—— & MOIR, G. (1984). 'Stone circles and megalithic mathematics', *PPS 50*, 197–216.

—— & PIERPOINT, S. (1983). 'Stone circles: observatories or ceremonial centres?', *SAR 2 (2)*, 101–16.

BARNES, REV. W. M. (1903), 'Poxwell circle', *PDNHAFC 21*, 150–7.

BARRETT, J. C. (1994). *Fragments from Antiquity. An Archaeology of Social Life in Britain. 2900–1200 BC*, Oxford.

BATEMAN, T. (1848). *Vestiges of the Antiquities of Derbyshire . . .*, London.

—— (1861). *Ten Years' Diggings in Celtic and Saxon Grave Hills in the Counties of Derby, Stafford and York from 1848 to 1858*, London.

BATT, M., GIOT P.-R., LECERF, Y., & LE ROUX, C. (1980). *Mégalithes au Pays de Carnac*, Châteaulin.

BAYNES, E. N. (1912). 'The megalithic remains of Anglesey', *Trans Soc Cymmrodorion*, 1911–12, 3–91.

BEALE, P. O. (1966). *The Anglo-Gambian Stone Circles Expedition, 1964/5. A Report*, Bathurst.

BEAU, LE B. (1894). *Catalogue du Musée à Carnac (Morbihan)*, Vannes.

BECKENSALL, S. (1983). *Northumberland's Prehistoric Rock Carvings. A Mystery Explained*, Rothbury.

—— (1986). *Rock Carvings of Northern Britain*, Princes Risborough.

—— (1992a). *Cumbrian Prehistoric Rock Art*, Hexham.

—— (1992b). *Prehistoric Rock Motifs of Northumberland, 2. Beanley to the Tyne*, Hexham.

—— (1999). British *Prehistoric Rock Art*. Brimscombe Port.

—— & LAURIE, T. (1998). *Prehistoric Rock Art of Co. Durham, Swaledale and Wensleydale*, Durham.

BENDER, B. (1986). *The Archaeology of Brittany, Normandy and the Channel Islands*, London.

BENNETT, P. (1995). *Circles, Standing Stones and Legendary Rocks of West Yorkshire*, Loughborough.

BENNETT, W. (1951). 'Report on excavations near Burnley', *TLCAS 62*, 204–8.

BERRIMAN, A. E. (1953). *Historical Metrology*, London.

BEVERIDGE, E. (1911). *North Uist. Archaeology & Topography*, Edinburgh.

BEWLEY, R. (1994). *English Heritage Book of Prehistoric Settlements*, London.

BIRD, A. J. (1977). *History on the Ground*, Cardiff.

BISHOP, A. see COLES, J. M.

BLIGHT, J. T. (1865). 'Barrows in Cornwall', *Gent's Mag. Archaeology, I, (1886)*, 90–4.

—— (1868). 'Stone circles and megalithic remains', *Gent's Mag. Archaeology, II (1886)*, 16–23.

BORD, J. & C. (1974). *Mysterious Britain*, St Albans.

—— (1987). *Ancient Mysteries of Britain*, London.

—— (1990). *Atlas of Magical Britain*, London.

BORLASE, W. (1769). *Antiquities, Historical and Monumental of the County of Cornwall* London.

BORLASE, W. C. (1872). *Naenia Cornubiae*, Truro.

—— (1897). *The Dolmens of Ireland. I–III*, London.

BOWEN, E. G. & GRESHAM, C. A. (1967). *History of Merioneth, I*, Dolgellau.

BRADLEY, R. (1978). *The Prehistoric Settlement of Britain*, London.

—— (1984). *The Social Foundations of Prehistoric Britain*, Harlow.

—— (1991). 'Rock art and the perception of landscape', *Cambridge Arch J I (1)*, 77–101.

—— (1993). *Altering the Earth*, Edinburgh.

—— (1996). 'Excavations at Clava', *Curr Arch 148*, 136–48.

—— (1997). *Rock Art and the Prehistory of Atlantic Europe. Signing the Land*, London.

—— (1998a). 'Stone circles and passage graves – a contested relationship', in Gibson, A. & Simpson, D.D.A. (eds), 2–13.

—— (1998b). *The Significance of Monuments. On the Shaping of Human Experience in Neolithic and Bronze Age Europe*, London.

—— & EDMONDS, M. (1993). *Interpreting the Axe Trade. Production and Exchange in Neolithic Britain*, Cambridge.

BRAILSFORD, J. W. (1938). 'The Bronze Age stone monuments of Dartmoor', *Ant 12*, 444–63.

BRETON, REV. H. H. (1931). *The Forest of Dartmoor, Pt 1*, Newton Abbot, 1990.

—— *ibid. Pt 2*, Newton Abbot, 1990.

BREWSTER, T.C.M. (1968). 'Kemp Howe, Yorkshire, E. R.', *Ann Exc. Rep*, 13.

BRIARD, J. (1987). *Mégalithes de Bretagne*, Rennes.

—— (1989). *Mégalithes de Haute Bretagne*, Paris.

—— (1990). *Dolmens et Menhirs*, Luçon.

—— & GIOT, P.-R. (1968). 'Le tumulus de Tossen-Keler en Penvenan (Côtes-du-Nord)', *L'Anthropologie 72*, 5–40.

BRIGGS, S. (1979). 'Ysbyty Cynfyn churchyard wall', *Arch Camb 128*, 138–46.

—— (1986). 'Druid's circles in Wales', *Landscape History 8*, 5–13.

BROWN, B. S. (1963). 'Neolithic engineering', *Ant 37*, 140–4.

BROWN, P. L. (1976). *Megaliths, Myths and Men. An Introduction to Astro-Archaeology*, London.

BROWNE, REV. G. F. (1921). *On Some Antiquities in the Neighbourhood of Dunecht House, Aberdeenshire*, Cambridge.

BRYCE, J. (1862). 'An account of excavations within the stone circles of Arran', *PSAS 4*, 499–524.

BRYCE, T. H. (1902). 'The cairns of Arran', *PSAS 36*, 1901–2, 73–173.

—— (1910). 'The sepulchral remains', in Balfour, J. A. (ed), *The Book of Arran. Archaeology*, Glasgow. 33–155.

BUCKLEY, V. M. (1986). *Archaeological Inventory of Co. Louth*, Dublin.

BU'LOCK, J. D. (1961). 'The Bronze Age in the north-west', *TLCAS 71*, 1–42.

BUNCH, B. & FELL, C. (1949). 'A stone axe factory at Pike of Stickle, Great Langdale, Westmorland', *PPS 15*, 1–20.

BURGESS, C. (1969). 'Chronology . . . in the British Bronze Age', *Ant J 49*, 22–9.

—— (1974). 'The Bronze Age', in ed. Renfrew, C. *British Prehistory. A New Outline*, London.

—— (1980). *The Age of Stonehenge*, London.

—— (1990). 'The chronology of cup- and cup-and-ring marks in Atlantic Europe', *Rev Archéol Ouest. Supplément no. 2*, 157–71. See also Lynch, F.

BURL, A. (1969a). 'Henges: internal features and regional groups', *Arch J 126*, 1–28.

—— (1969b). 'The great stone circle debate', *Curr Arch 12*, 27–8.

—— (1970). 'The stone circles of Britain and Ireland', unpublished M.A. thesis, University of Leicester.

—— (1971). 'Two "Scottish" stone circles in Northumberland', *Arch Ael 49*, 37–51.

—— (1972). 'Stone circles and ring-cairns', *SAF 4*, 31–47.

—— (1973). 'Dating the British stone circles', *Am Sci 61*, 167–74.

—— (1974a). 'The recumbent stone circles of north-east Scotland', *PSAS 102*, 56–81.

—— (1974b). 'Torhousekie stone circle, Wigtownshire', *TDGNHAS 49*, 24–34.

—— (1976a). *The Stone Circles of the British Isles*, New Haven & London.

—— (1976b). 'Intimations of numeracy in the Neolithic and Bronze Age societies of the British Isles', *Arch J 133*, 9–32.

—— (1979a). *Prehistoric Avebury*, New Haven & London.

—— (1979b). *Rings of Stone*, London.

—— (1980a). 'Science or symbolism: problems of archaeoastronomy', *Ant 54*, 191–200.

—— (1980b). see Thom, Thom & Burl.

—— (1981a). *Rites of the Gods*, London.

—— (1981b). 'Holes in the argument', *Archeoastronomy. The Bulletin of the Center for Archaeoastronomy, 4 (4)*, 19–25.

—— (1981c). 'The recumbent stone circles of Scotland', *Sci Am 245 (6)*, 50–6.

—— (1981d). 'By the light of the cinerary moon: chambered tombs and the astronomy of death', in Ruggles & Whittle (eds), 243–74.

—— (1982a). 'Pi in the sky', in Heggie, D. (ed), 141–69.

—— (1982b). 'John Aubrey's *Monumenta Britannica*. A review', *WAM 77*, 163–6.

—— (1983a). *Prehistoric Astronomy and Ritual*, Princes Risborough.

—— (1983b). 'An interim report on excavations and field studies on Machrie Moor and surroundings, Isle of Arran, 1978 and 1979', Scottish Development Department, Edinburgh.

—— (1984). 'Geoffrey of Monmouth and the Stonehenge bluestones', *WAM 79*, 178–83.

—— (1985a). *Megalithic Brittany: a Guide*, London.

—— (1985b). 'Stone circles: the Welsh problem', *CBA Report No. 35*, London.

—— (1987a). *The Stonehenge People*, London.

—— (1987b). 'The sun, the moon and megaliths', *UJA 50*, 7–21.

—— (1988a). *Four-Posters. Bronze Age Stone Circles of Western Europe*, Oxford.

—— (1988b). 'Without sharp north . . . Alexander Thom and the great stone circles of Cumbria', in Ruggles, C.L.N. (ed), 175–205.

—— (1988c). 'Coves: structural enigmas of the Neolithic', *WAM 82*, 1–18.

—— (1990). see Thom, Thom & Burl.

—— (1991a). 'The Devil's Arrows, Boroughbridge, North Yorkshire. The archaeology of a stone row', *YAJ 63*, 1–24.

—— (1991b). 'Megalithic myth or man the mover?', *Ant 65*, 297–8.

—— (1991c). 'The Heel Stone, Stonehenge: a study in misfortunes', *WAM 84*, 1–10.

—— (1991d). *Prehistoric Henges*, Princes Risborough.

—— (1992). 'Two early plans of Avebury', *WAM 85*, 163–72.

—— (1993). *From Carnac to Callanish*, New Haven & London.

—— (1994a). 'Long Meg & Her Daughters, Little Salkeld', *TCWAAS 94*, 1–11.

—— (1994b). 'Stonehenge: slaughter, sacrifice and sunshine', *WAM 87*, 85–95.

—— (1995). *A Guide to the Stone Circles of Britain, Ireland and Brittany*, New Haven & London.

—— (1996). 'Callanish meets the olde tea-shoppe', *British Archaeology*, September, 14.

—— (1997). 'The sarsen horseshoe at Stonehenge: a rider', *WAM 70*, 1–12.

—— (1998). 'Ever-increasing circles: exercises in duplicity', *3rd Stone 30*, 33–7.

—— (1999). *Great Stone Circles*, New Haven & London.

—— (2000). 'Myth – Conceptions', *3rd Stone 37*, 6–9.

BURL, A. & FREEMAN, P. (1977). 'Local units of measurement in prehistoric Britain', *Ant 51*, 152–4.

BURL, A. & JONES, N. (1972). 'The excavation of the Three Kings circle, Northumberland', *Arch Ael 50*, 1–14. See also Hatchwell & Burl; Milligan & Burl; Ruggles & Burl; Thom, Thom & Burl.

BURLEIGH, R., LONGWORTH, I. H., & WAINWRIGHT, G. J. (1972). 'Relative and absolute dating of four Late Neolithic enclosures', *PPS 38*, 389–407.

BURNARD, R. (1906). 'Stone circles', *VCH Devon, I*, 356–60.

BUSHELL, W. D. (1911). 'Among the Prescelly circles', *Arch Camb 11*, 287–333.

BUTLER, J. (1991a). *Dartmoor Atlas of Antiquities, I. East*, Exeter.

—— (1991b). *ibid, II. North*, Exeter.

—— (1993). *ibid, IV. South-east*, Exeter.

—— (1994). *ibid, III. South-west*, Exeter.

—— (1997). *ibid. V. The Second Millennium BC. And Index, I–V*, Exeter.

CALDER, C.S.T. (1950). 'Report on the excavation of a Neolithic temple at Stanydale in the parish of Sandsting, Shetland', *PSAS 84*, 185–205.

CAMDEN, W. (1610). *Britain*, trans. Holland, P., London.

—— (1697). *Britannia*, Gibson, E. (ed), London. See also Gough 1806.

CARPENTER, R. (1973). *Beyond the Pillars of Hercules*, London.

CARY, M. & WARMINGTON, E. H. (1963). *The Ancient Explorers*, London.

CASE, H. (1961). 'Irish Neolithic pottery: distribution and sequence', *PPS 27*, 174–233.

—— (1963). 'Foreign connections in the Irish Neolithic', *UJA 26*, 3–18.

—— (1967). 'Were beaker Folk the first metallurgists in Ireland?', *Palaeohistoria 12*, 141–77.

—— (1969). 'Settlement-patterns in the north Irish Neolithic', *UJA 32*, 3–27.

—— (1977). 'The beaker culture in Britain and Ireland', in Mercer, R. (ed), 1977, 71–101.

CASTLEDEN, R. (1992). *Neolithic Britain. New Stone Age Sites of England Scotland and Wales*, London.

—— (1993). *The Making of Stonehenge*, London.

CATHERALL, P. D. (1972). 'Henges in perspective', *Arch J 128*, 147–53.

CHADWICK, N. (1970). *The Celts*, London.

CHANTER, REV. J. F. & WORTH, R. H. (1905). 'The rude stone monuments of Exmoor and its borders, Pt 1', *TDA 37*, 375–97.

—— (1906). *'ibid*. Pt 2', *TDA 38*, 538–52.

CHART, D. A., EVANS, E. E. & LAWLOR, H. C. eds (1940). *A Preliminary Survey of the Ancient Monuments of Northern Ireland*, London.

CHATELLIER, P. DU. (1889). *Les Époques Préhistoriques et Gauloises dans le Finistère. Inventaire des Monuments de ce Département*, Quimper.

CHILDE, V. G. (1933). 'Trial excavations at the Old Keig stone circle, Aberdeenshire', *PSAS 67*, 37–53.

—— (1934). 'Final report on the excavation of the stone circle at Old Keig, Aberdeenshire', *PSAS 68*, 372–93.

—— (1935). *The Prehistory of Scotland*, London.

—— (1940). *The Prehistoric Communities of the British Isles*, London, 1940.

CHIPPINDALE, C. (1994). *Stonehenge Complete*, 2nd ed., London.

CHITTY, L. F. (1926). 'The Hoar Stone or Marsh Pool circle', *TSANHS 10*, 247–53.

—— (1963). 'The Clun-Clee Ridgeway', in Foster, I. L. & Alcock, L. (eds), 171–92.

CHRISTIE, P. M. (1967). 'A barrow-cemetery of the second millennium BC in Wiltshire', *PPS 33*, 336–66.

CHURCHER, I. (1985). 'A survey of stone circles in southern Leinster', unpublished BA dissertation, University of Durham.

CLARE, T. (1975). 'Some Cumbrian stone circles in perspective', *TCWAAS 75*, 1–16.

—— (1978). 'Recent work on the Shap "Avenue" ', *TCWAAS 78*, 5–15.

—— (1986). 'Towards a reappraisal of henge monuments', *PPS 52*, 281–316.

—— (1987). 'Towards a reappraisal of henge monuments: origins, evolution and hierarchies', *PPS 53*, 457–77.

CLARK, J.G.D. (1936). 'The timber monument at Arminghall and its affinities', *PPS 2 (1)*, 1–51.

CLARK, M. G. (n.d.). *Stone Circles of Buchan*, Peterhead.

CLARKE, D. L. (1970). *The Beaker Pottery of Great Britain & Ireland, I, II*, Cambridge.

CLARKE, D. V., COWIE, T. G. & FOXON, A. (1985). *Symbols of Power at the Time of Stonehenge*, Edinburgh.

CLEAL, R.M.J., WALKER, K. E. & MONTAGUE, R. (1995). *Stonehenge in its Landscape*, London.

CLES-REDEN, S. VON. (1961). *The Realm of the Great Goddess*, London.

CLOSE-BROOKS, J. (1986). *Exploring Scotland's Heritage. The Highlands*, Edinburgh.

CLOUGH, T. H. McK. (1968). 'The beaker period in Cumbria' *TCWAAS 68*, 1–21.

—— & CUMMINS, W. A. (1979). *Stone Axe Studies. Archaeological, Petrological, Experimental and Ethnographic*, London.

—— (1988). *Stone Axe Studies, 2. The Petrology of prehistoric stone implements in the British Isles*, London.

COLES, F. R. (1894). 'The "stone circle" at Holywood, Dumfriess', *PSAS 28*, 84–90.

—— (1895). 'The stone circles of the Stewartry of Kirkcudbright', *PSAS 29*, 301–16.

—— (1900). 'Stone circles in Kincardineshire (North) and part of Aberdeenshire', *PSAS 34*, 139–98.

—— (1901). 'Stone circles of the N.E. of Scotland, Inverurie district', *PSAS 35*, 187–248.

—— (1902). 'Stone circles of the N.E. of Scotland, Aberdeenshire', *PSAS 36*, 488–581.

—— (1903). 'Stone circles of the N.E. of Scotland, Auchterless and Forgue, *PSAS 37*, 82–142; 193–232.

—— (1904). 'Stone circles of the N.E. of Scotland, the Buchan district', *PSAS 38*, 256–305.

—— (1905a). 'Report of the excavation of two stone circles in Kincardine (1) in Garrol Wood, Durris, (2) in Glassel Wood, Banchory-Ternan', *PSAS 39*, 190–205.

—— (1905b). 'Stone circles in Aberdeenshire', *PSAS 39*, 206–18.

—— (1906). 'Stone circles, chiefly in Banffshire', *PSAS 40*, 164–206.

—— (1907). 'Stone circles, Banffshire and Moray, *PSAS 41*, 130–72.

—— (1908). 'Stone circles surveyed in Perthshire, N. E. Section', *PSAS 42*, 95–162.

—— (1909). 'Stone circles, S. E. district', *PSAS 43*, 93–130.

—— (1910). 'Stone circles, Aberfeldy district', *PSAS 44*, 117–68.

—— (1911). 'Stone circles, principally Strathearn', *PSAS 45*, 46–116.

COLES, J. M. (1965). 'Bronze Age metalwork in Dumfriess & Galloway', *TDGNHAS 42*, 61–98.

—— (1968). 'A Neolithic god-dolly from Somerset, England', *Ant 42*, 275–7.

—— (1971a). 'Scottish Early Bronze Age metalwork', *PSAS 101*, 1–110.

—— (1971b). 'Dowris and the Late Bronze Age of Ireland', *JRSAI 101*, 164–5.

—— (1973). *Archaeology by Experiment*, London.

—— (1979). *Experimental Archaeology*, London.

COLES, J. M., ORME, B. R., BISHOP, A. & WOOLLEY, A. R. (1974). 'A jade axe from the Somerset Levels', *Ant 48*, 216–20.

COLES, J. M. & SIMPSON, D.D.A. (1968) eds. *Studies in Ancient Europe*, Leicester.

COLLINS, A.E.P. (1956). 'A stone circle on Castle Mahon mountain, Co. Down', *UJA 19*, 1–10.

—— (1957). 'Excavations at the Giant's Ring, Ballynahatty', *UJA 20*, 44–50.

—— & WATERMAN, D. M. (1955). *Millin Bay: a Late Neolithic Cairn in Co. Down*, Belfast.

CONLON, J. P. (1916). 'Rude stone monuments of the northern portion of Cork County', *JRSAI 46*, 58–76, 136–62.

—— (1917). *JRSAI 47*, 153–64.

—— (1918a). *JRSAI 48*, 121–39.

—— (1918b). 'Cape Clear Island', *JCHAS 24*, 53–6.

COOKE, J. A., FEW, R. W., MORGAN, J. G. & RUGGLES, C.L.N. (1977). 'Indicated declinations at the Callanish megalithic sites', *JHA 8*, 113–33.

COONEY, G. & GROGAN, E. (1994). *Irish Prehistory: a Social Perspective*, Dublin.

CORBETT, D. M. see Pearson, G. W.

CORCORAN, J.X.W.P. (1969). 'The Cotswold-Severn group, I', in Powell, T., et al., 13–106, 273–95.

CORNWELL, I. W. see Ashbee, P.

COTTON, W. (1827). *Illustrations of Stone Circles, Cromlehs* [sic] *and Other Remains of the Aboriginal Britons in the West of Cornwall*, London.

COUTTS, H. (1970). *Ancient Monuments of Tayside*, Dundee.

COWAN, T. M. (1969). 'Megalithic rings: their design construction', *Sci 168*, 321–5.

—— (1988). 'Megalithic compound ring geometry', in, Ruggles, C.L.N. (ed), 378–91.

COWIE, T. G. (1978). *Bronze Age Food Vessel Urns*, Oxford.

COWLING, E. T. (1946). *Rombald's Way*, Otley.

COX, J. S. (1976). *Prehistoric Monuments of Guernsey and Associated Folklore*, St Peter Port.

CRAIG, J. (1956). 'The stone circles of the Ladieswell of Balronald and of Knocksoul', *Aberdeen Univ. Rev. 33*, 428–30.

CRAW, E. T. (1929). 'Appendix F', *PSAS 63*, 189.

—— (1930). 'Excavations at Dunadd and at other sites on the Poltalloch estates, Argyll. No. 2. Cist and stone circle, Temple Wood, Ri Cruin', *PSAS 64*, 130–1.

CRAWFORD, O.G.S. (1920). 'Account of the excavations at Hengwm, Merioneth, August and September, 1919', *Arch Camb*, 99–133.

CRONE, A. (1983). 'The Clochmabanestane, Gretna', *TDGNHAS 58*, 16–20.

CROSSING, W. (1912). *Guide to Dartmoor*, (1965 edition), Newton Abbot.

CUMMINS, W. A. (1974). 'The Neolithic stone axe trade in Britain', *Ant 48*, 201–5.

—— (1980). 'Stone axes as a guide to Neolithic communications and boundaries in England and Wales', *PPS 46*, 45–60. See also Clough, T. H. McK.

CUNNINGTON, M. E. (1929). *Woodhenge*, Devizes.

—— (1931). 'The "Sanctuary" on Overton Hill, near Avebury', *WAM 45*, 300–35.

CUPPAGE, J. (1986) ed. *Archaeological Survey of the Dingle Peninsula*, Ballyferriter.

CURTIS, M. R. & G. R. (1994a). *Callanish. Stones, Moon and Landscape*, Callanish.

—— (1994b). *Mini Guide to Druim Dubh Stone Circle*, Callanish. see also Ponting, M. R.

CURTIS, R. (1988). 'The geometry of some megalithic rings', in Ruggles, C.L.N. (ed) 1988a, 351–77.

DAICOVICIU, H. (1960). 'Le temple calendaire des Daces à Sarmizegetuza', *Dacia 4*, 231–54.

DALRYMPLE, C. E. (1884). 'Notes of the excavation at Crichie, Aberdeenshire', *PSAS 18*, 319–25.

DANIEL, G. E. (1950). *The Prehistoric Chamber Tombs of England & Wales*, Cambridge.

—— (1962). 'The megalith builders, in Piggott, S. (ed), 39–72.

—— (1966). 'Editorial', *Ant 40*, 169.

—— (1967). *The Origins and Growth of Archaeology*, London.

—— (1968). 'Editorial', *Ant 42*, 167–8.

DARVILL, T. (1987). *Prehistoric Britain*, London.

DAVIDSON, C. J. & SEABROOK, R.A.G. (1973). 'Stone rings on S. E. Dartmoor', *PDAS 31*, 22–44.

DAVIES, M. (1945). 'Types of megalithic monuments of the Irish Sea and North Channel coastlands: a study in distributions', *Ant J 25*, 125–46.

DAVIES, O. (1936). 'Excavations at Dun Ruadh, Co. Tyrone', *PBNHPS 1*, 50–75.

—— (1938). 'Excavations at Castledamph stone circle, Co. Tyrone', *JRSAI 68*, 106–12.

—— (1939a). 'Stone circles in Northern Ireland', *UJA 2 (1)*, 2–14.

—— (1939b). 'Excavation at Clogherny stone circles', *UJA 2 (1)*, 36–43. See also Paterson, T.G.F.

DAWKINS, W. B. (1900). 'On the excavation of prehistoric sepulchral remains of the Bronze Age at Bleasdale, by S. Jackson, Esq', *TLCAS 18*, 114–24.

DEANE, REV. J. B. (1934). 'Observations on dracontia', *Arch 25*, 188–229.

DEVOIR, A. (1911). 'Les grands ensembles mégalithiques de la presqu'île de Crozon et leur destination originelle', *Bull. de la Archéologique Finistère 38*, 3–38.

DICK, O. L. (1949). *Aubrey's "Brief Lives"*, London.

Dixon, J. A. & Fell, C. I. (1948). 'Some Bronze Age burial circles at Lacra near Kirksanton', *TCWAAS 48*, 1–22.

Dobson, D. P. (1931). *The Archaeology of Somerset*, London.

Donaldson-Blyth, I. (1995). *In Search of Prehistoric Skye*, Insch.

Duignan, M. V. see Killanin, Lord.

Duke, E. (1846). *The Druidical Temples of the County of Wiltshire*, Salisbury.

Dunkin, E.H.W. (1870). 'Remarks on the stone circles at Boscawen-Un and Boskednan in West Cornwall', *Reliquary Quarterly 10*, 1869–70, 97–102.

—— (1871). 'Some account of the megalithic remains in South Dorset', *Reliquary Quarterly 11*, 1870–1, 145–57.

Dunn, C. J. see Quinnell, N. V.

Dunning, G. C. (1943). 'A stone circle and cairn on Mynydd Epynt, Brecknockshire', *Arch Camb 97*, 169–94.

Dyer, J. (1981). *The Penguin Guide to Prehistoric England & Wales*, London.

Dymond, C. W. (1879). 'The Hurlers. Three stone circles near St. Cleer, Cornwall', *JBAA 35*, 297–307.

—— (1881). 'A group of Cumberland megaliths', *TCWAAS (O.S.), 5*, 39–57.

—— (1891). 'Mayburgh and King Arthur's Round Table', *TCWAAS (O.S.) 11*, 187–219.

—— (1896). *The Ancient Remains at Stanton Drew in the County of Somerset*, Bristol.

—— (1902). 'An exploration at the megalithic circle called Sunken Kirk at Swinside in the parish of Millom, Cumberland', *TCWAAS 2*, 53–63.

Dymond, D. P. (1966). 'Ritual monuments at Rudston, East Yorkshire, England', *PPS 32*, 86–95.

Eardley-Wilmot, H. (1983). *Ancient Exmoor*, Dulverton.

Edmonds, M. see Bradley, R.

Ekwall, E. (1959). *The Concise Oxford Dictionary of English Place-Names*, Oxford.

Elgee, F. (1930). *Early Man in North-East Yorkshire*, Gloucester.

Elgee, F. & H. W. (1933). *The Archaeology of Yorkshire*, London.

Ellice, E. (1860). 'Some pieces of charcoal dug up in a stone circle near Callernish in the Lewis', *PSAS 3*, 202–3.

Eochaidhe, O. see O'Riordan, 1965.

Eogan, G. (1964). 'The excavation of a stone alignment and circle at Cholwichtown, Lee Moor, Devonshire, England', *PPS 30*, 25–38.

—— (1986). *Knowth and the Passage-Tombs of Ireland*, London.

—— (1994). 'A Grooved Ware wooden structure at Knowth, Boyne Valley, Ireland', *Ant 68*, 322–9. See also Herity, M.

Evans, A. J. (1895). 'The Rollright Stones and their folklore', *Folklore 6*, 5–51.

Evans, E. D., Grinsell, L. V., Piggott, S. & Wallis, F. S. (1962). 'The fourth report of the sub-committee of the S. W. group of museums and art galleries on the petrological identification of stone axes', *PPS 28*, 209–66.

Evans, E. D., Smith, I. F. & Wallis, F. S. (1972). 'The petrological identification of stone implements from south-western England' *PPS 38*, 235–75.

Evans, E. E. (1953). *Lyles Hill, a Late Neolithic Site in Co. Antrim*, Belfast.

—— (1966). *Prehistoric and Early Christian Ireland*, London. See also Chart, D. A.

Evans, J. (1897). *The Ancient Stone Implements, Weapons and Ornaments of Great Britain and Ireland*, 2nd ed., London.

—— (1881). *The Ancient Bronze Implements, Weapons and Ornaments of Great Britain and Ireland*, London.

Evans, J. G. (1971). 'Habitat change on the calcareous soils of Britain: the impact of Neolithic man', in Simpson, D.D.A. (ed), 27–72.

—— (1972). *Land-Snails in Archaeology*, London.

—— (1975). *The Environment of Early Man in the British Isles*, London.

—— (1978). *An Introduction to Environmental Archaeology*, London.

Fahy, E. M. (1959). 'A recumbent stone circle at Drombeg, Co. Cork', *JCHAS 64*, 1–27.

—— (1960). 'A hut and cooking-places at Drombeg, Co. Cork', *JCHAS 65*, 1–17.

—— (1961). 'A stone circle, hut and dolmen at Bohonagh, Co. Cork', *JCHAS 66*, 93–104.

—— (1962). 'A recumbent stone circle at Reanascreena, Co. Cork', *JCHAS 67*, 59–69.

Feachem, R. (1965). *The North Britons: the Prehistory of a Border People*, London.

—— (1977). *Guide to Prehistoric Scotland*, 2nd ed., London.

Fell, C. I. (1950). 'The beaker period in Cumberland, Westmorland and Lancashire North of the Sands', in Fox, C. & Dickins, B. (eds), 43–50.

—— (1964a). 'Gamelands stone circle', *TCWAAS 64*, 408.

—— (1964b). 'The Cumbrian type of polished axe and its distribution in Britain', *PPS 30*, 39–55.

—— (1964c). 'Some cairns in High Furness', *TCWAAS 64*, 1–5.

—— (1967). 'Two enlarged food-vessels from How Hill, Thursby', *TCWAAS 67*, 17–25.

—— (1972). *Early Settlement in the Lake Counties*, Clapham. See also Bunch, B; Dixon, J. A.

Ferguson, R. S. (1895). 'On a tumulus at Old Parks, Kirkoswald', *TCWAAS (O.S.) 13*, 389–99.

—— (1906). 'Stone Circles', *VCH-Cumberland, I*, 245–9.

Fergusson, J. (1872). *Rude Stone Monuments of all Countries*, London.

Fleming, A. (1971a). 'Bronze Age agriculture on the marginal lands of NE Yorkshire', *Agricultural History Review 19 (1)*, 1–24.

—— (1971b). 'Territorial patterns in Bronze Age Wessex', *PPS 37*, 138–66.

—— (1972). 'Vision and design', *Man 7*, 57–73.

—— (1973a). 'Tombs for the living', *Man 8*, 177–93.

—— (1973b). 'Models for the development of the Wessex culture', in Renfrew, C. (ed), 571–85.

—— (1988). *The Dartmoor Reaves*, London.

Fletcher, W. (1958). 'Grey Croft stone circle, Seascale, Cumberland', *TCWAAS 57*, 1–8.

Fojut, N. (1981). *A Guide to Prehistoric Shetland*, Lerwick.

Foster, I. L. & Alcock, L. (1963). eds. *Culture and Environment. Essays in Honour of Sir Cyril Fox*, London.

Fowler, P. (1972). ed. *Archaeology and the Landscape*, London.

Fox, Lady A. (1948). 'A Broad Down (Farway) necropolis and the Wessex culture in Devon', *PDAES 4 (1)*, 1–9.

—— (1973). *South-West England*, Newton Abbot.

Fox, Sir C. (1938). *The Personality of Britain*, 3rd ed., Cardiff.

—— (1959). *Life and Death in the Bronze Age*, London.

Fox, Sir C. & Dickens, B. (1950). eds. *The Early Cultures of North-West Europe*, Cambridge.

Frazer, Sir J. G. (1912). *Spirits of the Corn and Wild, I, II*, London.

—— (1913a). *The Scapegoat*, London.

—— (1913b). *Balder the Beautiful, I, II*, London.

—— (1922). *The Golden Bough*, abridged version, London.

Freeman, P. R. (1976). 'A Bayesian analysis of the Megalithic Yard', *JRSS 139, Pt 1*, 20–35.

—— (1977). 'Thom's survey of the Avebury ring', *JHA 8*, 134–6. See also Burl, 1977.

Frodsham, P. (1996). 'Spirals in time: Morwick Mill and the spiral motif in the British Neolithic', *Northern Archaeology 13/14*, 101–38.

Gaffikin, W. see Paterson, T.G.F.

Gaillard, F. (1892). *Inventaire des Monuments Mégalithiques du Morbihan*, Paris.

Gelderd, C. (1912). 'Report on the excavations carried out at the "Druid's Circle" on Birkrigg, in the parish of Urswick, September, 1911', *TCWAAS 12*, 262–74.

Gelling, P. & Davidson, H. E. (1969). *Chariot of the Sun*, London.

Gerrard, S. (1997). *English Heritage Book of Dartmoor. Landscapes Through Time*, London.

Gibbon, G. (1989). *Explanation in Archaeology*, Cambridge.

Gibbons, M. & Higgins, J. (1988). Connemara's emerging pre-history', *Arch Ire 2*, 636.

Gibson, A. M. (1994). 'Excavations at the Sarn-y-bryn-caled cursus complex, Welshpool, Powys, and the timber circles of Great Britain & Ireland' *PPS 60*, 143–223.

—— (1998). *Stonehenge and Timber Circles*, Stroud.

Gibson, A. M. & Simpson, D.D.A. eds (1998). *Prehistoric Ritual & Religion. Essays in Honour of Aubrey Burl*, London.

Gibson, A. M. & Woods, A. (1990). *Prehistoric Pottery for the Archaeologist*, Leicester.

Gilbert, M. (1962). *Pierres Mégalithiques dans le Maine et Cromlechs en France*, Guernsey.

Giot, P.-R. (1960). *Brittany*, London.

—— (1983). *Les Alignements de Carnac*, Rennes.

—— (1988a). 'Stones in the landscape of Brittany', in Ruggles, C.L.N. (ed), 319–24.

—— (1988b). *Préhistoire en Bretagne*, Châteaulin.

Giot, P.-R., l'Helgouac'h, J., & Monnier, J. P. (1979). *Préhistoire de la Bretagne*, Rennes. See also Batt, M.; Briard, J.

Glentworth, R. & Muir, J. W. (1963). *The Soils of the Country around Aberdeen, Inverurie and Fraserburgh*, Edinburgh.

Glob, P. V. (1974). *The Mound People*, London.

Gogan, L. S. (1931). 'A small stone circle at Muisire Beag', *JCHAS 36*, 9–19.

Gosling, P. (1991). ed. *Archaeological Inventory of Co. Galway, I. West Galway*, Dublin.

Gouezin, P. (1998). *Le Site Mégalithique d'er Lannic*, Vannes?

Gough, R. (1806). *William Camden's 'Britannia', I–IV*, 2nd ed. London.

Gray, H. St G. (1903). 'On the excavations at Arbor Low, 1901–2', *Arch 58*, 461–98.

—— (1907). 'The stone circle at Withypool Hill, Exmoor', *PSANHS 52*, 42–50.

—— (1908). 'On the stone circles of East Cornwall', *Arch 61*, 1–60.

—— (1929). 'The Porlock stone circle, Exmoor', *PSANHS 77*, 71–7.

—— (1931). 'Rude stone monuments of Exmoor, III', *PSANHS 77*, 78–82.

—— (1935). 'The Avebury excavations, 1908–22', *Arch 84*, 99–162.

—— (1950). 'Porlock stone circle. A note', *Arch J 107*, 87.

Gray, M. (1975). 'The Devil's Quoits, Stanton Harcourt, Oxon'. *Oxon 39*, 96–7. See also Barclay, A.

Green, C. P. (1973). 'Pleistocene river-gravels and the Stonehenge problem', *Nature 243*, 214.

Green, M. (1991). *The Sun-Gods of Ancient Europe*, London.

—— (1992). *Dictionary of Celtic Myth and Legend*, London.

Greenfield, E. see ApSimon, A.

Gresham, C. A. see Bowen, E. G.

Griffiths, W. E. (1960). 'The excavation of stone circles near Penmaenmawr, North Wales', *PPS 26*, 303–39.

Grimes, W. F. (1938). 'Excavations at Meini-gwyr, Carmarthen', *PPS 4*, 324–5.

—— (1944). 'Excavations at Stanton Harcourt, 1940', *Oxon 8–9*, 19–63.

—— (1960). 'A "henge" monument and burial rings at Stanton Harcourt, Oxfordshire', *Excavations on Defence Sites, 1939–45, I. Mainly Neolithic and Bronze Age*, London, 140–69.

—— (1963). 'The stone circles and related monuments of Wales' in Foster, I, Ll. & Alcock, A. (eds), 93–152.

Grinsell, L. V. (1936). *The Ancient Burial-Mounds of England*, London.

—— (1957). 'Archaeological gazetteer', in Pugh, R. B. & Crittall, E. (eds) *A History of Wiltshire 1 (1)*, 21–279.

—— (1958). *The Archaeology of Wessex*, London.

—— (1959). *Dorset Barrows*, Dorchester.

—— (1970). *The Archaeology of Exmoor*, Newton Abbot.

—— (1971). 'Somerset barrows, II. North and East', *PSANHS 115*, 44–137.

—— (1973). *The Folklore of Stanton Drew*, St Peter Port.

—— (1975). *Legendary History and Folklore of Stonehenge*, St Peter Port.

—— (1976). *Folklore of Prehistoric Sites in Britain*, Newton Abbot.

—— (1977). *The Rollright Stones and their Folklore*, St Peter Port.

—— (1978a). 'Dartmoor barrows', *PDAS 36*, 85–180.

—— (1978b). *The Druids and Stonehenge. The Story of a Myth*, St Peter Port.

—— (1978c). *The Stonehenge Barrow Groups*, Salisbury.

—— (1981). *Mitchell's Fold Stone Circle and its Folklore*, St Peter Port.

—— (1994). *The Megalithic Monuments of Stanton Drew*, Bristol. See also Evans, E. D., 1962.

GROENMAN-VAN WAATERINGE & BUTLER, J. J. (1976). 'The Ballynoe stone circle. Excavations by A. E. van Giffen, 1937–8', *Palaeohistoria 18*, 105–10.

GROGAN, E. see Cooney, G.

GROGAN, E. & KILFEATHER, A. (1997). *Archaeological Inventory of Co. Wicklow*, Dublin.

GROSSMAN, N. (1970). 'Megalithic rings', *Sci 169*, 1228–9.

GUNN, G. (1915). 'The standing stones of Caithness', *Trans Inverness Sci Soc 7*, 337–60.

GUTTRIDGE, R., *Dorset Murders*, Wimborne, 1986. (Maumbury Rings, 9–24).

HADINGHAM, E. (1974). *Ancient Carvings in Britain. A Mystery*, London.

—— (1975). *Circles and Standing Stones*, London.

—— (1983). *Early Man and the Cosmos*, London.

HAGGARTY, A. (1991). 'Machrie Moor, Arran: recent excavations at two stone circles', *PSAS 121*, 51–94.

HAMOND, F. W. (1979). 'Settlement, economy and environment on prehistoric Dartmoor', in Maxwell, V. A. (ed), 146–75.

HARBISON, P. (1970). *Guide to the National Monuments in the Republic of Ireland*, Dublin.

—— (1988). *Pre-Christian Ireland*, London.

—— (1992). *Guide to National and Historic Monuments of Ireland*, Dublin. See also Killanin, Lord.

HARDING, A. (1981). 'Excavations in the prehistoric ritual complex near Milford, Northumberland', *PPS 47*, 87–135.

HARDING, A. with LEE, G. (1987). *Henge Monuments and Related Sites of Great Britain*, Oxford.

HARRISON, R. J. (1980). *The Beaker Folk. Copper Age Archaeology in Western Europe*, London.

HARRISON, W. J. (1901). 'A bibliography of the great stone monuments of Wiltshire – Stonehenge and Avebury', *WAM 32*, 1–169.

HARTSHORNE, REV. A. C. (1841). *Salopia Antiqua*, London.

HARTWELL, B. (1998). 'The Ballynahatty complex', in Gibson, A. & Simpson, D.D.A. (eds), 32–44.

HARVEY, J. H. (1948). 'A note on Long Meg, Salkeld', *Arch J 105*, addendum.

HATCHWELL, R. & BURL, A. (1998). 'The Commonplace Book of William Stukeley', *WAM 91*, 65–75.

HAWKES, J. (1937). *The Archaeology of the Channel Islands, II. The Bailiwick of Jersey*, Jersey.

HAWKES, J. with BAHN, P. (1986). *The Shell Guide to British Archaeology*, London.

HAWKINS, G. S. (1965). 'Callanish: a Scottish Stonehenge', *Sci 147*, 127–30.

—— (1966). *Astro-Archaeology*, Cambridge, Massachusetts.

—— (1977). *Beyond Stonehenge*, London.

HAWKINS, G. S. with WHITE, J. B. (1966). *Stonehenge Decoded*, London. See also Petrie, W. M. F.

HAWLEY, W. (1921). 'Stonehenge: interim report on the exploration', *Ant J 1*, 17–41.

—— (1922). 'Second report on the excavations at Stonehenge. *Ant J 2*, 36–52.

—— (1923). 'Third report on the excavations at Stonehenge', *Ant J 3*, 13–20.

—— (1924). 'Fourth report on the excavations at Stonehenge', *Ant J 4*, 30–9.

—— (1925). 'Report on the excavations at Stonehenge during the season of 1923', *Ant J 5*, 21–50.

—— (1926). 'Report on the excavations at Stonehenge during the season of 1926', *Ant J 6*, 1–25.

—— (1928). 'Report on the excavations at Stonehenge during 1925 and 1926', *Ant J 8*, 149–76.

HAYMAN, R. (1997). *Riddles in Stone. Myths, Archaeology and the Ancient Britons*, London.

HEGGIE, D. C. (1981). *Megalithic Science. Ancient Mathematics and Astronomy in Northwest Europe*, London.

—— (1982) ed. *Archaeoastronomy in the Old World*, Cambridge.

L'HELGOUAC'H, J. (1966). *Les Sépultures Mégalithiques en Armorique*, Rennes. See also Giot, P.-R.

L'HELGOUAC'H, J., LE ROUX, C. & LECORNEC, J eds (1997). *Arte et Symboles du Mégalithisme Européen*, Rennes.

HENCKEN, O'N. (1932). *The Archaeology of Cornwall and Scilly*, London.

HENSHALL, A. S. (1963). *The Chambered Tombs of Scotland, I*, Edinburgh.

—— (1972). *ibid, II*, Edinburgh.

HENSHALL, A. S. & STEWART, M.E.C. (1956). 'Excavations at Clach na Tiompan, West Glen Almond, Perthshire', *PSAS 88*, 112–24.

HERITY, M. (1970). 'The prehistoric people of Kerry', JKHAS 3, 5–14.

—— (1974). *Irish Passage-Graves*, Dublin.

HERITY, M. & EOGAN, G. (1977). *Ireland in Prehistory*, London.

HIBBS, J. (1984). 'The Neolithic of Brittany and Normandy', in Scarre, C. (ed), 271–323.

—— (1985). *Little Master Stonehenge*, St Helier.

HICKS, R. E. (1975). 'Some henges and hengiform earthworks in Ireland', unpublished PhD dissertation.

HICKS, R. E. (1977). 'Thom's Megalithic Yard and traditional measurements', *IARF 4 (1)*, 1–7.

HICKS, S. P. (1972). 'The impact of man on the East Moor of Derbyshire from Mesolithic times', *Arch J 129*, 1–21.

HOARE, SIR R. C. (1812). *The Ancient History of South Wiltshire*, London.

—— (1819). *The Ancient History of North Wiltshire*, London.

HODDER, I. (1990). *The Domestication of Europe*, London.

HODGSON, K. S. (1952). 'Further excavations at Broomrigg near Ainstable', *TCWAAS 52*, 1–8.

HODSON, F. R. (1974). *The place of Astronomy in the Ancient World*, London.

HOLLIER, J. (1989). *Nothing But Circles*, Crewkerne.

HOULDER, C. (1974). *Wales. An Archaeological Guide*, London.

HOULDER, C. & MANNING, W. H. (1966). *South Wales*, London.

HOWARTH, E. (1899). *Catalogue of the Bateman Collection of Antiquities in the Sheffield Museum*, London.

HUNTER, M. (1975). *John Aubrey and the Realm of Learning*, London.

HUTCHINSON, G. E. (1972). 'Long Meg Reconsidered, I, II', *Am Sci 60*, 24–31, 210–19.

HUTCHINSON, W. (1794). *The History & Antiquities of Cumberland, I, II*, Carlisle.

HUTTON, R. (1991). *The Pagan Religions of the Ancient British Isles*, London.

—— (1996). *The Stations of the Sun*, Oxford.

Hyslop, J. & R. (1912). *Langholm As It Was*, Langholm.

Innes, C. (1860). 'Notice of the stone circle called Callernish in the Lewis, and of a chamber tomb under the circle. Recently excavated', *PSAS 3*, 110–12.

Jackson, J. S. (1968). 'Bronze Age copper mines on Mount Gabriel, West County Cork, *Archaeologia Austriaca 43*, 92–114.

Jervise, A. (1882). *The History and Traditions of the Land of the Lindsays*, Edinburgh.

Jewitt, L. (1869). 'Stone circles', *Student 3*, 344–51.

—— (1870). *Grave Mounds and their Contents*, London.

Jobey, G. (1968). 'Excavation of cairns at Chatton Sandyford, Northumberland', *Arch Ael 46*, 5–50.

Johnson, N. & Rose, P. (1994). *Bodmin Moor. An Archaeological Survey, I. The Human Landscape to c.1800*, London.

Johnston, D. E. (1981). *The Channel Islands. An Archaeological Guide*, Chichester.

Jones, I. (1655). *The Most Noble Antiquity of Great Britain, Vulgarly Called Stone-Heng on Salisbury Plain*, London.

Jones, S. J. (1938). 'The excavation of Gorsey Bigbury', *PUBSS 5*, 3–56.

Jope, E. M. (1966) ed. *An Archaeological Survey of Co. Down*, Belfast.

Kains-Jackson, C. P. (1880). *Our Ancient Monuments and the Land Around Them*, London.

Kavanagh, R. M. (1973). 'The encrusted urn in Ireland', *PRIA 73C*, 507–617.

Keillar, I. (1972). 'Edinkillie stone circle, Moray', *D & E*, 30.

Keiller, A. (1934). *Megalithic Monuments of North-East Scotland*, London.

Keiller, A. & Piggott, S. (1936). 'The West Kennet avenue; excavations, 1934–5', *Ant 10*, 417–27.

Kellaway, G. A. (1971). 'Glaciation and the stones of Stonehenge', *Nature 233*, 30–5.

Kendrick, T. D. (1925). *The Axe Age. A Study in British Prehistory*, London.

—— (1927). *The Druids. A Study in Keltic Prehistory*, London.

—— (1928). *The Archaeology of the Channel Isles, I. The Bailiwick of Guernsey*, London.

Kenworthy, J. (1972). 'Ring-cairns in NE Scotland', *SAF 4*, 18–30.

Kermode, P.M.C. & Herdman, W. A. (1914). *Manks Antiquities*, Liverpool.

Kilbride-Jones, H. E. (1934). 'Stone circles: a new theory of the erection of the monoliths', *PSAS 68*, 81–99.

—— (1935). 'An account of the excavation of the stone circle at Loanhead of Daviot, and of the Standing Stones of Echt, Aberdeenshire', *PSAS 69*, 168–222.

—— (1950). 'The excavation of a composite Iron Age monument with "henge" features at Lugg, Co. Dublin', *PRIA 53C*, 311–32.

Killanin, Lord, & Duignan, M. V. (1969). *Shell Guide to Ireland*, 2nd ed., London.

—— (1989). *Shell Guide to Ireland*, revised and updated by P. Harbison, Dublin.

Kinnes, I. & Grant, J. A. (1983). *Les Fouillages and the Megalithic Monuments of Guernsey*, Alderney.

Kinnes & Hibbs, J. (1988). *The Dolmens of Jersey*, Jersey.

Kinnes, I. & Longworth, J. M. (1985). *Catalogue of the Excavated Prehistoric and Romano-British Material in the Greenwell Collection*, London.

Kirk, W. (1953). 'Prehistoric sites at the Sands of Forvie, Aberdeenshire', *Aberdeen University Review 33*, 150–71.

Kitchen, F. T. (1983). 'The Carrowmore megalithic cemetery, Co. Sligo', *PPS 49*, 151–75.

Knight, P. (1996). *Ancient Stones of Dorset*, Ferndown.

Lacy, B. (1983). *Archaeological Survey of Co. Donegal*, Lifford.

Laet, S. J. de, (1958). *The Low Countries*, London.

Lambrick, G. (1983). *The Rollright Stones. The Archaeology and Folklore of the Stones and their Surroundings. A Survey and Review*, Oxford.

—— (1988). *The Rollright Stones. Megaliths, Monuments and Settlement in the Prehistoric Landscape*, London. See also Barclay, A.

Lanting, J. N. & van der Waals, J. D. (1972). 'British beakers as seen from the continent', *Helinium 12*, 20–46.

Laurie, T. see Beckensall, S.

Lawlor, C. see Chart, D. A.

Leask, H. G. (1945). 'Stone circles, Castleruddery, Co. Wicklow', *JRSAI 75*, 266–7.

Lecerf, Y. see Batt, M.

Leeds, R. T. (1939). 'Early man, II. Mesolithic-Neolithic Age', *VCH Oxon, I*, 238–41.

Lees, D. (1999). 'The Sanctuary, Avebury. An architectural re-assessment', *WAM 92*, 1–6.

Leger-Gordon, R. (1994). *The Witchcraft and Folklore of Dartmoor*, Newton Abbot.

Legg, R. (1986). *Stonehenge Antiquaries*, Milborne Port.

Leland, J. (1535–43). *The Itinerary of John Leland, the Antiquary, Pts. I to III*, Smith, L. T. (ed), 5 vols, Carbondale, Southern Illinois, 1964.

Lewis, A. L. (1871). 'Megalithic monuments', *JRAI 1*, 286–96.

—— (1874). 'Arthurian theory', *Anth 1*, 282–99.

—— (1877). 'Stone monuments in Wales', *JRAI 7*, 118–23.

—— (1882a). 'Notice of two stone circles in Shropshire', *JRAI 11*, 3–7.

—— (1882b). 'Remarks on some archaic structures in Somersetshire and Dorsetshire', *JRAI 11*, 117–21.

—— (1883). 'On the relationship of stone circles to outlying stones or tumuli or neighbouring hills, with some inferences therefrom', *JRAI 12*, 176–91.

—— (1886). 'Three stone circles in Cumberland', *JRAI 15*, 471–81.

—— (1888). 'Stone circles near Aberdeen', *JRAI 17*, 44–57.

—— (1891). 'On the Wiltshire circles', *JRAI 20*, 277–88.

—— (1892a). 'Stone circles of Britain', *Arch J 49*, 136–54.

—— (1892b). 'Notes on the relative positions of certain hills and stone circles in England and Wales', *PSAL 14*, 150–4.

—— (1895). 'British stone circles', *Sci 21*, 161; *Sci 22*, 17.

—— (1896). 'Prehistoric remains in Cornwall, Pt. 1. East Cornwall', *JRAI 25*, 2–16.

—— (1898). 'Rude stone monuments on Bodmin Moor', *JRIC 13*, 107–13.

—— (1899a). 'The stone circles of Cornwall and Scotland', *JRIC 14*, 378–83.

—— (1899b). 'Circles of Stanton Drew', *British Assoc. Report*, 1014.

—— (1900). 'Stone circles of Scotland', *JRAI 30*, 56–73.

—— (1903). 'Stone circles in Derbyshire', *Man 3*, 133–6.

—— (1905). 'Prehistoric remains in Cornwall, Pt. II', *JRAI 35*, 427–34.

—— (1914). 'Standing stones and stone circles in Yorkshire', *Man 14*, 163–6.

LEWIS, G. (1966). 'Some radiocarbon dates for the Peak District', *JDANHS 86*, 115–17.

LEWIS, J. M. (1966). 'The standing stones of Pembrokeshire', *Pembr. Hist. 2*, 7–18.

Livret-Guide de l'Excursion à Bretagne, (1976). Union Internationale des Sciences Préhistoriques et Protohistoriques, Paris.

LOCKYER, SIR N. (1906). 'Notes on some Cornish circles', *Nature 73*, 366–8.

—— (1909). *Stonehenge and Other British Stone Monuments Astronomically Considered*, 2nd ed., London.

LOGAN, J. (1829). 'Observations on several stone circles in Scotland, presumed to be druidical', *Arch 22*, 198–203.

LOHAN, M. (1993). 'Moytura Conga: a mythical and ritual landscape', *J. Westport Hist Soc 3*, 16–31.

LONG, W. (1858a). *Abury Illustrated*, Devizes. (see also *WAM 4*, 1858, 307–63).

—— (1858b). 'The druidical temple at Stanton Drew, commonly called the Weddings', *Arch J 15*, 199–215.r.

LONGWORTH, I. H. (1984). *Collared Urns of the Bronze Age in Great Britain and Ireland*, Cambridge. See also Burleigh, R.

LOVE, R. (1876). 'The Four Stones, Beith', *PSAS 11*, 291–2.

LOVEDAY, R. (1998). 'Double entrance henges – routes to the past?', in Gibson, A. & Simpson, D.D.A. (eds), 14–31.

LUKIS, REV. W. C. (1870). *The Stone avenues of Carnac*, Salisbury. (See also *WAM 13*, 1872, 78–91).

—— (1875). *Guide to the Chambered Barrows etc of South Brittany*, Ripon.

—— (1882). *The Family Memoirs of the Rev. William Stukeley MD, and the Antiquarian and other Correspondence of William Stukeley, Roger and Samuel Gale etc, I*, Surtees Society 73, Durham, London and Edinburgh.

—— (1883). *The Family Memoirs of the Rev. William Stukeley MD, and the Antiquarian and other Correspondence of William Stukeley, Roger and Samuel Gale etc, II*, Surtees Society, 76, 1881.

—— (1885a). *Prehistoric Stone Monuments of the British Isles. Cornwall*, London.

—— (1885b). 'Megalithic monuments in Scotland, Cumberland and Westmorland', *PSAL 10*, 302–20.

—— (1887). *The Family Memoirs of the Rev. William Stukeley, MD . . . III*, Surtees Society 80, 1885.

LYNCH, A. (1981a). *Man and Environment in S. W. Ireland*, Oxford.

—— (1981b). 'Astronomical alignment or megalithic muddle?', in Corrain, D. O. (ed), *Irish Antiquity*, 23–7.

—— (1982). 'Astronomy and stone alignments in S. W. Ireland', in Heggie, D. C. (ed), 205–14.

LYNCH, F. (1969). 'The megalithic tombs of North Wales', in Powell et al., 296–308.

—— (1972). 'Ring-cairns and related monuments in Wales', *SAF 4*, 61–80.

—— (1979). 'Ring cairns in Britain and Ireland; their design and purpose', *UJA 42*, 1–19.

—— (1991). *Prehistoric Anglesey*, 2nd ed., Llanfegni.

—— (1998). 'Colour in prehistoric architecture', in Gibson, A. & Simpson, D.D.A. (eds), 62–67.

LYNCH, F. & BURGESS, C. (1972) eds. *Prehistoric Man in Wales and the West*, Bath.

MACALISTER, R.A.S. (1898). 'The gallans near Dingle', *JRSAI 28*, 161–4.

—— (1921). *Ireland in Pre-Celtic Times*, Dublin.

—— (1928). *The Archaeology of Ireland*, London.

—— (1935). *Ancient Ireland*, London.

MACCARTHY, C. (1996). 'Structural developments within megalithic monuments of the Clava group', *PSAS 126*, 87–102.

MACKIE, E. W. (1975). *Scotland. An Archaeological Guide*, London.

—— (1977a). *The Megalith Builders*, London.

—— (1977b). *Science and Society in Prehistoric Britain*, London.

MACLAGAN, C. (1875). *The Hill Forts, Stone Circles and Other Structural Remains of Ancient Scotland*, Edinburgh.

MACLEOD, F. T. (1912). 'Further notes on the antiquities of Skye, chiefly in the districts of Sleat and Strath', *PSAS 46*, 202–12.

MAITLAND, W. (1757). *History and Antiquities of Scotland, I*, London.

MALLORY, J. P. & McNEILL, T. E. (1991). *The Archaeology of Ulster*, Belfast.

MALONE, C. (1989). *English Heritage Book of Avebury*, London.

MANBY, T. (1965). 'The distribution of rough-cut "Cumbrian" axes, and related axes of Lake District origin in northern England', *TCWAAS 65*, 1–37.

—— (1988). *Archaeology in Yorkshire. Essays in Honour of T.C.M. Brewster*, Sheffield.

MANDAL, S. & COONEY, G. (1996). 'The Irish stone axe project: a second petrological report', *JAI 7*, 41–64.

MANNING, P. (1902). 'Stray notes on Oxfordshire folk-lore', *Folklore 13*, 288–97.

MANNING, W. H. see Houlder, C.

MANX MUSEUM. (1981). *The Ancient and Historic Monuments of the Isle of Man*, Douglas.

MARCH, H. C. (1888). 'A new theory of "Stone circles" ', *T. Lancs & Chesh Ant Soc 6* 98–111.

MARTIN. M. (1716). *A Description of the Western Islands of Scotland*, 2nd ed., London.

MARWICK, E. (1976). 'The Stone of Odin', in Ritchie, J.N.G., 28–34.

MASON, J. R. & VALENTINE, H. (1925). 'Studfold Gate circle', *TCWAAS 25*, 269.

MASTERS, L. (1977). 'Excavations at the Wren's Egg, Port William, Wigtown District', *TDGNHAS 52*, 28–43.

MAXFIELD, V. A. (1979) ed. *Prehistoric Dartmoor in its Context*, Torquay.

MAY, A. McL. (1945). 'Burial mound, circles and cairn, Gortcorbies, Co. Londonderry', *JRSAI 77*, 5–22.

—— (1953). 'Neolithic habitation site, stone circles and alignments at Beaghmore, Co. Tyrone', *JRSAI 83*, 174–97.

McCLELLAN, R. (1977). *Ancient Monuments of Arran*, Edinburgh.

McCLOUGH, T. W. & CUMMINS, W. A. (1979). eds. *Stone Axe Studies, 1*, London.

—— (1988). *Stone Axes Studies, 2*, London.

McCONKEY, R. (1987). 'Stone circles of Ulster, unpublished M.A. thesis, Queen's University of Belfast.

McNEILL, M. (1962). *The Festival of Lughnasa*, Oxford.

MERCER, R. J. (1981). 'The excavation of a Late Neolithic henge-type enclosure at Balfarg, Markinch, Fife, Scotland, 1977–8', *PSAS 111*, 63–171.

—— (1998). 'Recording orthostatic settings', in Gibson, A. & Simpson, D.D.A. (eds), 209–18.

MERCER, R. J., BARCLAY, R. J., JORDAN, G. J. & RUSSELL-WHITE, C. J. (1988), 'The Neolithic henge-type enclosure at Balfarg – a reassessment of the evidence for an incomplete ditch circuit', *PSAS 118*, 61–7.

MERLET, R. (jun.) (1974) ed. *Exposé du Système Solsticial Néolithique Reliant Entre Eux Certains Cromlechs et Menhirs Dans Le Golfe du Morbihan, par R. Merlet*, Rennes.

MERLET, R. (sen.) (1929). 'Peut-on calculer, à l'aide de l'astronomie, la date approximatif de certains monuments mégalithiques?', *Soc d'Histoire et d'Archéologie de Bretagne 10*, 13–26.

—— (1935). 'Valeur métrique du pied . . .', *Soc d'Histoire et d'Archéologie de Bretagne 16*, 133–45.

MICHELL, J. (1974). *The Old Stones of Land's End*, London.

—— (1982). *Megalithomania. Artists, Antiquarians and Archaeologists at the Old Stone Monuments*. London.

MILLIGAN, M. & BURL, A. (1999). *Circles of Stone*, London.

MILN, J. (1881). *Excavations at Carnac (Brittany). The Alignments of Kermario*, Edinburgh.

MINOT, R. S. (n.d., post-1961). *Les Monuments Mégalithiques du L'Ile aux Moines*, Vannes.

MITCHELL, F. (1990). *The Shell Guide to Reading the Irish Landscape*, Dublin.

MITCHELL, M.E.C. & YOUNG, A. (1939). 'Report on excavations at Monzie, Perthshire', *PSAS 73*, 62–71.

MOHEN, J.-P. (1989). *The World of Megaliths*, London.

MOIR, G. (1981). 'Some archaeological and astronomical objections in British prehistory', in Ruggles, C.L.N. & Whittle, A.W.R. (eds), 221–41.

MONTAGUE, R. see Cleal, R.M.J.

MOORE, D. (1970) ed. *The Irish Sea Province in Archaeology and History*, Cardiff.

MOORE, M. J. (1987). *Archaeological Inventory of Co. Meath*, Dublin.

—— (1995). 'A Bronze Age settlement in the Monavullagh mountains, Co. Waterford, Ireland', *PPS 61*, 191–243.

MOORE, P. D. (1973). 'Influence of prehistoric cultures upon the initiation and spread of blanket bog in upland Wales', *Nature 241*, 350–3.

MORGAN, C. L. (1887). 'The stones of Stanton Drew: their source and origin', *PSANHS 33*, 37–50.

MORRIS, R.W.B. (1977). *The Prehistoric Rock Art of Argyll*, Poole.

—— (1979). *The Prehistoric Rock Art of Galloway and the Isle of Man*, Poole.

—— (1981). *The Prehistoric Rock Art of South Scotland except Argyll and Galloway*, Oxford.

—— (1989). 'The prehistoric rock-art of Great Britain: a survey of all sites bearing motifs more complex than simple cup-marks', *PPS 55*, 45–88.

MORRISON, A. (1968). 'Cinerary urns and pygmy vessels in south-west Scotland', *TDGNHAS 45*, 80–140.

MUIR, R. (1985). *Shell Guide to Reading the Celtic Landscapes*, London.

MURRAY, J. (1981). 'The stone circles of Wigtownshire', *TDGNHAS 56*, 18–30.

MUSSON, C. R. (1971). 'A study of possible building forms at Durrington Walls, Woodhenge and the Sanctuary', in Wainwright, G. J. with Longworth, I. H. (eds), 363–77.

MYATT, L. J. (1973). 'Survey of an unrecorded stone setting near Broubster', *Bull. Caithness F.C. 1*, 9–10.

—— (1986). 'A survey of a stone setting and alignment at Dorrery, Caithness', priv. comm.

—— (1988a). 'The stone rows of northern Scotland', in Ruggles, C.L.N. (ed), 277–318.

—— (1988b). 'A megalithic winter solstice alignment at Dorrery, Caithness', *JHA 19*, S63–S68.

—— (1989). 'A stone setting at Achnagoul, Caithness', priv. comm.

NEWHAM, C. A. (1964). *The Enigma of Stonehenge and its Astronomical and Geometrical Significance*, Leeds.

—— (1966). 'Stonehenge – a Neolithic "Observatory"', *Nature 211*, 456–68.

—— (1972). *The Astronomical Significance of Stonehenge*, Leeds.

NICOLSON, J. & BURN, R. (1777). *The History and Antiquities of the Counties of Westmorland and Cumberland*, 2 vols, London.

NIEL, F. (1976). *Connaissance des Mégalithes*, Paris.

NORDEN, J. (1597–1604?). *A Topographical and Historical Description of Cornwall*, 2nd ed., London, 1728.

NORTH, J. (1996). *Stonehenge. Neolithic Man and the Cosmos*, London.

NORTH, O. H. & SPENCE, J. E. (1936). 'A stone circle at Summerhouse Hill, Yealand Conyers', *TCWAAS 36*, 69–70.

NSA ABERDEEN. (1845). *New Statistical Account of Scotland, XII*.

NSA ANGUS. (1843). *New Statistical Account of Scotland, XI*.

NSA DUMFRIESS. (1845). *New Statistical Account of Scotland, IV*.

O'BRIEN, W. (1994). *Mount Gabriel. Bronze Age Mining in Ireland*, Galway.

—— (1996). *Bronze Age Copper Mining in Britain and Ireland*, Princes Risborough.

O'DONOVAN, P. F. (1995). *Archaeological Inventory of Co. Cavan*, Dublin.

OGSTON, SIR A. (1931). *The Prehistoric Antiquities of the Howe of Cromar*, Aberdeen.

O'KELLY, C. (1969). 'Bryn Celli Ddu, Anglesey. A reinterpretation', *Arch Camb 118*, 17–48.

—— (1973). 'Passage-grave art in the Boyne Valley', *PPS 39*, 354–82.

—— (1978). *Illustrated Guide to Newgrange and the Other Boyne Monuments*, 3rd ed., Blackrock.

O'KELLY, M. J. (1952). 'Excavation of a cairn at Moneen, Co. Cork', *PRIA 54C*, 121–59.

—— (1982). *Newgrange. Archaeology, Art and Legend*, London.

—— (1989). *Early Ireland*, Cambridge.

O'KELLY, M. J. & C. (1978). *Illustrated Guide to Lough Gur, Co. Limerick*, Cork.

OMAND, D. (1987) ed. *The Grampian Book*, Golspie.

O'NUALLAIN, S. (1975). 'The stone circle complex of Cork and Kerry', *JRSAI 105*, 83–131.

—— (1978). 'Boulder-burials', *PRIA 78C*, 75–114.

—— (1984a). 'A survey of stone circles in Cork & Kerry', *PRIA 84C*, 1–77.

—— (1984b). 'Grouped standing stones, radial-stone cairns, and enclosures in the south of Ireland', *JRSAI 114*, 63–79.

—— (1988). 'Stone rows in the south of Ireland', *PRIA 88C*, 179–256.

—— (1995). *Stone Circles in Ireland*, Dublin. See also Valera, R. de

O'RIORDAIN, S. P. (1939). 'Excavation of a stone circle and cairn at Kealkil, Co. Cork', *JCHAS 44*, 46–9.

—— (1950). 'Excavations of some earthworks on the Curragh, Co. Kildare', *PRIA 53C*, 249–77.

—— (1951). 'Lough Gur excavations. The Great Circle (B) in Grange townland', *PRIA 54C*, 37–74.

—— (1954). 'Lough Gur excavations. Neolithic and Bronze Age houses on Knockadoon', *PRIA 56C*, 297–459.

—— (1965). *Antiquities of the Irish Countryside*, 4th ed., London.

O'RIORDAIN, S. P. & DANIEL, G. (1964). *New Grange and the Bend of the Boyne*, London.

O'RIORDAIN, S. P. & EOCHAIDHE, O. (1956). 'Trial excavation at Newgrange', *JRSAI 86*, 52–61.

ORME, B. J. see Coles, J. M.

PARKER, C. A. & COLLINGWOOD, W. G. (1926). *The Gosforth District: Its Antiquities and Places of Interest*, Kendal.

PASSMORE, A. D. (1894). 'Notes on an undescribed stone circle at Coate near Swindon', *WAM 27*, 171–4.

PATERSON, T.G.F., GAFFIKIN, W. & DAVIES, O. (1938). 'An account of Co. Cavan', *UJA 1*, 142–51.

PATRICK, J. (1974). 'Midwinter sunrise at Newgrange', *Nature 249*, 517–19.

—— (1979). 'A reassessment of the lunar observatory hypothesis for the Kilmartin stones', *Archaeoastronomy 1*, S78–S85.

PATRICK, J. & WALLACE, C. S. (1982). 'Stone circle geometries: an information theory approach', in Heggie, D. C. (ed), 231–64.

PATTON, M. (1987). *Jersey in Prehistory*, La Haule, Jersey.

—— (1992). 'Megalithic transport and territorial markers: evidence from the Channel Islands', *Ant 66*, 392–4.

—— (1993). *Statements in Stone. Monuments and Society in Neolithic Brittany*, London.

PEACOCK, D.P.S. (1969). 'Neolithic pottery production in Cornwall', *Ant 43*, 145–9.

PEARCE, S. M. (1981). *The Archaeology of South-West Britain*, London.

PEARSON, G. W., PILCHER, J. R., BAILLIE, M.G.L., CORBETT, D. M. & QUA, F. (1986). 'High precision 14C measurement of Irish oaks to show the natural 14C variations from AD 1840 to 5210 BC', *Radiocarbon 28*, 911–34.

PEARSON, M. P. (1993). *Bronze Age Britain*, London

PEARSON, W. (1970). 'Commondale stone circle', *YAJ 42*, 240.

PEET, T. E. (1912). *Rough Stone Monuments and Their Builders*, London.

PELTENBURG, E. G. (1974). 'Excavation of Culcharron cairn, Benderloch, Argyll, *PSAS 104*, 63–70.

PENNANT, T. (1774). *A Tour in Scotland*, 3rd ed., London.

—— (1784). *A Tour in Wales, I, II*, London.

PENNINGTON, W. (1970). 'Vegetation history in the north-west of England; a regional synthesis', in Walker, D. & West, R. G. (eds), 41–80.

PENNY, A. & WOOD, J. E., (1973). 'The Dorset cursus complex: a Neolithic astronomical observatory', *Arch J 130*, 44–76.

—— (1975). 'A megalithic observatory on Dartmoor', *Nature 257*, 205–7.

PÉQUART, M. & ST J. & ROUZIC, Z., LE (1927). *Corpus de Signes Gravés des Mégalithiques du Morbihan*, Paris.

PETERSON, F. (1972). 'Traditions of multiple burial in Later Neolithic and Early Bronze Age England', *Arch J 129*, 22–55.

PETRIE, W.M.F. & HAWKINS, G. S. (1989). *Stonehenge: Plans, Descriptions and Theories*, London. Reprint of Petrie, 1880. With Appendix by Hawkins: 'Stonehenge astronomy – an update', 41–80.

PETTIT, P. (1974). *Prehistoric Dartmoor*, Newton Abbot.

PIERPOINT, S. see Barnatt, J.

PIGGOTT, S. (1940). 'Timber circles: a re-examination', *Arch J 96*, 193–222.

—— (1948). 'The excavations at Cairnpapple Hill, West Lothian', *PSAS 82*, 68–123.

—— (1954). *Neolithic Cultures of the British Isles*, Cambridge.

—— (1956). 'Excavations in passage-graves and ring-cairns of the Clava group, 1952–3', *PSAS 88*, 173–207.

—— (1962a) ed. *Prehistoric Peoples of Scotland*, London.

—— (1962b). 'Traders and metalworkers', in Piggott (ed), 73–104.

—— (1962c). *The West Kennet Long Barrow Excavations, 1955–6*, London.

—— (1965). *Ancient Europe*, Edinburgh.

—— (1968). *The Druids*, London.

—— (1976). *Ruins in a Landscape*, Edinburgh.

—— (1985). *William Stukeley. An Eighteenth Century Antiquary*, 2nd ed., London.

—— (1989). *Ancient Britons and the Antiquarian Imagination*, London. See also Atkinson, R.J.C.; Evans, E. D., 1962; Keiller, A.

PILCHER, J. R. (1969). 'Archaeology, palaeoecology and C14 dating of the Beaghmore stone circle site', *UJA 32*, 73–91.

—— (1975). 'Finds at Beaghmore stone circles', *UJA 38*, 83–4. See also Pearson, G. W.

PITTS, M. W. (1982). 'On the road to Stonehenge: report on the investigations beside the A344 – 1968, 1979 and 1980', *PPS 48*, 75–132.

PITTS, M. W. & WHITTLE, A.W.R. (1992). 'The development and date of Avebury', *PPS 58*, 203–12.

PLINT, R. G. (1962). 'Stone axe factory sites in the Cumbrian Fells', *TCWAAS 62*, 1–26.

PONTING, G. & M. (1977). *The Standing Stones of Callanish*, Stornoway.

—— (1979). 'Callanish. The documentary record', unpublished MS, Callanish.

—— (1981a). 'Decoding the Callanish complex – some initial results', in Ruggles, C.L.N. & Whittle, A.W.R. (eds), 63–110.

—— (1981b). *Achmore Stone Circle*, Callanish.

—— (1982). 'Decoding the Callanish complex – a progress report', in Heggie, D.C. (ed), 191–203.

—— (1984a). *New Light on the Stones of Callanish*, Stornoway.

—— (1984b). *The Stones Around Callanish*, Stornoway.

PONTING, M. (1988). 'Megalithic Callanish', in Ruggles, C.L.N. (ed), 1988a, 423–41. See also Curtis, R.

PONTOIS, B. LE (1929). *Le Finistère Préhistorique*, Paris.

POWELL, A. (1949). *Brief Lives and Other Selected Writings by John Aubrey*, London.

—— (1988). *John Aubrey and His Friends*, 3rd ed., London.

POWELL, A. B. (1994). 'Newgrange – science or symbolism?', *PPS 60*, 85–96.

POWELL, T.G.E. (1969). 'Introductory to the field study of megalithic tombs', in Powell, T.G.E., et al., 1969, 1–12.

—— 'The Neolithic in the west of Europe and megalithic sepulture: some points and problems', in Powell, T.G.E. et al., 1969, 247–72.

POWELL, T.G.E., CORCORAN, J.X.W.P., LYNCH, F. & SCOTT, J. G. (1969). *Megalithic Enquiries in the West of Britain*, Liverpool.

POWER, D., BYRNE, E., EGAN, U., LANE, S. & SLEEMAN, M. (1992). *Archaeological Inventory of Co. Cork, I. West Cork*. Dublin.

—— (1994). *Archaeological Inventory of Co. Cork, II. East and South Cork*, Dublin.

—— (1997). *Archaeological Inventory of Co. Cork, III. Mid Cork*, Dublin.

PRICE, L. (1934). The ages of Stone and Bronze in County Wicklow', *PRIA 42C*, 31–64.

PRIOR, Dr (1872). 'Archaic stone monuments', *Proc. Beds. Arch. & Arch Soc*, 343–60.

PURDY, J. D. (1972). *The Church of All Saints and the Monolith, Rudston*, Bridlington.

QUA, F. see Pearson, G. W.

QUINE, R. H. (n.d.). *The Mystery of the Early British*, Douglas.

QUINNELL, N. V. (1992). Dunn, C. J. (ed) *Lithic Monuments within the Exmoor National Park. A New Survey for Management Purposes*, RCAHM-England.

RADFORD, C.A.R. (1938). 'The Hurlers, Cornwall. Notes on excavations', *PPS 4*, 319.

—— (1952). 'Prehistoric settlements on Dartmoor and the Cornish Moors', *PPS 18*, 55–84.

RADLEY, J. (1966). 'A Bronze Age ringwork on Totley Moor and other Bronze Age ringworks in the Pennines', *Arch J 123*, 1–26.

—— (1969a). 'The origins of the Arbor Low monument', *DAJ 88*, 100–3.

—— (1969b). 'A stone circle on Kirkmoor Beck farm, Fylingdales', *YAJ 42*, 250–1.

RAFTERY, J. (1951). *Prehistoric Ireland*, London.

RAISTRICK, A. (1929). 'The Bronze Age in West Yorkshire', *YAJ 29*, 354–65.

RALSTON, I.B.M. see SHEPHERD, I.A.G., 1979.

RAVENHILL, T. H. (1932). *The Rollright Stones and the Men who Erected Them*, 2nd ed., Birmingham.

RAY, K. & THOMAS, J. (1989). 'Banc Rhosgoch Fach. Trial excavations, 1989', interim report, Archaeology Unit, St David's College, Lampeter.

RAY, T. P. (1989). 'The winter solstice phenomenon at Newgrange, Ireland: accident or design?', *Nature 337*, 343–5.

RCAHM-E. (1936). *Westmorland*, London.

RCAHM-S. (1911a). *Caithness*, Edinburgh.

—— (1911b). *Sutherland*, Edinburgh.

—— (1912). *Galloway, I. Wigtownshire*, Edinburgh.

—— (1914). *Galloway, II. Kirkcudbrightshire*, Edinburgh.

—— (1915). *Berwickshire*, Edinburgh.

—— (1920). *Dumfriess-shire*, Edinburgh.

—— (1924). *East Lothian*, Edinburgh.

—— (1928). *Outer Hebrides*, Edinburgh.

—— (1929). *Midlothian and West Lothian*, Edinburgh.

—— (1922). *Fife, Kinross and Clackmannanshire*, Edinburgh.

—— (1946a). *Orkney and Shetland, I. Introduction*, Edinburgh.

—— (1946b). *Orkney and Shetland, II. Orkney*, Edinburgh.

—— (1946c). *Orkney and Shetland, III. Shetland*, Edinburgh.

—— (1956). *Roxburghshire, I, II*, Edinburgh.

—— (1967). *Peebles-shire*, Edinburgh.

—— (1971). *Argyll, I. Kintyre*, Edinburgh.

—— (1975). *Argyll, II. Lorn*, Edinburgh.

—— (1980). *Argyll, III. Mull, Tiree, Coll and North Argyll*, Edinburgh.

—— (1984). *Argyll, V. Islay, Jura, Colonsay and Oronsay*, Edinburgh.

—— (1988). *Argyll, VI. Mid-Argyll and Cowal*, Edinburgh.

RCAHM-W. (1911). *Montgomeryshire*, London.

—— (1912). *Flintshire*, London.

—— (1913). *Radnorshire*, London.

—— (1914). *Denbighshire*, London.

—— (1917). *Carmarthenshire*, London.

—— (1921). *Merioneth*, London.

—— (1925). *Pembrokeshire*, London.

—— (1937). *Anglesey*, London.

—— (1956). *Caernarvonshire, I*, London.

—— (1960). *Caernarvonshire, II*, London.

—— (1964). *Caernarvonshire, III*, London.

REID, M. L. (1993). *Prehistoric Houses in Britain*, Princes Risborough.

RENFREW, C. (1973a) ed. *The Explanation of Culture Change. Models in Prehistory*, London.

—— (1973b). *Before Civilisation*, London.

—— (1979). *Investigations in Orkney*, London.

RICHARDS, J. (1991). *The English Heritage Book of Stonehenge*, London.

RILEY, D. N. (1966). 'An Early Bronze Age cairn on Harland Edge, Beeley Moor, Derbyshire', *JDANHS 86*, 31–53.

RISKINE, A.-E. (1992). *Carnac: l'Armée de Pierres*, Paris.

RITCHIE, A. (1985). *Exploring Scotland's Heritage. Orkney & Shetland*, Edinburgh.

RITCHIE, J. (1918). 'Cupmarks on the stone circles and standing stones of Aberdeenshire and part of Banff', *PSAS 52*, 86–121.

—— (1919). 'Notes on some stone circles in the south of Aberdeenshire and north of Kincardineshire', *PSAS 53*, 64–75.

—— (1920). 'The stone circle at Broomend of Crichie', *PSAS 54*, 154–71.

—— (1923). 'Stone circles at Raedykes, near Stonehaven, Kincardineshire', *PSAS 53*, 20–8.

—— (1926). 'Folklore of the Aberdeenshire stone circles and standing stones', *PSAS 60*, 304–13.

RITCHIE, J.N.G. (1967). 'Balnabraid cairn, Kintyre, Argyll', *TDGNHAS 44*, 81–98.

—— (1971). 'Excavation of a cairn at Strontoiller, Lorn, Argyll', *GAJ 2*, 1–7.

—— (1974). 'Excavation of the stone circle and cairn at Balbirnie, Fife', *Arch J 131*, 1–32.

—— (1976). 'The Stones of Stenness, Orkney', *PSAS 107*, 337–50.

—— (1988). 'The Ring of Brodgar, Orkney', in Ruggles, C.L.N. (ed), 1988a, 337–50.

—— (1998) 'Tyrebagger recumbent stone circle, Aberdeenshire: a note on recording', in Gibson, A. & Simpson, D.D.A., 176–82.

RITCHIE, J.N.G. & A. (1972). *Regional Archaeologies. Edinburgh and South-East Scotland*, London.

RITCHIE, J.N.G. & Harman, M. (1985). *Exploring Scotland's Heritage. Argyll and the Western Isles*, Edinburgh.

RITCHIE, J.N.G. & MacLaren, A. C. (1972). 'Ring-cairns and related monuments in Scotland', *SAF 4*, 1–17.

RITCHIE, P. R. (1968). 'The stone implement trade in 3rd millennium Scotland', in Coles, J. M. & Simpson, D.D.A. (eds), 117–36.

ROBERTS, J. (1985). *Sketches of Ancient Carbery. The Megaliths of West Cork*, Dublin.

—— (1988). *Exploring West Cork*, Skibbereen.

—— (n.d.). *Antiquities of the Beara peninsula*, (with separate map), Skibbereen.

—— (n.d.). *Antiquities of West Cork. A Guide*, (with separate map), Skibbereen.

—— (n.d.). *The Stone Circles of Cork & Kerry. An Astronomical Guide*, (with separate map), Skibbereen.

—— (1996). *The Sacred Mythological Centres of Ireland*, Skibbereen.

ROBINSON, T. (1990). *Connemara*, Roundstone.

ROE, F.E.S. (1966). 'The battle-axe series in Britain', *PPS 32*, 199–245.

—— (1967). 'The battle-axes, mace-heads and axe-hammers from south-west Scotland', *TDGNHAS 44*, 57–80.

—— (1968). 'Stone mace-heads and the latest Neolithic cultures of the British Isles', in Coles, J. M. & Simpson, D.D.A. (eds), 145–72.

ROESE, H. E. (1980a). 'Some aspects of topographical locations of Neolithic and Bronze Age monuments in south-east Wales, I. Menhirs', *BBCS 28*, 645–55.

—— (1980b). 'Some aspects of topographical locations of Neolithic and Bronze Age monuments in south-east Wales, II. Henges and circles', *BBCS 29*, 264–70.

—— (1981). 'Some aspects of topographical locations of Neolithic and Bronze Age monuments in south-east Wales, III. Cairns and round barrows', *BBCS 29*, 575–87.

ROSE, P. see Johnson, N.

ROSS, A. (1970). *Pagan Celtic Britain*, London.

—— (1986). *The Pagan Celts*, London.

ROUX, C. LE see Batt, M.

ROUZIC, Z. LE. (1930). *Les Cromlechs de Er-Lannic*, Vannes.

—— (1935). *Les Monuments Mégalithiques de Carnac: Leur Destination – Leur Age*, 7th ed., Nantes.

—— (1939). *Carnac. Légendes, Traditions, Coutumes et Contes de Pays*, Vannes. See also Péquart, M. & St J.

ROY, A. E., McGRAIL, N. & CARMICHAEL, R. (1963). 'A new survey of the Tormore circles', *TGAS 51 (2)*, 59–67.

RUGGLES, C.L.N. (1981). 'A critical examination of the megalithic lunar observatories', in Ruggles, C.L.N. & Whittle, A.W.R. (eds), 153–209.

—— (1984a). *Megalithic Astronomy. A New Archaeological and Statistical Study of 300 Western Scottish Sites*, Oxford.

—— (1984b). 'A new study of the Aberdeenshire recumbent stone circles, 1. Site data', *JHA 15. Archaeoastronomy Supplement 19*, S55–S79.

—— (1988a) ed. *Records in Stone. Papers in Memory of Alexander Thom*, Cambridge.

—— (1988b). 'The stone alignments of Argyll and Mull: a perspective on the statistical approach in archaeoastronomy', in Ruggles, C.L.N. (ed), 1988a, 232–50.

—— (1994). 'The stone rows of south-west Ireland: a first reconnaissance', *JHA 25, Archaeoastronomy Supplement 19*, S1–S21.

—— (1998) 'Ritual astronomy in the Neolithic and Bronze Age British Isles: patterns of continuity and change', in Gibson, A. & Simpson, D.D.A., 203–8.

—— (1999) *Astronomy in Prehistoric Britain & Ireland*, New Haven & London.

RUGGLES, C.L.N. & BURL, A. (1985). 'A new survey of the Aberdeenshire recumbent stone circles, 2. Interpretation', *JHA 16*, S25–S60.

RUGGLES, C.L.N. & MARTLEW, R. D. (1989). 'The North Mull project (1): excavations at Glengorm, 1987–8', *JHA 20*, S137–S149.

RUGGLES, C.L.N. & MARTLEW, R. D. (1992). 'The North Mull project (3): prominent hill summits and their astronomical potential', *JHA 23*, S1–S13.

RUGGLES, C.L.N., Martlew, R. D. & HINGE, P. D. (1991). 'The

North Mull project (2): the wider astronomical potential of the sites', *JHA 22*, S52–S75.

RUGGLES, C.L.N. & WHITTLE, A.W.R. (1981). eds. *Astronomy and Society in Britain During the Period 4000–1500 BC*, Oxford.

RUSSELL-WHITE, C. J. see Barclay, G.

RYAN, M. (1991) ed. *The Illustrated Archaeology of Ireland*, Dublin.

RYNNE, E. (1969). 'A stone alignment and a stone circle near Rearcross, Co. Tipperary', *NMAJ 12*, 90.

RYNNE, E. & EAILIDHE, P. (1966). 'A group of prehistoric sites at Piperstown, Co. Dublin', *PRIA 64c*, 61–84.

ST LEGER-GORDON, R. E. (1965). *The Witchcraft and Folklore of Dartmoor*, London. Sandars, N. see Atkinson, R.J.C.

SAVORY, H. N. (1964). 'Excavations at a third round barrow at Pen-Dre, Letterston, (Pembrokeshire)', *BBCS 20 (3)*, 309–25.

—— (1965). 'The Bronze Age', in Foster & Alcock (eds), 71–107.

—— (1970). 'The later prehistoric migrations across the Irish Sea', in Moore, D. (ed), *The Irish Sea Province in Archaeology and Prehistory*, 38–49.

SCARRE, C. (1983) ed. *Ancient France*, Edinburgh.

SCARRE, C. & Healy, F. (1993) eds. *Trade and Exchange in Prehistoric Europe*, Oxford.

SCARTH, H. M. (1857). 'On ancient earthworks in the neighbourhood of Bath', *JBAA 13*, 98–113.

SCOTT, D. (n.d.). 'An astronomical assessment of the Clava cairns', unpublished paper, Tain, Ross-shire.

SCOTT, J. G. (1964). 'The chambered tomb at Beacharra, Kintyre, Argyll', *PPS 30*, 134–58.

—— (1969). 'The Neolithic period in Kintyre, Argyll', in Powell, T.G.E. et al., 175–246, 309–34.

—— (1989). 'The stone circles at Temple Wood, Kilmartin, Argyll', *GAJ 15*, 53–124.

SCOTT, SIR L. (1951). 'The colonisation of Scotland in the 2nd millennium BC', *PPS 17*, 16–82.

SCOTT-ELLIOTT, J. (1967). 'Whitestanes Muir (Sites 7 and 8)', *TDGNHAS 44*, 117–21.

SCOUËZEC, G. LE (1979). *Guide de la Bretagne Mystérieuse*, Paris.

SCOUËZEC, G. LE & MASSON, J.-R. (1987). *Bretagne Mégalithique*, Paris.

SEABROOK, R.A.G. see DAVIDSON, C. J.

SERVICE, A. & BRADBERY, J. (1993). *The Standing Stones of Europe*, London.

SHARPLES, N. & SHERIDAN, A. eds (1992). *Vessels for the Ancestors*, Edinburgh.

SHEE, E. (1981). *The Megalithic Art of Western Europe*, Oxford.

SHEE, E. & EVANS, E. E. (1965). 'A standing stone in the Townland of Newgrange, Co. Meath', *JCHAS 70*, 124–30. See also: Twohig, E. S.

SHEPHERD, I.A.G. (1986). *Powerful Pots. Beakers in North-East Prehistory*, Aberdeen.

—— (1987). 'The early peoples', in Omand, D. (ed), 119–30.

SHEPHERD, I.A.G. & Ralston, I.B.M. (1979). *Early Grampian. A Guide to the Archaeology*, Aberdeen.

SHERRATT, A. (1998) 'Points of exchange: the Later Neolithic monuments of the Morbihan', in Gibson, A. & Simpson, D.D.A., 119–38.

SIMMONS, I. G. (1961). 'Stallmoor Down stone row', *TDA 93*, 65.

—— (1962). 'An outline of the vegetational history of Dartmoor', *TDA 94*, 555.

—— (1969). 'Environment and early man on Dartmoor', *PPS 35*, 203–19.

SIMMONS, I. G. & TOOLEY, M. (1981) eds. *The Environment in British Prehistory*, New York.

SIMPSON, D.D.A. (1965). 'Food-vessels in south-west Scotland', *TDGNHAS 42*, 25–50.

—— (1968). 'Food-vessels: associations and chronology', in Coles & Simpson (eds), 197–211.

—— (1971) ed. *Economy and Settlement in Neolithic and Early Bronze Age Britain*, Leicester.

—— (1996). 'Excavation of a kerbed funerary monument at Stoneyfield, Raigmore, Highland, 1972–3', *PSAS 126*, 53–86.

SIMPSON, D.D.A. & THAWLEY, J. (1972). 'Single-grave art in Britain', *SAF 4*, 81–104. See also Coles, J. M.

SIMPSON, Sir J. Y. (1867). *Archaic Sculpturings of Cups, Circles etc*, Edinburgh.

SITWELL, BRIG-GEN, W. (1930). *Stones of Northumberland and Other Lands*, Newcastle.

SMITH, REV, A. C. (1885). *Guide to the British and Roman Antiquities of the North Wiltshire Downs*, Devizes.

SMITH, A. G. (1970). 'The influence of Mesolithic and Neolithic man on British vegetation', in Walker & West (eds), 81–96.

SMITH, I. F. (1965). *Windmill Hill & Avebury. Excavations by Alexander Keiller, 1929–35*, Oxford.

—— (1971). 'Causewayed enclosures', in Simpson, D.D.A. (ed), 89–112.

—— (1979). 'The chronology of British stone implements', in McKClough & Cummins (eds), 13–22. See also Evans, E. D., 1972.

SMITH, J. (1771). *Choir Gaur: the Grand Orrery of the Ancient Druids, Commonly called Stonehenge*, London.

SODEN-SMITH, R. H. (1870). 'Notice of circles of stones in the parish of Crosby Ravensworth, Westmorland', *TCWAAS 27 (O.S.)*, 200–3.

SOMERVILLE, H. B. (1909). 'Notes on a stone circle in Co. Cork', *JCHAS 15*, 105–8.

—— (1912). 'Prehistoric monuments in the Outer Hebrides, and their astronomical significance', *JRAI 42*, 23–52.

—— (1913). 'Astronomical indications in the megalithic monument at Callanish', *J. B. Astr. Assoc 23*, 68–71.

—— (1923). 'Instances of orientation in prehistoric monuments of the British Isles', *Arch 73*, 193–224.

—— (1928). 'Prehistorics', *JCHAS 33*, 57–68.

—— (1930). 'Five stone circles of West Cork', *JCHAS 35*, 70–85.

SPENCE, L. (1917). *Legends and Romances of Brittany*, London.

SPOONER, G. M. & RUSSELL, F. S. (1967) eds. *Worth's Dartmoor*, Newton Abbot.

STELL, G. (1986). *Exploring Scotland's Heritage. Dumfriess & Galloway*, Edinburgh.

STEVENS, F. (1936). *Stonehenge Today and Yesterday*, revised ed., London.

STEVENSON, J. B. (1985). *Exploring Scotland's Heritage. The Clyde Estuary and Central Region*, Edinburgh.

STEWART, M.E.C. (1959). 'Strathtay in the 2nd millennium BC', *PSAS 92*, 71–84.

—— (1966a). 'Excavation of a circle of standing stones at Sandy Road, Scone, Perthshire', *TPPSNS 11*, 7–23.

—— (1966b). 'The excavation of a setting of standing stones at Lundin Farm, near Aberfeldy, Perthshire', *PSAS 98*, 126–49.

—— (1985). 'The excavation of a henge, stone circles and metal-working area at Moncreiffe, Perthshire', *PSAS 115*, 125–50. See also Henshall, A. S.

STONE, E. H. (1924) *The Stones of Stonehenge*, London.

STONE, J.F.S. & WALLIS, F. S. (1951). 'Third report . . . on the petrological determination of stone axes, *PPS 17*, 99–158.

STOUT, H. B. (1961). 'Three stone circles at Gretigate Sides, Cumberland, *TCWAAS 61*, 1–6.

STRAFFON, C. (1992). *Ancient Sites in West Penwith*, St Just.

—— (1993). *Bodmin Moor and North Cornwall, including Tintagel*, St Just.

—— (1994). *Mid Cornwall and the Lizard*, St Just.

STUART, J. (1856). *The Sculptured Stones of Scotland, I*, Aberdeen.

—— (1860). 'Note of incised marks on one of a circle of standing stones in the island of Lewis', *PSAS 3*, 212–14.

—— (1867). *The Sculptured Stones of Scotland, II*, Edinburgh.

STUKELEY, W. (1723). 'The history of the temples and religion of the antient Celts', MS 4, 253, Cardiff Public Library.

—— (1740). *Stonehenge. A Temple Restor'd to the British Druids*, London.

—— (1743). *Abury, a Temple of the British Druids*, London.

—— (1776a). *Itinerarium Curiosum, I*, London.

—— (1776b). *Itinerarium Curiosum, II*, London.

SWEETMAN, P. D. (1985). 'A Late Neolithic/Early Bronze Age pit circle at Newgrange, Co. Meath', *PRIA 85C*, 195–221.

—— (1987). 'Excavation of a Late Neolithic/Early Bronze Age site at Newgrange, Co. Meath', *PRIA 87C*, 283–98.

SWIRE, O. F. (1963). *The Highlands and their Legends*, Edinburgh.

—— (1966). *The Outer Hebrides and their Legends*, Edinburgh.

TAIT, J. (1965). *Beakers From Northumberland*, Newcastle.

TAYLOR, C. (1979). *Roads and Tracks of Britain*, London.

TAYLOR, J. J. (1980). *Bronze Age Goldwork of the British Isles*, Cambridge.

TAYLOR, M. W. (1886). 'The prehistoric remains on Moordivock, near Ullswater', *TCWAAS 8 (O.S.)*, 323–47.

TAYLOR, T. (1996). *The Prehistory of Sex*, London.

THOM, A. (1955). 'A statistical examination of the megalithic sites in Britain', *JRSS 118*, 275–95.

—— (1961a). 'The geometry of megalithic man', *Math Gaz 45*, 83–93.

—— (1961b). 'The egg-shaped standing stone rings of Britain', *Archs Int Hist Sci 14*, 291–303.

—— (1966a). 'Megalithic astronomy: indications in standing stones', *Vistas in Astronomy 7*, 1–57.

—— (1966b). 'The lunar observatories of megalithic man', *Nature 212*, 1527–8.

—— (1966c). 'Megaliths and mathematics', *Ant 40*, 121–8.

—— (1967). *Megalithic Sites in Britain*, Oxford.

—— (1971). *Megalithic Lunar Observatories*, Oxford.

—— (1972). 'The Carnac alignments', *JHA 3*, 11–26.

—— (1984). 'Moving and erecting the menhirs', *PPS 50*, 382–4.

THOM, A. & THOM, A. S. (1973). 'A megalithic lunar observatory in Orkney: the Ring of Brogar and its cairns', *JHA 4*, 111–23.

—— (1974). 'The Kermario alignments', *JHA 5*, 30–47.

—— (1976). 'Avebury (2): the West Kennet avenue', *JHA 7*, 193–7. See also: (1) Thom, A., A. S. & Foord , T. R. (1976).

—— (1977). *La Géometrie des Alignements de Carnac (suivi de plans comparatifs*, Rennes.

—— (1978). *Megalithic Remains in Britain and Brittany*, Oxford.

—— (1974). 'Stonehenge', *JHA 5 (2)*, 71–90.

—— (1975). 'Stonehenge as a possible lunar observatory', *JHA 6 (1)*, 19–30.

THOM, A., THOM, A. S., & BURL, A. (1980). *Megalithic Rings: Plans and Data for 229 Sites*, Oxford.

—— (1990). *Stone Rows and Standing Stones. Britain, Ireland and Brittany, I, II*, Oxford.

THOM, A., THOM, A. S. & FOORD, T. R. (1976). 'Avebury (1). A new assessment of the geometry and metrology of the ring', *JHA 7*, 183–92. See also (2) Thom, A. & Thom, A. S. (1976).

THOM, A. S. (1980). 'The Stone rings of Beaghmore: geometry and astronomy', *UJA 43*, 15–19.

—— (1995). *Walking in All of the Squares. A Biography of Alexander Thom*, Glendaruel.

THOM, A. S., MERRITT, R. L. & MERRITT, A. L. (1973). 'The astronomical significance of the Crucuno stone rectangle', *Curr Anthr 14*, 450–4.

THOMAS, A. C. (1969). 'The Bronze Age in the South-West', *Arch Review 4*, 3–12.

THOMAS, J. (1991). *Rethinking the Neolithic*, Cambridge.

THOMAS, N. (1976). *Guide to Prehistoric England*, 2nd ed., London.

THOMPSON, D. (1963). *Guide to Arbor Low*, London.

THORPE, L. (1966) trans. *Geoffrey of Monmouth, 'The History of the Kings of Britain'*, Harmondsworth.

THORPE, R. S., WILLIAMS-THORPE, O., JENKINS, D. G. & WATSON, J. S. (1991), 'The geological sources and transport of the bluestones of Stonehenge, Wiltshire, U.K.', *PPS 57 (2)*, 103–57.

TILLEY, C. (1995) 'Rocks as resources: landscape and power', *Corn Arch 34*, 5–57.

TIZARD, T. H. (1909). *The Tides and Tidal Streams of the British Islands, the North Sea and the North Coast of France*, London.

TOAL, C. (1995) *North Kerry Archaeological Survey*, Dingle.

TOLAND, J. (c. 1726). *A Critical History of the Celtic Religion and Learning, containing an Account of the Druids*, 1814 edition, London.

TOPPING, G. (1981) 'Hethpool', *Northern Archaeology 2 (2)*, 3–10.

TRATMAN, E. K. (1958). 'The lost stone circles of Somerset', *PUBSS 11 (1)*, 110–18.

—— (1966). 'Investigations at Stanton Drew stone circles, Somerset', *PUBSS 11 (2)*, 40–2.

—— (1967). 'The Priddy circles, Mendip, Somerset, henge monuments', *PUBSS 11 (2)*, 97–125.

TREGELLES, G. F. (1906). 'The stone circles', *VCH Cornwall, I*, 379–406.

TUCKWELL, A. (1975). 'Patterns of burial orientation in the round barrows of Yorkshire', *Bull. Inst. Archaeology 12*, 95–123.

TULLOCH, A. (1983). 'The recumbent stone circle tradition of the north-east of Scotland', unpublished BA dissertation, University of Edinburgh.

TURNER, J. (1965). 'A contribution to the history of forest clearance', *PRS B161*, 343–54.

—— (1970). 'Post-Neolithic disturbance of British vegetation', in Walker & West (eds), 97–116.

TURNER, J. R. (1990). 'Ring cairns, stone circles and related monuments on Dartmoor', *PDAS 48*, 27–86.

TWOHIG, E. S. (1981) *The Megalithic Art of Western Europe*, Oxford.

—— (1990) *Irish Megalithic Tombs*, Princes Risborough. See also Shee, E. (Twohig).

TWOHIG, E. S. & RONAYNE, M. (1993) eds. *Past Perceptions. The Prehistoric Archaeology of South-West Ireland*, Cork.

UCKO, P. J., HUNTER, M., CLARK, A. J. & DAVID, A. (1991). *Avebury Reconsidered. From the 1660s to the 1990s*, London.

VALERA, R. DE (1960). 'The court cairns of Ireland', *PRIA 60C*, 9–140.

VALERA, R. DE & O'NUALLAIN, S. (1964). *Survey of the Megalithic Tombs of Ireland, II. Co. Mayo*, Dublin.

—— (1982). *Survey of the Megalithic Tombs of Ireland, IV. Cos. Cork, Kerry, Limerick, Tipperary*, Dublin.

—— (1989). *Survey of the Megalithic Tombs of Ireland, V. Co. Sligo*, Dublin.

VAN HOEK, M.A.M. (1988). 'The prehistoric rock art of Co. Donegal, II', *UJA 51*, 21–47.

VARLEY, W. J. (1938). 'The Bleasdale circle', *Ant J 18*, 154–71.

VATCHER, F. DE M. (1969). 'Two incised chalk plaques near Stonehenge Bottom', *Ant 43*, 310–11.

VATCHER, F. & L. (1975). 'Excavation of three postholes in Stonehenge carpark', *WAM 68*, 57–63.

WADDELL, J. (1970). 'Irish Bronze Age cists: a survey', *JRSAI 100*, 91–139.

—— (1990). *The Bronze Age Burials of Ireland*, Galway.

WAINWRIGHT, G. J. (1967). 'The excavation of Hampton stone circle, Portesham, Dorset', *PDNHAS 88*, 122–7.

—— (1971). 'The excavation of a Late Neolithic enclosure at Marden, Wiltshire', *Ant J 51*, 177–239.

—— (1979). *Mount Pleasant, Dorset: Excavations, 1970–1*, London.

—— (1989). *The Henge Monuments. Ceremony and Society in Prehistoric Britain*, London.

WAINWRIGHT, G. J. with LONGWORTH, I. H. (1971). *Durrington Walls: Excavations, 1966–8*, London. See also Burleigh, R.

WALKER, B. & RITCHIE, J.N.G. (1987). *Exploring Scotland's Heritage. Fife & Tayside*, Edinburgh.

WALKER, D. & WEST, R. G. (1970) eds. *Studies in the Vegetational History of the British Isles*, Cambridge.

WALKER, K. E. see Cleal, R.M.J.

WALLACE, C. S. see Patrick, J., 1982.

WALLIS, F. S. see Evans, E. D., 1962; 1972.

WALSH, P. T. (1931). 'Antiquities of the Dunlavin-Donard district', *JRSAI 61*, 127–30.

WARD, J. (1905). 'The stone circles', *VCH Derbyshire, I*, 181–4.

WARD, J. C. (1876). 'Archaeological remains in the Lake District', *TCWAAS 3 9O.S.*, 243–55.

WARDEN, A. J. (1885). *Angus or Forfarshire, V*, Dundee.

WARNE, C. (1865). *Dorsetshire: Its Vestiges, Celtic, Roman, Saxon and Danish*, London.

—— (1872). *Ancient Dorset*, London.

WATERHOUSE, J. (1985). *The Stone Circles of Cumbria*, Chichester.

WATERMAN, D. M. (1964). 'The stone circle, cairn and alignment at Drumskinny, Co. Fermanagh', *UJA 27*, 23–30. See also Collins, A.E.P.

WATKINS, A. (1925). *The Old Straight Track*, London.

WATSON, G. (1908). 'The stone circles of Roxburghshire', *T. Hawick Arch Soc*, 20–8.

WEATHERHILL, C. (1981). *Belerion. Ancient Sites of Land's End*, Penzance.

—— (1985). *Cornovia. Ancient Sites of Cornwall and Scilly*, Penzance.

WEATHERHILL, C. & DEVEREUX, P. (1994). *Myths and Legends of Cornwall*, Wilmslow.

WEBLEY, D. P. (1969). 'Some aspects of Neolithic and Bronze Age agriculture in South Wales', *BBCS 23*, 285–90.

WELSH, T. C. (1971). 'Clachtoll stone circle', *D & E*, 45.

WESTWOOD, J. (1987). *Albion. A Guide to Legendary Britain*, London.

WHITTLE, A.W.R., (1993) 'The Neolithic of the Avebury area: sequence, environment, settlement and monuments', *OJA 12 (1)*, 29–53.

WHITTLE, A.W.R. et al. (1997). *Sacred Mound, Holy Rings. Silbury Hill and the West Kennet Palisade Enclosures: a Later Neolithic Complex in north Wiltshire*, Oxford.

WHYBROW, C. (1966). 'The discovery of an Exmoor stone row', *Exmoor Review 7*, 69–70.

—— (1970). *Antiquary's Exmoor*, Dulverton.

WILLIAMS, B. (1856a). 'On some ancient monuments in the county of Cumberland', *PSAL 3*, 224.

—— (1856b). 'Notice of an excavation on Burnmoor', *PSAL 3*, 225–6.

WILLIAMS, G. (1988). *The Standing Stones of Wales and South-West England*, Oxford.

WILLIAMS, J. (1970). 'Neolithic axes in Dumfriess and Galloway', *TDGNHAS 47*, 111–22.

WILLIAMS, J. G. see BARBER, C.

WILSON, D. (1851) *The Prehistoric Annals of Scotland*, London.

—— (1863). *Prehistoric Annals of Scotland, I, II*, London & Cambridge.

WILSON, J. S. & GARFITT, G. A. (1920). 'Stone circle, Eyam Moor', *Man 20*, 34–6.

WINDLE, B.C.A. (1912). 'Megalithic remains surrounding Lough Gur, Co. Limerick', *PRIA 30*, 283–306.

WOOD, E. H. (1947). 'The grooves on the Devil's Arrows, Boroughbridge, Yorks', *PPS 13*, 180–2.

WOOD, J. (1747). *Choir Gaure, Vulgarly Called Stonehenge*, Oxford.

—— (1765). *A Description of Bath, I*, Oxford.

WOOD, J. E. (1978). *Sun, Moon and Standing Stones*, Oxford.

WOODWARD, A. (1992). *England Heritage Book of Shrines and Sacrifice*, London.

WOODWARD, A. & P. J. (1996). 'The topography of some barrow cemeteries in Bronze Age Wessex', *PPS 62*, 275–92.

WOOLACOTT, D. (1909). 'Note on the rocks of the stone circles at Keswick and Long Meg near Penrith', *University of Durham Phil. Soc. Proc 3*, 12–13.

WOOLLEY, A. R. see COLES, J. M.

WORSFOLD, T. C. (1898). *The French Stonehenge, an Account of the Principal Megalithic Remains in the Morbihan Archipelago*, London.

WORTH, R. H. (1932). 'The prehistoric monuments of Scorhill, Buttern Hill and Shuggledown', *TDA 64*, 279–87.

—— (1939). 'Two stone circles on Dartmoor, Swincombe Valley, and West Dart Valley, with a note on the "Grey Wethers" ', *TDA 71*, 321–8.

—— (1941). 'Retaining-circles associated with stone rows, Dartmoor', *TDA 73*, 227–38.

—— (1942). 'A stone circle in the Plym Valley', *TDA 74*, 207–10.

—— (1946). 'The stone rows of Dartmoor, I', *TDA 78*, 285–315.

—— (1947), 'The stone rows of Dartmoor, II', *TDA 79*, 175–86.

—— (1967). *Worth's Dartmoor*, see Spooner & Russell. See also Chanter, Rev. J. F.

YOUNG, A.M.A., LACAILLE, A. D. & ZEUNER, F. E. (1943). 'Report on standing stones and other remains near Fowlis Wester, Perthshire', *PSAS 77*, 174–84.

Index